HIROSHIGE

Hiroshige

Meisho
Edo
hyakkei

*One
Hundred
Famous
Views
of Edo*

*Hundert
berühmte
Ansichten
von Edo*

*Cent
Vues
célèbres
d'Edo*

OTA
MEMORIAL
MUSEUM
OF ART,
TOKYO

texts by
Texte von
textes par

MELANIE TREDE &
LORENZ BICHLER

TASCHEN

HONG KONG KÖLN LONDON LOS ANGELES MADRID PARIS TOKYO

Images of a City between Visual Poetry and Idealized Reality

Bilder einer Stadt zwischen visueller Poesie und idealisierter Wirklichkeit

Images d'une ville entre poésie visuelle et réalité idéale

In the second month of 1856, the censors approved five prints by Utagawa Hiroshige (1797–1858) with the series title *One Hundred Famous Views of Edo* (*Meisho Edo hyakkei*). And so began the story of one of the most famous landscape series in the history of Japanese woodblock printing. While the city of Edo, renamed Tokyo in 1868, had already been chosen as the subject of numerous paintings, printed books and other woodcut series, there had never been a series with so many views as was promised in the title of this one. The promise was more than kept: by the time of the appearance of the final pictures in the tenth month of 1858, a total of 120 individual prints, issued in instalments, did indeed constitute the most comprehensive topographical series among *ukiyo-e*, "pictures of the floating, fleeting world".

The term *ukiyo* goes back to the Buddhist notion of the world's illusory and transitory nature. In the course of the late 17th century, the term was extended to secular contexts, referring now not only to the pleasures of the theatres, teahouses and brothels, but also to other popular entertainments in the cities of Kyoto, Osaka and Edo. The last part of the word, *e*, simply means picture. Many ukiyo-e functioned as advertisements for theatrical performances or sumo tournaments, or they fêted the celebrities of entertainment culture. Portraits of actors in their latest roles, along with those of the most popular, trend-setting courtesans, were among the best-selling motifs.

These purely urban amusements had been joined since the 1760s by landscapes. The increasingly mobile population were familiar with many of the places depicted at first hand, but even when they were not, they could use the printed "views" to form an impression of the places they had heard about in stories and poems. The lay members of poets' circles in the field of *haikai* and *kyōka* satirical poems – Hiroshige was one – often used privately distributed prints or illustrated books to depict sites or districts known for their seasonal attractions, and they worked together with woodblock print artists to this end.

Some luxury editions of poetry from the 1820s concentrated on Edo, and soon afterwards views of this city, with its one million inhabitants and respected culture, became one of the central themes of ukiyo-e prints. Hiroshige was the undisputed master of this art form. The colours, sites and compositional principles he selected in the *One Hundred Famous Views of Edo* fascinated the local clientele to such an extent that each print had to be reprinted between ten and fifteen thousand times. As the posthumously compiled table of contents (page 51) mentions in its title cartouche (on a red ground), the series is the artist's most prestigious achievement (*issei ichidai*).

Hiroshige's predominance in the landscape genre was quickly recognized by European painters and art dealers. The print *Bamboo Quay by Kyōbashi Bridge* (ill. 2, plate 76) inspired, among others, the painter James Abbott McNeill Whistler (1834–1903), who was a collector of Japanese objects in general and Hiroshige's prints in particular. The oil painting *Nocturne in*

Im zweiten Monat des Jahres 1856 genehmigten Zensoren fünf Entwürfe von Utagawa Hiroshige (1797–1858) mit dem Serientitel *Hundert berühmte Ansichten von Edo* (*Meisho Edo hyakkei*). Damit begann die Erfolgsgeschichte einer der berühmtesten Landschaftsserien des japanischen Holzschnitts. Die 1868 in Tokyo umbenannte Stadt Edo war zwar bereits in zahlreichen Malereien, gedruckten Büchern und anderen Holzschnittserien zum Bildthema gewählt worden, aber eine Serie mit so vielen Ansichten, wie im Titel versprochen, hatte es noch nie gegeben. Aus den bis zum zehnten Monat 1858 nach und nach gedruckten insgesamt 120 Einzelblättern entstand denn auch die umfassendste Serie im Landschaftsgenre der Bilder der fließenden, vergänglichen Welt, *ukiyoe*.

Der Begriff *ukiyo* geht auf die buddhistische Vorstellung von der illusionären und vergänglichen Existenz im Diesseits zurück. Im Laufe des späten 17. Jahrhunderts wurde diese Bedeutung aber weltlich gewendet. Der Begriff bezog sich nun auf die Vergnügungen in den Theatern, Teehäusern und einschlägigen Etablissements, aber auch auf andere populäre Unterhaltungen in den Städten Kyoto, Osaka und Edo. Viele Ukiyoe-Bilder fungierten wie Werbungen für Theateraufführungen oder Sumo-Turniere, oder sie feierten die Stars der Unterhaltungskultur. Bildnisse von Schauspielern in ihren neuen Rollen gehörten wie die beliebtesten, modisch tonangebenden Kurtisanen zu den meist verkauften Bildsujets.

Neben die urbanen Amüsements trat seit den 1760er Jahren die Faszination für Landschaften. Wenn die zunehmend mobilere Bevölkerung diese nicht sogar aus eigener Anschauung kannte, so konnte sie sich doch anhand von Ansichten vorstellen, wie die aus Erzählungen und Gedichten bekannten Orte aussahen. Die Laienmitglieder von Dichterkreisen im Bereich der Haikai- und Kyōka-Scherzgedichte – auch Hiroshige gehörte zu ihnen – thematisierten in privat vertriebenen Drucken oder illustrierten Büchern oft Sehenswürdigkeiten oder für ihre jahreszeitlichen Attraktionen bekannte Gegenden und arbeiteten dafür mit Holzschnittmeistern zusammen.

Einige luxuriöse Gedichtbände aus den 1820er Jahren konzentrierten sich auf Edo, und bald darauf wurden die Ansichten der auch wegen ihrer Kultur geschätzten Millionenstadt zu einem der zentralen Bildthemen der Ukiyoe-Drucke. Ihr unbestrittener Meister war Hiroshige. Die von ihm gewählten Farben, Kompositionsprinzipien und Orte in den *Hundert Ansichten* faszinierten die einheimische Klientel derart, dass jeder Holzschnitt zwischen 10 000 und 15 000 Mal nachgedruckt werden musste. Wie das posthum gefertigte Inhaltsverzeichnis (S. 51) in seinem rot unterlegten Titelstreifen erwähnt, war die Serie das repräsentativste Werk (*issei ichidai*) des Künstlers.

Hiroshiges Vormachtstellung im Metier der Landschaften wurde schnell von europäischen Malern und Kunsthändlern erkannt. Das Blatt *Bambusquai an der Brücke Kyōbashi* (Abb. 2, Tafel 76) inspirierte u. a. den Maler James Abbott McNeill Whistler (1834–1903), der japanische Objekte und insbesondere Hiroshiges Drucke sammelte. Das zwischen 1872 und 1875 entstandene Ölbild *Nocturne in Blue and Gold: Old Battersea Bridge* (Abb. 1)

Au deuxième mois de l'année 1856, les censeurs approuvaient cinq projets d'Utagawa Hiroshige (1797–1858) portant le titre générique *Cent Vues célèbres d'Edo* (*Meisho Edo hyakkei*). Ainsi commençait la *success-story* d'une des plus célèbres séries paysagères de l'estampe japonaise. Si la ville d'Edo – rebaptisée Tokyo en 1868 – avait déjà été le sujet de nombreuses peintures, publications livresques et autres séries d'estampes, une série aussi nombreuse que l'annonçait le titre était un fait inédit. Du reste, les 120 feuilles individuelles imprimées successivement jusqu'au dixième mois de l'année 1858 allaient composer le plus vaste ensemble du genre paysager des images du monde flottant et éphémère – l'*ukiyo-e*.

Le terme *ukiyo* remonte à la conception bouddhiste de l'existence illusoire et fugace de ce monde. Au cours de la fin du XVIIᵉ siècle, le mot allait prendre un sens plus mondain pour se référer au monde des loisirs, des théâtres, des maisons de thé et établissements du genre, mais aussi à d'autres divertissements proposés par les villes de Kyoto, d'Osaka et d'Edo. De nombreuses images ukiyo-e servaient de réclames pour des représentations théâtrales et des tournois de sumo, ou célébraient les stars de la culture des loisirs. Les portraits d'acteurs incarnant un nouveau rôle faisaient partie des sujets les plus vendus, tout comme ceux, très prisés, des courtisanes en vogue.

À côté des distractions urbaines, une fascination pour le paysage apparaît peu à peu à partir des années 1760. Grâce aux vues paysagères imprimées, la population de plus en plus mobile qui ne connaissait pas *de visu* les lieux célèbres décrits dans la prose et la poésie pouvait au moins s'en faire une idée tangible. Au travers de gravures ou de livres diffusés dans un cadre privé, les amateurs de *haïkaïs* et de poèmes comiques *kyōka* réunis en cercles poétiques – Hiroshige en fit lui-même partie – illustraient souvent des sites célèbres ou des régions connues pour leur charme saisonnier, et travaillaient pour cela avec des maîtres de l'estampe.

Dans les années 1820, certains recueils de poésie luxueux commencent à se concentrer sur Edo; un peu plus tard, les vues de la capitale, dont la population dépassait le million et qui commençait aussi à rayonner sur le plan culturel, devinrent un des principaux sujets de l'estampe ukiyo-e. Hiroshige sera leur maître incontesté. Les couleurs, les principes de composition et les sites des *Cent Vues* choisis par l'artiste suscitèrent un tel engouement parmi la clientèle locale qu'après le premier tirage, chaque estampe dut être réimprimée à 10 000 et jusqu'à 15 000 exemplaires. Comme la table des matières compilée à titre posthume (p. 51) l'indique dans son bandeau de titre imprimé sur fond rouge, la série était l'œuvre la plus représentative (*issei ichidai*) de l'artiste.

La position dominante de Hiroshige au sein du genre paysager fut rapidement reconnue par les peintres et les marchands d'art européens. C'est ainsi que la feuille *Le quai au bambou près du pont Kyōbashi* (ill. 2, pl. 76) inspirera un peintre comme James Abbott McNeill Whistler (1834–1903), collectionneur de japoniaiseries, et en particulier des estampes de Hiroshige. La peinture à l'huile

1

2

Blue and Gold: Old Battersea Bridge (ill. 1), created between 1872 and 1875, bears witness to Whistler's confrontation with the atmospheric evening mood, the low vantage point and the marked feeling for colour combinations that we find in Hiroshige.

In 1887, Vincent van Gogh (1853–1890) copied the prints *Plum Park in Kameido* (ill. 3, plate 30) and *Sudden Shower over Shin-Ōhashi Bridge and Atake* (ill. 4, plate 58). Hiroshige, who himself confronted the principles of Western linear perspective in his work, thus became a dual protagonist in the artistic dialogue between Japan and Europe of the late 19th century.

The success of the *One Hundred Famous Views of Edo* is not due to Hiroshige alone. Thanks to the technical sophistication of the wood cutters and printers, the first impressions achieved an altogether painterly quality, and the publisher Sakanaya Eikichi (life dates unknown) played his key role by commissioning the series in the first place, advancing the materials and fees, and then distributing the prints, all at considerable financial risk to himself.

While the *One Hundred Famous Views of Edo* sold extremely well, this success was not altogether positive. Numerous later impressions (*atozuri*) found their way to Europe, and, being printed with fewer colour woodblocks, did not display the typical elaborate and time-consuming colour gradations as did the first impressions (*shozuri*). They were in fact merely cheap copies of the original masterpieces. Thus the *One Hundred Famous Views of Edo* as a whole, or individual prints, were occasionally described in the art literature as garish trivialities, heralding the end of the ukiyo-e woodblock print as an art form. The magnitude of the discrepancy between first and later impressions became apparent to a broader public only when high-quality colour reproductions became available in the second half of the 20th century. The series in the Ota Memorial Museum of Art in Tokyo, which is that reproduced in the present volume, is one of the few complete series consisting entirely of impressions from the first print run.

The Subjects of the Woodblock Prints

The popularity of the *One Hundred Famous Views of Edo* is due not least to the selection of sites. Temple and shrine precincts (plates 10, 11, 117) are to be found along with busy streets (ill. 6, plate 8), public parks (plate 17) and pure landscapes (plate 22), often with a background extending into the far distance (plate 24) and featuring many rivers, canals and bridges (plates 1, 59). Not quite 40 per cent of the prints show places never previously depicted. Hiroshige and his publishers hoped to use this element of surprise to increase sales. In this sense, Hiroshige invented "new traditions" and with his own series at the same time recalled "pictures of famous places" (*meishoe*), a tradition that extended back to the 10th century. These pictures, which had circulated among the elite since the Heian period (794–1185), took up poetic allusions to seasonal specialities of the places in question, an aspect

zeugt von der Auseinandersetzung des Künstlers mit der atmosphärischen Abendstimmung, dem niedrigen Betrachterstandpunkt und dem ausgeprägten Gefühl für Farbkombinationen bei Hiroshige.

1887 kopierte Vincent van Gogh (1853–1890) die Holzschnitte *Pflaumenpark Kameido* (Abb. 3, Tafel 30) und *Plötzlicher Schauer über der Brücke Shin-Ōhashi und Atake* (Abb. 4, Tafel 58). Hiroshige, der sich selbst in seinem Werk mit den Prinzipien westlicher Linearperspektive auseinandersetzte, wurde so in doppelter Hinsicht zu einem Protagonisten im japanisch-europäischen Kunstdialog des späten 19. Jahrhunderts.

Der Erfolg der *Hundert Ansichten* ist nicht allein Hiroshige zuzuschreiben. Dank der technischen Raffinesse von Holzschneidern und Druckern erhielten die Erstabzüge eine geradezu malerische Qualität, und der Verleger Sakanaya Eikichi (Lebensdaten unbekannt) trug dazu sein Teil bei, indem er mit großem finanziellen Risiko die Serie in Auftrag gab, Materialien und Honorar vorstreckte und die Holzschnitte vertrieb.

Der reißende Absatz der *Hundert Ansichten* hatte auch negative Folgen. Denn die zahlreichen Nachdrucke (*atozuri*), die ihren Weg auch nach Europa fanden, waren mit weniger Farbplatten gedruckt und wiesen nicht die typischen aufwändigen Farbgradierungen auf wie die Erstabzüge (*shozuri*) – sie waren einfach billige Abklatsche der ursprünglichen Meisterwerke. So wurden die *Hundert Ansichten* oder einzelne Blätter in der frühen Kunstliteratur gelegentlich als farbig-knallige Trivialitäten bezeichnet, die das Ende des Ukiyoe-Holzschnittes ankündigten. Wie groß die Diskrepanz zwischen einem Nachdruck und einem Erstabzug tatsächlich ist, konnte einem breiteren Publikum erst mit hochwertigen Farbreproduktionen in der zweiten Hälfte des 20. Jahrhunderts vor Augen geführt werden. Die Serie des Ota Memorial Museum of Art in Tokyo, die im vorliegenden Band reproduziert ist, gehört zu den wenigen kompletten Serien, die durchweg aus Erstabzügen bestehen.

Themen der Holzschnitte

Die Beliebtheit der *Hundert Ansichten* ist nicht zuletzt der Auswahl der Orte zuzuschreiben. Tempel- und Schreinbezirke (Tafeln 10, 11, 117) stehen neben belebten Straßen (Abb. 6, Tafel 8) sowie öffentlichen Parks (Tafel 17) und reinen Landschaftsszenen (Tafel 22), häufig mit einem weit in die Ferne reichenden Hintergrund (Tafel 24) und vielen Flüssen, Kanälen und Brücken (Tafeln 1, 59). In knapp 40 Prozent der Blätter sind Gegenden vorgestellt, die zuvor noch nie thematisiert worden waren. Mit diesem Überraschungsmoment wollten Hiroshige und sein Verleger den Absatz der Serie steigern. Hiroshige erfand somit „neue Traditionen" und ließ mit seiner Serie gleichzeitig an die bis ins 10. Jahrhundert zurückreichenden „Bilder berühmter Orte" (*meishoe*) denken. Diese seit der Heian-Zeit (794–1185) in Kreisen der Elite verbreiteten Bilder griffen aus der Lyrik bekannte Anspielungen auf jahreszeitliche Besonderheiten der Orte auf – ein Aspekt, der in Hiro-

Nocturne in Blue and Gold : Old Battersea Bridge (1872–1875; ill. 1) illustre la confrontation de l'artiste avec l'atmosphère vespérale, le point de vue surbaissé et le sens très marqué des combinaisons chromatiques chez Hiroshige.

En 1887, Vincent van Gogh (1853–1890) copie les estampes *Le parc de pruniers à Kameido* (ill. 3, pl. 30) et *Averse soudaine sur le pont Shin-Ōhashi et Atake* (ill. 4, pl. 58). Hiroshige, qui avait lui-même étudié les lois de la perspective occidentale, devint ainsi à double titre le protagoniste du dialogue artistique nippo-européen de la fin du XIXe siècle.

Cela dit, le succès des *Cent Vues* ne se doit pas au seul talent de Hiroshige. Grâce aux prouesses et à la subtilité technique des graveurs sur bois et des imprimeurs, les premiers tirages purent présenter une qualité proche de la peinture, et l'éditeur Sakanaya Eikichi (dates inconnues) contribua lui aussi fortement à ce succès en prenant des risques financiers considérables, passant commande de la série, avançant l'argent des matériaux et des honoraires et prenant en charge la diffusion des estampes.

Les très fortes ventes des *Cent Vues* eurent aussi des conséquences négatives. Les nombreuses réimpressions (*atozuri*) qui entrèrent en Europe furent en effet imprimées avec un moins grand nombre de « bois à colorier » et ne présentaient pas la caractéristique richesse de dégradés des premiers tirages (*shozuri*) – il s'agissait de simples copies des chef-d'œuvres originaux. C'est ainsi que dans un premier temps, la littérature spécialisée qualifia les *Cent Vues célèbres d'Edo* ou des feuilles isolées de trivialités criardes annonçant la fin de l'estampe ukiyo-e, et il faudra attendre les reproductions en couleur de haute qualité réalisées à partir de la seconde moitié du XXe siècle pour voir la différence éclatante entre une réimpression et un premier tirage entrer dans la conscience d'un large public. La série de l'Ota Memorial Museum of Art à Tokyo reproduite dans la présente publication fait partie des rares séries complètes exclusivement composées de tirages originaux.

Thèmes des estampes

La popularité des *Cent Vues* se doit en bonne partie au choix des lieux représentés. Les domaines des temples et des sanctuaires (pl. 10, 11, 117) y côtoient des scènes de rues (ill. 6, pl. 8), des parcs publics (pl. 17) et de purs paysages (pl. 22). Ces sujets sont souvent placés devant un arrière-plan s'étendant dans le lointain (pl. 24), avec de nombreux fleuves, canaux et ponts (pl. 1, 59). Dans presque 40 pour cent des feuilles apparaissent des régions qui n'avaient encore jamais été représentées par l'estampe. Avec ce facteur de surprise, Hiroshige et son éditeur voulaient évidemment augmenter les ventes de la série. Hiroshige inventa ainsi de « nouvelles traditions », tout en s'appuyant sur les « vues célèbres » (*meishoe*), qui pouvaient se prévaloir d'une tradition remontant au Xe siècle. Ces images diffusées dans les cercles de l'élite depuis l'ère Heian (794–1185) étaient truffées de références aux particularités saisonnières popularisées par la poésie – un aspect qui n'apparaît

3

VINCENT VAN GOGH
(1853–1890)

*Japonaiserie:
Flowering Plum Tree
(after Hiroshige)*

*Japonaiserie:
Blühender
Pflaumenbaum
(nach Hiroshige)*

*Japonaiserie :
prunier en fleurs
(d'après Hiroshige)*

September–October
1887, oil on canvas,
55 x 46 cm, F 371,
JH 1296

Amsterdam,
Van Gogh Museum,
Vincent van Gogh
Foundation

4

VINCENT VAN GOGH
(1853–1890)

*Japonaiserie:
Bridge in the Rain
(after Hiroshige)*

*Japonaiserie:
Brücke im Regen
(nach Hiroshige)*

*Japonaiserie :
pont sous
la pluie (d'après
Hiroshige)*

September–October
1887, oil on canvas,
73 x 54 cm, F 372,
JH 1297

Amsterdam,
Van Gogh Museum,
Vincent van Gogh
Foundation

P. 10

Detail from plate 15

Detail aus Tafel 15

Détail de planche 15

3

4

which in Hiroshige's newly chosen views is not very prominent. However, every educated Japanese would immediately have linked "one hundred", in the context of famous places, with *One Hundred Poets, One Poem Each (Hyakunin isshu)*, a widely disseminated collection dating from the early 13th century and known quite generally in the 19th century through numerous imitations and parodies.

As Tsuzumi Tsuneyoshi (1887–1981) remarks in his 1929 book *Die Kunst Japans* (The Art of Japan), it was "an invention of the ukiyo-e painters, in particular Hiroshige, to represent densely populated areas as landscape pictures". Indeed, almost every print either includes human figures, or else hints at their presence (for example, in plates 3, 4). In these pictures, Hiroshige, unlike his famous older contemporary Katsushika Hokusai (1760–1849), rarely focuses on labour. Instead, he depicts Edo's different social classes and sometimes also visitors to the city, especially on the occasion of seasonal customs and festivities (plates 2, 51) and when engaging in tourist or leisure activities (plates 11, 72). Even though a certain melancholy emanates from some scenes, Hiroshige presents an Edo of manifold attractions, unspoilt idylls and prosperity.

A compositional, seasonal or colour role was often played by vegetation, in particular trees (plate 68), which sometimes bear names (plates 89, 97). The blossoming cherry trees we see on 15 prints express more than just a season, however. The reference was to an Edo blossoming once more following the catastrophic earthquake of 1855. Less frequently, certain areas are symbolized by animals (plates 56, 118), while birds are often used to enliven broad areas of sky and lend depth to them.

Almost all the prints are characterized by clear weather, a red horizon hinting at sunrise or sunset. Only three rainy scenes (plates 47, 58, 119) and seven snowscapes (e.g. plates 99, 111) interrupt the run of good weather. This picture-postcard atmosphere can be understood as a commercial strategy.

Strict edicts forbade the depiction of Edo Castle or any of the other buildings or installations of the shogun. It is true that places occupied by the military regime were sometimes concealed from the censors by being given an innocuous title (plate 108 with the title *View of Shiba Coast*), or else the castle appears in the background (plate 1), or its outer ramparts and moats are integrated into the composition (plate 54). Yet there remains a huge void in the centre of Edo: 2.4 square kilometres (less than one square mile) are largely hidden from the eyes of the viewer.

shiges neu gewählten Ansichten kaum hervorsticht. Allerdings dachte jeder gebildete Japaner bei der Zahl hundert in Verbindung mit berühmten Orten an *Hundert Gedichte von hundert Dichtern (Hyakunin isshu)*, eine weit verbreitete Sammlung des frühen 13. Jahrhunderts, deren Gedichte im 19. Jahrhundert in zahlreichen Variationen und Parodien allgemein bekannt waren.

Wie Tsuzumi Tsuneyoshi (1887–1981) in seinem Buch *Die Kunst Japans* (1929) bemerkt, war es „eine Erfindung der Ukiyoe-Maler, besonders Hiroshiges, starkbewohnte Gegenden als Landschaftsbild darzustellen". In der Tat erscheinen auf fast allen Blättern Menschen, oder ihre unmittelbare Präsenz wird angedeutet (etwa in den Tafeln 3, 4). Hiroshige stellt dabei – anders als sein berühmter älterer Zeitgenosse Katsushika Hokusai (1760–1849) – selten die Arbeit in den Vordergrund. Stattdessen zeigt er unterschiedliche soziale Schichten von Edo und gelegentlich auch seine Besucher vor allem bei jahreszeitlichen Bräuchen und Festen (Tafeln 2, 51) und bei touristischen oder Freizeitvergnügungen (Tafeln 11, 72). Auch wenn manche Blätter eine gewisse Melancholie ausstrahlen, stellt Hiroshige doch ein Edo der variationsreichen Attraktionen, der ungetrübten Idylle und des Wohlstands vor.

Häufig spielt die Vegetation, allen voran Bäume (Tafel 68) – die zuweilen sogar Namen tragen (Tafeln 89, 97) –, eine kompositorische, farbliche oder auch jahreszeitliche Rolle. Mit den blühenden Kirschbäumen auf 15 Holzschnitten wird aber mehr ausgedrückt als nur eine Jahreszeit. Sicherlich soll damit auch das nach dem verheerenden Erdbeben von 1855 wieder aufblühende Edo präsentiert werden. Weniger häufig werden bestimmte Gegenden durch Tiere symbolisiert (Tafeln 56, 118), dagegen beleben Vögel häufig den weiten Himmel und verleihen ihm Tiefe.

Auf fast allen Holzschnitten herrscht klares, strahlendes Wetter, wobei ein roter Horizont auf den Sonnenauf- oder -untergang hindeuten kann. Nur drei Regenszenen (Tafeln 47, 58, 119) und sieben Schneelandschaften (u. a. Tafeln 99, 111) unterbrechen die Gutwetterstimmung. Diese Ansichtskartenatmosphäre kann als kommerzielle Strategie verstanden werden.

Strenge Gesetze verboten die Darstellung des Edo-Schlosses und aller anderen Gebäude und Einrichtungen des Shoguns. Zwar wird die Darstellung von Orten, die vom Militärherrscher vereinnahmt waren, gelegentlich durch einen harmlosen Titel vor den Zensoren verborgen (Tafel 108 mit dem Titel *Die Landschaft an der Küste Shibaura*), das Schloss taucht im Hintergrund auf (Tafel 1), oder seine äußeren Wälle und Gräben sind in die Kompositionen integriert (Tafel 54). Und doch bleibt dieses gigantische „leere" Zentrum Edos mit einem Areal von etwa 2.4 Quadratkilometern dem Betrachter weitgehend verborgen.

guère dans les nouvelles vues choisies par Hiroshige. Il est vrai qu'en entendant le nombre cent associé à des vues célèbres, tout Japonais cultivé songeait immédiatement aux *Cent poèmes de cent poètes (Hyakunin isshu)*, un recueil du XIIIe siècle largement répandu dont les poèmes étaient connus de tous au XIXe siècle par de nombreuses variantes et parodies.

Comme le fait observer Tsuzumi Tsuneyoshi (1887–1981) dans son livre *Die Kunst Japans* (1929 ; L'art du Japon), ce fut une « invention des peintres ukiyo-e, et particulièrement de Hiroshige, que de représenter sous forme de paysages des zones urbaines fortement peuplées ». Presque toutes les feuilles sont en effet marquées par la présence humaine – parfois seulement évoquée de manière indirecte, comme on le voit par exemple dans les planches 3 et 4. À la différence de son aîné et contemporain Katsushika Hokusai (1760–1849), Hiroshige ne met que rarement en avant le travail de l'homme, mais montre en revanche les différentes couches sociales d'Edo, parfois aussi les visiteurs de la capitale, surtout lors des fêtes et usages saisonniers (pl. 2, 51), divertissements touristiques ou ludiques (pl. 11, 72). Si quelques feuilles sont empreintes d'une certaine mélancolie, dans l'ensemble, Hiroshige représente un Edo prospère aux attractions diverses et variées – une idylle intacte.

La végétation, et en tout premier lieu les arbres (pl. 68) – qui portent parfois même des noms (pl. 89, 97) –, joue souvent un rôle important dans la composition ou dans le coloris, mais aussi pour caractériser l'époque de l'année. Avec les cerisiers en fleurs présents dans rien moins que 15 estampes, Hiroshige exprime encore quelque chose d'autre qu'une caractéristique saisonnière. En définitive, un des propos majeurs de l'artiste était en effet de présenter la renaissance de la capitale après le séisme dévastateur de 1855. En revanche, les différents lieux des *Cent Vues* sont moins souvent représentés par des animaux (pl. 56, 118), à l'exception des oiseaux qui animent très souvent la vastitude du ciel et lui confèrent sa profondeur.

Enfin, dans presque toutes les estampes règne un splendide beau temps, sachant qu'un horizon rougeoyant peut indiquer le lever ou le coucher du soleil. Trois scènes de pluie seulement (pl. 47, 58, 119) et sept paysages enneigés (p. ex. pl. 99, 111) interrompent cette radieuse ambiance de carte postale qui peut être comprise comme une stratégie commerciale.

Des lois strictes interdisaient rigoureusement toute représentation du château d'Edo et de tout autre bâtiment et dispositif shogunal. Dans quelques estampes, la représentation de sites réquisitionnés par l'autorité militaire a certes été cachée aux censeurs sous le titre anodin de la planche 108 (*La côte à Shibaura*), et si dans la planche 54 le château apparaît à l'arrière-plan, ou si ses remblais fortifiés sont noyés dans la composition, avec une aire d'environ 2.4 kilomètres carrés, ce gigantesque « vide » en plein Edo n'en reste pas moins largement caché au spectateur.

Pictorial Innovations

The choice of the *ōban* format, i.e. a vertical format, in the present series measuring 36.5–37.7 cm (approx. 14.3–14.8 in.) by 24.9–26.4 cm (approx. 9.8–10.4 in.) for the *One Hundred Famous Views of Edo* was novel for landscape prints. The choice of this format was not entirely unrelated to the success of Hiroshige's vertical-format series, printed between 1853 and 1856, entitled *Famous Views of Sixty-Odd Provinces* (*Rokujū yoshū meisho zue*, ills. 20, 21). By using the vertical format, Hiroshige was also harking back to the tradition of vertical hanging scrolls often employed for landscape paintings.

With their fine colour gradations and other special printing techniques, these woodblock prints resemble painted pictures. The use of the vigorous and contrasting colours blue, red and green, and sometimes also yellow, but often also subtly composed related hues, such as the blue-to-black shadings in *Fireworks by Ryōgoku Bridge* (ill. 9, plate 98) was by the mid-19th century part of the repertoire of ukiyo-e printmakers. At the same time, they reveal Hiroshige's familiarity with the established painting schools of his age.

The eclecticism of Japanese painting at this time is also reflected in the principles of picture composition we see in the *One Hundred Famous Views of Edo*. Three important techniques of pictorial composition go back to different sources. In numerous prints, Hiroshige chooses the bird's-eye view anchored in the Japanese painting tradition. But while our gaze falls on to a landscape from above, at the same time the overlayering of pictorial planes generates space and depth. Typical in the use of this technique are, for example, the prints *Moto-Hachiman Shrine in Sunamura* (ill. 5, plate 29) and *Senju Great Bridge* (plate 103). There is no fixed point to define a picture's centre; we are encouraged instead to let our gaze wander.

Another technique is Western linear perspective. Its optical realism had made it a widespread feature in the popular medium of the woodblock print since the mid-18th century, and Hiroshige used it for prominent street scenes, among other things. One or two house fronts run from the sides of the picture at an acute angle towards an often undepicted vanishing point. Sometimes he combines this relatively schematic grid with the bird's-eye view. In the view of *Suruga-chō* (ill. 6, plate 8), for example, we look down on the street in which people are going about their business; those in the middle distance are reduced to schematic figures of men and women. In the distance, precisely above the imaginary vanishing point, Mount Fuji rises majestically from a broad band of cloud.

The third compositional principle to contribute to the fame of this series is that of a motif seen close up and usually cropped by the margin of the print; through the motif, or to one side, the actual scene is situated in the middle distance and background. The stimulus for this technique, which was certainly unusual and occasionally comes across as contrived, originates also in Western vanishing-point perspective. But Hiroshige emphasizes the

Visuelle Innovationen

Die Wahl des sogenannten Ōban-Blattes im Hochformat für die *Hundert berühmten Ansichten von Edo* – in der vorliegenden Serie 36,5–37,7 cm x 24,9–26,4 cm – war für gedruckte Landschaftsansichten eine Neuerung. Sicherlich hat die Entscheidung für dieses Format mit dem Erfolg der von Hiroshige zwischen 1853 und 1856 entworfenen, ebenfalls hochformatigen Serie *Berühmte Ansichten von über sechzig Provinzen* (*Rokujū yoshū meisho zue*, Abb. 20, 21) zu tun. Hiroshige knüpfte mit dem Hochformat auch an die für Landschaften häufig eingesetzte vertikale Hängerolle an.

Mit den feinen Farbgradierungen und anderen speziellen Drucktechniken ähneln die Holzschnitte gemalten Bildern. Die kräftigen und kontrastreich eingesetzten Farben Blau, Rot und Grün, zuweilen auch Gelb, oft aber auch subtil zusammengestellte verwandte Farbtöne wie etwa die Blau- bis Schwarzschattierungen im Blatt *Feuerwerk bei der Brücke Ryogokubashi* (Abb. 9, Tafel 98) gehören Mitte des 19. Jahrhunderts zu den Stilmitteln des Ukiyoe-Holzschnittes. Gleichzeitig verraten sie Hiroshiges Kenntnis von etablierten Malschulen seiner Zeit.

Der Eklektizismus der damaligen japanischen Malerei spiegelt sich u. a. in den Prinzipien des Bildaufbaus der *Hundert Ansichten*: Die drei wesentlichen Techniken der Bildkomposition gehen auf unterschiedliche Quellen zurück. Hiroshige wählt in zahlreichen Blättern die in der japanischen Maltradition verankerte Vogelperspektive. Dabei fällt der Blick von oben auf eine Landschaft, gleichzeitig aber wird durch ein Übereinanderschichten von Bildebenen Raum und Tiefe erzeugt. Typisch für diese Technik sind z. B. die Blätter *Der Schrein Moto-Hachiman in Sunamura* (Abb. 5, Tafel 29) und *Die Große Brücke in Senju* (Tafel 103). Kein Fixpunkt definiert ein Bildzentrum. Der Betrachter wird stattdessen aufgefordert, seinen Blick im Bild wandern zu lassen.

Ein weiterer Modus ist die westliche Linearperspektive. Sie war wegen ihres optischen Verismus seit der Mitte des 18. Jahrhunderts im populären Medium des Holzschnittes verbreitet, und Hiroshige wendete sie u. a. bei prominenten Straßenszenen an. Eine oder zwei Häuserfronten laufen von den Bildseiten im spitzen Winkel auf einen oft nicht dargestellten Fluchtpunkt zu. Gelegentlich kombiniert er dieses relativ schematisch eingesetzte Raster auch mit der Vogelperspektive. Im Falle der Ansicht von *Suruga-chō* (Abb. 6, Tafel 8) etwa blickt der Betrachter auf die Straße herab, auf der sich bis in den Mittelgrund zu Strichmännchen verkleinerte Menschen tummeln. Genau über dem imaginären Fluchtpunkt und oberhalb einer breiten Wolkenbank aber erhebt sich in der Ferne majestätisch der Berg Fuji.

Das dritte Kompositionsprinzip, das zum Ruhm dieser Serie beitrug, ist ein nah an den Betrachter herangerücktes und meist von einem der Bildränder abgeschnittenes Motiv, durch das hindurch oder an dem vorbei sich eine Szene im Mittel- und Hintergrund abspielt. Die Anregung für diese ungewöhnliche und gelegentlich forciert angewendete Methode ist zwar ebenfalls in einer west-

Innovations visuelles

Le format vertical dit *ōban* choisi pour les *Cent Vues célèbres d'Edo* – dans la présente série, 36,5 à 37,7 cm x 24,9 à 26,4 cm – fut une innovation dans le domaine des vues paysagères imprimées. Les raisons qui ont motivé ce format sont sans doute liées au succès de la série des *Vues célèbres des 60 et quelques provinces* (*Rokujū yoshū meisho zue*, ill. 20,21) que Hiroshige avait conçue entre 1853 et 1856, série qui avait également été imprimée dans un format vertical. De plus, ce format permettait à Hiroshige de s'inscrire dans la tradition du rouleau suspendu souvent utilisé dans la peinture de paysages.

Avec ses subtils dégradés de couleurs et autres techniques d'impression spécifiques, les estampes se rapprochent fortement de la peinture. Depuis le milieu du XIXᵉ siècle, les bleus, rouges et verts, parfois aussi le jaune, utilisés en ton direct pour obtenir des contrastes aussi variés que possible, mais aussi des demi-tons subtilement composés, tels les ombrages de bleu jusqu'au noir dans une feuille comme *Feu d'artifice au-dessus du pont Ryogokubashi* (ill. 9, pl. 98), faisaient partie du vocabulaire stylistique de l'estampe ukiyo-e. En même temps, ils révèlent l'excellente connaissance que Hiroshige a eue des écoles de peinture établies de son temps.

Dans les *Cent Vues*, la présence éclectique de la peinture japonaise de l'époque se manifeste aussi au niveau des principes de composition. Dans ce domaine, les trois principales techniques utilisées remontent à plusieurs sources. Dans de nombreuses feuilles, Hiroshige choisit la vue d'oiseau profondément ancrée dans la tradition picturale japonaise. Le regard y plonge d'un point élevé dans un paysage dont l'espace et la profondeur sont générés par la stratification des niveaux visuels. Des illustrations caractéristiques en sont par exemple les feuilles *Le sanctuaire de Moto-Hachiman à Sunamura* (ill. 5, pl. 29) ou *Le grand pont à Senju* (pl. 103). Si aucun point fixe n'y détermine un centre visuel, le spectateur est en revanche invité à promener son regard dans l'image.

Un autre mode de composition ressort de la perspective linéaire occidentale. Du fait de son caractère vériste, celle-ci s'était surtout répandue, depuis le milieu du XVIIIᵉ siècle, dans le médium populaire de l'estampe, et Hiroshige s'en est notamment servi pour les principales scènes de rue. Une ou deux rangées de façades y partent des bords latéraux de l'image pour mener en angle aigu vers un point de fuite qui souvent n'est pas représenté. Ce mode de représentation relativement schématique est parfois associé à la vue d'oiseau. Dans le cas de la vue de *Suruga-chō* par exemple (ill. 6, pl. 8), le regard du spectateur plonge dans une rue où se promènent des hommes progressivement réduits jusqu'à des bonshommes dessinés au trait. Dans le lointain, au-dessus d'un large banc de nuages, très exactement au-dessus du point de fuite imaginaire, trône en revanche, majestueux, le mont Fuji.

Le troisième principe de composition qui a contribué à la célébrité de la série consiste en un motif fortement rapproché du spectateur,

7

8

P. 14

Detail from plate 19

Detail aus Tafel 19

Détail de planche 19

7
UTAGAWA HIROSHIGE

*Bakuro-chō
Hatsune no baba*

*Hatsune Riding
Ground in
Bakuro-chō*

*Der Reitplatz
Hatsune no baba in
Bakuro-chō*

*Le manège équestre
Hatsune no baba à
Bakuro-chō*

Plate/Tafel/planche 6

8
UTAGAWA HIROSHIGE

*Asakusa
Kinryūzan*

*Kinryūzan
Temple
in Asakusa*

*Der Tempel
Kinryūzan in
Asakusa*

*Le temple
Kinryūzan à
Asakusa*

Plate/Tafel/planche 99

---

contrast between the large object in the foreground, known as a *repoussoir*, and a background pushed far further into the distance than would have been conceivable in mid-19th-century European art. The extreme cropping of the motifs was also unusual amongst Hiroshige's Japanese predecessors; this is true, for example, of the "pictures in the Dutch style" (*ranga*) painted since the end of the 18th century. The apparent randomness of the cropping suggests that a certain moment in the course of an action is being captured.

In the *Plum Orchard in Kamada* (plate 27), for example, the empty palanquin encourages us to imagine the coming and going of the visitors. Suggestive details such as these were intended to provide contemporary buyers of the prints with something to discuss. The well-known Hiroshige scholar Suzuki Jūzō described this technique as photographic, while the most influential connoisseur of the *One Hundred Famous Views of Edo* in the West, Henry D. Smith, referred to them as proto-filmic, since they included the element of time.

The earliest prints in the series with this surprising perspective date from the seventh month of 1856. They include *Kinryūzan Temple in Asakusa* (ill. 8, plate 99) where we feel the "eye catcher" is literally within our grasp: the temple's emblem, the red lantern hanging from the Kaminarimon "Thunder Gate". Together with the cropped left-hand bay, it provides a compositional frame through which we can look into the sanctuary with the temple gate (*sanmon*) and the pagoda. The viewer has the feeling of standing in the gateway like a pilgrim.

Production of the Series

An edict dating from the fifth month of 1790 required the publishing houses, organized into guilds, to appoint censors from their own ranks on a rotating basis. Their job was to apply to compositions laid before them government-defined criteria relating to limits on luxury as well as to sensitive political material, and they were called to account in case of contravention. The earliest censors' seals still extant, with the character *kiwame* ("approved"), date from 1790/91. In 1842 this system was replaced by a censor appointed by the government and known as the "overseer of pictures" (*e'nanushi*). His seal, the character *aratame* ("examined"), can be found on draft compositions, alone or in various combinations, until about 1875. In the case of the *One Hundred Famous Views of Edo*, it was joined by the oval date seal, established in 1852, which gives the characters for the year and the month. This allowed the prints to be dated by their composition, and to be put in chronological order.

Hiroshige presented 37 prints in 1856, to be followed by a further 71 the next year and another 7 in 1858, the year of his death. Evidently, Hiroshige and his publisher already intended in the seventh month of 1858 to bring the series to an end, for two prints with this date seal bear the alternative series title *Entertaining Supplements to the Hundred Views of Edo* (*Edo hyakkei yokyō*,

---

lichen Fluchtpunktperspektive zu suchen. Hiroshige betont aber den Gegensatz zwischen großem Gegenstand im Vordergrund, dem sogenannten Repoussoir, und klein in die Ferne gerücktem Hintergrund so sehr, wie es Mitte des 19. Jahrhunderts in Europa nicht denkbar gewesen wäre. Das extreme Anschneiden der Bildmotive war allerdings auch in den japanischen Vorläufern unüblich; dies gilt z. B. für die seit Ende des 18. Jahrhunderts entstandenen „Bilder im holländischen Stil" (*ranga*). Die scheinbare Zufälligkeit des Bildausschnitts suggeriert, dass ein gewisser Moment in einem Handlungsablauf dargestellt ist; in dem Blatt *Pflaumengarten in Kamada* (Tafel 27) verleitet z. B. die leere Sänfte dazu, sich das Herankommen und Sich-Entfernen der Besucher vorzustellen. Die Blätter sollten den zeitgenössischen Käufern gerade durch solche Suggestionen Anlass zu Gesprächen bieten. Der bekannte Hiroshige-Forscher Suzuki Jūzō beschrieb diese Technik als fotografisches Mittel, während der maßgebliche Kenner der *Hundert Ansichten* im Westen, Henry D. Smith, sie als proto-filmisch bezeichnete, da sie das Element der Zeit einkalkuliere.

Die frühesten Blätter der Serie mit dieser überraschenden Blickführung entstanden ab dem siebten Monat 1856. Dazu gehört *Der Tempel Kinryūzan in Asakusa* (Abb. 8, Tafel 99) mit der zum Greifen nahe vom „Donnertor" Kaminarimon herabhängenden roten Laterne, dem Wahrzeichen des Tempels, als Blickfang. Zusammen mit dem angeschnittenen linken Joch des Tores bildet sie einen Kompositionsrahmen, durch den hindurch man in das sakrale Zentrum mit dem Tempeltor (*sanmon*) und der Pagode blickt. Dem Betrachter wird das Gefühl vermittelt, selbst als Pilger im Tor zu stehen.

Herstellungsverlauf der Serie

Ein Edikt vom fünften Monat des Jahres 1790 forderte die zu Gilden zusammengeschlossenen Verlagshäuser auf, rotierende Zensoren aus den eigenen Reihen zu stellen. Diese sollten die vorgelegten Entwürfe auf von der Regierung definierte Luxusbeschränkungen und politisch sensibles Material hin untersuchen und wurden bei Verstößen gegen diese Auflagen zur Rechenschaft gezogen. Die frühest erhaltenen Zensorensiegel mit dem Zeichen *kiwame* („genehmigt") stammen von 1790/91. Im Jahr 1842 wurde dieses System abgelöst von einem durch die Regierung bestimmten *e'nanushi* („Vorsteher von Bildern"). Sein Siegel *aratame* („geprüft") findet sich auf den Entwürfen allein oder in verschiedenen Kombinationen bis um das Jahr 1875. Im Falle der *Hundert Ansichten* kam das seit 1852 etablierte ovale Datumssiegel hinzu, das das zyklische Zeichen des Jahres und den Monat angibt. Dies erlaubt es, die Blätter in ihrem Entwurfsstadium zu datieren und in eine chronologische Reihenfolge zu bringen.

37 Blätter stellte Hiroshige 1856 vor, im nächsten Jahr folgten 71 Holzschnitte, und in seinem Todesjahr 1858 kamen 7 weitere Entwürfe hinzu. Offensichtlich hatten Hiroshige und sein Verleger schon im siebten Monat des Jahres 1858 vor, die Serie zu beenden, denn zwei Blätter mit diesem Datumssiegel tragen den abweichen-

---

le plus souvent coupé par un des bords de l'image, et à travers lequel – ou l'évitant – le regard accède à une scène qui se déroule au second ou à l'arrière-plan. Si l'origine de cette méthode inusitée et parfois même forcée, doit également être recherchée dans la perspective centrale occidentale, Hiroshige pousse l'opposition entre grand objet au premier plan, dit « repoussoir », et arrière-plan fortement relégué dans le lointain – jusqu'à un point qui n'aurait pas été concevable dans l'art européen du milieu du XIXᵉ siècle. Côté oriental, la coupure abrupte des motifs par les bords de l'image n'était pas un fait inhabituel chez les précurseurs japonais de Hiroshige. Ceci vaut en particulier pour les « images de style hollandais » (*ranga*) apparues au Japon depuis la fin du XVIIIᵉ siècle. L'aspect fortuit du cadrage suggère qu'un certain moment est représenté dans le déroulement de l'action. Dans la feuille *Prunelaie à Kamada* par exemple (pl. 27), le palanquin vide invite à imaginer l'approche et l'éloignement des visiteurs du jardin. Avec ce genre de suggestions, les feuilles concernées devaient précisément fournir des sujets de conversation aux acheteurs contemporains. Suzuki Jūzō, le célèbre spécialiste de Hiroshige, a décrit cette technique comme un artifice photographique, tandis que le grand connaisseur occidental des *Cent Vues* Henry D. Smith, l'a qualifiée de procédé proto-filmique dans la mesure où elle prend en compte un facteur temporel.

Les premières feuilles de la série présentant ce guidage surprenant du regard ont vu le jour à partir du septième mois de l'année 1856. En fait partie *Le temple Kinryūzan à Asakusa* (ill. 8, pl. 99), avec l'accroche visuelle de la lanterne rouge suspendue à la « porte du dragon » Kaminarimon, signe distinctif du temple que l'on croit pouvoir toucher du doigt. Avec le montant gauche de la porte, la lanterne donne son cadre à la composition, cadre à travers lequel le regard pénètre par la porte d'entrée pour apercevoir le centre sacré avec la porte du temple (*sanmon*) et sa pagode. Le spectateur a ainsi l'impression d'être lui-même un pèlerin franchissant l'entrée du temple.

Production de la série

Un édit du cinquième mois de l'année 1790 imposait aux maisons d'édition constituées en corporations de nommer des censeurs issus de leurs propres rangs. Ces censeurs devaient examiner les projets d'estampes sous le signe des restrictions au luxe et des questions politiquement sensibles définies par le gouvernement, et pouvaient être convoqués en cas d'infraction. Les premiers cachets de censeurs conservés montrant l'idéogramme *kiwame* (« approuvé ») datent de 1790/91. En 1842, ce système fut remplacé par des censeurs (*e'nanushi*, « directeur d'images ») directement nommés par le gouvernement. Leur sceau *aratame* (« vérifié ») se retrouve sur tous les projets, soit seul, soit dans diverses combinaisons jusqu'à l'année 1875. Dans le cas des *Cent Vues* vint s'y ajouter le cachet de datation ovale imposé à partir de 1852, cachet qui présente l'idéogramme cyclique de l'année et du mois et qui permet de déterminer l'époque de conception et donc la succession chronologique des feuilles.

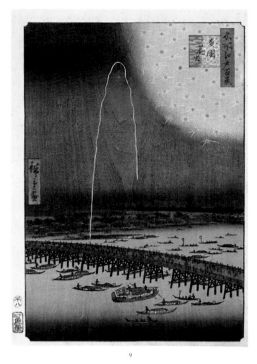

9

UTAGAWA HIROSHIGE

Ryōgoku hanabi

*Fireworks by
Ryōgoku Bridge*

*Feuerwerk bei der
Brücke Ryōgokubashi*

*Feu d'artifice
au-dessus du pont
Ryōgokubashi*

Plate/Tafel/planche 98

P. 17

Detail from plate 24

Detail aus Tafel 24

Détail de planche 24

9

plates 78, 79). The following month, however, three further prints were added, which once more bear the original title *Meisho Edo hyakkei* (plates 44, 72, 98). This total of 115 prints was further supplemented by three prints bearing the date seal of the tenth month of 1858 (plates 12, 41, 114), all of them approved by the censors after Hiroshige's death on the sixth day of the ninth month. Recent research by the ukiyo-e specialist Asano Shūgō assumes that Hiroshige's pupil Shigenobu (1826–1869) executed these prints at the publisher's behest on the basis of sketches prepared by the master. Shortly afterwards, Sakanaya commissioned a table of contents from the designer Baisotei Gengyo (1817–1880), who was well known for his book illustrations.

Shigenobu became Hiroshige's successor and adopted his name and seal in the spring of 1859. According to Asano, he may have celebrated the adoption of the name of Hiroshige II with a final composition for the series, which bears the date seal of the fourth month of 1859 (plate 119). Asano presumes that the publisher retained some of the first impressions of this print for himself, selling them with the table of contents as an album when the whole series was complete.

The Version in the Ota Memorial Museum of Art

The present series, kept in the Ota Memorial Museum of Art in Tokyo, consists exclusively of early impressions and was a rare bound album, recognizable as such by the holes for the binding threads and the worm-eaten creases outside the picture area. All the prints in this album evince the characteristics, highly esteemed by connoisseurs, of the early impressions. These include the colour gradations (*bokashi*) often used in considerable numbers on a single print as well as the different coloured square title cartouches in the format of poem prints (*shikishi*), which often take up the colours of the print, or suggest stylized cloud formations; sometimes these also allude to the theme of the picture, as in the print *Atagoshita and Yabu Lane* (plate 112), with yellow dabs as snowflakes. The quality of the paper, too, which can hardly be appreciated in photographic reproductions, is the best throughout. For these reasons the Ota series has been reproduced in its entirety many times in specialist Japanese publications.

The Order of the Individual Prints

The 118 individual prints, with the exception of Shigenobu's added print of 1859 (plate 119), were doubtless arranged retrospectively by Gengyo together with Sakanaya according to the four seasons. Fourty-two prints were assigned to spring, 30 to summer, 26 to autumn and a mere 20 to winter. Within the seasons, the arrangement is topographical and thematic. The first print had to depict Edo's hallmark, the Nihonbashi Bridge, which, in combination with

den Serientitel *Unterhaltsame Ergänzungen zu den Hundert Ansichten von Edo (Edo hyakkei yokyo*, Tafeln 78, 79). Im folgenden Monat kamen aber noch drei weitere Drucke hinzu, die wieder den üblichen Titel *Meisho Edo hyakkei* trugen (Tafeln 44, 72, 98). Diese insgesamt 115 Blätter werden von drei Holzschnitten mit einem Datumssiegel vom zehnten Monat des Jahres 1858 ergänzt (Tafeln 12, 41, 114), die allesamt nach Hiroshiges Tod am sechsten Tag des neunten Monats von den Zensoren gebilligt wurden. Neuere Forschungen des Ukiyoe-Spezialisten Asano Shūgō gehen davon aus, dass sein Schüler Shigenobu (1826–1869) diese Blätter auf Geheiß des Verlegers anhand von Skizzen Hiroshiges anfertigte. Kurz danach gab Sakanaya bei dem für seine Bucheinschläge bekannten Designer Baisotei Gengyo (1817–1880) ein Inhaltsverzeichnis in Auftrag.

Shigenobu wurde Hiroshiges Nachfolger und übernahm dessen Namen und Siegel im Frühjahr 1859. Laut Asano soll der nun als Hiroshige II auftretende Holzschnittmeister dieses Ereignis mit einem letzten Entwurf für die Serie gefeiert haben, der ein Datumssiegel des vierten Monats 1859 trägt (Tafel 119). Asano vermutet, dass der Verleger selbst einige der ersten Abzüge zurückhielt und sie nach Fertigstellung der gesamten Serie mit dem Inhaltsverzeichnis als Album verkaufte.

Das Exemplar des Ota Memorial Museum of Art

Die vorliegende Serie des Ota Memorial Museum of Art in Tokyo mit den durchweg frühen Drucken gehört zu solch einem seltenen, gebundenen Album, erkennbar an den Bindelöchern und wurmstichigen Falzen außerhalb des Bildes. Alle Blätter weisen die unter Kennern geschätzten Charakteristika der ersten Abzüge auf. Dazu gehören die – häufig auf einem einzigen Blatt – zahlreich angewendeten Farbgradierungen (*bokashi*) und die immer wieder unterschiedlich gefärbte quadratische Titelkartusche im Format eines Gedichtblattes (*shikishi*), die oft die Farben des Blattes aufnimmt, stilisierte Wolkenformationen suggeriert oder auch zuweilen auf das Bildthema anspielt. Im Blatt *Atagoshita und die Straße Yabukoji* (Tafel 112) etwa mit gelben Tupfen auf Schneeflocken. Auch die Qualität des Papiers, die sich in fotografischen Reproduktionen kaum nachvollziehen lässt, ist durchweg die allerbeste. Die Ota-Serie wurde denn auch in einschlägigen japanischen Publikationen in ihrer Gesamtheit mehrfach reproduziert.

Anordnung der Einzelblätter

Gengyo ordnete wohl zusammen mit Sakanaya retrospektiv die 118 Einzelblätter – mit Ausnahme von Shigenobus hinzugefügtem Blatt von 1859 (Tafel 119) – nach den vier Jahreszeiten. 42 Blätter schrieben sie dem Frühling zu, der Sommer umfasst 30, der Herbst 26 und der Winter lediglich 20 Blätter. Die Anordnung der Jahreszeiten folgt regionalen und thematischen Gesichtspunkten. Das erste Blatt musste die als Wahrzeichen Edos bekannte Brücke

Hiroshige a présenté 37 feuilles en 1856, l'année suivante, ce nombre passe à 71, et en 1858, année de la mort de l'artiste, 7 autres projets viendront encore s'y ajouter. Selon toute apparence, au septième mois de l'année 1858, Hiroshige et son éditeur avaient déjà prévu de clore la série, car deux feuilles revêtues du cachet correspondant à cette date portent un nouveau titre de série : *Compléments ludiques aux Cent Vues d'Edo* (*Edo hyakkei yokyo*, pl. 78, 79). Le mois suivant ne viendront plus s'ajouter que trois estampes portant à nouveau le titre habituel *Meisho Edo hyakkei* (pl. 44, 72, 98). Ce total de 115 feuilles est complété par trois estampes portant un cachet daté du dixième mois de l'année 1858 (pl. 12, 41, 114). Ces feuilles ont donc toutes été approuvées après la mort de Hiroshige le sixième jour du neuvième mois de cette année. Les recherches récentes du spécialiste de l'ukiyo-e Asano Shūgō permettent de penser que son élève Shigenobu (1826–1869) créa ces feuilles à la demande de l'éditeur en s'appuyant sur des esquisses de Hiroshige. Peu après, Sakanaya commanda une table des matières au designer Baisotei Gengyo (1817–1880), célèbre pour ses pages de garde.

Après la mort de Hiroshige, Shigenobu lui succéda, reprenant son nom et son sceau au printemps 1859. Selon Asano, le maître estampiste apparaissant désormais sous le nom « Hiroshige II » aurait célébré l'évènement en créant une dernière estampe pour la série, estampe qui porte un cachet de datation du quatrième mois de l'année 1859 (pl. 119). Asano suppose par ailleurs que l'éditeur conserva quelques-uns des premiers tirages et qu'il les vendit une fois la série achevée sous forme d'album augmenté de la table des matières.

L'exemplaire de l'Ota Memorial Museum of Art

Composée exclusivement des premiers tirages, la série de l'Ota Memorial Museum of Art de Tokyo reproduite dans le présent ouvrage est un de ces rares albums reliés, reconnaissable aux percements de la reliure et aux pliures piquées en bordure de feuille. Toutes les feuilles dénotent les caractéristiques des premiers tirages si prisés des connaisseurs. Font partie de ces caractéristiques les dégradés de couleurs souvent nombreux utilisés dans une seule et même feuille (*bokashi*) et les différents tons des cartouches de titre gravés au format d'une feuille de poésie (*shikishi*). Ces cartouches font souvent écho aux couleurs de la feuille, suggérant une formation nuageuse ou se référant parfois directement au sujet, comme on le voit par exemple dans la feuille *Atagoshita et la rue Yabukōji* (pl. 112), où de petites touches jaunes évoquent les flocons de neige. La qualité du papier, presque imperceptible dans les reproductions photographiques, est uniment la meilleure. La série de l'Ota Museum a de ce fait été reproduite plusieurs fois intégralement dans les ouvrages spécialisés japonais.

10

10

Edo Castle and Mount Fuji in the background, is one of Edo's best-known views. Four excursion destinations in the north of Edo (plates 14–17), five views of the northern stretch of the Sumida River (plates 34–37, 39) and three conspicuously flowering plants in the foreground (plates 63–65) are, for instance, collated to create subseries. But often enough, two prints that show the same motif from different viewpoints are placed adjacent to each other: in the first the motif is in the distance, and in the second it is in the foreground, as in the case of the Kanda Myōjin shrine on *Yatsukōji, Inside Sujikai Gate* and *Sunrise at Kanda Myōjin Shrine* (ill. 10, plates 9, 10). This was how the prints were ordered in the albums bound together shortly after the completion of the series, in other words also in the copy presented here, and this is the order generally still adhered to today.

It must be said, however, that Hiroshige oriented himself neither to the seasons nor to topography when creating the series. In numerous compositions, it is impossible to determine with certainty what the season is. Indeed, Gengyo and Sakanaya assigned the print *The Original Fuji in Meguro* (ills. 26, 27, plate 25) to spring, although it shows autumn foliage and not cherry blossoms. It is apparent, then, that even by the mid-19th century, the conventional ways of depicting the four seasons with their lyrical associations had already lost some of their importance.

The City of Edo and its People

When the founder of the Tokugawa dynasty, Ieyasu (1542–1616), occupied Edo in 1590, the city was still a country town surrounded by marshy land. After becoming shogun in 1603, he had the local castle comprehensively rebuilt, and soon the city began to develop into a political centre, and increasingly a place of commercial importance. Its cultural achievements began to unfold only after the catastrophic Meireki fire of 1657, which claimed more than 100,000 lives and razed both the city and the castle to the ground in a matter of hours. Reconstruction, however, proceeded rapidly and in a well-organized fashion.

Edo at this time covered 44 square kilometres (17 square miles), making it more than twice the size of Japan's second-biggest city, Kyoto. By 1725, it had become half as big again, while its population, at more than a million, was the largest of any city in the world. By the mid-19th century, when the *One Hundred Famous Views of Edo* appeared, it had an area of almost 80 square kilometres (30 square miles) and an estimated population of up to two million.

More than half of these people were craftsmen and merchants, but they inhabited only 21 per cent of the total area. These two estates were regarded as the lowest ranking in the Confucian four-estate system (*shinōkōshō*) introduced by the Tokugawa dynasty, the top rank of the social hierarchy comprising the warrior

Nihonbashi zeigen, die in Kombination mit dem Edo-Schloss und dem Berg Fuji im Hintergrund zu den bekanntesten Ansichten Edos gehört. Vier Ausflugsziele im nördlichen Edo (Tafeln 14–17), fünf Blicke auf den nördlichen Fluss Sumidagawa (Tafeln 34–37, 39) oder drei auffällig blühende Pflanzen im Vordergrund (Tafeln 63–65) werden zu Bildgruppen zusammengestellt. Häufig aber sind zwei Blätter nacheinander angeordnet, die ein Gebäude oder Objekt aus verschiedenen Perspektiven darstellen: zunächst in der Ferne, dann als Vordergrundmotiv, wie im Falle des Schreins Kanda Myōjin auf den Blättern *Die Straße Yatsukōji innerhalb des Tores Sujikai* und *Sonnenaufgang am Schrein Kanda Myōjin* (Abb. 10, Tafeln 9, 10). In dieser Reihenfolge wurden die Blätter in den kurz nach Fertigstellung der Serie gebundenen Alben angeordnet, also auch in dem hier vorgestellten Exemplar, angeordnet, und so hat sie sich bis heute durchgesetzt.

Allerdings orientierte sich Hiroshige bei seiner Arbeit weder an Jahreszeiten noch an regionalen Gesichtspunkten. Die Jahreszeiten können in zahlreichen Kompositionen denn auch nicht eindeutig identifiziert werden. Tatsächlich ignorierten Gengyo und Sakanaya in ihrer Einteilung das Herbstlaub im Blatt *Der Ursprüngliche Fuji in Meguro* (Abb. 26, 27, Tafel 25) und interpretierten es als Kirschblüten. Folglich schrieben sie den Holzschnitt dem Frühling statt dem Herbst zu. Es zeigt sich also, dass schon Mitte des 19. Jahrhunderts die konventionellen Darstellungsformen der vier Jahreszeiten mit ihren lyrischen Assoziationen an Bedeutung verloren hatten.

Die Stadt Edo und ihre Bevölkerung

Nachdem der Gründer der Tokugawa-Dynastie, Ieyasu (1542–1616), 1590 in das noch ländliche und von sumpfigem Flachland umgebene Edo eingezogen war und bald nach seiner Ernennung zum Shogun 1603 das dortige Schloss grundlegend hatte umbauen lassen, entwickelte sich die Stadt zu einem politischen Zentrum mit zunehmend auch wirtschaftlicher Bedeutung. Ihre kulturelle Ausstrahlungskraft entfaltete die Stadt erst nach dem verheerenden Meireki-Feuer von 1657. Es forderte mehr als 100 000 Tote und legte die Stadt und das große Edo-Schloss binnen weniger Stunden in Schutt und Asche. Der Wiederaufbau erfolgte jedoch schnell und gut organisiert.

Edo war in dieser Zeit mit 44 Quadratkilometern Fläche mehr als doppelt so groß wie die zweitgrößte japanische Stadt Kyoto. 1725 zählte Edo auf der anderthalbfachen Fläche über eine Million Einwohner und war damit die größte Stadt weltweit. Mitte des 19. Jahrhunderts, als die *Hundert Ansichten* erschienen, lebten auf knapp 80 Quadratkilometern Schätzungen zufolge anderthalb bis zwei Millionen Menschen.

Mehr als die Hälfte waren Handwerker und Kaufleute, die sich auf nur 21 Prozent der Stadtfläche drängten. Sie galten als die beiden

Organisation des Cent Vues

C'est sans doute avec la collaboration de Sakanaya que Gengyo a organisé rétrospectivement l'ensemble des 118 vues selon les quatre saisons – exceptée la feuille ajoutée en 1859 par Shigenobu (pl. 119). 42 estampes ont ainsi été attribuées au printemps, 30 à l'été, 26 à l'automne et 20 seulement à l'hiver. L'organisation au sein de ces sections suit des points de vue régionaux et thématiques. La première feuille de chaque section devait présenter le pont Nihonbashi, emblème d'Edo qui, combiné avec le château d'Edo et le mont Fuji à l'arrière-plan, fait partie des vues les plus célèbres de la série. Quatre buts d'excursions au nord d'Edo (pl. 14–17), cinq vues du cours nord de la rivière Sumidagawa (pl. 34–37, 39) ou trois plantes en fleurs remarquables au premier plan (pl. 63–65) forment des sous-groupes. On trouve toutefois souvent réunies deux feuilles successives montrant un édifice ou un sujet à partir de points de vue différents : de loin d'abord, puis comme motif au premier plan, comme c'est par exemple le cas du sanctuaire Kanda Myōjin dans les feuilles *La rue Yatsukōji dans l'enceinte de la porte Sujikai* et *Le sanctuaire Kanda Myōjin au soleil levant* (ill. 10, pl. 9, 10). C'est dans cet ordre que les feuilles furent classées dans les albums reliés une fois la série close, et donc aussi dans l'exemplaire reproduit dans le présent ouvrage ; enfin, c'est aussi cet ordre qui s'est imposé aujourd'hui.

Reste que Hiroshige n'a nullement travaillé en fonction des saisons ou de points de vue régionalistes. D'ailleurs, dans bien des feuilles, les saisons restent difficiles à déterminer. De fait, dans leur classement, Gengyo et Sakanaya ont ignoré le feuillage d'automne qu'on peut voir dans la feuille *Le Fuji original à Meguro* (ill. 26, 27; pl. 25), l'interprétant comme des fleurs de cerisiers, et c'est ainsi que l'estampe a été intégrée dans la section printemps au lieu de la section automne. On voit donc que dès le milieu du XIXᵉ siècle, les formes traditionnelles de représentation des quatre saisons et de leurs associations poétiques avaient perdu de leur validité.

La ville d'Edo et sa population

Après que le fondateur de la dynastie Tokugawa Ieyasu (1542–1616) se fut établi à Edo en 1590, région rurale entourée d'une plaine marécageuse, et qu'il eut fait transformer de fond en comble le château local une fois nommé shogun en 1603, la ville devint progressivement un centre politique et prit aussi une importance croissante comme centre économique. En revanche, le rayonnement culturel d'Edo ne débutera qu'après l'incendie dévastateur de Meireki (1657). En quelques heures à peine, cet incendie réduisit en cendres la ville et le grand château, faisant plus de 100 000 victimes. La reconstruction fut toutefois bien organisée et menée tambour battant.

S'étendant sur une superficie de 44 kilomètres carrés, Edo était alors plus de deux fois plus grande que Kyoto, la deuxième ville du Japon. En 1725, la surface d'Edo s'était étendue de 50 pour cent, et

11

UTAGAWA HIROSHIGE

Yamashita-chō
Hibiya
Soto-Sakurada

Hibiya and
Soto-Sakurada
Seen from
Yamashita-chō

Hibiya und
Soto-Sakurada
von Yamashita-chō
aus

Vue de Hibiya et de
Soto-Sakurada
depuis Yamashita-chō

Plate/Tafel/planche 3

P. 21
Detail from plate 49
Detail aus Tafel 49
Détail de planche 49

11

caste and the second the farmers. The system did not extend to either the imperial court aristocracy or to the *hinin* and *eta*, who were classified as "non-human". Officially, importance was attached to rigid separation of the estates, and sumptuary laws were passed to keep the merchants, who were becoming de facto ever more dominant both culturally and economically, in check. In fact, however, the system was permeable, and the estates were broadly based in respect of the social and economic status of their members. The craftsmen and merchants of Edo were settled in the quarters named after their particular trade or profession. These were largely situated to the east and north-east of Edo Castle and the indigo dyers, for example, lived in the quarters known as *kon'ya-chō* (plate 6).

In 1635, the government instituted a system of alternate residence duty (*sankin kōtai*) in Edo. The feudal lords (*daimyō*) were required to spend every second year in the city and to leave their families there, in effect as possible hostages. Thus this pre-modern city also became a centre of cultural innovation.

The lords were obliged to maintain more than one residence in Edo, the number depending on the size of their fiefs. These residences often occupy a prominent position in the prints of this series, e.g. that of Nabeshima Kansō (1814–1871), one of the richest daimyōs, whose feudal estate was on the island of Kyūshū (ill. 11, plate 3). The daimyōs were thus prevented from forging any political or military alliances in the provinces, and were forced to spend a great deal of money, which also benefitted the city. Depending on a daimyō's status and financial resources, the processions, which led him from his provincial fief to Edo, could comprise several thousand retainers and last for weeks. Thus there developed along the main highways a flourishing economy with guest houses, hotels, brothels and stations where horses could be changed.

The warrior estate (*buke*) likewise comprised a broad spectrum of ranks, privileges and economic power. Lower-ranking samurai inhabited almost a quarter of the city of Edo, while the shogun and the daimyō military aristocracy occupied more than two-fifths of the municipal area, while nearly 15 per cent of the total area of the city was taken up by temples, like the extensive Kan'eiji in Ueno to the north of Edo Castle, which was under the shogun's protection, and the Zōjōji in the south of the city, along with numerous other religious sites.

One Hundred Famous Views of Edo *as Pictures of Current Affairs*

In agreement with his publisher, Hiroshige reacted to current events in the city in many prints. In his latest investigations, the ukiyo-e scholar Harashida Minoru characterizes the woodblock prints as "images of current affairs". The series was created in the middle of the politically and socially most turbulent years in Japan-

niedersten Stände des mit der Tokugawa-Dynastie eingerichteten konfuzianischen Vierständesystems (*shinōkōshō*), das dem Kriegerstand den obersten Rang und den Bauern den zweiten Rang in der Gesellschaftshierarchie einräumte. Ausgeschlossen waren dabei die kaiserliche Hofaristokratie und die als „Nicht-Menschen" klassifizierten *hinin* und *eta*. Offiziell wurde zwar auf die Trennung der Stände geachtet, und es wurden Luxusgesetze erlassen, um die de facto ökonomisch und kulturell immer dominierendere Kaufmannsschicht in Schranken zu halten. Tatsächlich aber waren die Stände durchlässig und hinsichtlich der gesellschaftlichen und wirtschaftlichen Stellung ihrer Angehörigen von großer Bandbreite. Die Handwerker und Kaufleute waren in Edo je nach Berufsgruppe in nach ihnen benannten Quartieren angesiedelt, die Indigofärber z. B. in den sogenannten Färbervierteln, den *kon'ya-chō* (Tafel 6). Diese lagen großenteils östlich und nordöstlich des Edo-Schlosses.

Im Jahr 1635 richtete die Regierung ein System der alternierenden Residenzpflicht (*sankin kōtai*) in Edo ein. Die Feudalfürsten (*daimyo*) mussten demnach jedes zweite Jahr in Edo verbringen und ihre Familien dort quasi als Geiseln zurücklassen. So wurde diese vormoderne Megastadt auch zum Umschlagplatz kultureller Neuerungen.

Die Fürsten waren je nach Größe ihres Feudalgebietes gezwungen, mehrere Residenzen in Edo zu unterhalten; sie sind auf den Holzschnitten der Serie häufig prominent zu sehen, z. B. diejenige von Nabeshima Kansō (1814–1871), einem der reichsten Daimyō auf der Insel Kyūshū (Abb. 11, Tafel 3). Die Daimyō konnten so keine militärischen oder politischen Allianzen in den Regionen schmieden und waren gezwungen, viel Geld ausgeben, was auch der Stadt Edo zugute kam. Je nach Rang und finanzieller Potenz des Daimyō konnten die Prozessionen, die ihn aus seiner Provinz nach Edo führten, mehrere tausend Gefolgsleute umfassen und Wochen dauern. So entwickelte sich entlang der Hauptverkehrswege eine blühende Wirtschaft mit Gaststätten, Hotels, Freudenhäusern und Pferdeaustauschstationen.

Der Kriegerstand (*buke*) umfasste ebenfalls eine große Bandbreite an Rängen, Privilegien und Wirtschaftskraft. Niedere Samurai nahmen fast 24 Prozent der Stadt Edo ein, während der Shogun und die Militäraristokratie der Feudalherren über 40 Prozent des Stadtraumes besetzten. Tempel wie der vom Shogun protegierte weiträumige Kan'eiji in Ueno nördlich des Edo-Schlosses und der Zōjōji im Süden belegten zusammen mit den zahlreichen anderen religiösen Stätten Edos knapp 15 Prozent der Fläche.

Die Hundert Ansichten *als Bilder von Tagesereignissen*

Im Einvernehmen mit seinem Verleger reagierte Hiroshige in vielen Blättern auf aktuelle Ereignisse in der Stadt. Der Ukiyoe-Forscher Harashida Minoru charakterisiert die Holzschnitte in seinen neues-

sa population de plus d'un million d'habitants en faisait la plus grande ville du monde. Au milieu du XIXᵉ siècle, c'est-à-dire à l'époque de la parution des *Cent Vues*, un million et demi à deux millions d'habitants – selon les estimations – vivent sur une superficie de quelque 80 kilomètres carrés.

Plus de la moitié sont des artisans et des marchands qui n'occupent que 21 pour cent de cette surface. Ils appartiennent aux deux classes inférieures dans le système à quatre classes (*shinōkōshō*) institué par la dynastie Tokugawa selon la doctrine confucianiste, système dans lequel la classe des guerriers est au sommet de la hiérarchie sociale, les paysans occupant le deuxième rang. Sont exclus de ce système l'aristocratie de la cour impériale ainsi que les *hinin* et *eta* considérés comme des « non hommes ». Officiellement, la division des classes était respectée, et des lois restreignant le luxe furent promulguées pour empêcher l'ascension d'une classe marchande de plus en plus influente à la fois économiquement et culturellement. Dans les faits, les classes étaient toutefois perméables et couvraient un vaste éventail en termes de position sociale et économique. Selon leur branche particulière, les artisans et les marchands résidaient dans des quartiers d'Edo nommés d'après les différents métiers ; ainsi, les teinturiers de l'indigo vivaient dans celui appelé *kon'ya-chō* (pl. 6). Ces quartiers majoritairement situés à l'est et au nord-est du château d'Edo.

En 1635, le gouvernement instaura un système d'obligation de résidence alternée (*sankin kōtai*) à Edo : les seigneurs féodaux (*daimyō*) devaient vivre une année sur deux dans la capitale et en quelque sorte laisser leur famille en otage à Edo. C'est ainsi que la mégalopole proto-moderne devint aussi une plaque tournante des innovations culturelles.

Selon l'importance de leur fief, les seigneurs étaient aussi contraints d'entretenir plusieurs résidences à Edo ; celles-ci apparaissent souvent en place proéminente dans les *Cent Vues* – par exemple celle de Nabeshima Kansō (1814–1871), un des plus riches daimyōs, sur l'île de Kyūshū (ill. 11, pl. 3). Toutes ces dispositions étaient destinées à empêcher les daimyōs de forger des alliances politiques ou militaires et les contraignaient à dépenser des fortunes, ce qui profita aussi à l'essor de la ville. Selon le rang et la puissance financière des daimyos, les cortèges qui les accompagnaient entre leur province et Edo pouvaient compter plusieurs milliers de personnes et le voyage prendre plusieurs semaines. Une économie florissante allait ainsi se développer tout au long des principales voies de circulation, avec des restaurants, des hôtels, maisons de tolérance et relais de poste.

La classe des guerriers (*buke*) comprenait elle-même toute une série de rangs, de privilèges et de puissance économique. Les samouraïs inférieurs occupaient presque 24 pour cent de la superficie d'Edo, tandis que le shogun et l'aristocratie militaire des seigneurs féodaux en occupaient 40 pour cent. Avec les nombreux autres lieux sacrés, les temples protégés par le shogun – par exemple le vaste Kan'eiji d'Ueno, au nord du château d'Edo – ou des temples comme le Zōjōji au sud occupaient presque 15 pour cent de la surface totale de la ville.

12

UTAGAWA HIROSHIGE

P. 22

Detail from plate 45

Detail aus Tafel 45

Détail de planche 45

Takanawa Ushimachi

Ushimachi in Takanawa

Ushimachi in Takanawa

Ushimachi à Takanawa

Plate/Tafel/planche 81

12

ese history, and it would be surprising if the epoch-making events of this period had not been reflected in the prints.

Only three years before the series was launched, in July 1853, the American commodore Matthew Perry (1794–1858) had landed his fleet in Uraga (in what is today the city of Yokosuka in Kanagawa Prefecture) and presented the Tokugawa government with a letter from the American president Millard Fillmore (1800–1874) with the demand that after more than 200 years, Japanese harbours be opened to foreign commercial traffic once more. Just one year later, he returned to neighbouring Yokohama and concluded a "peace treaty" that ultimately led to the "unequal treaties" of the seventh month of 1858. This "Treaty of Amity and Commerce" of the Ansei era, also referred to as the "Harris Treaty" after the US negotiator, which sanctioned the opening of five harbours to trade, was followed by similar treaties with Holland, Russia, Great Britain and Italy. Perry's arrival triggered fears of a military conflict, and some prints depict preparations for just such an eventuality. These included the earth ramparts (*daiba*) surmounted by cannons that were rapidly erected around Edo Bay, which Hiroshige skilfully integrated into individual compositions without focusing on them (ill. 12, plates 81, 83, 108).

Then, in 1854, the area around Osaka and the imperial capital Kyoto was shaken by a major earthquake, and the island of Shikoku by another. Finally, on the evening of the second day of the tenth month of 1855, just four months before the first five designs for the *One Hundred Famous Views of Edo*, Edo itself was struck by the so-called Ansei earthquake, which had an estimated strength of nearly 7 on the Richter scale: its epicentre was directly beneath the densely populated merchant and craftsman neighbourhoods in the east of the city. Some 10,000 people lost their lives as a result of falling debris and the firestorm that followed. Almost half of those killed were merchants and craftsmen. One-tenth of the victims were in the city's most densely populated area: the pleasure quarter Shin-Yoshiwara, with its 10,000 or so prostitutes and their clients, was completely razed to the ground. The quarters to the south of Hiroshige's house on Kano Shindō street were likewise destroyed by the flames, as were the buildings around Sakanaya's shop.

The printing industry reacted immediately to the disaster. Sakanaya is said to have made his money with prints dating from this period, before venturing to issue the *One Hundred Famous Views of Edo*, his first large-scale publication. Numerous single prints with illustrated novelties, known as *kawaraban*, a prototype of modern newspapers, were already selling very well among the inhabitants of Edo. They wanted information about the state of the various neighbourhoods, and were looking for reasons for the disaster, which in some prints was explained by the absence or the influence of certain deities. Many woodblock prints contained hidden political allusions. In order to deliver this "news", but also out of political considerations, the publishers circumvented the censors. The sensitivity of these depictions of the devastation can be judged by the fate of the three-volume illustrated book *Reports of Things*

ten Untersuchungen denn auch als „Bilder von Tagesereignissen". Die Entstehung der Serie fällt in die politisch und sozial turbulentesten Jahre der Geschichte Japans, und es wäre verwunderlich, wenn die epochemachenden Begebenheiten dieser Zeit nicht Eingang in die Blätter gefunden hätten.

Nur drei Jahre vor Beginn der Serie, im Juli 1853, war der amerikanische Admiral Matthew Perry (1794–1858) mit seiner Flotte in Uraga (in der heutigen Stadt Yokosuka, Präfektur Kanagawa) an Land gegangen und hatte der Tokugawa-Regierung einen Brief des amerikanischen Präsidenten Millard Fillmore (1800–1874) mit der Forderung überreicht, nach mehr als 200 Jahren der Abschottung die Häfen für den Handel zu öffnen. Schon ein Jahr danach kam er zurück in das benachbarte Yokohama und schloss einen „Friedensvertrag", der schließlich zu den „Ungleichen Verträgen" vom siebten Monat des Jahres 1858 führte. Diesen sogenannten Fünfländervertrag der Ära Ansei, mit dem fünf Häfen für den Handel geöffnet wurden, schloss das Shogunat mit Amerika, Holland, Russland, Großbritannien und Italien. Die Ankunft Perrys löste Angst vor einem militärischen Konflikt aus, und in einigen Blättern sind die Vorkehrungen gegen einen Angriff zu erkennen. Dazu gehören die mit Kanonen bestückten Erdwälle (*daiba*), die man schnell in der Edo-Bucht aufbaute und die Hiroshige geschickt in einzelne Kompositionen integrierte, ohne sie in den Vordergrund zu stellen (Abb. 12, Tafeln 81, 83, 108).

1854 erschütterten dann zwei schwere Erdbeben die Gegend um die Kaiserhauptstadt Kyoto und Osaka sowie Shikoku. Am Abend des zweiten Tages des zehnten Monats im Jahr 1855, nur vier Monate vor den ersten fünf Entwürfen der *Hundert Ansichten*, folgte schließlich das Ansei-Erdbeben von Edo mit einer geschätzten Stärke von knapp 7 auf der Richterskala und dem Epizentrum direkt unter den von Kaufleuten und Handwerkern dicht besiedelten Stadtvierteln im Osten. An die 10 000 Menschen fanden in den Trümmern und bei der folgenden Feuersbrunst den Tod. Knapp die Hälfte aller Opfer waren Händler und Kaufleute. Das wohl am dichtesten bevölkerte Freudenviertel Shin-Yoshiwara mit seinen um die 10 000 Prostituierten – und ihren zahlreichen Kunden – brannte völlig ab; dabei kam ein Zehntel der Erdbebenopfer ums Leben. Die südlich von Hiroshiges Domizil an der Straße Kano Shindō gelegenen Quartiere wurden ebenfalls Opfer der Flammen, und auch um den Laden Sakanayas herum lagen Gebäude in Schutt und Asche.

Die Druckindustrie reagierte sofort auf das Desaster. Von Sakanaya heißt es, er habe mit Drucken aus dieser Zeit sein Geld gemacht, bevor er sich an die *Hundert berühmten Ansichten von Edo* als erste große Publikation wagte. Zahlreiche *kawaraban* genannte Einblattdrucke mit illustrierten Neuigkeiten – ein Prototyp der modernen Zeitungen – fanden reißenden Absatz unter den Bewohnern von Edo. Sie wollten sich über den Zustand der verschiedenen Stadtviertel informieren und suchten nach Gründen für die Katastrophe, die in einigen Drucken mit der Abwesenheit oder dem Wirken bestimmter Gottheiten erklärt wird. Viele Holzschnitte enthalten versteckte politische Anspielungen. Um aktuell diese

Les Cent Vues *comme images d'actualité*

En concertation avec son éditeur, Hiroshige a réagi dans bien des feuilles à des faits d'actualité de la capitale. Dans ses dernières recherches, le spécialiste de l'ukiyo-e Harashida Minoru qualifie les estampes d'« images d'actualité ». La réalisation de la série coïncide avec les années les plus turbulentes de l'histoire du Japon, et il serait bien étonnant que les événements les plus marquants de l'époque n'y aient laissé aucune trace.

Trois ans seulement avant le début de la série, en juillet 1853, le commodore américain Matthew Perry (1794–1858) avait débarqué à Uraga (aujourd'hui Yokohama, préfecture de Kanagawa) avec sa flotte, et avait transmis au gouvernement Tokugawa une missive du président des États-Unis Millard Fillmore (1800–1874) qui exigeait l'ouverture au commerce des ports japonais fermés depuis plus de deux siècles. Un an plus tard, il revenait à Yokohama et concluait un « traité de paix » qui allait déboucher sur les « traités inégaux » du septième mois de l'année 1858. Ce traité dit « des cinq nations » de l'ère Ansei, par lequel cinq ports furent ouverts au commerce étranger, fut conclu entre le shogunat d'une part, et les États-Unis, la Hollande, la Russie, le Portugal, la Grande-Bretagne et l'Italie d'autre part. L'arrivée de Perry déclencha la crainte d'un conflit militaire, et c'est ainsi que quelques feuilles montrent les mesures défensives prises en prévision d'une éventuelle attaque. En font partie les levées de terre (*daiba*) armées de canons qui furent édifiées à la hâte dans la baie d'Edo et que Hiroshige intégra habilement dans certaines compositions – sans toutefois jamais les présenter au premier plan (ill. 12, pl. 81, 83, 108).

De plus, en 1854, deux séismes de forte magnitude secouèrent les régions de Kyoto, la ville impériale, d'Osaka et de Shikoku. Dans la soirée du deuxième jour du dixième mois de l'année 1855 enfin, quatre mois seulement après les cinq premiers projets réalisés pour les *Cent Vues*, suivit le séisme dit de l'ère Ansei à Edo, d'une magnitude estimée de 7 sur l'échelle de Richter, avec un épicentre situé directement sous les quartiers des marchands et artisans fortement peuplés de la ville. Quelque 10 000 personnes trouvèrent la mort dans les décombres et les incendies consécutifs au séisme. Une petite moitié étaient des marchands et des commerçants. Le quartier des plaisirs Shin-Yoshiwara, le plus peuplé avec ses quelque 10 000 prostituées – et leurs nombreux clients –, fut entièrement dévasté par les flammes, faisant un dixième des victimes. Les quartiers situés au sud du domicile de Hiroshige, près de la rue Kano Shindō, furent également ravagés par des incendies, et autour de la boutique de Sakanaya, de nombreuses maisons furent réduites en cendres.

L'industrie de l'imprimerie réagit immédiatement au désastre. De Sakanaya, on dit qu'il aurait fait sa fortune avec des estampes datant de cette époque – avant de se lancer dans sa première grande publication avec les *Cent Vues célèbres d'Edo*. De nombreux tirages isolés montrant des nouvelles illustrées, appelées *kawaraban* – prototypes des journaux modernes – se vendirent

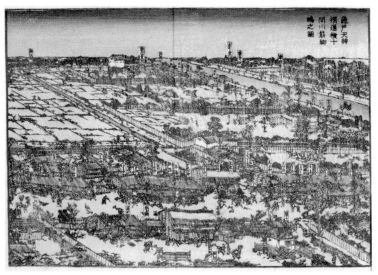

13

14

Seen and Heard in the Ansei Era (Ansei kenmonshi), which appeared in the fourth month of 1856 (ills. 13, 14). The text, compiled by the writer Kanagaki Robun (1829–1894), contains reports of damage, earthquake measurements, passages dealing with heroic rescues, announcements of business openings and advertisements for remedies of all kinds. The illustrations by the woodblock masters are correspondingly varied. In a panorama on the folding picture at the end of volume I, reproduced here, Utagawa Kunichika (1835–1900) strikingly depicts the destruction east of the Sumida River, including the neighbourhoods of Kameido-chō, Yanagishima-machi and Daichi-chō to Oshiagemura. The names and places given in the cartouches lend a degree of reality designed to illustrate vividly the devastating extent of the disaster. At the same time, Kunichika depicts the range of human reactions to the events: some people are fleeing, others are trying to help each other, others again have sat down to await the end. The publication became an immediate bestseller, whereupon the very next month all those involved in the production were summoned to the responsible official and subjected to a heavy fine. The owner of the woodblocks from which the prints were made was even banished from the city. The authorities classified the book as opposition to the Tokugawa, as it showed the government in a bad light: according to Confucian principles, good governance was in harmony with nature.

Earthquakes were not experienced only as disasters. For certain trades, such as carpenters, they provided a chance for a new start. While nothing of the human tragedy is to be seen in the *One Hundred Famous Views of Edo*, this is partly because Hiroshige is presenting a reconstructed Edo, not least in order to inform citizens about new events (plates 13, 58, 99). However, he rarely places the repaired or newly constructed buildings in the centre, preferring to arrange them in the background. The shogunate's boathouses in Atake, for example, which had been rebuilt only in the eighth month of 1857, a month before the date of the famous print *Sudden Shower over Shin-Ōhashi Bridge and Atake* (plate 58), are merely hinted at as three white triangles on the opposite bank. With pictures like these, Hiroshige was challenging the knowledge of the local population, providing them with something to talk about, while at the same time showing outsiders an intact Edo. Commercial interests may have been an important motive, but any opposition to the shogunate would have been alien to Hiroshige, the conservative samurai.

In the eighth month of 1856, while reconstruction was in full swing, the city was struck by a devastating typhoon. While this claimed "only" 60 lives and left another 90 or so injured, large areas of the city adjoining Edo Bay were flooded, numerous rivers and canals burst their banks and took with them buildings that had escaped the earthquake and resulting firestorm. Edo's waterways, which in Hiroshige's series play a central role, not least from the point of view of colour, doubtless did not always look so idyllic or well cared-for as the prints would have us believe.

Neuigkeiten zu liefern, aber auch aus politischen Überlegungen heraus umgingen die Verleger die Zensoren. Wie brisant die Darstellungen der Zerstörung waren, lässt sich aus dem Schicksal des im vierten Monat 1856 erschienenen dreibändigen illustrierten Buches *Berichte über Gesehenes und Gehörtes aus der Ära Ansei (Ansei kenmonshi)* ersehen (Abb. 13, 14). Der vom Schriftsteller Kanagaki Robun (1829–1894) zusammengestellte Text enthält Schadensberichte, Erdbebenmessungen, Passagen über heldenhafte Retter, Ankündigungen von Geschäftseröffnungen und Werbung für allerlei Heilmittel. Die Illustrationen der beteiligten Holzschnittmeister sind entsprechend variationsreich. Auf den hier abgebildeten ausfaltbaren Seiten am Ende des ersten Bandes gibt Utagawa Kunichika (1835–1900) in einem Panorama die Zerstörungen östlich des Flusses Sumidagawa mit den Vierteln Kameidochō, Yanagishima-machi und Daichi-chō bis Oshiagemura eindrücklich wieder. Die auf den Kartuschen angegebenen Namen und Orte verleihen dem Anblick einen Realitätsgrad, der das verheerende Ausmaß der Katastrophe plastisch vor Augen führen soll. Gleichzeitig schildert Kunichika die unterschiedlichen menschlichen Reaktionen auf das Desaster: Einige fliehen, andere versuchen sich gegenseitig zu helfen oder setzen sich hin und warten das Ende ab. Die Publikation wurde sofort zum Kassenschlager, woraufhin es bereits im fünften Monat zu einer Vorladung des zuständigen Dienstleiters und einer empfindlichen Geldstrafe für alle an der Produktion Beteiligten kam. Der Besitzer der Holzplatten wurde gar der Stadt verwiesen. Die Behörden werteten das Buch als Äußerung gegen die Tokugawa, denn es warf ein schlechtes Licht auf die Regierung: Nach konfuzianischen Prinzipien stand eine gute Herrschaft im Einklang mit der Natur.

Erdbeben wurden nicht nur als Naturkatastrophen erlebt, sie boten auch verschiedenen Berufen, u. a. den Zimmerleuten, eine Chance zum Neuanfang. Während von der menschlichen Tragödie in den *Hundert Ansichten* nichts zu sehen ist, präsentiert Hiroshige darin auch ein wieder aufgebautes Edo, nicht zuletzt, um die Bevölkerung über neue Ereignisse zu unterrichten (Tafeln 13, 58, 99). Er stellt die reparierten oder neu errichteten Gebäude jedoch selten ins Zentrum, sondern rückt sie in den Hintergrund. Die shogunalen Bootshäuser in Atake etwa, die erst im achten Monat 1857, einen Monat vor dem Zensorensiegel des berühmten Blattes *Plötzlicher Schauer über die Brücke Shin-Ōhashi und Atake* (Tafel 58), wiedererrichtet worden waren sind als drei weiße Dreiecke am gegenüberliegenden Ufer nur schemenhaft angedeutet. Mit solchen Bildern forderte Hiroshige das Wissen der örtlichen Bevölkerung heraus und bot ihnen Gesprächsstoff, während er den Auswärtigen das unversehrte Edo vor Augen führte. Kommerzielle Interessen mögen ein wichtiger Beweggrund gewesen sein, aber dem konservativen Samurai Hiroshige war wohl auch eine oppositionelle Haltung gegenüber dem Shogunat fremd.

Mitten in den Wiederaufbauarbeiten wurde die Millionenstadt im achten Monat des Jahres 1856 von einem vernichtenden Taifun heimgesucht. Dieser ließ zwar „nur" um die 60 Tote und etwa 90 Verletzte zurück, aber weite Teile der an die Edo-Bucht grenzenden

comme des petits pains parmi les habitants d'Edo qui voulaient s'informer de l'état des différents quartiers de la ville et qui cherchaient des raisons à la catastrophe, raisons que les dites feuilles expliquaient par l'absence ou la volonté de certaines divinités. De nombreuses estampes de cette époque contiennent aussi des allusions politiques voilées. Pour pouvoir livrer des nouvelles fraîches, mais aussi pour des raisons politiques, les éditeurs contournèrent la censure. La teneur hautement explosive de ces images ressort notamment des rapports sur l'étendue des dégâts, des mesures d'intensité du séisme, des récits d'actions héroïques, des annonces d'ouvertures de magasins et des réclames pour toutes sortes de remèdes. La diversité des illustrations réalisées par les maîtres estampistes qui participèrent à l'ouvrage est à l'avenant. Dans les pages en accordéon qui referment le premier tome et que nous reproduisons ici, Utagawa Kunichika (1835–1900) livre un panorama impressionnant des dévastations à l'est de la rivière Sumidagawa, avec les quartiers Kameido-chō, Yanagishima-machi et Daichi-chō jusqu'à Oshiagemura. Les noms de personnes et de lieux indiqués dans les cartouches confèrent au paysage un degré de réalisme qui devait permettre au spectateur de se faire une idée très concrète de l'étendue des dégâts. En même temps, Kunichika dépeint aussi les différentes réactions humaines au désastre : certains prennent la fuite, d'autres tentent de s'entraider ou restent assis en attendant la fin. Du jour au lendemain, cette publication devint un best-seller, sur quoi, dès le mois suivant, le directeur de publication fut convoqué par les autorités, qui infligèrent de lourdes amendes à tous ceux qui avaient participé à sa production. Le propriétaire des bois d'impression fut même banni de la ville. Les autorités considéraient le livre comme une rébellion contre les Tokugawa, car il jetait un piètre éclairage sur le gouvernement : selon les principes de la doctrine confucianiste, un bon gouvernement agissait en effet en accord avec la nature.

Les séismes ne furent pas seulement vécus comme des catastrophes naturelles, ils offrirent aussi la possibilité à différents corps de métiers, notamment aux charpentiers, de se refaire une santé florissante. Si les *Cent Vues* ne montrent rien de la tragédie humaine, Hiroshige y présente aussi un Edo rénové, notamment pour informer la population de l'avancement des travaux de reconstruction (pl. 13, 58, 99). Mais Hiroshige ne met que rarement en avant les constructions réparées ou rebâties et les relègue plutôt à l'arrière-plan. Ainsi, sur la rive opposée de la rivière, la représentation des maisons flottantes du shogun à Atake, qui n'avaient été reconstruites qu'au huitième mois de l'année 1857 – un mois avant la date du cachet de censure de la célèbre feuille *Averse soudaine sur le pont Shin-Ōhashi et Atake* (pl. 58) – se borne à une indication schématique sous la forme de trois triangles blancs. Avec ce genre d'images, Hiroshige suscitait l'intérêt de la population locale et lui fournissait des sujets de conversation tout en présentant aux visiteurs extérieurs une capitale intacte. Les intérêts commerciaux auront sans doute joué un rôle important, mais le samouraï conser-

15

Other current events are reflected in the prints, including the excursions organized within the city by the thirteenth Tokugawa shogun, Iesada (1824–1858). In 1856 and 1857, he undertook 20 such excursions, to which at least ten of Hiroshige's prints probably make some reference. They gave rise to new "famous views" of Edo by Hiroshige's definition, including three plates rich in cherry blossom (plates 15, 16, 17), all of which bear the censors' seal for the fifth month of 1856, and reflect a trip by the shogun on the 13th day of the third month.

Finally, other important occasions for the production of woodblock prints were festivals, above all the famous Sannō and Sumiyoshi processions (plates 51, 55), and exhibitions (known as *kaichō*: "opening of the curtain") of the treasures of temples both in Edo and in other regions. Such events attracted numerous visitors, and the demand for souvenirs was accordingly great. For example, the censors approved four compositions relating to the Meguro neighbourhood in the fourth month of 1857 (plates 24, 25, 84, 111). This was the month in which the Fudō image of Rōzenji Temple – popularly known as Meguro Fudō – was put on display, in precisely this neighbourhood. The icon was venerated not least because it offered protection against fire.

Utagawa Hiroshige and his Images of Edo

Alongside numerous paintings, Hiroshige created more than 120 illustrated books and between 4,000 and 4,500 individual prints. The largest group, of almost 1,000, comprises views of Edo, and he devoted some 800 prints each to the stations on the Tōkaidō (Eastern Sea Road, the main highway between Edo and Kyoto) and the various provinces. In addition, he made 600 prints of actors, beautiful women and other people, as well as 300 for fans and more than 200 in the genre of bird-and-flower pictures. These numbers show that Hiroshige's focus was on topographical views, and it was with this genre that he made a name for himself in the 1830s.

Hiroshige's year of birth can be deduced from the inscription on his memorial portrait (*shinie*, ill. 15). By Japanese convention, a newborn child is one year old, and thus the age given in the inscription, 62, indicates that he was born in 1797. This portrait, the only one we have of him, was executed shortly after his death in the ninth month of 1858 by Utagawa Kunisada (1786–1864). It shows the artist in formal dress with the geometrical monogram *hiro*, prayer beads in his right hand, and a shaven head. On the occasion of his 60th birthday on the 28th day of the third month of 1856, Hiroshige became a monk, a formal act that had virtually no effect on his professional life.

The inscription, signed by Kunisada "with tear-drenched sleeves", says that Hiroshige was by far the most important pupil of Toyohiro (Utagawa Toyohiro, 1763?–1825), and that he was, alongside Toyokuni (in the third generation, i.e. Kunisada himself) and

Stadtteile wurden überschwemmt, zahlreiche Flüsse und Kanäle traten über die Ufer und rissen die Gebäude mit sich, die das Beben und die Feuersbrunst verschont hatten. Die Wasserwege Edos, die in Hiroshiges Serie auch farblich eine zentrale Rolle spielen, sahen sicherlich nicht immer so idyllisch oder wohlgepflegt aus, wie sie in den Ansichten vorgeführt werden.

Auch andere aktuelle Begebenheiten spiegeln sich in den Blättern. Dazu gehören die innerhalb Edos veranstalteten Ausflüge des damals herrschenden 13. Shoguns der Tokugawa-Dynastie, Iesada (1824–1858). In den Jahren 1856 und 1857 unternahm er 20 solcher Ausflüge, auf die wenigstens zehn Blätter Hiroshiges zurückgehen dürften. Sie brachten neue, von Hiroshige definierte „berühmte Ansichten" von Edo hervor, darunter die drei durchweg mit blühenden Kirschbäumen geschmückten Tafeln 15, 16 und 17, die allesamt ein Zensorensiegel vom fünften Monat 1856 zeigen und auf einer Ausfahrt des Shogun am 13. Tag des dritten Monats basieren.

Schließlich waren Festivals, vor allem die berühmten Sannō- und Sumiyoshi-Umzüge (Tafeln 51, 55), und Ausstellungen von Tempelschätzen in Edo (sogenanntes *kaichō*: „Öffnen des Vorhangs") und von Tempeln anderer Regionen wichtige Anlässe für die Entstehung von Holzschnitten. Solche Ereignisse zogen zahlreiche Besucher an, und entsprechend groß war die Nachfrage nach einer Wiedergabe der Orte. Die Zensoren gaben z. B. im vierten Monat des Jahres 1857 vier Entwürfe über den Stadtteil Meguro frei (Tafeln 24, 25, 84, 111). In diesem Monat lief die Ausstellung der Fudō-Ikone des Tempels Rōzenji – populär auch Meguro Fudō genannt – in eben diesem Stadtviertel. Die Ikone wurde u. a. verehrt, weil sie Schutz vor Feuergefahren bot.

Utagawa Hiroshige und seine Bilder von Edo

Hiroshige schuf neben zahlreichen Malereien mehr als 120 illustrierte Bücher und zwischen 4000 und 4500 Einzeldrucke. Die größte Gruppe von knapp 1000 bilden die Ansichten von Edo, etwa je 800 Blätter entwarf er zu den Stationen des Hauptverkehrsweges Tōkaidō und den verschiedenen Provinzen. 600 Drucke mit Schauspielern, schönen Frauen und anderen Figurendarstellungen stehen neben etwa 300 Drucken für Fächer und mehr als 200 im Genre der Vogel- und Blumenbilder. Schon diese Zahlen belegen, dass Hiroshiges Schwerpunkt auf den Landschaften lag, und mit diesem Genre wurde er auch in den 1830er Jahren bekannt.

Hiroshiges Geburtsjahr geht aus der Aufschrift auf dem Totenbildnis (*shinie*) hervor (Abb. 15). Nach japanischer Konvention wird mit der Geburt bereits das erste Lebensjahr begonnen, und so kann man aus dem genannten Alter von 62 Jahren seine Geburt auf 1797 zurückrechnen. Utagawa Kunisada (1786–1864) entwarf das einzige Porträt Hiroshiges kurz nach dessen Tod im neunten Monat 1858. Er zeigt Hiroshige in formellem Gewand mit geometrisch abstrahiertem Monogramm *hiro*, einer Gebetskette in der Rechten und rasier-

vateur Hiroshige n'était sans doute pas trop enclin à prendre position contre le shogunat.

Au huitième mois de l'année 1856, alors que les travaux de reconstruction battaient leur plein, la ville de plus d'un million d'habitants fut frappée par un typhon qui fit sans doute « seulement » une soixantaine de morts et une petite centaine de blessés, mais qui provoqua l'inondation de grandes parties de la ville aux abords de la baie ; de nombreuses rivières et canaux débordèrent, emportant sur leur passage les constructions épargnées par le séisme. Les voies fluviales d'Edo qui jouent un rôle central notamment dans le coloris de la série, ne présentaient alors plus rien de l'aspect idyllique et soigné qu'on relève dans les *Cent Vues*.

D'autres événements d'actualité se reflètent encore dans les feuilles de la série. En font partie les excursions organisées dans le domaine d'Edo par Iesada (1824–1858), 13ème shogun de la dynastie Tokugawa. Dans les années 1856 et 1857, le shogun entreprit une vingtaine d'excursions de ce genre, auxquelles se réfèrent sans doute au moins une dizaine de feuilles des *Cent Vues*. Ces feuilles présentent de nouvelles « vues célèbres » d'Edo définies par Hiroshige, notamment les planches 15, 16 et 17 parées de cerisiers en fleurs, lesquelles portent toutes un cachet de censure datant du cinquième mois 1856 et qui font référence à une excursion du shogun entreprise le 13ème jour du troisième mois de cette année.

Enfin, les grandes festivités, en particulier les célèbres transferts de Sannō et Sumiyoshi (pl. 51, 55), les dévoilements de trésors de certains temples d'Edo (appelés *kaichō* : « ouverture du rideau ») ou d'autres régions – fournissaient des prétextes importants pour la création d'estampes. Ces événements attiraient les foules, et la demande d'images de lieux qui leur servaient de cadre était bien sûr à l'avenant. Au quatrième mois de l'année 1857, les censeurs ont approuvé quatre projets décrivant le quartier Meguro (pl. 24, 25, 84, 111) ; c'est précisément en ce mois que l'icône de Fudō du temple Rōzenji – que l'usage populaire appelait aussi Meguro Fudō – fut exposée dans ce quartier. L'icône était vénérée entre autres parce qu'elle attirait la protection contre les incendies.

Utagawa Hiroshige et ses images d'Edo

À côté de ses nombreuses peintures, Hiroshige a illustré plus de 120 livres et créé entre 4000 et 4500 estampes individuelles. Le groupe le plus important – environ un millier – est celui des vues d'Edo. 800 feuilles sont consacrées aux étapes de la Tōkaidō, la plus grande voie de circulation du Japon, et à différentes provinces. 600 estampes représentant des acteurs, des beautés féminines ou d'autres figures, côtoient en outre quelque 300 œuvres gravées dédiées à des éventails ; enfin, plus de 200 relèvent de la peinture d'oiseaux et de fleurs. Ces chiffres montrent à eux seuls que Hiroshige fut avant tout peintre de paysages, et c'est aussi ce genre qui l'a rendu célèbre à partir des années 1830.

Kuniyoshi, one of the three great living masters of ukiyo-e. In saying this, Kunisada was repeating the assessment found in a list of woodblock print masters dating from 1853.

Finally, he emphasizes Hiroshige's mastery of landscape painting and mentions the *One Hundred Famous Views of Edo* in particular. These gave the impression, he said, that "one had the very landscapes before one's eyes". This observation takes up a remark made by Hiroshige himself, who, in the preface to the fourth volume of his work *Illustrated Souvenirs of Edo* (*Ehon Edo miyage*), printed in 1850, stated: "I intend above all to depict accurately (*shashin*) the famous areas of Edo ... and to draw landscapes such as one would see them with one's own eyes."

The concept of reproducing reality (*shashin*) goes back to the confrontation with Western painting techniques at the end of the 18th century. From 1852, the word *shashin* was also used to denote the first daguerreotypes made in Japan, mostly portraits, albeit on a small scale. In the world of painting in Hiroshige's day, however, *shashin* referred not so much to the accurate reproduction of a landscape, but was used, rather, in contrast to the ideal of the "reproduction of an idea" (*shai*) pursued by the literati painters. Even though Hiroshige's views doubtless seemed to contemporaries as uncommonly real, on account of their colour and use of perspective, they were for the most part based less on his own observations than on models.

The inscription on the memorial portrait ends with the death poem composed by Hiroshige himself:

Azumaji e On the way to the east
fude wo nokoshite I lay down my brush;
tabi no sora the goal of the journey:
nishi no mikuni no the famous places
nadokoro wo min of the Western Paradise to see.
Hiroshige Hiroshige

Hiroshige integrates the central motifs of the *One Hundred Famous Views of Edo* into this verse: his (life-) journey, which he intends to extend from Edo (Azumaji) to the Western Paradise of the Amida Buddha, where too he imagines there to be "famous places" (*nadokoro*, an alternative reading of the characters would be: *meisho*).

Hiroshige's father was a member of the warrior estate and was employed as a captain of the fire brigade that was charged with protecting Edo Castle and the residences of the shogun's vassals. It is because of his social background that we owe a few sparse biographical details that, in the case of woodblock print masters of lower social status, we often do not have. Hiroshige grew up in the central district of Yayosugashi, now known as Marunouchi, in the Chiyoda quarter of the city. While he belonged to the highest estate, like many samurai he had to perform a craft or mercantile occupation to make ends meet.

tem Kopf. Anlässlich seines 60. Geburtstags am 28. Tag des dritten Monats 1856 war Hiroshige in den Mönchsstand übergetreten, ein formeller Akt, der beruflich kaum Änderungen mit sich brachte.

Die von Kunisada „mit tränendurchtränkten Ärmeln" signierte Aufschrift besagt, dass Hiroshige der weitaus bedeutendste Schüler des Toyohiro (Utagawa Toyohiro, 1763?–1825) war und neben Toyokuni (in der dritten Generation, nämlich Kunisada selbst) und Kuniyoshi zu den drei größten lebenden Ukiyoe-Meistern gehörte. Damit wiederholt Kunisada die Beurteilung einer Liste von Holzschnittmeistern von 1853.

Schließlich hebt er Hiroshiges Meisterschaft in der Landschafts-malerei hervor und erwähnt speziell die *Hundert Ansichten von Edo*. Diese seien „so, als ob man die Landschaften vor den eigenen Augen sehen würde". Die Bemerkung schließt an Hiroshiges Bild-auffassung an, die er selbst im Vorwort zum 1850 erschienenen vierten Band seines Werkes *Illustrierte Mitbringsel aus Edo* (*Ehon Edo miyage*) formuliert hatte: „Ich beabsichtige vor allem die berühmten Gegenden von Edo genau abzumalen (*shashin*) ... und Landschaften zu zeichnen, wie man sie jetzt mit eigenen Augen sehen kann."

Das Konzept des Wiedergebens der Wirklichkeit (*shashin*) geht auf die Beschäftigung mit westlichen Malmethoden Ende des 18. Jahrhunderts zurück. Ab 1852 wurden mit dem Wort *shashin* denn auch die ersten vereinzelt in Japan entstandenen Daguerreo-typien, meist Porträts, bezeichnet. In der Malerei zur Zeit Hiro-shiges deutet *shashin* aber weniger auf das mimetische Abbilden einer Landschaft hin, sondern ist als Gegensatz zum Ideal des „Wiedergebens einer Idee" (*shai*) der Literatenmaler zu verstehen. Auch wenn Hiroshiges Ansichten wegen ihrer Farbigkeit und der perspektivischen Kompositionen auf zeitgenössische Betrachter sicherlich ungemein echt wirkten, basierten sie doch größtenteils weniger auf eigenen Beobachtungen denn auf Modellen.

Die Aufschrift auf dem Totenbildnis endet mit Hiroshiges selbst verfasstem Sterbegedicht:

Azumaji e Auf dem Weg nach Osten
fude wo nokoshite lege ich den Pinsel nieder;
tabi no sora das Reiseziel:
nishi no mikuni no die berühmten Orte
nadokoro wo min des westlichen Paradieses
zu schauen.
Hiroshige Hiroshige

Hiroshige integriert die zentralen Motive der *Hundert Ansichten* in dieses Gedicht: seine (Lebens-)Reise, die er von Edo (Azumaji) auf das Westliche Paradies des Amida Buddha aus-zudehnen gedenkt, wo er auch „berühmte Orte" (*nadokoro*, nach einer anderen Lesung: *meisho*) vermutet.

Hiroshiges Vater stammte aus dem Kriegerstand und war als Feuerwehrhauptmann zum Schutz des Edo-Schlosses und der

L'année de naissance de Hiroshige découle de l'inscription portée sur son portrait funèbre (*shinie*, ill. 15). La convention japonaise fait naître les enfants à l'âge d'un an, de sorte que l'âge de 62 ans cité dans l'inscription permet de fixer l'année de sa naissance à 1797. Utagawa Kunisada (1786–1864) a peint le seul portrait connu de Hiroshige peu après sa mort au neuvième mois 1858. Ce portrait montre Hiroshige en habit formel arborant le monogramme géo-métriquement abstrait *hiro*, un chapelet dans la main droite et le crâne rasé. À l'occasion de son 60ème anniversaire le 28ème jour du troisième mois 1856, Hiroshige avait pris l'état de moine, acte for-mel qui ne changeait pas grand-chose à son activité professionnelle.

L'inscription du portrait, que Kunisada signe des mots « les manches trempées de larmes », indique que Hiroshige fut, et de loin, l'élève le plus célèbre de Toyohiro (Utagawa Toyohiro, 1763?–1825), et qu'il avait été l'un des trois plus grands maîtres vivants de l'ukiyo-e avec Toyokuni (troisième du nom, c'est-à-dire Kunisada lui-même) et Kuniyoshi. Kunisada confirme ainsi l'appré-ciation d'une liste de maîtres de l'estampe établie en 1853.

Enfin, Kunisada souligne la maîtrise de Hiroshige dans la peinture de paysages et évoque en particulier les *Cent Vues célèbres d'Edo*, qui donnaient le sentiment « de voir les paysages de ses propres yeux ». Cette observation s'inscrit dans le sillage de la conception picturale que Hiroshige formulait dans la préface au quatrième tome (1850) de ses *Souvenirs illustrés d'Edo* (*Ehon Edo miyage*) : « Mon intention est surtout de dépeindre exactement (*shashin*) les lieux célèbres d'Edo ... et de dessiner des paysages tels qu'on peut les voir aujourd'hui de ses propres yeux. »

Ce concept de reproduction du réel (*shashin*) remonte à l'intérêt pour les méthodes picturales occidentales apparu vers la fin du XVIIIᵉ siècle. À partir de 1852, le terme *shashin* désigne notamment les premiers daguerréotypes réalisés au Japon, le plus souvent des por-traits. Dans la peinture de l'époque, le *shashin* se définit toutefois moins comme la représentation mimétique d'un paysage que par son opposition à l'idéal de la peinture érudite, qui consistait à « rendre une idée » (*shai*). Reste que si le spectateur percevait les vues créées par Hiroshige comme extrêmement réalistes en raison du coloris et de la perspective, elles reposaient moins sur des obser-vations de première main que sur des modèles existants.

L'inscription du portrait funèbre s'achève sur le propre poème funèbre de Hiroshige :

Azumaji e Sur la route de l'est,
fude wo nokoshite je dépose mon pinceau ;
tabi no sora le but de ce voyage :
nishi no mikuni no contempler les lieux célèbres
nadokoro wo min du paradis de l'ouest.
Hiroshige Hiroshige

Dans ce poème, Hiroshige évoque donc le motif central des *Cent Vues*, à savoir le voyage (de sa vie) qu'il entend poursuivre d'Edo (Azumaji) jusqu'au paradis occidental d'Amida Bouddha.

16

KATSUSHIKA HOKUSAI
(1779–1849)

*Tōto Asakusa
Honganji*

P. 30
Detail from plate 90
Detail aus Tafel 90
Détail de planche 90

*Honganji Temple
in Asakusa in the
Eastern Capital*

*Der Tempel Honganji
in Asakusa in der
östlichen Hauptstadt*

*Le temple Honganji à
Asakusa dans
la capitale de l'est*

From/aus/de:
Fugaku sanjūrokkei,
1830–1832

*The Thirty-Six Views
of Mount Fuji*

*Die 36 Ansichten
des Berges Fuji*

*Les 36 Vues
du mont Fuji*

Colour woodblock print,
25.5 x 38.2 cm
Publisher: Eijudō
Madison (WI), Chazen
Museum of Art, Bequest
of John H. van Vleck,
1980.2393

Hiroshige was probably only 13 when he began to study painting. The occasion was the death of his father in 1809 and his inheriting the office of fire-brigade captain. The same year, he abandoned his childhood name Tokutarō in favour of Jūeimon, finally taking the name Hiroshige in 1819, from which year we have a New Year print bearing the signature "Ichiyūsai Hiroshige". The character for *hiro* is evidence of his apprenticeship, mentioned on his memorial portrait, to the not very well-known ukiyo-e master Utagawa Toyohiro. In addition to the character for *hiro*, his teacher gave him the school-name Utagawa. His work shows virtually no similarities with that of his master; his style typically evinces the eclectic mixture of the various painting schools in which he studied until 1829. It is said, for example, that Hiroshige was the pupil of Okashima Rinsai, a representative of the Kano School officially patronized by the shogunate. This school was esteemed for its synthesis of Chinese stylistic elements with domestic painting in the tradition of the Tosa School. Ōoka Unpō (1765–1848), known for his literati painting inspired by Chinese models, was doubtless also one of Hiroshige's teachers at this time, as were representatives of the Maruyama-Shijō School in Edo, which combined Western techniques of expressing space and volume with Japanese forms and picture formats. Thus Hiroshige's training exposed him to various Chinese, Japanese and Western painting techniques, all of which are reflected in his *One Hundred Famous Views of Edo*.

With the death of Toyohiro in 1829, and following a number of unsuccessful book illustrations, Hiroshige seems to have undergone a fundamental reorientation. A year later, Hokusai designed his exquisite series *Thirty-Six Views of Mount Fuji (Fugaku sanjūrokkei)* to great acclaim. He was one of the first to choose the *ōban* format for purely landscape depictions, and so topographical views, which on ukiyo-e prints since the mid-18th century had merely provided backgrounds to figural scenes, became a genre in their own right. On the print reproduced here, *Honganji Temple in Asakusa in the Eastern Capital* (ill. 16), we see the triangle of Mount Fuji in the distance, depicted with the reduced palette typical of the series. It forms an echo of the close-up view of the roof of Honganji Temple in Edo.

In 1831 or 1832, Hiroshige, who at the time was signing himself Ichiyūsai, produced ten woodblock prints in the series *Famous Places in the Eastern Capital (Tōto meisho)*, meaning Edo. These prints marked the start of his specialization as a landscape painter. In collaboration with the publishers Hōeidō and Senkakudō, he enjoyed his great breakthrough in the early 1830s with the series *Fifty-Three Stations of the Tōkaidō (Tōkaidō gojūsan tsugi no uchi)*. There is no documentary evidence to determine whether, as is often asserted, a purported official trip to the imperial capital had given Hiroshige first-hand knowledge of the Tōkaidō, the important highway between Edo and Kyoto. His compositions could also be based on models, as two later series on Kyoto and Osaka might suggest. However, he enriched any models he may have had with unusual and varied perspectives, humorous figures, a concentration on atmosphere resulting from the time of day and natural phenomena, as well as the first regular application of the printing

Vasallenresidenzen des Shogun eingesetzt. Diesem Umstand verdanken wir einige spärliche biografische Daten, die bei Holzschnittmeistern aus einfacheren sozialen Umständen oft fehlen. Hiroshige wuchs im zentralen Distrikt Yayosugashi, dem heutigen Marunouchi im Stadtteil Chiyoda, auf. Er gehörte zwar zum höchsten Stand, musste sich aber wie viele gleichgestellte Samurai für den Lebensunterhalt auf Nebenverdienste im handwerklichen oder kaufmännischen Bereich verlegen.

Hiroshige begann wohl schon als 13-Jähriger mit dem Studium der Malerei. Anlass war der Tod seines Vaters im Jahr 1809 und sein Erbe des offiziellen Amtes als Feuerwehrhauptmann. Seinen Kindernamen Tokutarō legte er im selben Jahr zugunsten von Jūeimon ab, 1819 nahm er schließlich den Namen Hiroshige an. Aus diesem Jahr ist ein Neujahrsdruck mit der Signatur „Ichiyūsai Hiroshige" erhalten. Das Zeichen für *hiro* ist Beleg für die im Totenbildnis genannte Ausbildung bei dem weniger bekannten Ukiyoe-Meister Utagawa Toyohiro. Neben dem Zeichen für *hiro* erhielt er von seinem Lehrer auch den Schulnamen Utagawa. Ähnlichkeiten mit dem Werk seines Lehrers sind kaum auszumachen, dafür weist sein Stil das typische eklektische Nebeneinander verschiedener Malschulen auf, bei denen er bis zum Jahr 1829 studierte. So soll Hiroshige bei einem Vertreter der offiziell vom Shogunat geförderten Kano-Schule, Okashima Rinsai, gelernt haben. Diese Schule war für ihre Synthese chinesischer Stilelemente mit der einheimischen Malerei in der Tradition der Tosa-Schule geschätzt. Der für seine von chinesischen Modellen inspirierte Literatenmalerei bekannte Ōoka Unpō (1765–1848) war in dieser Zeit wohl ebenso Hiroshiges Lehrer wie Vertreter der Maruyama-Shijō-Schule in Edo. Diese kombinierte westliche Raumauffassung und Volumendarstellung mit einheimischen Farben und Bildformaten. So fließt schon in Hiroshiges Ausbildung eine Vielzahl einheimischer, chinesischer und westlicher Maltechniken ein, die sich auch in seinen *Hundert berühmten Ansichten von Edo* manifestieren.

Mit dem Tod Toyohiros im Jahr 1829 und als Folge einiger erfolgloser Buchillustrationen scheint sich Hiroshige grundlegend umorientiert zu haben. Ein Jahr später legte Hokusai seine exquisite Serie *Die 36 Ansichten des Berges Fuji (Fugaku sanjurokkei)* mit großem Erfolg vor. Er hatte als einer der Ersten das Ōban-Format für reine Landschaftsdarstellungen gewählt und die Ansichten, die seit Mitte des 18. Jahrhunderts auf den Ukiyoe-Holzschnitten meist als bloßer Hintergrund von figürlichen Szenen erschienen waren, aus dieser Funktion gelöst und als eigenständiges Bildgenre etabliert. Auf dem hier abgebildeten Druck *Der Tempel Honganji in Asakusa in der östlichen Hauptstadt* ist mit der für die Serie typischen reduzierten Palette in der Ferne das Dreieck des Fuji zu sehen (Abb. 16). Er bildet das Echo zu dem nah an den Betrachter gerückten Dach des Tempels Honganji in Edo.

1831 oder 1832 erschienen von Hiroshige, der damals mit Ichiyūsai signierte, zehn Holzschnitte der Serie *Berühmte Orte der östlichen Hauptstadt (Tōto meisho)*, gemeint ist Edo. Mit diesen Blättern begann er, sich auf Landschaftsansichten zu spezialisieren. In Zusammenarbeit mit den Verlegern Hōeidō und Senkakudō

où il suppose aussi l'existence de « lieux célèbres » (*nadokoro*, qu'une autre lecture permet de lire aussi : *meisho*).

Le père de Hiroshige appartenait à la classe des guerriers et servait en qualité de capitaine de la brigade du feu dédiée à la protection du château d'Edo et des résidences vassales du shogun. C'est à cette circonstance que nous devons les rares données biographiques qui manquent le plus souvent dans le cas des maîtres issus de classes inférieures. Hiroshige a grandi dans le district central de Yayosugashi (aujourd'hui Marunouchi), dans le quartier Chiyoda. Bien qu'il appartînt à la classe sociale supérieure, Hiroshige dut assurer sa subsistance par des revenus annexes dans le domaine artisanal ou marchand, comme c'était alors le cas de nombreux samouraïs qui se trouvaient dans une situation comparable.

Hiroshige a sans doute commencé l'étude de la peinture dès sa treizième année, suite à la mort de son père en 1809, qui le fit hériter de la charge officielle de capitaine du feu. La même année, il abandonne son nom d'enfant Tokutarō au profit du nom Jūeimon. En 1819 enfin, il adopte le nom Hiroshige. De cette année date en effet une estampe de Nouvel An portant la signature « Ichiyūsai Hiroshige ». Le signe *hiro* atteste sa formation – évoquée dans son portrait funèbre – chez Utagawa Toyohiro, un maître moins important de l'ukiyo-e. À côté du signe *hiro*, il reçut encore de son maître le nom d'école Utagawa. Si l'on ne relève guère de similitudes entre l'œuvre de Hiroshige et celle de son maître, sa manière présente en revanche la juxtaposition éclectique des styles de peinture qu'il étudia jusqu'en 1829 dans différentes écoles. Hiroshige est en effet censé avoir étudié chez Okashima Rinsai, un représentant de l'école Kano officiellement soutenue par le shogunat. Cette école était reconnue pour sa synthèse d'éléments stylistiques chinois et de la peinture japonaise dans la tradition de l'école Tosa. À la même époque, Ōoka Unpō (1765–1848), célèbre pour sa peinture érudite inspirée de modèles chinois, fut lui aussi le maître de Hiroshige, tout comme quelques représentants de l'école Maruyama-Shijō installée à Edo, école qui associait une conception et une représentation spatiale occidentalisante à des coloris et des formats japonais. Ainsi voit-on déjà entrer dans la formation de Hiroshige un grand nombre de techniques picturales japonaises, chinoises et occidentales dont on relève aussi la trace dans les *Cent Vues*.

Sous le coup de la mort de Toyohiro en 1829 et suite à l'insuccès de quelques illustrations de livres, Hiroshige semble avoir procédé à une profonde réorientation. Un an plus tard, Hokusai connaissait un succès retentissant avec son exquise série *36 Vues du mont Fuji (Fugaku sanjurokkei)*. Hokusai avait été un des premiers artistes à choisir le format *ōban* pour de purs paysages, libérant aussi ses vues de la fonction habituelle que l'estampe ukiyo-e avait eue depuis le milieu du XVIIIe siècle, fonction qui faisait le plus souvent du paysage une simple toile de fond pour des scènes figurées, et établissant le paysage comme un genre à part entière. Dans l'estampe *Le temple Honganji à Asakusa dans la capitale de l'est* reproduite ici (ill. 16), on peut voir au loin le triangle du Fuji traité dans la palette réduite caractéristique de la série et faisant écho au toit du temple Honganji d'Edo fortement rapproché du spectateur.

Plate/Tafel/planche 12
from/aus/de:
*Tōkaidō gojūsan tsugi
no uchi,*
1833

17
UTAGAWA HIROSHIGE
Mishima asagiri

*Morning Mist at
Mishima*

*Morgennebel in
Mishima*

*Les brouillards
matinaux à Mishima*

*The Fifty-Three
Stations of the
Tōkaidō, in the
early 1830s*

*Die 53 Stationen der
Ostmeerstraße,
Anfang 1830er Jahre*

*Les 53 Étapes de
la Tōkaidō, début
des années 1830*

P. 33
Detail from plate 95
Detail aus Tafel 95
Détail de planche 95

Colour woodblock print,
approx. 23 x 25 cm
Publisher: Hōeidō
and Senkakudō
Madison (WI), Chazen
Museum of Art, Bequest
of John H. van Vleck,
1980.793

technique involving colour gradation at the top margin of the print (*ichimonji bokashi*). In his depiction of the twelfth station at Mishima in the province of Izu, several travellers in the foreground are passing the famous shrine on the right as they journey to Edo (ill. 17). Its buildings disappear into the morning mist just like the people and houses of the town behind the travellers. This print is the only one to depict fog, an aspect particularly emphasized in subsequent impressions, where the contours in the middle distance are in some cases blurred to the point of unrecognizability. The labour of the palanquin bearers is evident, and the fact that the faces both of the gentleman in the palanquin and of the horseman are hidden by their travelling hats gives rise to speculation as to their identity.

In 1832, he relinquished his office of fire-brigade captain to his son (or adoptive son) Nakajirō, in order to devote himself entirely to painting and the composition of woodcuts. Since the 1830s, he had been producing depictions of Edo on painted hanging scrolls, in book illustrations, and on individual woodblock prints. Some views of Edo were evidently particularly sought-after: he produced more than 50 prints of Ryōgoku Bridge, more than 40 of Ueno, Takanawa and Kinryūzan Temple in Asakusa and more than 30 of Susaki, Gotenyama and the Yoshiwara pleasure district, each combined with time-of-the-day atmospherics or seasonal attributes, such as morning scenes in Yoshiwara (plate 38), cherry blossoms in Gotenyama (plate 28), fireworks over Ryōgoku Bridge (ill. 9, plate 98) and snow in Asakusa (ill. 8, plate 99).

Among the most important visual preconditions for a major series of pictures of Edo like the *One Hundred Famous Views of Edo* was the long-awaited publication of the *Illustrated Guide to Famous Views of Edo (Edo meisho zue)* dating from 1834–1836. This seven-volume work was doubtless the most popular in the guide-to-famous-views genre, which since 1780 had embraced various cities and regions. Hasegawa Settan (1778–1843) illustrated the *Edo meisho zue*, which since 1791 had been written by three generations of authors, Saitō Yukio, Yukitaka and finally Yukinari (also known as Gesshin, 1804–1878). These volumes introduced the traveller to the city through pictures and information about their history and religious significance. One of the first illustrations in the first volume is of the Suruga-chō quarter, with the Mitsui store on both sides of the road against a backdrop of a majestic Mount Fuji (ill. 18). This depiction was evidently known to Hiroshige, as evidenced by his own version of the view, dating from the ninth month of 1856 (ill. 6, plate 8).

Against the background of the *Edo meisho zue*, Hiroshige composed the ten-volume *Illustrated Souvenirs of Edo*, which can be seen as the most comprehensive preliminary work to the *One Hundred Famous Views of Edo*. The illustrations in this work take the form of double-page spreads, and the first four volumes, arranged according to the points of the compass, appeared in 1850; three more appeared by 1857, while the remaining three were added by Hiroshige II before 1867. Short explanatory texts on the

schaffte er Anfang der 1830er Jahre den Durchbruch mit der Serie *Die 53 Stationen der Ostmeerstraße (Tokaido gojūsan tsugi no uchi)*. Ob Hiroshige diesen wichtigsten Hauptverkehrsweg zwischen Edo und Kyoto, den Tōkaidō, anlässlich einer offiziellen Reise in die Kaiserhauptstadt aus erster Hand kannte, wie oft behauptet wird, lässt sich anhand der Dokumentenlage nicht entscheiden. Seine Entwürfe könnten auch auf Modellen basieren, wie zwei spätere Serien über Kyoto und Osaka nahelegen. Die Vorlagen bereicherte er aber mit ungewöhnlichen und abwechslungsreichen Blickwinkeln, humoristischen Figurendarstellungen, der Konzentration auf Tagesstimmungen und Naturphänomene sowie mit der zum ersten Mal regelmäßig angewendeten Drucktechnik der Farbgradierung am oberen Bildrand (*ichimonji bokashi*). In der Darstellung der zwölften Station in Mishima in der Provinz Izu zieht im Vordergrund eine Gruppe Reisender vorbei an dem berühmten Schrein rechter Hand in Richtung Edo (Abb. 17). Seine Gebäude verschwinden ebenso im Morgennebel wie die Menschen und Häuser der Stadt hinter den Reisenden. Dieser Druck ist der einzige mit einer Nebeldarstellung, ein Aspekt, der in den folgenden Abzügen besonders herausgestrichen wurde und die Konturen des Mittelgrunds zum Teil bis zur Unkenntlichkeit verschwimmen ließ. Die Mühsal der Sänftenträger ist deutlich zu erkennen, und die mit Reisehüten verdeckten Gesichter des in der Sänfte sitzenden Herrn und des Reiters geben Anlass zu Spekulationen, um wen es sich handeln könnte.

1832 gab Hiroshige das Amt als Feuerwehrhauptmann an seinen Sohn (oder Adoptivsohn) Nakajirō ab, um sich ganz der Malerei und dem Entwerfen von Holzschnitten zuzuwenden. Seit den 1830er Jahren verarbeitete er Darstellungen von Edo auf gemalten Hängerollen, in Illustrationen zu Büchern und auf Einzelblattholzschnitten. Einige Ansichten von Edo waren offenbar besonders gefragt: Es erschienen von ihm mehr als 50 Drucke zur Brücke Ryōgokubashi, mehr als 40 über Ueno, Takanawa und den Tempel Kinryūzan in Asakusa und mehr als 30 über Susaki, Gotenyama und das Freudenviertel Yoshiwara, jeweils kombiniert mit Tagesstimmungen oder jahreszeitlichen Attributen, wie Morgenszenen in Yoshiwara (Tafel 38), Kirschblüte in Gotenyama (Tafel 28), Feuerwerk über der Brücke Ryōgokubashi (Abb. 9, Tafel 98) und Schnee in Asakusa (Abb. 8, Tafel 99).

Zu den wichtigen visuellen Voraussetzungen für eine große Serie mit Bildern von Edo wie die *Hundert berühmten Ansichten von Edo* gehörte zunächst die lang erwartete Publikation des *Illustrierten Führers zu berühmten Ansichten von Edo (Edo meisho zue)* von 1834–1836. Dieses siebenbändige Werk war wohl das beliebteste im Genre der Führer berühmter Ansichten, das seit 1780 viele verschiedene Städte und Regionen umfasste. Hasegawa Settan (1778–1843) illustrierte das *Edo meisho zue*, das seit 1791 über die drei Generationen der Autoren Saitō Yukio, Yukitaka und schließlich Yukinari (auch Gesshin genannt, 1804–1878) verfasst worden war. Diese Bände führten den Reisenden anhand von Bildern sowie historischen und religiösen Hintergrundinformationen in die Stadt ein. Als eine der ersten Illustrationen im ersten Band ist das Stadtviertel Suruga-chō mit dem Handelshaus Mitsui zu bei-

En 1831 ou 1832 paraissent encore sous la signature Ichiyūsai dix estampes de la série *Lieux célèbres de la capitale de l'est (Tōto meisho)*, c'est-à-dire d'Edo. Avec ces feuilles, Hiroshige commençait à se spécialiser dans les vues paysagères. En collaboration avec les éditeurs Hōeidō et Senkakudō, au début des années 1830, il réalise une percée avec la série des *53 Étapes de la Tōkaidō (Tōkaidō gojūsan tsugi no uchi)*. Quant à savoir si Hiroshige, comme on l'a souvent affirmé, a connu par lui-même la grande voie de circulation entre Edo et Kyoto dans le cadre d'un voyage officiel dans la ville impériale, la chose ne peut être tranchée en l'état des documents disponibles. Ses projets peuvent tout aussi bien s'être appuyés sur des modèles, comme pourraient le laisser penser deux séries ultérieures ayant pour sujet Kyoto et Osaka. Mais Hiroshige a enrichi ses modèles par des angles de vue inhabituels et variés, des figures humoristiques, une prédilection pour certains phénomènes naturels et ambiances du jour, enfin, fait jusqu'alors inédit, par l'emploi régulier des dégradés de couleurs contre le bord supérieur (*ichimonji bokashi*). Au premier plan de la représentation de la douzième étape, celle de Mishima dans la province d'Izu, un groupe de voyageurs passe à côté du célèbre sanctuaire à droite en direction d'Edo (ill. 17). Les bâtiments du sanctuaire disparaissent dans les brouillards matinaux, tout comme les hommes et les maisons de la ville représentés derrière les voyageurs. Cette estampe est la seule à montrer des brouillards, un aspect qui sera fortement souligné dans les tirages ultérieurs et qui rendait flous, jusqu'à les rendre en partie méconnaissables, les contours du second plan. Les rudes efforts des porteurs de palanquin se reconnaissent clairement et les visages cachés sous les chapeaux du cavalier et des messieurs assis dans le palanquin se prêtent aux spéculations sur l'identité des personnages.

En 1832, Hiroshige transmet sa charge de capitaine de la brigade du feu à son fils (ou fils adoptif) Nakajirō afin de pouvoir se consacrer entièrement à la peinture et à l'estampe. À partir des années 1830, il travaille à des représentations d'Edo sur des rouleaux suspendus, dans des illustrations de livres ou des estampes individuelles. Plusieurs vues d'Edo suscitèrent apparemment une forte demande : de Hiroshige paraissent plus de 50 estampes autour du pont Ryōgokubashi, plus de 40 sur Ueno, Takanawa et le temple Kinryūzan à Asakusa, et plus de 30 sur Susaki, Gotenyama et le quartier des plaisirs Yoshiwara, combinées chaque fois avec des ambiances diurnes ou des caractéristiques saisonnières, telles que les montrent par exemple la scène matinale à Yoshiwara (pl. 38), la floraison des cerisiers à Gotenyama (pl. 28), le feu d'artifice sur le pont Ryōgokubashi (ill. 9, pl. 98) et la neige à Asakusa (ill. 8, pl. 99).

En 1834–1836, parmi les conditions qui ont permis de présenter une série d'images d'Edo aussi nombreuse que les *Cent Vues*, il y eut d'abord la publication longtemps attendue du *Guide illustré des vues célèbres d'Edo (Edo meisho zue)*. Cet ouvrage en sept volumes fut sans doute le plus populaire dans le genre des guides de vues célèbres qui, depuis 1780, couvraient de nombreuses villes et régions. Hasegawa Settan (1778–1843) fut l'illustrateur de l'*Edo meisho zue*, pour lequel à partir de 1791 travaillèrent trois généra-

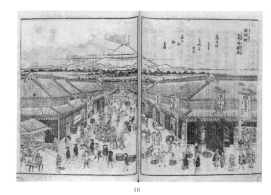

18

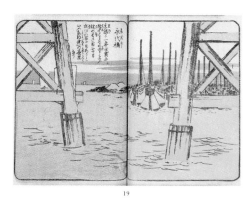

19

history or importance of the places explain why they were famous. Thus the picture of Eitai Bridge in volume II is accompanied by the following explanation (ill. 19):

"Eitaibashi. It is said that the bridge was first built in the eleventh year of the Genroku era [1698] in the cyclical year *tsuchinoe tora*. The bridge is 120 or 110 bays in length. It is the longest bridge in the eastern capital."

When we compare this print with *Tsukudajima and Eitai Bridge* (plate 4), it is clear how Hiroshige used his earlier composition to bring out the vertical format by means of an impressive reduction of motifs and palette and integration of the nocturnal atmosphere.

In addition, in the illustrations to his book Hiroshige was already experimenting with similar compositional techniques to those he was employing six years later, including placing large motifs in the foreground that take up much of the picture, while the rest retreats into the distance.

One crucial woodblock print series for the *One Hundred Famous Views of Edo* was the *Famous Views of Sixty-Odd Provinces*, which was composed between 1853 and the eleventh month of 1856. This was Hiroshige's first use of the *ōban* vertical format, and in the colourfulness of the prints and in the compositions we also see the earliest use of some of the techniques used in the *One Hundred Famous Views of Edo* (ills. 20, 21). The views are largely borrowed from existing models, but skilfully worked, giving him the reputation of a "lyrical painter", a judgement that was based not least on the outstanding craftsmanship of the wood cutters and printers who also worked on the *One Hundred Famous Views of Edo*. On Whistler's oil painting *Caprice in Purple and Gold*, dating from 1864 (ill. 22), the model, wrapped in Japanese textiles, is depicted looking at one of the prints of this series, while others are lying scattered around the floor. This reception dates from just eight years after the completion of the series, and is evidence of Hiroshige's immediate success in Europe.

Hiroshige's Impact

In a printed ranking of ukiyo-e masters dating from as early as 1849, Hiroshige was listed second in his speciality, "landscapes" (*keshiki*). Four years later, he was placed third in a similar ranking after Kunisada (portrait) and Kuniyoshi (depictions of warriors), with the additional remark "famous places" (*meisho*). It is conceivable that it was on marketing grounds that Hiroshige and Sakanaya used this word, *meisho*, in a grammatically unusual and unprecedented initial position in the series title *Meisho Edo hyakkei*.

Even while the *One Hundred Famous Views of Edo* was still incomplete, various publishers were capitalizing on its success. In 1857/58 they issued a print series by Kunisada with the similar title

den Straßenseiten und dem hoch darüber thronenden Berg Fuji zu sehen (Abb. 18). Diese Darstellung kannte Hiroshige offenbar, wie seine Version der Ansicht vom neunten Monat 1856 belegt (Abb. 6, Tafel 8).

Vor dem Hintergrund des *Edo meisho zue* verfasste Hiroshige das zehnbändige Werk *Illustrierte Mitbringsel aus Edo*, das als die umfassendste Vorarbeit zu den *Hundert Ansichten* gelten kann. Die ersten vier nach Himmelsrichtungen angeordneten Bände dieser mit doppelseitigen Illustrationen versehenen Bücher erschienen 1850, die weiteren drei bis 1857, und die restlichen drei Bände vervollständigte Hiroshige II bis 1867. Kurze Erklärungstexte zur Geschichte oder Bedeutung der Orte machen deutlich, wofür sie bekannt wurden. So steht etwa zur Darstellung der Brücke Eitaibashi im zweiten Band folgende Erläuterung (Abb. 19):

„Eitaibashi. Es ist überliefert, dass im elften Jahr der Ära Genroku [1698] mit den zyklischen Jahreszeichen *tsuchinoe tora* die Brücke erstmals erbaut wurde. Die Länge der Brücke umfasst 120 oder 110 Joche. Es ist die längste Brücke in der östlichen Hauptstadt."

Im Vergleich mit dem Blatt *Tsukudajima und die Brücke Eitaibashi* (Tafel 4) wird deutlich, wie Hiroshige seinen früheren Entwurf benutzte, um durch eine eindrucksvolle Reduktion der Motive und die Farbwahl unter Einbeziehung der nächtlichen Stimmung das Hochformat gut zur Geltung zu bringen.

Außerdem experimentierte Hiroshige in den Illustrationen zu seinem Buch schon mit ähnlichen Kompositionsmitteln wie sechs Jahre später, darunter große Gegenstände im Vordergrund, die das Bildfeld umspannen und das dahinter Dargestellte verkleinert in die Ferne rücken.

Eine für die *Hundert Ansichten* maßgebliche Holzschnittserie waren die zwischen 1853 und dem elften Monat 1856 entworfenen *Berühmten Ansichten von über sechzig Provinzen*. Hiroshige setzte hier zum ersten Mal das Ōban-Hochformat ein, und in der Farbigkeit der Blätter sowie in der Komposition kommen einige Mittel der *Hundert Ansichten* zum ersten Mal zum Einsatz (Abb. 20, 21). Die Ansichten sind weitgehend aus Vorlagen entlehnt, aber geschickt verarbeitet, sodass sie ihm den Ruf eines „lyrischen Malers" einbrachten – ein Urteil, das nicht zuletzt auf der überragenden Technik der Holzschneider und Drucker basiert, die im Übrigen auch für die *Hundert Ansichten* gearbeitet haben. Auf Whistlers Ölbild *Caprice in Purple and Gold* von 1864 (Abb. 22), betrachtet das in japanische Textilien gehüllte Modell eines der Blätter aus dieser Serie, während andere auf dem Boden verstreut herumliegen. Diese nur acht Jahre nach Fertigstellung der Serie erfolgte Rezeption belegt Hiroshiges unmittelbaren Erfolg in Europa.

tions d'auteurs : Saitō Yukio, Yukitaka et finalement Yukinari (aussi appelé Gesshin, 1804–1878). Par le truchement d'images et d'informations décrivant les contextes historique et religieux de chaque site, ces volumes permettaient au voyageur de se familiariser avec la capitale. Une des premières illustrations du tome I montre le quartier Suruga-chō avec le grand magasin Mitsui des deux côtés de la rue et le mont Fuji trônant au-dessus de la scène (ill. 18). Hiroshige a assurément connu cette représentation, comme l'atteste sa version de la même vue datée du neuvième mois de l'année 1856 (ill. 6, pl. 8).

Sur la toile de fond de l'*Edo meisho zue*, Hiroshige réalisa l'ouvrage en dix volumes *Souvenirs illustrés d'Edo*, qui peut être considéré comme le plus vaste travail préliminaire aux *Cent Vues*. Consacrés respectivement aux quatre points cardinaux, les quatre premiers tomes de cet ouvrage illustré en doubles pages parurent en 1850 ; les trois suivants furent publiés jusqu'en 1857 ; les trois derniers complétés jusqu'en 1867 par Hiroshige II. De courts textes sur l'histoire ou la signification des lieux expliquent les raisons de leur célébrité. À titre d'exemple, dans le deuxième tome, la représentation du pont Eitaibashi est assortie du commentaire suivant (ill. 19) :

« Eitaibashi. On rapporte que le pont fut construit pour la première fois pendant la onzième année de l'ère Genroku [1698] avec les signes cycliques annuels *tsuchinoe tora*. Sa longueur est de 120 ou 110 travées. Ce pont est le plus long de la capitale de l'est. »

Une comparaison avec l'estampe *Tsukudajima et le pont Eitaibashi* (pl. 4) éclaire la manière dont Hiroshige a exploité son projet antérieur pour mettre en valeur le format vertical de la feuille, mais aussi l'ambiance nocturne de la scène par la réduction des motifs et le choix des couleurs.

Dans les illustrations de son livre, Hiroshige travaillait déjà avec des moyens de composition qu'on retrouvera six ans plus tard dans les *Cent Vues*, notamment avec des objets de grande taille placés au premier plan, couvrant tout le champ de l'image et repoussant dans le lointain les motifs réduits placés derrière.

Une autre série d'estampes déterminante pour les *Cent Vues* fut celle des *Vues célèbres des 60 et quelques provinces* conçues entre 1853 et le onzième mois 1856. Hiroshige y utilisait pour la première fois le format vertical *ōban*, et les coloris et composition présentaient pour la première fois certains moyens visuels utilisés dans les *Cent Vues* (ill. 20, 21). Si la plupart des vues sont dérivées de modèles existants, elles ont été habilement remaniées et ont valu à Hiroshige la réputation d'un « peintre poétique » – jugement qui se doit pour une bonne part à l'extraordinaire savoir-faire technique des graveurs et des imprimeurs, qui travailleront aussi pour les *Cent Vues*. Dans la peinture à l'huile de Whistler *Caprice in Purple and Gold* de 1864 (ill. 22), le modèle vêtu de tissus japonais contemple une des feuilles de cette série, d'autres feuilles gisent éparses sur le sol. Cette réception picturale, qui eut lieu huit ans seulement après l'achèvement de la série, illustre le succès immédiat de Hiroshige en Europe.

20

21

20
UTAGAWA HIROSHIGE
Edo: Asakusa no ichi
Edo: Market
in Asakusa
*Edo: Der Markt
in Asakusa*
*Edo: Le marché
à Asakusa*
Plate/Tafel/ planche 17
from/aus/de:
*Rokujū yoshū meisho
zue, 1853–1856*
Famous Views
of Sixty-Odd
Provinces
*Berühmte Ansichten
von über sechzig
Provinzen*
*Vues célèbres des 60 et
quelques provinces*
Colour woodblock print,
34.5 x 23.2 cm
Publisher: Koshihei
Madison (WI), Chazen
Museum of Art, Bequest
of John H. van Vleck,
1980.1312

21
UTAGAWA HIROSHIGE
*Satsuma: Bō no ura
Sōkenseki*
Satsuma Province:
The Twin Sword Rocks
in Bō Bay
*Die Provinz Satsuma:
Die zwei Schwertfelsen
in der Bucht von Bō*
*La province Satsuma :
les deux rochers de l'épée
dans la baie de Bō*
Plate/Tafel/ planche 67
from/aus/de: *Rokujū
yoshū meisho zue,
1853–1856*
Famous Views of
Sixty-Odd Provinces
*Berühmte Ansichten
von über sechzig
Provinzen*
*Vues célèbres des 60
et quelques provinces*
Colour woodblock print,
34.2 x 28.7 cm
Publisher: Koshihei
Madison (WI), Chazen
Museum of Art, Bequest
of John H. van Vleck,
1980.1364

P. 37
Detail from plate 98
Detail aus Tafel 98
Détail de planche 98

Famous Views of Edo with a Hundred Beauties (Edo meisho hyakunin bijo), in which large-format depictions of beautiful women were combined with scenic vignettes of Edo.

In 1917, a memorial exhibition of Hiroshige's works, was held in Tokyo, and two years later the Japanese Hiroshige Society published a comparison of his *One Hundred Famous Views of Edo* with contemporary photographs intended to show the same places from approximately the same viewpoints. This undertaking was repeated in 1963 in the first completely coloured publication of the series in top quality, and again in 2003 for an exhibition catalogue by the Ota Memorial Museum of Art. These comparisons may, for some lovers of woodblock prints, demonstrate the painful incursion of the modern age into an unspoilt bygone Japan. The comparison between the woodblock prints and the photographs, however, also highlights how little one can trust Hiroshige's assertion that the prints represented depictions of the actual topography.

At first, Japanese Hiroshige studies were devoted above all to the establishment of biographical details, from the series of articles by Iijima Kyōshin in 1894 to the central monograph of Uchida Minoru in 1932 and finally the still definitive *Hiroshige* (1970) by Suzuki Jūzō. In the meantime, though, some ukiyo-e scholars have also turned their attention to individual pictures or groups of works by Hiroshige, among them Asano Shūgō, Harashida Minoru, Kobayashi Tadashi and Orii Takae.

In Europe, exhibitions of Hiroshige's work were organized, and articles about him published, within just a few years of his death. The magazine *Le Japon Artistique*, which was published from 1888 to 1891 by the dealer in Japanese art objects Samuel Bing (1838–1905), had a wide distribution. In the July and August issues of 1889, the British doctor William Anderson published an article on Hiroshige, and some of his prints were reproduced as drawings. Shortly afterwards, on 3 February 1893, Camille Pissarro (1830–1903), on the occasion of an exhibition of Utamaro and Hiroshige prints organized by Bing at Durand's gallery, wrote to his son Lucien:

"The Japanese exhibition is magnificent: Hiroshige is a wonderful Impressionist. Monet, Rodin and I are enthusiastic. How glad I am to have painted the effects of snow and floods. These Japanese artists have confirmed me in our visual judgement."

Pissarro emphasizes in particular Hiroshige's ability to reproduce natural atmospheres and moments. It is precisely this aspect of Hiroshige's œuvre that gives Mary Fenollosa's 1901 monograph on Hiroshige (the world's first) its title, *Hiroshige: The Master of Mist, Snow and Rain*. The subsequent specialist literature praised his landscapes, for instance Friedrich Perzynski in his book *Der Japanische Farbenholzschnitt* (1903), in which, however, he delivers a damning judgement on Hiroshige's treatment of the human figure. Further important early monographs in Europe were written by the collector John Steward Happer (1909) and Edward Strange (1925). A monographic exhibition in 1997

Hiroshiges Wirkung

Schon 1849 wurde Hiroshige in einer gedruckten Rangliste von Ukiyoe-Meistern als Zweiter mit seiner Spezialität, den „Landschaften" (keshiki), genannt. Vier Jahre später stand er in einem ähnlichen Ranking nach Kunisada (Porträt) und Kuniyoshi (Kriegerdarstellungen) an dritter Stelle mit dem Zusatz „berühmte Orte" (meisho). Es ist daher denkbar, dass Hiroshige und Sakanaya aus verkaufsstrategischen Gründen dieses Markenzeichen meisho grammatikalisch ungewöhnlich und ohne Präzedenzfall im Serientitel *Meisho Edo hyakkei* an den Anfang stellten.

Bereits während der Entstehung der *Hundert berühmten Ansichten von Edo* schlugen unterschiedliche Verleger aus deren Erfolg Kapital. Sie druckten 1857/58 eine Holzschnittserie von Kunisada mit dem abgewandelten Titel *Berühmte Ansichten von Edo mit hundert Schönheiten (Edo meisho hyakunin bijo)*, in der großfigurige schöne Frauen mit Landschaftsvignetten von Edo kombiniert sind.

1917 fand eine Hiroshige-Gedächtnisausstellung in Tokyo statt, zwei Jahre später publizierte die japanische Hiroshige-Gesellschaft eine Gegenüberstellung seiner *Hundert Ansichten* mit zeitgenössischen Fotografien, die dieselben Orte aus etwa demselben Blickwinkel wiedergeben sollten. Dieses Unterfangen wurde 1963 in der ersten komplett farbig publizierten Serie von bester Qualität und 2003 in einem Ausstellungskatalog des Ota Memorial Museum of Art wiederholt. Diese Gegenüberstellungen mögen für einige Holzschnittliebhaber die schmerzlichen Eingriffe der Moderne in ein heiles vergangenes Japan demonstrieren. Der Vergleich zwischen den Holzschnitten und den Fotografien macht aber deutlich, wie wenig man Hiroshiges Bekenntnis Glauben schenken sollte, die Holzschnitte stellten die tatsächliche Landschaft vor Augen.

Die japanische Hiroshige-Forschung widmete sich zunächst vor allem biografischen Details, wie die Artikelserie des Iijima Kyōshin von 1894 verdeutlicht, bis die zentrale Monografie von Uchida Minoru im Jahr 1932 und schließlich das auch heute noch gültige Buch *Hiroshige* (1970) von Suzuki Jūzō erschienen. Inzwischen haben sich einige Ukiyo-Forscher auch auf einzelne Bilder oder Werkgruppen Hiroshiges konzentriert, darunter Asano Shūgō, Harashida Minoru, Kobayashi Tadashi und Orii Takae.

In Europa wurden schon wenige Jahre nach Hiroshiges Tod Ausstellungen zu seinem Werk organisiert und Artikel publiziert. Weite Verbreitung fand etwa die Zeitschrift *Le Japon Artistique* des Kunsthändlers japanischer Objekte, Samuel Bing (1838–1905), die 1888–1891 erschien. In den Juli- und Augustnummern von 1889 verfasste der Brite William Anderson einen Artikel zu Hiroshige, und einige Holzschnitte wurden in Umzeichnungen abgebildet. Kurz darauf, am 3. Februar 1893, schrieb Camille Pissarro (1830–1903) anlässlich einer Ausstellung von Utamaro- und Hiroshige-Holzschnitten, die Bing bei Durand organisiert hatte, an seinen Sohn Lucien:

L'effet Hiroshige

Dès 1849, dans une liste de maîtres de l'ukiyo-e, Hiroshige était cité en seconde place pour sa spécialité, les « paysages » (keshiki). Quatre ans plus tard, dans un classement similaire, il apparaissait en troisième position après Kunisada (portrait) et Kuniyoshi (représentations de guerriers), avec la mention « lieux célèbres » (meisho). On peut penser que pour le titre de la série (Meisho Edo hyakkei), Hiroshige et Sakanaya utilisèrent le terme meisho, inédit et grammaticalement inhabituel, pour des raisons de stratégie commerciale.

Dès la parution successive des *Cent Vues*, différents éditeurs cherchèrent à tirer parti du succès de la série. En 1857/58 fut imprimée une série d'estampes de Kunisada ayant pour titre *Vues célèbres d'Edo avec cent beautés (Edo meisho hyakunin bijo)*, série dans laquelle de belles femmes représentées de près étaient combinées avec des vignettes paysagères d'Edo.

En 1917, une exposition commémorative Hiroshige fut organisée à Tokyo ; deux ans plus tard, la société Hiroshige japonaise publiait un livre dans lequel les *Cent Vues* étaient présentées à côté de photographies contemporaines montrant les mêmes lieux à partir d'un point de vue proche. Cette entreprise fut réitérée en 1963 dans la première publication intégrale de la série en couleurs de haute qualité, puis en 2003 dans un catalogue de l'Ota Memorial Museum of Art. Certains amateurs d'estampes ne pourront sans doute s'empêcher de regretter dans ces rapprochements les effets cruels de la modernité sur le Japon idyllique d'autrefois. Reste que la comparaison entre les estampes et les photographies montre clairement qu'on ne peut guère prêter foi à l'affirmation de Hiroshige selon laquelle les estampes présentaient le paysage réel au spectateur.

Jusqu'à la parution de la monographie de référence d'Uchida Minoru (1932) et plus récemment du livre *Hiroshige* (1970) de Suzuki Jūzō, lequel conserve toute sa pertinence jusqu'à ce jour, la recherche japonaise sur Hiroshige s'est surtout attachée à réunir un maximum d'informations biographiques, comme le montre notamment la série d'articles publiée en 1894 par Iijima Kyōshin. Depuis, quelques spécialistes de l'ukiyo-e se sont aussi concentrés sur des images isolées ou des groupes d'estampes de l'artiste. Citons ici à titre d'exemple Asano Shūgō, Harashida Minoru, Kobayashi Tadashi et Orii Takae.

En Europe, quelques années seulement après la mort de Hiroshige, des expositions autour de son œuvre allaient être organisées et des articles publiés. La revue *Le Japon Artistique* de Samuel Bing (1838–1905), marchand d'objets japonais, connut une large diffusion entre 1888 et 1891. L'Anglais William Anderson écrivit un article sur Hiroshige pour les numéros de juillet et d'août 1899, et quelques estampes furent publiées sous forme de contours en noir et blanc. Un peu plus tard, le 3 février 1893, à l'occasion d'une exposition d'estampes d'Utamaro et de Hiroshige que Bing organisa chez Durand-Ruel, Camille Pissarro (1830–1903) écrivait à son fils Lucien :

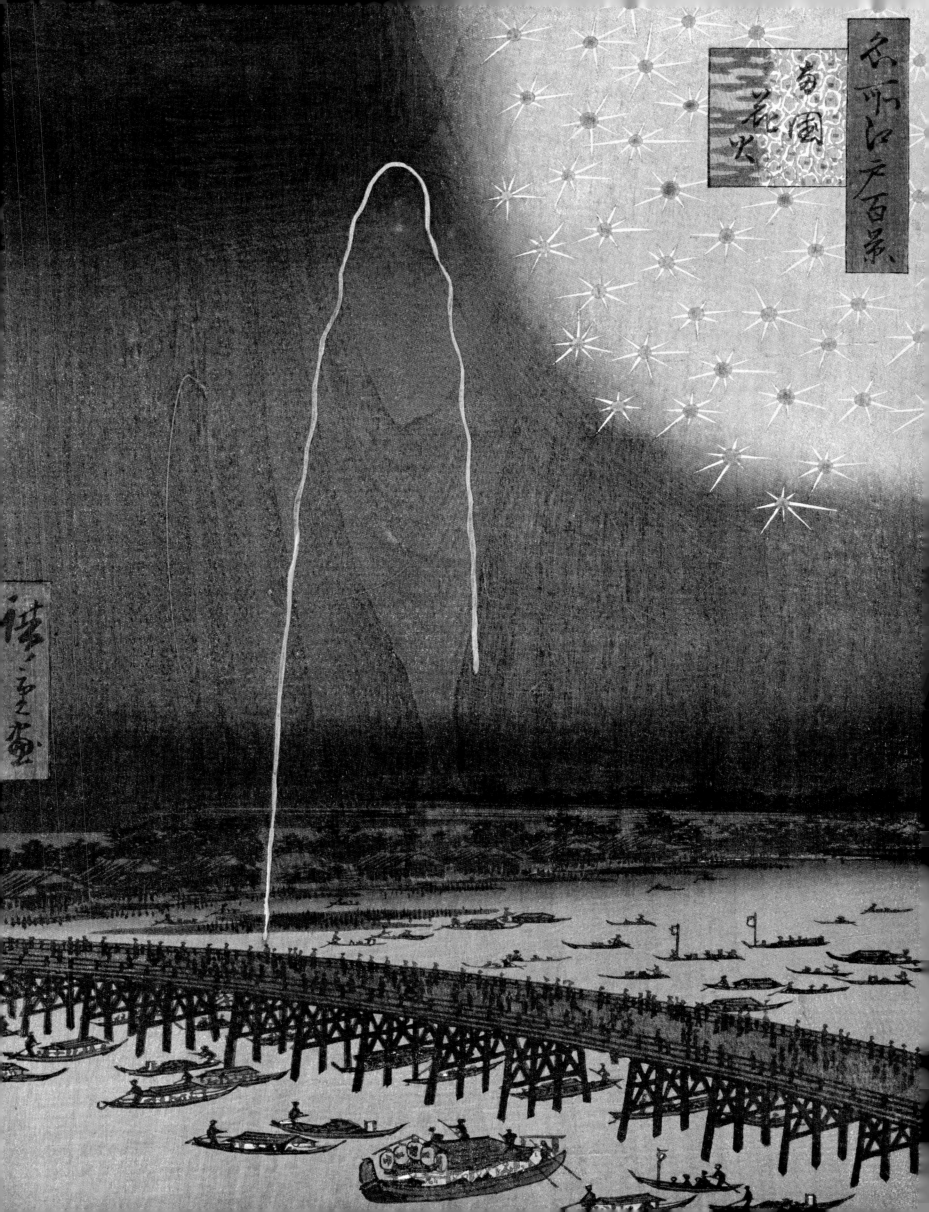

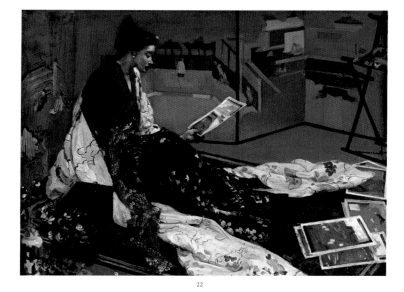

22

22

JAMES ABBOTT McNEILL
WHISTLER
(1834–1903)
*Caprice in Purple
and Gold No. 2:
The Golden Screen,*
1864
Oil on wood,
49.8 x 68.9 cm
Washington (DC),
Smithsonian
Institution,
Freer Gallery of Art,
Gift of Charles Lang
Freer, F1904.75

P. 38

Detail from plate 112
Detail aus Tafel 112
Détail de planche 112

organized by the ukiyo-e specialist Matthi Forrer presented the results of new research, including precise descriptions of the state of preservation of the selected prints.

Since the first complete high-quality colour reproduction of the *One Hundred Famous Views of Edo* in Japan in 1963, there have been a number of such collected editions, with sometimes substantial scholarly contributions. These include that produced by Henry D. Smith and Amy Poster in 1986, and the volume published by Suzuki Jūzō in 1991; the present publication owes much to both.

The Publisher Sakanaya Eikichi

Hiroshige worked with Sakanaya Eikichi only in connection with the *One Hundred Famous Views of Edo*. Publishers were the key figures in book and print production. They commissioned the pictures from the artists, paid the woodblock cutters and the printers, procured the material for the woodblocks, the paper and the paint, and finally organized distribution and sales. This required a considerable investment before the printed products could be sold. Occasionally, several publishers issued one and the same series in order to share the cost. Takenouchi Magohachi and Tsuruya Kiemon, for example, collaborated in this way on Hiroshige's *Fifty-Three Stations of the Tōkaidō*.

Sakanaya, hitherto mostly known by another reading of the characters of his name as Uoya Eikichi ("Uoei" for short), was largely unknown in the publishing sector before the publication of the *One Hundred Famous Views of Edo*. He is said to have joined the publishers of illustrated books (*ezōshi mon'ya*) shortly before the great Ansei earthquake of 1855. The *One Hundred Famous Views of Edo* represented his major debut in this fiercely contested market and made him one of the most successful publishers of the age. In Kunisada's triptych *Present-day Parody of the Four Estates of Warriors, Farmers, Artisans and Merchants: Merchants (Imayō mitate shinōkōshō – akindo)*, dated the eighth month of 1857, he proudly displays his flourishing business (ill. 23). The triptychs and individual woodblock prints show beautiful women, heroic warriors, narrative scenes and actors as represented by Kunisada and other masters. Piled up on the floor in the foreground of the middle and left-hand prints are books from his own publishing house. On the far left of the left-hand print, an advertising poster emphasizes the *One Hundred Famous Views of Edo*. To its right can be seen two prints from the series: *Kinryūzan Temple in Asakusa* (ill. 8, plate 99) and *Cherry Blossoms on the Banks of the Tama River* (plate 42).

Sakanaya's shop was situated, as we can gather from various seals on the prints (*Shitaya Uoei* or *Shitaya Shinkuro Uoei*, e.g. on plate 62), in Shinkuromon-chō in Shitaya, a neighbourhood to the north of the city centre and not far from Ueno, a popular destination for visitors. Forrer has compared the addresses of various publishers with the number and formats of Hiroshige's pictures of

„Großartig die japanische Ausstellung: Hiroshige ist ein wunderbarer Impressionist. Monet, Rodin und ich sind begeistert. Wie froh bin ich, die Wirkung von Schnee und Überschwemmungen gemalt zu haben. Diese japanischen Künstler bestätigen mich in unserem visuellen Urteil."

Pissarro hebt besonders Hiroshiges Fähigkeit hervor, Naturstimmungen und Augenblicke wiederzugeben. Genau dieser Aspekt in Hiroshiges Œuvre geht bei Mary Fenollosas weltweit erster Monografie zu Hiroshige (1901) in den Titel ein, *Hiroshige: Meister von Nebel, Schnee und Regen*. Die einschlägige Literatur lobt danach seine Landschaften, wie etwa Friedrich Perzynski in seinem Buch *Der Japanische Farbenholzschnitt* (1903), in dem er Hiroshiges Figurenmalerei allerdings vernichtend kritisiert. Weitere wichtige frühe Monografien in Europa stammen von dem Sammler John Steward Happer (1909) und von Edward Strange (1925). Eine monografische Ausstellung von 1997 unter Federführung des Ukiyoe-Spezialisten Matthi Forrer legte neue, u. a. in genaue Zustandsbeschreibungen der ausgewählten Drucke eingegangene Forschungsergebnisse vor.

Seit der ersten kompletten qualitätvollen Farbreproduktion zu den *Hundert Ansichten* von 1963 in Japan gibt es einige solcher Gesamtpublikationen mit zum Teil substantiellen Forschungsbeiträgen. Dazu zählen das von Henry D. Smith und Amy Poster 1986 verfasste Buch und der von Suzuki Jūzō 1991 herausgegebene Band, denen die vorliegende Publikation viel verdankt.

Der Verleger Sakanaya Eikichi

Hiroshige arbeitete für Sakanaya Eikichi nur im Rahmen der *Hundert Ansichten*. Verleger waren die Dreh- und Angelpunkte einer Buch- oder Holzschnittproduktion. Sie vergaben die Aufträge an den Designer, bezahlten die Arbeit der Holzschneider und Drucker, stellten das Material für Holzplatten, Papier und Farben bereit und übernahmen schließlich auch den Vertrieb. Dies bedeutete ein erhebliches Investment, bevor die gedruckten Produkte verkauft werden konnten. Gelegentlich gaben auch mehrere Verleger eine Serie heraus, um sich die Kosten zu teilen. Bei Hiroshiges *Die 53 Stationen der Ostmeerstraße* arbeiteten z. B. die Verleger Takenouchi Magohachi und Tsuruya Kiemon zusammen.

Der bisher meist in einer anderen Lesung als Uoya Eikichi bezeichnete Verleger (abgekürzt „Uoei") Sakanaya war bis zur Produktion der *Hundert berühmten Ansichten von Edo* in der Verlagsbranche weitgehend unbekannt. Er soll sich kurz vor dem großen Ansei-Erdbeben von 1855 den Verlegern von illustrierten Büchern (*ezōshi mon'ya*) angeschlossen haben. Die *Hundert Ansichten* sind sein großes Debüt auf dem umkämpften Markt der Druckindustrie und machten ihn zu einem der erfolgreichsten Verleger seiner Zeit. In dem auf den achten Monat 1857 datierten Triptychon *Gegenwärtige Travestie auf die vier Stände Krieger, Bauern,*

« Admirable, l'exposition japonaise : Hiroshige est un impressionniste merveilleux. Moi, Monet et Rodin en sommes enthousiasmés. Je suis content d'avoir fait mes effets de neige et d'inondation, ces artistes japonais me confirment dans notre parti-pris visuel. »

Pissarro souligne tout particulièrement l'aptitude de Hiroshige à rendre des atmosphères et des phénomènes naturels, et c'est précisément cet aspect qui entrera dans le titre de la toute première monographie jamais consacrée à Hiroshige que Mary Fenollosa publiera en 1901 : *Hiroshige : Maître du brouillard, de la neige et de la pluie*. La littérature spécialisée loue ensuite les paysages de Hiroshige, comme le fera par exemple Friedrich Perzynski dans son livre *Der Japanische Farbenholzschnitt* (1903), dans lequel l'auteur émet en revanche de vives critiques sur la peinture de figures de Hiroshige. D'autres grandes monographies européennes seront celles du collectionneur John Steward Happer (1909) et d'Edward Strange (1925). Plus récemment, une exposition monographique de 1997 placée sous le commissariat du spécialiste de l'ukiyo-e Matthi Forrer a pu présenter les derniers résultats de la recherche, qui s'attachent notamment à donner des descriptions précises de l'état des estampes sélectionnées.

Depuis la première reproduction complète en couleur de haute qualité des *Cent Vues* publiée en 1963 au Japon, quelques éditions intégrales sont parues avec des contributions parfois substantielles. Parmi celles-ci, citons les livres d'Henry D. Smith et Amy Poster de 1986 et l'ouvrage publié en 1991 par Suzuki Jūzō, auxquels la présente publication doit beaucoup.

L'éditeur Sakanaya Eikichi

Hiroshige n'a travaillé pour Sakanaya Eikichi que dans le cadre des *Cent Vues*. Les éditeurs étaient les pivots de toute publication de livres ou d'estampes. Il passaient les commandes au concepteur, payaient le travail des graveurs et des imprimeurs, fournissaient les matériaux pour les bois, le papier et les couleurs et prenaient aussi en charge la diffusion. Tout cela nécessitait de gros investissements avant que les feuilles pussent être mises sur le marché. Dans certains cas, plusieurs éditeurs se regroupaient pour partager les frais de production. C'est ainsi que les *53 Étapes de la Tōkaidō* purent être publiées grâce à la collaboration des éditeurs Takenouchi Magohachi et Tsuruya Kiemon.

L'éditeur Sakanaya, plus connu dans une autre lecture de son nom, Uoya Eikichi (abréviation « Uoei »), était largement inconnu dans le secteur de l'édition jusqu'au moment où il produisit les *Cent Vues célèbres d'Edo*. Sakanaya est censé avoir rejoint les éditeurs de livres illustrés (*ezōshi mon'ya*) peu avant le grand séisme d'Ansei (1855). Les *Cent Vues* ont marqué son grand début sur le marché très concurrentiel de l'imprimerie et lui ont valu un des plus grands succès éditoriaux de son époque. Dans le triptyque de Kunisada daté du huitième mois 1857, *Parodie contemporaine des quatre classes des guerriers, paysans, artisans et marchands : marchands (Imayō mitate shinōkōshō – akindo)*, il présente

23
UTAGAWA KUNISADA
(1786–1864)

*Imayō mitate
shinokōshō — akindo,
8/1857*

P. 41
Detail from plate 114
Detail aus Tafel 114
Détail de planche 114

*Present-day Parody
of the Four Estates of
Warriors, Farmers,
Artisans and
Merchants: Merchants*

*Gegenwärtige
Travestie auf die
vier Stände Krieger,
Bauern, Handwerker
und Kaufleute:
Kaufleute*

*Parodie contempo-
raine des quatre
classes des guerriers,
paysans, artisans
et marchands :
marchands*

Woodblock print:
triptych, each print
approx. 37 x 25.7 cm.
Publisher:
Sakanaya Eikichi,
Geneva, Collections
Baur

23

famous views of Edo. He concludes that almost three-quarters of prints in the most frequently – in the *One Hundred Famous Views of Edo* exclusively – represented format, the *ōban*, were produced by publishers from Shitaya together with those from the Shiba district to the south of the centre. The remaining quarter were produced by publishers based in the city centre. Forrer argues that these prints were aimed primarily at tourists passing along the main roads leading out of the city, namely the Nikkō kaidō leading north to Nikkō and the Tōkaidō leading to the south.

Sakanaya was interested in continuing with Hiroshige II the great success he had enjoyed with the *One Hundred Famous Views of Edo*. Between 1859 and 1861 he commissioned from Hiroshige II compositions for *One Hundred Famous Views of All Provinces* (*Shokoku meisho hyakkei*), which use comparable compositional techniques and the same *ōban* format. He also commissioned portraits from Kunisada, which include the *Illustrated Guide to Toyokuni's Sketches* (*Toyokuni manga zue*) dating from 1859 and 1860, a two-part series of half-length portraits of actors and kabuki scenes.

The publisher Fujiokaya Yoshizō (1793–after 1868?) reports in his diary *Fujiokaya nikki*, which he kept between 1804 and 1868, that each print run of a woodblock print consisted of 1,000 impressions. This was doubtless the minimum, and further editions depended on its success. The discrepancy between the considerable production costs and the low sales price of a print, which in the case of the *One Hundred Famous Views of Edo* was no more than 16 to 26 *mon* and thus about the same as a bowl of rice, meant that the publishers were dependent on selling large quantities. Especially from the 1850s onwards, the quality and cost of the first print run could be vastly different from later ones, which suggested an average-cost calculation: if the first print runs proved successful, a cheaper version would be produced – corresponding to the modern publishing practice of following up a hardback first edition with a paperback. The *One Hundred Famous Views of Edo* can be seen as a prime example of such a publishing strategy.

The Production of a Woodblock Print

One characteristic of the *One Hundred Famous Views of Edo* is the outstanding quality of the woodblock cutters (*horishi*) and printers (*surishi*) employed on the project. Their work was given pride of place in Kunisada's illustration of the artisan's estate, approved in the eighth month of 1857 (ill. 24). After the publisher had commissioned the print, the ink drawing had, following a decree of 1790, to be submitted to the censors and given the round seal of approval. In the *One Hundred Famous Views of Edo*, this seal is placed, together with a date seal, either at the top of the print or on the left, outside the image. Only the print added by Shigenobu (plate 119) shows the combined *aratame*/date seal usual between 1859 and 1871. Following the appearance of a print with 72 different colours the previous year, a

Handwerker und Kaufleute: Kaufleute (*Imayō mitate shinokōshō — akindo*) von Kunisada stellt er stolz seinen geschäftigen Betrieb zur Schau (Abb. 23). Die dargestellten Triptychen und Einzelholzschnitte zeigen schöne Frauen, Kriegerhelden, narrative Szenen sowie Schauspieler von Kunisada und anderen Holzschnittmeistern. Im Vordergrund des mittleren und linken Blattes sind Bücher auf dem Boden gestapelt, die Sakanaya ebenso verlegte. Ganz links auf dem linken Holzschnitt hebt ein Werbeplakat die *Hundert berühmten Ansichten von Edo* hervor. Rechts daneben sind zuoberst zwei Drucke aus den *Hundert Ansichten* zu sehen, *Der Tempel Kinryuzan in Asakusa* (Abb. 8, Tafel 99) und *Kirschblüten am Ufer des Flusses Tamagawa* (Tafel 42).

Sakanayas Laden stand, wie aus einigen Siegeln auf den Holzschnitten hervorgeht (*Shitaya Uoei* oder *Shitaya Shinkuro Uoei*, z. B. auf Tafel 62), in Shinkuromon-chō in Shitaya, einem nördlich des Zentrums und nahe dem frequentierten Ausflugsort Ueno gelegenen Stadtviertel. Forrer verglich die Adressen verschiedener Verleger mit der Anzahl und den Formaten von Hiroshiges Bildern berühmter Ansichten von Edo. Er kommt zu dem Schluss, dass bei dem zahlenmäßig am stärksten vertretenen – und in den *Hundert Ansichten* durchgängig verwendeten – Ōban-Format die Verleger aus Shitaya zusammen mit dem südlich des Zentrums gelegenen Shiba fast drei Viertel der Produktion bestritten. Das restliche Viertel entfällt auf die Verleger im Stadtzentrum. Forrer argumentiert, dass diese Drucke vor allem auf Touristen abzielten, die nahe der Ausfallstraßen nach Nikkō (Nikkō kaidō) im Norden bzw. der Ostmeerstraße (Tōkaidō) im Süden vorbeikamen.

Sakanaya war daran interessiert, seinen großen Erfolg mit den *Hundert Ansichten* mit Hiroshige II fortzusetzen. Bei ihm bestellte er zwischen 1859 und 1861 Entwürfe für *Hundert berühmte Ansichten aller Provinzen* (*Shokoku meisho hyakkei*), die mit vergleichbaren Kompositionstechniken angelegt sind und ebenso im Ōban-Hochformat gedruckt wurden. Er gab ferner bei Kunisada Figurenbildnisse in Auftrag, zu denen der 1859 und 1860 entworfene *Illustrierte Führer zu Toyokunis Skizzen* (*Toyokuni manga zue*) gehört, eine zweiteilige Serie aus Halbfigurenporträts von Schauspielern und Kabuki-Szenen.

Der Verleger Fujiokaya Yoshizō (1793–nach 1868?) berichtet in seinem zwischen 1804 und 1868 geführten Tagebuch *Fujiokaya nikki*, dass der Entwurf für einen Holzschnitt in Einheiten von 1000 Abzügen gedruckt wurde. Dies war wohl das Minimum, von dessen Erfolg die weiteren Auflagen abhingen. Wegen der Diskrepanz zwischen den beträchtlichen Produktionskosten und dem niedrigen Verkaufspreis eines Holzschnitts, der im Falle der *Hundert Ansichten* nicht mehr als zwischen 16 und 26 *mon* und damit etwa so viel wie eine Schale Reis kostete, waren die Verleger auf eine hohe Auflage angewiesen. Dabei konnten besonders seit den 1850er Jahren die Qualität und die Kosten der Erstdrucke von denjenigen der späteren Abzüge stark abweichen, was eine Mischkalkulation nahelegte: Erwiesen sich die Erstdrucke als gut verkäuflich, folgte – vergleichbar der Taschenbuchausgabe eines gebundenen Buches – eine billigere

fièrement sa maison d'édition très affairée (ill. 23). Les triptyques et estampes individuelles de cette série montrent de belles femmes, des héros militaires, des scènes anecdotiques et des acteurs créés par Kunisada et d'autres maîtres de l'estampe. Au premier plan des feuilles centrale et gauche s'empilent des livres que Sakanaya a également édités. À l'extrême gauche de l'estampe de gauche, une affiche met en exergue les *Cent Vues célèbres d'Edo*. À côté, tout en haut à droite, on peut voir deux estampes des *Cent Vues*, *Le temple Kinryūzan à Asakusa* (ill. 8, pl. 99) et *Fleurs de cerisiers au bord de la Tamagawa* (pl. 42).

Comme il ressort de quelques cachets figurant sur les estampes (*Shitaya Uoei* ou *Shitaya Shinkuro Uoei*, p. ex. pl. 62), la maison d'édition de Sakanaya était située dans le quartier Shinkuromon-chō, à Shitaya, au nord du centre, tout près d'Ueno, lieu d'excursion très fréquenté. Forrer a comparé les adresses de différents éditeurs avec les nombre et format des images de Hiroshige montrant des vues célèbres d'Edo et en a déduit que pour le format *ōban* le plus souvent utilisé – et pour toutes les estampes des *Cent Vues* –, les éditeurs de Shitaya et de Shiba, au sud du centre, couvraient pratiquement les trois quarts de la production, le quatrième quart revenant aux éditeurs du centre. Forrer considère que ces estampes s'adressaient surtout aux touristes qui, à la sortie d'Edo, empruntaient la route du nord vers Nikkō (Nikkō kaidō), et la Tōkaidō (route de la mer orientale) vers le sud.

Sakanaya voulut évidemment réitérer l'immense succès des *Cent Vues* avec Hiroshige II. Entre 1859 et 1861, il commanda au successeur de Hiroshige des projets pour *Cent Vues célèbres de toutes les provinces* (*Shokoku meisho hyakkei*) qui reprenaient les mêmes techniques de composition et qui furent également imprimées au format vertical dit *ōban*. Il commanda en outre à Kunisada des portraits en figure parmi lesquels on trouve le *Guide illustré des esquisses de Toyokuni* (*Toyokuni manga zue*), série en deux parties de portraits en demi-figure d'acteurs et de scènes de théâtre kabuki.

Dans son journal tenu entre 1804 et 1868 *Fujiokaya nikki*, l'éditeur Fujiokaya Yoshizō (1793–après 1868 ?) explique que le premier tirage des estampes comptait mille exemplaires. C'était sans doute là le minimum requis pour décider des tirages ultérieurs en fonction du succès obtenu. Du fait de l'écart entre les coûts de production élevés et un prix de vente très faible n'excédant pas 16 à 26 *mon* par feuille dans le cas des *Cent Vues* –, les éditeurs étaient obligés d'imprimer un fort tirage. À partir des années 1850 en particulier, la qualité et les coûts des premiers tirages pouvaient diminuer fortement avec les tirages suivants, ce qui obligeait à un double calcul : si les premiers tirages se vendaient bien, suivait alors une version meilleur marché – tout comme une édition de poche suit aujourd'hui le livre relié. Les *Cent Vues célèbres d'Edo* peuvent être considérées comme une illustration exemplaire de ce genre de calcul.

24

UTAGAWA KUNISADA
(1786–1864)

*Imayō mitate
shinokōshō —
shokunin, 8/1857*

P. 42

Detail from plate 111

Detail aus Tafel 111

Détail de planche 111

*Present-day Parody
of the Four Estates
of Warriors, Farmers,
Artisans and
Merchants: Artisans*

*Gegenwärtige
Travestie auf die
vier Stände Krieger,
Bauern, Handwerker
und Kaufleute:
Handwerker*

*Parodie contempo-
raine des quatre
classes des guerriers,
paysans, artisans et
marchands : artisans*

Woodblock print:
triptych, each print
approx. 37 x 25.7 cm
Publisher:
Sakanaya Eikichi,
Geneva, Collections
Baur

24

censorship law of 1842 restricted the number of colours to eight. Hiroshige's series demonstrates that the colour limitation also had its positive sides.

Once it had been given the censors' seal of approval, the drawing, together with the master's colouring instructions, was passed to the woodblock engraver. He placed the drawing face down on a prepared block of wood about 2.5 centimetres (1 inch) thick, which had been seasoned for a number of years. The grain of the wild cherry (*yamazakura*) wood was used to decorative purpose, for example in *The Sannō Festival Procession at Kōjimachi itchōme* (plate 51). In order to bring out the contours of the original draft, the redundant areas of paper were carefully scraped off. Using a fine knife, the craftsman cut the lines to stand proud of the block and cut out all the empty areas with a chisel. As there was only one original draft, which was destroyed in the engraving process, he had to proceed with great care. Only at the end of the process was a register mark or *kentō* notched into the outer edge to act as a guide to the correct alignment of the paper when the eventual print was produced. From this outline block, a number of prints were printed in black ink: this number corresponded to the number of different colours required for the picture. Each colour was noted individually on each of these proofs; each was used to create a "colour plate" (*irohan*), which was engraved in the same way as the plate for the black outlines.

The plates were now passed on to the printer (*surishi*), whose first job was to cut the handmade *kōzo* paper to size. For the *ōban* format used in this series, he had to halve the sheets of tear-proof and absorbent paper obtained from the mulberry tree and produced in the *ōbōsho* size. In order to bind the fibres of the paper and prevent the colours from running, the paper was prepared with a size consisting of animal glue (*dōsa*) diluted with alum. The printer now moistened three sheets, one over the other, with a broad paintbrush, rubbed the woodblock with a brush soaked in ink and placed a sheet on the register mark. Using a disc known as a *baren* – consisting of plaited cords with a bamboo leaf around them – the printer then rubbed the paper against the block. Then he laid this paper, which now bore the contours of the design, on to the *irohan* blocks (which by now had had the different colours rubbed on to them) one after the other, starting with the palest colour. The rubbing movements produced a pattern that was sometimes consciously integrated as a visible element into the finished product, as can be clearly seen on *Kumano Jūnisha Shrine at Tsunohazu, known as "Jūnisō"* (plate 50). With the exception of the ink, which was obtained from pinewood soot, and the chemically produced Prussian blue (*beroai*), which had been introduced to Japan by the Dutch in 1820 and been used in Japanese woodblock prints since 1829, the colours in the *One Hundred Famous Views of Edo* are natural mineral or vegetable dyes. Sometimes mixed and sometimes by a process of overprinting, these created the variety of colours for which the series is so famous.

The complex nature of the printing process becomes clear when we consider the sequence of one outline-block and 15 colour-blocks

Version. Die *Hundert berühmten Ansichten von Edo* können als Paradebeispiel einer solchen Kalkulation gelten.

Die Herstellung eines Holzschnittes

Ein Charakteristikum der *Hundert berühmten Ansichten von Edo* ist, wie erwähnt, die herausragende Qualität der Holz- oder Plattenschneider (*horishi*) und Drucker (*surishi*). Ihre Tätigkeit wird in der am achten Monat 1857 genehmigten und von Kunisada entworfenen Travestie auf die Handwerkskunst in den Vordergrund gestellt (Abb. 24). Nachdem der Verleger dem Holzschnittmeister den Auftrag vergeben hatte, musste die entworfene Tuschzeichnung seit 1790 der Zensurbehörde vorgelegt und mit dem runden Zensursiegel genehmigt werden. In den *Hundert Ansichten* ist dieses Siegel zusammen mit einem Datumssiegel entweder oben oder links außerhalb des Bildes angesetzt. Nur das eine von Shigenobu hinzugefügte Blatt (Tafel 119) zeigt das zwischen 1859 und 1871 übliche Kombinationssiegel aus *aratame* und Datum. Einem Zensurgesetz von 1842 zufolge war die Zahl der Farben auf acht beschränkt, nachdem im Jahr zuvor ein Druck mit 72 Farbtönen erschienen war. Dass die Farbbeschränkung auch ihre positiven Seiten hatte, belegt Hiroshiges Serie.

Das zum Druck freigegebene Blatt gelangt mit Farbanweisungen des Meisters zum Holzschneider, der den Entwurf mit der Vorderseite auf die mehrere Jahre abgelagerte und dreifach präparierte Holzplatte mit einer Stärke von ca. 2,5 cm klebt. Die Maserung der dazu verwendeten Wildkirsche (*yamazakura*) wird dabei durchaus dekorativ eingesetzt, etwa in *Die Sannō-Festprozession bei Kōjimachi itchōme* (Tafel 51). Um die Umrisslinien des Entwurfs gut sichtbar zu machen, werden die überflüssigen Schichten des Papiers vorsichtig abgeschabt. Mit einem feinen Messer legt der Holzschneider nun die Linien aus dem Block frei und hämmert alle leer gebliebenen Flächen mit einem groben Grabstichel heraus. Da nur ein einziges, beim Gravieren zerstörtes Entwurfsblatt besteht, muss er äußerst sorgsam vorgehen. Erst am Schluss wird eine *kentō* genannte Passmarke am äußeren Rand eingeritzt, an der das später zu druckende Papier im richtigen Winkel angelegt werden kann. Nun werden von dieser Konturenplatte so viele Blätter mit schwarzer Tusche gedruckt, wie unterschiedliche Farben für ein Blatt vorgesehen sind. Jede Farbe wird auf diesen Andrucken einzeln markiert, auf jeweils eine „Farbplatte" (*irohan*) aufgelegt und wie bei den schwarzen Konturen eingraviert.

Die Platten werden an den Drucker (*surishi*) weitergegeben, der zunächst das handgeschöpfte Kozo-Papier zuschneidet. Für das Ōban-Format der Serie musste dieses vom Maulbeerbaum gewonnene reißfeste und saugfähige Papier in der Größe *ōbōsho* gehälftet werden. Um die Papierfasern zu binden und das Verlaufen der Farben zu verhindern, wird das Papier mit Tierleim (*dōsa*) präpariert, der mit Alaun verdünnt ist. Drei Blätter übereinander feuchtet der Drucker nun mit einem breiten Pinsel an, die Druckplatte reibt er mit einer in Tusche getränkten Bürste ein und legt

Production d'une estampe

Comme on l'a évoqué plus haut, une des caractéristiques des *Cent Vues célèbres d'Edo* est le savoir-faire exceptionnel des graveurs (*horishi*) et des imprimeurs (*surishi*). Leur activité est le sujet de la feuille de Kunisada approuvée au huitième mois 1857 (ill. 24) qui traite de la parodie de l'artisanat. À partir de 1790, une fois que l'éditeur avait passé la commande au maître estampiste, le dessin à l'encre de Chine dut être soumis à la censure et recevoir le cachet de censure rond. Dans les *Cent Vues*, ce cachet est apposé à côté d'un cachet de datation placé hors de l'image, soit en haut, soit à gauche. Seule la feuille ajoutée par Shigenobu (pl. 119) présente le cachet en vigueur entre 1859 et 1871 qui combine l'*aratame* et la date. Suite à un décret de 1842, le nombre des couleurs était limité à huit – après qu'un an plus tôt, une estampe eut été imprimée avec 72 tons différents. Le fait que la limitation du nombre des couleurs ait aussi eu des aspects positifs ressort très clairement de la série de Hiroshige.

Après ces démarches administratives, une fois approuvée par la censure et dotée des indications de tons du maître, la feuille parvient au graveur qui la colle face avant contre la plaque de bois d'environ 2,5 cm d'épaisseur ayant séché plusieurs années avant de recevoir une triple préparation. Les veinures du merisier (*yamazakura*) utilisé pour les bois d'impression sont mises à profit comme élément résolument décoratif, comme on le voit par exemple dans *La procession solennelle de Sannō près de Kōjimachi itchōme* (pl. 51). Pour rendre nettement visibles les contours du dessin à graver, les couches superflues du verso de la feuille sont soigneusement grattées. Avec un fin ciseau, le graveur dégage alors les lignes du bois et ôte à la gouge et au marteau toutes les surfaces devant être épargnées. Dans la mesure où il n'existe qu'un seul dessin original et que celui-ci est détruit lors de ce premier travail de gravure, le graveur doit procéder de manière particulièrement méticuleuse. Ce n'est qu'au terme de ce travail qu'une marque appelée *kentō* est alors gravée le long du bord extérieur de l'image afin de pouvoir caler correctement la feuille au moment de l'imprimer. Cette première plaque de contours sert alors à imprimer à l'encre noire autant de feuilles qu'ont été prévues de couleurs pour l'estampe concernée. Chaque ton est indiqué séparément sur chacune des épreuves et appliqué sur un « bois à colorier » (*irohan*) par couleur, lequel est gravé à son tour comme l'ont été les contours noirs du premier bois.

Les plaques sont ensuite remises à l'imprimeur (*surishi*) qui découpe d'abord un papier de type *kōzo* puisé à la main. Pour le format *ōban* de la série, ce papier en fibres de mûrier indéchirable et absorbant devait être coupé en deux à partir d'une feuille de format *ōbōsho*. Pour lier les fibres du papier et éviter les bavures, le papier était préparé à l'aide d'une colle animale (*dōsa*) diluée d'alun. Avec un large pinceau, l'imprimeur humecte alors trois feuilles superposées, il enduit le bois à l'aide d'une brosse trempée d'encre d'imprimerie et applique une feuille le long de la marque de calage. Avec un tampon appelé *baren* – fait d'un tressage de ficelles enveloppé dans une feuille de bambou –, l'imprimeur frotte alors le papier fortement contre la plaque. Commençant par la

25

Tōkyō Dentō
Mokuhanga Kōgei
Kyōdō Kumiai (Tōkyō
Traditional Woodblock
Craft Society)

Reconstructed
sequence of the
printing process of
one printing block
with contour outlines
and 15 colour blocks
(to be viewed from
right to left)

Rekonstruierte Abfolge
des Druckprozesses von
einer Konturenplatte
und 15 Farbplatten
(von rechts nach
links zu betrachten)

Reconstitution des
étapes successives de
l'impression d'une
plaque de contours et de
15 plaques dédiées aux
couleurs (à considérer
de la droite vers la
gauche)

of/für/de:
Plate/Tafel/planche 44
*Nihonbashi tōri
itchōme ryakuzu,
8/1858*
*View of Nihonbashi
itchōme Street*

*Ansicht von der Straße
Nihonbashi itchōme*

*Vue de la rue Nihon-
bashi itchōme*

Courtesy Fukushima
Kiyotake, Unsōdō
Publishers,
Tokyo/Kyoto

P. 45
Detail from plate 113
Detail aus Tafel 113
Détail de planche 113

---

for the print *View of Nihonbashi itchōme Street* (ill. 25, plate 44). On the occasion of the Hiroshige's bicentenary in 1997, the then still young Tōkyō Traditional Woodblock Craft Society (Tōkyō Dentō Mokuhanga Kōgei Kyōdō Kumiai) embarked on a project of recutting and printing the *One Hundred Famous Views of Edo*. The production process, which spread over a period of six years, was meticulously recorded by the artists. Their documentation provided the source of these illustrations. The project allowed detailed insights into the sophisticated technical implementation of Hiroshige's compositions.

It is to the printers that the series owes numerous visual effects, such as the subtle gradations, known as *bokashi*, which give volume to an area of colour, or express effects of perspective or light, and make each print unique. There are various forms of *bokashi*, for example *atenashi bokashi* ("not-indicated colour gradation"), frequently used in this series, in which the cloudlike colour gradation is applied to an area of the woodblock not indicated by the artist, for example in the sky or water surfaces. The print *Sudden Shower over Shin-Ōhashi Bridge and Atake* (plate 58) was famous for a particularly elaborate application of this technique. The horizontal stroke of the *ichimonji bokashi* ("bokashi in the form of the figure one" – the figure one being horizontal in Japanese writing) can often be seen at the top margin of a print, for example on *Nihonbashi and Edobashi Bridges* (plate 43).

Another technique was the silver mica print (*kirazuri*), which can be seen, for example, on the scales of the fish on the carp banner on plate 48. And sometimes even both sides of the paper were printed (*ryōmenzuri*) in order to enhance the intensity of the colour. The technique of blind printing, i.e. without any colour (*karazuri*), raises the surface of the paper and was intended to emphasize particular elements of the scene. The effect can normally only be seen by looking at an original print in good light. One of the favourite uses of blind printing was to reproduce a textile structure by pressing a piece of cloth on to the paper (*nunomezuri*) within the contours of a particular motif, as indicated by the artist. This technique was used to good effect in the detail of the white length of cloth in *Hatsune Riding Ground in Bakuro-chō* (ill. 7, plate 6).

The importance of the printer for the quality of a woodblock print can be clearly seen by comparing a print from the first print run at the Ota Memorial Museum with a later edition of the print *The Original Fuji in Meguro* from the Chazen Museum (ills. 26, 27). A typical feature of later editions is the simpler coloration of the square title cartouches. Here, the originally intended colour scheme of brown, green and yellow was restricted to yellow. The long, drawn-out colour gradation of the sky from deep blue to white is much reduced, and the same is true of other areas, such as in the green of the hill in the foreground or on Fuji in the background, where the three-dimensional effect of the *bokashi* technique is less pronounced. Some of the artist's colour instructions were simply not followed in the later edition, for example, the thin yellow veil of cloud beneath the summit of Mount Fuji, or else different

---

ein Blatt an der Passmarke an. Mit dem *baren* genannten Scheibe – bestehend aus geflochtenen Schnüren, die von einem Bambusblatt umfasst sind – reibt der Drucker das Papier gegen die Platte. Danach legt er dieses Konturenblatt mit der hellsten Farbe angefangen nacheinander auf die mit den jeweiligen Farben eingeriebenen Irohan-Platten und setzt teilweise die Druckbewegungen als sichtbares Element des Endproduktes ein, wie auf dem Blatt *Der Schrein Kumano Junisha in Tsunohazu, bekannt unter dem Namen „Junisō"* (Tafel 50) deutlich zu erkennen. Mit Ausnahme der aus Kiefernruß gewonnenen Tusche und des chemisch hergestellten Preußischblaus (*beroai*) – das 1820 von den Holländern in Japan eingeführt und seit 1829 in japanischen Holzschnitten eingesetzt wurde – sind in den *Hundert Ansichten* wohl nur Pflanzen- und Mineralfarben verwendet worden. Diese erzeugten, zum Teil miteinander gemischt oder übereinandergedruckt, die Farbenpracht, für die die Serie so bekannt ist.

Wie kompliziert das Druckverfahren sein kann, wird aus der Abfolge von einer Konturenplatte und 15 Druckstadien für das Blatt *Ansicht von der Straße Nihonbashi itchome* deutlich (Abb. 25, Tafel 44). Aus Anlass des 200. Geburtstages von Hiroshige im Jahr 1997 begann die noch junge Handwerkergesellschaft traditioneller Holzschnitte Tokyo (Tōkyō Dentō Mokuhanga Kōgei Kyōdō Kumiai), die *Hundert Ansichten* nachzuschneiden und zu drucken. Den sich über sechs Jahre hinziehenden Herstellungsprozess haben die Künstler in einer minutiösen Dokumentation festgehalten, der diese Abbildungen entnommen sind. Sie lieferte detaillierte Erkenntnisse über die raffinierte technische Umsetzung von Hiroshiges Entwürfen.

Den Druckern verdankt die Serie zahlreiche visuelle Effekte wie die subtilen, *bokashi* genannten Gradierungen, die einer Farbfläche Volumen verleihen, Perspektive oder Lichteffekte ausdrücken können und jedes Blatt zum Unikat machen. Es gibt verschiedene Formen des *bokashi*, wie etwa das in dieser Serie besonders häufig angewendete *atenashi bokashi* („nicht angegebene Farbgradierung"), bei dem die wolkenartige Farbgradierung auf einem von der Holzplatte nicht vorgeschriebenem Bereich aufgebracht wird, etwa bei Wasserflächen oder dem Himmel. Für eine besonders elaborierte Version dieser Technik wurde das Blatt *Plötzlicher Schauer über der Brücke Shin-Ohashi und Atake* (Tafel 58) berühmt. Der waagerechte Strich des *ichimonji bokashi* („bokashi in Gestalt der Zahl Eins") ist häufig am oberen Bildrand zu sehen, etwa auf dem Blatt *Die Brücken Nihonbashi und Edobashi* (Tafel 43).

Daneben kamen aber auch der silberfarbene Glimmerdruck (*kirazuri*), z. B. auf den Fischschuppen des Karpfenbanners von Tafel 48, und sogar die Technik des beidseitigen Bedruckens (*ryōmenzuri*) zur Steigerung der Farbintensität zur Anwendung. Die Technik des Blinddrucks ohne Farbhinzufügung (*karazuri*) bewirkte eine Erhöhung der Blattoberfläche und sollte bestimmte Bildelemente betonen. Der Effekt ist fast nur beim Betrachten des Originals unter guten Lichtverhältnissen auszumachen. Unter den verschiedenen Blinddruckmethoden wird die Wiedergabe einer Stoffstruktur durch Aufdrucken eines Gewebes (*nunomezuri*)

---

couleur la plus claire, il applique ensuite cette feuille de contours successivement sur les plaques de merisier enduites de la couleur respective et exploite en partie les mouvements de pression comme élément visible du produit final, comme le montre très clairement l'estampe *Le sanctuaire de Kumano Junisha à Tsunohazu, aussi connu sous le nom « Junisō »* (pl. 50). À l'exception de l'encre noire, obtenue à partir de suie de pin, et du bleu de Prusse (*beroai*) obtenu par voie chimique – cette couleur avait été introduite au Japon par les Hollandais en 1820 et fut employée dans l'estampe japonaise à partir de 1829 –, seules des couleurs végétales ou minérales ont été utilisées pour les *Cent Vues*. Mélangées parfois entre elles ou imprimées l'une sur l'autre, celles-ci produisent la diversité de tons qui a contribué à la célébrité de la série.

L'extrême complexité du processus d'impression ressort par exemple de la plaque de contours suivie des 15 étapes d'impression qui ont été nécessaires pour réaliser la feuille *Vue de la rue Nihonbashi itchôme* (ill. 25, pl. 44). En 1997, à l'occasion du bicentenaire de la naissance de Hiroshige, la toute jeune société des artisans de l'estampe traditionnelle de Tokyo (Tōkyō Dentō Mokuhanga Kōgei Kyōdō Kumiai) a commencé à regraver et imprimer les *Cent Vues*. Le processus de fabrication, qui s'est étendu sur plus de six ans, a été minutieusement documenté par les artistes. Les reproductions concernées proviennent de cette documentation, qui a pu livrer des informations détaillées sur les raffinements techniques ayant permis de traduire les projets de Hiroshige dans l'estampe.

La série doit aux imprimeurs de nombreux effets visuels, tels les subtils dégradés appelés *bokashi*, qui servent à donner son volume à une surface de couleur, à traduire un effet de profondeur ou d'éclairage, et qui font de chaque feuille un exemplaire unique. Il existe différentes formes de *bokashi*, notamment l'*atenashi bokashi* (« dégradé de couleur non indiqué ») particulièrement fréquent dans les *Cent Vues*, grâce auquel le dégradé nuageux est appliqué dans un domaine non prescrit de la plaque de bois, par exemple pour le ciel ou les plans d'eau. La feuille *Averse soudaine sur le pont Shin-Ōhashi et Atake* (pl. 58) a ainsi été rendue célèbre par une version particulièrement élaborée de cette technique. Le trait horizontal de l'*ichimonji bokashi* (« bokashi sous la forme du nombre un ») apparaît souvent près du bord supérieur ; à titre d'exemple, on se reportera à la feuille *Les ponts Nihonbashi et Edobashi* (pl. 43).

À côté de cette technique ont aussi été employées l'estampage de particules de mica (*kirazuri*), par exemple pour les écailles de la carpe dans la bannière de la planche 48, ou encore l'estampage des deux côtés de la feuille (*ryōmenzuri*), qui permettait d'augmenter l'intensité des couleurs. La technique d'estampage à sec, c'est-à-dire sans encrage (*karazuri*), produisait un rehaut du plan de la feuille permettant d'accentuer certains éléments visuels. L'effet n'en est perceptible qu'en présence des originaux et dans de bonnes conditions d'éclairage. Parmi les différentes méthodes d'estampage à sec, un moyen particulièrement prisé est le rendu d'une trame textile par application d'un tissu (*nunomezuri*) à

26

27

colours were used, such as the light green of the hill or the blue-grey of the mountain range in the background.

The name of the woodblock engraver is occasionally given on the print itself. In the series *Famous Views of Sixty-Odd Provinces*, almost two-thirds of the prints bear the name "Horitake", often in a prominent position beside Hiroshige's signature. Even the technically skilled printers are occasionally mentioned by name. In the *One Hundred Famous Views of Edo*, though, no printer is named on any print, and the name of the woodblock engraver "Horisen" (i. e. Hori Sennosuke, probably the same person as Sugawa Sennosuke) appears only on *View of Shiba Coast* (plate 108), where it is integrated into the bottom left-hand half of the picture, and on a further three occasions in the left-hand margin (plates 17, 28, 83). The name "Horitake" (Yokogawa Takejirō) by contrast turns up on one print only, and then somewhat hidden: *Bamboo Quay by Kyōbashi Bridge* (ill. 2, plate 76). Horitake had engraved woodblocks for Hiroshige as early as 1847, and also worked for Kunisada.

Sakanaya not only largely suppressed the names of the wood engravers and printers, but also, unlike many of his fellow publishers, indicated his own name only outside the field of the print, where it was abbreviated to "Uoei" or, with the address "Shitaya (Shinkuro) Uoei."

By doing so, he gave undivided prominence to the print itself and to its creator, Hiroshige.

innerhalb eines angegebenen Motivs besonders gerne angewendet. Diese Technik kommt im Detail der weißen Stoffbahn auf dem Blatt *Der Reitplatz Hatsune no baba in Bakuro-chō* (Abb. 7, Tafel 6) gut zum Ausdruck.

Wie wichtig die Drucker für die Qualität eines Holzschnitts waren, wird anhand eines Vergleiches zwischen einem Erstdruck des Ota Memorial Museums und einem späteren Druck des Blattes *Der Ursprüngliche Fuji in Meguro* aus dem Chazen Art Museum deutlich (Abb. 26, 27). Typisch für die Nachdrucke sind die farblich einfacher gestalteten quadratischen Titelkartuschen. Hier wurde der ursprünglich beabsichtigte Farbakkord von Braun, Grün und Gelb nur auf das Gelb beschränkt. Die langgezogene Farbgradierung des Himmels von einem Tiefblau zum Weiß hin ist stark reduziert, wie auch an anderen Stellen, etwa im Grün des Hügels im Vordergrund oder im Fuji im Hintergrund, die volumengebende Wirkung der Bokashi-Technik vermindert ist. Einige Farbanweisungen wurden im Nachdruck nicht befolgt, wie der dünne gelbe Wolkenschleier unterhalb des Fuji-Gipfels, oder es kamen andere Farben zum Einsatz wie das Hellgrün des Hügels oder das Blaugrau der Bergkette im Hintergrund.

Der Name des Plattenschneiders wird gelegentlich auf den Holzschnitten selbst angegeben. Im Falle der Serie *Berühmte Ansichten von über sechzig Provinzen* sind mehr als 60 Prozent der Holzschnitte mit dem Namen „Horitake" versehen – oft sogar prominent neben Hiroshiges Signatur. Selbst die technisch versierten Drucker werden zuweilen namentlich erwähnt. Im Falle der *Hundert Ansichten* dagegen wird auf keinem Blatt ein Drucker genannt, und der Name des Holzschneiders „Horisen" – Hori Sennosuke (wohl identisch mit Sugawa Sennosuke) – erscheint nur auf der *Landschaft an der Küste Shibaura* (Tafel 108) integriert in der unteren linken Bildhälfte und weitere drei Mal außerhalb des linken Blattrandes (Tafeln 17, 28, 83). Derjenige von „Horitake" (Yokogawa Takejirō) taucht dagegen nur ein einziges Mal versteckt im Blatt *Bambusquai an der Brücke Kyobashi* auf (Abb. 2, Tafel 76). Horitake hatte schon 1847 für Hiroshiges Entwürfe die Platten geschnitten und war auch für Kunisada tätig.

Sakanaya hat nicht nur die Namen der Holzschneider und Drucker weitgehend verschwiegen, sondern – anders als viele seiner Kollegen – auch seinen eigenen Namen nur außerhalb des Bildrandes angegeben, abgekürzt zu „Uoei" oder mit der Adresse „Shitaya (Shinkuro) Uoei".

Damit hat er dem Bild selbst sowie seinem Schöpfer Hiroshige ungeteilte Geltung eingeräumt.

l'intérieur d'un motif indiqué. Cette technique se relève par exemple très bien dans le détail de la grande bande de drap blanc de la feuille *Le manège équestre Hatsune no baba à Bakuro-chō* (ill. 7, pl. 6).

L'extrême importance de l'imprimeur pour la qualité d'une estampe ressort très clairement de la comparaison entre un tirage des débuts comme celui du *Fuji original à Meguro* de l'Ota Memorial Museum et le tirage ultérieur de la même feuille conservé au Chazen Museum (ill. 26, 27). Sont caractéristiques des réimpressions les cartouches de titre carrés de coloris moins élaboré. Ici, l'accord initialement prévu de brun, de vert et de jaune a été réduit au seul jaune ; au niveau du ciel, le long dégradé du bleu profond au blanc a été fortement réduit ; de même, l'effet de volume produit par le *bokashi* est également moindre au niveau du ton vert de la colline au premier plan ou du mont Fuji à l'arrière-plan. Dans les tirages ultérieurs, certaines indications de couleurs n'ont pas été respectées, comme le subtil voile nuageux jaune sous le sommet du Fuji, ou encore, des tons différents ont été utilisés, comme pour le vert de la colline ou le bleu-gris du massif montagneux à l'arrière-plan.

Le nom du graveur est parfois gravé sur les plaques mêmes. Dans le cas de la série des *Vues célèbres des 60 et quelques provinces*, plus de 60 pour cent des bois portent le nom « Horitake » – souvent même en place proéminente à côté de la signature de Hiroshige. Les meilleurs imprimeurs sont parfois eux-mêmes cités nommément. Mais dans le cas des *Cent Vues*, aucun nom d'imprimeur ne figure sur les feuilles, et celui du graveur « Horisen » – Hori Sennosuke (sans doute identique avec Sugawa Sennosuke) – n'apparaît que dans *La côte à Shibaura* (pl. 108), dans la moitié inférieure gauche de l'image, et par trois fois dans la marge gauche des feuilles 17, 28, 83. Celui de « Horitake » (Yokogawa Takejirō) n'apparaît en revanche qu'une seule fois, caché dans la feuille *Le quai au bambou près du pont Kyōbashi* (ill. 2, pl. 76). Dès 1847, Horitake avait déjà gravé des plaques pour des projets de Hiroshige, et il a aussi travaillé pour le compte de Kunisada.

Sakanaya n'a pas seulement largement passé sous silence les noms des graveurs et des imprimeurs, mais – à la différence de nombreux collègues – n'a fait figurer son propre nom qu'en marge, abrévié en « Uoei » ou avec l'adresse « Shitaya (Shinkuro) Uoei ».

Il a ainsi donné une valeur sans partage aux image elles-mêmes et à leur créateur Hiroshige.

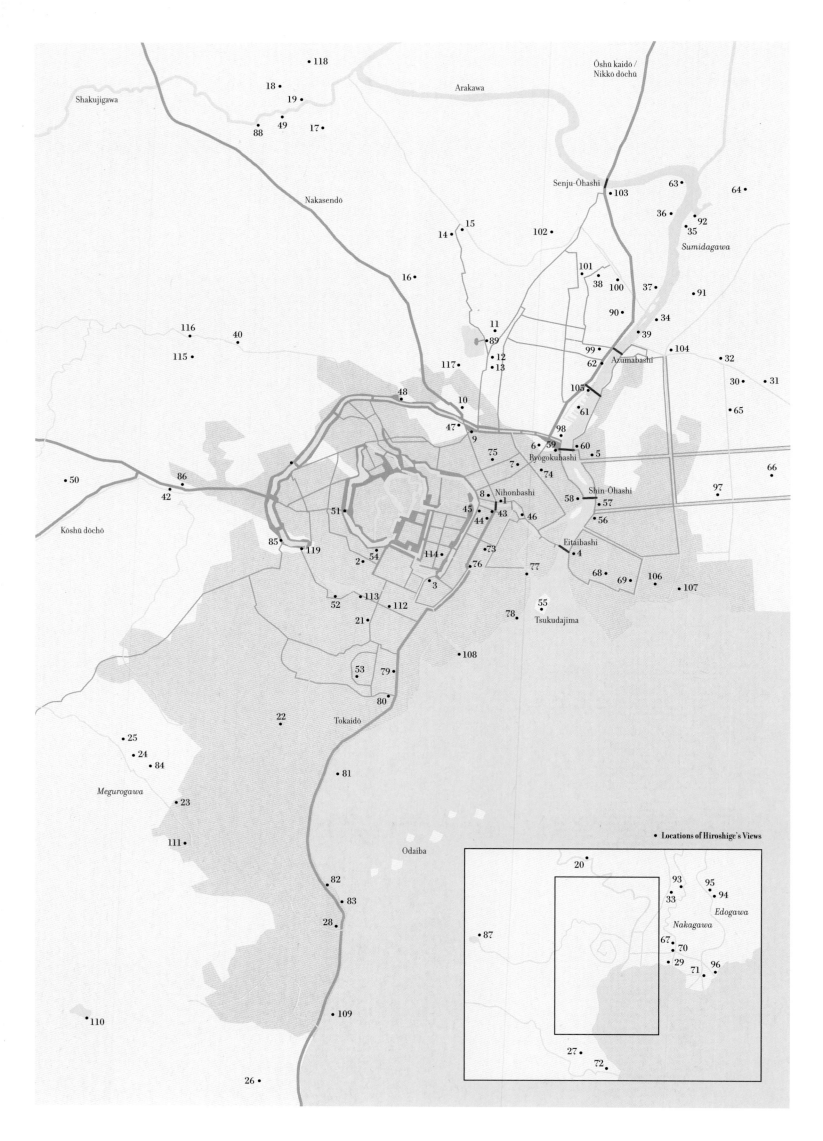

MEISHO
EDO
HYAKKEI

One
Hundred
Famous
Views
of Edo

Hundert
berühmte
Ansichten
von Edo

Cent
Vues
célèbres
d'Edo

Table of Contents

Known as a designer of bookbindings, Baisotei Gengyo (1817–1880) presents the titles of the 118 prints of the *One Hundred Famous Views of Edo*, which appeared by the tenth month of 1858, in a colourful and decorative woodblock print. Gengyo, whose lozenge-shaped seal appears bottom right, had already designed the far simpler table of contents for Hiroshige's series *Famous Views of Sixty-Odd Provinces* (*Rokujū yoshū meisho zue*) in the ninth month of 1856, in which he used seven regions as his structuring principle. For the *One Hundred Famous Views of Edo*, and doubtless after consultation with the publisher of the series, Sakanaya Eikichi (life dates unknown), he arranged the prints by the seasons of the year.

The two rectangular fields at the top relate to prints with the theme of spring. The abbreviated picture titles are arranged in two rows, each of which is to be read from right to left. With 42 titles, spring is the best represented season, followed by summer with 30, which are listed on a blue-and-green graduated fan. By arranging the titles into three groups, Gengyo elegantly exploited the asymmetrical fan format. The first title in each group begins at the top with a powerfully written character; the second is to its left, while the third is somewhat lower. The titles of the 26 autumn and 20 winter prints are set off by textile blind printing, like the spring cartouches, and the titles are printed over decorations reminiscent of traditional calligraphy paper.

The red title cartouche (left) contains four large characters that read *Edo hyakkei* (*One Hundred Views of Edo*). The word *meisho* ("famous"), with which the series title starts, was omitted, probably because it was already well known. Above the title to the right is the name "Ichiryūsai Hiroshige", while to the left of the name the series is acclaimed as the most representative work of the master (*issei ichidai*). Beneath the title, and almost as prominent, is the name of the publisher Sakanaya Eikichi, with his address in the vicinity of the Kan'eiji Temple in Ueno, called "Tōeizan Hirokōji".

The poetic connotations of the formats of the titles, and the common method of "scattered writing" (*chirashigaki*) in calligraphy on the fan are stylistic means that correspond to the seasonal ordering of the prints: this method had been used in numerous anthologies of poems since the Heian period (794–1185). The background to the title cartouches also displays seasonal motifs: a blossoming plumtree for spring, the Hototogisu bird against the white disc of the moon for summer and the seven different plants on a haystack for autumn.

The table of contents lists 118 prints and excludes only the composition by Hiroshige's successor, Shigenobu (Hiroshige II, plate 119), approved in the fourth month of 1859. Sakanaya Eikichi commissioned it because he wanted to bind a complete series of prints in albums in a rational order. The present series from the Ota Memorial Museum of Art belongs to such an early complete album.

By arranging the prints according to the four seasons, Gengyo and the publisher took a decision with far-reaching consequences. Not only the contemporary albums, but also subsequent publications, as well as books and articles on the series, all follow the same principle. The lack of any seasonal import in many of the prints is usually overlooked, however. Hiroshige has had narrative intentions imputed to him as a result of identifying a sequence based on a region or motif. If the series were to be ordered chronologically, by the date seals of the censors, a quite different picture would emerge, namely one that focused on the historical background of the creation of the series. Even so, in this publication we have followed the convention of ordering the prints according to Gengyo's table of contents, as that is how the Ota series has been handed down to us.

Inhaltsverzeichnis

Der als Entwerfer von Bucheinschlägen bekannte Baisotei Gengyo (1817–1880) präsentiert die Titel der bis zum zehnten Monat 1858 erschienenen 118 Drucke der *Hundert berühmten Ansichten von Edo* in einem farbenfrohen, dekorativen Holzschnitt. Gengyo, dessen rautenförmiges Siegel rechts unten angebracht ist, hatte bereits im neunten Monat 1856 das viel schlichter gehaltene Inhaltsverzeichnis für Hiroshiges Serie *Berühmte Ansichten von über sechzig Provinzen* (*Rokujū yoshū meisho zue*) entworfen, in dem er sieben Regionen zum Ordnungsprinzip erhob. Bei den *Hundert Ansichten* teilte er, sicherlich nach Absprache mit dem Verleger der Serie, Sakanaya Eikichi (Lebensdaten unbekannt), die Blätter nach den vier Jahreszeiten ein.

Die oberen beiden rechteckigen Formate beziehen sich auf die Holzschnitte zum Thema Frühling. Die abgekürzten Bildtitel sind in zwei Reihen angeordnet, die jeweils von rechts nach links zu lesen sind. Mit 42 Titeln ist der Frühling die am stärksten vertretene Jahreszeit, gefolgt von 30 Titeln für den Sommer, die auf einem blaugrün changierenden Fächer aufgelistet sind. Indem Gengyo sie zu Dreiergruppen zusammenfasst, nutzt er das asymmetrische Fächerformat elegant aus. Der erste Titel beginnt jeweils oben mit einem kräftig geschriebenen Zeichen; der zweite steht links daneben, während der dritte etwas nach unten versetzt ist. Die 26 Herbst- und 20 Winterblätter sind, wie die Frühlingskartuschen mit Stoffblinddruck abgesetzt, auf Dekore aufgebracht, die an traditionelle Kalligrafiepapiere erinnern.

In der roten Titelkartusche steht *Edo hyakkei* (*Hundert Ansichten von Edo*) in vier großen Zeichen. Das *meisho*, mit dem der Serientitel beginnt, hat Gengyo, wohl wegen hinlänglicher Bekanntheit, weggelassen. Darüber befindet sich rechts der Name „Ichiryūsai Hiroshige", daneben wird die Serie als das repräsentativste Werk des Holzschnittmeisters (*issei ichidai*) angepriesen. Unterhalb des Titels ist, fast ebenso prominent, der Name des Verlegers Sakanaya Eikichi mit seiner Adresse nahe dem Tempel Kan'eiji in Ueno, „Tōeizan Hirokōji", genannt.

Durch die lyrisch konnotierten Bildformate für die Titel und die in der Kalligrafie gebräuchliche Methode des „gestreuten Schreibens" (*chirashigaki*) auf dem Fächer greift Gengyo Stilmittel auf, die dem Ordnungsprinzip nach den vier Jahreszeiten entsprechen: Seit der Heian-Zeit (794–1185) wurde es in zahlreichen Gedichtanthologien angewendet. Auch der Hintergrund, gegen den die Titelblätter gesetzt sind, weist jahreszeitliche Motive auf: Der Frühling ist durch einen blühenden Pflaumenbaum, der Sommer durch den Vogel Hototogisu vor der weißen Mondscheibe und der Herbst durch seine sieben verschiedenen Gräser an einem Heuhaufen repräsentiert.

Das Inhaltsverzeichnis umfasst 118 Blätter und schließt nur den im vierten Monat 1859 genehmigten Entwurf von Hiroshiges Nachfolger Shigenobu (Hiroshige II, Tafel 119) aus. Sakanaya Eikichi gab es in Auftrag, weil er komplette Serien von Blättern, die er möglicherweise schon von Beginn an zurückhielt, sinnvoll geordnet in Alben binden wollte. Zu solch einem frühen kompletten Album gehört das vorliegende des Ota Memorial Museum of Art.

Mit der Anordnung der Blätter nach den vier Jahreszeiten haben Gengyo und der Verleger der Serie eine folgenreiche Entscheidung getroffen. Nicht nur die zeitgleichen Alben, auch die folgenden Publikationen und Schriften über diese Serie richten sich nach diesem Prinzip. Dabei wird meist übersehen, wie unerheblich für zahlreiche Blätter jahreszeitliche Motive sind; auch werden so Hiroshige narrative Absichten durch die Abfolge der Blätter mit ihren regionalen oder motivischen Bezügen unterstellt. Würde man die Serie nach den Datumssiegeln der Zensoren anordnen, ergäbe sich ein anderes Bild, eines, das die historischen Hintergründe ihrer Entstehung in den Vordergrund rückte. In dieser Publikation folgen wir dennoch der Konvention, die Blätter nach Gengyos Inhaltsverzeichnis anzuordnen, da die Ota-Serie so überliefert wurde.

La table des matières

Baisotei Gengyo (1817–1880), connu comme concepteur de pages de garde, présente les titres des 118 estampes des *Cent Vues célèbres d'Edo* parues jusqu'au dixième mois 1858 dans une feuille décorative très colorée – son sceau en forme de losange figure en bas à droite de la page. Au neuvième mois 1856, Gengyo avait déjà créé la table des matières beaucoup plus sobre de la série des *Vues célèbres des soixante et quelques provinces* (*Rokujū yoshū meisho zue*), qu'il avait classées en sept régions principales. En concertation avec l'éditeur Sakanaya Eikichi (dates inconnues), il allait répartir les feuilles des *Cent Vues* en fonction des quatre saisons.

Les deux rectangles en haut de page recensent les estampes de la section printemps. Les titres abrévíés ont été disposés sur deux rangées qui se lisent de droite à gauche. Avec 42 titres, le printemps est la saison la plus représentée, suivie de l'été avec 30 titres listés sur un éventail chatoyant dans des tons bleu-vert. En les regroupant par groupes de trois, Gengyo exploite élégamment le format asymétrique de l'éventail. Le premier titre débute toujours en haut avec un caractère écrit en gras, le deuxième est placé à sa gauche, tandis que le troisième est légèrement décalé vers le bas. Tout comme les deux cartouches du printemps, les 26 et 20 feuilles des sections automne et hiver se distinguent par un estampage à sec à motif textile, le tout sur des décors rappelant les papiers traditionnellement utilisés pour la calligraphie.

Dans le cartouche de titre à fond rouge, on peut lire *Edo hyakkei* (*Cent Vues d'Edo*) en quatre grands caractères. Le terme *meisho* qui ouvre le titre de la série a été laissé de côté par Gengyo, sans doute parce qu'il était de notoriété publique. À droite en revanche, on trouve le nom « Ichiryūsai Hiroshige », à côté, la série est célébrée comme l'œuvre la plus représentative du maître estampiste (*issei ichidai*). Sous le titre figure de manière presque aussi proéminente, le nom de l'éditeur Sakanaya Eikichi avec l'adresse de la maison d'édition près du temple Kan'eiji à Ueno, appelé « Tōeizan Hirokōji ».

Du fait de la connotation poétique des formats utilisés pour les titres et de la méthode usuelle en calligraphie de « l'écriture éparse » (*chirashigaki*) dans l'éventail, Gengyo utilise des moyens stylistiques dont le principe de classement correspond aux quatre saisons : depuis l'ère Heian (794–1185), ce style était en effet couramment utilisé dans bien des anthologies poétiques. L'arrière-plan sur lequel sont posées les présentations des titres, comporte lui aussi des motifs saisonniers : le printemps est représenté par un prunier en fleurs, l'été par l'oiseau Hototogisu devant le disque lunaire blanc et l'automne par ses sept différentes herbes près d'une meule de foin.

La table des matières comprend 118 feuilles et exclut uniquement le projet du successeur de Hiroshige (Shigenobu, dit Hiroshige II, pl. 119), projet qui ne fut approuvé qu'au quatrième mois 1859. Sakanaya Eikichi a commandé cette table des matières pour relier sous forme d'album des séries complètes qu'il mit sans doute de côté dès le début de la publication. L'exemplaire de l'Ota Mémorial Museum of Art reproduit dans le présent ouvrage est un de ces albums complets de la première heure.

Avec le classement des feuilles selon les quatre saisons, Gengyo et l'éditeur de la série ont pris une décision lourde de conséquences. Les autres albums de la même époque, mais aussi les écrits et publications sur les *Cent Vues* ont entériné ce principe de classement. Pourtant, on oublie généralement que les motifs saisonniers jouent un rôle plutôt secondaire dans bien des feuilles ; qui plus est, cet ordre et ses références régionales ou thématiques prêtent à Hiroshige des intentions narratives qu'il n'a pas eues. Si les feuilles étaient classées en fonction des cachets de datation des censeurs, on obtiendrait une tout autre image de la série, image qui mettrait en avant la toile de fond historique de sa genèse. Dans la présente publication, nous n'en suivons pas moins la convention qui classe les feuilles dans l'ordre indiqué par la table des matières de Gengyo. Une des raisons en est que c'est dans cet ordre que nous parvient aujourd'hui la série de l'Ota.

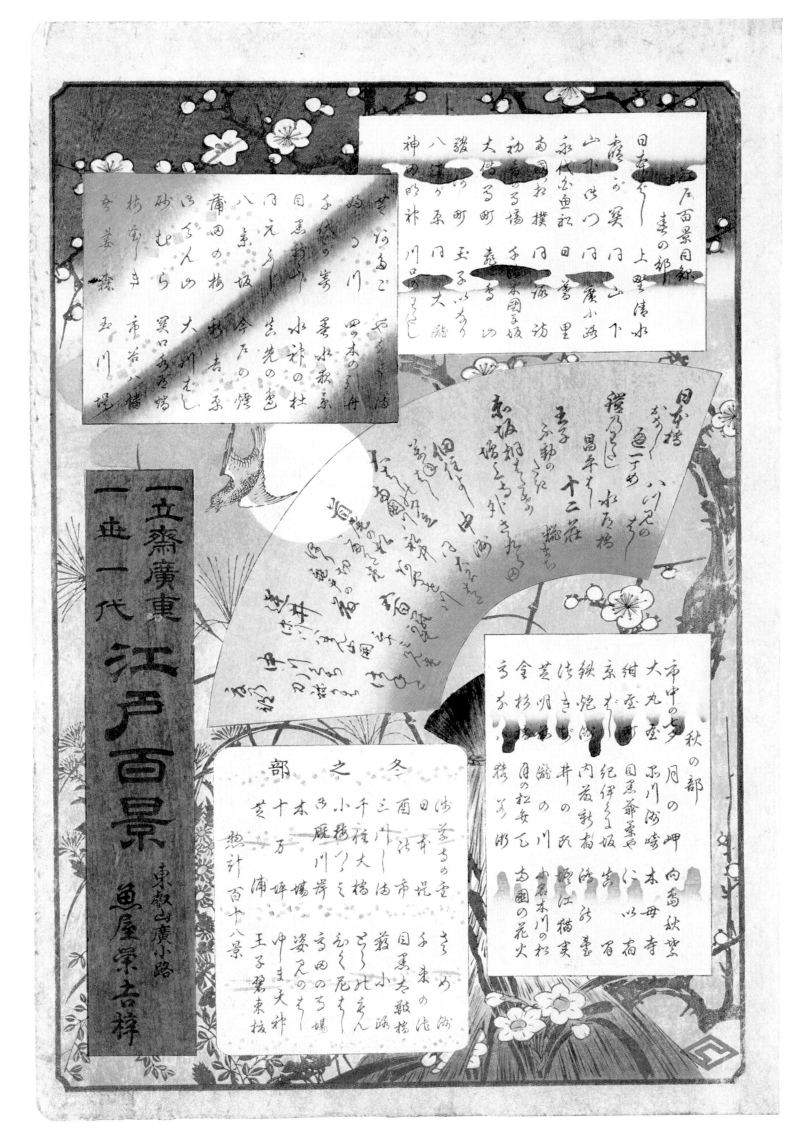

日本橋
雪晴

Nihonbashi yukibare
5–1856

Nihonbashi: Clearing after Snow

In the very first print of the series, Hiroshige unfolds the whole range of his vision: the lofty and sublime are shown side by side with the profane and the everyday. Its base covered by a layer of mist, snow-covered Mount Fuji rises majestically above the horizon and dominates the scene. On the right, schematically indicated in monochrome, is the Edo castle of the Tokugawa dynasty, which had ruled Japan since the beginning of the 17th century.

The lower half of the print, characterized by the fresh and strong blue of the river, depicts the hustle and bustle of the great fish market on the northern bank. The Nihonbashi, the large, crowded bridge in the centre of the picture, was built in 1603; literally the "Bridge of Japan", it had since 1605 been the official point from which all distances in the country were measured.

This combination of the Nihonbashi Bridge, the shogun's castle and Mount Fuji had become one of Edo's most celebrated and iconic views. Since the 18th century, various painters and printmakers, including the famous Katsushika Hokusai (1760–1849) and Shiba Kōkan (1747–1818), the latter well known for his engagement with the rules of Western perspective, had tried time and again to find new ways of capturing these key motifs. Hiroshige was one of the few to choose the vertical format.

In this print we witness the culmination of the craftsmanship of the very best printers, who were responsible for the subtle gradation of the blue from a deep, almost blue-black shade in the middle of the river to the pale blue of the water near both banks of the river. This effect, known as *bokashi*, was achieved by the careful wiping away of pigment from parts of the printing block. The degree of *bokashi* is what determines the quality of a print.

Die Brücke Nihonbashi: Aufklaren nach dem Schneefall

Schon auf dem ersten Blatt zeigt uns Hiroshige die ganze Spannbreite seiner Vision: Das Hohe und Erhabene wird gleichzeitig mit dem Profanen und Alltäglichen in unser Blickfeld gerückt.

So thront durch Schichten von Nebelschwaden abgetrennt der schneebedeckte Berg Fuji am Horizont über der gesamten Szene. Am rechten Rand schwebt, schemenhaft und monochrom gehalten, das Schloss der Tokugawa, der japanischen Herrscherdynastie seit Beginn des 17. Jahrhunderts.

Die untere Bildhälfte wird vom frischen, kräftigen Blau des Flusses geprägt. Sie zeigt das emsige Treiben auf dem Fisch-Großmarkt am Nordufer. Die Nihonbashi, die große belebte Brücke in der Bildmitte, wurde 1603 erbaut. Die sogenannte „Japan-Brücke" war seit 1605 der offizielle Kilometer Null, von dem aus alle Distanzen in Japan gemessen wurden.

Die Tafel zeigt die Brücke Nihonbashi zusammen mit dem shogunalen Schloss und dem Berg Fuji. Diese Bildkomposition wurde zu einer der wichtigsten und bekanntesten Ansichten von Edo. Seit dem 18. Jahrhundert hatten unterschiedliche Maler und Grafiker, darunter der für die Auseinandersetzung mit westlichen Perspektivregeln bekannte Shiba Kōkan (1747–1818) und der berühmte Katsushika Hokusai (1760–1849), immer wieder versucht, diese Bildelemente visuell neu umzusetzen. Aber nur wenige Künstler wählten wie Hiroshige das Hochformat.

Auf diesem Holzschnitt sehen wir einen Höhepunkt in der Meisterschaft der besten Drucker, die für die sanfte Gradierung der Farbe Blau, von einem tiefen, ins Blauschwarz reichenden Ton in der Flussmitte bis zum Blassblau der Ufernähe, verantwortlich zeichnen. Dieses sogenannte *bokashi* wird durch das sorgfältige, stellenweise Entfernen von Farbe auf dem Druckstock erzielt. Der Grad der Abstufungen des *bokashi* ist maßgeblich für die Qualität eines Blattes.

Éclaircie après la chute de neige – le pont Nihonbashi

Dès la première feuille de la série, Hiroshige nous montre toute l'étendue de sa vision : dans notre champ de vision, le noble et le sublime côtoient le profane et le quotidien.

Ainsi, à l'horizon, isolé par des nappes de brouillard, le mont Fuji sous la neige domine un vaste panorama. Près du bord droit apparaît la silhouette schématique et monochrome du château d'Edo, résidence, depuis le début du XVIIe siècle, des Tokugawa, la grande dynastie seigneuriale du Japon.

La moitié inférieure de l'image est marquée par la fraîcheur bleu vif de la rivière. L'on y voit s'affairer le grand marché aux poissons de la rive nord. La construction du Nihonbashi, le grand pont très animé au centre de l'image, remonte à 1603. À partir de 1605, le « Pont du Japon » devint le kilomètre zéro officiel d'où étaient mesurées toutes les distances du pays.

En regroupant le pont Nihonbashi, le château shogunal et le mont Fuji, cette composition devint l'une des vues les plus importantes et les plus célèbres d'Edo. Depuis le XVIIIe siècle, différents peintres et graveurs, notamment Shiba Kōkan (1747–1818), connu pour son travail sur les lois de la perspective, et le célèbre Katsushika Hokusai (1760–1849), ont sans cesse tenté de donner de nouvelles transpositions visuelles de ces éléments iconiques. Rares sont toutefois les artistes qui ont choisi pour cela le format en hauteur utilisé par Hiroshige dans les *Cent Vues célèbres d'Edo*.

L'estampe nous présente aussi la plus haute maîtrise technique des meilleurs imprimeurs, auxquels se doivent les subtils dégradés de bleu – du profond bleu-noir au centre de la rivière jusqu'au bleu pâle près des deux rives. Cette technique appelée *bokashi* s'obtient par la suppression soigneuse de l'encre sur le bois d'impression. La finesse du camaïeu du *bokashi* est un facteur d'appréciation décisif de la qualité d'une feuille.

霞
か
せ
き

Kasumigaseki
1–1857

Kasumigaseki

This view is characterized by brilliant horizontal bands of blue, white, red, green and grey. In order not to diminish the effect of these colour zones, the two daimyō residences have been placed at the extreme left and right of the scene. The wide street in the middle, which descends steeply to Edo Bay, seems cut off by the green colour zone; the linear perspective used to depict the street appears somewhat schematic, for the flat areas of colour create a predominantly two-dimensional impression.

The guardhouse of the residence of Asano, the feudal lord of Hiroshima, is on the left, while on the right are the grey barracks of the samurai serving the daimyō Kuroda from Fukuoka on Kyūshū Island. They lay strategically on the fringes of the complex, so that their walls protected the feudal lords, whose residence was at its centre.

The *kadomatsu* ("gate pines") standing on both sides of the street indicate a change of season, for they were traditionally set up in front of houses for the New Year's festival. Deities were supposed to settle on them and so bring good fortune to a household during the coming year.

The paths of different sorts of people cross on the broad street. An inhabitant of Edo and her daughter, together with two *manzai* dancers (who for a small offering at New Year bring good fortune and prosperity during the coming year), are watching a group of *kashima* dancers approach, led by a man dressed as a shrine priest – they proclaim the oracle of the Kashima deity at New Year. Behind them are a few samurai, dressed in ceremonial costume, also climbing the slope from the city; a linking element, they guide our gaze across the roofs of the city to Edo Bay, which is punctuated with the white sails of distant boats.

High in the sky, cropped by the top margin of the print, hovers a kite with the character for "fish" (*sakana*). This is a reference to the first character in the name of the publisher of this series, Sakanaya Eikichi; his abbreviated signature, "Uoei," appears outside the left-hand picture frame. The censors approved the design of this print in the first month of 1857 – and we can assume that the publisher also hoped for continuing success in the second year of the series.

Kasumigaseki

In Blau, Weiß, Rot, Grün und Grau leuchten dem Betrachter horizontale, unterschiedlich breite Farbzonen entgegen und prägen den ersten Bildeindruck. Um die Wirkung dieser Farbräume nicht zu schmälern, liegen die beiden Daimyō-Residenzen an den äußersten linken und rechten Bildrand gerückt. Die breite Straße in der Bildmitte fällt zur Bucht von Edo stark ab und wirkt durch die grünliche Farbzone wie abgeschnitten. Die Linearperspektive leitet den Blick, erhält jedoch durch die flächige Anordnung der Farben eine schematische Komponente.

Das Wächterhaus der Residenz von Asano, des Feudalherrn von Hiroshima, ist auf der linken Seite angeordnet, während sich rechts die grauen Kasernen der Samurai, die dem Daimyō Kuroda aus Fukuoka auf Kyūshū dienten, befinden. Sie lagen strategisch an den Außenseiten des Anwesens, um den im Inneren der Anlage residierenden Daimyō durch ihre Mauern zu schützen.

Die an beiden Straßenseiten stehenden *kadomatsu*, „Kiefern am Tor", verweisen auf den Zeitpunkt des Jahreswechsels, denn sie wurden traditionell zum Neujahrsfest vor den Häusern aufgestellt. Die Götter sollten sich in ihnen einnisten, um dem dahinterliegenden Haus für das neue Jahr Glück zu bringen.

Auf der breiten Straße kreuzen sich die Wege verschiedener Menschen. Eine Städterin und ihre Tochter betrachten zusammen mit zwei Manzai-Tänzern, die gegen einen Obolus zu Neujahr Wohlstand verheißen, eine Gruppe von Kashima-Tänzern. Ein als Schreinpriester gekleideter Mann führt die Tänzergruppe an, die an Neujahr das Orakel der Kashima-Gottheit verkündet. Hinter ihnen sind Samurai zu erkennen, die in Festtagstracht von der Stadt aus den Hang hinaufsteigen. Als verbindendes Element leiten sie den Blick über die Dächer der Stadt auf die durch Segelboote akzentuierte Bucht von Edo.

Hoch am Himmel, vom Bildrand angeschnitten, schwebt der Drachen mit dem Schriftzeichen „Fisch" (*sakana*). Es verweist auf das erste Zeichen im Namen des Verlegers dieses Werkes, Sakanaya Eikichi, während sich dessen abgekürzte Signatur „Uoei" außerhalb des linken Bildrandes befindet. Die Veröffentlichung des Blattes wurde von den Zensoren im ersten Monat des Jahres 1857 genehmigt – sicherlich erhoffte sich der Verleger auch für das zweite Entstehungsjahr der Serie die Fortsetzung ihres Erfolg.

Kasumigaseki

Des bandes horizontales de différentes largeurs et couleurs – bleu, blanc, rouge, vert et gris – illuminent le regard du spectateur et déterminent la première impression visuelle. Pour ne pas diminuer l'effet de ces plans chromatiques, les deux résidences de daimyōs ont été reléguées contre les bords gauche et droit de l'image. Au centre, la large route qui plonge vers la baie d'Edo semble traversée par la zone de couleur verdâtre. La perspective linéaire dirige le regard vers la profondeur, cependant que l'organisation des couleurs dans le plan lui confère une apparence schématique.

La maison du gardien de la résidence d'Asano, le seigneur féodal d'Hiroshima, est placée du côté gauche de l'image, tandis qu'à droite se trouvent les casernes grises des samouraïs placés au service du daimyō Kuroda de Fukuoka à Kyūshū. Elles étaient adossées stratégiquement contre l'enceinte extérieure du complexe pour protéger le daimyō vivant à l'intérieur.

Les deux *kadomatsu*, les « pins de porte » qui se dressent de part et d'autre de la rue, renvoient à l'époque du changement d'année, car ils étaient traditionnellement installés devant les maisons pour le Nouvel An.

Les dieux devaient venir s'y nicher pour apporter fortune et bonheur aux foyers pendant l'année nouvelle.

Dans la large rue se croisent les routes de différentes personnes. Une habitante d'Edo et sa fille regardent un groupe de danseurs *kashima* accompagnés de deux danseurs de *manzai* qui promettent la prospérité pour la nouvelle année en échange d'une obole. Un homme vêtu en prêtre d'un sanctuaire anime le groupe de danseurs qui répand l'oracle de la divinité Kashima pour l'année à venir. Derrière eux, des samouraïs en habit de cérémonie gravissent la côte depuis la ville. Ils servent d'élément de transition et dirigent le regard des toits de la ville vers la baie d'Edo ponctuée de voiliers.

Haut dans le ciel, coupé par le bord de l'image, vole le dragon arborant l'idéogramme « poisson » (*sakana*). Il renvoie au premier signe du nom de Sakanaya Eikichi, l'éditeur de cet ouvrage, dont la signature abréviée « Uoei » figure à gauche dans la marge de la feuille. La publication de cette estampe a été approuvée par la censure au premier mois de l'année 1857 – après un an de succès, l'éditeur espérait assurément voir se répéter les ventes de la série pendant la deuxième année.

山下町
日比谷外
さくら田

Yamashita-chō, Hibiya Soto-Sakurada
12–1857

Hibiya and
Soto-Sakurada from
Yamashita-chō

The main theme of this print is again the New Year, the symbols of which are brought even more emphatically into the foreground than in the previous print.

The middle distance is dominated by the finely gradated blue of the water. On the right-hand margin of the print, a high stone wall topped by trees rises from the outer moat of Edo Castle, while on the left there is a *kadomatsu* pine (see plate 2), set up for the New Year, its upper branches reaching up to Mount Fuji.

Two large *hagoita* bats, used to play the Japanese version of badminton known as *hanetsuki*, project from the left and right margins, by which they are abruptly cropped. These decorated bats were sold in the precincts of the Sensōji Temple in Asakusa every year in the middle of the twelfth month on the occasion of the imminent New Year.

High up in the sky we can see a shuttlecock, propelled there by one of the *hagoita* bats. The game is in full swing, but the players cannot be seen: we are encouraged to cast our gaze beyond the confines of the print, and to imagine the players for ourselves.

Another favourite New Year's activity was kite flying. In this print, the lines are seen rising into the air some way off, but there is no sign of those who are actually flying the paper kites.

In the middle of the scene is the broad red gate (in form and colour almost identical to the title and signature cartouches) of the imposing residence of the very wealthy daimyō Nabeshima Kansō (1814–1871) from the fief of Saga on Kyūshū Island. This feudal lord was one of the first producers of Western artillery pieces in Japan and served the emperor after the Meiji Restoration of 1868. As a high official, he was responsible during this period for, among other things, the development of the northern, main island of Hokkaidō.

Hibiya und
Soto-Sakurada von
Yamashita-chō aus

Hauptthema des Blattes ist der Jahreswechsel, wobei die Neujahrssymbole noch stärker als auf der vorhergehenden Tafel an den Betrachter herangerückt werden. Das fein abgestufte Blau des Wassers bestimmt das Zentrum des Bildes. Eine hohe, mit Bäumen bewachsene Steinmauer erhebt sich am rechten Bildrand aus dem äußeren Wassergraben des Edo-Schlosses, während links der Blick über die Zweige einer zu Neujahr aufgestellten Kadomatsu-Kiefer (siehe Tafel 2) bis zur Spitze des Fuji schweift.

Zwei Hagoita-Schläger, die beim japanischen Federballspiel *hanetsuki* zum Einsatz kommen, ragen angeschnitten von den Bildrändern in die Komposition. Die mit bambusähnlichen Ornamenten verzierten Schläger wurden jedes Jahr in der Mitte des zwölften Monats, anlässlich des bevorstehenden Jahreswechsels, auf dem Gelände des Tempels Sensōji in Asakusa verkauft.

Hoch am Himmel schwebt der Federball, den die Hagoita-Schläger hinauf befördert

haben. Das Spiel ist in vollem Lauf, doch die Spieler sind nicht zu sehen. So wird der Betrachter angeregt, seinen Blick nach rechts und links zu wenden, um sich die Identität der Spielpartner vorstellen zu können. Eine weitere zu Neujahr bevorzugte Aktivität ist das Drachensteigen. Auf dem Holzschnitt steigen die Leinen von weit her in den Himmel, aber auch hier ist nicht zu sehen, wer die Papierdrachen aufsteigen lässt.

In Form und Farbe fast identisch mit dem Titelstreifen und der Signaturenkartusche ist das breite rote Tor der beeindruckenden Residenz, die das Bildzentrum beherrscht. Sie war das Anwesen eines der reichsten Daimyōs, Nabeshima Kansō (1814–1871) aus dem Feudalgebiet Saga auf Kyūshū. Der Feudalherr gehörte zu den ersten Produzenten westlicher Artilleriegeschosse in Japan und diente nach der Meiji-Restauration von 1868 dem Kaiser. Als hoher Beamter war er in dieser Zeit unter anderem für die Erschließung der nördlichen Hauptinsel Hokkaidō zuständig.

Vue de Hibiya
et de Soto-Sakurada depuis
Yamashita-chō

Le sujet principal de cette feuille est le changement de saison, sachant que les symboles du Nouvel An ont été rapprochés du spectateur plus encore que dans la feuille précédente.

Le subtil dégradé de bleu au niveau de l'eau régit le centre de la composition. Près du bord droit de l'image, une haute muraille plantée d'arbres en son sommet s'élève d'une des douves du château d'Edo, tandis qu'à gauche, la vue passe le long des branches d'un pin *kadomatsu* dressé à l'époque du Nouvel An (cf. pl. 2) et s'étend au loin jusqu'au sommet du mont Fuji.

Deux raquettes de *hagoita* servant au jeu de volant *hanetsuki* japonais entrent dans la composition par les bords latéraux de l'image qui les coupent. En prévision du Nouvel An, les raquettes décorées de motifs de bambous se vendaient au milieu du douzième mois de chaque année sur l'aire du temple Sensōji à Asakusa.

Haut dans le ciel, on aperçoit le volant que les raquettes de *hagoita* ont propulsé dans les

airs. Si le jeu bat son plein, les joueurs restent cachés. Le spectateur est ainsi convié à parcourir l'image de droite et de gauche pour imaginer leur identité.

Une autre activité très prisée à l'époque du Nouvel An est le lancer de cerfs-volants. Dans cette estampe, on voit monter leurs fils très haut dans le ciel, mais ceux qui manient les dragons de papier ne sont pas non plus visibles.

La large porte de l'impressionnante résidence qui domine le centre de la composition présente une forme et des couleurs presque identiques au bandeau de titre et au cartouche de signature. Elle était la propriété d'un des plus riches daimyōs, Nabeshima Kansō (1814–1871), du fief de Saga à Kyūshū. Kansō fut un des premiers fabricants de pièces d'artillerie occidentales au Japon ; après la restauration Meiji de 1868, il se mit au service de l'empereur. En tant que haut fonctionnaire, il fut à alors notamment responsable de l'aménagement du territoire d'Hokkaidō, la plus grande île du nord.

永代橋
佃しま

Eitaibashi Tsukudajima
2–1857

Tsukudajima
and Eitai Bridge

In bright moonlight under a starry sky, we see from a viewpoint under Eitai Bridge the little island of Tsukudajima in Edo Bay. In this atmospheric nocturnal scene, Hiroshige plays with light and shade in virtuoso fashion, deploying the whole spectrum of the woodblock-print techniques available in his day.

The dark *bokashi* around the unrigged sailing boats suggests the shadows of the small vessels in the moonlight, while the gradations on the lower margin of the print indicate the shadow of Eitai Bridge, of which we see just one huge post; a greenish hue hints that algae are growing there. Traces of a delicate glimmer on the masts of the boats – the reflection of the moonlight – represent a special feature that is included only in the much sought-after early impressions of this print, such as the one reproduced here.

The Eitaibashi ("Bridge of Eternity"), built in 1698, was Edo's longest bridge, crossing the Sumida River shortly before it flows into Edo Bay. When the first Tokugawa shogun Ieyasu (1542–1616) came to Edo, he brought fishermen from Tsukudamura (in today's Osaka Prefecture) with him, and settled them on an island in Edo Bay that from then on bore the name Tsukudajima, mentioned in the title of this print. The fishermen were required to supply the shogun with fresh fish every day, and their catch was to include the *shirauo* ("white fish") for which the shogun had an especial fondness. These transparent little fish were lured at night by lanterns like those we can see just beyond the post of the bridge. What was not required by the shogun could be sold by the fishermen of Tsukudajima at the markets alongside Nihonbashi Bridge (see plate 1).

In the almost identical composition, *Eitaibashi*, included in the second volume of his *Illustrated Souvenirs of Edo (Ehon Edo miyage)*, begun in 1850, Hiroshige refers to *shirauo* fishing on winter and early-spring nights, with torches and nets hung from bamboo rods (*yotsudeami*), as the ideal inspiration for landscape poetry. Without including figures, he succeeded in capturing the poetic mood of this scene in masterly fashion.

Tsukudajima
und die Brücke Eitaibashi

Im hellen Mondschein, bei sternenklarer Nacht ist von der Brücke Eitaibashi aus die kleine Insel Tsukudajima in der Bucht von Edo zu erkennen. In der atmosphärisch dichten Nachtszene spielt Hiroshige virtuos mit Licht und Schatten, indem er die gesamte Bandbreite der Holzdrucktechnik seiner Zeit einsetzt.

Das dunkle *bokashi* um die abgetakelten Segelboote suggeriert die Schatten der kleinen Schiffe im Mondschein, während die Gradierungen am unteren Bildrand die Schatten der Brücke Eitaibashi wiedergeben, von der nur ein Brückenpfeiler zu sehen ist. An diesem haben sich, in grünlichem Farbton hervorgehoben, Algen abgesetzt. Spuren von feinem Glimmer an den Bootsmasten als zarte Reflexionen des Mondlichtes stellen ein besonderes Gestaltungsmerkmal dar, das nur in den begehrten frühen Drucken wie diesem zu sehen ist.

Die 1698 erbaute Eitaibashi („Brücke der Ewigkeit") war die längste Brücke von Edo, sie überspannt den Fluss Sumidagawa kurz vor seiner Mündung in die Edo-Bucht. Als der erste Tokugawa-Shogun Ieyasu (1542–1616) nach Edo kam, brachte er Fischer aus Tsukudamura (in der heutigen Präfektur Osaka) mit und siedelte sie auf einer Insel in Ufernähe an, die fortan den im Titel des Blattes erwähnten Namen Tsukudajima trug. Die Fischer waren verpflichtet, dem Shogun täglich frischen Fisch zu liefern. Sie sollten unter anderem auch den vom Shogun besonders geschätzten *shirauo* („Weiß-Fisch") fangen. Dieser durchsichtige kleine Fisch wurde vor allem nachts mit Hilfe von Laternen angelockt, wie sie im Bild hinter dem Brückenpfeiler hervorragen. Was von den Fängen übrig blieb, konnten die Fischer von Tsukudajima auf den Märkten an der Brücke Nihonbashi (siehe Tafel 1) verkaufen.

Im zweiten Band seines 1850 begonnenen Werkes *Illustrierte Mitbringsel aus Edo (Ehon Edo miyage)* verweist Hiroshige im Kontext der nahezu identischen Komposition *Eitaibashi* auf die Darstellung des Shirauo-Fischens, das in den Winter- und Vorfrühlingsnächten mit Fackeln und an Bambusstangen aufgehängten Netzen (*yotsudeami*) durchgeführt wurde. Dieses poetische Motiv fand Eingang in die Landschaftslyrik. Es gelingt ihm meisterhaft, die poetische Stimmung dieser Szenerie ohne figürliche Darstellungen zu visualisieren.

Tsukudajima et
le pont Eitaibashi

Au clair de lune, par une nuit étoilée, on aperçoit depuis le pont Eitaibashi la petite île de Tsukudajima dans la baie d'Edo. Dans cette scène nocturne à l'atmosphère dense, Hiroshige joue magistralement avec l'ombre et la lumière, exploitant pour cela toutes les ressources techniques de l'estampe.

Le *bokashi* sombre autour des voiliers dégréés suggère les ombres des petits navires au clair de lune, tandis qu'en bas de l'image, les dégradés traduisent les ombres du pont Eitaibashi, dont on n'aperçoit qu'une seule pile, sur laquelle poussent des algues indiquées par un ton verdâtre. De fines traces de poussière de mica sur les mâts des voiliers figurent les tendres chatoiements du clair de lune ; ce moyen de représentation n'existe que dans les premiers tirages très recherchés.

Construit en 1698, l'Eitaibashi (« pont de l'Éternité ») était le plus long pont d'Edo ; il enjambait la rivière Sumidagawa peu avant son embouchure dans la baie d'Edo. Quand le premier shogun Tokugawa Ieyasu (1542–1616) s'installa à Edo, il fit venir avec lui des pêcheurs de Tsukudamura (dans l'actuelle préfecture d'Osaka) et leur fit coloniser l'île côtière qui porte depuis le nom Tsukudajima cité dans le titre de cette feuille. Les pêcheurs avaient l'obligation de livrer quotidiennement du poisson frais au shogun, et notamment de pêcher le *shirauo* (« poisson blanc ») particulièrement prisé par le shogun. Ce petit poisson transparent se pêchait surtout la nuit à la lueur des lanternes, telles qu'on les voit derrière la pile du pont. Les pêcheurs de Tsukudajima pouvaient vendre le surplus de la pêche sur les proches marchés du pont Nihonbashi (cf. pl. 1).

Dans le contexte de la composition presque identique *Eitaibashi* du deuxième tome des *Souvenirs illustrés d'Edo (Ehon Edo miyage)* commencés en 1850, Hiroshige évoque la pêche du *shirauo* comme l'inspiration idéale du paysage poétique – avec des flambeaux et des filets suspendus à des perches de bambou (*yotsudeami*) pendant les nuits d'hiver et au début du printemps. Il parvient à visualiser magistralement, sans la moindre représentation figurée, l'atmosphère poétique du décor.

両ごく
回向院
元柳橋

Ryōgoku Ekōin Moto-Yanagibashi
i5–1857

Ekōin Temple
in Ryōgoku and
Moto-Yanagi Bridge

At the very bottom of the print we see the roofs of the neighbourhood of Honjo, which is located on the banks of a broad river; on the opposite bank is the residence of Matsudaira, the feudal lord of Tanba, and, on the right, the Moto-Yanagi Bridge. In the distance is the snow-covered peak of Mount Fuji.

The flatness of the landscape extending to Mount Fuji is accentuated by the tower-like scaffolding in the foreground. We can put ourselves in the shoes of an imaginary drummer ascending the tower, and thus we are on a level with the sacred mountain.

The thematic focal point of the print is the Ekōin, a temple of the Pure Land School (Jōdo) of Buddhism. It was built in 1657, after the worst fire in Edo's history, on the instructions of the fourth Tokugawa shogun, Ietsuna (1641–1680). The temple served as a place of prayer for the more than 100,000 victims, who were buried in Honjo to the east of the Sumida River.

In 1768, it was the venue for the first sumo tournament, which soon established itself as a biannual event. Not until the

National Sumō Stadium was built in Ryōgoku in 1909 did Ekōin lose its status as the prime venue.

Even today, the high-pitched sumo drums are beaten from scaffolding such as this, which is rebuilt for every competition, to announce the start of every tournament day.

Two months prior to the date of the censors' seal on this print, the Ekōin was the site of a spectacular exhibition of the treasures of other temples. This displayed the eleven-headed Kannon statue and other sacred objects from the Kannonji Temple in Shibayama in Kazusa (today's Chiba Prefecture). The crowds that bid the temple treasures welcome in a procession through the city included sumo wrestlers, the Yoshiwara Pilgrims' Group (*Yoshiwara jūnin kō*) and the mountain ascetics known as *yamabushi*. The exhibition was inaugurated by a Kanjin sumo tournament dedicated to various deities.

The date seal clearly shows that Hiroshige and his publisher had deliberately chosen to create this print when the memory of the exhibition was still fresh in people's minds.

Der Tempel Ekōin
in Ryōgoku und
die Brücke Moto-Yanagibashi

Der Blick schweift von den Dächern des Stadtteils Honjo über den Fluss, an dessen gegenüberliegendem Ufer sich die Nebenresidenz des Matsudaira, Feudalherr von Tanba, und die Brücke Moto-Yanagibashi erstrecken, bis in die Ferne zum schneebedeckten Berg Fuji.

Die bis auf den Fuji flach verlaufende Stadt- und Flusslandschaft ist der nicht abgebildete Zensorensiegels auf diesem turmartige Gerüst im Vordergrund akzentuiert. So sieht sich der Betrachter auf Augenhöhe mit dem heiligen Berg und vermag sich wie der imaginäre Trommler zu fühlen, der das hochaufragende Gerüst besteigt.

Ausgangspunkt der Blickrichtung ist der abgebildete Ekōin, ein Tempel der Reinen-Land-Schule (Jōdo) des Buddhismus. Er wurde nach der größten Feuerkatastrophe in der Geschichte Edos im Jahr 1657 auf Anweisung des vierten Tokugawa-Shogun Ietsuna (1641–1680) errichtet. Der Tempel diente als Gebetsstätte für die Totenruhe der über 100 000 Opfer, die in Honjo, östlich des Flusses Sumidagawa, begraben wurden.

1768 fand hier das erste Sumo-Turnier statt, das sich rasch zu einem zwei Mal jährlich organisierten Spektakel etablierte.

Erst als man 1909 das Nationale Sumo-Stadion in Ryōgoku erbaute, wurde der Ekōin als Austragungsort abgelöst.

Auch jetzt noch werden von einem zu jedem Wettkampf neu aufgebauten Turmgerüst herab die Sumo-Trommeln geschlagen, um den Beginn jedes Turniertages anzukündigen.

Zwei Monate vor dem Datum des Zensorensiegels auf diesem Blatt fand im Tempel Ekōin eine jener aufsehenerregenden Ausstellungen von Schätzen auswärtiger Tempel statt, bei der die elfköpfige Kannon-Statue und andere Heiligtümer des Tempels Kannonji aus Shibayama in Kazusa gezeigt wurden. Unter der Menschenmenge, die die Tempelschätze in einer Prozession durch die Stadt willkommen hieß, befanden sich auch Sumo-Ringer, die Pilgergruppe von Yoshiwara (*Yoshiwara jūnin kō*) und die Bergasketen (*yamabushi*). Zur Eröffnung der Ausstellung fand ein den Gottheiten gewidmetes Kanjin-Sumo-Turnier statt.

Derartige Anlässe weisen im Kontext mit der Zensurdatierung darauf hin, dass sich Hiroshige und sein Verleger bewusst für den aktuellen Zeitpunkt entschieden, um den Tempel Ekōin als Gegenstand eines Blattes zu wählen.

Le temple Ekōin
à Ryōgoku et le
pont Moto-Yanagibashi

Des toits du quartier de Honjo, le regard glisse au-delà de la rivière, sur la rive opposée de laquelle on aperçoit la résidence secondaire de Matsudaira, seigneur féodal de Tanba, et le pont Moto-Yanagibashi – jusqu'au lointain où s'élève le mont Fuji enneigé.

La planéité du paysage urbain et fluvial qui s'étend jusqu'au mont Fuji est encore accentuée par la structure en forme de tour qui se dresse au premier plan. Le point de vue est ainsi placé à la hauteur de la montagne sacrée et le spectateur peut s'identifier au batteur de tambour imaginaire qui gravit l'échafaudage.

La vue est prise à partir du temple Ekōin, un sanctuaire de l'école bouddhiste de la Terre Pure (Jōdo), temple qui reste ici invisible. Le temple fut édifié en 1657 à l'initiative du quatrième shogun Tokugawa Ietsuna (1641–1680) après l'incendie le plus dévastateur de toute l'histoire d'Edo. Il servit de lieu de prière pour le repos des quelque 100 000 victimes qui furent enterrées à Honjo, à l'est de la rivière Sumidagawa.

En 1768 s'y tint le premier championnat de sumo, qui devint bientôt un événement semestriel. Ce n'est qu'après la construction du stade national

de sumo à Ryōgoku en 1909 que l'Ekōin cessa de servir de cadre à ces championnats.

L'on y bat aujourd'hui encore du haut d'un échafaudage reconstruit à neuf pour chaque nouveau championnat, les tambours sumo qui annoncent l'ouverture de chaque journée de la compétition.

Deux mois avant la date du cachet de la censure figurant sur cette feuille, l'Ekōin présentait une des expositions spectaculaires de trésors d'autres temples, expositions lors desquelles étaient exhibés la statue à onze têtes de Kannon et d'autres trésors du Kannonji de Shibayama, dans la province de Kazusa. Dans la foule qui les accueillait en procession se trouvaient aussi des lutteurs de sumo, le groupe de pèlerins de Yoshiwara (*Yoshiwara jūnin kō*) et les *yamabushi*, des ascètes des montagnes. L'exposition était inaugurée par un championnat de kanjin-sumo dédié aux dieux.

La datation de la feuille par la censure montre que Hiroshige et son éditeur ont délibérément pris cet événement comme prétexte pour publier en temps opportun une estampe montrant le temple Ekōin.

6

馬喰町
初音の
馬場

Bakuro-chō Hatsune no baba
9–1857

Hatsune Riding Ground in Bakuro-chō

Four lengths of fabric stretched out horizontally wave gently in the breeze, their ochre, white and violet colours harmonizing with the background. The dyers from the nearby district of Kon'ya-chō have used the wide-open spaces of Edo's oldest riding ground, Hatsune, to dry their cloth.

On the elaborately printed early impressions, the length of white cloth displays a technique known as *nunomezuri*, which creates the embossed impression of a piece of fabric. This textured effect, which can hardly be seen in photographic reproductions, was achieved by pressing the paper against a piece of cloth over an area of the print during the printing process; the paper remained white, but took on the texture of the cloth. The same technique was also used on plate 115.

The background is dominated by the district fire-watch tower. On the left, beneath its roof, hangs the bell that was rung to warn the public in case of fire. Different signals were sounded, depending on the size of the fire.

As early as 1809, Hiroshige had inherited his father's official position of captain of the fire brigade responsible for Edo Castle and the houses of the shogun's vassals. In 1832, he passed on this office to his adopted son, in order to devote himself entirely to painting and printmaking.

Der Reitplatz Hatsune no baba in Bakuro-chō

Quer gespannte Stoffbahnen wehen sacht im lauen Wind und harmonieren in ihren Ocker-, Weiß- und Violetttönen mit dem Hintergrund. Die Färber des nahegelegenen Bezirks Kon'ya-chō haben ihre Tücher auf der großen Fläche des ältesten Reitplatzes von Edo, Hatsune no baba, zum Trocknen aufgehängt.

Die weiße Stoffbahn ist auf den aufwändig hergestellten frühen Abzügen mit dem *nunomezuri* genannten Abdruck eines Gewebestücks versehen. Dieser auf fotografischen Reproduktionen kaum auszumachende Effekt der Textilstruktur wurde erzielt, indem der Holzschneider den entsprechenden Bildteil auf einem Druckstock freilegte, der Drucker dann einen Stoff über diese Stelle legte und das Papier kräftig dagegenrieb. So entstand der Abdruck des Textilgewebes auf dem weiß gebliebenen Papier. Dieselbe reizvolle Technik wurde zum Beispiel auch auf Tafel 115 angewendet.

Im Hintergrund ragt der Feuerwachturm des Bezirks empor. Links unter seinem Dach hängt die Glocke, die bei Bränden geläutet wurde, um die Bevölkerung zu warnen. Je nach Größe des Brandes ertönten unterschiedliche Signale.

Hiroshige hatte schon 1809, nach dem Tod seines Vaters, das offizielle Amt eines Feuerwehrhauptmanns zum Schutze des Edo-Schlosses und der Vasallenresidenzen des Shogun geerbt. 1832 gab er dieses Amt an seinen Adoptivsohn weiter, um sich fortan ganz der Malerei und Holzschnittkunst zu widmen.

Le manège équestre Hatsune no baba à Bakuro-chō

De longues bandes de drap tendues transversalement flottent doucement dans la tiédeur du vent et forment une tendre harmonie avec les tons blancs et violets de l'arrière-plan. Les teinturiers du proche quartier Kon'ya-chō ont étendu leurs draps à sécher sur la grande aire du plus ancien manège équestre d'Edo, Hatsune no baba.

Dans les précieux premiers tirages de cette feuille, la bande blanche a été réalisée par estampage à sec d'une pièce de tissu – une technique appelée *nunomezuri*. Le graveur de la planche d'impression obtenait cet effet presque indiscernable dans les reproductions photographiques en épargnant la zone concernée ; l'imprimeur apposait ensuite une trame textile dans la dite zone et la frottait fortement contre le papier, laissant imprimée dans le papier la structure du tissu. Cette technique se retrouve par exemple aussi dans la planche 115.

À l'arrière-plan s'élève la tour de garde de la brigade du feu du quartier. À gauche sous son toit est suspendue la cloche qui servait à alerter la population en cas d'incendie. Les signaux variaient en intensité selon la gravité du sinistre.

Dès après la mort de son père en 1809, Hiroshige avait hérité de la charge officielle de capitaine de la brigade affectée à la protection du château d'Edo et des résidences des vassaux du shogun. En 1832, l'artiste transmettra cette charge à son fils adoptif pour pouvoir se consacrer entièrement à la peinture et à l'estampe.

7

大てんま
町
木綿店

Ōdenma-chō momendana
4–1858

Shops with Cotton Goods in Ōdenma-chō

Two geishas on high *geta* sandals walk past the cotton shops in Ōdenma-chō. It is evening and the neighbourhood gate on the left, of which only one post can be seen, is still open. We can see two merchants sitting in a shop alongside their bales of cloth calculating their day's takings.

The geishas are holding up their grey kimonos decorated with white dragonflies to allow a glimpse of their red undergarments. Hiroshige enlivens their faces with just a few well-placed lines. Immediately behind the two women, the almost hidden face of their maid shows one raised eyebrow. In this detail, too, Hiroshige achieves a maximum of expression with a minimum of pictorial means.

Hiroshige used Western linear perspective to depict this street of shops: from right to left, the lines of the roofs and the ground run in an acute angle to meet at a vanishing point outside the left-hand margin of the print.

The shop roofs display fixtures for pots that served to catch rainwater. In this way, there was always water on hand to extinguish the frequent fires, big and small.

The various characters and company logos denote, from right to left, the names of the shops Tahataya, Masuya and Shimaya.

The various shades of blue play a key role in this print, possibly because the deep indigo of the shop panels, taken up in the decorative sashes (*obi*) of the geishas, was one of the most popular colours for dyeing cotton.

Ōdenma-chō ("Great Relay-Horse Quarter") was the most important postal station in Edo. All mercantile traffic on the five highways was handled in Ōdenma-chō, where the relay horses (*tenma*) were kept ready. The postal stations coordinated a complex system of courier services that was able to convey goods the 600 kilometres (370 miles) from Edo to Kyoto in less than 60 hours.

This print was approved by the censors in the fourth month of 1858, five months before Hiroshige's death. It was the last but ten of the woodblock prints for his *One Hundred Famous Views of Edo*.

Läden mit Baumwollwaren in Ōdenma-chō

Auf ihren hohen Geta-Sandalen schreiten zwei Geishas an den Läden mit Baumwollwaren in Ōdenma-chō auf das noch geöffnete Tor des Stadtviertels zu, von dem nur ein Pfosten am linken Bildrand zu sehen ist. Es ist Abend, und zwei Händler sitzen im Geschäft neben ihren Stoffballen und verrechnen die Tageseinnahmen.

Die Geishas haben ihre grauen, mit weißen Libellen dekorierten Kimonos hochgerafft und geben dabei den Blick auf ihre roten Untergewänder frei. Mit wenigen wohlgesetzten Strichen verleiht Hiroshige ihren Gesichtern Lebendigkeit. Hinter den beiden Frauen ist das fast verdeckte Gesicht einer Dienerin zu erkennen, die eine Augenbraue hebt. Auch in diesem Detail erzielt Hiroshige mit geringem grafischen Aufwand maximalen Ausdruck.

Hiroshige komponiert die Ladenstraße in einer an westlicher Linearperspektive geschulten Technik: Von rechts laufen die Dach- und Bodenlinien in spitzem Winkel auf einen imaginären Fluchtpunkt außerhalb des linken Bildrandes zu.

Auf den Ladendächern sind Halterungen für Töpfe befestigt, die dem Auffangen von Regenwasser dienten. So hatte man bei den häufig auftretenden kleineren und größeren Bränden stets Löschwasser zur Hand. Die verschiedenen Schriftzeichen und Firmenmarken bezeichnen von rechts nach links die Namen der Geschäfte Tahataya, Masuya und Shimaya.

Eine besondere Rolle spielt auf diesem Blatt die Farbe Blau in diversen Schattierungen, möglicherweise weil das tiefe Indigoblau der Ladenvorhänge, das sich in den Obi-Schmuckgürteln der Geishas widerspiegelt, einer der beliebtesten Töne für das Färben von Baumwolle war.

Das Viertel Ōdenma-chō ("Großes Postpferdeviertel") war die wichtigste Poststation in Edo. Hier wurden die Postpferde (*tenma*) bereitgehalten und der gesamte Frachtverkehr der fünf großen Transportwege abgewickelt. Die Poststationen koordinierten ein komplexes System von Kurierdiensten, das imstande war, innerhalb von sechzig Stunden Pakete über die rund 600 Kilometer lange Distanz von Edo nach Kyoto zu befördern.

Das Blatt wurde von den Zensoren fünf Monate vor Hiroshiges Tod im vierten Monat 1858 zum Druck freigegeben. Es folgten lediglich noch zehn weitere Holzschnitte für die *Hundert berühmten Ansichten von Edo*.

Boutiques de cotonnades à Ōdenma-chō

Deux geishas perchées sur leurs getas longent les boutiques de cotonnades d'Ōdenma-chō et se dirigent vers la porte encore ouverte du quartier, porte dont on ne voit qu'un seul poteau parallèle au bord gauche de l'image. La scène se déroule à la tombée de la nuit : deux marchands sont assis dans leur boutique à côté de ballots de tissus et font les comptes de la journée.

Les geishas relèvent leurs kimonos gris à motifs de libellules, découvrant leur combinaison rouge au spectateur. Hiroshige a animé leurs visages à l'aide de quelques traits bien posés. Derrière les deux femmes apparaît le visage presque caché d'une servante au sourcil levé. Par ce simple détail aussi, Hiroshige obtient une expressivité maximale avec des moyens graphiques réduits à l'extrême.

Hiroshige a composé la scène de rue commerçante dans une technique empruntée à la perspective occidentale : de la droite, les lignes des toits et du sol convergent vers un point de fuite imaginaire placé à gauche hors de l'image.

Sur les toits des boutiques sont fixées toute une série de corbeilles accueillant des pots destinés à recevoir les eaux de pluie. L'on avait ainsi toujours à disposition une certaine quantité d'eau pour éteindre les feux et départs d'incendies très fréquents dans ces quartiers.

Les différents sigles et idéogrammes indiquent, de gauche à droite, les noms des boutiques Tahataya, Masuya et Shimaya.

Dans cette feuille, la déclinaison du bleu en différentes teintes et ombrages joue un rôle particulier, peut-être parce que le profond indigo des boutiques qui se reflète dans les ceintures ornementales (*obi*) des geishas était une des teintures préférées du coton.

Le quartier Ōdenma-chō (« Grand quartier des chevaux de poste ») était le plus important relais de poste d'Edo. Des chevaux de poste (*tenma*) y étaient disponibles à toute heure et l'on y organisait l'ensemble du transport de marchandises des cinq voies de circulation principales. Les relais coordonnaient un complexe réseau de courriers capable d'acheminer des paquets en soixante heures sur la distance de quelque 600 kilomètres séparant Edo de Kyoto.

Cette feuille a été approuvée par la censure au quatrième mois de l'année 1858, cinq mois avant la mort de Hiroshige. Elle ne sera plus suivie que de dix autres estampes destinées à la série des *Cent Vues*.

8

する
賀て
ふ

Suruga-chō
9–1856

Suruga-chō

From a high vantage point we are looking down on a long, bustling street lined by shops with tiled roofs. Depicted with linear perspective, the straight road tapers away sharply before dissolving in a broad, traditionally shaped Japanese bank of clouds.

Floating majestically high above the clouds is Mount Fuji with a surreal appearance that is unique in this series.

The name of the quarter depicted here, Suruga-chō, corresponds to the old name of the province in which Mount Fuji is located. It is possible that those who planned Edo deliberately laid out this street so that the mountain, 80 kilometres (50 miles) distant, could be seen at its south-west end – and that the street might appear to lead right up to it.

The Mitsui textile store extends along both sides of the street: on the right-hand side is the main store, opposite the cotton shop (*watadana*). On the indigo-dyed panels is a symbol consisting of a circle enclosing the character for the number three (*mittsu*) and the word "well (as in water)" (*i*), which together form the name "Mitsui". In Edo, this textile-retailing business, which had stores in many parts of Japan, also bore the name "Echigoya". This name can be seen in small, exuberant *hiragana* characters to the left and right of the main logo on each panel.

Echigoya was the predecessor of the modern Mitsukoshi chain of department stores. The success of the Mitsui shops was based on a clever marketing strategy. The goods appealed to a broad clientele, and for the first time customers were able to buy goods at a fixed price. The large number of customers allowed not only for lower prices but also for more rapid delivery than usual: those in a hurry could even take the finished kimono home with them after a short wait.

The depiction of Mount Fuji with Echigoya in Suruga-chō was an iconic motif. In 1792, Torii Kiyonaga (1752–1815) designed a woodblock print almost twice the size of the present one. Around 1790, his workshop also produced a hanging scroll with the same subject painted on silk; it is still in the Mitsui Collection. Comparable to this composition by Hiroshige is a double-page spread in the first volume of his *Illustrated Guide to Famous Views of Edo (Edo meisho zue)*, which appeared between 1834 and 1836.

Suruga-chō

Von oben fällt der Blick auf eine lange belebte Straße, die von ziegelgedeckten Geschäftshäusern gesäumt wird. Schnurgerade sich verjüngend verläuft sie in Linearperspektive bis sie sich dem Blick entzieht und sich in einer breiten, traditionell japanisch gestalteten Nebel- und Wolkenbank aufzulösen scheint. Hoch über den Wolken thront der Berg Fuji, eine unwirklich anmutende, majestätische Erscheinung.

Der Name des hier dargestellten Viertels, Suruga-chō, entspricht dem alten Namen für die Provinz, in der sich der Berg Fuji befindet. Möglicherweise hatten die Stadtplaner Edos die Straße bewusst so angelegt, dass man am südwestlichen Ende den rund 80 Kilometer entfernten Berg sehen konnte und sie auf ihn zuzuführen schien.

Der Mitsui-Textilhandel erstreckt sich an beiden Seiten der Straße: Auf der rechten Seite liegt das Hauptgeschäft, gegenüber der Baumwollladen (*watadana*). Auf den indigoblau gefärbten Ladenvorhängen sind innerhalb eines Kreises grafisch abstrahierte Schriftzeichen für die Zahl drei (*mittsu*) und das Wort Brunnen (*i*) angeordnet, die verbunden den Namen „Mitsui" bilden. In Edo trug der überregionale Textilhandel Mitsui zusätzlich den Namen „Echigoya". Dieser Geschäftsname findet sich in kleinen schwungvollen Hiragana-Schriftzeichen jeweils links und rechts des Kreises auf jedem Vorhang.

Echigoya ist der Vorläufer der heutigen Warenhauskette Mitsukoshi. Sein Erfolg basierte auf einer klugen Marktstrategie. Das Angebot sprach eine breite Klientel an, und erstmals konnten Kunden die Waren zu einem festgelegten Preis erwerben. Der große Kundenkreis ermöglichte es, die Waren günstiger und schneller anzubieten. Wer es besonders eilig hatte, konnte nach einer kurzen Wartezeit den fertigen Kimono sogleich mit nach Hause nehmen.

Die Darstellung des Berges Fuji mit dem Echigoya im Stadtviertel Suruga-chō war ein beliebtes Bildthema. Torii Kiyonaga (1752–1815) schuf 1792 einen fast doppelt so großen Holzschnitt wie den vorliegenden. Aus seiner Werkstatt stammt auch eine um 1790 entstandene Hängerolle, die das Sujet zeigt und sich heute in der Sammlung Mitsui befindet. Vergleichbar mit dieser Komposition Hiroshiges ist eine Doppelseite im ersten Band des zwischen 1834 und 1836 erschienenen *Illustrierten Führers zu berühmten Ansichten von Edo (Edo meisho zue)*.

Suruga-chō

La vue plonge dans une longue rue animée bordée de boutiques aux toits couverts de tuiles. Présentée toute droite en perspective linéaire, la rue s'étire à perte de vue et semble se dissoudre dans un banc de nuages et de brouillards de facture japonaise traditionnelle.

Haut au-dessus des nuages trône le mont Fuji, apparition irréelle et majestueuse.

Suruga-chō, le quartier représenté, correspond à l'ancien nom de la province où se trouve le mont Fuji. On peut penser que les urbanistes d'Edo en aménagèrent délibérément la rue centrale de manière à faire apparaître à son extrémité sud-ouest la montagne distante de quelque 80 kilomètres, vers laquelle elle pouvait ainsi sembler mener.

Le magasin de tissus Mitsui borde les deux côtés de la rue : à droite se trouve la boutique mère, en face le comptoir du coton (*watadana*). Sur les rideaux de l'établissement teintés à l'indigo sont disposés, à l'intérieur d'un cercle, les idéogrammes abstraits du nombre trois (*mittsu*) et du mot puits (*i*) qui forment le nom « Mitsui ». À Edo, le commerce interrégional du textile Mitsui portait aussi le nom « Echigoya » ; ce nom commercial se retrouve en petits caractères cursifs *hiragana*, respectivement à gauche et à droite du cercle de chaque rideau.

L'Echigoya a été le précurseur de l'actuelle chaîne de grands magasins Mitsukoshi. Son succès se devait à une stratégie commerciale avisée : l'offre s'adressait à une large clientèle et l'établissement avait été le premier à proposer des articles à prix fixes. La vaste clientèle pouvait ainsi les acheter moins cher et plus rapidement. Après une courte attente, les acheteurs les plus pressés pouvaient aussi emporter chez eux les kimonos tout prêt confectionnés.

La représentation du mont Fuji avec l'Echigoya à Suruga-chō était un sujet très populaire. En 1792, Torii Kiyonaga (1752–1815) créa une estampe presque deux fois plus grande que celle-ci. De son atelier provient vraisemblablement aussi une peinture de même sujet que la collection Mitsui conserve encore aujourd'hui. La présente composition de Hiroshige peut par ailleurs être aussi rapprochée d'une double page du premier tome du *Guide illustré des vues célèbres d'Edo (Edo meisho zue)* paru entre 1834 et 1836.

9

筋違内八ツ小路

Sujikai uchi Yatsukōji
11–1857

Yatsukōji,
Inside
Sujikai Gate

The Yatsukōji runs in a broad diagonal from the bottom right corner of the print to the mid left, where it is closed off by the dark-grey buildings of the daimyō residence. Yatsukōji means "Eight Streets", a number that is not meant to be taken literally, but simply indicates "many".

The Sujikai Gate was built in 1636 and, as an important traffic intersection, was always open. Within the gate, numerous streets joined the Nakasendō, one of the region's main highways.

What we see here is one of the few open spaces in Edo – none of which looks anything like the grand piazzas of the kind we admire in the views of Venice by Canaletto (1697–1768). The few large squares in Edo were created as firebreaks after the major fires, and served primarily as thoroughfares for the traffic

that already in 18th-century Edo was considerable.

The large area of light grey representing this open space is enlivened by the print's delicate browns and greens, which testify to the brilliant craftsmanship of the printer. Deeper shades of green and brown are also used for the garments of the stylized figures.

Above red banks of mist hovering over the Kanda River, we can see the Kanda Myōjin Shrine and its associated buildings. The red roof of the palanquin at the bottom of the print indicates that a high-ranking lady is being escorted home. At both the top and bottom of the print, the intense red accents take up and emphasize the red of the title cartouche, with its unusual tortoiseshell pattern, the series title and the signature.

Die Straße Yatsukōji
innerhalb des Tores
Sujikai

In einer breiten Diagonale verläuft die Straße Yatsukōji von der rechten unteren Bildecke nach links und wird dort durch die dunkelgrauen Gebäude einer Daimyō-Residenz begrenzt. Yatsukōji bedeutet „Acht Straßen", wobei diese Zahl nicht wörtlich zu verstehen ist, sondern nur eine große Anzahl andeutet.

Das Tor Sujikai wurde 1636 errichtet und stand als wichtiger Verkehrsknotenpunkt immer offen. Innerhalb des Tores vereinigten sich zahlreiche Straßen mit einem der Hauptverkehrswege, der Straße Nakasendō.

Dargestellt ist auf dem Holzschnitt eine der wenigen unbebauten Flächen Edos, die jedoch keineswegs einer grandiosen Piazza ähneln, wie man sie in den venezianischen Veduten von Canaletto (1697–1768) bewundern kann. Die wenigen offenen Plätze in Edo entstanden nach den großen Feuerkatastrophen als Brandschutzzonen und dienten in erster Linie als Durchgang für den schon im

Edo des 18. Jahrhunderts beträchtlichen Verkehr.

Die weitgehend leere Fläche des Platzes wird durch eine Vielfalt von zartesten Braun-, Grün- und Grautönen belebt und zeugt so von der brillanten handwerklichen Kunst des Druckers. In kräftigeren Schattierungen werden die Farben Grün und Braun auch für die Gewänder der stilisiert dargestellten Figuren verwendet.

Oberhalb von roten Nebelschwaden, die über dem Fluss Kandagawa schweben, erhebt sich der Schrein Kanda Myōjin mit den zugehörigen Gebäuden. Das rote Dach der Sänfte am unteren Bildrand deutet darauf hin, dass hier eine Dame von hohem Rang nach Hause eskortiert wird. An beiden Bildrändern leuchten intensive rote Akzente, die das Rot der im seltenen Schildkrötenmuster gehaltenen Titelkartusche, des Serientitels sowie der Signatur wiederaufnehmen und hervorheben.

La rue Yatsukōji
dans l'enceinte de la
porte Sujikai

La rue Yatsukōji traverse l'image en une large diagonale partant du coin inférieur droit vers la gauche, où elle est limitée par les bâtiments gris sombre de la résidence d'un daimyō. Yatsukōji signifie « huit voies », sachant que le nombre « huit » ne s'entend pas au sens littéral mais renvoie simplement à un grand nombre de rues.

Bâtie en 1636, la porte Sujikai restait toujours ouverte comme grand carrefour de circulation. Dans son enceinte se croisaient de nombreuses rues et un des plus grands axes du Japon, la Nakasendō.

L'estampe présente une des rares aires dégagées d'Edo ; celle-ci ne ressemble en rien aux admirables *piazza* que montrent les védutes vénitiennes de Canaletto (1697–1768). Les quelques places ouvertes d'Edo ont été créées comme pare-feux après de grands incendies et servaient avant tout comme lieu

transitaire pour le trafic déjà très dense au XVIIIe siècle à Edo.

L'aire largement vide de la place est animée d'un grand nombre de tons bruns, verts et gris et illustre le savoir-faire magistral de l'imprimeur. Des tons plus fortement ombrés de vert et de brun servent aussi à décrire les habits des figures représentées sous une forme stylisée.

Au-dessus des bancs de brouillard rouges qui flottent sur la rivière Kandagawa s'élèvent le sanctuaire Kanda Myōjin et ses annexes. Le toit rouge du palanquin qu'on voit près du bord inférieur indique qu'une haute dame se fait escorter sur le chemin du retour vers sa demeure. Les deux bords de l'image sont éclairés d'accents rouge vif qui soulignent et font écho aux tons rouges des cartouches de titre de l'estampe, qui présente une motif de tortue très rare, du titre de la série et de la signature.

10

神田
明神
曙
之
景

Kanda Myōjin akebono no kei
9–1857

Sunrise at
Kanda Myōjin Shrine

In the previous print we saw the Kanda Myōjin Shrine from a distance, while in this view we find ourselves in the grounds of the shrine overlooking the roofs of Edo. As in this case, the prints of the series are often ordered in such a way that there is a zooming-in from a distant view to a close-up of an element in that view in the next print.

In the centre, a tall cedar trunk rises from the saturated green of the ground; it functions as an axis of symmetry for the dark tree trunks to the left and right. In contrast to the schematic arrangement of the trees, the garments of the priest on the left, and the temple servant and her assistant on the right, are decidedly colourful and composed with extraordinary care. The three colours of the priest's robe, which blur into each other, derive from Hiroshige's imagination, and represent a variation of the dominant blue and green of the print. The white areas on the garments of the other two figures reveal the same successful application of the embossing technique that creates the texture of fabric (*nunomezuri*) as in plates 6 and 115.

Although the shrine itself is not depicted, its well-known name in the title of this print evokes numerous associations. The shrine was established as early as AD 730 and represents one of the oldest and most important sacred sites in Edo. It was moved to the Kanda district in 1616, and was revered as a guardian shrine by the city's rapidly growing population. During the biennial shrine festival, which alternated with the Sannō Festival (see plate 51), the citizens of Edo proceeded through the Tayasu Gate into the shogun's castle and paid homage to the ruler before leaving the centre of power in Japan through the Takebashi Gate.

The festival took place on the 15th day of the ninth month, in memory of the decisive Battle of Sekigahara in 1600, in which the Tokugawa secured their power over the Japanese estates. Hiroshige probably composed this print as a souvenir of this festival, as it was approved by the censors in the ninth month of 1857 and must have been ready to be sold shortly afterwards.

Sonnenaufgang
am Schrein Kanda Myōjin

Während der Schrein Kanda Myōjin auf der vorhergehenden Tafel am oberen Bildrand in Fernsicht zu sehen ist, befindet sich der Betrachter nun direkt auf dem Gelände des Schreins mit Blick über die Dächer Edos. Die Tafeln sind innerhalb der Serie häufig so angeordnet, dass – wie in diesem Fall – eine Bewegung von der Fernsicht hin zu einem ausgewählten Motiv erfolgt.

Zentral im Vordergrund erhebt sich aus dem satten Grün des Bodens ein hochaufragender Zedernstamm, der gleichsam als Spiegelachse der dunklen Baumstämme links und rechts fungiert. Im Kontrast zu der schematischen Anordnung der Bäume sind die Gewänder des Priesters und der Tempeldienerin und ihres Gehilfen betont farbig und mit außergewöhnlichem Aufwand gestaltet. Die dreifarbig abgestufte Robe des Priesters entspringt der Farbfantasie Hiroshiges und nimmt das Blau und Grün des gesamten Blattes in variierter Form auf. Die weißen Flächen in den Kleidern der beiden anderen Figuren offenbaren die gleiche gelungene Anwendung des Blinddrucks mit Textilmuster (*nunomezuri*) wie in den Tafeln 6 und 115.

Obwohl der Schrein selbst nicht abgebildet ist, ruft sein bekannter Name im Titel des Blattes zahlreiche Assoziationen hervor. Der Schrein wurde bereits im Jahr 730 gegründet und stellt eines der ältesten und bedeutendsten Heiligtümer Edos dar. Er gelangte erst 1616 nach Kanda und wurde von der rasch wachsenden Bevölkerung Edos als Schutzheiligtum verehrt. Während des alle zwei Jahre ausgerichteten Schreinfests, das alternierend mit dem Sannō-Fest (siehe Tafel 51) stattfand, betraten die städtischen Bewohner Edos das Schloss des Shoguns in einer Prozession durch das Tor Tayasumon, erwiesen dem Herrscher die Ehre und verließen das Machtzentrum des damaligen Japan anschließend wieder durch das Tor Takebashimon.

Das Fest fiel auf den 15. Tag des neunten Monats, in Erinnerung an die Entscheidungsschlacht bei Sekigahara im Jahr 1600, mit der sich die Tokugawa ihre Macht über Japan sicherten. Hiroshige entwarf dieses Blatt wohl auch als Andenken an dieses Fest, denn es wurde im neunten Monat 1857 von den Zensoren genehmigt und muss bald darauf zum Verkauf fertiggestellt worden sein.

Le sanctuaire
Kanda Myōjin au soleil levant

Alors que l'estampe précédente ne montrait qu'une vue éloignée du sanctuaire Kanda Myōjin placé près du bord supérieur de l'image, le spectateur se trouve maintenant sur l'aire du sanctuaire lui-même et jouit d'une vue des toits d'Edo. Dans les *Cent Vues*, les planches sont souvent organisées de manière à faire effectuer, comme ici, à partir d'une vue éloignée, un mouvement d'approche d'un motif choisi.

Au premier plan, en place centrale, le tronc d'un cèdre jaillit du sol vert saturé et sert en même temps d'axe de symétrie pour les troncs sombres qui jouxtent les bords droit et gauche de l'image. Contrastant avec la disposition schématique des arbres, les habits du prêtre figuré près du bord gauche et, à droite, de la servante et son assistant, présentent des couleurs vives et une grande diversité de facture. La robe au dégradé tricolore du prêtre est issue de l'imagination coloriste de l'artiste et reprend le bleu et le vert de l'estampe. Les surfaces blanches des habits des deux autres figures dénotent le même emploi magistral de l'estampage à motif textile (*nunomezuri*) que les planches 6 et 115.

Bien que le sanctuaire ne soit pas lui-même représenté, son nom célèbre indiqué dans le titre de la feuille incite à de nombreuses associations. Le sanctuaire avait été fondé dès 730 et était un des temples les plus anciens et les plus célèbres d'Edo. Il ne fut transféré à Kanda qu'en 1616 et rapidement vénéré comme sanctuaire protecteur par la population fortement croissante d'Edo. Pendant la fête du temple célébrée tous les deux ans et s'accompagnant une fois sur deux d'une fête de Sannō (cf. pl. 51), les habitants d'Edo défilaient en procession par la porte Tayasumon du château du shogun, à qui ils rendaient les honneurs avant de quitter le centre du pouvoir du Japon par la porte Takebashimon.

La fête était célébrée le 15ème jour du neuvième mois en souvenir de la bataille de Sekigahara qui permit aux Tokugawa d'établir définitivement leur domination sur le Japon en l'an 1600. Hiroshige a sans doute aussi conçu cette feuille comme un rappel de cette fête, car elle fut approuvée par la censure au neuvième mois de l'année 1857 et fut vraisemblablement mise en vente peu après.

11

上野
清水堂
不忍ノ池

Ueno Kiyomizudō Shinobazu no ike
4–1856

Kiyomizu Hall and Shinobazu Pond at Ueno

A large, red balcony projects like the prow of a boat into a sea of blossoming cherry trees. Its two strong reds contrast with the delicate blue of Shinobazu Pond, the *ichimonji bokashi* reduced to a narrow strip on the opposite bank.

The numerous cherry trees of the *higanzakura* variety growing around the Kiyomizu Hall were famous for their blossoms, which were both early and luxuriant. By comparison, the pines on the banks of the pond are tall and slender. This depiction of the trees, which in reality were smaller, possibly derive from a desire to balance the vertical composition. The row of pines is rounded off on the left by the unusual "Moon Pine", which is the main motif of plate 89.

On the balcony and on the shore of the lake we see people strolling along. Among the figures at the bottom of the print is a man in a light-blue garment with his face half covered; he is probably a client of the prostitutes who worked in Ueno, and does not want to be recognized.

The buildings and landscape depicted in this print are copies of buildings and sites in the imperial city of Kyoto. Thus the – actually much smaller – balcony is a replica of the celebrated "stage" of the Kiyomizudera Temple in Kyoto; its construction in the eastern mountains is famous to this day. Shinobazu Pond was laid out as a counterpart of Lake Biwa to the northeast of Kyoto. As the counterpart of Chikubushima Island in Lake Biwa, an island was provided with a Benten shrine in 1625. The island is not visible in this print apart from the narrow causeway on the left-hand margin of the print, beyond the moon pine. Duplicating well-known Kyoto sights in Edo served to legitimize the latter as the "new" capital.

Die Halle Kiyomizudō und der Teich Shinobazu no ike in Ueno

Ein großer roter Balkon ragt keilförmig in ein Meer aus blühenden Kirschbäumen. Reizvoll kontrastieren seine beiden kräftigen Rottöne mit der, bis auf ein strichförmiges *ichimonji bokashi* am gegenüberliegenden Ufer, zartblauen Fläche des Teiches Shinobazu no ike.

Die zahlreichen hohen Kirschbäume der Art *higanzakura* neben der Halle Kiyomizudō waren berühmt für ihre frühzeitige und üppige Blüte. Hoch und schlank erheben sich im Vergleich dazu die Kiefern am Ufer des Gewässers. Möglicherweise entsprang diese Darstellung der Bäume, die in der Realität viel niedriger waren, dem Wunsch, das Hochformat zu füllen. Abgeschlossen wird die Kiefernreihe am linken Bildrand von der außergewöhnlichen „Mondkiefer", die auf Tafel 89 zum bestimmenden Motiv wird.

Auf dem Balkon und am Seeufer flanieren vereinzelt Passanten. Unter den Figuren befindet sich am unteren Bildrand ein Mann in hellblauem Gewand mit halb verhülltem Gesicht. Er ist wahrscheinlich ein Kunde der in Ueno tätigen Prostituierten, der sein Antlitz verbergen will.

Die abgebildeten Gebäude und Landschaftselemente in diesem Druck stellen Kopien von Bauwerken und Orten dar, die sich in der Kaiserstadt Kyoto und ihrer Umgebung befanden. So handelt es sich etwa bei dem – in der Realität viel niedrigeren – Balkon um eine Replik der in Japan bis heute berühmten „Bühne" des gewagt in die Ostberge gebauten Tempels Kiyomizudera in Kyoto. Der Teich Shinobazu no ike wurde als Pendant zum nordöstlich von Kyoto gelegenen Biwako-See künstlich angelegt. Im Jahr 1625 wurde die Insel, von der hier nur der schmale Zugangsweg am linken Bildrand, unterhalb der Mondkiefer, sichtbar ist, als Gegenstück zur Insel Chikubushima des Biwako-Sees mit einem Benten-Heiligtum ausgestattet. Das Duplizieren bekannter Sehenswürdigkeiten aus Kyoto diente der Legitimierung Edos als „neuer" Hauptstadt.

Le pavillon Kiyomizudō et l'étang Shinobazu no ike à Ueno

Un grand balcon rouge s'enfonce comme un coin dans des nuages de cerisiers en fleurs. Ses deux tons rouge vif contrastent avec l'étang Shinobazu et sa surface bleu pâle – à l'exception de l'*ichimonji bokashi* linéaire qui longe la rive opposée.

Les nombreux hauts cerisiers *higanzakura* figurés à côté du pavillon Kiyomizudō étaient célèbres pour leur abondante et précoce floraison. Sont en revanche comparativement plus hauts et plus sveltes les pins plantés sur les rives de l'étang. Il se peut que ce mode de représentation des arbres, qui étaient en fait beaucoup moins hauts, répondait au besoin de combler la hauteur du format de l'image. Près du bord gauche, la rangée de pins s'achève sur l'inhabituel « Pin de la lune » qui sera le motif principal de la feuille 89.

Sur la terrasse et le long de l'étang s'attardent ou flânent des passants isolés. Près du bord inférieur, on peut voir un homme en habit bleu clair au visage à moitié masqué. Il s'agit sans doute d'un client des filles de joie travaillant à Ueno qui voulait cacher son identité.

Les bâtiments et éléments paysagers de cette estampe sont des reconstitutions d'édifices et de lieux situés à l'intérieur aux environs de Kyoto, la ville impériale. Concernant la terrasse en réalité beaucoup plus basse, il s'agit d'une réplique de la « scène » aujourd'hui encore célèbre du temple Kiyomizudera, avec son audacieuse avancée en surplomb dans les monts de l'est à Kyoto. Quant à l'étang artificiel Shinobazu no ike, il fut aménagé comme pendant du lac Biwako situé au nord-est de Kyoto. En 1625, sur l'île de l'étang, dont seule l'étroite bande d'accès apparaît près du bord gauche, sous le Pin de la lune, fut construit un sanctuaire de Benten faisant pendant à l'île de Chikubushima du lac Biwako. Ce genre de répliques d'attractions célèbres de Kyoto servait à la légitimation d'Edo dans sa fonction de « nouvelle » capitale.

12

上野
山した

Ueno Yamashita
10—1858

Ueno Yamashita

High in the pale sky, crows circle over the Ueno Temple district; even today, their loud cawing is a feature of this area. Red and yellow bands of cloud hang between the temple buildings, which are hidden in heavy green foliage, and separate them from the crowded street with its shops in the foreground. Here, elegantly clothed ladies with large parasols walk by, followed by the inquisitive looks of the plainly dressed citizens, who are depicted smaller by comparison.

The busy Iseya restaurant dominates the scene. In exuberant characters, its dark blue frontage advertises *shisomeshi*, a dish of rice with *shiso* leaves. The name of the restaurant can be seen on the right in Chinese characters; it is repeated on the left in the simpler characters of the Japanese *hiragana* syllabary. The latter enabled the generally less well educated to read the name, too. Hiroshige places his own red signature cartouche on the right-hand margin, as though he saw his own profession as a trade like any other.

The censors approved this print in the tenth month of 1858, the month following Hiroshige's death. The composition is presumably based on his sketches, but was probably completed by his pupil Shigenobu (1826–1869), also known as Hiroshige II.

Ueno Yamashita

Hoch oben am blassen Himmel zieht ein Schwarm Krähen seine Kreise über dem Tempelbezirk von Ueno. Noch heute prägt das laute Krächzen dieser Vögel das Gebiet. Rotgelbe Wolkenbänder schweben zwischen den im satten Grün verborgenen Tempelgebäuden und trennen diese von der belebten Straße mit Ladenlokalen im Bildvordergrund ab. Dort flanieren, dicht am Betrachter vorbei, vornehm gewandete Damen mit großen Sonnenschirmen, gefolgt von den neugierigen Blicken unscheinbar gekleideter Städter, die im Verhältnis kleiner dargestellt sind.

Das gut besuchte Imbiss-Restaurant Iseya beherrscht die Szenerie. Sein blau-schwarzes Ladenbanner bietet in schwungvollen Schriftzeichen *shiso-meshi* an, ein Gericht aus Reis mit Shiso-Blättern. Der Name des Geschäfts steht einmal rechts in chinesischen Schriftzeichen und am linken Rand in den einfacheren Hiragana-Silben. Somit konnten auch weniger Gebildete den Namen lesen. Wie ein weiteres Restaurantschild platziert Hiroshige seine eigene rote Signaturenkartusche ebenfalls am rechten Rand, ganz so, als verstünde er sein Gewerbe auch als Dienstleistung.

Dieser Holzschnitt wurde im zehnten Monat 1858, einen Monat nach dem Tod Hiroshiges, von den Zensoren genehmigt. Er basiert vermutlich auf seinen Skizzen, wurde aber wohl von seinem Schüler Shigenobu (1826–1869), auch Hiroshige II genannt, vollendet.

Ueno Yamashita

Haut dans le ciel pâle, un vol de corbeaux trace ses cercles audessus du temple d'Ueno. Aujourd'hui encore, leurs croassements sonores donnent son caractère à cette partie de la ville. Des bancs de nuages rouge-jaune flottent parmi les bâtiments du temple cachés dans le vert saturé, les séparant de la rue marchande animée du premier plan. Des dames élégamment vêtues, munies de grandes ombrelles y flânent tout près du spectateur, suivies par les regards curieux d'habitants humblement vêtus représentés dans une taille relativement plus petite.

La cantine bien fréquentée Iseya domine la scène. Les idéogrammes cursifs de son enseigne bleu-noir proposent du *shisomeshi*, plat composé d'un mélange de riz et de feuilles de *shiso*. Le nom de l'établissement est écrit à droite en idéogrammes chinois, et à gauche en caractères *hiragana* plus simples, permettant aux moins cultivés de lire le nom de l'établissement. Près du bord droit de l'image, Hiroshige a aussi apposé son propre cartouche de signature rouge – comme s'il s'agissait d'une autre enseigne de restaurant, et comme s'il comprenait lui-même son activité artistique comme une prestation de service.

L'estampe a été approuvée par la censure au dixième mois de l'année 1858, un mois après la mort de Hiroshige. Elle repose vraisemblablement sur des esquisses de l'artiste et fut sans doute achevée par son élève Shigenobu (1826–1869), dit Hiroshige II.

下谷
広小路

Shitaya Hirokōji
9–1856

Shitaya Hirokōji

Several samurai in the foreground are watching a long procession of women whose uni-
formly patterned parasols are
glowing in red and white. They
are passing a row of shops lining
the right-hand side of the busy
"Broadway" (Hirokōji). This
street leads to the wooded temple precinct of Kan'eiji in Ueno,
which is covered by a stylized
cloud. The view shown here is
very similar to that depicted by
the preceding print (plate 12),
which was, however, made
two years later.

With its large, grey roof, the
imposing premises of the textile
retailer Matsuzakaya dominate

the composition. The censors
approved this print in the same
month (9/1856) in which the
store reopened after its total
destruction in the earthquake of
1855. Not far from "Broadway"
was the premises of Hiroshige's
publisher, Sakanaya Eikichi. He
not only witnessed the reopening of the store from nearby, but
as a businessman also benefited
from the lively retail trade in
his neighbourhood. It was therefore very much in his interest
to have Hiroshige depict this
quarter. Already in the late
1830s, Hiroshige had designed
advertising material for the
Matsuzakaya store, which still
occupies the same site today.

Shitaya Hirokōji

Eine Gruppe von Samurai im
Vordergrund schaut einer langen Prozession von Frauen nach,
deren gleichförmig gemusterte
Sonnenschirme in Rot und Weiß
leuchten. Sie ziehen auf der
belebten „Breiten Straße"
(Hirokōji) an einer Reihe von
Läden vorbei, die die rechte
Seite säumen. Die Straße führt
zu dem bewaldeten Tempel-
bezirk des Kan'eiji in Ueno, der
von einer stilisierten Wolke
verdeckt wird. Der hier abgebildete Ort liegt ganz nah an demjenigen, den die vorhergehende
Tafel zeigt. Allerdings entstand
Tafel 12 erst zwei Jahre später.

Das imposante Gebäude des
Textilwarenhandels Matsu-
zakaya dominiert mit seinem
großen grauen Dach die Bildkomposition. Der Zensor geneh-

migte die Veröffentlichung im
gleichen Monat (9/1856), in
dem das vom Erdbeben 1855
völlig zerstörte Geschäft neu
eröffnet wurde. Unweit der
„Breiten Straße" befand sich
außerdem das Verlagshaus von
Sakanaya Eikichi. Hiroshiges
Verleger konnte die Neueröffnung also nicht nur aus nächster
Nähe miterleben, sondern hatte
als Geschäftsmann auch ein
Interesse am regen Einkaufs-
betrieb in seinem Quartier. Es
war ihm daher sicher sehr daran
gelegen, diese Gegend von
Hiroshige ins Bild setzen zu
lassen. Hiroshige selbst
hatte zudem schon Ende
der 1830er Jahre für das
noch heute am selben Ort
befindliche Warenhaus
Matsuzakaya Reklamebilder
entworfen.

Shitaya Hirokōji

Au premier plan, un groupe de
samouraïs suit du regard un long
cortège de femmes dont les
ombrelles aux motifs identiques
chatoient en rouge et blanc.
Elles passent le long d'une
enfilade de boutiques qui
bordent le côté droit de la rue
très animée appelée « Rue
large » (Hirokōji). Cette rue
mène au domaine boisé du
temple Kan'eiji à Ueno, caché ici
par un banc de nuages stylisé. Le
site représenté est situé tout
près de celui de l'estampe précédente, sachant toutefois que la
planche 12 n'a été réalisée que
deux ans après celle-ci.

Avec son grand toit gris, l'imposant bâtiment du magasin de
tissus Matsuzakaya domine la
composition de l'image. Le cen-

seur a approuvé la feuille le mois
même (9/1856) de la réouverture du magasin après sa destruction totale lors du séisme de
1855. Non loin de la « Rue
large » se trouvait aussi la
maison d'édition de Sakanaya
Eikichi. Si l'éditeur de Hiroshige
a donc pu assister *de visu* à la
réouverture du magasin, en tant
qu'homme d'affaires, il avait
tout intérêt à ce que son quartier
reprenne une vie commerçante
aussi intense que possible. Il lui
importait donc sûrement d'illus-
trer les alentours de son magasin par une image. Du reste, à la
fin des années 1830, Hiroshige
avait déjà conçu des réclames
pour le magasin Matsuzakaya,
qui occupe aujourd'hui encore le
même emplacement que dans
cette estampe.

14

日暮里
寺院の
林泉

Nippori jiin no rinsen
2–1857

Temple Gardens in Nippori

Men, women and children form colourful accents as they stroll around a blossoming garden landscape. What is artificial about this landscape is the simultaneous flowering of the cherry trees and azaleas – impossible because they bloom at different times, though attractive for Hiroshige, as this juxtaposition allowed him to show off different shades of red. Also artificial is the curious topiary on the right-hand margin of the print, a tree in the shape of a sailing boat. This, though, while manmade, was at least real: it would have enabled the inhabitants of Edo (and Hiroshige's customers) to recognize this elaborately landscaped garden immediately.

The unnaturally truncated pale pink of the two cherry trees in the foreground, by contrast, is due to a misunderstanding of the colour instructions on the part of the printers when producing the first impressions. This error was corrected in later impressions, in which a more organic, delicate pink appears behind the branches. However, for these later impressions, the printers chose for the ground in the middle of the print not the bluish colour we see here, but a pale yellow (which was also used for the title cartouche), while dispensing with it for the garments of the figures. The result is a garish contrast of pink, yellow and green, which has nothing in common with the more refined colour harmonies of this early impression.

The area depicted here belonged to three 18th-century temples whose unusual garden landscaping, with its artificial mounds and bizarrely shaped rocks, attracted numerous visitors, in particular from the middle of the second month, as we are told in the fifth volume of the *Illustrated Guide to Famous Views of Edo (Edo meisho zue)*, dating from 1836. Buddhist temples stood here in close proximity to shrines devoted to the veneration of native deities, forming an indissoluble unity. Eleven years after this print was made, however, the new Meiji government proclaimed Shinto the state religion and, as a result, Buddhist institutions and cult objects were destroyed, and the monks forcibly laicized.

Tempelgärten in Nippori

Männer, Frauen und Kinder wandeln als farbenfrohe Kontrastpunkte in einer blühenden Gartenlandschaft. Künstlich an dieser Landschaft ist dabei nicht nur das für Hiroshige wegen seiner Rotschattierungen attraktive, in der Natur aber – aufgrund unterschiedlicher Blütezeiten – unmögliche Nebeneinander von Kirsch- und Azaleenblüten. Auch der am rechten Rand sichtbare, wie ein barockes Gartengewächs gestutzte Baum in Gestalt eines Segelbootes gehört in diese kunstvoll gestalteten Gärten; er hatte für die Bewohner Edos und für Hiroshiges Kunden einen großen Wiedererkennungswert.

Das unnatürlich abgeschnittene Hellrosa der beiden Kirschbäume im Vordergrund basiert dagegen auf einer missverstandenen Farbanweisung bei den ersten Abzügen. Bei den Nachdrucken wurde dieser Fehler denn auch durchweg mit einem organischeren Zartrosa hinter den Zweigen korrigiert. Allerdings wählten die Drucker für diese späteren Abzüge statt der bläulichen Bodenfarbe im Mittelgrund ein Hellgelb, das auch für die Titelkartusche verwendet wurde und auf das sie dafür bei den Gewändern der Figuren verzichteten. Ein greller Kontrast von Rosa, Gelb und Grün war das Ergebnis, das mit der edleren Farbkomposition dieses frühen Abzuges nichts mehr gemein hatte.

Das hier dargestellte Areal gehörte zu drei Tempeln aus dem 18. Jahrhundert, die wegen ihrer ungewöhnlichen Gartenarchitektur mit artifiziellen Bergen und bizarr geformten Felsen vor allem ab Mitte des zweiten Monats zahlreiche Besucher anlockten, wie aus den Erläuterungen im fünften Band des *Illustrierten Führers zu berühmten Ansichten von Edo (Edo meisho zue)* von 1836 hervorgeht. Buddhistische Tempel und shintoistische Schreine zur Verehrung einheimischer Schutzgottheiten standen hier dicht gedrängt nebeneinander und bildeten eine unauflösliche Einheit. Elf Jahre nach Entstehung dieses Druckes rief die neue Meiji-Regierung (1868–1912) per Dekret den Shintoismus als Staatsreligion aus. In der Folge wurden buddhistische Einrichtungen sowie Kultobjekte zerstört und Mönche gezwungen, in den Laienstand überzutreten.

Jardins d'un temple à Nippori

Des hommes, des femmes et des enfants formant des accents contrastés très colorés se promènent dans un jardin paysager tout en fleurs. Ce jardin n'est pas seulement artificiel en tant que tel, mais aussi du fait de la juxtaposition, sans doute attrayante pour Hiroshige en raison des différents effets de rouge, mais impossible du fait des différentes époques de floraison des cerisiers et des azalées. L'arbre taillé comme une plante baroque en forme de voilier qu'on peut voir près du bord droit de l'image fait également partie de ce jardin paysager ; pour les habitants d'Edo et les clients de Hiroshige, il avait une forte valeur de reconnaissance du lieu.

L'interruption artificielle du rose clair des deux cerisiers du premier plan se doit en revanche à une mauvaise interprétation des indications de ton lors des premiers tirages. Les tirages suivants corrigent uniment cette erreur par un rose délicat plus organique apparaissant parmi les branchages. En revanche, pour ces tirages ultérieurs, les imprimeurs choisirent un jaune clair au lieu du sol bleuâtre au second plan, jaune qu'ils utilisèrent aussi pour le cartouche de titre, mais en y renonçant pour les habits des figures. Il en résulta un contraste strident de rose, de jaune et de vert qui n'a plus rien à voir avec la noble composition de couleurs des premiers tirages qu'on peut voir ici.

L'aire représentée dans cette estampe appartenait à trois temples du XVIIIe siècle dont l'architecture paysagère inhabituelle avec ses monts artificiels et ses rochers aux formes singulières attirait de nombreux visiteurs, plus particulièrement à partir du deuxième mois de l'année, comme l'explique le cinquième tome (1836) du *Guide illustré des vues célèbres d'Edo (Edo meisho zue)*. Les temples bouddhistes et les sanctuaires consacrés à la vénération des divinités locales s'y côtoyaient en paix et constituaient une unité indissociable. Onze ans après la réalisation de cette estampe, le nouveau gouvernement Meiji (1868–1912) allait décréter le shintoïsme religion d'État. Ceci eut pour conséquence que les temples et les instruments de culte bouddhistes furent détruits et que les moines furent contraints d'adopter l'état laïque.

15

日暮里
諏訪の臺

Nippori Suwanodai
5–1856

Suwa Bluff
in Nippori

The dense crowns of two slender cedar trunks rise into the sky, the varied green nuances of the treetops being continued in the grassy surface of the slope beneath the trees. In the distance on the right, we can see the silhouette of the twin peaks of Mount Tsukuba. The view of this well-known mountain was one of the attractions for which the citizens of Edo used to visit the grounds of the Suwa Myōjin Shrine. They could enjoy the panorama while strolling beneath blossoming cherry trees and drinking tea, as the visitors in this print do.

The shrine was founded in the 12th century; in the 15th century, the warlord Ōta Dōkan (1432–1486) donated the surrounding land to the shrine, which in the 17th century, after the entry of the Tokugawa into Edo, quickly became a popular destination for outings. The Suwa Myōjin was located in the countryside, but was close to the densely populated districts of Asakusa and Ueno. The inhabitants of the nearby district of Nippori visited the shrine regularly in order to offer gifts to the patron deities of their district, who were venerated at the shrine. This attractive landscape lent itself to combining religious obligations with leisure and recreation.

Suwa-Abhang
in Nippori

Zwei schlanke Zedernstämme und ihre dichten grünen Kronen ragen in den Himmel empor. Die vielfältigen Grünnuancen der Wipfel setzen sich in den Grasflächen des Abhangs unterhalb der Bäume fort. In der Ferne ist am rechten Bildrand die doppelte Gipfelsilhouette des Berges Tsukubasan zu erkennen. Der Ausblick auf diesen bekannten Berg gehörte zu den Attraktionen, für die sich die Städter auf das Gelände des Schreins Suwa Myōjin begaben. Sie genossen die Aussicht, während sie – wie hier abgebildet – unter blühenden Kirschbäumen spazieren gingen und Tee tranken.

Das Heiligtum wurde im 12. Jahrhundert errichtet. Im 15. Jahrhundert übertrug der Feldherr Ōta Dōkan (1432–1486) das Gelände dem Schrein, der im 17. Jahrhundert, nach dem Einzug der Tokugawa in Edo, rasch zu einem beliebten Ausflugsziel wurde. Der Suwa Myōjin befand sich mitten im Grünen, lag aber dennoch in der Nähe der dicht besiedelten Stadtteile Asakusa und Ueno. Auch die Bewohner aus dem umliegenden Bezirk Nippori begaben sich regelmäßig dorthin, um den Schutzgottheiten ihres Stadtteils, die sich in dem Schrein befanden, ihre Gaben darzubringen. In dieser schönen Landschaft ließen sich auf angenehme Weise die religiösen Pflichten mit Freizeit und Erholung verbinden.

La montée de Suwa
à Nippori

Les troncs légers de deux cèdres au feuillage touffu et verdoyant s'élancent dans le ciel. Les multiples nuances de vert de leurs faîtes se prolongent dans les surfaces herbeuses de la montée sous les arbres. Au loin, près du bord droit de l'image, on reconnaît la silhouette du mont Tsukubasan caractérisé par ses deux sommets. La vue sur cette montagne célèbre était une des attractions pour lesquelles les citadins se rendaient dans le domaine du sanctuaire Suwa Myōjin. Ils pouvaient y jouir du panorama en se promenant – comme on le voit ici – ou en buvant du thé sous des cerisiers en fleurs.

La construction du sanctuaire remonte au XIIe siècle. Au XVe siècle, le général Ōta Dōkan (1432–1486) offrit ce terrain au sanctuaire. Au XVIIe siècle, après l'installation des Tokugawa à Edo, le sanctuaire devint un lieu d'excursion populaire pour les habitants de la nouvelle capitale. Situé en pleine campagne, le Suwa Myōjin restait néanmoins proche des quartiers populeux d'Asakusa et d'Edo. Les habitants de Nippori, le district environnant, s'y rendaient eux aussi régulièrement pour apporter des offrandes aux divinités tutélaires du quartier abritées par le sanctuaire. Ce beau paysage permettait ainsi de joindre l'utile à l'agréable en accomplissant ses devoirs religieux tout en profitant des distractions et du délassement offert par le cadre.

16

千駄木
団子坂
花屋敷

Sendagi Dangozaka Hanayashiki
5–1856

Flower Park and Dangozaka Slope in Sendagi

This print is divided into two parts, both in terms of composition and colour. Beneath a green, white and red *genji* cloud, a splendid cherry orchard in blossom spreads out beside a pond. As in the preceding and following prints, which were all approved by the censors in the same month, colourfully dressed park visitors are depicted sitting down or walking around to enjoy the brief period during which the cherry trees are in bloom. Above the stylized cloud, three small figures climb steep steps lined by bizarre rock formations, a large stone lantern and a thatched pavilion. At the top, the "Pavilion of the Violet Spring" (Shisentei) offers a spectacular view across the luxuriant green foliage of Shinobazu Pond and the neighbourhood of Ueno to the south-west.

This flower park had been laid out just four years earlier by the gardener Kusuda Uheiji. It was therefore a new "famous place" (*meisho*), which Hiroshige immortalized in two more views in the seventh volume of his *Illustrated Souvenirs of Edo* (*Ehon Edo miyage*), printed in 1857. The first of the two illustrations resembles the one reproduced here. Its inscription states that in the park, which had originally belonged to a gardener, "a great variety of flowers had recently been planted, providing a year-round attraction".

Towards the end of the Tokugawa period (1615–1868), garden design enjoyed great popularity, with famous gardens attracting numerous visitors, as illustrated in the *One Hundred Famous Views of Edo* (see plate 14). According to a contemporary account, the "three-storey building" escaped damage during the great Ansei earthquake in the tenth month of 1855, while the "tea pavilion" was destroyed. In this print, Hiroshige depicts the already reconstructed pavilion, and at the same time immortalizes the memory of a day trip, organized two months earlier, by the ruling shogun Tokugawa Iesada (1824–1858), who took the opportunity to enjoy the blossom spectacle (see plate 17).

Blumenpark und der Abhang Dangozaka in Sendagi

Zwei kompositorisch wie farblich getrennte Sphären bestimmen diesen Holzschnitt. Unterhalb einer grün-weiß-rot changierenden Genji-Wolke breitet sich ein prächtig blühender Kirschbaumpark am Ufer eines Teiches aus. Wie schon im vorangegangenen und im folgenden Blatt, die alle im gleichen Monat von den Zensoren genehmigt wurden, erfreuen sich bunt gekleidete Parkbesucher im Sitzen und beim Spazierengehen an der kurzen Zeit der Kirschblüte. Oberhalb der stilisierten Wolke steigen drei Figuren eine steile Treppe hinauf, die von bizarren Felsformationen, einer Steinlaterne und einem strohgedeckten Pavillon gesäumt ist. Oben erwartet sie vom „Pavillon der Violetten Quelle" (Shisentei) aus ein spektakulärer Blick über üppiges Grün hinweg auf das Stadtviertel Ueno im Südwesten und den Teich Shinobazu no ike.

Dieser Blumenpark war erst vier Jahre zuvor vom Gärtner Kusuda Uheiji gegründet worden, ein neuer „berühmter Ort" (*meisho*) also, den Hiroshige denn auch 1857 im siebten Band seiner *Illustrierten Mitbringsel aus Edo* (*Ehon Edo miyage*) noch einmal in zwei Ansichten verewigte. Die erste der beiden Kompositionen ähnelt der vorliegenden. Ihre Aufschrift besagt, dass in dem Park, der ursprünglich einem Gärtner gehörte, „in jüngster Zeit die unterschiedlichsten Blumen angepflanzt wurden, die sich das ganze Jahr über als Attraktion anbieten".

Gegen Ende der Tokugawa-Zeit (1615–1868) erfreute sich die Gartenkunst großer Beliebtheit und lockte – wie auch in den *Hundert Ansichten von Edo* dargestellt (siehe Tafel 14) – zahlreiche Besucher an. Gemäß dem Bericht eines zeitgenössischen Beobachters blieb das „dreistöckige Gebäude" zwar vom großen Ansei-Erdbeben im zehnten Monat 1855 verschont, aber der „Teepavillon" wurde zerstört. Hiroshige zeigt auf dem Blatt das bereits wiederhergestellte Gebäude und verewigt zugleich die Erinnerung an den zwei Monate zuvor organisierten Ausflug des regierenden Shogun Tokugawa Iesada (1824–1858), der sich den Genuss der Blütenpracht nicht entgehen lassen wollte (siehe Tafel 17).

Le parc floral et la montée Dangozaka à Sendagi

Deux sphères distinctes par la composition comme par le coloris déterminent cette estampe. Sous un nuage *genji* chatoyant du vert au blanc et au rouge, un parc de cerisiers en fleurs s'étend au bord d'un étang. Comme dans les feuilles précédente et suivante, qui furent approuvées au même mois par la censure, des visiteurs du parc portant des habits colorés, assis ou se promenant, se réjouissent de la brève floraison des cerisiers. Au-dessus du nuage stylisé, trois figures gravissent un escalier pentu bordé de rochers aux formes bizarres, d'une lanterne de pierre et d'un pavillon couvert de chaume. En haut, depuis le « Pavillon de la source violette » (Shisentei), les attend une vue spectaculaire sur la verdure foisonnante et le quartier d'Ueno au sud-ouest d'Edo, ainsi que de l'étang Shinobazu no ike.

Ce parc floral avait été créé seulement quatre ans plus tôt par le jardinier Kusada Uheiji ; il s'agissait donc d'un nouveau « lieu célèbre » (*meisho*) que Hiroshige a encore immortalisé dans deux vues du septième tome (1857) de ses *Souvenirs illustrés d'Edo* (*Ehon Edo miyage*). La première ressemble à celle-ci, et son inscription indique que dans ce parc, qui appartient initialement à un jardinier, « les fleurs les plus diverses ont été plantées récemment, qui proposent une attraction pendant toute l'année. »

Vers la fin de l'ère Tokugawa (1615–1868), l'art du jardin connut une forte popularité et attirait de nombreux visiteurs, comme le montrent d'ailleurs les *Cent Vues* (cf. pl. 14). Conformément au récit d'un spectateur de l'époque, le « bâtiment à trois étages » était resté intact après le grand séisme d'Ansei du dixième mois 1855, alors que le « pavillon du thé » avait été détruit. Dans cette feuille, Hiroshige nous montre le pavillon déjà restauré et immortalise en même temps le souvenir de l'excursion entreprise deux mois plus tôt par le shogun régnant Iesada (1824–1858), qui ne voulait pas se priver du spectacle de toute cette splendeur florale (cf. pl. 17).

17

飛鳥山
北の
眺望

Asukayama kita no chōbō
5–1856

View to the North
from Asukayama

The area around Asukayama was famous for its splendid cherry trees, and in this scene we see numerous visitors strolling around and picnicking on blankets beneath blossoming branches.

Beyond the precincts of this park extends a broad, light-green, almost featureless plain of rice paddies. Hiroshige uses fine grey blurring to indicate the water in which the young plants, suggested by black dots, are growing. Extending over the horizon are the thinly outlined twin peaks of the sacred Mount Tsukuba. Hiroshige simplifies and exaggerates the contour in order render the mountain easily recognizable, but changes the relative heights of the two peaks. In contrast to this depiction, the left-hand peak is in reality lower, though by tradition it was usually depicted as the higher of the two, as it was regarded as the male peak.

Yoshimune (1684–1751), the eighth Tokugawa shogun, donated this land to the Kinrinji Monastery in 1737 on condition that the park be made freely accessible to the public. In 1873, the Meiji government (1868–1912), fully intent on pursuing Westernizing reforms, created here what was modern Japan's first public park.

This print was executed shortly after Tokugawa Iesada (1824–1858), the 13th shogun of the Tokugawa dynasty, had made an excursion to Asukayama in the third month of 1856 and had enjoyed precisely this view. The event led the art historian Harashida Minoru to assume that the choice of this landscape motif by Hiroshige was based on Iesada's visit, and that this print, like many others in the series, was inspired by contemporary events.

Blick nach Norden
vom Berg Asukayama

Das Gebiet um den Berg Asukayama war für seine prächtigen Kirschbäume berühmt. Unter blühenden Zweigen gehen zahlreiche Besucher spazieren und picknicken auf Decken.

Hinter dem Gelände erstreckt sich eine weite hellgrüne, fast strukturlose Ebene aus Reisfeldern. Durch feine graue Schleier deutet Hiroshige das Wasser an, in dem die noch jungen, als schwarze Punkte angedeuteten Reispflanzen wachsen. Am Horizont erheben sich die feinen Umrisslinien des heiligen Berges Tsukubasan mit seinen zwei Gipfeln. Hiroshige vereinfacht und überhöht die Konturen, um den Wiedererkennungseffekt zu steigern, vertauscht jedoch die reale Höhe der Bergspitzen. Im Gegensatz zu der Darstellung ist der linke der beiden Gipfel in Wirklichkeit der niedrigere. Da er jedoch traditionell als der männliche Gipfel galt, stellte man ihn meistens als den höheren dar.

Der achte Tokugawa-Shogun Yoshimune (1684–1751) schenkte das Land 1737 dem Tempel Kinrinji mit der Auflage, die Grünanlagen frei zugänglich zu machen. Im Jahr 1873 richtete die Meiji-Regierung (1868–1912), ganz auf westliche Reformen bedacht, hier den ersten öffentlichen Park des modernen Japans ein.

Das Blatt entstand kurz nachdem Tokugawa Iesada (1824–1858), der 13. Shogun der Tokugawa-Dynastie, im dritten Monat 1856 einen Ausflug zum Tempel Kinrinji unternommen und das hier dargestellte Panorama vom Berg Asukayama aus genossen hatte. Dieser Umstand veranlasste den Kunsthistoriker Harashida Minoru zu der Vermutung, dass die Wahl des Landschaftssujets auf den Besuch Iesadas zurückzuführen sei und dieser Holzschnitt somit, wie viele andere der Serie, auch dokumentarischen Charakter habe.

Vue nord depuis
le mont Asukayama

Les environs du mont Asukayama étaient célèbres pour la splendeur des cerisiers en fleurs. Sous leurs branches fleuries, de nombreux visiteurs se promènent et pique-niquent sur des couvertures.

Derrière le domaine s'étend une vaste plaine de rizières verdoyantes presque entièrement dépourvue de structure. Hiroshige indique l'eau dans laquelle poussent les jeunes plants de riz évoqués par des points noirs, en se servant comme d'un léger voile gris. À l'horizon s'élèvent les fins contours de la montagne sacrée Tsukubasan avec son double sommet. Hiroshige en a simplifié et surhaussé le dessin pour accroître l'effet d'identification, mais a inversé la hauteur réelle des deux sommets. En fait, contrairement à ce que montre l'image, le sommet de gauche est le moins haut. Dans la mesure où il était traditionnellement considéré comme le sommet mâle, on le représentait généralement comme le plus haut.

Yoshimune (1684–1751), le huitième shogun Tokugawa, a offert ce domaine au temple Kinrinji en 1737, sous la condition que les espaces verts en fussent ouverts au public. En 1873, le gouvernement Meiji (1868–1912), soucieux de réaliser des réformes à l'occidentale, y aménagea le premier parc public du Japon moderne.

Cette feuille a vu le jour peu après que Iesada (1824–1858), 13ème shogun de la dynastie Tokugawa, eut entrepris une excursion sur ces lieux au troisième mois 1856 et qu'il y eut contemplé le panorama représenté ici depuis l'Asukayama. L'événement a conduit l'historien de l'art Harashida Minoru à supposer que le choix du sujet se devait précisément à la visite d'Iesada, et que cette estampe, comme beaucoup de la même série, n'est pas dénuée d'un certain aspect documentaire.

18

王子
稲荷
の社

Ōji Inari no yashiro
9–1857

The Ōji Inari Shrine

The Ōji Inari Shrine, a branch of the Fushimi Inari Shrine in Kyoto, which was founded at the beginning of the 8th century AD, was the oldest of all the shrines in the Kantō district.

Situated on a wooded hill near the village of Ōji, the shrine was dedicated to the rice deity Inari and dominated the fertile plain to the north of Edo. Among the pilgrims were not just farmers, but also the shogun (see plate 19), who went there every autumn to give thanks for a good harvest, and at New Year to ask for health and prosperity in the coming year. Inari (also Oinari) was the most popular of Japan's native deities, with more than 10,000 cult sites dedicated to him. His shrines were often guarded by a pair of foxes (*kitsune*), for according to legend foxes gathered around an old tree at the Ōji Shrine on New Year's Eve as ghostly messengers of the deities (see plate 118). In contrast to that eerie scene, this print, which was also approved by the censors in the ninth month of 1857, depicts a humane aspect of the Inari cult.

The close-up of the shrine's red portico, cropped by the right-hand margin of the print, fixes our gaze on a level approximately that of the shrine servant on the veranda. He is turning towards the pilgrims, who, laden with sacrificial offerings of rice-wine (*sake*) and baked tofu (*inari sushi*), are climbing a steep flight of steps. Beyond the imposing cedars in the shrine precinct, we can see the saddle-shaped silhouette of Mount Tsukuba on the horizon. The budding plum trees along the village street at the foot of the hill indicate that Inari will soon be turning wintry nature green once more.

Der Schrein Ōji Inari

Der Schrein Ōji Inari, eine Dependance des zu Beginn des 8. Jahrhunderts gegründeten Schreins Fushimi Inari in Kyoto, war unter allen Schreinen im Kantō-Gebiet der älteste.

Auf einem bewaldeten Hügel nahe bei dem Dorf Ōji gelegen, überragte das Heiligtum des Reis-Gottes Inari die fruchtbare Ebene im Norden Edos. Zu dem Schrein pilgerten nicht nur Bauern, sondern selbst der Shogun (siehe Tafel 19), um im Herbst für eine gute Ernte zu danken oder an Neujahr um Reichtum und Gesundheit zu bitten. Inari (auch Oinari) stellte mit über 10.000 Kultstätten die populärste einheimische Gottheit Japans dar. Seine Schreine werden oft von Füchsen (*kitsune*) bewacht, die sich der Legende nach als gespenstische Götterboten am Neujahrsabend um einen alten Baum beim Schrein Ōji versammelt haben sollen (siehe Tafel 118). Im Gegensatz zu jener unheimlichen Versammlung der Füchse zeigt das vorliegende Blatt, das ebenfalls im neunten Monat 1857 von den Zensoren genehmigt wurde, einen humanen Aspekt des Inari-Kultes.

Die Nahansicht auf den angeschnittenen, roten Vorbau des Heiligtums am rechten Bildrand fixiert den Blickwinkel des Betrachters etwa auf Höhe des Schreindieners auf der Veranda. Dieser wendet sich den Pilgern zu, die – mit Opfergaben wie Reiswein (*sake*) und gebratenen Tofutaschen (*inari sushi*) beladen – über eine steile Treppe heraneilen. Jenseits der mächtigen Zedern des Schreinbezirks erstreckt sich am Horizont die sattelförmige Silhouette des Berges Tsukubasan. Die blühenden Pflaumenbäumchen entlang der Dorfstraße am Fuß des Hügels lassen erahnen, dass die Gottheit Inari die winterliche Natur bald wieder ergrünen lassen wird.

Le sanctuaire Ōji Inari

Le sanctuaire Ōji Inari, une dépendance du sanctuaire Fushimi Inari fondé à Kyoto au début du VIIIe siècle, était le plus ancien de tous les sanctuaires du domaine de Kantō.

Situé sur une colline boisée près du village d'Ōji, le sanctuaire d'Inari, le dieu du riz, surplombait la plaine fertile qui s'étendait au nord d'Edo. Le sanctuaire n'était pas seulement un lieu de pèlerinage pour les paysans, mais aussi pour le shogun lui-même (cf. pl. 19), qui allait y prier à l'automne pour les bonnes récoltes ou à l'époque du Nouvel An pour la santé et la prospérité du pays. Avec plus de 10 000 lieux de culte, Inari (ou Oinari) est la divinité la plus populaire du Japon. Ses sanctuaires sont souvent gardés par un couple de renards (*kitsune*), messagers du dieu dont la légende rapporte qu'il se réunissent la veille du Nouvel An autour d'un vieil arbre des environs du sanctuaire d'Ōji (cf. pl. 118). Contrairement à cette réunion mystérieuse des renards, la présente feuille, qui fut elle aussi approuvée par la censure au neuvième mois 1857, présente plutôt l'aspect humain du culte d'Inari.

La vue rapprochée d'un angle rouge du sanctuaire coupé par le bord droit de l'image, fixe la hauteur du regard à peu près à la hauteur de l'homme qui se tient sur la véranda. Le serviteur du temple se tourne vers les pèlerins porteurs d'offrandes – alcool de riz (*sake*), tofu grillé (*inari sushi*) – qui s'approchent du sanctuaire par un escalier escarpé. À l'horizon, au-delà des puissants cèdres du domaine du sanctuaire, se dresse la silhouette en forme de selle du mont Tsukubasan. Les arbustes fleuris qui bordent la route du village au pied de la colline annoncent que la divinité Inari va bientôt faire reverdir la nature hivernale.

19

王子音無
川堰壕
世俗大瀧
卜唱

Ôji Otonashigawa entai, sezoku Ôtaki to tonau
2–1857

Dam on the Otonashi River at Ôji, known as "The Great Waterfall"

In the middle of this scene, a waterfall gushes into the Otonashi River ("Noiseless River"), the banks of which are lined with cedars and cherry trees with delicate pink blossoms. Following a gentle curve, the river flows out of the scene on the left. A few men have dared to step into the icy waters and the most courageous are even taking a shower under the waterfall. Directly above we can see, in a grove, the roof of the Amida Buddha Hall in the Kinrinji Temple.

The narrow band of blue *bokashi* at the top margin of the print, which indicates the sky, echoes the colour of the river.

This woodblock print was made shortly after the ruling shogun Iesada (1824–1858) went on a day trip to Ôji to the north of Edo on the 21st day of the first month of 1857. He ate at the Kinrinji Temple, then passed by Takata-chô before returning to his castle in Edo. The temple buildings the shogun visited are depicted inconspicuously. As in other prints, Hiroshige here conceals the most important place in the middle distance. Two views of Takata (see plates 115, 116) were approved by the censors in the first and second months, and likewise indicate that Hiroshige created the three prints specifically to mark the occasion of the shogun's visit.

Der Damm des Flusses Otonashigawa in Ôji, bekannt unter dem Namen „Der große Wasserfall"

Ein Wasserfall in der Bildmitte speist den von Zedern und zartrosa erblühten Kirschbäumen gesäumten Fluss Otonashigawa („lautloser Fluss"). Mit einer sanften Biegung fließt das Wasser nach links aus dem Bild. Einige Männer haben es gewagt, in das eisige Wasser zu steigen, und die mutigsten nehmen sogar eine Dusche unter dem Wasserfall. Über ihnen ist in einem Hain das Dach der Halle des Amida-Buddha im Tempel Kinrinji zu erkennen. Die schmale blaue Farbgradierung (*bokashi*) am oberen Bildrand deutet den Himmel an und bildet ein Farbecho auf den Fluss.

Dieser Holzschnitt entstand kurz nachdem der amtierende Shogun Tokugawa Iesada (1824–1858) am 21. Tag des ersten Monats 1857 einen Ausflug zu dem im Norden Edos gelegenen Ôji unternahm. Am Kinrinji hatte er zu Mittag gegessen und war nach einer Zwischenstation in Takata-chô in sein Schloss zurückgekehrt. Die Tempelgebäude, in denen sich der Shogun aufhielt, sind nur unscheinbar dargestellt. Wie schon in anderen Blättern versteckt Hiroshige auch hier den wesentlichen Ort im Mittelgrund des Blattes. Zwei Ansichten von der Gegend um Takata (siehe Tafeln 115, 116) sind, wie dieser Druck, im ersten und zweiten Monat von den Zensoren genehmigt worden und weisen darauf hin, dass Hiroshige die drei Holzschnitte aus Anlass des shogunalen Ausfluges entworfen hat.

La digue de la rivière Otonashigawa à Ôji, connue sous le nom « La Grande chute d'eau »

Une chute d'eau au milieu de l'image alimente la rivière Otonashigawa (« rivière silencieuse ») bordée de cyprès et de cerisiers en fleurs aux couleurs délicatement rosées. Le cours d'eau sort de l'image par la gauche en suivant une courbe douce. Quelques hommes ont osé entrer dans l'eau glacée, les plus téméraires prennent même une douche sous la cascade. Directement au-dessus, le toit du pavillon d'Amida-Buddha du temple Kinrinji émerge d'un bois. Le fin *bokashi* bleu près du bord supérieur de l'image indique le ciel et fait un écho chromatique à la rivière.

Cette estampe a vu le jour un peu après le 21ème jour du premier mois de l'année 1857. À cette date, le shogun Tokugawa régnant Iesada (1824–1858) avait entrepris une excursion à Ôji, au nord d'Edo. Il y déjeuna au Kinrinji et retourna dans son château d'Edo après avoir fait étape à Takata. Les bâtiments du temple qui ont reçu la visite du shogun sont seulement représentés accessoirement. Comme dans d'autres feuilles, Hiroshige cache une fois de plus le site principal au second plan de l'image. Deux vues de Takata (cf. pl. 115, 116) ont été approuvées par les censeurs aux premier et deuxième mois, tout comme cette feuille ; Hiroshige a donc conçu les trois estampes dans le contexte de l'excursion du shogun.

20

川口の
わたし
善光寺

Kawaguchi no watashi Zenkōji
2–1857

The Kawaguchi Ferry and Zenkōji Temple

With this view, Hiroshige marks the northern limit of "his" Edo, whose imaginary boundary is formed by the Sumida River; in this middle part of its course, it is called the Arakawa, "Wild River" (see plate 103).

The scene is dominated by the diagonal, deep-blue central section of the river, which is accentuated by the rafts. A pale-yellow thatched roof on this side of the river, as well as those on the opposite bank, provide glowing colour accents.

Hiroshige was primarily concerned with composition and colour, and not with an exact reproduction of the landscape, yet details play an important role. For example, he manages to convey the effort taken to punt the rafts of timber upstream. The Kawaguchi ferryman, by contrast, has a much easier time getting his passengers to the opposite bank of the river. Cropped by the right-hand margin of the print, the ferry that gives the picture its title skilfully leads us into the scene.

The "secret Buddha" (*hibutsu*) Amida in the Zenkōji Temple at the top of the print is the subject of a sophisticated pictorial pun by the artist. A year after Hiroshige designed this print, the Buddha was due to be exhibited publicly for the first time in 13 years; a longer interval of 17 years was customary. This event, known as the "opening of the curtain" (*kaichō*), is documented for the first time in 1757, and was a major spectacle that had a significant commercial impact. Just as the image is usually hidden from the eyes of the faithful, so Hiroshige uses the square title cartouche partially to hide the Golden Hall of the temple in which the Amida statue is housed.

Die Fähre in Kawaguchi und der Tempel Zenkōji

Hiroshige steckt mit diesem Blatt das nördliche Ende „seines" Edo ab, dessen imaginäre Grenze der Fluss Sumidagawa bildet. Er wird in seinem hier dargestellten Mittellauf Arakawa („Wilder Fluss") genannt (siehe Tafel 103).

Der diagonal verlaufende, tiefblaue Flusskern dominiert die Bildmitte, die von den parallel versetzten Flößen akzentuiert wird. Die hellgelben, strohgedeckten Dächer am unteren Bildrand und am gegenüberliegenden Flussufer setzen Farbakzente und bringen das Bild zum Leuchten.

Primär ging es Hiroshige bei diesem Blatt um die Wirkung von Komposition und Farbgebung und nicht um die mimetische Abbildung der Landschaft, dennoch spielen Details eine wichtige Rolle. Es ist deutlich zu erkennen, wie die Flößer sich anstrengen müssen, das Bauholz flussaufwärts zu staken. Der Bootsmann der Kawaguchi-Fähre hat es dagegen viel leichter, seine Passagiere an das gegenüberliegende Ufer zu befördern. Angeschnitten, am rechten Bildrand positioniert, leitet die Fähre, die dem Blatt den Titel gibt, bildwirksam in das Blatt hinein.

Der „geheime Buddha" (*hibutsu*) Amida des am oberen Bildrand dargestellten Tempels Zenkōji ist Gegenstand eines raffinierten Versteckspiels des Künstlers. Ein Jahr nachdem Hiroshige das Blatt geschaffen hatte, sollte der Buddha erstmals nach 13 Jahren wieder der Öffentlichkeit gezeigt werden. Üblich war normalerweise ein größeres Intervall von 17 Jahren. Dieses als „Öffnen des Vorhangs" (*kaichō*) bezeichnete Ereignis, das zum ersten Mal aus dem Jahr 1757 überliefert ist, war von großem Unterhaltungswert mit stark kommerziellen Aspekten. Da die Ikone üblicherweise vor den Augen der Gläubigen verborgen ist, verdeckte Hiroshige hier die Goldene Halle des Tempels, die die Amida-Statue beherbergte, teilweise mit der quadratischen Titelkartusche.

Le bac de Kawaguchi et le temple Zenkōji

Dans cette feuille, Hiroshige marque l'extrême limite nord de « son » Edo, dont la rivière Sumidagawa dessine la frontière. La rivière est ici représentée en son cours moyen, appelé Arakawa, c'est-à-dire le « Fleuve sauvage » (cf. pl. 103).

Le milieu bleu profond de la rivière domine le centre de l'image de sa large diagonale, renforcée encore par les deux zones parallèles plus claires qui le flanquent. Les toits de chaume jaune clair posent des accents de couleur et donnent sa lumière à l'image.

Hiroshige a moins recherché ici une représentation mimétique du paysage que l'efficacité de la composition et du coloris. Certains détails anecdotiques n'en jouent pas moins un rôle important. On comprend clairement que les pilotes des radeaux doivent travailler dur pour faire remonter le cours d'eau au bois de construction. Pour le batelier du bac de Kawaguchi, le transfert des passagers sur l'autre rive est en revanche beaucoup plus aisé. Coupé par le bord droit de l'image, le bac qui donne son titre à l'estampe fait une entrée spectaculaire dans l'image.

Amida, le « Bouddha secret » (*hibutsu*) du temple Zenkōji représenté près du bord supérieur, est ici l'objet d'un jeu de cache-cache raffiné de la part de l'artiste. Un an après la création de cette feuille, le Bouddha devait être à nouveau présenté au public – la première fois après 13 ans. L'intervalle entre deux présentations était normalement de 17 ans. Cet événement appelé *kaichō* (ouverture du rideau), et dont la première occurrence est attestée en 1757, avait une forte valeur événementielle dans laquelle entraient aussi des considérations commerciales. De même que l'icône est habituellement cachée aux yeux des croyants, de même Hiroshige s'est servi du cartouche de titre carré pour occulter en partie la salle dorée abritant la statue d'Amida.

21

芝愛宕山

Shiba Atagoyama
8–1857

Mount Atago in Shiba

An old man in ceremonial dress and an elaborate headgear is climbing the steps to the Atago Shrine. Far below him, a grey expanse of buildings lines the blue waters of Edo Bay, which is punctuated with the white sails of boats. On the horizon, a red glow heralds the rising sun.

Cropped by the margins of the print in the top left-hand corner, from the roof of the shrine hangs a black-framed votive picture on which we can read only the dateline: "an auspicious day, in the [not specified], Ansei 4 [1857]". The unusually yellow signature cartouche contains a more precise date and explains the figure: "On the third day of the first month, an emissary of Bishamon (*shōgatsu mikka, Bishamon tsukai*)."

In accordance with New Year customs, on the third day of the year a messenger from the Enpukuji Temple went to Mount Atago and performed a ceremony designed to bring good fortune, health and success, and to avert hunger and disease. The large rice-paddle in the emissary's hand symbolizes abundance. The seaweed around his neck will be cut up after the ceremony and distributed to the faithful, who will use it to brew an infusion supposed to cure colds. The brown garment of the messenger is decorated with white wheels, symbols of Buddhist teachings. The club in his left hand symbolizes the violence that Bishamon is capable of using in defence of Buddhism.

Mount Atago rises a mere 26 metres (85 feet) above Edo Bay to the south of Edo Castle. It owes its description of "mountain" (*yama*) to its namesake in Kyoto, which is 924 metres (3,030 feet) high.

The first volume of *Illustrated Guide to Famous Views of Edo* (*Edo meisho zue*), dating from 1834, praises this little replica of Mount Atago: "… a steep cliff rises into the sky, so mightily that its 68 stone steps seem to touch the clouds … looking down, one sees the neat rows of roof tiles of the countless houses and gates on the broad streets. The sea extends infinitely to the far horizon, a truly splendid view."

Hiroshige succeeds in masterly fashion in rendering a visual equivalent to this description.

Der Berg Atagoyama in Shiba

Ein zeremoniell gekleideter alter Mann, mit prächtiger Kopfbedeckung, erklimmt die Stufen zum Schrein Atago. Tief unter ihm säumt ein graues Häusermeer die Bucht von Edo, aus der die Segel der Boote als weiße Farbakzente hervorleuchten. Die aufgehende Sonne schickt vom Horizont her ihren roten Schein voraus.

Vom Dach des Schreines, in der linken oberen Ecke des Blattes, hängt ein angeschnittenes, schwarz gerahmtes Votivbild, von dem nur die Datierung „… ein glückbringender Tag, Monat [nicht angegeben] Ansei 4 [1857] …" zu lesen ist. Die gelb gestaltete Signaturenkartusche darunter enthält ein weiteres Datum und erläutert die Figur: „Am dritten Tag des ersten Monats, ein Abgesandter des Bishamon (*shōgatsu mikka, Bishamon tsukai*)".

Gemäß den Neujahrsbräuchen begibt sich am dritten Tag ein Bote aus dem Tempel Enpukuji auf den Berg Atagoyama und führt eine Glück verheißende Zeremonie durch, die Gesundheit und Erfolg im Leben verspricht und vor Hunger und Krankheit schützen soll. Die große Reiskelle in der Hand des Gesandten symbolisiert Überfluss, und die Algenblätter um seinen Hals werden nach der Zeremonie zerschnitten und an die Gläubigen verteilt, die sich daraus einen Erkältungstee zubereiten. Weiße Räder als Symbol der buddhistischen Lehre zieren das Gewand des Boten. Der Knüppel in seiner Linken deutet auf die Gewalt hin, die Bishamon als Verteidiger der buddhistischen Lehre anzuwenden im Stande ist.

Der Berg Atagoyama erhebt sich südlich des Edo-Schlosses nur 26 Meter über die Edo-Bucht. Die Bezeichnung „Berg" (*yama*) verdankt er dem gleichnamigen Vorbild in Kyoto, das immerhin 924 Meter über dem Meeresspiegel liegt.

Der *Illustrierte Führer zu berühmten Ansichten von Edo* (*Edo meisho zue*) rühmt in seinem ersten Band aus dem Jahr 1834 die kleine Replik des Berges Atagoyama: „… eine steile Klippe erhebt sich in den Himmel, so mächtig, dass seine 68 Steinstufen die Wolken zu berühren scheinen (…) schaut man hinunter, sieht man die aneinandergereihten Dachziegel der zahllosen Häuser und Tore an den großen Straßen. Das Meer dehnt sich unendlich am Horizont aus, eine wahrlich prächtige Aussicht."

Hiroshige gelingt es meisterhaft, diesem so eindrucksvoll beschriebenen Ort ein visuelles Denkmal zu setzen.

Le mont Atagoyama à Shiba

Un vieil homme en habit de cérémonie portant une coiffe sophistiquée gravit les marches accédant au sanctuaire d'Atago. Loin au-dessous de lui, une mer grise de maisons borde la baie d'Edo où miroitent les blancs accents des voiliers. Le rougeoiement du soleil levant annonce le jour à l'horizon.

Du toit du sanctuaire, dans le coin supérieur gauche de la feuille, est suspendue une image votive encadrée de noir et coupée par le bord de l'image, sur laquelle on lit seulement la date « un jour annonciateur de bonheur le mois [non indiqué] Ansei 4 [1857] ». Plus bas, le cartouche de signature sur fond jaune présente une autre date et fournit une explication de la figure de l'estampe : « troisième jour du premier mois, un envoyé de Bishamon (*shōgatsu mikka, Bishamon tsukai*) ».

Les coutumes du Nouvel An veulent que le troisième jour de l'année, un émissaire du temple Enpukuji se rende sur le mont Atagoyama et y exécute une cérémonie dispensatrice de bonheur, de santé et de succès devant protéger de la faim et de la maladie. La grande cuiller plate dans la main de l'émissaire symbolise l'abondance. Après la cérémonie, son collier de feuilles d'algues est découpé et répartie entre les fidèles, qui en font une infusion contre le refroidissement. Des roues blanches, symboles de la doctrine bouddhique, décorent l'habit de l'envoyé. Le bâton dans sa main gauche renvoie à la force dont dispose Bishamon, le gardien de l'enseignement bouddhique.

Le mont Atagoyama se dresse au sud du château d'Edo à seulement 26 mètres au-dessus du niveau de la mer. Il doit son appellation de « mont » (*yama*) à l'original du même nom qui se trouve à Kyoto et qui culmine à 924 mètres au-dessus du niveau de la mer.

Dans le premier tome (1834) de son *Guide illustré des vues célèbres d'Edo* (*Edo meisho zue*), Hiroshige loue la petite réplique du mont Atagoyama en ces termes : « … un versant escarpé se dresse dans le ciel, si puissant que ses 68 degrés de pierre semblent toucher le ciel … quand on jette un regard en contrebas, on peut voir les rangées de tuiles des innombrables maisons et portes qui bordent les grandes rues. La mer s'étend à l'infini à l'horizon, une vue splendide en vérité. »

Hiroshige a su dresser un monument visuel magistral à ce site décrit de manière si impressionnante.

22

広尾
ふる川

Hiroo Furukawa
7–1856

Hiroo on Furukawa River

The little Furukawa River meanders into the foreground, where it is spanned by a wooden bridge that leads to a hamlet on the left bank. By the roadside, a restaurant invites travellers to rest awhile. As we learn from the seventh volume of Hiroshige's *Illustrated Souvenirs of Edo (Ehon Edo miyage)*, printed in 1857, this is the "Fox" restaurant (Kitsune), which had become famous for its speciality of fried freshwater eels (*unagi*).

Many of the scenes depicted in Hiroshige's *One Hundred Famous Views of Edo* allude to famous local specialities (*meibutsu*). The centres of Edo's material culture were often marked by restaurants located next to bridges or religious sites (plates 12, 114); silk and cloth shops and dye works (plates 7, 13, 74, 75); or places celebrated for bamboo or wood crafts (plates 76, 106). Thanks to the diligence and business acumen of its inhabitants, the city surpassed Osaka and Kyoto, to become first among Japan's three major cities. The pale-blue river flowing across the green plain creates an idyllic meadow landscape that never existed in this form in southern Edo. Today, this area around Azabu and Hiroo is Tokyo's most exclusive district, replete with expensive apartment blocks and embassy buildings. Even though the Furukawa was first canalized and then built over, this quarter is still famous for its luxurious restaurants and *kaiseki* cuisine, featuring in particular eel specialities.

It was one of the inventions of the ukiyo-e print industry to combine famous views (*meisho*) and local products (*meibutsu*) with the more attractive portraits of kabuki actors or courtesans depicted in cartouches, thus paving the way for the amalgamation of seemingly incongruous motifs typical of present-day advertising. However, in his *One Hundred Famous Views of Edo*, Hiroshige almost never incorporated figures from the pleasure world of the theatre and the brothels. His compositions were to focus on extreme contrasts between near and far, and on eye-catching abstract areas of colour and shapes. This novel style was a major inspiration for printmakers working in the Art Nouveau style.

Hiroo am Fluss Furukawa

Das Flüsschen Furukawa schlängelt sich aus der Bildtiefe in den Vordergrund, wo es von einer Holzbrücke überspannt wird, die zu einer Siedlung am linken Ufer führt. Am Wegrand lädt eine Gaststätte den Wanderer zum Verweilen ein. Wie aus Band 7 von Hiroshiges 1857 erschienenem Werk *Illustrierte Mitbringsel aus Edo (Ehon Edo miyage)* hervorgeht, handelt es sich um das Gasthaus „Zum Fuchs" (Kitsune), das sich mit seiner Spezialität, gebratenem Süßwasser-Aal (*unagi*), einen Namen gemacht hat.

Auf vielen von Hiroshiges *Hundert Ansichten* wird Bezug auf berühmte lokale Spezialitäten (*meibutsu*) genommen. Die oft an religiösen Stätten und Brücken gelegenen Gasthäuser (siehe Tafeln 12, 114), die Seiden- und Stoffgeschäfte und Färbereien (siehe Tafeln 7, 13, 74, 75), aber auch die durch die Verarbeitung von Bambus oder Holz bekannten Orte (siehe Tafeln 76, 106) markierten die Zentren der materiellen Kultur Edos. Dank des Fleißes und Geschäftssinns seiner Bewohner stieg die Stadt neben Osaka und Kyoto zur größten der drei Metropolen Japans auf. Der hellblaue Fluss in der grünen Ebene suggeriert eine idyllische Wiesenlandschaft, die es im südlichen Edo so nie gegeben hat. Heute befindet sich an dieser Stelle, rund um Azabu und Hiroo, das vornehmste Viertel Tokyos mit teuren Apartmenthäusern und Botschaftsgebäuden. Auch wenn der Fluss Furukawa erst kanalisiert und schließlich überbaut worden ist, blieb dieser Stadtteil für seine exklusiven Restaurants und die auf Aal spezialisierte Kaiseki-Küche bekannt.

Es gehörte zu den Erfindungen der Ukiyoe-Druckindustrie, berühmte Ansichten (*meisho*) und lokale Produkte (*meibutsu*) in Bildkartuschen mit den attraktiveren Porträts von Kabuki-Schauspielern oder Kurtisanen zu verbinden und so die noch für die Bildreklame der Gegenwart typische Kombination scheinbar artfremder Motive vorzubereiten. Hiroshige verzichtete in den *Hundert Ansichten* allerdings fast vollständig auf Figuren aus der Vergnügungswelt des Theaters und der Bordelle. Gestalterisch arbeitete er mit extremen Kontrasten zwischen nah und fern und setzte abstrakte und plakativ wirkende Farbflächen und Formen als Blickfang ein. Nicht zuletzt durch diesen neuartigen Stil visueller Werbung inspirierte er in hohem Maße die Grafik des Jugendstils und Art Nouveau.

Hiroo au bord de la Furukawa

La petite rivière Furukawa serpente de la profondeur de l'image jusqu'au premier plan où l'enjambe un pont menant à un petit hameau situé sur la rive gauche. Au bord du chemin, un restaurant invite le promeneur à faire une halte. Comme il ressort du septième tome (1857) des *Souvenirs illustrés d'Edo (Ehon Edo miyage)* de Hiroshige, il s'agit de l'auberge « Au renard » (Kitsune), qui s'était taillé une solide réputation en raison d'une spécialité gastronomique : l'anguille d'eau douce (*unagi*) grillée.

De nombreuses planches des *Cent Vues* se réfèrent à des activités locales (*meibutsu*). Les auberges souvent situées près des lieux saints et des ponts (cf. pl. 12, 114), les boutiques de soieries et de tissus et les teintureries (cf. pl. 7, 13, 74, 75), mais aussi les lieux réputés pour la transformation du bois ou du bambou (cf. pl. 76, 106), étaient les centres de la culture matérielle d'Edo. Grâce au travail et au sens commercial de ses habitants, la ville devint la plus grande des trois métropoles japonaises que sont Edo, Osaka et Kyoto. La rivière bleu clair qui serpente dans la plaine verdoyante suggère un paysage de prairies idyllique qui n'a jamais existé sous cette forme au sud d'Edo. Au même endroit, tout autour d'Abazu et de Hiroo, s'étendent aujourd'hui les quartiers résidentiels de Tokyo, avec leurs ambassades et leurs luxueux appartements. Bien que la rivière Furukawa ait été canalisée et finalement recouverte par des constructions, cette partie de la ville est aujourd'hui encore réputée pour ses restaurants exclusifs et sa gastronomie *kaiseki* spécialisée dans l'anguille.

Une des inventions de l'industrie de l'estampe ukiyo-e est d'avoir regroupé dans ses formules visuelles des vues célèbres (*meisho*) et des produits locaux (*meibutsu*), associés aux portraits attractifs de courtisanes ou d'acteurs de kabuki, et d'avoir ainsi préparé la combinaison de motifs apparemment étrangers qui caractérise aujourd'hui la publicité japonaise. Dans les *Cent Vues*, il est vrai que Hiroshige a presque entièrement renoncé aux figures issues du monde des théâtres et des plaisirs de la chair. Du point de vue de la composition, il mise sur de forts contrastes entre le proche et le lointain, utilisant comme accroche visuelle des surfaces de couleurs et des formes abstraites qui confèrent un fort impact aux images. Par ce nouveau style de réclame visuelle, il est un des artistes qui ont exercé la plus forte influence sur le graphisme de l'art nouveau.

目黒
千代か池

Meguro Chiyogaike
7–1856

Chiyogaike Pond in Meguro

In blue-and-white cascades, a waterfall descends a green hillside lined with blossoming cherry trees to flow into Chiyogaike Pond. The print is structured with reddish banks of cloud in the traditional Japanese manner. One woman is walking towards the little island in the pond, on which another woman and a girl are standing, watching the waterfall.

The trees are reflected in the water of the pond, creating an idyllic atmosphere. This technique is very unusual for Hiroshige and is rarely used in *One Hundred Famous Views of Edo*. Japanese painters had already experimented with the depiction of reflections in water in the early 18th century, but it was not until Western painting techniques were studied decades later that it became more common. Ukiyo-e artists were among those to adapt this unusual effect in their pictures and woodblock prints in order both to surprise and delight the viewer. The fascination of this pictorial device lay not in exact depiction of objects, but in the subtle allusion to them – as in this example of the blossoming cherry tree rendered in the delicate pink shimmer on the water.

A legend is associated with Chiyogaike Pond ("Chiyo's Pond"). In the 14th century, a woman called Chiyo – in despair following the death of her warrior husband Nitta Yoshioki (1331–1358) – is said to have taken her own life by throwing herself into the pond. According to the legend, there used to be a pine tree here, where Chiyo hung her clothes before drowning herself.

Der Teich Chiyogaike in Meguro

In blau-weißen Kaskaden ergießt sich ein Wasserfall zwischen blühenden Kirschbäumen und grünen Hügeln in den Teich Chiyogaike. Rötliche Wolkenfelder gliedern die Szenerie in klassisch japanischer Manier. Eine Frau geht auf die kleine Insel im Teich zu, auf der bereits eine Dame und ein Mädchen stehen und die hinabstürzenden Wassermassen betrachten.

Stimmungsvoll spiegeln sich die Bäume in den Wellen des Teichs. Diese Darstellung ist für Hiroshige und die *Hundert berühmten Ansichten von Edo* ungewöhnlich. Schon im frühen 18. Jahrhundert hatten einige Maler mit der Darstellung von Wasserspiegelungen experimentiert, aber erst die Rezeption westlicher Maltechniken, die Jahrzehnte später einsetzte, begünstigte deren Verbreitung. Auch Ukiyoe-Maler nahmen den unüblichen Effekt in ihren Bildern und Holzschnitten auf, um den Betrachter zu erstaunen und zu erfreuen. Wie hier am Beispiel der Kirschbäume erkennbar, lag der Reiz solcher Bildelemente nicht in der exakten Reflexion des Gegenstandes, sondern in seiner feinen Andeutung – dem zarten rosa Schimmer der Blüten auf dem Wasser.

Um den Teich Chiyogaike („Teich der Chiyo") rankt sich eine Sage. Im 14. Jahrhundert soll sich Chiyo aus Verzweiflung über den Tod ihres Mannes, des Kriegers Nitta Yoshioki (1331–1358), in diesen Teich gestürzt und sich das Leben genommen haben. Der Legende nach soll dort eine Kiefer gestanden haben, an der Chiyo vor ihrem Selbstmord die Gewänder aufhängte.

L'étang Chiyogaike à Meguro

Parmi des cerisiers en fleurs et des collines verdoyantes, une chute d'eau se jette dans le lac Chiyogaike en cascades bleublanc. Des bancs de nuages rouges structurent la scène dans le style classiquement japonais. Une femme marche vers une petite île de l'étang sur laquelle se trouvent déjà une dame et une jeune fille qui contemplent la chute des masses d'eau.

Les arbres se reflètent dans les vaguelettes de l'étang, conférant une atmosphère particulière à l'image. Ce genre de représentation est inhabituel pour Hiroshige en général et dans la série des *Cent Vues* en particulier. Dès le début du XVIIIe siècle, quelques peintres avaient travaillé sur la représentation des reflets dans l'eau, mais il faudra attendre la réception des techniques de peinture occidentales quelques décennies plus tard pour voir se propager leur utilisation. Des peintres de l'école ukiyo-e reprirent cet effet inusité dans leurs tableaux et leurs estampes pour surprendre et réjouir le spectateur. Comme on voit avec les cerisiers, l'attrait de la chose ne résidait pas dans l'exactitude de l'image reflétée, mais dans la subtilité de l'allusion, exprimée ici par le chatoiement rosé des fleurs dans l'eau.

Une légende s'est tissée autour de l'étang Chiyogaike (« étang de Chiyo »). Au XIVe siècle, Chiyo, poussée au désespoir par la mort de son mari, le valeureux Nitta Yoshioki (1331–1358), se serait jetée dans l'étang pour mettre fin à ses jours. Selon la légende, un pin se dressait autrefois à cet endroit, auquel Chiyo accrocha ses habits avant de se suicider.

24

目黒
新富
士

Meguro Shin-Fuji
4–1857

New Fuji in Meguro

The water of the Mita Aqueduct meanders gently between blossoming cherry trees and green meadows. Several visitors are enjoying the beauty of the landscape, in which a path leads to the summit of a replica of Mount Fuji. Others have already made it to the top, from where they admire the picturesque view of the real Fuji. A pink and yellow bank of cloud separates the two mountains, creating a greater sense of pictorial depth.

This artificial Fuji was constructed in 1829 on territory belonging to Kondō Jūzō (1771–1829), a vassal of the shogun. As early as 1780, adherents of Fuji worship (*Fuji shinkō*) had erected a first replica of the sacred mountain in the city's Takata quarter. Countless others were to follow (see plates 25, 68).

Religious rituals and veneration of the volcano were performed because of its unpredictability and thus the danger it presented. Mount Fuji had already erupted 18 times in recorded history, and its worshippers hoped to prevent further eruptions by placating it with prayers and gifts. Long before the Tokugawa period (1615–1868), the emperor had bestowed court honours on the mountain, which was subsequently venerated as a deity.

The subtle green shading reflects the special feature of this particular Fuji replica in Meguro: it was one of the few imitations covered in grass and having smooth contours. Usually, these replicas were constructed with blocks of lava from the real Mount Fuji, which were then piled up into a shapeless mass. For the worshippers of the mountain, blocks of lava were essential components of an artificial Fuji, because only with their help could the mountain be pacified.

Der Neue Berg Fuji in Meguro

Sanft windet sich der Wasserlauf des Mita-Aquädukts zwischen blühenden Kirschbäumen und grünen Wiesen. Mehrere Besucher genießen die Schönheit der Landschaft, in der ein Weg bis zum Gipfel eines künstlich angelegten Fuji hinaufführt. Einige Spaziergänger haben bereits den Gipfel erklommen und bewundern von dort aus die pittoreske Aussicht auf den echten Berg Fuji. Rosa-gelb changierende Wolkenfelder liegen zwischen den beiden Gipfeln und verleihen dem Bildhintergrund Tiefe.

Der hier abgebildete künstliche Fuji wurde 1829 auf dem Gelände eines Vasallen des Shoguns, Kondō Jūzō (1771–1829), angelegt. Bereits 1780 hatten Anhänger des Fuji-Glaubens (*Fuji shinkō*) erstmals eine Nachbildung des heiligen Berges im Stadtteil Takata-chō errichtet. Unzählige weitere sollten folgen (siehe Tafeln 25, 68).

Der Glaube an den Vulkan und die damit verbundenen religiösen Riten gingen auf seine Unberechenbarkeit und damit auf die von ihm ausgehende Gefahr zurück. 18 Mal war er bereits ausgebrochen, daher hofften seine Anhänger, den Berg durch Anbetung und Gaben zu beruhigen, um weitere Ausbrüche zu verhindern. Schon lange vor der Tokugawa-Zeit (1615–1868) hatte der Kaiser dem Berg Hofrang verliehen, und er wurde seitdem als Gottheit verehrt.

Die subtilen Grünschattierungen geben die Besonderheit dieser Fuji-Replik in Meguro wieder: sie gehörte zu den wenigen grasbewachsenen Imitationen mit weichen Konturen. Üblicherweise verwandte man sonst Lavabrocken des echten Berges Fuji, die zu unförmigen Massen aufeinandergetürmt wurden. Für die Gläubigen des Berges waren Lavasteine als Bestandteile der künstlichen Fuji unverzichtbar, weil man mit ihrer Hilfe den Berg zu besänftigen hoffte.

Le nouveau Fuji à Meguro

L'eau de l'aqueduc de Mita serpente doucement parmi des cerisiers en fleurs et des prés verdoyants. Plusieurs visiteurs contemplent la beauté du paysage dans lequel un sentier mène au sommet d'un Fuji artificiel. Quelques promeneurs sont déjà arrivés au sommet pour admirer la vue pittoresque du vrai Fuji. Des bancs de nuages aux chatoiements rose-jaune s'intercalent entre les massifs montagneux et confèrent sa profondeur à l'arrière-plan de l'image.

Le Fuji artificiel représenté dans cette estampe fut édifié en 1829 sur les terres de Kondō Jūzō (1771–1829), un vassal du shogun. Dès 1780, des adeptes de la religion du Fuji (*Fuji shinkō*) avaient commencé d'élever une réplique de la montagne sacrée dans le quartier Takata-chō. D'innombrables autres répliques allaient suivre (cf. pl. 25, 68).

La croyance au volcan et les rites qui y étaient associés découlaient de son caractère imprévisible et donc à la menace qu'il représentait. Le volcan avait déjà été dix-huit fois en éruption et ses adeptes espéraient l'apaiser par toutes sortes de rituels et d'offrandes destinés à éviter d'autres catastrophes.

Bien avant l'ère Tokugawa (1615–1868), l'empereur avait déjà conféré à la montagne une dignité à la cour, où elle était vénérée comme une divinité.

Les subtils ombrages de vert restituent la singularité à cette réplique du Fuji à Meguro : elle faisait partie des rares imitations aux contours doux semés d'herbe. Habituellement, on utilisait des blocs de lave du vrai Fuji qu'on amoncelait en masses informes. Pour les adeptes de la montagne, les blocs de lave étaient la composante indispensable de tout authentique Fuji artificiel, parce qu'ils permettaient d'apaiser la montagne.

25

目黒
元不
二

Meguro Moto-Fuji
4–1857

The Original Fuji in Meguro

Two men are climbing a replica of Mount Fuji. One of them is pointing to the real Fuji on the western horizon, rising above a broad plain. Constructed in 1812, this Fuji, at almost twelve metres (39 feet) high, was the tallest replica in Edo. Immediately below, other visitors sit on benches to chat over a cup of tea. The planting of pine trees in regular rows was unusual among the imitations of the sacred mountain.

The artificial Fuji depicted here was constructed 17 years before that shown in the preceding plate, and was therefore called "Original Fuji." The censors approved both prints in the same month, which is why the publisher Sakanaya Eikichi and the designer of the table of contents, Baisotei Gengyo (1817–1880), placed them one after the other. In the process, they may have overlooked the fact – or perhaps it was intentional – that the cherry trees in this scene are not in bloom, as in the previous plate, but are already in their autumnal foliage, represented by the

pigment *tan* ("cinnabar"). As a consequence, this print does not belong to those assigned to the spring section. The iconographical similarity between the two prints, as well as the geographical closeness of the two artificial Fujis, however, may have motivated the publisher to put them together.

An ironic pun creates a further link between the two views. In the title of the present print, Hiroshige uses the characters for "not two" (*fu-ji*) to refer to the mountain. The characters can also mean "unique". This was an alternative way of writing the mountain's name, and reflects the attitude that the real and the artificial Fujis were one and the same mountain. But the choice of written characters is not without a certain humorous aspect, for what is depicted in these two prints are two imitations of the same mountain. To this extent, the juxtaposition of the prints conveys a hidden meaning, not least regarding this subtly alluded to doubling of the real Fuji.

Der Ursprüngliche Fuji in Meguro

Zwei Männer besteigen eine Nachbildung des Berges Fuji. Einer der beiden weist mit ausgestrecktem Arm auf den echten Fuji am westlichen Horizont, der sich über einer weiten Ebene erhebt. Unmittelbar unterhalb des 1812 konstruierten Fuji, der mit fast 17 Metern die höchste Fuji-Replik in Edo war, haben sich weitere Besucher auf niedrigen Tischbänken zu einem Plausch bei einer Schale Tee niedergelassen. Die Bepflanzung mit Kiefern in regelmäßigen Abständen stellte eine Seltenheit bei den Imitationen des heiligen Berges dar.

Der hier abgebildete künstliche Fuji war 17 Jahre vor der vorangegangenen Tafel angelegt worden und wurde daher als der „Ursprüngliche Fuji" bezeichnet. Die Zensoren genehmigten beide Entwürfe im selben Monat, weshalb sie von dem Verleger Sakanaya Eikichi und dem Entwerfer des Inhaltsverzeichnisses, Baisotei Gengyo (1817–1880), nacheinander angeordnet worden sind. Dabei übersahen sie möglicherweise – oder vielleicht war es Absicht –, dass die Bäume auf diesem Druck keine Kirschblüten tragen wie auf der vorherigen Tafel, sondern bräunliches Herbstlaub, das mit der Farbe *tan* („Zinnober") aufgetragen

wurde. Das Blatt gehört deshalb eigentlich nicht in die dem Frühling zugeordnete Gruppe. Die ikonografische Ähnlichkeit der beiden Holzschnitte sowie die geografische Nähe der beiden künstlichen Fujis haben den Verleger aber wohl zu einer Aneinanderreihung der beiden Blätter veranlasst.

Ein ironisches Wortspiel schafft eine weitere Verbindung zwischen den beiden Drucken. In der Titelkartusche des hier gezeigten Holzschnitts wählt Hiroshige als Schreibweise für den Bergnamen die beiden Schriftzeichen für „nicht" (*fu*) und für „zwei" (*ji*), die zusammen auch „einzigartig" bedeuten. Diese durchaus übliche Schreibweise für den künstlichen Berg spiegelt die Auffassung wider, es handele sich bei dem echten und dem künstlichen Fuji um ein und denselben Berg – womit auch die Imitation als echter Fuji zu verstehen ist. Die Wahl der Schriftzeichen entbehrt nicht einer gewissen Komik, da es hier um zwei Nachbildungen desselben Berges geht. Insofern gibt die Zusammenstellung der beiden Tafeln auch im Hinblick auf diese subtil angedeutete Verdopplung des echten Berges Fuji einen durchaus hintergründigen Sinn.

Le Fuji original à Meguro

Deux hommes gravissent une réplique du mont Fuji. L'un d'entre eux tend le bras vers l'horizon ouest où le vrai Fuji trône au-dessus d'une immense plaine. Immédiatement sous ce Fuji élevé en 1812 – la plus haute réplique du Fuji à Edo avec ses presque douze mètres de hauteur –, d'autres visiteurs se sont assis sur des tables basses pour s'entretenir autour d'une tasse de thé. La plantation régulière de pins était une rareté dans le contexte des imitations de la montagne sacrée.

Le Fuji artificiel représenté ici fut aménagé 17 ans avant celui de l'estampe précédente et était de ce fait appelé le « Fuji original ». Les censeurs ont approuvé les deux estampes au même mois, et c'est la raison pour laquelle l'éditeur Sakanaya et Baisotei Gengyo (1817–1880), le concepteur de la table des matières, les ont placées l'une après l'autre. Dans ce contexte, il se peut qu'ils aient omis – peut-être volontairement – de tenir compte du fait qu'ici, les arbres ne présentent pas des fleurs de cerisiers comme dans la feuille précédente, mais un feuillage d'automne brunâtre

imprimé avec la couleur *tan* (« cinabre »). À l'origine, cette feuille n'avait donc pas sa place dans la section printemps. La similitude iconographique entre les deux estampes et la proximité géographique des Fuji artificiels sont sans doute les raisons qui ont poussé à regrouper les deux feuilles.

Un jeu de mots ironique crée encore un autre lien entre les deux feuilles. Dans le titre de cette estampe, pour la graphie du nom de la montagne, Hiroshige a choisi deux caractères qui se lisent « non deux » (*fu-ji*) et signifient donc aussi « unique ». Cette graphie inusitée pour désigner la montagne traduit l'idée qu'il s'agissait d'une seule et même montagne dans le cas du vrai comme du « faux » Fuji – c'est-à-dire que la réplique devait également être comprise comme un vrai Fuji. Le choix de cette graphie n'est pas dénué d'un certain humour attendu que nous sommes ici en présence de deux imitations de la même montagne. Le regroupement des deux planches génère donc aussi un sens caché au regard de la subtile évocation du redoublement du vrai Fuji.

26

八景坂
鎧掛松

Hakkeizaka Yoroikakematsu
5–1856

The "Armour-Hanging Pine" at Hakkeizaka Bluff

\ monumental pine with broadly spreading branches stands on a bluff overlooking Edo Bay, which is animated by a number of sailing boats. On the Tōkaidō highway (Eastern Sea Road), which linked Edo with Kyoto, small silhouettes of travellers can be made out. From the plain below, some of them are climbing the Hakkeizaka, the "Bluff of the Eight Views", to enjoy the picturesque panorama of the bay. Those who can afford it have had themselves transported in a palanquin. Woodcuts like this were perhaps made as souvenirs for those who enjoyed tea or *sake* next to the celebrated pine.

The composition is based on Hiroshige's illustration for the third volume of *Illustrated Souvenirs of Edo (Ehon Edo miyage)*, dating from 1850. According to the text, the *hakkei* ("eight views") refer to the famous eight views in this area. The expression goes back to the "Eight Views of Xiao and Xiang" (in Japanese *Shōshō hakkei*), a subject of Chinese poetry and painting that had been depicted in Japanese landscape paintings since the 14th century.

Apart from the notable view, it was also the legendary pine that made Hakkeizaka attractive as a destination for travellers. The warrior Minamoto no Yoshiie (1039–1106) is said to have hung his armour on this tree while resting before subduing the Abe clan in the Mutsu Province (today's Aomori Prefecture) in 1062, after twelve years of armed conflict. This victory led to the consolidation of the position of the Minamoto warriors in the north of Japan. They set up the first military regime in the Kamakura period (1185–1333), and the Tokugawa shoguns as well as other warrior families traced their lineage back to them.

Hiroshige adapts the shape of the tree to this story so that only a giant could have hung his armour on the twisted trunk. According to contemporary reports of the 19th century, the pine was indeed some 20 metres (65.5 feet) tall and had a substantial girth. But the majestic tree is said to have died during the Meiji period (1868–1912).

Die „Kiefer zum Aufhängen einer Rüstung" und der Abhang Hakkeizaka

Eine monumentale Kiefer mit weit ausladenden Ästen steht an einem Abhang über der mit Segelbooten belebten Bucht von Edo. Entlang der Küstenlinie sind auf der Ostmeerstraße (Tōkaidō), die Edo mit Kyoto verbindet, kleine Silhouetten von Reisenden zu erkennen. Einige von ihnen steigen aus der Ebene den Hakkeizaka, den „Abhang der Acht Ansichten", hinauf, um die malerische Aussicht auf die Bucht zu genießen. Wer es sich leisten kann, lässt sich in einer Sänfte hinauftragen. Wohl für Reisende, die neben der Kiefer Tee oder Sake tranken, wurden solche Holzschnitte als Souvenir angefertigt.

Die Komposition basiert auf Hiroshiges Illustration für den dritten Band seines *Illustrierte Mitbringsel aus Edo (Ehon Edo miyage)* von 1850. Laut Aufschrift leitet sich *hakkei* („Acht Ansichten") von den in dieser Gegend berühmten acht Landschaften ab. Der Ausdruck geht auf die „Acht Ansichten von Xiao und Xiang" (Japanisch *Shōshō hakkei*) zurück, ein chinesisches Lyrik- und Bildthema, das in Japan seit dem 14. Jahrhundert Eingang in die Darstellung pittoresker Landschaften

fand. Neben der Aussicht machte auch die sagenumwobene Kiefer Hakkeizaka zu einem attraktiven Ausflugsort. Der Krieger Minamoto no Yoshiie (1039–1106) soll während einer Rast seine Rüstung an diesem Baum aufgehängt haben, bevor er im Jahr 1062 den Klan der Abe in der Provinz Mutsu (heutige Präfektur Aomori) nach zwölf Jahren kriegerischer Auseinandersetzungen unterwarf. Diese Entwicklung führte zur Festigung der Stellung des Minamoto-Clans im Norden Japans, die das erste Militärregime der Kamakura-Zeit (1185–1333) errichteten und auf die die Tokugawa-Shogune und andere Kriegerfamilien ihre Genealogien zurückführten.

Hiroshige passt die Form des Baumes dieser Geschichte an, indem er den Stamm mit einer Biegung ausstattet, an der nur ein Riese seine Rüstung hätte aufhängen können. Die Kiefer war im 19. Jahrhundert laut zeitgenössischen Berichten tatsächlich circa zwanzig Meter hoch und hatte einen beträchtlichen Umfang, doch während der Meiji-Ära (1868–1912) soll der stattliche Baum eingegangen sein.

Le « Pin pour accrocher une armure » et la montée Hakkeizaka

Un pin monumental aux branches largement déployées se dresse au bord d'un précipice au-dessus de la baie d'Edo ponctuée de voiliers. Le long de la côte, on aperçoit de petites silhouettes de voyageurs sur la Tōkaidō (route de la mer orientale) qui relie Edo à Kyoto. Depuis la plaine, quelques-uns gravissent la Hakkeizaka, la « montée des huit vues » pour jouir du panorama pittoresque. Ceux qui peuvent se le permettre se font porter en palanquin. Ce genre d'estampe a sans doute été réalisé à l'intention des voyageurs qui venaient boire du thé ou du saké sous ce pin.

La composition de cette feuille s'appuie sur les illustrations que Hiroshige avait créées pour le troisième tome (1850) de ses *Souvenirs illustrés d'Edo (Ehon Edo miyage)*. Selon l'inscription, le mot *hakkei* (« huit vues ») se doit aux huit paysages célèbres dans la région. L'expression remonte aux « Huit vues du Xiao et du Xiang » (japonais *Shōshō hakkei*), un thème poétique et pictural chinois avec lequel l'art japonais accéda à la représentation de paysages pittoresques à partir du XIVe siècle.

Indépendamment de la vue, le pin légendaire fait lui aussi de Hakkeizaka un lieu d'excursion attractif. Y faisant une halte en 1062, le guerrier Minamoto no Yoshiie (1039–1106) est censé y avoir suspendu son armure avant de soumettre le clan des Abe dans la province de Mutsu (actuelle préfecture d'Aomori) après douze ans de conflits militaires. Cette évolution des rapports de forces conduisit à renforcer la position, au nord du Japon, des Minamoto qui mirent en place le premier régime militaire de l'ère Kamakura (1185–1333), et auxquels les shoguns Tokugawa et d'autres familles de guerriers faisaient remonter leur généalogie.

Hiroshige a adapté la forme du pin à l'histoire en le dotant d'une courbure permettant à un géant d'y accrocher son armure. D'après les récits d'époque, au XIXe siècle, le pin mesurait en effet une vingtaine de mètres de haut et la base du tronc présentait une circonférence impressionnante. Il aurait toutefois dépéri pendant l'ère Meiji (1868–1912).

蒲
田
の
梅
園

Kamada no umezono
2–1857

Plum Orchard in Kamada

A traveller has ordered the bearers to put down his palanquin; he has flung his green overgarment casually on the top, and is now mingling with the admirers of the countless blossoming plum trees. Some drink *sake* to fend off the chill in the air, others contemplate the calligraphy on the stone stelae being admired along with the blooming trees.

The red-to-white hues of the blossoms are reproduced in the colouring of the sky. The sky, which is gradated with skilled perfection, takes up more than half of the print. It frames this famous view above, just as the green shading encloses the scene below.

The empty palanquin in the foreground draws us directly into the scene. Like the person who has just alighted – maybe he is taking a short break while travelling along the nearby Tōkaidō, the main highway from Edo to Kyoto – we are invited to wander around the garden and discover the stelae hidden among the trees. The degree to which Hiroshige was interested in viewer participation in this print is demonstrated by his quite differently composed double spread with the same title in the second volume of his *Illustrated Souvenirs of Edo (Ehon Edo miyage)*, dating from 1850. In that album, he depicts the stone stelae such that they are clearly recognizable, one by one, and the bird's-eye view reveals every detail of the orchard.

Here, by contrast, Hiroshige has selected a much lower vantage point and has chosen to capture a particular moment in time, in what Henry D. Smith has described as a "proto-filmic technique". This technique left a deep impression on the contemporary European avant-garde, as demonstrated, for example, by a remark made by the French artist Camille Pissarro (1830–1903) in 1893: "Hiroshige is a wonderful Impressionist."

Pflaumengarten in Kamada

Ein Reisender hat seine Sänfte anhalten lassen und sein grünes Übergewand etwas achtlos auf das Dach geworfen. Er ist ausgestiegen und hat sich unter die Bewunderer der zahlosen blühenden Pflaumenbäume gemischt. Man trinkt Sake, um die noch beträchtliche Kälte abzuwehren, sinniert über die Kalligrafien auf den Steinstelen oder bestaunt die Blüten.

Ihre weißen bis rötlichen Töne nimmt Hiroshige in der Farbgebung des Himmels auf. Das virtuos gradierte und mehr als die Hälfte des Blattes einnehmende Rot sowie das Grün des Bodens fassen diesen berühmten Holzschnitt von oben und unten ein.

Die in den Vordergrund gerückte leere Sänfte bezieht den Betrachter unmittelbar in das Bildgeschehen ein. Wie der ihr Entstiegene – vielleicht legt er, unterwegs auf dem nahe gelegenen Hauptverkehrsweg Tōkaidō, eine kleine Rast ein – ist er versucht, im Garten umherzuwandern, auf Entdeckungsreise zu gehen und die von den Bäumen verdeckten Stelen aufzustöbern. Wie sehr es Hiroshige auf eine Beteiligung des Betrachters ankam, belegt seine ganz anders gestaltete doppelseitige Illustration mit gleichem Titel im zweiten Band des 1850 erschienenen Werks *Illustrierte Mitbringsel aus Edo (Ehon Edo miyage)*. Hiroshige zeigt dort die Steinstelen einzeln und deutlich erkennbar – die Vogelperspektive gibt den Blick frei auf alle Details des Gartens.

Hier hingegen hat Hiroshige einen niedrigen Betrachterstandpunkt gewählt und es darauf angelegt, einen bestimmten Augenblick einzufangen – eine von Henry D. Smith als protofilmisch bezeichnete Technik, die bei der zeitgenössischen europäischen Avantgarde tiefen Eindruck hinterließ. Dies belegt z. B. Camille Pissarros (1830–1903) Bemerkung aus dem Jahr 1893: „Hiroshige ist ein wunderbarer Impressionist."

Prunelaie à Kamada

Un voyageur a fait arrêter son palanquin sur lequel il a jeté un peu négligemment son vêtement de dessus. Il en est descendu et s'est mêlé aux admirateurs des innombrables pruniers en fleurs. On boit du saké pour se protéger du froid encore vif en cette saison, on médite sur les calligraphies gravées dans la pierre des stèles ou l'on s'émerveille de la floraison.

Hiroshige a repris les tons blancs jusqu'à rougeâtres des fleurs de pruniers dans le coloris du ciel. Le magistral dégradé de rouge qui occupe plus de la moitié de l'image et le vert du sol encadrent cette estampe célèbre par le haut et le bas.

Le palanquin rapproché du premier plan permet au spectateur d'entrer directement dans la scène. Tout comme l'homme qui vient d'en sortir – peut-être fait-il une petite halte en ce lieu lors d'un voyage sur la grande Tōkaidō –, il est invité à parcourir le jardin, à partir en exploration et à découvrir les stèles cachées par les arbres. L'importance que Hiroshige accordait à la participation du spectateur est attestée par l'illustration homonyme du deuxième tome (1850) de ses *Souvenirs illustrés d'Edo (Ehon Edo miyage)*, illustration dont la composition en double page s'écarte fortement de celle-ci. Hiroshige y montre les stèles de pierre isolément, clairement reconnaissables, et une perspective d'oiseau ouvre la vue sur tous les détails du jardin.

Ici en revanche, Hiroshige a choisi un point de vue bas et tout mis en œuvre pour saisir un instant particulier – technique que Henry D. Smith a qualifiée de protofilmique et qui a fait profonde impression sur l'avant-garde de l'époque, comme l'atteste le commentaire de Camille Pissarro (1830–1903) en 1893 : « Hiroshige est un impressionniste merveilleux. »

28

品川
御殿やま

Shinagawa Gotenyama
4–1856

Palace Hill in Shinagawa

One of the most famous sites for admiring cherry blossoms in Edo was Palace Hill (Gotenyama). Legend attributes the palace that gives the hill its name to the warrior Ōta Dōkan (1432–1486), who built the first castle in Edo, in 1457.

The Tokugawa shoguns still used this residence as a country residence in the early 17th century. When it burnt to ashes in the Genroku era (1688–1704), however, it was not rebuilt.

Hiroshige's *One Hundred Famous Views of Edo* includes 35 prints depicting Gotenyama and its magnificent cherry trees. In this view, however, Hiroshige appears as a chronicler of the drastic intrusions into the otherwise untainted countryside around Edo resulting from what were regarded as necessary national defence measures. The American commodore Matthew Perry (1794–1858) arrived in Edo Bay with his Black Ships in 1853 and announced that he would return the following year in order to open up Japanese ports to international trade. Immediately after Perry's departure, the *daiba* were erected. These earthen ramparts built

into the sea as fortifications were reinforced with stones and equipped with cannons.

In this print, the scars of the disfigured hillsides have not yet healed even three years after the hasty removal of earth to erect the ramparts. Oblivious, the cherry-blossom enthusiasts are not daunted by this: little schematic figures walk up the hill in a loose procession and stroll beneath the blossoming trees.

Hiroshige shows in this view a traditional "famous landscape" (*meisho*), and at the same time its destruction through modern technology. This print therefore exhibits thematic links with Paul Cézanne's (1839–1906) 1870 painting *The Railway Cutting*, now in the Neue Pinakothek in Munich. In this painting, we see a hill that looks as if it had been cut open with a carving knife, this time in order to make way for a railway line. The depiction of the glaring contrast produced by modern interventions in picturesque landscapes was a concern of Cézanne and Hiroshige alike, and makes both appear "modern" even today.

Palasthügel in Shinagawa

Einer der berühmtesten Orte der Kirschblütenschau in Edo ist der Palasthügel (Gotenyama). Legenden schreiben den Palast, der dem Hügel seinen Namen gab, dem Krieger Ōta Dōkan (1432–1486) zu, der 1457 das erste Schloss in Edo baute.

Im frühen 17. Jahrhundert benutzten die Tokugawa-Shogune diese Residenz noch als Landhaus. Als sie in der Ära Genroku (1688–1704) abbrannte, baute man sie aber nicht wieder auf.

Es gibt in Hiroshiges *Hundert berühmten Ansichten von Edo* allein 35 Blätter, welche den Gotenyama mit seinen prächtigen Kirschbäumen darstellen. In dieser Komposition hingegen tritt Hiroshige als Chronist der drastischen Einschnitte in die unversehrte Landschaft auf, die rund um Edo im Dienste einer als notwendig erachteten Landesverteidigung vorgenommen wurden. Der amerikanische Admiral Matthew Perry (1794–1858) hatte nach seiner Landung in der Bucht von Edo mit den Schwarzen Schiffen 1853 angekündigt, im folgenden Jahr wiederzukommen, um die Öffnung der japanischen Häfen für den internationalen Handel durchzusetzen. Sofort nach Perrys Abreise wurden die sogenannten *daiba* errichtet. Diese als eine Art Befestigungsanlage

ins Meer gebauten Erdwälle waren mit Steinen befestigt und mit Kanonen bestückt.

Auf diesem Blatt ist an den geschundenen und aufgerissenen Hügelflanken zu erkennen, wie auch drei Jahre nach dem hastigen Erdabbau zur Konstruktion der Erdwälle die Grasnarben noch nicht verheilt sind. Die Kirschblütenliebhaber lassen sich davon freilich nicht beirren. Die kleinen schematischen Figuren ziehen wie in einer losen Prozession den Hügel hinauf und spazieren unter den blühenden Bäumen umher.

Hiroshige zeigt auf dem Blatt eine traditionelle „berühmte Landschaft" (*meisho*) und zugleich deren Zerstörung durch die Anforderungen moderner Technik. Das Werk rückt damit in die Nähe von Paul Cézannes (1839–1906) Gemälde *Bahndurchstich* aus dem Jahr 1870 in der Neuen Pinakothek in München. Auch hier sehen wir einen Hügel, der wie mit einem Tranchiermesser durchschnitten wurde, um einer Eisenbahnlinie Platz zu machen. Die Darstellung des starken Kontrasts moderner Eingriffe in malerische Landschaften lag Cézanne und Hiroshige gleichermaßen am Herzen und lässt beide auch heute noch „modern" erscheinen.

La Colline du palais à Shinagawa

À Edo, la Colline du palais (Gotenyama) est un des lieux les plus populaires pour s'adonner à la contemplation des cerisiers en fleurs. C'est au guerrier Ōta Dōkan (1432–1486), fondateur du premier château d'Edo, que la légende attribue la construction du palais qui donne son nom à la colline.

Au début du XVIIe siècle, le palais servait encore de résidence de campagne aux shoguns Tokugawa. Après sa destruction par un incendie pendant l'ère Genroku (1688–1704), il ne fut pas reconstruit.

Le Gotenyama et ses splendides cerisiers n'apparaissent pas moins de 35 fois dans la série des *Cent Vues célèbres d'Edo* de Hiroshige. Ici, Hiroshige fait plutôt office de chroniqueur des transformations drastiques de la topographie naturelle qui furent jugées nécessaires au nom de la défense du pays. Après avoir débarqué dans la baie d'Edo avec ses « bateaux noirs » en 1853, le commodore américain Matthew Perry (1794–1858) avait fait savoir qu'il reviendrait l'année suivante pour forcer l'ouverture des ports japonais au commerce international. Les *daiba* furent édifiées immédiatement après le départ de Perry. Ces remblais de terre conçus comme des

ouvrages fortifiés s'avançant dans la mer étaient consolidés de pierres et armés de canons.

Dans la présente feuille, les flancs ravagés de la colline montrent que trois ans après les creusements hâtifs réalisés pour l'édification des remblais, les cicatrices laissées dans la végétation ne se sont pas encore refermées. Mais les amateurs de la floraison des cerisiers n'en sont pas pour autant perturbés. Leurs petites figures schématiques gravissent la colline en procession dissoute et déambulent sous les arbres en fleurs.

Hiroshige nous présente ici à la fois un traditionnel « paysage célèbre » (*meisho*) et sa destruction par les impératifs de la technologie moderne. Cette estampe peut ainsi être rapprochée du tableau *La Tranchée* peint par Cézanne en 1870 (Nouvelle Pinacothèque, Munich). Ce tableau montre lui aussi une colline comme tailladée au couteau, en l'occurrence pour ouvrir une ligne de chemin de fer. La représentation du fort contraste induit par les interventions pratiquées sur des paysages pittoresques importait au cœur de Cézanne comme à celui de Hiroshige et fait aujourd'hui encore apparaître les deux artistes comme des « modernes ».

29

砂
む
ら
元
八
ま
ん

Sunamura Moto-Hachiman
4–1856

Moto-Hachiman Shrine in Sunamura

From a high vantage point, we look down on blooming cherry trees and tall pines lining a causeway that forms an acute angle across the width of the print. Beyond, the marshy reedbeds of Edo Bay define the middle of the image and the water stretches out to a high horizon. Small figures walk the causeway, hardly distinguishable from the grey of the dike. However, the upper parts of their bodies stand out against the background, rendering them easier to discern; even small details characterizing these visitors are visible, for example the pipe of the man with a yellow hat in the foreground. The depiction of the lone boatman rowing his boat through the reeds betrays Hiroshige's training in Chinese-inspired literati painting, which he had studied under Ôoka Unpô (1765–1848). With the choice of a reduced palette, Hiroshige succeeds in creating a lyrical atmosphere in masterly fashion.

At the lower right-hand margin, a *torii* entrance gate to a shrine reveals the fact that the Moto-Hachiman Shrine of the title is not far away. Hiroshige explicitly avoids depicting the building itself; instead we have to imagine that we are looking out from the shrine, which is located above Edo Bay in the eastern suburbs of the city.

After the Tokugawa settled in Edo, it did not take long for the rapidly increasing population to outgrow the neighbourhoods around the shogun's castle. By the mid-17th century, land was drained to cultivate rice, among other things. The Sunamura district was among the areas created that way, and in Hiroshige's day it was still on the shores of Edo Bay. Today it is a part of Tokyo's Kôtô-ku district.

Der Schrein Moto-Hachiman in Sunamura

Von einem hohen Betrachterstandpunkt aus fällt der Blick auf eine mit blühenden Kirschbäumen und hohen Kiefern gesäumte Deichstraße, die in einem spitzen Winkel die Bildbreite durchmisst. Darüber breitet sich die Edo-Bucht, von Schilf bewachsenem Sumpf durchzogen, bis zum hohen Horizont aus. Auf der Straße sind kleine Figuren zu sehen, die sich kaum vom Grau des Deiches abheben. Mit ihrem Oberkörper überschneiden sie jedoch den unmittelbaren Hintergrund und sind dadurch leichter zu erkennen. So fallen auch winzige Details ins Auge, die die Spaziergänger charakterisieren, wie etwa die Pfeife des Mannes mit dem gelben Hut. Die besondere Darstellung des einsamen Bootsmannes, der seinen Kahn durch das Ried rudert, verrät Hiroshiges Schulung in der – von chinesischen Vorbildern inspirierten – Literatenmalerei, die er bei Ôoka Unpô (1765–1848) studiert hatte. Mit der Wahl einer reduzierten Farbpalette gelingt es

Hiroshige meisterhaft, den Eindruck einer lyrischen Stimmung zu erzeugen.

Am rechten unteren Rand verrät ein *torii*, das Eingangstor zu einem Schrein, dass sich der im Titel angekündigte Moto-Hachiman ganz in der Nähe befindet. Hiroshige verzichtet explizit auf die Darstellung des Gebäudes und versetzt stattdessen den Betrachter an den Standort des Schreins oberhalb der Edo-Bucht in den östlichen Vorort der Stadt.

Schon bald nachdem die Tokugawa sich in Edo niedergelassen hatten, wurden die Bezirke um das Schloss des Shoguns zu eng für die rasch wachsende Bevölkerung. Mitte des 17. Jahrhunderts begann man daher, Land trocken zu legen, das auch für den Reisanbau genutzt wurde. Das Gebiet Sunamura gehörte zu dem neu aufgeschütteten Gelände und lag zu Hiroshiges Zeiten noch direkt an der Edo-Bucht. Heute ist es Teil des Stadtbezirks Kôtô-ku von Tokyo.

Le sanctuaire de Moto-Hachiman à Sunamura

Depuis un point de vue très haut placé, le regard plonge sur une digue et sur sa route bordée de pins hauts et de cerisiers en fleurs, qui traversent à angle aigu toute la largeur de l'image. Au-dessus de la digue s'étend à perte de vue la baie marécageuse d'Edo où foisonnent les roseaux. Sur la route, on aperçoit de petites figures qui se détachent à peine du ton gris de la digue. En se démarquant du fond verdoyant du marécage environnant, leurs torses les rendent toutefois mieux reconnaissables. D'infimes détails qui caractérisent les promeneurs sautent alors aux yeux, comme la pipe de l'homme au chapeau jaune. La représentation particulière d'un batelier qui fait avancer sa barque à la rame, trahit la formation de Hiroshige à la peinture littéraire d'inspiration chinoise qu'il avait étudiée auprès d'Ôoka Unpô (1765–1848). Avec le choix d'une palette réduite, Hiroshige parvient magistralement à produire l'impression d'une ambiance poétique.

Près du bord droit de l'image, une *torii*, porte d'entrée d'un sanctuaire, révèle que le sanctuaire de Moto-Hachiman indiqué par le titre est tout proche. Hiroshige a délibérément renoncé la représentation du bâtiment, plaçant en revanche le point de vue du spectateur sur l'aire même du sanctuaire au-dessus de la baie d'Edo, dans les faubourgs est de la ville.

Peu après que les Tokugawa se furent installés à Edo, les abords immédiats du château shogunal s'avérèrent par trop exigus pour la population en forte croissance. Au milieu du XVIIᵉ siècle, on commença donc à assécher des terres qui servaient notamment à la riziculture. Le domaine de Sunamura faisait partie des terrains récemment assainis ; à l'époque de Hiroshige, il était encore situé tout près de la baie d'Edo. Il fait aujourd'hui partie du quartier Kôtô-ku à Tokyo.

50

亀
戸
梅
屋
舖

Kameido Umeyashiki
11—1857

Plum Park in Kameido

This close-up of the trunk of a plum tree with its bizarrely shaped branches and roundish white blossoms marks one of the most famous prints in the entire series. The printer achieved a three-dimensionality with the grey gradation of the trunk that could not have been surpassed by a painter. This strangely shaped tree was called Garyūbai ("Sleeping Dragon") and was mentioned in all guide books of Edo. In the top left-hand corner of the print is the back of the sign that bears the name of this famous tree. Through the branches we see numerous plum trees in blossom and, behind a fence, strolling visitors admiring them.

The Plum Park in Kameido is located in the north-east of the city, behind the Kameido Tenjinsha Shrine. Both in colour and theme, the motif of this picture is closely related to the print designed nine months earlier, *Plum Orchard in Kamada* (plate 27). There, too, a red *bokashi* covers almost the entire top half of the picture, highlighting the glowing white blossoms.

In a number of his compositions after the fifth month of 1856, Hiroshige employed a *repoussoir* – an object placed in the foreground that helps to push the background motifs farther into the distance and so lends greater depth to the pictorial space. While this device seems sometimes contrived, it was very popular at the time, as evidenced in Vincent van Gogh's (1853–1890) 1887 painting (see ill. 3) based on this print, *Japonaiserie: Flowering Plum Tree (after Hiroshige)*.

Pflaumenpark Kameido

Mit der extremen Nahansicht auf den Stamm eines Pflaumenbaums mit bizarren Zweigen und runden, weißen Knospen gelingt Hiroshige eines der berühmtesten Bilder der ganzen Serie. Der Drucker erreichte mit der organischen Graugradierung des Stammes eine Volumendarstellung, wie sie in der Malerei nicht besser hätte erzielt werden können. Wegen seiner exzentrischen Form nannte man diesen in allen Edo-Führern erwähnten Baum Garyūbai („Ruhender Drache"). In der linken oberen Bildecke ist die Rückseite des Schildes zu sehen, das den Namen des berühmten Baumes trägt. Durch das Geäst hindurch sind zahlreiche blühende Pflaumenbäume zu sehen, und hinter einem Zaun im Mittelgrund flanieren Besucher und betrachten sie bewundernd.

Der Pflaumenpark Kameido befindet sich im Nordosten hinter dem Schrein Kameido Tenjinsha. Das Bildmotiv steht offensichtlich in enger thematischer und farblicher Beziehung zum neun Monate zuvor entstandenen Holzschnitt *Pflaumengarten in Kamada* (siehe Tafel 27). Auch dort bedeckt ein rotes *bokashi* fast die gesamte obere Bildhälfte und bringt die weißen Blüten durch seine feinen Farbabstufungen zum Leuchten.

Hiroshige arbeitete in einigen Entwürfen nach dem fünften Monat 1856 gerne mit Repoussoirs, die das Hauptmotiv in den Vordergrund stellen und die dahinter liegenden Bereiche in die Ferne rücken lassen, wodurch der gesamte Bildraum Tiefe erhält. Dieser Effekt wirkte zwar zuweilen künstlich, war jedoch beim zeitgenössischen Publikum sehr beliebt. Davon zeugt unter anderem Vincent van Goghs (1853–1890) Kopie *Japonaiserie: Der blühende Pflaumenbaum (nach Hiroshige)* von 1887 (siehe Abb. 3).

Le parc de pruniers à Kameido

Avec cette vue fortement rapprochée d'un tronc de prunier aux branches bizarrement conformées et ponctuées de fleurs rondes et blanches, Hiroshige a créé une des images les plus célèbres de toute la série. Dans le dégradé gris organique du tronc, l'imprimeur est parvenu à une représentation du volume tel que la peinture n'aurait pu mieux la rendre. Du fait de sa forme inhabituelle, cet arbre évoqué dans tous les guides d'Edo était appelé Garyubai (« dragon au repos »). Dans le coin supérieur gauche, on aperçoit la face arrière du panneau où est inscrit le nom de cette célébrité. À travers les branches apparaissent de nombreux pruniers en fleurs ; des visiteurs admiratifs les contemplent derrière la clôture qu'on aperçoit au second plan.

Le parc de pruniers de Kameido est situé au nord-est et derrière le sanctuaire Kameido Tenjinsha. Du point de vue thématique autant que chromatique, le sujet de cette feuille entretient un lien manifeste avec l'estampe *Prunelaie à Kamada* (cf. pl. 27) réalisée neuf mois plus tôt. Dans cette estampe aussi, un *bokashi* rouge occupe la quasi totalité de la moitié supérieure de l'image et vient renforcer la lumineuse blancheur des fleurs.

Dans quelques projets réalisés après le cinquième mois 1856, Hiroshige s'est volontiers servi de repoussoirs – le motif principal au premier plan – qui relèguent au loin les domaines placés au second ou à l'arrière-plan. Ce procédé confère une profondeur particulière à tout l'espace de l'image. L'effet relève parfois de l'artifice, mais il était très apprécié du public de l'époque, comme l'illustre notamment la copie réalisée en 1887 (cf. ill. 3) par Vincent van Gogh (1853–1890) *Japonaiserie : prunier en fleurs (d'après Hiroshige)*.

51

吾嬬の森
連理の梓

Azuma no mori Renri no azusa
7–1856

Azuma no mori Shrine and the Entwined Camphor

The "Entwined Camphor" of the title rises high above a red horizon into a pale sky enlivened by a small flock of birds. The right-hand side of the tree's bushy crown was seen as the "male" part, its curving contour towering over the lower "female" part on the left. This unusual tree was a symbol of the mythical prince Yamato Takeru no Mikoto (known as the "Brave Prince of Yamato") and his wife Ototachibana Hime. The prince's father, the legendary emperor Keikō, had sent his son into battle against the northern barbarians. But the tempestuous young man aroused the anger of the gods, who determined to sink his ship in a storm. At the critical moment, however, Princess Ototachibana Hime threw herself into the waves, her self-sacrifice thus propitiating the gods. After a few days, her comb was washed ashore and buried by the prince under a small hill.

Distraught following his loss, the prince stuck a few chopsticks of camphor wood into the symbolic grave, from which the "Entwined Camphor" is said to have grown.

According to legend, the name Azuma goes back to the cry of the prince "Ah, tsuma!" ("Oh, my wife!"), but Azuma can also simply mean "east", referring to the area around Edo. In Hiroshige's picture, the Azuma no mori Shrine buildings erected around the famous tree almost disappear in the dark, dense grove, but to compensate he uses an intense yellow to emphasize the tree and banner-lined path leading to the sanctuary. The dark grey of the fields acts as a contrast to the striking yellow of the path and the pale pink of the cherry blossoms, which are being admired not only by pilgrims – men, women and a child – but also by travellers in the two boats.

Der Schrein Azuma no mori und der Zwillings-Kampfer

Die Baumkrone des im Titel genannten Zwillings-Kampfers ragt hoch über den roten Horizont in den von einem kleinen Vogelschwarm belebten hellen Himmel. Die rechte Krone wurde als männlicher Teil verstanden, der mit einer kurvigen Kontur über sein flacheres weibliches Pendant links daneben hinausragt. Dieser ungewöhnliche Baum war ein Symbol für den mythischen Prinzen Yamato Takeru no Mikoto und seine Frau Ototachibana Hime. Der Vater des Prinzen, der legendäre Kaiser Keikō, schickte seinen Sohn in den Norden zum Kampf gegen die Barbaren. Der ungestüme Prinz erregte den Zorn der Götter, welche sein Schiff in einem Sturm untergehen lassen wollten. In diesem Moment warf sich Prinzessin Ototachibana Hime in die Fluten und beschwichtigte durch ihr Opfer die Götter. Nach einigen Tagen wurde ihr Kamm an Land gespült und vom Prinzen unter einem kleinen Hügel begraben. Verzweifelt über seinen Verlust, steckte der Prinz ein paar Essstäbchen aus Kampferholz in das symbolische Grabmal, aus denen der Zwillings-Kampfer gewachsen sein soll.

Der Name Azuma geht der Legende nach auf den Ausruf des Prinzen „Aa, tsuma!" („Oh, meine Frau!") zurück, bedeutet aber auch einfach nur „Osten" und bezieht sich auf das Gebiet um Edo. Bei Hiroshige verschwinden die um den berühmten Baum errichteten Schreingebäude des Azuma no mori fast in dem dichten, dunklen Wäldchen, dafür hebt er mit einem intensiven Gelb den zum Heiligtum führenden und von Bäumen und Bannern gesäumten Weg hervor. Das dunkle Grau der Felder bringt nicht nur den Weg, sondern auch die zartrosa blühenden Kirschbäume zum Leuchten. Pilgernde Frauen, Männer und ein Kind sowie die Reisenden auf zwei Booten bewundern die Blütenpracht.

Le sanctuaire Azuma no mori et le camphrier jumeau

Le faîte du camphrier jumeau évoqué dans le titre s'élève haut au-dessus de l'horizon rougeoyant dans un ciel encore clair animé par un petit vol d'oiseaux. Le faîte de droite était compris comme partie masculine, dont le contour ondoyant s'élève au-dessus de son pendant féminin plus plat. Cet arbre peu commun était un symbole du prince mythique Yamato Takeru no Mikoto (le valeureux prince de Yamato) et de son épouse Ototachibana Hime. Le père du prince, le légendaire empereur Keikō, avait envoyé son fils au nord du pays pour combattre les barbares. La férocité du prince provoqua la colère des dieux qui résolurent de faire sombrer son navire dans une tempête. Au moment prévu, la princesse Ototachibana Hime se jeta dans les flots, apaisant ainsi la colère des dieux. Après quelques jours, son peigne fut rejeté par la mer et le prince l'enterra sous une petite colline. Désespéré par la perte de la princesse, le prince planta une paire de baguettes de camphrier dans le tombeau symbolique, d'où aurait alors poussé le camphrier jumeau.

Selon la légende, le nom Azuma remonte à l'exclamation « Aa, tsuma ! » (« O mon épouse ! »), mais signifie en fait simplement « est » et se réfère au domaine autour d'Edo. Chez Hiroshige, les bâtiments du sanctuaire Azuma no mori édifiés autour de cet arbre célèbre disparaissent presque entièrement dans une forêt dense et sombre, tandis que Hiroshige utilise un jaune vif pour faire ressortir le chemin bordé d'arbres et de bannières qui mène au sanctuaire. Le gris sombre des champs ne confère pas seulement sa luminosité au chemin, mais aussi aux cerisiers tout en fleurs délicatement rosées. Des pèlerins – femmes, hommes et un enfant – et les voyageurs de deux barques admirent la splendeur florale.

52

柳
し
ま

Yanagishima
4—1857

The Yanagishima Island

The Hashimotoya restaurant ("At the Foot of the Bridge") was situated on Yanagishima, the "Willow Island", on the north-east edge of Edo. Guests either had themselves rowed out to the island, or else walked across the "Willow Bridge".

The brightly lit interior of the restaurant, which remained in business until 1923, marks the brightest point of the lower half of the print. To the left of the restaurant is the Myōken Hall of the Nichiren Temple of Hōshōji. "Our Myōken of Yanagishima" was what the long-established residents of Edo lovingly called the main icon in this building. As the embodiment of the constellation of the Great Bear, the Bodhisattva Myōken was invoked to protect against fires, to defend the country and to bestow wealth and longevity.

This Nichiren temple was the centre of the Myōken cult in Edo and included among its worshippers such famous characters as the master printmaker Katsushika Hokusai (1760—1849).

Sacred and profane spheres are often found in close proximity in Japan, as in medieval Europe, where markets and taverns sprang up around churches and cathedrals. However, it is unlikely that in the past the sacred and the profane spheres were clearly distinguished from each other in the way they are today. In Japan as in Europe, boundaries were far more fluid, and so it was common to see monks and nuns preaching at fairgrounds as though at stalls selling all kinds of food, and souvenirs abounded in temple and shrine districts.

Die Insel Yanagishima

Das Restaurant Hashimotoya („Am Brückenfuß") liegt auf Yanagishima, der „Weideninsel" am nordöstlichen Stadtrand von Edo. Die Gäste lassen sich im Boot zum Restaurant rudern oder überqueren die „Weidenbrücke".

Das hell erleuchtete Interieur der bis 1923 betriebenen Gaststätte markiert den hellsten Punkt der unteren Blatthälfte. Links neben dem Lokal erstreckt sich die Halle Myōkendō des Nichiren-Tempels Hōshōji. „Unser Myōken von Yanagishima" nannten die alteingesessenen Städter von Edo liebevoll die Hauptikone in diesem Gebäude. Der Bodhisattva Myōken war die Verkörperung des Sternbilds „Großer Wagen" und wurde zum Schutz des Landes, gegen Feuersbrünste sowie für Reichtum und langes Leben angebetet. Der Nichiren-Tempel war das Zentrum des Myōken-Kultes in Edo und hatte solch berühmte Gläubige wie den Holzschnittmeister Katsushika Hokusai (1760—1849).

Sakrales und Profanes sind in Japan oft in unmittelbarer Nähe zueinander angesiedelt, vergleichbar den Märkten und Gaststätten, die in Europa seit dem Mittelalter um Kirchen herum entstanden. Allerdings ist die Frage berechtigt, ob die heute als „sakral" und „profan" bezeichneten Bereiche früher überhaupt in ähnlicher Weise getrennt wurden. Wie auch in vielen europäischen Kulturen waren die Grenzen fließend, und so fand man predigende Nonnen und Mönche auf Jahrmärkten ebenso wie Verkaufsstände mit allerlei Esswaren und Andenken in Tempel- und Schreinbezirken.

L'île Yanagishima

Le restaurant Hashimotoya, littéralement « Au pied du pont », est situé sur Yanagishima, c'est-à-dire « l'île aux Saules », à la limite nord-est d'Edo. Pour accéder au restaurant, les clients se font passer en barque ou franchissent le « pont aux Saules ».

L'intérieur fortement éclairé de l'auberge, qui restera ouverte au public jusqu'en 1923, marque le point le plus clair de la moitié inférieure de l'image. À gauche derrière le restaurant s'étend le pavillon Myōkendō du temple nichiren Hōshōji. « Notre Myōken de Yanagishima », tel était le nom affectueux que les anciens habitants d'Edo donnaient à l'icône principale de l'édifice. Le bodhisattva Myōken était l'incarnation de la Grande Ourse, il était vénéré comme protecteur du pays contre les incendies et dispensateur de richesse et de longévité. Le temple nichiren était le centre du culte de Myōken à Edo et a eu des adorateurs aussi célèbres que le maître estampiste Katsushika Hokusai (1760—1849).

Au Japon, les domaines sacré et profane sont souvent contigus, tout comme les marchés et les restaurants foisonnent aux abords des églises européennes depuis le Moyen Âge. Il est vrai qu'on peut se demander légitimement si les domaines dits « sacré » et « profane » ont jamais été aussi fortement séparés que nous les concevons aujourd'hui. Comme dans bien des cultures européennes, la frontière entre les deux domaines était fluide, et c'est ainsi qu'on pouvait trouver dans les foires annuelles des nonnes et des moines, de même qu'on trouve dans les lieux saints des étals présentant toutes sortes de produits alimentaires ou de souvenirs.

四ツ木通
用水
引ふね

Yotsugi dōri yōsui hikifune
2–1857

Towboats on the Yotsugi dōri Canal

The Yotsugi dōri Canal to the east of the Sumida River was constructed at the beginning of the 17th century as part of the system that provided Edo with drinking water. It was not needed as such for very long, however, and thenceforth served as an irrigation channel and as a waterway for freight. It was so shallow and narrow that only small boats could travel along it, pulled from the towpath by ropes. As we see in this print, it also became a waterway for passengers on their way to north-east Japan.

Hiroshige depicted the canal in a bold S-shaped curve, though in fact it was absolutely straight. In this meandering composition, the blue of the canal tapers far less strongly towards the top of the picture than it does in the more "accurate" (from the point of view of perspective) oblong depiction of the same scene in the seventh volume of his *Illustrated Souvenirs of Edo (Ehon Edo miyage)* dating from the same year, 1857. The text accompanying that picture states that it is more elegant to be towed in a boat than rowed.

As so often, Hiroshige gave priority to artistic intention rather than topographical accuracy in this print. He wanted to present something striking, and offer the viewer an unusual impression of a familiar scene.

Some Japanese experts regard this print as one of the finest in the entire series. The colour combination of saturated blue, ochre and green, together with the broad view, have been described as "comparable to an oil painting". But when passing such a judgement, these critics not only make a positive assessment of Western painting techniques, but also underestimate Japanese traditions. Interestingly, the British woodcut aficionado Basil Stewart (1880–?), by contrast, in his 1922 book *Subjects Portrayed in Japanese Colour-Prints*, simply wrote off this print as "worthless".

Schleppkähne am Kanal Yotsugi dōri

Der Kanal Yotsugi dōri östlich des Flusses Sumidagawa wurde zu Beginn des 17. Jahrhunderts als Teil des Trinkwasserversorgungssystems von Edo gebaut. Schon bald aber wurde er nicht mehr benötigt und diente nur noch als Bewässerungskanal und Transportweg. Der Kanal war aber so seicht und schmal, dass auf ihm nur kleine Boote verkehrten, die vom Ufer aus mit Seilen gezogen wurden. Schließlich nutzte man den Kanal, wie in diesem Holzschnitt dargestellt, auch als Wasserweg für Passagiere, die sich auf dem Weg nach Nordostjapan befanden.

Hiroshige zeigt uns den Kanal als ein schwungvoll verlaufendes „S", obwohl er schnurgerade verlief. In dieser gewundenen Komposition verjüngt sich das Blau der Wasseroberfläche wesentlich weniger stark nach oben hin als in Hiroshiges perspektivisch „exakter" herausgearbeiteten, querformatigen Darstellung dieser Szene im siebten Band von *Illustrierte Mitbringsel aus Edo (Ehon Edo miyage)* aus dem gleichen Jahr 1857. In der Beschreibung dort wird hervorgehoben, dass es eleganter sei, sich in einem Boot ziehen zu lassen, als gerudert zu werden.

Auch im vorliegenden Holzschnitt stellte Hiroshige demnach seine künstlerischen Ansprüche über die geografischen Gegebenheiten. Er wollte dem Betrachter die bekannte Szene neu ins Blickfeld rücken und etwas Ungewohntes präsentieren.

Einige japanische Experten halten diesen Holzschnitt für eines der besten Blätter der ganzen Serie. Die Farbkombination des satten Blau, Ockergelb und Grün zusammen mit dem weit ausgreifenden Blick wurden als „so gut wie auf einem Ölbild" beschrieben. Mit dieser Beurteilung bringen die Kritiker eine positive Wertschätzung der westlichen Maltechniken bei gleichzeitiger Unterschätzung der eigenen Tradition zum Ausdruck. Interessanterweise hielt dagegen der britische Holzschnittliebhaber Basil Stewart (1880–?) in seinem *Subjects Portrayed in Japanese Colour-Prints* von 1922 das Blatt schlicht für „wertlos".

Chalands sur le canal Yotsugi dōri

Le canal Yotsugi dōri, à l'est de la rivière Sumidagawa, fut creusé au début du XVIIᵉ siècle comme partie du système de distribution d'eau potable d'Edo. Mais il perdit bientôt son utilité et ne servit plus que comme canal d'irrigation et comme voie de transport. Le canal était toutefois si étroit et peu profond que seules de petites barques pouvaient y circuler – on les tirait depuis la berge à l'aide de cordes. Pour finir, le canal fut aussi utilisé comme voie fluviale pour des passagers voyageant vers le nord-est du Japon, comme on le voit dans la présente estampe.

Hiroshige nous montre le canal décrivant une ligne serpentine alors qu'il était en réalité rectiligne. Dans cette composition en « S », le bleu de la surface de l'eau s'amincit beaucoup moins fortement vers le haut que dans la représentation horizontale de la même scène qui figure dans le septième volume des *Souvenirs illustrés d'Edo (Ehon Edo miyage)* de la même année 1857, représentation qui est plus « exacte » en termes de perspective. La description qui l'accompagne souligne qu'il est plus élégant de se déplacer dans une barque tirée depuis la berge que dans une barque mue par des rameurs.

Dans la présente estampe aussi, Hiroshige a donc subordonné les données topographiques à ses exigences artistiques. Son propos était de donner une vision nouvelle de cette scène célèbre et de présenter quelque chose d'inhabituel.

Certains experts japonais considèrent cette feuille comme une des meilleures de toute la série. La combinaison entre le bleu saturé, l'ocre jaune et le vert associée à un vaste panorama a été décrite comme « aussi excellente que dans une peinture à l'huile ». Les critiques émettent ainsi une appréciation positive des techniques de peinture occidentales, non sans sous-estimer leur propre tradition. Fait intéressant, dans son ouvrage *Subjects Portrayed in Japanese Colour-Prints* de 1922, l'amateur d'estampes anglais Basil Stewart (1880–?) considérait en revanche que cette feuille n'avait tout bonnement « pas la moindre valeur ».

真乳山
山谷堀
夜景

Matsuchiyama San'yabori yakei
8–1857

Night View of Matsuchiyama and the San'ya Canal

This print is an exception in the series, which is primarily famous for its landscapes, as it is the only image in the *One Hundred Famous Views of Edo* to depict a large human figure. To great effect, Hiroshige places the profile of a woman, her face snow-white, against a night sky sprinkled with stars that are reflected in the calm waters of the Sumida River. The grain of the wood, clearly visible in the sky, is also evident in the river. In the assured depiction of the various textiles and the woman's coiffure, Hiroshige proves himself to be an outstanding woodblock designer, superbly skilled at depicting people. The hint of uncertainty in the geisha's gait as she walks along on her high *geta* sandals suggests she has been drinking. According to Miyao Shigeo, contemporary gossip had it that Hiroshige had made a portrait of a geisha called Koman, whose services he is said to have favoured.

The lantern cropped by the left-hand margin of the print, which is intended to illuminate the path for the lady, forms luminous red accents together with her undergarment and the signature bottom right. Red is echoed in the title cartouches on the top right and emphasizes the darkness of the scene.

On the opposite west bank of the Sumida River, we can see a brightly lit establishment at the foot of a hill known as Matsuchiyama, the summit of which is crowned by the faintly discernible Shōten Shrine. At the base of the hill on the right, the little San'ya Canal flows into the Sumida River. From here, small boats plied up and down the San'ya with customers bound for the Shin-Yoshiwara pleasure district.

Nachtansicht von Matsuchiyama mit dem Kanal San'yabori

Dieser Holzschnitt bildet eine Ausnahme in der Serie, die in erster Linie für ihre Landschaften berühmt ist: Es handelt sich um die einzige große Figurendarstellung in den *Hundert Ansichten*. Hiroshige setzt das Profil einer schneeweiß geschminkten Frau effektvoll gegen einen Nachthimmel, dessen Sterne sich im ruhigen Wasser des Flusses Sumidagawa spiegeln. Auch die den Himmel strukturierende Holzmaserung taucht im Fluss wieder auf. In der souveränen Ausgestaltung der verschiedenen Textilien und der Haartracht der Protagonistin zeigt Hiroshige sich auch als talentierter Figurendarsteller und Werbegrafiker, der er ja ebenfalls war. Die angedeutete leichte Unsicherheit der Geisha auf ihren hohen Geta-Sandalen lässt an Alkoholgenuss bei einem Bankett denken. Laut Miyao Shigeo kolportierte der zeitgenössische Klatsch, dass Hiroshige ein Bildnis der Geisha Koman geschaffen habe, deren Dienste er selbst bevorzugt in Anspruch genommen haben soll.

Der vom linken Bildrand abgeschnittene Lampion, der der Dame den Weg erhellen soll, bildet mit dem Untergewand und der Signatur einen leuchtenden roten Dreiklang, der vom Rot der Titelkartuschen oben rechts aufgenommen wird und das Dunkel dieses Druckes betont.

Am gegenüberliegenden Westufer des Sumidagawa ist ein hell erleuchtetes Etablissement unterhalb eines Hügels zu sehen. Diese Erhebung ist der Matsuchiyama, auf dessen Spitze der Schrein Shōten schemenhaft angedeutet ist. Am Fuß des Hügels fließt rechts der kleine Kanal San'yabori in den Sumidagawa. Von dieser Stelle aus fuhren kleine Boote den San'yabori hoch und beförderten ihre Kunden zum Freudenviertel Shin-Yoshiwara.

Vue rapprochée du Matsuchiyama et du canal San'yabori

Cette estampe marque une exception notoire au sein d'une série qui doit sa célébrité en premier lieu à ses vues paysagères : il s'agit de la seule planche des *Cent Vues* montrant une figure en grand format. Hiroshige a placé spectaculairement le profil d'une femme au visage fardé de blanc contre un ciel de nuit dont les étoiles se reflètent dans l'eau calme de la rivière Sumidagawa. Les veinures du bois qui structurent le ciel apparaissent également au niveau de la rivière. Par la facture souveraine des différentes textures d'étoffes et de la coiffure de la protagoniste, Hiroshige apparaît aussi comme un portraitiste et un graphiste publicitaire de talent – que d'ailleurs il fut. L'imperceptible manque d'assurance de la geisha perchée sur ses *getas* suggère la consommation de boissons alcoolisées lors d'un banquet. Selon Miyao Shigeo, la rumeur circulait alors que Hiroshige aurait fait ici le portrait de la geisha Koman, dont il n'aurait du reste nullement dédaigné les services.

Le lampion coupé par le bord droit de l'image qui doit éclairer le chemin de la maîtresse forme avec ses vêtements de dessous et la signature un triple et lumineux accord repris par le ton rouge du cartouche de titre, en haut à droite, accord que renforce encore l'obscurité de la scène.

Au pied d'une colline de la rive opposée de la Sumidagawa, on aperçoit un établissement fortement éclairé. La colline en question est le Matsuchiyama, au sommet duquel est indiqué schématiquement le sanctuaire Shōten. À droite au pied de la colline, le petit canal San'yabori se jette dans la Sumidagawa. De cet endroit partaient alors de petites barques qui remontaient le canal pour déposer les clients dans le quartier des plaisirs Shin-Yoshiwara.

55

隅田川
水神の
森真崎

Sumidagawa Suijin no mori Massaki
8–1856

The Grove at the Suijin Shrine and Massaki on the Sumida River

Framed by a cherry-tree trunk and its luxuriant blossoms, a view dominated by the broad Sumida River opens before us. On the distant opposite bank, the district of Massaki is hinted at, and on the horizon the stylized outline of Mount Tsukuba rises out of the mist. In the foreground, a few people are making their way to the Hashiba ferry, which is depicted on plate 37. On the right, a gate known as a *torii* leads to the Suijin ("water deity") shrine in its wooded setting, where the deity of the Sumida River was venerated.

The cherry blossoms dominating the picture cover the sky, which is depicted with an elongated blue *bokashi* gradation, and the grain of the wood has been effectively used by the printer.

In the case of the two-colour blossoms, the printer used the *kimedashi* ("push out") technique, though this is difficult to appreciate in a reproduction. In order to create a certain three-dimensionality, the paper was pressed from behind into the carved hollows in the woodblock, usually with the elbow, a technique also known as *nikuzuri* (flesh print).

The restricted palette of gentle greens and blues, enriched only with sparingly used bright red, was employed by Hiroshige in some of his early woodblock prints. It accords here with the characterization of this region in the first volume of his *Illustrated Souvenirs of Edo (Ehon Edo miyage)*, printed in 1850, in which he observed that this landscape is tranquil and elegant and it was often eulogized by poets.

Der Wald am Schrein Suijin und die Gegend um Massaki am Sumidagawa

Von einem Kirschbaumstamm und seinen üppigen Blüten gerahmt öffnet sich eine Ebene mit dem breiten Fluss Sumidagawa, der schemenhaft angedeuteten Gegend um Massaki am gegenüberliegenden Ufer und der stilisierten Kontur des Berges Tsukubasan am Horizont. Im Vordergrund laufen einige Menschen auf die Fähre von Hashiba zu, die in Tafel 37 gezeigt wird. Rechts führt ein Tor (*torii*) zu dem von einem Wald umgebenen Schrein Suijin ("Wasser-Gottheit"), in dem die Gottheit des Flusses Sumidagawa verehrt wird.

Die das Bild dominierenden Kirschblüten bedecken den Himmel mit seiner langgezogenen blauen Farbgradierung (*bokashi*) und der wirkungsvoll beim Druck eingesetzten Holzmaserung.

Bei den zweifarbigen Blüten wendeten die Drucker die Technik des *kimedashi* ("Herausdrücken") an, die auf Reproduktionen nur schwer erkennbar ist. Um eine gewisse Dreidimensionalität zu erzeugen, wurde das Papier von hinten in die geschnitzten Vertiefungen der Holzplatte gepresst. Weil dabei meist der Ellenbogen benutzt wurde, nannte man diese Technik auch *nikuzuri* (Fleisch-Druck).

Die begrenzte Farbpalette von zarten Grün- und Blautönen, angereichert nur durch ein spärlich verwendetes helles Rot, hat Hiroshige in einigen der frühen Holzschnitte eingesetzt. Sie entspricht hier der Charakterisierung dieser Gegend im ersten Band seines Werkes *Illustrierte Mitbringsel aus Edo (Ehon Edo miyage)* von 1850, in der er betont, diese Landschaft sei still, elegant und häufig von Dichtern besungen worden.

La forêt près du sanctuaire Suijin et Massaki au bord de la Sumidagawa

Dans le cadre formé par le tronc et les branches abondamment fleuries d'un cerisier s'étend une vaste plaine où coule largement la rivière Sumidagawa, la région de Massaki, seulement indiquée schématiquement sur la rive opposée, et le contour stylisé du mont Tsukubasan à l'horizon. Au premier plan, quelques personnages descendent vers le village de Hashiba de la planche 37. À droite, une porte dite *torii* marque l'accès au sanctuaire Suijin (« divinité de l'eau ») entouré d'une forêt, et dans lequel est vénérée la divinité fluviale de la Sumidagawa.

Les fleurs de cerisiers qui dominent l'image recouvrent le ciel avec son dégradé de bleus en longueur (*bokashi*) et la veinure mise en valeur lors de l'estampage.

Pour les fleurs en deux couleurs, les imprimeurs ont utilisé la technique dite *kimedashi* (« gaufrage ») qu'on ne décèle guère dans les reproductions. Pour produire un certain effet de relief, le papier est pressé par derrière dans les creux de la plaque. Comme ceci se faisait le plus souvent avec le coude, cette technique était aussi appelée *nikuzuri* (impression à chair).

La palette réduite de tons délicats de vert et de bleu, enrichie seulement par l'utilisation parcimonieuse d'un rouge clair, avait déjà été utilisée pour quelques estampes de jeunesse de Hiroshige. Elle répond ici à la caractérisation de la contrée dans le premier tome (1850) de ses *Souvenirs illustrés d'Edo (Ehon Edo miyage)*, où est précisé que « ce paysage paisible et élégant a souvent été chanté par les poètes ».

56

真崎辺よ
り水神の
森内川
関屋の里
を見る図

Massaki atari yori Suijin no mori Uchigawa Sekiya no sato wo miru zu
8–1857

View from Massaki on the Grove near
Suijin Shrine, the Uchigawa Inlet and
Sekiya Village

A round window bisected by a
sliding door reveals a view to the
north-east, where we see the
Sumida River as it passes
through the district of Massaki,
to the north of the Shin-Yoshiwara pleasure district. On the
river are various forms of waterborne transport, including a
barge, a sailing boat and in the
foreground a "roof boat"
(*yanebune*). On the distant
horizon stands Mount Tsukuba,
and to the right is a grove in
which we can just make out the
gate of the Suijin Shrine
(see plate 35).

Japanese and Western critics
alike have enthused over the
aesthetic confidence with which
Hiroshige allows a plum branch
to project into the evening sky. A
formation of flying birds creates
a slightly curved, branch-like
line that seems to extend the
slender tree into the infinity of

the sky. Even though the drafts
for this print and the preceding
one were separated by an interval of a year, and depict periods
some weeks apart, it was doubtless on account of the geographical proximity of the subjects,
and the similarity of the frame-
like compositions, that the publisher and the designer of the
table of contents placed them
next to each other.

The cropped view is designed to
convey the feeling that viewers
are guests enjoying refresh-
ments on the second floor of an
elegant teahouse, to whose wall
on the left has been attached a
vase with a flowering magnolia.
Massaki was well known for the
numerous restaurants of this
kind around the Inari shrine.
For some visitors, they offered
a welcome chance to fortify
themselves on the way to nearby
Shin-Yoshiwara.

Blick von der Gegend um Massaki auf den
Wald am Schrein Suijin, die kleine Bucht des
Uchigawa und das Dorf Sekiya no sato

Ein rundes, von einer Schiebe-
tür begrenztes Fenster gewährt
Ausblick nach Nordosten auf
den Fluss Sumidagawa. Ein Last-
kahn, ein Segelschiff und ein
sogenanntes „Dachboot" (*yane-*
bune) beleben den Fluss an
dieser nördlich des Freuden-
viertels Shin-Yoshiwara gelegenen Gegend von Massaki. Am
Horizont erscheint der Berg
Tsukubasan und rechts ist der
Wald mit dem Tor des Schreins
Suijin von Tafel 35 zu sehen.

Die ästhetische Sicherheit, mit
der Hiroshige einen Pflaumen-
zweig in den Abendhimmel
ragen lässt, hat japanische und
westliche Kritiker gleichermaßen begeistert. Eine Formation
fliegender Vögel bildet eine
leicht gebogene Linie und ver-
längert optisch den Zweig ins
Unendliche des Himmels. Auch
wenn die Entwürfe für dieses

und für das vorangegangene
Blatt ein Jahr und die auf ihnen
dargestellten Jahreszeiten
einige Wochen auseinander-
liegen, so ordneten der Verleger
und Entwerfer des Inhaltsverzeichnisses sie wohl wegen ihrer
geografischen Nähe und der
rahmenden Komposition
nacheinander an.

Der Bildausschnitt soll dem
Betrachter das Gefühl vermitteln, selbst als Gast eine Erfri-
schung im zweiten Stock eines
eleganten Teehauses zu genießen, an dessen Wand links eine
Blumenvase mit blühender Mag-
nolie angebracht ist. Es gab zahlreiche solcher Gaststätten am
Inari-Schrein, für den die
Gegend um Massaki bekannt
war. Für so manchen Besucher
boten sie eine willkommene
Stärkung auf dem Weg zum
nahegelegenen Shin-Yoshiwara.

La forêt près du sanctuaire Suijin, la petite baie
de l'Uchigawa et le village Sekiya no sato vus de
la région de Massaki

Le demi-cercle d'une fenêtre
ronde délimité par une porte
coulissante offre une vue de la
rivière Sumidagawa orientée au
nord-est. Un chaland, un voilier
et une « barque couverte »
(*yanebune*) animent la rivière
dans cette région de Massaki
située au nord du quartier des
plaisirs Shin-Yoshiwara. À l'horizon apparaît le mont Tsukubasan, à droite, on peut voir la forêt
avec la porte du sanctuaire
Suijin de la planche 35.

La grande assurance esthétique
avec laquelle Hiroshige fait
monter une branche de prunier
dans le ciel a suscité l'enthou-
siasme des critiques japonais
aussi bien qu'occidentaux. Un
vol d'oiseaux forme une ligne
légèrement courbe et prolonge
visuellement la branche dans
l'infini du ciel. Bien que les projets réalisés pour la présente
estampe et la précédente aient
vu le jour à un an d'intervalle et

que les saisons qu'elles évoquent
soient distantes de plusieurs
semaines, l'éditeur et le concepteur de la table des matières les
ont vraisemblablement placées
l'une après l'autre en raison
de leur proximité
géographique comme de
la parenté de composition.

L'ouverture qui définit ici la vue
doit donner au spectateur le sentiment de goûter lui-même un
rafraîchissement comme client
installé au deuxième étage d'une
élégante maison de thé, contre
le mur gauche de laquelle apparaît un vase de fleurs de magno-
lias. Aux abords du sanctuaire
du dieu Inari, il existait de nombreuses auberges du même
genre qui faisaient la célébrité
de Massaki. Pour bien des
visiteurs, elles offraient un
fortifiant bienvenu sur la
route du proche quartier
de Shin-Yoshiwara.

57

墨田河橋
場の渡
かわら竈

Sumidagawa hashiba no watashi kawaragama
4–1857

Kilns and the Hashiba Ferry on the Sumida River

A tall column of blackish-grey smoke, turning white as it rises, wafts over the Sumida River. On the opposite bank are woods and, amid them, the Suijin Shrine. Curiously, the smoke does not dissipate even high in the sky. The shape of the column is reflected, in reverse, in the grain of the woodblock where the river is depicted.

The smoke emanating from one of the round kilns in the foreground is both an eye-catcher and an element of the subject of the print. It has been created by burning pine needles, a supply of which is seen piled up between the kilns. These kilns were used for firing not only utilitarian items like tiles, but also figurines representing cats, foxes and racoons. The ever-popular *maneki neko* (cats with a raised paw), a favourite decoration for shops, were first fired here; they were bought by tourists and pilgrims, who at times donated them to temples and shrines.

Two boats operating the ferry service mentioned in the title are approaching each other in the middle of the river, while in the foreground small gulls of the *miyakodori* ("capital birds") type are rocking on the waves. In the printed book illustrated by Katsushika Hokusai

(1760–1849) *Views of Both Banks of the Sumida River (Sumidagawa ryōgan ichiran)*, which dates from the first decade of the 19th century, the appended satirical poems link the settlement of Hashiba with the *miyakodori* of the Sumida River. The allusion is to a verse in the ninth chapter of the 10th-century *Tales of Ise (Ise monogatari)*, in which travellers, when told the name of the bird by the ferryman, are reminded of the loved ones they have left behind in Kyoto, the capital (*miyako*).

This print depicts the same area as plates 35 and 36, and here, too, our gaze is directed towards the north. This time, though, the famous silhouette of Mount Tsukuba, shown on the left, is depicted in its authentic shape: the right-hand peak is a little higher than the left.

Only in the very early impressions from this woodblock, such as the one reproduced here, is the sky enlivened by yellow and blue stripes above the horizon by means of a technique known as *atenashi bokashi*: these effects are not indicated on the woodblock itself, but were added by the printer. Another such gradation in the case of the gulls emphasizes their slight bobbing movement on the water.

Die Brennöfen und die Hashiba-Fähre am Fluss Sumidagawa

Eine langgezogene schwarzgraue Rauchwolke zieht über den Fluss Sumidagawa und am Wald mit dem Schrein Suijin auf dem gegenüberliegenden Ufer vorbei. Sie löst sich seltsamerweise auch im Himmel nicht auf. Die Form des Rauches wird von der Holzmaserung der Druckplatte auf dem Fluss in umgekehrter Richtung wieder aufgenommen.

Der Rauch ist Blickfang und Teil des Bildthemas zugleich. Er stammt von einem der runden Brennöfen im unmittelbaren Vordergrund. Die Kiefernzweige, mit denen sie befeuert wurden, sorgten dafür, dass es ständig rauchte. Den Vorrat an Brennmaterial sehen wir zwischen den Öfen aufgehäuft. In den Brennöfen wurden neben Ziegeln auch kleine Figürchen von Katzen, Füchsen und Waschbären produziert. Die bis heute populären *maneki neko*, Katzen mit einladend erhobener Tatze, die man gerne in Geschäften aufstellt, wurden erstmals in diesen Öfen gebrannt. Touristen und Gläubige kauften sie und ließen sie teilweise als Opfergaben in Tempeln und Schreinen zurück.

Zwei Boote der im Titel genannten Fähre begegnen einander in der Mitte des Flusses, während im Vordergrund Möwen der Art *miyakodori* („Hauptstadtvogel") auf den Wellen schaukeln. In

dem von Katsushika Hokusai (1760–1849) illustrierten Buch *Blick auf die beiden Ufer des Sumidagawa (Sumidagawa ryōgan ichiran)* aus der ersten Dekade des 19. Jahrhunderts bringen die beigefügten Scherzgedichte den Ort Hashiba mit den *miyakodori* des Sumidagawa in Verbindung. Damit beziehen sie sich auf ein Gedicht der neunten Episode aus den *Geschichten von Ise (Ise monogatari)* des 10. Jahrhunderts. Darin befragen Reisende einen Fährmann nach dem Namen des Vogels und denken daraufhin an ihre Geliebte, die in der Hauptstadt (*miyako*) Kyoto geblieben ist.

Auf dem Holzschnitt ist dieselbe Gegend, mit Blick nach Norden, dargestellt wie auf den Tafeln 35 und 36. Hier ist die Silhouette des Bergs Tsukubasan am linken Bildrand so dargestellt, wie sie sich in Wirklichkeit präsentiert: Der rechte Gipfel ist ein wenig höher als der linke.

Nur in den ganz frühen Abzügen wie dem hier abgebildeten wird der Himmel von einem gelben und einem blauen Streifen über dem Horizont belebt, der auf der Druckplatte nicht angegeben ist, entsprechend der *atenashi bokashi* genannten Technik. Eine weitere solche Gradierung bei den Möwen betont ihr leichtes Schaukeln auf dem Wasser.

Les fours à tuiles et le bac de Hashiba sur la rive de la Sumidagawa

Un long nuage de fumée gris-noir s'étire au-dessus de la rivière Sumidagawa, passant le long de la forêt et du sanctuaire Suijin sur la rive opposée de la rivière – fait singulier, sans se dissoudre aucunement dans le ciel. Dans la rivière, la forme de la fumée est reprise en sens opposé par les veinures du bois d'impression.

L'immense volute de fumée joue à la fois le rôle d'accroche visuelle et de sujet de l'image. Elle sort d'un des fours qu'on aperçoit au tout premier plan. Les aiguilles de pin qui les alimentaient fumaient continuellement. Le matériau de combustion apparaît entassé parmi les fours. Outre les tuiles, on y cuisait aussi de petites figurines de chats, de renards et de ratons laveurs. Ces *maneki neko* restés populaires jusqu'à nos jours – des chats engageants donnant la patte que l'on aimait exposer dans les magasins –, occupaient le haut du four au moment de la cuisson. Les touristes et les fidèles les achetaient et les laissaient parfois comme offrandes dans les temples et les sanctuaires.

Deux barques de la ligne citée dans le titre se croisent au milieu de la rivière, tandis qu'au premier plan, des mouettes de l'espèce *miyakodori* (« oiseaux de la capitale ») voguent sur l'eau. Dans le livre imprimé illustré par Katsushika Hokusai

(1760–1849) *Regard sur les deux rives de la Sumidagawa (Sumidagawa ryōgan ichiran*, années 1810), les poèmes humoristiques qui accompagnent l'ouvrage mettent la ville de Hashiba en rapport avec les *miyakodori* de la Sumidagawa. Ils se réfèrent ainsi à un poème du neuvième épisode des *Histoires d'Ise (Ise monogatari)* du Xᵉ siècle, dans lesquelles, après avoir demandé le nom des oiseaux à un passeur, des voyageurs songent ensuite à leurs amoureuses restées à Kyoto, la capitale (*miyako*).

Cette estampe montre la même contrée que les planches 35 et 36, et la vue est orientée au nord. Ici la célèbre silhouette du mont Tsukubasan, près du bord gauche de l'image, est représentée telle qu'elle apparaît réellement : le sommet de droite est un peu plus élevé que celui de gauche.

Seuls les tout premiers tirages comme celui que nous reproduisons ici montrent un ciel animé, juste au-dessus de l'horizon, par deux bandes, l'une jaune, l'autre bleue, bandes qui n'avaient pas été indiquées sur le bois d'impression conformément à la technique dite *atenashi bokashi*. Un autre dégradé de ce genre apparaît aussi au niveau des mouettes pour souligner leur léger balancement sur l'eau.

58

廓中東雲

Kakuchū shinonome
4–1857

Dawn in Yoshiwara

Government-controlled pleasure districts had existed in Edo since the second decade of the 17th century. The Yoshiwara district was originally located in Nihonbashi, very close to the shogun's castle, but was destroyed in the disastrous Meireki fire of 1657 and moved to a remote area near Kinryūzan Temple ("Temple of the Golden Dragon") in Asakusa (see plate 39).

The newly built quarter, now called Shin-Yoshiwara, or New Yoshiwara, was strictly regulated by the government. The intention was not, however, to limit "immoral" behaviour, but rather to raise taxes and keep sexually transmitted diseases in check.

This depiction exhibits subtle colour variations. The delicate green beneath the cherry trees, which are already blossoming, suggests both spring and an early morning. It is in harmony with the merest hint of rosy-fingered dawn at the bottom edge of the still largely blue-black night sky.

The men and women are schematically depicted and yet provided with accessories that allow the experienced viewer to read the picture. Thus, for example, the men in dark clothes in the foreground cover their heads and cheeks, and thus conceal their identities as they leave the quarter. The courtesan in the bright red gown accompanies her clients to the gate. She wears the black-lacquered *geta* sandals reserved for high-ranking prostitutes.

Shin-Yoshiwara had burnt to ashes in the wake of the Ansei earthquake of 1855. Its gates opened again only in the sixth month of 1857. Hiroshige may have submitted a design of the pleasure district to the censors two months prior to the reopening as a result of one of the most dramatic incidents in the history of the quarter: two courtesans had committed suicide with their two lovers in the same room in one of the temporary establishments on the 19th day of this very month. This happened at dawn between two and four o'clock in the morning. Hiroshige referred to this time of day in the title and rendered the atmosphere of daybreak effectively in this print. The colour nuances and the few people on the street at the main entrance to the quarter create an uncanny mood and allude to the ominous event.

Morgengrauen in Yoshiwara

Von der Regierung kontrollierte Vergnügungsviertel gab es in Edo bereits seit den 1610er Jahren. Das Viertel Yoshiwara lag ursprünglich im Stadtteil Nihonbashi, ganz in der Nähe des shogunalen Schlosses, wurde aber im desaströsen Meireki-Feuer von 1657 zerstört und in eine abgelegene Gegend in der Nähe des Tempels Kinryūzan (Tempel des Goldenen Drachens) im Stadtteil Asakusa verlegt (siehe Tafel 39).

Die Regierung hatte ein strenges Auge auf das neu erbaute Viertel, das nun Shin-("Neu"-) Yoshiwara hieß. Damit sollte nicht etwa „unmoralisches" Treiben eingedämmt werden, es ging vielmehr darum, Steuern zu erheben und Geschlechtskrankheiten in Schach zu halten.

Auf diesem Blatt sind subtile Farbschattierungen zu sehen: Das zarte Grün am Boden unter den schon erblühten Kirschbäumen deutet den Frühling und die frühe Morgenstunde an. Es harmoniert mit dem Hauch von Morgenröte am unteren Rand des noch weitgehend nachtschwarzen Himmels.

Die Männer und Frauen sind zwar schematisch gestaltet, aber mit Accessoires ausgestattet, die es dem erfahrenen Betrachter erlauben, das Bild auf einer anderen Ebene zu verstehen. So tragen etwa die dunkel gekleideten Männer im Vordergrund beim Verlassen einer Seitenstraße des Viertels ein Tuch um Kopf und Wangen, mit dem sie ihre Identität verhüllen. Die Kurtisane im leuchtend roten Übergewand begleitet ihren Kunden bis ans Tor. Sie trägt die schwarz lackierten Geta-Sandalen einer hochrangigen Prostituierten.

Das während des Ansei-Erdbebens von 1855 völlig abgebrannte Shin-Yoshiwara konnte erst im sechsten Monat 1857 wieder seine Tore öffnen. Warum Hiroshige den Zensoren schon zwei Monate zuvor einen Entwurf für diesen Holzschnitt vorlegte, mag an einem der dramatischsten Zwischenfälle in der Geschichte dieses Viertels gelegen haben: Zwei Kurtisanen hatten mit ihren beiden Freiern am 19. Tag jenes Monats in demselben Raum eines temporären Freudenhauses Selbstmord begangen. Das geschah zwischen zwei und vier Uhr früh, im Morgengrauen also, das Hiroshige im Titel aufgegriffen und hier effektvoll in Szene gesetzt hat. Auch die durch die Farbnuancen und die wenigen Menschen erzeugte unheimliche Stimmung der Straße am Haupteingang zum Viertel spielt auf das unheilvolle Geschehen an.

Premières lueurs de l'aube à Yoshiwara

Les quartiers des plaisirs contrôlés par le gouvernement ont existé à Edo dès les années 1610. Le quartier de Yoshiwara fut d'abord situé à Nihonbashi, aux abords immédiats du château shogunal, mais après sa dévastation par l'incendie de Meireki en 1657, il fut transféré dans une zone éloignée située aux environs du temple Kinryūzan (le temple du Dragon d'or) à Asakusa (cf. pl. 39).

Le gouvernement exerçait un contrôle sévère sur le nouveau quartier désormais appelé Shin(« nouveau »)-Yoshiwara. En l'occurrence, il s'agissait moins d'endiguer des activités éventuellement considérées comme « immorales » que de lever des impôts et de tenir les maladies vénériennes en échec.

Cette feuille présente de subtils ombrages : sous les cerisiers clôturés et déjà fleuris, le vert délicat du sol annonce le printemps et l'heure matinale et s'harmonise avec la couleur diaphane de l'aurore près du bord inférieur du ciel nocturne encore largement plongé dans l'obscurité.

Les hommes et les femmes sont certes représentés schématiquement, mais arborent aussi des accessoires qui permettent au spectateur averti de comprendre l'image à un autre niveau. Ainsi, au premier plan, les hommes vêtus d'habits sombres qui quittent une rue latérale du quartier portent un tissu couvrant la tête et les joues pour cacher leur identité. La courtisane en habit de dessus rouge vif raccompagne son client jusqu'à la porte du quartier. Elle porte des getas, sandales laquées de noir réservées au prostituées de haut rang.

Shin-Yoshiwara, qui fut entièrement détruit par un incendie pendant le séisme d'Ansei de 1855, ne put rouvrir ses portes qu'au sixième mois 1857. La raison pour laquelle Hiroshige soumit un projet pour cette estampe à la censure deux mois avant cette date peut être liée à un des faits divers les plus dramatiques de l'histoire du quartier. Le 19ème jour du même mois, deux prostituées et leurs clients s'étaient suicidés dans la même chambre d'un établissement temporaire. Ceci eut lieu entre deux et quatre heures du matin, aux premières lueurs de l'aube donc, comme Hiroshige l'évoque dans le titre et le met en scène de manière spectaculaire. L'ambiance étrange près de l'entrée principale du quartier, telle qu'elle est générée par les subtilités chromatiques et les rares passants de la rue, est une allusion à cet événement funeste.

59

吾妻橋
金龍山
遠望

Azumabashi Kinryūzan enbō
8–1857

Distant View of Kinryūzan Temple in Asakusa and the Azuma Bridge

This view is dominated by the pleasure boat that bisects the picture in the foreground. A geisha, whose elegant coiffure is held in place by a gold hairpin, is sitting in the boat; she is cropped so severely that only a part of her hairdo and gown are visible. The red of her collar and *obi*, a decorative sash, provide an effective colour contrast to the grey of her elegant, patterned over-garment. She is probably on her way to the nearby pleasure district with companions and a guest.

In this print, Hiroshige creates a variation on the play of hints and symbols. In spite of the dating to the eighth month in the date seal at the top right-hand corner, the scene is transferred to the second or third month of the lunar calendar.

The season is indicated by the cherry-blossom petals wafting decoratively across the scene, as well as by the remnants of snow on Mount Fuji. The mountain rises above the distant horizon, framed by the superstructure of the boat as it glides by. Centre right, a five-storey pagoda rises into the sky, and next to it we see the main building of the most important temple in the district of Asakusa, the Kinryūzan, the "Temple of the Golden Dragon" (see plate 99).

The contrast between the transitory and the eternal can be understood as the theme of the picture: the cherry-blossom petals, falling from the trees after just a brief period of splendour, and the ephemeral erotic pleasures enjoyed in Yoshiwara, both contrast with the static sacred mountain and the two temple buildings.

Der Tempel Kinryūzan in Asakusa und die Brücke Azumabashi aus der Ferne

Bildbestimmend durchschneidet ein Vergnügungsboot das Blatt. Eine Geisha, deren elegante Frisur von einer goldfarbenen Haarnadel zusammengehalten wird, sitzt links im Boot. Sie ist so scharf angeschnitten, dass nur ein Teil der Haartracht und des Gewandes zu sehen ist. Zu ihrem edlen, graugemusterten Übergewand bieten der rot gewirkte Kragen und ihr Obi-Schmuckgürtel einen reizvollen Farbkontrast. Wahrscheinlich befindet sie sich zusammen mit Begleiterinnen und einem Gast auf dem Weg ins nahegelegene Vergnügungsviertel Yoshiwara.

Hiroshige variiert auf diesem Blatt das Spiel mit Andeutungen und Symbolen. Entgegen der Datierung auf den achten Monat im Datumssiegel am oberen Rand ist hier die Szene in den zweiten oder dritten Monat des Mondkalenders verlegt.

Die Jahreszeit wird durch die dekorativ über das Blatt wehenden Kirschblütenblätter sowie den mit einem Rest von Schnee bekrönten Berg Fuji angegeben. Der Berg erhebt sich am Horizont, gerahmt vom Dachaufbau des vorbeigleitenden Bootes. Rechts im Mittelgrund ragt die fünfstöckige Pagode in den Himmel empor und daneben erstreckt sich das Hauptgebäude des wichtigsten Tempels im Stadtteil Asakusa, des Kinryūzan ("Tempel des Goldenen Drachen", siehe Tafel 99).

Der Gegensatz zwischen Vergänglichkeit und Ewigem kann als Thema der Komposition verstanden werden: Die nach nur kurzer, prachtvoller Blütezeit herabfallenden Kirschblütenblätter sowie das ephemere Liebesabenteuer in Yoshiwara kontrastieren mit dem statischen heiligen Berg und den beiden Tempelgebäuden.

Vue lointaine du temple Kinryūzan à Asakusa et du pont Azumabashi

Une barque d'agrément détermine la composition de l'image qu'elle coupe par sa diagonale. À gauche dans la barque est assise une geisha dont l'élégante coiffure est maintenue par une épingle à cheveux dorée. Elle est coupée si abruptement par le bord de l'image qu'on ne peut voir qu'une partie de la coiffure et de l'habit. Son col à passementeries rouges et sa ceinture ornementale (*obi*) forment un charmant contraste avec les dessins gris de son noble vêtement de dessus. La geisha, ses compagnes et un invité se rendent vraisemblablement à Yoshiwara, le proche quartier des plaisirs.

Dans cette feuille, Hiroshige joue de toutes sortes d'allusions et de symboles. Contrairement à l'époque du huitième mois indiquée par le cachet de datation apposé près du bord supérieur de l'image, la présente scène se déroule pendant le deuxième ou troisième mois du calendrier lunaire.

La saison est en effet indiquée par les pétales de fleurs de cerisiers qui passent à travers la feuille sous l'effet du vent et par le reste de neige qui blanchit encore le mont Fuji. La montagne se dresse à l'horizon, encadrée par la structure du toit de la barque qui glisse à travers l'image. Au second plan à droite, une pagode à cinq étages s'élève dans le ciel, à côté d'elle s'étend le bâtiment principal du Kinryūzan (« Temple du Dragon d'or » ; cf. pl. 99), le plus grand temple d'Asakusa.

Le thème principal qu'il convient de voir dans cette composition est l'opposition entre la fugacité et l'éternité : les pétales de fleurs de cerisiers bientôt emportés par le vent et le caractère éphémère de l'aventure amoureuse à Yoshiwara y contrastent avec le statisme de la montagne sacrée et des bâtiments du temple.

せ
き
口
上
水
端
は
せ
を
庵
椿
や
ま

Sekiguchi jōsuibata Bashōan Tsubakiyama
4–1857

Bashō's Hermitage on Camellia Hill beside the Aqueduct at Sekiguchi

The meandering Sekiguchi Aqueduct was one of Edo's oldest means of supplying water to the city. The elevated vantage point is approximately on the same level as Bashō's Hermitage mentioned in the title, which is situated on the hill to the right. This structure was erected in memory of the great haiku poet Matsuo Bashō (1644–1694) by his pupils on the occasion of the 50th anniversary of his death, which by traditional Japanese reckoning was 1743 in the Western calendar.

The Sekiguchi Aqueduct was built at the beginning of the 17th century, and was maintained and extended by an annual levy to which all inhabitants of Edo were subjected, irrespective of their position in society.

The Camellia Hill (Tsubakiyama) on the right still looks much as it did in Hiroshige's day. The Hosokawa, then a powerful daimyō family – whose members include Prime Minister Hosokawa Morihiro (in office 1993/94) – own this land to this day. The hill is one of the few green retreats in densely populated Greater Tokyo still in private hands.

Bashō-Klause und der Kamelienhügel neben dem Aquädukt bei Sekiguchi

Das in einer S-Kurve verlaufende Sekiguchi-Aquädukt gehört zur ältesten Wasserversorgungsanlage von Edo. Etwa auf Augenhöhe des erhöhten Betrachterstandpunktes präsentiert Hiroshige rechter Hand auf einem Hügel liegend die im Titel erwähnte Bashō-Klause. Schüler des großen Haiku-Dichters Matsuo Bashō (1644–1694) hatten das Gebäude zum Gedenken an den Dichter anlässlich seines fünfzigsten Todesjahres errichtet, das im Jahr 1743 des Gregorianischen Sonnenkalenders lag.

Das Sekiguchi-Aquädukt wurde zu Beginn des 17. Jahrhunderts gebaut und durch eine jährlich zu entrichtende Abgabe instandgehalten und erweitert. Alle Bewohner von Edo, unabhängig von ihrem Stand, hatten diese Steuer zu entrichten.

Der den rechten Bildrand einnehmende „Kamelienhügel" (Tsubakiyama) sieht noch heute aus wie zur Zeit Hiroshiges. Die mächtige Daimyō-Familie Hosokawa, die noch 1993–1994 den Premierminister Hosokawa Morihiro stellte, besitzt dieses Land nach wie vor. Der Hügel ist im dicht besiedelten Großraum Tokyo eine der wenigen grünen Oasen, die sich noch in privater Hand befinden.

La cellule de Bashō et la Colline aux camélias au bord de l'aqueduc près de Sekiguchi

Avec sa forme serpentine, l'aqueduc de Sekiguchi est un des plus anciens dispositifs d'alimentation en eau d'Edo. À droite, à peu près à la hauteur du point de vue légèrement surélevé du spectateur, Hiroshige nous présente, logée à flanc de colline, la cellule de Bashō évoquée par le titre. Cette construction fut édifiée par des disciples en mémoire de Matsuo Bashō (1644–1694), le grand poète de haïkus, à l'occasion du cinquantenaire de sa mort, en l'an 1743 du calendrier grégorien.

La construction de l'aqueduc de Sekiguchi remonte au début du XVIIe siècle. Son entretien et son agrandissement étaient financés par un impôt annuel auquel étaient soumis tous les habitants d'Edo sans distinction de classe sociale.

La « Colline aux camélias » (Tsubakiyama) conserve aujourd'hui encore l'aspect qu'elle avait à l'époque de Hiroshige. La puissante famille de daimyōs Hosokawa, dont fut notamment issu le premier ministre du Japon (1993–1994) Hosokawa Morihiro, possède encore cette terre comme par le passé. La colline située en pleine ville dans une zone fortement bâtie est une des rares oasis de verdure à être encore propriété privée à Tokyo.

市
ケ
谷
八
幡

Ichigaya Hachiman
10–1858

Hachiman Shrine in Ichigaya

In a bird's-eye view of the Hachiman Shrine in Ichigaya in the fourth volume of Hiroshige's *Illustrated Guide to Famous Views of Edo* (*Edo meisho zue*) of 1836, the extensive shrine precincts, with its little shrine and temple buildings, takes up almost the entire double-spread composition.

In the present view, however, Hiroshige has emphasized the contrast between the lively shopping and amusement street in the foreground and the main building of the Hachiman Shrine, which rises majestically above stylized clouds. A steep and deserted flight of steps leads to the shrine, which stands on a wooded hill amongst cherry trees in full blossom. To the left and right of the steps are the leaves of tea bushes, indicated by little dots, for which the fox deity Inari, venerated in the same shrine, was famous.

Ichigaya today is an unspectacular station on East Japan Railway, but in the mid-19th century it was famous for its teahouses and prostitutes.

The censors dated this print to the tenth month of the fifth year of the Ansei era (1858). Hiroshige had died a month earlier, probably of cholera. Some art historians have therefore suggested attributing the print to Shigenobu (1826–1869), also known as Hiroshige II (see also plates 12, 114).

Hachiman-Schrein in Ichigaya

In einer Darstellung des Hachiman-Schreins in Ichigaya im vierten Band des *Illustrierten Führers zu berühmten Ansichten von Edo* (*Edo meisho zue*) von 1836 nimmt der weitläufige Schreinbezirk mit seinen vielen kleinen Schrein- und Tempelgebäuden von einer Vogelperspektive aus gesehen fast die gesamte querformatige Komposition ein.

Im vorliegenden Blatt hingegen hat Hiroshige den Gegensatz zwischen der belebten Geschäfts- und Vergnügungsstraße im Vordergrund und dem oberhalb der stilisierten Wolkenbänder thronenden Hauptgebäude des Hachiman-Schreins hervorgehoben. Eine menschenleere, steile Treppe führt zu dem Schrein, der auf einem bewaldeten Hügel zwischen hell erblühten Kirschbäumen steht. Links und rechts neben der Treppe sind die mit kleinen Punkten aufgetragenen Blätter von Teepflanzen zu sehen, für die die im selben Heiligtum verehrte Fuchsgottheit Inari berühmt war.

Ichigaya ist heute ein eher unspektakulärer Bahnhof des Liniennetzes der East Japan Railway in Tokyo, war aber Mitte des 19. Jahrhunderts berühmt für seine Teehäuser und Prostituierten.

Dieses Blatt wurde von den Zensoren auf den zehnten Monat des fünften Jahres der Ära Ansei (1858) datiert. Einen Monat zuvor war Hiroshige, vermutlich an Cholera, gestorben. Einige Kunsthistoriker schreiben das Blatt daher Shigenobu (1826–1869), auch Hiroshige II genannt, zu (ebenso wie Tafeln 12, 114).

Le sanctuaire de Hachiman à Ichigaya

Dans le quatrième tome (1836) du *Guide illustré des vues célèbres d'Edo* (*Edo meisho zue*), une représentation du même sanctuaire montre le vaste domaine sacré avec ses nombreux temples et dépendances occupant la quasi totalité de la composition de format horizontal.

Dans la présente feuille, Hiroshige a en revanche souligné l'opposition entre la rue marchande et de plaisirs au premier plan et le bâtiment principal du sanctuaire Hachiman qui trône au-dessus de bancs de nuages stylisés. Un escalier escarpé et désert conduit au sanctuaire bâti sur une colline boisée parmi de clairs cerisiers en fleurs. À gauche et à droite de l'escalier, indiquées par de petits points, on peut voir les feuilles de théiers dont la réputation se devait notamment au dieu renard Inari vénéré dans le sanctuaire.

Ichigaya est aujourd'hui une station peu spectaculaire du réseau ferroviaire de la East Japan Railway à Tokyo, mais était célèbre au XIXᵉ siècle pour ses maisons de thé et ses prostituées.

Les censeurs ont daté cette feuille du dixième mois de la cinquième année de l'ère Ansei (1858). Hiroshige était mort un mois plus tôt du choléra. Quelques historiens ont de ce fait proposé d'attribuer l'estampe à Shigenobu (1826–1869), dit Hiroshige II (cf. aussi pl. 12, 114).

玉
川
堤
の
花

Tamagawa tsutsumi no hana
2–1856

Cherry Blossoms on the Banks of the Tama River

This splendid avenue of cherry trees along the Tama River was laid out under the eighth shogun Tokugawa Yoshimune (1684–1751), around 1730. He was responsible for the first public parks, such as the Asukayama Park (plate 17), which were designed to provide Edo citizens with spaces for relaxation. The planting of cherry trees along the Tama River also served to strengthen the banks of this channel, which was an important part of the city's water supply, and the leaves and blossoms of the cherry tree were believed to purify the water.

In this scene, there is not a single petal either on the bank or drifting on the water. Thus Hiroshige points to the brevity of the early blossom time, a magical period, lasting at most just a few days. All places known for cherry trees then provided the occasion for alcohol-fuelled conviviality.

The brothel district of Shinjuku, hinted at in the guise of the brightly lit interior on the far right, contrasts with the relaxed strollers. On the second floor of one establishment, two prostitutes with elaborate hairstyles are dressed in red, and together with a maid they are seeing to the requirements of a guest in blue clothing.

The censors sanctioned this print, one of the first five in the series, in the second month of 1856. While the remaining four were integrated into the autumn and winter sections (plates 96, 103, 108, 110), only this one focuses on the springtime motif of blossoming cherry trees.

Kirschblüten am Ufer des Flusses Tamagawa

Die prachtvolle Kirschbaumallee am Fluss Tamagawa wurde unter dem achten Shogun Tokugawa Yoshimune (1684–1751) um 1730 angelegt. Yoshimune zeichnet verantwortlich für die Einrichtung der ersten öffentlichen Parks, wie etwa auch des Asukayama-Parks (siehe Tafel 17), die dem Vergnügen der Städter in Edo dienten. Durch die Bepflanzung mit Kirschbäumen wurden die Ufer dieses wichtigen Wasserversorgungskanals aber zugleich befestigt. Man war zudem der Überzeugung, dass Blätter und Blüten des Kirschbaums eine reinigende Wirkung auf das Wasser hätten.

Der Holzschnitt gehört zu den ersten fünf Kompositionen der Serie, die allesamt im zweiten Monat des Jahres 1856 von den Zensoren abgesegnet worden waren. Während die anderen Blätter im Nachhinein in die Herbst- und Wintersektionen eingegliedert wurden (siehe Tafeln 96, 103, 108, 110), thematisiert nur dieser das Frühlingsmotiv der blühenden Kirschbäume.

Kein einziges Blütenblatt liegt am Ufer des Flusses, keines treibt auf dem Wasser. Hiroshige deutet dadurch die meist nur wenige Tage andauernde magische Zeit des ersten Aufblühens an, das an allen bekannten Orten mit Kirschbäumen Anlass für geselliges, oft auch feucht-fröhliches Zusammensein bot.

Im Gegensatz zu den vergnüglichen Flaneuren wird das Prostituiertenviertel von Shinjuku in Form des hell erleuchteten Interieurs ganz rechts am Blattrand nur angedeutet. Im ersten Stock eines Etablissements bemühen sich zwei rotgewandete Prostituierte mit aufwändigen Frisuren und eine Bedienstete um ihren Gast in blauem Gewand.

Fleurs de cerisiers au bord de la Tamagawa

La splendide allée de cerisiers qui borde la rivière Tamagawa a été aménagée vers 1730 sous le huitième shogun Yoshimune (1684–1751). Yoshimune fut aussi à l'origine des premiers parcs publics d'Edo, comme le parc Asukayama de la planche 17, parcs qui furent créés pour le délassement des citadins. En même temps, la plantation de cerisiers servait aussi à consolider les berges de l'indispensable canal d'alimentation en eau. De plus, on croyait que les feuilles et les fleurs de cerisiers avaient des vertus purificatrices pour l'eau.

Aucun pétale de fleur de cerisier ne jonche la berge, aucun ne dérive sur l'eau. Hiroshige dépeint donc l'époque magique de la toute première floraison des cerisiers, qui ne dure que quelques jours et qui donne lieu à de joyeuses parties de promenade, souvent bien arrosées, dans tous les endroits célèbres.

Contrairement aux flâneurs enjoués, l'évocation de Shinjuku, le quartier des prostituées, est figurée par un intérieur fortement éclairé tout à fait à droite dans l'image. Au premier étage de l'établissement, une servante et deux prostituées richement coiffées, vêtues de rouge, s'attachent à égayer de leur mieux le client vêtu de bleu.

Cette estampe est une des cinq premières compositions de la série qui furent approuvées par la censure au deuxième mois de l'année 1856. Alors que les quatre autres furent insérées après-coup dans les sections automne et hiver (cf. pl. 96, 103, 108, 110), seule celle-ci illustre le motif printanier des cerisiers en fleurs.

日本橋
江戸ばし

Nihonbashi Edobashi
12–1857

Nihonbashi and Edobashi Bridges

The 42 springtime prints, and the 30 views arranged in the summer section, both begin with a depiction of the Nihonbashi Bridge, the point from which all distances in Japan were measured. In contrast to plate 1, however, only a section of the balustrade of the pivotal bridge is visible in this composition. Three horizontal beams at first glance block our view, but then guide it past the fishing boats and the schematically indicated Edobashi Bridge to the sun rising on the horizon behind white warehouses. The name "Nihonbashi" means "Bridge of the Rising Sun" – the rising sun stands for Japan (the word "Nihon" means "origin of the sun"), and is symbolized as a red disc on a white background on the Japanese national flag.

The ornamental metal top of the vertical post on the left, the *giboshi* (see plates 65, 76), was reserved for the most important bridges and underlined the significance of the Nihonbashi.

The laws of linear perspective demand that we see the top surface of the upper horizontal beam, but Hiroshige does not show it. He subordinated Western techniques to his own compositional needs, and used them only when appropriate to the design of a specific image.

Unlike the first print, this view is directed towards the east: in other words, the vantage point has shifted 180 degrees. The fish market of plate 1 is situated behind us to the left, on the north bank of the river, and is hinted at by a severely cropped wooden barrel in which a fishmonger is transporting the prohibitively expensive first *bonitos* of the season. Culinary habits in Edo were strongly influenced by the seasons, and the first *bonito* represented early summer.

Die Brücken Nihonbashi und Edobashi

Die 42 Frühlingsblätter beginnen mit der Darstellung der Brücke Nihonbashi, und auch die 30 dem Sommer gewidmeten Ansichten werden mit einem Blick auf diesen Ausgangspunkt aller geografischen Messungen eingeläutet. Im Vergleich zur ersten Tafel ist nur ein Geländersegment der Brücke zu sehen. Drei Querbalken versperren den Blick zunächst und leiten ihn dann vorbei an den Fischerbooten und der schemenhaften Edobashi-Brücke, direkt in die über den weißen Lagerhäusern aufgehende Sonne am Horizont. Der Name „Nihonbashi" wurde als „die Brücke der aufgehenden Sonne" gedeutet. Die aufgehende Sonne steht für Japan („Nihon" bedeutet wörtlich „Ursprung der Sonne") und wird als roter Kreis vor weißem Grund in der japanischen Nationalflagge symbolisiert. Die metallene Bekrönung des Brückenpfeilers, *giboshi* (siehe Tafeln 65, 76), auf der linken Bildseite ist nur den wichtigsten Brücken vorbehalten und unter-streicht die Bedeutung der Nihonbashi.

Hiroshige nimmt sich die Freiheit, am obersten Geländerbalken keine Aufsicht auf den Balken darzustellen, wie es die Gesetze der Linearperspektive verlangen würden. Er ordnet das westliche Kompositionsmittel der Perspektive seinem Gestaltungswillen unter und setzt es immer dann ein, wenn es sich für den Aufbau eines bestimmten Blattes eignet.

Im Gegensatz zum ersten Blatt blicken wir hier nach Osten, der Betrachterstandpunkt ist also um 180 Grad gewendet. Der Fischmarkt von Tafel 1 liegt links hinter dem Betrachter am nördlichen Flussufer und wird durch einen angeschnittenen Holzbottich angedeutet, in dem ein Fischhändler die sündhaft teuren ersten Bonitos (Thunfische) der Saison transportiert. Die kulinarischen Gepflogenheiten waren in Edo von den Jahreszeiten geprägt, und der erste Bonito steht für den Frühsommer.

Les ponts Nihonbashi et Edobashi

Tout comme la section hiver, les 42 feuilles qui composent la section printemps débutent avec la représentation du pont Nihonbashi. Il en va de même pour les trente vues consacrées à l'été, qui sont également inaugurées par le point zéro de toutes les distances géographiques du Japon. Contrairement à la première estampe, seul un segment du parapet est ici représenté. Trois poutres transversales barrent la vue avant de la diriger – le long des barques de pêche et de la lointaine silhouette du pont Edobashi – directement à l'horizon et au soleil levant sur les entrepôts blancs. Le nom « Nihonbashi » a été interprété comme « pont du Soleil levant ». Le soleil levant est lui-même l'emblème du Japon symbolisé par le cercle rouge sur fond blanc du drapeau national (littéralement, « Nihon » signifie « origine du soleil »).

Dans la partie gauche de l'image apparaît un *giboshi*. Ce couronnement métallique des piliers de support du pont (cf. pl. 65, 76) n'était réservé qu'aux ouvrages de première impor-tance et souligne ici le rang du Nihonbashi.

Contrairement aux exigences de la perspective linéaire, l'artiste a pris la liberté de ne pas représenter la poutre supérieure du parapet en vue plongeante. Chez Hiroshige, la perspective, moyen de composition importé d'Occident, reste soumise à la volonté créatrice de l'artiste, qui ne l'emploie que lorsqu'elle se prête à la composition d'une feuille particulière.

Contrairement à la première planche de la série, la vue est ici dirigée vers l'est ; le point de vue est donc tourné de 180 degrés. Ici, le marché aux poissons de la planche 1 est donc situé à gauche derrière le spectateur, près de la rive nord du fleuve ; il est indiqué par le bac en bois coupé par le bord de l'image, et dans lequel un marchand de poisson industrieux propose les premiers *bonitos* (thons) de la saison. À Edo, les usages culinaires étaient entièrement liés aux saisons, et le premier *bonito* marque ici le début de l'été.

Nihonbashi tōri itchōme ryakuzu
8–1858

View of Nihonbashi itchōme Street

Bustling activity characterizes the main street of the Nihonbashi quarter, a district of Edo/ Tokyo known then, as now, for the magnificence of its traditional stores.

In close and closed formation, a colourful group of dancers is walking along the street, protected from the searing summer sun by a richly decorated double parasol. This Sumiyoshi ensemble, though native to Edo, took its name from one of the most famous shrines in Osaka and its members earned their livelihood through regular street performances. They are followed by a shamisen player in a dark-blue garment.

Outside the shop named, Shirokiya ("White Tree") on the right, an elderly man in a bright yellow hat is taking a hearty bite out of a small melon. To his immediate left, the scantily clad deliveryman of the Tōkyōan *soba* restaurant is carrying a tray with a small bottle of *sake* and two cups, along with a lacquered multi-tiered box filled with buckwheat noodles (*soba*). These deliverymen still constitute an important feature of life in a city where people often cannot leave their workplace even for a short lunch break.

The Shirokiya shop was founded in 1662 and developed over the centuries into one of the city's largest department stores, finally becoming part of the Tōkyū chain. Other large businesses such as Matsuzakaya and Daimaru look back on traditions just as long. Their modern flagship stores are still in the immediate vicinity of the sites they occupied in the 19th century, when Hiroshige composed this print.

Ansicht von der Straße Nihonbashi itchōme

Geschäftiges Treiben herrscht auf der Hauptstraße des Viertels Nihonbashi, eines bis heute wegen seiner prachtvollen und traditionsreichen Läden bekannten Stadtteils von Edo beziehungsweise Tokyo.

In geschlossener Formation zieht eine farbenfrohe Tanzgruppe durch die Straße, die sich vor der brütenden Sommerhitze durch einen reich verzierten, zweilagigen Sonnenschirm schützt. Die Sumiyoshi-Truppe, die mit regelmäßigen Straßenaufführungen ihren Unterhalt verdiente, stammte aus Edo, trug aber den Namen einer der bekanntesten Schreine in Osaka. Den Tänzern folgt eine Shamisen-Spielerin in dunkelblauem Gewand.

Vor dem Laden Shirokiya („Weißbaum") am rechten Bildrand beißt ein älterer Herr mit leuchtend gelbem Hut herzhaft in eine kleine Honigmelone. Links neben ihm balanciert der luftig gekleidete Lieferant des Soba-Restaurants Tōkyōan ein Tablett mit einer kleinen Sakeflasche und zwei Bechern sowie einem lackierten Stapelkasten, der mit Buchweizennudeln gefüllt ist. Diese Lieferanten bilden auch heute noch einen integralen Bestandteil des Stadtlebens, das es häufig nicht zulässt, den Arbeitsplatz für ein kurzes Mittagessen zu verlassen.

Das Geschäft Shirokiya wurde im Jahr 1662 gegründet und entwickelte sich über die Jahrhunderte hinweg zu einem der größten Warenhäuser der Stadt, bis es Teil der Handelskette Tōkyū wurde. Andere große Unternehmen wie Matsuzakaya und Daimaru verfügen über eine ähnlich lange Tradition. Ihre modernen Hauptfilialen befinden sich auch heute noch in unmittelbarer Nähe der Standorte des 19. Jahrhunderts, als Hiroshige diesen Holzschnitt schuf.

Vue de la rue Nihonbashi itchōme

Une forte activité règne dans la rue principale de Nihonbashi, un quartier d'Edo (aujourd'hui Tokyo) aujourd'hui encore réputé pour ses traditionnelles boutiques de luxe.

Un groupe de danseurs riche en couleurs passe dans la rue en formation serrée, se protégeant de l'étouffante chaleur estivale avec une double ombrelle richement décorée. La troupe Sumiyoshi, qui gagnait sa vie par des spectacles de rue réguliers, était originaire d'Edo, mais portait le nom d'un des plus célèbres sanctuaires d'Osaka. Les danseurs sont suivis par une joueuse de shamisen en habit sombre.

Devant la boutique Shirokiya (« boutique de l'arbre blanc ») près du bord droit de l'image, un homme âgé coiffé d'un chapeau jaune vif mord goulûment dans un melon. À sa gauche, le livreur légèrement vêtu du restaurant Tōkyōan spécialisé dans les nouilles soba, tient un plateau en équilibre sur lequel on peut voir un flacon de saké et un empilement de paniers à vapeur laqués pleins de nouilles de blé. Ces livreurs font aujourd'hui encore partie intégrante de la vie trépidante de Tokyo, dans laquelle le poste de travail ne peut souvent être quitté même pour un court déjeuner.

La boutique Shirokiya a été fondée en 1662. Au fil des siècles, elle est devenue un des grands magasins les plus importants de la ville avant d'être intégrée au groupe Tōkyū. Aujourd'hui, seules quelques grandes entreprises comme Daimaru et Matsuzakaya peuvent également se prévaloir d'une aussi longue tradition. Leurs principales filiales modernes se trouvent encore tout près de leur emplacement au XIXᵉ siècle, à l'époque où Hiroshige créa cette estampe.

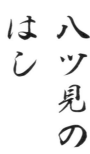

45

八ッ見の
はし

Yatsumi no hashi
8–1856

Yatsumi Bridge

The name of this bridge, *Yatsumi no hashi*, derives from the fact that a total of eight (*yatsu*) bridges (*hashi*) could be seen (*mi*) from it (this figure includes the Yatsumi Bridge itself).

As in plate 1, Hiroshige deliberately presents the contrast between a sacred symbol such as Mount Fuji and scenes from everyday life. The mountain rises majestically above the distant horizon, while in the middle distance we can see the precincts of the shogun's castle.

Two overlapping sunshades in the bottom left-hand corner, cropped by the margin of the print, indicate the dense throng of people crossing Yatsumi Bridge. As the bridge was heavily used, children often got lost in the crowd. There was a signboard, still extant, at the southern end of the structure, on which the names of missing children could be written.

The scene is framed top and bottom by a masterly application of blue *bokashi* gradation for the river and the sky, which are linked by the luxuriant branches of the willow in the foreground.

Die Brücke Yatsumi no hashi

Die Bezeichnung der Brücke *Yatsumi no hashi* entsprang dem Umstand, dass man von ihr aus – sie selbst eingeschlossen – insgesamt acht (*yatsu*) Brücken (*hashi*) sehen (*mi*) konnte.

Ähnlich wie in der ersten Tafel präsentiert Hiroshige bewusst den Kontrast zwischen einem heiligen Symbol wie dem Berg Fuji und Szenen aus dem Alltagsleben. Majestätisch ragt der Berg in der Ferne über den Horizont hinaus, während sich vor ihm weitläufig der Schlossbezirk des Shoguns erstreckt.

Zwei sich überlappende, nur angeschnitten dargestellte Sonnenschirme in der unteren linken Bildecke deuten auf das dichte Menschengedränge auf der Brücke Yatsumi no hashi hin, das in unmittelbarer Nähe des Betrachters vorbeizieht. Die Brücke wurde so stark genutzt, dass in dem Gedränge häufig Kinder verloren gingen. Aus diesem Grund stand am Südende des Bauwerkes eine heute noch erhaltene Tafel, auf der vermisste Kinder eingetragen werden konnten.

In meisterhafter Technik angewendet leuchtet in der Flussmitte die Farbgradierung, so dass die hellblaue, großflächige Ausdehnung des Gewässers eindrucksvoll mit den Farben des Abendhimmels korrespondiert. Dieses Farbenspiel wird durch die üppigen Weidenzweige verstärkt, die ganz im Vordergrund die Motive des Bildes verbinden.

Le pont Yatsumi no hashi

Le terme désignant le pont *Yatsumi no hashi* se doit au fait que l'on pouvait voir (*mi*) en tout huit (*yatsu*) ponts (*hashi*) à partir de celui-ci et en l'incluant.

Un peu comme dans la première estampe de la série, Hiroshige dépeint ici le contraste entre un symbole sacré comme le mont Fuji et quelques scènes de la vie quotidienne. La montagne se dresse majestueuse au loin sur l'horizon, tandis que devant lui s'étend le vaste domaine du château shogunal.

Dans le coin inférieur gauche, deux ombrelles légèrement superposées, coupées par le bord de l'image, renvoient à la foule qui empruntait le pont Yatsumi no hashi et que l'on voit passer ici tout près du spectateur. Le pont était si fréquenté que des enfants se perdaient souvent dans la multitude. C'est pourquoi un panneau encore visible aujourd'hui était placé à son extrémité sud, sur lequel on pouvait inscrire le nom des enfants égarés.

Un magistral dégradé de bleu éclaire le milieu de la rivière, de sorte que la vaste étendue des eaux fait un impressionnant écho aux couleurs du crépuscule. Ce jeu de couleurs est encore renforcé par les foisonnantes branches de saule pleureur au premier plan, qui relient entre eux les différents motifs de l'image.

46

鎧の渡し　小網町

Yoroi no watashi Koami-chō
10–1857

Yoroi Ferry and Koami-chō

Depicted in yellows ranging from delicate to deep, a cloud glows in the unusually designed, almost white sky. A long row of food warehouses, represented only by their outlines, conveys a strong impression of the prosperity and material abundance of Edo. Their lack of colour and their sharp linear recession into the distance contrast with the close-up of an elegant lady in an elaborately patterned and colourful garment on the right.

In front of the warehouses, the bow of a cargo boat projects into the scene from the left. The echo of the bow's shape in the lady's parasol creates a formal link between the opposite banks of the river. Between the two, a man is propelling a small boat in a manner reminiscent of that of a Venetian gondolier. Indeed, like Venice, the Queen of the Adriatic, Edo was characterized by the ubiquitous presence of water, numerous canals and waterborne traffic.

On the left bank of the Nihonbashi River we can see the Yoroi ferry. Ferries were for a long time the preferred means of crossing rivers and above all the waterways that formed part of the system of moats around the shogun's castle, as they were important for defence.

In 1639, the country was largely cut off from the outside world by government decree, enabling the political stability under the Tokugawa regime to grow. Both of these factors contributed to a greater sense of security and to an increase in the number of bridges, for they were now perceived as less of a threat. This in turn meant more mobility and therefore a great improvement in trade.

Die Yoroi-Fähre und Koami-chō

In zarten bis kräftigen Gelbtönen leuchtet eine Wolke am fast weißen, außergewöhnlich gestalteten Himmel. Die lange Reihe der nur in ihren Konturen abgebildeten Lagerhäuser für Lebensmittel vermittelt einen Eindruck von dem Reichtum und der materiellen Fülle der Stadt Edo. Ihre Farblosigkeit und perspektivische Verkleinerung in der Ferne kontrastiert wirkungsvoll mit der Nahansicht einer edlen Dame in aufwändig gemustertem, farbigem Gewand.

Vor den Lagerhäusern ragt von links der Bug eines Transportschiffes in das Bild. Dieser Schiffsbug und der Sonnenschirm der Dame stehen sich versetzt gegenüber und bilden eine formale Verbindung der beiden Ufer. Zwischen ihnen rudert stehend ein Mann, dessen Haltung einem venezianischen Gondoliere gleicht. Ebenso wie Venedig, die italienische Serenissima, wurde Edo maßgeblich geprägt von der Allgegenwart des Wassers, zahlreicher Kanäle und des Schiffsverkehrs.

Am linken Flussufer des Nihonbashigawa ist die Yoroi-Fähre erkennbar. Fähren dienten lange Zeit als bevorzugtes Mittel zur Flussüberquerung, insbesondere bei Gewässern, die zum Wassergrabensystem um das Schloss des Shoguns gehörten und daher wichtig für die Verteidigung waren.

Die im Jahr 1639 von der Regierung initiierte weitgehende Abschottung des Landes sowie die unter den Tokugawa sich entwickelnde politische Stabilität stärkte das Sicherheitsgefühl und führte zur zunehmenden Errichtung von Brücken, da diese nun weniger als Bedrohung empfunden wurden. Sie erleichterten das Überqueren des Wassers und führten zu einer wachsenden Mobilität, die dem Handel zugute kam.

Le bac de Yoroi et Koami-chō

Un nuage jaune dégradé du pâle au vif illumine un ciel presque blanc de facture inhabituelle. La longue rangée d'entrepôts alimentaires représentés seulement en leurs contours schématiques donne une idée de la prospérité matérielle d'Edo. L'absence de couleur et la perspective raccourcie vers le lointain contrastent de manière spectaculaire avec la vue rapprochée d'une noble dame vêtue d'un kimono coloré et richement décoré.

Devant les entrepôts, venant de la gauche, la proue d'une jonque entre dans l'image. Avec leurs formes légèrement décalées, la proue de la jonque et l'ombrelle de la dame se font pendant et réalisent le lien formel entre les deux rives. Entre elles se tient un rameur dont la position rappelle celle d'un gondolier vénitien. Tout comme Venise, la Sérénissime italienne, l'aspect de la ville d'Edo était fortement marqué par l'omniprésence de l'eau, de nombreux canaux et d'une forte circulation fluviale.

Sur la rive gauche du Nihonbashigawa, on reconnaît le bac de Yoroi. Les bacs ont longtemps servi de moyen de transport privilégié pour traverser fleuves et rivières, en particulier pour les eaux du système de douves entourant le château shogunal, qui jouaient un rôle important pour sa défense.

Le fort repli du pays sur lui-même initié par le gouvernement en 1639 et la stabilité politique qui s'était développée sous les Tokugawa confortaient le sentiment de sécurité et conduisirent à la construction de ponts de plus en plus nombreux dans lesquels le pouvoir central cessa peu à peu de voir une menace. Ils facilitaient la traversée de l'eau et conduisirent à une mobilité accrue dont bénéficia notamment le commerce.

昌平橋
聖堂
神田川

Seidō Shrine and the Kanda River from Shōhei Bridge

The steeply curved diagonal of a hillside leads the eye into the scene from the left. Beyond the Shōhei Bridge and the Kanda River, porters and passers-by can be seen by the wall of the Seidō Shrine on the opposite bank. The Seidō ("Sacred Hall") was erected as a Confucian shrine by the fifth Tokugawa shogun, Tsunayoshi (1648–1709), in 1690, and is still extant today.

Both Shōhei Bridge and Shōheizaka Hill take their name from the Japanese pronunciation – "Shōhei" – of the birthplace of Confucius (Chinese: "Changping") in the Shandong Province, pointing to the establishment of Confucianism as the state ethic in Tokugawa Japan (1615–1868). The Ministry of Education, established in 1871 under the Meiji government (1868–1912), turned the main hall of the Daiseiden Confucian temple into the venue for the government's first official exhibition, in 1872; after all, scholarship and education were associated with Confucius and his veneration.

Thus the Kansei Reforms (1787–1793) launched by the regent Matsudaira Sadanobu (1758–1829), which were strongly marked by Confucian ideals, led in 1797 to the establishment of the Confucian Shōheizaka Gakumonjo School, within the precincts of the Confucian shrine. The school was overseen by the shogunate.

In order to lend drama to his composition, Hiroshige exaggerated the size of the hill on the left, on which the rain is beating down, and at the same time placed the crown of the hill on the right farther away than it really is. The *bokashi* effect on both hills is used by Hiroshige to make the grass, now luxuriant after warm summer rain, look particularly dense. The boatmen transporting timber are wearing raincoats made of straw, as are two pedestrians on the opposite hill.

The reproduction of the extremely thin lines of rain, running across the print like a grid, demanded all the exceptional skills of the woodblock cutter (*horishi*). He had to carve the wood from the block in such a way that the fine lines ran absolutely straight without breaking off.

The typical Japanese summer rain is depicted only three times in the entire series (see plates 58, 62), in contrast to the many decorative depictions of snow in the winter scenes.

Die Halle Seidō und der Fluss Kandagawa von der Brücke Shōheibashi aus

Als steil geschwungene Diagonale leitet der Hügel links in das Bild hinein. Hinter dem Fluss Kandagawa und der Brücke Shōheibashi sieht man am gegenüberliegenden Ufer Träger und Passanten an der Mauer der Seidō („Heilige Halle") vorbeiziehen. Sie wurde 1690 als Heiligtum der Konfuzius-Verehrung vom fünften Tokugawa-Shogun Tsunayoshi (1648–1709) errichtet und ist heute noch intakt.

Auch die Brücke Shōheibashi und der Hügel Shōheizaka, deren Namensbestandteil „Shōhei" auf die japanische Aussprache des Geburtsorts von Konfuzius (chinesisch „Changping") in der Provinz Shandong zurückgehen, verweisen auf die Etablierung des Konfuzianismus als Staatsethik im Japan der Tokugawa-Zeit (1615–1868). Das 1871 gegründete Erziehungsministerium der Meiji-Regierung (1868–1912) machte die Haupthalle des Konfuziustempels Daiseiden 1872 zum Ort der ersten öffentlichen Ausstellung der Regierung, verband man doch mit Konfuzius und dessen Verehrung Gelehrsamkeit und Bildung.

So hatten die unter dem Regenten Matsudaira Sadanobu (1758–1829) durchgeführten, stark von konfuzianischen Idealen geprägten Kansei-Reformen (1787–1793) zur Folge, dass 1797 im Bezirk des Konfuziustempels die vom Shogunat kontrollierte konfuzianische Schule Shōheizaka Gakumonjo errichtet wurde.

Um seiner Komposition Dramatik zu verleihen, übertreibt Hiroshige die Höhe des linken Hügels, der dem Regenschauer entgegentritt und gleichzeitig die Hügelkuppe rechts weiter in die Ferne rücken lässt. Die Farbgradierung (*bokashi*) auf den beiden Hügelkuppen lässt das durch den warmen Sommerregen noch üppiger wachsende Gras besonders dicht erscheinen. Die Bauholz befördernden Bootsleute tragen Regenmäntel aus Stroh, wie auch zwei Fußgänger auf dem gegenüberliegenden Hügel.

Die Wiedergabe der extrem dünnen, das Blatt wie ein Raster durchziehenden Regenlinien erforderte das ganze Können des Holzschneiders (*horishi*). Ihm musste es gelingen, das Holz vom Block so wegzuschneiden, dass die feinen erhabenen Linien zwar schnurgerade verliefen, aber nicht wegbrachen.

Der typische japanische Sommerregen wird in der ganzen Serie nur dreimal dargestellt (siehe Tafeln 58, 62), ganz im Gegensatz zu den vielen dekorativen Schneedarstellungen der Winterbilder.

Vue du pavillon Seidō et de la rivière Kandagawa depuis le pont Shōheibashi

À gauche, la colline fait entrer le regard dans l'image par une diagonale abrupte et élancée. Après le pont Shōheibashi, sur la rive opposée de la Kandagawa, des porteurs et des passants longent le mur du Seidō. Le Seidō (« Pavillon sacré ») qui fut bâti en 1690 par Tsunayoshi, le cinquième shogun (1648–1709), comme sanctuaire dédié à la vénération de Confucius, s'est conservé en l'état jusqu'à nos jours.

Le pont Shōheibashi et la colline Shōheizaka, dont les noms reprennent la forme japonaise « Shōhei » du lieu de naissance de Confucius (chinois « Changping ») dans la province du Shandong, rappellent l'instauration du confucianisme comme éthique d'État dans le Japon des Tokugawa (1615–1868). Le ministère de l'éducation du gouvernement Meiji (1868–1912), fondé en 1871) fit de la halle principale du temple Daiseiden le cadre de la première exposition gouvernementale en 1872, car Confucius et sa vénération étaient associés à l'érudition et la culture.

C'est ainsi que dans le cadre des réformes de l'ère Kansei (1787–1793) fortement marquées par les idéaux confucianistes menées par le régent Matsudaira Sadanobu (1758–1829), l'école confucianiste Shōheizaka Gakumonjo contrôlée par le shogunat fut construite en 1797 dans l'enceinte du temple.

Pour conférer une note dramatique à sa composition, Hiroshige a exagéré la hauteur de la colline de gauche qui fait front à l'averse et contribue à reléguer plus fortement dans le lointain le sommet de la colline de droite. Grâce au *bokashi* réalisé au sommet des deux collines, Hiroshige fait apparaître l'herbe comme particulièrement dense et encore plus abondante pendant la mousson d'été. Les bateliers transportant du bois de construction portent des manteaux de pluie en paille, tout comme les deux piétons qu'on voit sur la colline de la rive opposée.

Le rendu des lignes de pluie extrêmement fines qui sillonnent la feuille en s'y superposant comme une trame, exigeait un grand savoir-faire de la part du graveur (*horishi*), qui devait en effet parvenir à ôter le bois de la planche d'impression de manière à ce que les fines arêtes soient totalement droites et ne se brisent pas.

La pluie d'été typiquement japonaise n'est d'ailleurs représentée que trois fois dans toute la série (cf. pl. 58, 62), contrairement aux nombreuses représentations décoratives des paysages d'hiver enneigés.

8

水道橋
駿河台

Suidōbashi Surugadai
15–1857

Suidō Bridge and the Surugadai Quarter

Three huge carp banners (*koi nobori*) flutter on high flagpoles over the roofs of the city. In the distance, we can see snow-capped Mount Fuji between the two fins of the carp, which is twisting in the wind.

The waving banners, depicted with a concern for maximum pictorial effect rather than correct perspective, were part of the decorations for the Boys' Festival on the 5th day of the fifth month. It was also in this month that Hiroshige's print was approved by the censors. By dint of their ability to swim upstream, carp are regarded in Japan as fish of particular strength and stamina. This strength and determination to overcome obstacles made them a symbol of courage and masculinity, and thus a key part of the festivities for families with sons aged around six or seven. The fish scales are emphasized with a print technique employing mica dust (*kirazuri*) that creates a silvery shimmer.

Other accoutrements of the Boys' Day Festival included armour, such as the over-sized helmet being carried by the boy in green in the bottom right-hand corner. Across the Suidō Bridge a procession of the warrior aristocracy is making its way to the samurai quarter of Surugadai on the opposite bank. Their tall, white, vertical banners were also associated with the Boys' Day Festival. On one of them is decorated with the depiction of the demon-vanquisher Shōki from a Chinese legend, who embodies the qualities of courage, loyalty and strength, and is a symbol of good luck throughout East Asia.

Die Brücke Suidōbashi und das Viertel Surugadai

Drei riesige Karpfenbanner (*koi nobori*) flattern an hohen Fahnenmasten über den Dächern der Stadt. In der Ferne erblickt man, zwischen den beiden Bauchflossen des sich im Wind biegenden Karpfens, den schneebedeckten Gipfel des Berges Fuji.

Die wehenden Banner, deren Darstellung weniger auf die korrekte Wiedergabe der Perspektive als vielmehr auf größtmögliche Wirkung abzielt, gehörten zu der Ausstattung des Knabenfestes am 5. Tag des fünften Monats. In diesem Monat wurde Hiroshiges Entwurf auch von den Zensoren genehmigt. Aufgrund ihrer Fähigkeit, stromaufwärts zu schwimmen, gelten in Japan Karpfen als besonders kräftige und ausdauernde Fische. Ihre Stärke und Entschlossenheit, Hindernisse zu überwinden, machen sie zu einem Symbol für Mut und Männlichkeit und damit zu einem Bestandteil dieses Festes für Familien mit Söhnen im Alter von sechs oder sieben Jahren. Die Schuppen des Fisches sind mit der Glimmerdruck-Technik (*kirazuri*) hervorgehoben, bei der ein silbrig glänzender Effekt erzeugt wird.

Zur Festtagsausstattung gehörten auch Rüstungen, wie sie der übergroße Helm andeutet, den der grün gekleidete Junge in der Bildecke rechts unten vor sich herträgt. Über die Brücke Suidōbashi zieht eine Prozession des Kriegeradels zum Samurai-Viertel Surugadai am gegenüberliegenden Ufer. Die dort emporragenden weißen Banner stellen weitere Dekorationen anlässlich des Knabenfestes dar. Eines zeigt den Dämonenbezwinger Shōki aus einer chinesischen Legende, der die Eigenschaften Mut, Loyalität und Kraft verkörpert und in ganz Ostasien als Symbol für Glück verbreitet ist.

Le pont Suidōbashi et le quartier Surugadai

Trois immenses bannières en forme de carpe (*koi nobori*) flottent au gré du vent, suspendues à de hauts mâts au-dessus des toits de la ville. Au loin, entre les deux nageoires ventrales de la carpe tordue sous l'effet du vent, on aperçoit le sommet enneigé du mont Fuji.

Les bannières flottant au vent, dont la représentation vise moins à la restitution correcte de la perspective qu'au maximum d'impact visuel, faisaient partie des décorations de la fête des garçons du 5ème jour du cinquième mois de chaque année. C'est d'ailleurs en ce même mois que le projet de Hiroshige reçut l'approbation de la censure. Au Japon, l'aptitude de la carpe à remonter les cours d'eau la fait considérer comme un poisson particulièrement fort et endurant. Sa force et sa détermination à surmonter les obstacles lui ont valu d'être un symbole du courage et de la virilité et donc un élément des festivités célébrées par les familles ayant un garçon âgé de six ou sept ans. Les écailles du poisson sont soulignées par la technique d'estampage de poussière de mica (*kirazuri*), qui permet d'obtenir un effet argenté et brillant.

Du décor de la même fête font aussi partie des éléments d'armure comme le casque surdimensionné que tient dans ses mains le garçon représenté dans le coin inférieur droit. Sur le pont Suidōbashi passe une procession de la noblesse d'épée qui se rend à Surugadai, le quartier des samouraïs situé sur la rive opposée. Les bannières qui s'y dressent sont d'autres décorations exhibées lors de la fête des garçons. Sous celles-ci, on aperçoit Shōki, le triomphateur des démons d'une légende chinoise, qui incarne les vertus du courage, de la loyauté et de la force et qui est un symbole du bonheur dans toute l'Asie.

王子
不動之瀧

Ōji Fudō no taki
9–1857

Fudō Falls in Ōji

In the deep blue of the mighty column of water at the Fudō Falls, Hiroshige employs the *bokashi* technique in no less masterly a fashion than in the gradations of the green surfaces of the forest, which appear as abstract colour elements.

A hempen rope with tassels (*shimenawa*) hangs high up over the waterfall. The rope is not merely decorative; it also has a religious connotation, for it identifies the site as sacred. Waterfalls are venerated throughout East Asia as miracles of nature with religious and mystical aspects and medicinal properties.

This particular waterfall, situated in the north of Edo, was named after Fudō Myōō, the king of esoteric knowledge in the Buddhist pantheon. According to a famous legend involving Fudō Myōō, a young girl prayed naked for a hundred days beneath a waterfall for her father to be healed – and her wishes were granted, for bathing in the Fudō Falls promised the healing of bodily ailments.

Hiroshige provides glimpses of the everyday activities of visitors to the Fudō Falls. While two elegantly dressed ladies approach the waterfall, a man is hesitantly stepping into the cold water. A hunchbacked old woman has set up the utensils for preparing tea, and is now offering a cup to a man who has just emerged from the water and is impatiently reaching out to take it.

Der Fudō-Wasserfall in Ōji

Im tiefen Blau der mächtigen, Gischt aufschäumenden Wassersäule des Fudō-Wasserfalls setzt Hiroshige das *bokashi* ebenso meisterhaft ein wie bei den Gradierungen der grünen Flächen des Waldbodens, die wie abstrakte Farbelemente erscheinen.

In der Höhe ist ein Hanfseil mit Troddeln (*shimenawa*) vor den Wasserfall gespannt, das nicht nur der Dekoration dient, sondern auch auf die Heiligkeit des Ortes verweist. Wasserfälle werden als Naturwunder in ganz Ostasien verehrt, wobei religiöse, mystische und medizinische Aspekte eine Rolle spielen.

Der im Norden Edos gelegene Wasserfall wurde nach Fudō Myōō benannt, dem König esoterischen Wissens im buddhistischen Pantheon. Einer berühmten Legende um Fudō Myōō zufolge betete ein junges Mädchen hundert Tage lang nackt unter einem Wasserfall für die Genesung ihres Vaters – ihre Gebete wurden erhört, denn ein Bad im Fudō-Wasserfall verhieß, körperliche Gebrechen zu heilen.

Hiroshige gewährt Einblicke in das Alltagsgeschehen der Besucher am Fudō-Wasserfall. Während zwei edel gekleidete Damen sich dem Wasserfall nähern, steigt ein Mann zögerlich in das kalte Gewässer. Eine alte Frau mit krummem Rücken hat ihre Utensilien für die Teezubereitung aufgebaut und bietet einem soeben dem Wasser entstiegenen Herrn eine Schale Tee an, der ihr bereits ungeduldig die Hand entgegenstreckt.

La cascade de Fudō à Ōji

Dans le bleu profond de la puissante colonne d'eau de la cascade de Fudō, au-dessus des embruns, Hiroshige a appliqué la technique du *bokashi* de manière tout aussi magistrale que dans les dégradés des surfaces vertes du sol de la forêt apparaissant comme des éléments de couleur abstraits.

Une corde à houppes (*shimenawa*) est tendue devant le haut de la chute d'eau ; elle ne sert pas seulement de décoration mais indique aussi la sainteté du lieu. Les cascades sont vénérées dans tout l'Extrême-Orient comme des merveilles naturelles, sachant que des aspects religieux, mystiques et médicaux interviennent dans cette vénération.

Le nom de la cascade située au nord d'Edo est dérivé de Fudō Myōō, le roi de la connaissance ésotérique du panthéon bouddhiste. Selon une légende tissée autour de Fudō Myōō, une jeune fille pria pendant cent jours entièrement nue pour la guérison de son père – et ses prières furent exaucées, car un bain dans la cascade promettait aussi de guérir les infirmités.

Hiroshige nous offre un petit aperçu quotidien des visiteurs de la cascade de Fudō. Deux dames noblement vêtues s'approchent de la cascade, tandis qu'un homme hésite à entrer dans l'eau froide. Une vieille femme au dos voûté a disposé ses ustensiles pour la préparation du thé et offre un bol de thé à une homme qui vient de sortir de l'eau et qui lui tend une main empressée.

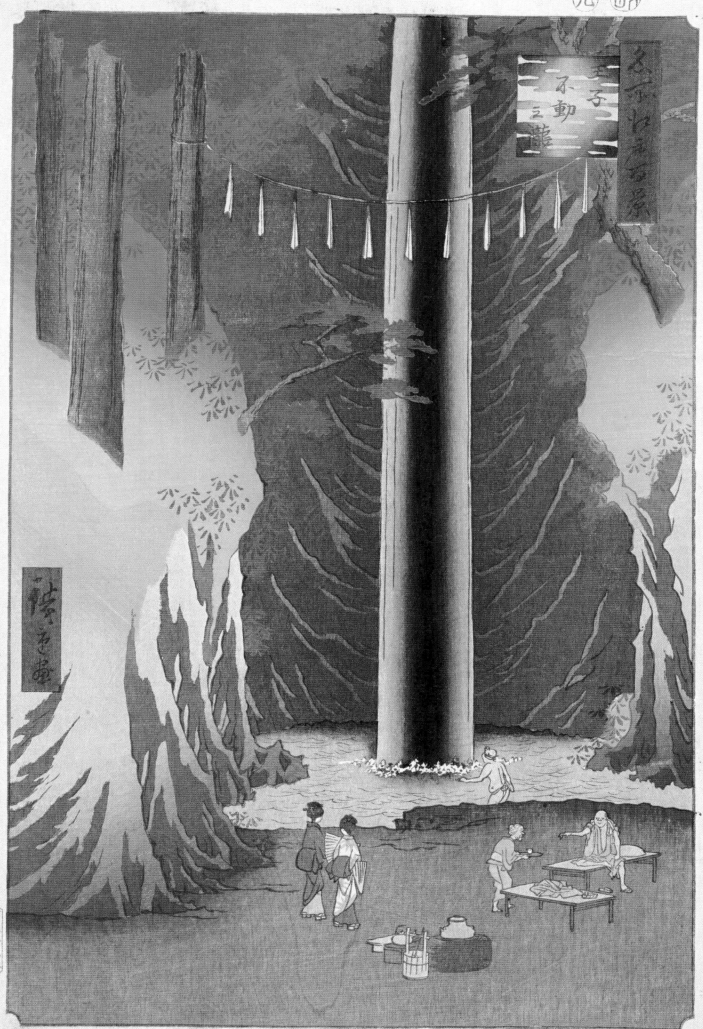

50

角答
熊野十二社
俗称
十二そう

Tsunohazu Kumano Jūnisha zokushō Jūnisō
7–1856

Kumano Jūnisha Shrine at Tsunohazu, known as "Jūnisō"

In this view towards the south-west, we look down on a pond from a high vantage point. Scratches intentionally applied by the printer during the printing process animate the calm surface of the pond. On its banks, people are strolling or drinking tea beneath covered pavilions, and pine trees are reflected in the water. In the bottom left-hand corner is a two-storey teahouse, and nearby the unassuming buildings of the Kumano Jūnisha Shrine mentioned in the title. In the almost identical idyllic composition included in the third volume of Hiroshige's *Illustrated Souvenirs of Edo (Ehon Edo miyage)*, published in 1850, he mentions the beauty of the landscape, along with the venerable age and the various names of this sanctuary.

The shrine was founded by a certain Suzuki Kurō in the village of Tsunohazu in the Ōei era (1394–1428). He came from the Kii Province (today Wakayama Prefecture), where the main Kumano shrine is located. Suzuki Kurō invited twelve different deities of the Kumano, and thus the shrine was also known as the "Twelve Shrines" (Jūnisha). Like many other sanctuaries in Edo in the mid-19th century, the shrine enjoyed enormous popularity, not least because of the charms of the surrounding landscape. The village of Tsunohazu, which at that time lay well to the west of the capital, was just a stone's throw from Kōshū kaidō, one of the five main highways: it led to today's Nagano Prefecture to the west of Edo. Tsunohazu is now part of Shinjuku, one of Tokyo's main centres, with numerous skyscrapers, constant traffic and a vibrant nightlife.

Der Schrein Kumano Jūnisha in Tsunohazu, bekannt unter dem Namen „Jūnisō"

Von einem hohen Betrachterstandpunkt aus bietet Hiroshige einen Blick nach Südwesten auf die große, stille Wasserfläche eines Teiches, die nur von den absichtlich angebrachten Kratzspuren der Reibescheibe beim Drucken belebt wird. Der Teich, an dessen Ufer Menschen promenieren oder sich auf überdachten Sitzgelegenheiten zum Teetrinken niedergelassen haben, ist gesäumt von sich im Wasser spiegelnden Kiefern, einem zweistöckigen Teehaus am linken Rand und schließlich von den unscheinbaren Gebäuden des im Titel angegebenen Schreins Kumano Jūnisha unten. In der fast identischen idyllischen Komposition in Hiroshiges Werk *Illustrierte Mitbringsel aus Edo (Ehon Edo miyage)* von 1850 (Band 3) werden neben der schönen Landschaft das beträchtliche Alter und die verschiedenen Namen dieser Kultstätte erwähnt.

Der Schrein wurde bereits in der Ära Ōei (1394–1428) im Dorf Tsunohazu von einem gewissen Suzuki Kurō gegründet. Er stammte aus der Provinz Kii (heutige Präfektur Wakayama), in welcher der Hauptschrein Kumano angesiedelt ist. Suzuki Kurō lud zwölf unterschiedliche Gottheiten des Kumano ein, und so wurde der Schrein auch als „Zwölf Schreine" (Jūnisha) bezeichnet. Mitte des 19. Jahrhunderts genoss er, wie viele andere religiöse Stätten in Edo, ungemeine Popularität – nicht zuletzt wegen der landschaftlichen Reize der Umgebung. Der damals weit westlich der Stadt gelegene Ort Tsunohazu war ein Katzensprung entfernt vom Kōshū kaidō, einem der fünf wichtigen Hauptverkehrswege, der bis zur heutigen Präfektur Nagano westlich von Edo führte. Heute ist Tsunohazu Teil von Shinjuku, einem der größten Zentren innerhalb Tokyos mit zahlreichen Hochhäusern, brausendem Verkehr und lebendigem Nachtleben.

Le sanctuaire de Kumano Jūnisha à Tsunohazu, aussi connu sous le nom « Jūnisō »

D'un point de vue élevé, Hiroshige nous offre une vue orientée au sud-est sur la paisible étendue d'un étang animé par les seule traces de grattage délibérément créées par l'imprimeur. L'étang, sur les rives duquel des hommes se promènent ou sont assis sous des auvents pour boire du thé, est bordé de pins reflétés dans son eau, une maison de thé à deux niveaux près du bord gauche de l'image et enfin, les modestes bâtiments du sanctuaire Kumano Jūnisha mentionné par le titre. Dans la composition idyllique presque identique que Hiroshige a donnée dans le troisième tome (1850) de ses *Souvenirs illustrés d'Edo (Ehon Edo miyage)* sont évoqués, outre la beauté du paysage, l'âge canonique et les différents noms du lieu saint.

Le sanctuaire fut en effet construit pendant l'ère Ōei (1394–1428) dans le village de Tsunohazu par un certain Suzuki Kurō. Celui-ci était originaire de la province de Kii (actuelle préfecture de Wakayama), dans laquelle se trouve le siège principal du sanctuaire de Kumano. Suzuki Kurō y invita douze divinités différentes du Kumano, d'où vient que le sanctuaire fut aussi appelé « douze sanctuaires » (Jūnisha). Au milieu du XIXᵉ siècle, comme bien d'autres sites religieux, le lieu saint jouissait d'une extraordinaire popularité – due en bonne partie aussi aux charmes paysagers des environs. La localité Tsunohazu, alors située assez loin à l'ouest de la ville, n'était qu'à un jet de pierre de la Kōshū kaidō – une des cinq voies de circulation principales – qui menait à l'actuelle préfecture de Nagano à l'ouest d'Edo. Tsunohazu fait aujourd'hui partie de Shinjuku, un des grands centres urbains de Tokyo, avec ses nombreuses tours, son trafic très dense et sa vibrante vie nocturne.

51

糀町　一丁目　山王祭　ねり込

Kōjimachi itchōme Sannō Matsuri nerikomi
7–1856

The Sannō Festival Procession at Kōjimachi itchōme

A festival procession is moving towards the Hanzōmon Gate of Edo Castle, headed by a float (*mikoshi*) topped by a monkey as the messenger of the deity Hiei Sannō. Another float is depicted in close-up in the left foreground, above the blue castle moat. The white cockerel sitting on the big Chinese "drum of admonition" (*kankadori*) is represented by just a few of its tail feathers. The cloth bands mounted on a bamboo rod beneath the drum swell out like a broad sail. This ensemble fixes our gaze on the foreground, while at the same time the golden disc at the end of the rod points imploringly to the palace. Those accompanying the drum float, wearing white hats decorated with red flowers, are marching in close formation towards the palace.

This print was approved in the seventh month of 1856, and depicts the procession of the Sannō Festival held a month earlier, on 15 June, by order of the shogunate and against the wishes of the people. Hiroshige was thus reacting very promptly – as so often in his *One Hundred Famous Views of Edo* – to a current event in the life of Edo, which had been thrown out of balance by the great earthquake of 1855. In so doing, he was making a statement on behalf of the established order. The procession consisted of more than 50 floats and 500 participants dressed in costumes of the Heian period (794–1185). The festival had been celebrated biennially since 1681, and the procession proceeded from the Hiei Sannō Shrine behind the shogun's castle through the centre of Edo. The Hiei Sannō was erected in the early 17th century to protect the newly built Edo Castle against demons. The deity originally housed in the Hiei Jinja Shrine near Kyoto was worshipped in the Edo Hiei Sannō.

All Sannō processions led through a part of the outer fortification of Edo Castle, where they were watched by the shogun himself. This fact underlines the particular significance of the procession, since apart from the shogun's vassals and the feudal lords with their entourages, normally no one was allowed to enter the castle fortifications. The Sannō Festival thus uniquely demonstrates the bonds between the ruler, the ruled and the native religion.

Die Sannō-Festprozession bei Kōjimachi itchōme

Angeführt von einem Festwagen (*mikoshi*) mit der Figur eines Affen als Boten des Gottes Hiei Sannō, bewegt sich eine Festprozession auf das Schlosstor Hanzōmon zu. Ein weiterer Festwagen ist im Close-up links von dem blauen Burggraben in den Vordergrund gestellt. Von dem weiß gefiederten Hahn, der auf der großen chinesischen „Trommel der Ermahnung" (*kankadori*) sitzt, sind nur wenige Schwanzfedern zu sehen. Wie ein breites Segel bauschen sich unterhalb der Trommel die auf eine Bambusstange montierten Bänder. Dieses Ensemble fixiert den Blick auf den Vordergrund und weist zugleich mit dem goldenen Knopf am Ende der Stange wie beschwörend auf den Palast. Die Begleiter des Trommelwagens tragen mit roten Blumen geschmückte weiße Hüte und marschieren in dichter Formation auf den Palast zu.

Das Blatt erschien im siebten Monat des Jahres 1856 und thematisiert die einen Monat zuvor, am 15. Juni, auf Anordnung des Shogunats entgegen dem Wunsch des Volkes abgehaltene Prozession des Sannō-Festes. Hiroshige reagiert mit seinem Holzschnitt also – wie so häufig in den *Hundert Ansichten* – überraschend schnell auf ein aktuelles Ereignis in dem durch das große Erdbeben von 1855 aus dem Gleichgewicht gebrachten Leben in Edo, und er gibt mit ihm ein Statement für die überkommene Ordnung ab. Die von über 50 Festwagen und 500 Statisten in heian-zeitlichen Kostümen (794–1185) begleitete Prozession führte seit 1681 jedes zweite Jahr vom Schrein Hiei Sannō hinter dem Schloss des Shoguns durch das Zentrum Edos. Der Hiei Sannō wurde im frühen 17. Jahrhundert zum Schutz des neu erbauten Edo-Schlosses gegen böse Dämonen errichtet. In ihm wird die ursprünglich im Schrein Hiei Jinja bei Kyoto beheimatete Gottheit verehrt. Alle Sannō-Prozessionen führten durch einen Teil der äußeren Befestigung des Edo-Schlosses und wurden dort vom Shogun selbst besichtigt. Dieser Umstand bezeugt die besondere Bedeutung der Prozession, da abgesehen von Vasallen des Shoguns und Feudalherren mit ihrer Entourage üblicherweise niemand diesen Befestigungsgürtel des Schlosses überschreiten durfte. Das Sannō-Fest demonstriert dadurch wie kein anderes die Verbundenheit von Herrscher, einheimischem Glauben und Volk.

La procession solennelle de Sannō près de Kōjimachi itchōme

Devancé par un char d'apparat (*mikoshi*) arborant la figure d'un singe messager du dieu Hiei Sannō, une procession solennelle se dirige vers la porte du château Hanzōmon. Un autre char est montré en gros plan à gauche devant la douve du château. Du coq à plumes blanches posté sur le grand « tambour de la mise en garde » (*kankadori*) d'origine chinoise, le spectateur n'aperçoit que quelques plumes de la queue. Sous le tambour, telle une voilure, les banderoles fixées à une hampe en bambou flottent au gré du vent. Cet ensemble d'éléments fixe le regard au premier plan, tout en renvoyant au château avec le bouton doré qui termine la hampe comme un clair signal. Les membres du cortège qui accompagne le char au tambour portent des chapeaux blancs décorés de fleurs rouges et marchent en rangs serrés vers le palais.

Cette feuille publiée au septième mois 1856 illustre la procession de la fête de Sannō qui s'était déroulée un mois plus tôt sur ordre de l'autorité shogunale et contre le désir du peuple. Hiroshige réagit donc de manière étonnamment rapide – comme si souvent dans les *Cent Vues* – à un événement d'actualité qui eut lieu dans le désordre consécutif au grand séisme de 1855, et passe un message sur l'ordre traditionnel.

Depuis 1681, la procession accompagnée de plus de 50 chars et 500 participants en costumes de l'ère Heian (794–1185) partait tous les deux ans du sanctuaire Hiei Sannō situé derrière le château shogunal et traversait le centre d'Edo. Le Hiei Sannō avait été construit au début du XVIIᵉ siècle pour protéger le nouveau château des mauvais démons. C'est là qu'est vénérée la divinité dont le siège original était le sanctuaire Hiei Jinja situé près de Kyoto. Toutes les processions de Sannō passaient par une section des fortifications extérieures du château d'Edo, où elles étaient inspectées par le shogun en personne. Cette circonstance illustre l'importance toute particulière de la procession, notamment dans la mesure où personne, hormis les vassaux du shogun et les seigneurs féodaux accompagnés de leur entourage, n'était autorisé à fouler l'enceinte fortifiée du château. Plus qu'aucune autre, la fête de Sannō devait ainsi démontrer le lien de solidarité qui unissait le souverain et le peuple au travers des croyances propres au Japon.

52

赤坂桐畑

Akasaka Kiribatake
4–1856

The Paulownia Garden at Akasaka

Against the backdrop of Tameike, the "Reservoir Pond", two paulownias in the immediate foreground dominate the composition.

The leaves, seen in close up, are of a green gradation that harmonizes elegantly with the greys of the tree trunks and the deep blue of the night sky. The water of this pond was brackish, so that the lotus plants, indicated here by black dots, grew particularly well.

The buildings on the opposite bank belong to temples that were part of the Hiei Sannō Shrine. Not visible here, the shrine stood on the hill on the left and was the focus of an annual summer festival (see plate 51).

On the bank is the residence of a powerful ally of the Tokugawa shogunate, the feudal lord Kuroda, from the fiefdom of Fukuoka in northern Kyūshū. His estate in Edo was lined by paulownias (*kiri*), which is the origin of the print's title, *kiribatake*, "Paulownia Garden".

The decorative and scented paulownia blossoms as well as the leaves, which repelled insects, were combined into a motif of a crest that was also used by the imperial dynasty. While the bark of the paulownia was useful as a dye, the pale, lightweight and fire-resistant timber of this tree, which can grow to 10 metres (well over 30 feet) in height, was valued for making furniture, storage chests, *geta* sandals and the Japanese zither, the *koto*.

The memory of the Tameike Pond is kept alive today solely by the name of a station on the Ginza subway line. The first Tokugawa shogun, Ieyasu (1542–1616), had drinking-water reservoirs built in Akasaka and Kanda shortly after 1600, but already by the middle of the 17th century the population was growing so quickly that larger sources in the hinterland had to be exploited. The reservoirs were then integrated into the outer moats of the shogun's castle and finally, in 1910, completely filled in.

Paulowniengarten in Akasaka

Vor Tameike, dem hier dargestellten „Teichreservoir", sind zwei Paulownien-Bäume in den unmittelbaren Vordergrund gerückt, welche die Bildkomposition bestimmen.

Die wie herangezoomt wirkenden Blätter zeigen eine grüne Farbgradierung, die mit den Grautönen der Baumstämme und dem nachtblauen Himmel elegant harmonieren. Die Wasserqualität des Teiches Tameike war brackig, sodass die mit schwarzen Punkten angedeuteten Lotuspflanzen besonders gut gedeihen konnten.

Die Gebäude am gegenüberliegenden Ufer gehörten zu Tempeln, die Bestandteil des Hiei-Sannō-Schreins waren. Dieser thronte, hier nicht sichtbar, auf dem Hügel und war das Zentrum des jährlichen Sommerfestes (siehe Tafel 51).

Am diesseitigen Ufer stand die Residenz des mächtigen, dem Tokugawa-Shogunat nahestehenden Feudalfürsten Kuroda aus dem Lehnsgebiet Fukuoka in Nord-Kyūshū. Sein Landbesitz in Edo war gesäumt von Paulownien (*kiri*), von denen sich die Bezeichnung *kiribatake*, Paulowniengarten, ableitet. Die dekorativen und duftenden Paulownienblüten und die Insekten abwehrenden Blätter wurden zu einem Wappenmotiv kombiniert, das auch vom Kaiserhaus verwendet wurde. Während sich die Rinde der Paulownien zum Färben eignete, schätzte man das helle, leichte und feuerresistente Holz dieses bis zu zehn Metern hoch wachsenden Baumes als Material für Möbel, Aufbewahrungsschachteln, Geta-Sandalen oder die japanische Zither (*koto*).

Vom Wasserreservoir Tameike zeugt heute nur noch der Name einer U-Bahn-Station der Ginza-Linie. Der erste Tokugawa-Shogun Ieyasu (1542–1616) ließ schon kurz nach 1600 Vorratsbecken für Trinkwasser in den Stadtteilen Akasaka und Kanda bauen. Aber bereits um die Mitte des 17. Jahrhunderts wuchs die Bevölkerung so schnell, dass ergiebigere Quellen im Umland erschlossen werden mussten. Die Reservoirs wurden nun in den äußeren Wassergraben um das Schloss des Shoguns integriert und schließlich 1910 ganz zugeschüttet.

Jardin de paulownias à Akasaka

Devant Tameike, le « réservoir » à ciel ouvert représenté dans cette estampe, deux paulownias se dressent au tout premier plan et déterminent la composition. Les feuilles agrandies comme au zoom présentent un dégradé de vert qui s'harmonise élégamment avec les gris des troncs et le ciel bleu nuit. L'eau de l'étang Tameike était saumâtre, et les lotus indiqués ici par des points noirs pouvaient donc s'y développer tout à leur aise. Les bâtiments de la rive opposée font partie des temples qui composent le sanctuaire de Hiei Sannō, centre de l'annuelle fête de l'été (cf. pl. 51), sanctuaire qui trône, invisible ici, sur la colline.

Sur la rive où sont plantés les paulownias se dressait aussi la résidence du puissant seigneur féodal Kuroda de Fukuoka, dans le Nord-Kyūshū, lequel était un proche du shogunat Tokugawa. À Edo, ses propriétés étaient bordées de paulownias (*kiri*), d'où se dérive le nom *kiribatake* – jardin de paulownias. Les odorantes et décoratives fleurs de paulownias et leurs feuilles insectifuges formaient un motif héraldique également utilisé par la maison impériale. L'écorce du paulownia servait à la teinture ; le bois clair, résistant et ignifuge du même arbre – qui peut atteindre jusqu'à 10 mètres de haut –, était très apprécié comme matériau pour la confection de meubles, de boîtes, de *getas* ou de la cithare japonaise (*koto*).

Du réservoir de Tameike, il ne reste plus aujourd'hui que le nom d'une station de métro de la ligne Ginza. Peu après 1600, Ieyasu (1542–1616), le premier shogun Tokugawa, avait fait construire à Akasaka et à Kanda des bassins collecteurs d'eau potable. Dès le milieu du XVIIe siècle, avec la forte croissance démographique, des sources plus abondantes durent être exploitées dans la région. Les réservoirs furent alors intégrés aux systèmes des douves extérieures du château shogunal avant d'être définitivement comblés en 1910.

増
上
寺
塔

赤
羽
根

Zōjōjitō Akabane
1–1857

The Pagoda of Zōjōji Temple and Akabane

While today the pagoda of the Zōjōji Temple is surrounded by skyscrapers, in the mid-19th century it towered above all the surrounding buildings. Its impressive size underscored the importance of the structure, which was built by the founder of the Tokugawa dynasty, Ieyasu (1542–1616), as the main temple of the Pure Land School (*Jōdo*) of Buddhism in the Kantō region. The top two roofs of the five-storey pagoda express sublime clarity. The projecting red brackets depicted in great detail seem to be growing out of the green treetops.

This close-up of the pagoda faces a distant watchtower to the left. Its thin halo of cloud is Hiroshige's way of expressing its size and hence its status as the tallest watchtower in Edo. The tower stood on the estate of the daimyō Arima from the fief of Kurume on Kyūshū, whose residence, with its very long façade, lines the broad, bright yellow street on the opposite bank, reached by the Akabane Bridge.

The constant growth of the urban population of Edo brought considerable prosperity to those quarters where shrines and temples were situated, which lay on major highways. While the Kinryūzan Sensōji Temple (plates 39, 99) attracted travellers bound for the north along the Ōshū dōchū, Zōjōji lay to the south-west of the city centre near the important Eastern Sea Road (Tōkaidō), which led to Kyoto, the imperial capital.

In Hiroshige's day, the Zōjōji, as the Tokugawa family temple, had an annual income of more than 10,000 *koku* of rice, which corresponded to that of a minor feudal territory. The interior had a floor area of 25,000 tatami (the straw mats that also serve as a unit of area) or slightly more than four hectares (ten acres), and accommodated 3,000 monks. The social and economic importance of the Zōjōji, even in present-day Tokyo, can still be measured by its generously proportioned, luxuriously green precincts, which occupy a prime location.

Die Pagode des Tempels Zōjōji und Akabane

Während die Pagode des Tempels Zōjōji heute von Wolkenkratzern überragt wird, erhob sie sich Mitte des 19. Jahrhunderts über alle Gebäude der Umgebung hoch in den Himmel. Die beeindruckende Größe betonte die Bedeutung des Bauwerkes als Haupttempel der Reinen-Land-Schule (Jōdo) des Buddhismus im Kantō-Gebiet, da sie vom Gründer der Tokugawa-Dynastie, Ieyasu (1542–1616), erbaut worden war. Die oberen beiden Dächer der fünfstöckigen Pagode drücken Klarheit und Erhabenheit aus. Das detailliert wiedergegebene, rote Kraggebälk scheint geradezu aus den grünen Baumwipfeln herauszuwachsen.

Dem nah an den Betrachter gerückten Ausschnitt der Pagode steht am linken Bildrand ein Wachturm gegenüber. Er ist von einem dünnen Wolkenschleier umgeben, wodurch Hiroshige seine besondere Größe und damit seinen Rang als höchster Wachturm in Edo zum Ausdruck bringt. Der Turm gehörte zum Areal der Feudalfürsten Arima vom Lehen in Kurume auf Kyūshū, deren Residenz mit ihrer lang gezogenen Fassade die breite, hellgelbe Straße am gegenüberliegenden Ufer des Flusses Akabanegawa säumt.

Das stete Wachstum der städtischen Bevölkerung in Edo verhalf den Stadtvierteln, in denen Schreine und Tempel lagen, zu besonderem Reichtum. Diese sakralen Bezirke lagen städtebaulich gesehen an wichtigen Transportwegen und Verkehrsadern. Während der Tempel Kinryūzan Sensōji (siehe Tafeln 39, 99) Reisende anzog, die auf der Ōshū dōchū, der Straße nach Norden, unterwegs waren, lag der Zōjōji südwestlich des Stadtkerns nahe der wichtigen Tōkaidō (Ostmeerstraße) zur Kaiserhauptstadt Kyoto.

Zur Zeit Hiroshiges bezog der Zōjōji als Familientempel der Tokugawa eine Jahressumme von über 10 000 *koku* Reis, was dem Einkommen eines kleinen Feudalgebietes entsprach. Die Innenräume hatten eine Fläche von 25 000 Tatami-Matten und beherbergten 3000 Mönche. Die bis heute anhaltende wirtschaftliche und gesellschaftliche Bedeutung des Zōjōji in Tokyo lässt sich nach wie vor an dem großen, luxuriös begrünten Tempelbezirk in bester Lage erkennen.

La pagode du temple Zōjōji et Akabane

Alors que la pagode du temple Zōjōji est aujourd'hui environnée de gratte-ciel qui la dépassent de beaucoup, au milieu du XIXᵉ siècle, elle s'élevait haut dans le ciel au-dessus de tous les édifices de la zone. Cette hauteur impressionnante soulignait l'importance de l'édifice comme temple principal de l'école bouddhiste de la Terre pure dans le domaine de Kantō, temple qui avait été institué par Ieyasu (1542–1616), le fondateur de la dynastie Tokugawa. Les deux toits supérieurs de la pagode à cinq étages expriment la clarté et le sublime. L'encorbellement rouge traité en détail semble pousser directement sur le faîte des arbres verdoyants.

Au détail de la pagode représenté en vue fortement rapprochée fait écho la tour de garde qu'on aperçoit près du bord gauche de l'image. La tour est entourée d'un léger voile de brume par lequel Hiroshige souligne sa hauteur et donc son rang comme plus haute tour de garde d'Edo. Elle faisait partie du domaine des seigneurs féodaux Arima, du fief de Kurume à Kyūshū, seigneurs dont la résidence, avec sa longue façade étirée, borde la large rue jaune clair qu'on aperçoit sur la rive opposée de la rivière.

La croissance démographique constante d'Edo a contribué à la richesse particulière des quartiers situés aux abords des temples et des sanctuaires. Du point de vue urbanistique, les domaines sacrés étaient en effet situés près des voies de transport et des artères de circulation. Alors que le temple Kinryūzan Sensōji (cf. pl. 39, 99) attirait les voyageurs qui se rendaient vers le nord par la route Ōshū dōchū, le Zōjōji était situé au sud-ouest du centre-ville, près de l'importante Tōkaidō (route de la mer orientale) qui permettait de relier Kyoto, la ville impériale.

À l'époque de Hiroshige, le Zōjōji, temple familial des Tokugawa, recevait une dotation annuelle de plus de 10 000 *koku* de riz, ce qui correspondait au rendement d'un fief de petite importance. Les espaces intérieurs avaient une surface de 25 000 tatamis et hébergeaient quelque 3000 moines. À Tokyo, l'importance économique et sociale du Zōjōji, qui n'a en rien diminué jusqu'à nos jours, se reconnaît aujourd'hui encore au grand domaine luxuriant et verdoyant situé à l'un des meilleurs emplacements de la ville.

外桜田
弁慶堀
糀町

Soto-Sakurada Benkeibori Kōjimachi
5–1856

The Benkei Moat from Soto-Sakurada to Kōjimachi

In this print, Hiroshige depicts the spatial power relations between the shogun and his vassals. On the right we see the south-west embankment of the shogun's castle (today's Imperial Palace) descending steeply to the moat. The entrance to this centre and symbol of power was guarded by sentries and gates.

On a path in the bottom left, several men and women walk along the side of the moat towards a guardhouse, to the right of which is the "Cherry Well", famous for its simultaneous use of three buckets to lift water.

By the guardhouse, schematically rendered figures are standing in front of the red entrance to the residence of the feudal lord Ii, from Hikone domain in today's Shiga Prefecture. The Ii were among the vassals who supported the Tokugawa against the armies of the Toyotomi in the Battle of Sekigahara in 1600. These most trustworthy and loyal of subjects enjoyed numerous privileges and were permitted to protect the shogun by erecting their residences in the immediate vicinity of the castle, while all others had quite literally to keep their distance.

Directly beneath the series title, in the top right-hand corner, the Kōjimachi watchtower rises above the horizon. It had burnt down in the great Ansei earthquake of the tenth month of 1855, and its reconstruction was completed only two months before the censors approved this print.

In today's Tokyo, too, the clear deep-blue waters at the foot of the walls surrounding the Imperial Palace still evoke a strong impression. Even now, as in Hiroshige's day, one is amazed at how quiet it can sometimes be in the middle of one of the world's largest cities.

In his book *Empire of Signs*, sometimes criticized as Orientalist, Roland Barthes describes the Imperial Palace in the middle of Tokyo as a "void". At the time of the real-estate boom during the late 1980s, the value of the land occupied by the palace was calculated as matching that of the total area of California. Something of this "symbolic extravagance" was already visible in the mid-19th century.

Der Benkei-Graben von Soto-Sakurada bis Kōjimachi

Auf diesem Blatt zeigt uns Hiroshige die räumlichen Machtverhältnisse des Shoguns und seiner Vasallen. Am rechten Bildrand fällt die im Südwesten liegende Mauer des shogunalen Schlosses (des heutigen Kaiserpalasts) steil ins Wasser ab. Der Zugang zu diesem Arkanum der symbolischen Macht war damals ebenso wie heute von Wachtposten und Toren versperrt.

Auf dem Weg unten links bewegt sich eine Gruppe von Menschen entlang dem Graben auf ein Wächterhäuschen zu, neben dem weiter rechts der berühmte Brunnen „Kirschquelle" zu sehen ist. Er war für die gleichzeitige Förderung von Wasser aus drei Eimern bekannt.

Am Häuschen sind schemenhaft Menschen vor dem roten Eingang zur Residenz des Feudalfürsten Ii von Hikone in der heutigen Präfektur Shiga zu erkennen. Die Ii gehörten zu denjenigen Vasallen, welche die Tokugawa in der Schlacht von Sekigahara im Jahr 1600 gegen die Armeen der Toyotomi unterstützt hatten. Diese zuverlässigsten und treuesten Untergebenen genossen zahlreiche Privilegien und durften zum Schutz des Shoguns ihre Residenzen in nächster Nähe zu dessen Schloss errichten, während

alle anderen buchstäblich auf Distanz gehen mussten.

Direkt unter dem Serientitel ragt der Wachturm des Stadtteils Kōjimachi über den Horizont hinaus. Er war während des großen Ansei-Erdbebens im zehnten Monat des Jahres 1855 abgebrannt, und sein Wiederaufbau war nur zwei Monate bevor der Holzschnitt zensiert wurde erfolgt.

Auch im heutigen Tokyo hinterlässt die tiefblaue, klare Wasserfläche am Fuß der den Kaiserpalast umgebenden Mauer einen starken Eindruck. Und man kann noch, wie zur Zeit Hiroshiges, darüber staunen, wie ruhig es mitten im Zentrum einer der größten Städte der Welt manchmal sein kann.

Roland Barthes bezeichnet in seinem gelegentlich als orientalistisch kritisierten Buch *Das Reich der Zeichen* den Kaiserpalast in Tokyos Zentrum als eine Leerstelle. Zur Zeit des Immobilienbooms Ende der 1980er Jahre wurde ausgerechnet, dass der hypothetische Wert des kaiserlichen Bodens demjenigen des gesamten Bodens von Kalifornien entspricht. Etwas von dieser „Verschwendung an ein Symbol" ist schon in der Mitte des 19. Jahrhunderts sichtbar.

La douve dite Benkei de Soto-Sakurada à Kōjimachi

Dans cette feuille, Hiroshige nous montre un des leviers du pouvoir exercé par le shogun et ses vassaux. Près du bord droit de l'image, le mur d'enceinte sud-est du château shogunal (actuel palais impérial) tombe à pic dans l'eau. Tout comme aujourd'hui, l'accès à cet arcane du pouvoir symbolique était alors fermé par des gardes et des portes.

Sur le chemin qui apparaît dans le coin inférieur gauche, un groupe d'hommes longe la douve et se dirige vers la cahute du gardien à côté de laquelle, un peu plus loin à droite, on aperçoit la célèbre « source aux cerisiers », un puits qui était aussi réputé pour l'eau qu'on y puisait avec trois seaux.

Près de la cahute, on reconnaît la silhouette schématique de gens postés à l'entrée de la résidence du seigneur féodal Ii de Hikone (actuelle préfecture de Shiga). Les Ii avaient été du nombre des vassaux qui avaient soutenu les Tokugawa en l'an 1600 lors de la bataille de Sekigahara qui les opposait aux armées des Toyotomi. Ces sujets les plus loyaux et dévoués jouissaient de nombreux privilèges particuliers, notamment celui de pouvoir bâtir leurs résidences aux abords immédiats du château pour assurer sa protection, tan-

dis que tous les autres vassaux devaient littéralement se maintenir à distance.

Directement sous le titre de la série, la tour de garde de Kōjimachi se dresse au-dessus de l'horizon. Elle avait été détruite par un incendie lors du grand séisme d'Ansei au dixième mois 1855, et sa reconstruction ne fut achevée que deux mois avant l'approbation de cette estampe par la censure.

De nos jours encore, la limpide surface bleu sombre au pied de l'enceinte du palais impérial fait une profonde impression sur le visiteur. Et comme à l'époque de Hiroshige, celui-ci peut encore s'étonner de la paix qui peut régner en plein centre d'une des grandes métropoles du monde.

Dans *L'empire des signes*, dont la tendance orientalisante a parfois été critiquée, Roland Barthes qualifie le palais impérial au centre de Tokyo comme un vide. À l'époque du boom immobilier de la fin des années 1980, la valeur hypothétique des terrains impériaux a été estimée équivalente à celle de l'ensemble des terres de Californie. Quelque chose de ce « gaspillage au nom d'un symbole » apparaît déjà au milieu du XIXe siècle.

55

佃しま
住吉の祭

Tsukudajima Sumiyoshi no matsuri
7–1857

The Sumiyoshi Festival at Tsukudajima

Framed by a red-and-white festive lantern and a pine tree, this print also features a white banner in the immediate foreground, which spans the entire height of the image. It is decorated with prominent Chinese characters and its impact is enhanced by a textile embossing technique known as *nunomezuri*. The five characters written in seal script can be read from a distance and identify the subject of the print: "Sumiyoshi daimyōjin" ("Great Sumiyoshi Deity"). To the right, the year (the fourth year of the Ansei era, i.e. 1857) and the month of the Sumiyoshi Festival (held annually on the 29th day of the sixth month) are rendered in smaller characters.

The central event of the Sumiyoshi Festival was a long procession featuring a large palanquin crowned with a phoenix as a symbol of the deity. The palanquin is just to the left of the banner. It was carried once around the island of Tsukudajima by young men wading through the sea along the shore, before being returned to the shrine at the north-east end of the coast. This ritual, which continued until 1963, goes back to the Tsukudamura fishermen's veneration of Sumiyoshi, who was also the patron deity of fish-

ermen and sailors. At the beginning of the Tokugawa period (1615–1868) these fishermen had been settled on the island of Tsukudajima in Edo Bay by the shogun (see plate 4), but had kept their own ancient rituals. At the foot of the banner, the congregation of the Tsukudajima Sumiyoshi Shrine is immortalized as its sponsor. The banner is said to still exist.

Chinese and Japanese characters, although seen routinely by the Japanese every day, have a high identification value when presented aesthetically. Underscored by an unusual or witty design, their particular quality was employed not only by temples and shrines, but also by shops and restaurants (see plates 7, 8, 12, 13). Eye-catching calligraphy meant that a sanctuary or business could be quickly identified.

In East Asia, calligraphy is seen as the direct trace of its creator and has therefore traditionally been the most esteemed among the arts. The writer of this inscription is identified in the middle of the banner next to the bamboo pole: it is the creator of the table of contents of the *One Hundred Famous Views of Edo*, referred to in this print as Seikengū Gengyo.

Das Sumiyoshi-Fest in Tsukudajima

Gerahmt von einer rot-weißen Festlaterne und einer Kiefer, dient ein mit prominenten chinesischen Schriftzeichen dekoriertes weißes Banner als Blickfang im unmittelbaren Vordergrund. Seine Größe wird durch die Blinddrucktechnik mit Stoffstruktur (*nunomezuri*) noch hervorgehoben. Die fünf weithin sichtbaren Zeichen in Siegelschrift geben das Thema des Blattes an: „Sumiyoshi daimyōjin" („Große Gottheit Sumiyoshi"). Rechts daneben sind in kleinen Zeichen Jahr (viertes Jahr der Ära Ansei, also 1857) und Monat des Sumiyoshi-Festes angegeben, das jährlich am 29. Tag des sechsten Monats stattfand.

Zentrales Ereignis des Sumiyoshi-Festes ist die lange Prozession mit einer tragbaren Sänfte, die – als Symbol für die Gottheit – von einem Phönix bekrönt ist. Diese auf dem Holzschnitt links vom Banner im Hintergrund sichtbare Sänfte wird von jungen Männern im Wasser einmal um die Insel Tsukudajima getragen und schließlich in den Schrein am Nordostende der Küste zurückgebracht. Das bis 1963 durchgeführte Ritual geht auf die Verehrung der Fischer aus Tsukudamura für Sumiyoshi zurück, der auch als Schutzgottheit der Fischer und Seeleute galt. Die Fischer waren zu Beginn der Tokugawa-Zeit

(1615–1868) vom Shogun auf der Insel Tsukudajima vor der Bucht von Edo angesiedelt worden (siehe Tafel 4), hielten aber an ihren ursprünglichen Ritualen fest. Auf dem Banner ganz unten verewigt sich denn auch die Gemeinde des Sumiyoshi-Schreins von Tsukudajima als deren Stifter. Das Banner soll bis heute erhalten sein.

Obwohl die Menschen in Japan täglich chinesische und japanische Schriftzeichen vor Augen haben, verbindet sich mit ihnen, wenn sie ästhetisch gestaltet sind, ein hoher Identifikationswert. Tempel und Schreine, aber auch Laden- und Restaurantbesitzer nutzen ihren Signalcharakter (siehe Tafeln 7, 8, 12, 13), der durch ein ausgefallenes oder witziges Design noch unterstrichen wird. Ein gelungener Schriftzug bringt einen schnellen Wiedererkennungseffekt für die jeweiligen religiösen Stätten oder Geschäfte mit sich.

In Ostasien gelten Kalligrafien als direkte Spuren ihrer Schöpfer und wurden unter den Künsten am meisten geschätzt. Der Schreiber dieser Inschrift wird direkt neben der Bambusstange des Banners identifiziert: Es ist kein anderer als der Entwerfer des Inhaltsverzeichnisses der *Hundert berühmten Ansichten von Edo*, der hier als Seikengū Gengyo bezeichnet wird.

La fête de Sumiyoshi à Tsukudajima

Encadrée par une lanterne de fête rouge et blanc et un pin, une bannière blanche décorée d'idéogrammes chinois proéminents sert d'accroche visuelle au tout premier plan de cette vue. Sa grande taille est encore accentuée par la technique d'estampage à sec avec impression d'une trame textile (*nunomezuri*). Les cinq idéogrammes très visibles en écriture sigillaire indiquent le sujet de la feuille : « Sumiyoshi daimyōjin » (« Grande divinité Sumiyoshi »). À droite à côté de la bannière sont indiqués en petits caractères l'année (quatrième année de l'ère Ansei, c'est-à-dire 1857) et le mois de la fête de Sumiyoshi célébrée le 29ᵉᵐᵉ jour du sixième mois de chaque année.

L'événement central de la fête de Sumiyoshi est la longue procession d'un palanquin, symbole de la divinité couronné d'un phénix. Ce palanquin qu'on aperçoit à l'arrière-plan à gauche de la bannière est porté par de jeunes hommes qui traversent l'eau pour le porter jusqu'à l'île Tsukudajima avant de le rapporter au sanctuaire qui l'abrite à l'extrémité nord-est de la côte. Ce rituel qui fut accompli jusqu'en 1963 remonte à la dévotion des pêcheurs de Tsukudamura pour Sumiyoshi, qui était aussi considérée comme la divinité protectrice des pêcheurs et des marins. Au début de l'ère Tokugawa

(1615–1868), le shogun avait installé les pêcheurs sur l'île Tsukudajima dans la baie d'Edo (cf. pl. 4), mais ceux-ci étaient restés fidèles à leurs anciens rites. Sur la bannière tout en bas de l'image, la communauté du sanctuaire de Sumiyoshi à Tsukudajima s'immortalise ainsi comme fondatrice du sanctuaire. La bannière est réputée s'être conservée jusqu'à nos jours.

Bien que les idéogrammes chinois et japonais fassent partie de leur vie quotidienne, les Japonais y associent une haute valeur d'identification dès lors qu'ils sont esthétisés. Les temples et les sanctuaires, mais aussi les propriétaires de boutiques et de restaurants en exploitent le caractère signalétique (cf. pl. 7, 8, 12, 13) que renforce encore un dessin original ou plaisant. Un caractère réussi produit un fort effet de reconnaissabilité pour les sites religieux ou les boutiques concernées.

En Asie, la calligraphie est considérée comme une trace directe de son créateur et était le plus prisé de tous les arts. L'auteur de la présente inscription est identifié directement à côté de la perche en bambou de la bannière : il s'agit de nul autre que du concepteur de la table des matières des *Cent Vues célèbres d'Edo*, qui est ici désigné comme Seikengū Gengyo.

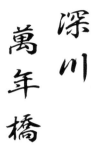

56

深川
萬年橋

Fukagawa Mannenbashi
11–1857

Mannen Bridge in Fukagawa

Exhibiting one of the most exciting compositions of the series, this print shows Mount Fuji as symbol of the eternal and sacred contrasted with the seemingly everyday world of commerce: a turtle is being offered for sale. Hanging in a noose from the handle of an ochre-coloured wooden tub, it hovers freely in the air. Compositionally, the turtle is framed by the light wood of the tub and the dark beams of a bridge.

This is Mannen Bridge, the "Bridge of Ten Thousand Years". In East Asia, the number 10,000 – like the turtle – symbolizes longevity.

Turtles and other aquatic animals were offered for sale at the foot of Mannen Bridge to give buyers the opportunity of setting them free. This Buddhist custom was widespread in East Asia: it was hoped that by granting life, one could improve one's own karma.

The striking contrast between the motifs and their symbolic significance, between the concrete and the abstract, is among the particular attractions of Hiroshige's late work. As a result, this print became one of the best-known in the series, and it served in a monochrome outline as an eye-catching motif in Samuel Bing's (1838–1905) *Le Japon Artistique*.

Die Brücke Mannenbashi in Fukagawa

Eine der aufregendsten Bildkompositionen der Serie zeigt den Berg Fuji als Symbol des Ewigen und Heiligen im Kontrast zum vermeintlich alltäglichen Geschäftsleben: Eine Schildkröte wird zum Verkauf angeboten. Sie hängt in einer Schlinge vom Tragegriff eines ockerfarbenen Holzbottichs herab und schwebt nahezu frei in der Luft. Kompositorisch wird die Schildkröte von dem hellen Holz des Bottichs und den dunklen Balken des Brückengeländers eingerahmt.

Bei dem im unmittelbaren Vordergrund angedeuteten Bauwerk handelt es sich um die Brücke Mannenbashi, „die Brücke der zehntausend Jahre". In Ostasien versinnbildlicht die Zahl 10 000 – ebenso wie die Schildkröte – Langlebigkeit.

Schildkröten und andere Wassertiere bot man am Fuß der Brücke Mannenbashi zum Kauf an und gab den Käufern die Gelegenheit, die Tiere wieder freizulassen. Dieser buddhistische Brauch war in Ostasien weit verbreitet, denn man erhoffte sich eine Verbesserung des eigenen Karmas, indem man Leben schenkte.

Der markante Kontrast zwischen den dargestellten Motiven und ihrer symbolischen Bedeutung, das Spannungsverhältnis zwischen Visualität und Abstraktion machen einen besonderen Reiz von Hiroshiges Spätwerk aus. So wurde diese Tafel eine der bekanntesten der Serie und diente in einer schwarz-weißen Umzeichnung als Blickfang in Samuel Bing's (1838–1905) *Le Japon Artistique*.

Le pont Mannenbashi à Fukagawa

Une des compositions les plus passionnantes de la série montre le mont Fuji comme symbole de l'éternité et de la sainteté contrastant avec la vie dite quotidienne des marchands : une tortue y est proposée à la vente. Attachée par une ficelle, elle pend à l'anse d'un grand bac en bois couleur ocre et semble en quelque sorte flotter au gré du vent. Du point de vue de la composition, la tortue est encadrée par le bois clair du bac et les poutres sombres du parapet du pont.

L'ouvrage évoqué au tout premier plan est le pont Mannenbashi, à savoir, le « pont des dix mille ans ». En Extrême-Orient – tout comme la tortue – le nombre 10 000 symbolise la longévité.

Les tortues et d'autres animaux aquatiques étaient proposés à la vente au pied du pont Mannenbashi et permettaient aux acheteurs de les relâcher. Cet usage bouddhiste était largement répandu en Extrême-Orient, car on en attendait une amélioration du karma personnel en donnant ou, mieux, en rendant la vie.

Le contraste appuyé entre les motifs représentés et leur sens symbolique, la tension entre fait visuel et abstraction font le charme particulier de l'œuvre tardif de Hiroshige. Et c'est ainsi que cette estampe est devenue l'une des plus célèbres de la série et que son dessin en noir et blanc a servi d'accroche visuelle pour la revue de Samuel Bing (1838–1905), *Le Japon Artistique*.

57

淵 の わかれた つまた ミ

Mitsumata Wakarenofuchi
2–1857

Mitsumata Wakarenofuchi

Beyond the broad Sumida River, animated by a number of fishing and cargo boats, rises Mount Fuji in the distance. The two white sails direct our gaze into the depth of the scene, and together with the mountain form the lightest areas of the composition. The unusual white coloration of the cone of the mountain, crowned by a bluish-black summit, doubtless serves primarily to set off the well-known silhouette of Japan's most famous peak from its surroundings. If we compare this print with the previous plate, and bear in mind that the two depict Mount Fuji from almost identical viewpoints, we can see how freely, and how well adapted to the respective composition, Hiroshige "stages" Japan's most famous landmark.

Not shown in this print, but well known, was the island of Nakazu, which Hiroshige merely alludes to in the form of a large reed-covered sandbank in the foreground. When this artificial island was created in 1775, an attractive pleasure district was established, with numerous restaurants, teahouses and bathhouses. The new quarter was so popular that it very soon came to be seen as a threat to public morals, and was demolished in 1789 as part of the restrictive Kansei Reforms (1787–1793). When this print was created, almost 70 years later, the one-time pleasure district was still vivid in the collective memory. In the second volume of his *Illustrated Souvenirs of Edo (Ehon Edo miyage)*, printed in 1850, Hiroshige writes:

"Nakazu lies to the south of Shin-Ōhashi Bridge. There used to be teahouses, and everyone spoke of the liveliness of the place. Now the island has become marshland, and looks particularly attractive in the snow."

Mitsumata Wakarenofuchi

Über den mit Lasten- und Fischerbooten belebten breiten Fluss Sumidagawa erhebt sich in der Ferne der Berg Fuji. Die beiden weißen Segel leiten den Blick in die Raumtiefe und bilden gemeinsam mit dem Berg die hellsten Punkte der Komposition. Die ungewöhnliche Farbgestaltung des blauschwarz bekrönten, weißen Kegels dient wohl in erster Linie dazu, die bekannte Form des berühmtesten Berges Japans aus seiner Umgebung hervorzuheben. Vergleicht man das Blatt mit dem vorhergehenden und bedenkt, dass beide Holzschnitte den Berg Fuji von nahezu identischen Standpunkten aus abbilden, wird deutlich, wie frei und der jeweiligen Komposition angepasst Hiroshige das wichtigste Wahrzeichen Japans in Szene setzte.

Bekannt war die auf dem Holzschnitt nicht gezeigte Insel Nakazu, die Hiroshige nur durch eine mit Schilf bewachsene große Sandbank im Vordergrund andeutet. Als die Insel 1775 künstlich angelegt wurde, entstand darauf ein attraktives Vergnügungsviertel mit zahlreichen Restaurants, Tee- und Badehäusern. Das neue Viertel erfreute sich solcher Beliebtheit, dass es schon bald als Bedrohung der sittlichen Ordnung galt und bereits 1789 im Zuge der restriktiven Kansei-Reformen (1787–1793) abgerissen wurde. Zur Zeit der Entstehung dieses Holzschnittes knapp 70 Jahre später war die einstige Vergnügungsinsel dennoch Vielen immer noch bekannt. So schreibt Hiroshige im zweiten Band seines Werkes *Illustrierte Mitbringsel aus Edo (Ehon Edo miyage)* von 1850 zu diesem Ort:

„Nakazu liegt im Süden der Brücke Shin-Ōhashi. Früher gab es hier Teehäuser und alle haben über die Lebendigkeit des Ortes geredet. Jetzt ist diese Insel zu einem Sumpfgelände geworden, und sie sieht bei Schnee besonders schön aus."

Mitsumata Wakarenofuchi

Au-dessus de la rivière Sumidagawa animée de chalands et de barques de pêche s'élève au loin le mont Fuji. Les deux voiles blanches font entrer le regard dans la profondeur de l'image et forment avec la montagne sacrée les accents les plus clairs de la composition. Le chromatisme inhabituel du cône blanc couronné d'un bleu-noir a sans doute été choisi avant tout pour démarquer de son environnement la forme connue de la montagne la plus célèbre du Japon. Quand on compare cette feuille avec la précédente et quand on songe que les deux estampes montrent le mont Fuji à partir d'un point de vue quasiment identique, on réalise avec quelle liberté et quel sens de la composition de chaque estampe individuelle Hiroshige a su mettre en scène le premier symbole du Japon.

Était aussi très connue l'île Nakazu qui n'apparaît pas ici, et que Hiroshige n'indique au premier plan qu'à l'aide d'un grand banc de sable planté de roseaux. À partir de 1775, l'année où fut créée cette île artificielle, un attrayant quartier des plaisirs y vit le jour avec de nombreux restaurants, maisons de thé et de bains. La vogue du nouveau quartier était telle que le gouvernement y vit bientôt une menace pour l'ordre moral et qu'il fut rasé dès 1789 dans le cadre des réformes de l'ère Kansei (1787–1793). Presque 70 ans plus tard, au moment où Hiroshige créait cette estampe, l'ancien quartier des plaisirs n'en restait pas moins un lieu très fréquenté. Dans le deuxième tome (1850) de ses *Souvenirs illustrés d'Edo (Ehon Edo miyage)*, Hiroshige écrivait :

« Nakazu est situé au sud du pont Shin-Ōhashi. L'on y trouvait autrefois des maisons de thé et tout le monde parlait de la vie animée du quartier. Aujourd'hui, l'île est devenue une zone marécageuse particulièrement belle sous la neige. »

58

大
は
し
あ
た
け
の
夕
立

Ōhashi Atake no yūdachi
9–1857

Sudden Shower over
Shin-Ōhashi Bridge and Atake

Rain falling from dark clouds forms a curtain of vertical, crisscrossing lines, some lighter, some darker. Through the rain we can see the imposing Shin-Ōhashi Bridge. Men and women are hurrying across, trying to protect themselves from the cloudburst with umbrellas, a straw mat or a hat, while a boatman poles his raft of timber down the Sumida River. The Atake district on the opposite bank is rendered in a silhouette of grey and blue tones. Hiroshige conveys an impression of saturated dampness, which, coupled with the evening atmosphere, is taken up, for example, in the *Nocturnes* of James Abbott McNeill Whistler (1834–1903) and his pictures of *Old Battersea Bridge*, painted in the 1860s and 1870s (see ill. 1).

The three light triangles in the middle of the forest in the left background hint at the boathouses. Their restoration was necessitated by the destructive Ansei earthquake of 1855 as well as by a number of typhoons, and had been completed a month before this print was approved. We can assume that Hiroshige produced different versions of this composition: the first, very rare, impressions show the boathouse triangles in brilliant white, and also two more boats near the bank towards the right margin of the print. For reasons unknown, shortly after the first impressions were made, the composition had to be changed to the present version. The *bokashi* seen here on the bridge is a characteristic element of this much sought-after second version.

Sudden Shower is one of the few prints in this series that all experts agree to be a masterpiece. It is the best-known print in the series and possibly Hiroshige's most famous work, comparable to the *Wave* by Katsushika Hokusai (1760–1849). In 1887, 30 years after this print was made, Vincent van Gogh (1853–1890) was also inspired to paint a copy in oils (see ill. 4).

The charm of this composition lies not least in the sophistication of the technical details. Thus, paradoxically, the naturalism allows the printer scope for his own creativity. The irregularly dabbed black clouds at the top margin of the print are slightly different in every impression. The woodblock cutter, on the other hand, needed to employ all his skills in order to produce the extremely thin hairlines representing the rain – a competence that continues to amaze copyists today.

Plötzlicher Schauer über der
Brücke Shin-Ōhashi und Atake

Aus dunklen Wolken fallender Regen bildet einen Vorhang aus vertikalen, einander kreuzenden, teils helleren, teils dunkleren Linien. Durch ihn hindurch blicken wir auf die imposante Brücke Shin-Ōhashi. Männer und Frauen überqueren sie, indem sie sich mit Schirmen, Strohmatten oder einem Hut gegen den Wolkenbruch schützen, während ein Bootsmann sein Bauholz den Fluss Sumidagawa hinunterstakt. Die Gegend Atake am gegenüberliegenden Ufer ist nur schemenhaft in Grau- und Blautönen angedeutet. Hiroshige vermittelt so den Eindruck satter Feuchtigkeit, der, gepaart mit der abendlichen Atmosphäre, etwa in James Abbott McNeill Whistlers (1834–1903) *Nocturnes* und seinen Bildern der *Old Battersea Bridge* der 1860er und 1870er Jahre wiederkehrt (siehe Abb. 1).

Die drei hellen Dreiecke inmitten des Waldes am linken Blattrand deuten die Bootshäuser an, deren Restaurierung nach dem zerstörerischen Ansei-Erdbeben von 1855 und mehreren Taifunen einen Monat vor Entstehung des Holzschnittes abgeschlossen worden war. Vermutlich fertigte Hiroshige verschiedene Versionen dieser Komposition an, denn der erste, sehr seltene Zustand zeigt die Dreiecke der Bootshäuser in leuchtendem Weiß und zwei weitere Boote nahe dem Ufer am rechten Bildrand. Kurz nach den ersten Abzügen des Entwurfs muss die Komposition zu der vorliegenden Version verändert worden sein. Die Farbgradierung (*bokashi*) auf der Brücke ist ein Kennzeichen dieser begehrten zweiten Version.

Plötzlicher Schauer ist eines der Blätter, bei denen sich alle Experten einig sind: ein Meisterwerk. Dieser bekannteste Holzschnitt der Serie ist zugleich vielleicht Hiroshiges berühmtestes Werk, vergleichbar mit der *Welle* von Katsushika Hokusai (1760–1849). So ließ sich Vincent van Gogh (1853–1890) im Jahr 1887, 30 Jahre nach Entstehung des Holzschnitts, zu einer Kopie in Öl inspirieren (siehe Abb. 4).

Der Reiz dieser Komposition liegt in raffinierten technischen Details begründet. So bietet ein auf die Spitze getriebener Naturalismus dem Drucker Spielraum für eigene Kreativität: Die unregelmäßig hingetupften schwarzen Wolken am oberen Bildrand fallen auf jedem Abzug etwas anders aus, und der Holzschneider musste sein ganzes Können einsetzen, um die extrem dünnen Stege für die Darstellung des Regens aus der Holzplatte freizulegen – eine Fertigkeit, die noch heute Kopisten in Erstaunen versetzt.

Averse soudaine sur le pont
Shin-Ōhashi et Atake

Une forte averse éclate sous de sombres nuages et forme un rideau de verticales entrecroisées tantôt claires, tantôt sombres. À travers elles, la vue tombe sur l'imposant pont Shin-Ōhashi, que des hommes et des femmes traversent en s'abritant de la pluie avec des parapluies, des paillasses ou un chapeau, tandis qu'un batelier descend la rivière sur son radeau de bois de construction. La contrée d'Atake sur la rive opposée n'est indiquée que schématiquement à l'aide de tons gris et bleus. Hiroshige communique ainsi l'impression d'une humidité saturée que l'on retrouve par exemple, associée à l'atmosphère vespérale, dans les *Nocturnes* de James Abbott McNeill Whistler (1834–1903) et dans ses tableaux de l'*Old Battersea Bridge* (cf. ill. 1) des années 1860 et 1870.

L'attrait de cette composition réside dans le raffinement technique des détails. Un naturalisme poussé à l'extrême n'en laisse pas moins au graveur une certaine latitude pour faire preuve de créativité : les touches irrégulières des nuages noirs sont un peu différentes dans chaque tirage. Le graveur devait en outre faire appel à toute son habileté pour dégager du bois d'impression les finissimes arêtes permettant de représenter la pluie, un savoir-faire qui suscite aujourd'hui encore l'admiration des copistes.

barques figurées près de la rive, côté droit de l'image. Peu après le tirage des premières épreuves du projet, la composition a dû être modifiée pour aboutir à la présente version. Le *bokashi* réalisé sur le pont est un signe distinctif de cette seconde version très recherchée.

Averse soudaine est une des rares feuilles sur lesquelles tous les experts sont d'accord : un chef-d'œuvre. Du reste, l'estampe la plus célèbre des *Cent Vues* est peut-être aussi la plus célèbre de tout l'œuvre de Hiroshige, comparable en cela à la *Vague* de Katsushika Hokusai (1760–1849). Elle inspira aussi Vincent van Gogh (1853–1890) qui en réalisa une copie à l'huile en 1887 (cf. ill. 4), trente ans après sa création.

Les trois triangles clairs au milieu de la forêt près du bord gauche de l'image indiquent les maisons flottantes, dont la restauration, après le séisme dévastateur de l'ère Ansei en 1855 et une série de typhons, avait été achevée un mois avant la création de cette estampe. Hiroshige a sans doute réalisé plusieurs versions de cette composition. Un premier état très rare présente en effet les triangles des maisons flottantes dans un ton blanc lumineux, avec deux autres

59

両国橋
大川ばた

Ryōgokubashi Ōkawabata
8–1856

Ryōgoku Bridge and the Great Riverbank

In this print, Hiroshige depicts the monumental Ryōgoku Bridge in a strong pictorial diagonal spanning the width of the print. At both ends of the bridge were teahouses and pleasure districts.

The ochre-coloured opposite bank, the bridge and the bamboo-pole roofs at the lower margin of the print form a clear Z-shaped composition that is emphasized by the dark-blue *bokashi*. Some parasols visible on the bridge at the near end are in the same light blue as the water, evidently a carelessness on the part of the printer.

Ryōgoku means "Two Lands", the two lands in question being the provinces linked by the bridge, Shimōsa and Musashi (in today's prefectures of Chiba, Saitama and Tokyo). The first Ryōgoku Bridge was completed in 1660, making it the oldest of the fixed crossings of the Sumida River. For a long time, therefore, it was simply called the "Great Bridge" (Ōhashi). The bridge shown in plate 58 was not built until 1693, and was consequently called the "New Great Bridge" (Shin-Ōhashi).

It was the building of this bridge that helped Edo to develop from a provincial centre into a metropolis dominating all Japanese islands. With a span of 160 metres (525 feet) and a breadth that – at seven metres (23 feet) – was enormous by the standards of the time, the Ryōgokubashi was Japan's largest bridge.

Die Brücke Ryōgokubashi mit großem Flussufer

Hiroshige zeigt auf diesem Blatt die monumentale, die Bilddiagonale durchmessende Brücke Ryōgokubashi mit den Teehäusern und Vergnügungsvierteln an den beiden Brückenköpfen.

Das ockerfarbene gegenüberliegende Ufer, die Brücke und die Dächer aus Bambusstangen am unteren Bildrand bilden eine klare Z-förmige Komposition, die durch ein dunkelblaues *bokashi* noch unterstrichen wird. Einige am linken Ende der Brücke erkennbare Schirme sind im Hellblau des Wassers gehalten, offensichtlich eine Nachlässigkeit des Druckers.

Ryōgoku heißt übersetzt „zwei Länder". Damit waren die durch die Brücke miteinander verbundenen Provinzen Shimōsa und Musashi in den heutigen Präfekturen Chiba, Saitama und Tokyo gemeint. Die Brücke Ryōgokubashi wurde 1660 fertiggestellt und war damit der älteste den Fluss Sumidagawa überquerende Transportweg. Lange Zeit nannte man sie deshalb einfach nur „Die Große Brücke" (Ōhashi). Die in Tafel 58 gezeigte Brücke entstand erst 1693 und wurde folglich „Neue Große Brücke" (Shin-Ōhashi) genannt.

Erst durch den Brückenbau konnte sich die Stadt Edo von einem Provinzzentrum zu einer alle japanischen Inseln beherrschenden Metropole entwickeln. Mit einer Spannweite von 160 Metern und einer für damalige Verhältnisse enormen Breite von sieben Metern war die Ryōgokubashi die größte Brücke Japans.

Le pont Ryōgokubashi et la grande rive

Hiroshige nous offre ici une vue du monumental pont Ryōgokubashi traversant à l'oblique toute la largeur de l'image, avec les maisons de thé et les quartiers des plaisirs des deux rives.

La rive opposée couleur ocre, le pont et les toits de bambou près du bord inférieur de l'image marquent une claire composition en « Z » que souligne encore le *bokashi* bleu sombre des deux rives et du pont. Quelques parapluies apparaissant à l'extrémité gauche du pont présentent le ton bleu clair de l'eau – apparemment une négligence de l'imprimeur.

Ryōgoku signifie « deux terres », ce qui renvoyait au fait que le pont reliait entre elles les provinces de Shimōsa et de Musashi (dans les actuelles préfectures de Chiba, de Saitama et de Tokyo). La construction du pont Ryōgokubashi fut achevé en 1660 et était donc la plus ancienne voie de communication franchissant la Sumidagawa. Pendant longtemps, il fut appelé simplement le « grand pont » (Ōhashi). Le pont de la planche 58 ne fut construit qu'en 1693 et était de ce fait appelé le « nouveau grand pont » (Shin-Ōhashi).

Ce n'est qu'avec la construction des ponts que la ville d'Edo put accéder du rang de centre provincial à celui de métropole exerçant sa domination sur toutes les îles japonaises. Avec une longueur de 160 mètres et une largeur de sept mètres, dimensions impressionnantes pour l'époque, le Ryōgokubashi était alors le plus grand pont du Japon.

60

浅草川
大川端
宮戸川

Asakusagawa Ōkawabata Miyatogawa
7–1857

Asakusa River, Miyato River, Great Riverbank

Beyond the heads of pilgrims in the foreground, we see a broad river animated by numerous small boats. The pale and expansive blue sky, reaching from the red of the low horizon to the dark *bokashi* gradations at the top margin of the print, is given a striking texture by the effective use of the grain of the woodblock.

The large red-and-white paper decorations on the left, and their distant counterparts on the right, stand symbolically for the theme of the picture: pilgrimage. The paper strips were among the requisites for pilgrims on the way to Mount Ōyama, which is some 60 kilometres (37 miles) south of Edo in today's Kanagawa Prefecture. The mountain was officially opened to pilgrims on the 27th day of the sixth month. Before starting out, pilgrims underwent a ritual cleansing on the eastern bank of the Sumida River beneath Ryōgoku Bridge, which is not depicted here (see plate 59).

The travellers in the immediate foreground have already completed the purification ceremony and are crossing the river in a boat. In their simple blue-and-white headcloths, they can be recognized as craftsmen distributing the colourful paper ribbons to the inhabitants of Edo as talismans against disease. This pilgrimage was so popular among craftsmen that in the very year this print was made, 1857, the popular story *Journey on Foot to Ōyama (Ōyama dōchū hizakurige)* also appeared.

Less homogeneous, colourfully dressed pilgrims are taking a boat towards the mouth of the Kanda River in the west. They are headed by a mountain ascetic, known as a *yamabushi*, who is blowing into a typical spiral conch. It was the mountain ascetics who had introduced the cult of ascending Mount Ōyama.

After their trip to Ōyama, the pilgrims can be seen on their way home to Edo on plate 76.

Over the years, three different names had come into common use for this section of the Sumida River, all of which feature in the title of this print. In subsequent print runs, the confusing title was changed to the more easily comprehensible *In Boats at Ryōgoku with a Distant View of Asakusa (Ryōgoku senchū Asakusa enkei)*.

Die Flüsse Asakusagawa und Miyatogawa und das Ufer des Ōkawa

Über die Köpfe von Pilgern hinweg fällt der Blick auf die von zahlreichen Booten belebte Flusslandschaft. Der sich vom roten Horizont bis zu den dunklen Bokashi-Gradierungen am oberen Bildrand spannende fahlblaue Himmel erhält durch die wirkungsvoll eingesetzte Holzmaserung der Druckplatte eine markante Strukturierung.

Das monumentale, rot-weiße Papiergesteck am linken Bildrand und sein Pendant auf der gegenüberliegenden Seite stehen symbolisch für das Thema des Blattes, eine Pilgerreise. Die Papierstreifen gehörten zur Ausstattung der Pilger auf dem Weg zum Berg Ōyama, der etwa 60 Kilometer südlich von Edo in der heutigen Präfektur Kanagawa liegt. Der Berg wurde offiziell am 27. Tag des sechsten Monats für die Pilger geöffnet. Vor Antritt der Reise unterzogen sich die Pilger einer rituellen Reinigung am Ostufer des Sumidagawa unterhalb der Brücke Ryōgokubashi, die außerhalb des Bildes liegt.

Die Reisenden im Vordergrund haben die Reinigungszeremonie bereits abgeschlossen und überqueren den Fluss in einem Boot. Sie sind an ihren einfachen weiß-blauen, um den Kopf gebundenen Tüchern als Handwerker zu erkennen, welche die bunten Papierbänder als Talismane gegen Krankheiten an die Bewohner von Edo verteilten. Diese Pilgerreise war bei Handwerkern so beliebt, dass im gleichen Jahr 1857 die populäre Erzählung *Zu Fuß auf dem Weg zum Ōyama (Ōyama dōchū hizakurige)* erschien.

Eine weniger homogene, bunt gekleidete Pilgergruppe fährt mit ihrem Boot auf die Mündung des Flusses Kandagawa im Westen zu. An ihrer Spitze bläst ein Bergasket (*yamabushi*) in das typische Instrument der Spiralmuschel. Die Bergasketen führten auch den Kult ein, den Berg Ōyama zu besteigen.

Auf Tafel 76 sind die Pilger – nach beendeter Reise zum Ōyama – auf ihrer Heimkehr nach Edo zu sehen.

Für den Fluss Sumidagawa hatten sich an der hier abgebildeten Stelle im Laufe der Zeit drei unterschiedliche Namen eingebürgert, die alle im Titel des Blattes genannt sind. In Nachdrucken änderte man den verwirrenden Titel zu dem einfacher verständlichen *Von Booten bei Ryōgoku aus mit Blick auf Asakusa in der Ferne (Ryōgoku senchū Asakusa enkei)*.

Les rivières Asakusagawa et Miyatogawa et la rive de l'Ōkawa

Au-dessus des têtes de quelques pèlerins, la vue s'ouvre sur un paysage fluvial animé de nombreuses barques. Le ciel bleu pâle qui se tend de l'horizon rouge jusqu'aux dégradés sombres (*bokashi*) près du bord supérieur de l'image, reçoit sa forte texture des veinures du bois d'impression efficacement exploitées par l'imprimeur.

La composition monumentale de papiers rouges et blancs qu'on aperçoit près du bord gauche de l'image et son pendant du côté opposé figurent symboliquement le sujet de la feuille, à savoir un pèlerinage. Les bandes de papier faisaient partie de l'équipement des pèlerins qui se rendaient au mont Ōyama situé à quelque 60 kilomètres au sud d'Edo dans l'actuelle préfecture de Kanagawa. Cette montagne était officiellement ouverte aux pèlerins le 27ème jour du sixième mois. Avant le départ, les pèlerins accomplissaient une ablution rituelle sur la rive est de la Sumidagawa, sous le pont Ryōgokubashi qui n'apparaît pas ici dans le champ de l'image.

Les voyageurs au premier plan ont déjà terminé leurs ablutions et traversent la rivière dans une barque. Les simples tissus blanc et bleu qui ceignent leurs têtes permettent de les identifier comme des artisans qui distribuaient aux habitants d'Edo des bandes de papier coloré servant de talismans contre les maladies. Ce pèlerinage était si apprécié parmi les artisans qu'en cette année 1857 parut le récit très populaire *À pied sur la route du mont Ōyama (Ōyama dōchū hizakurige)*.

Un groupe moins homogène de pèlerins vêtus d'habits de toutes les couleurs se dirige en barque vers l'embouchure de la rivière Kandagawa à l'ouest. À leur tête, un ascète des montagnes (*yamabushi*) souffle dans l'instrument typique d'une conque spiraliforme. Les ascètes des montagnes furent aussi ceux qui inaugurèrent le culte consistant à gravir le mont Ōyama. Dans la planche 76, on peut voir des pèlerins revenant à Edo après leur voyage au mont Ōyama.

À l'endroit représenté dans cette estampe, trois noms différents étaient entrés dans l'usage pour désigner la Sumidagawa, noms qui sont intégralement cités dans le titre de la feuille. Dans les tirages ultérieurs, ce titre prêtant à confusion sera rendu plus compréhensible par sa simplification en *Des barques près de Ryōgoku, avec une vue d'Asakusa dans le lointain (Ryōgoku senchū Asakusa enkei)*.

61

浅草川
首尾の松
御厩河岸

Asakusagawa Shubi no matsu Oumayagashi
8–1856

The "Pine of Success" and Oumayagashi on the Asakusa River

The "Pine of Success" (Shubi no matsu), which spreads its branches from the left over the Sumida River, stood by a landing quay near the Asakusa district's rice storage. This storage was administered by the shogunate and is said to have suffered serious damage in the 1855 earthquake. From here, the Oumayagashi ferry took passengers to the Shin-Yoshiwara pleasure district north of Asakusa. Stars are already twinkling in the darkening evening sky, while the horizon is still bathed in the golden light of the sun, which has set behind the Azuma Bridge. Boats glide through the dusk, and guests are coming and going. A roofed pleasure boat (*yanebune*) has moored in front of the bamboo palisade on the bank at the left. It is said that below the ancient pine was the place where lovers met secretly.

In a later version of this print, in Hiroshige's *Illustrated Souvenirs of Edo* (*Ehon Edo miyage*, volume seven, 1857), we find a mirror image of the same view, but with a woman standing upright in the boat and apparently gazing across to the opposite bank. Why did Hiroshige reject this erotically unambiguous element in the version for his *One Hundred Famous Views of Edo*? He opted for a more subtle pictorial solution: behind the lowered green blind, we can just guess the silhouette of a woman. In later impressions of this print, the contrast is much stronger. Has she found a secret love-nest where she is waiting for her lover? In any case, the sophisticated printing technique and the unusual colour combination of green with the yellow and gradated blues of the evening sky lend a romantic air to the scene.

Die „Kiefer des Erfolgs" und Oumayagashi am Fluss Asakusagawa

Die „Kiefer des Erfolgs" (Shubi no matsu), die ihre Äste von links über den Fluss Sumidagawa ausbreitet, stand auf einem Landungssteg in der Nähe des vom Shogunat verwalteten Reisspeichers für den Bezirk Asakusa. Dieser Speicher soll in dem Erdbeben von 1855 zu großem Schaden gekommen sein. Von dort verkehrte die Oumayagashi-Fähre zum Freudenviertel Shin-Yoshiwara nördlich von Asakusa. Am dunklen Abendhimmel funkeln bereits Sterne, während der Horizont noch in das goldgelbe Licht des Sonnenuntergangs über der Brücke Azumabashi getaucht ist. Durch die Dämmerung gleiten Boote mit kommenden und gehenden Gästen. Ein überdachtes Vergnügungsboot (*yanebune*) hat links vor der Bambuspalisade am Ufer festgemacht. Hier unter der alten Kiefer soll der Ort gewesen sein, an dem sich Liebespaare heimlich trafen.

In einer späteren Version zu diesem Blatt in Hiroshiges Werk

Illustrierte Mitbringsel aus Edo (*Ehon Edo miyage*), Band 7 von 1857, findet sich die gleiche Komposition seitenverkehrt, aber mit einer aufrecht im Boot stehenden Frau, die auf das gegenüberliegende Ufer zu blicken scheint. Warum hat Hiroshige auf diese erotisch eindeutige Komponente bei den *Hundert Ansichten* verzichtet? Er hat sich für eine subtilere Lösung entschieden: Hinter der heruntergelassenen grünen Jalousie verbirgt sich die Silhouette einer weiblichen Person, die in den Nachdrucken erheblich kontrastreicher herausgearbeitet wurde. Hat sie sich dort zu einem Stelldichein eingefunden und wartet, im Boot verborgen, auf ihren Liebhaber? Jedenfalls verleihen die raffinierte Drucktechnik und die ungewöhnliche Farbenkomposition von Gelb, Grün und gradiertem Blau der Nachtszene einen unvergleichlichen romantischen Zauber.

Le « Pin du succès » et Oumayagashi sur les rives de l'Asakusagawa

Le « Pin du succès » (Shubi no matsu) qui déploie une de ses branches à gauche au-dessus de la rivière Sumidagawa, était planté sur un débarcadère proche de l'entrepôt de riz de la zone d'Asakusa administré par le shogunat. Cet entrepôt est réputé avoir subi de graves dommages lors du grand séisme de 1855. De là, le bac d'Oumayagashi partait vers le quartier des plaisirs Shin-Yoshiwara situé au nord d'Asakusa. Au firmament brillent déjà des étoiles, tandis qu'au-dessus du pont Azumabashi, l'horizon est encore plongé dans la lumière dorée du couchant. Des barques chargées de passagers vont et viennent à travers le crépuscule. Une barque d'agrément couverte (*yanebune*) s'est amarrée à gauche devant la palissade de bambou. La rumeur dit que c'est ici sous le vieux pin que les amants se retrouvaient en secret.

Dans une version plus tardive de cette feuille parue dans le septième tome (1857) des *Souvenirs illustrés d'Edo* (*Ehon Edo miyage*), la même composition est présentée inversée en miroir, mais dans la barque, une femme debout semble scruter la rive opposée. Pourquoi Hiroshige a-t-il renoncé à cet élément romanesque dans les *Cent Vues* ? En fait, l'artiste a opté pour une solution plus subtile : derrière le store vert abaissé se cache la silhouette d'une personne féminine que les tirages ultérieurs font ressortir beaucoup plus fortement. Cette femme s'est-elle rendue ici à un rendez-vous amoureux, attendant cachée dans la barque la venue de son amant ? Quoi qu'il en soit, le raffinement technique et la combinaison de jaune, de vert et d'un dégradé bleu, confèrent à cette scène nocturne un charme romanesque incomparable.

駒形堂
吾嬬橋

Komakatadō Azumabashi
1–1857

Komakata Hall and Azuma Bridge

The "famous place" that gives this print its title is the square-shaped Komakata Hall, bottom left. Beyond its tent roof we survey a broad expanse of the Sumida River, with the Azuma Bridge on the far left and the Asakusa district stretching along the far bank (see plate 61). This small temple, which exists today only in the form of a replica built in concrete, once housed a statue of the Bodhisattva Kannon with a Horse's Head (*Batō Kannon*).

The eye-catching focal points, however, are a red flag fluttering in the wind, presumably outside a cosmetics shop, and a black-and-white bird, a *hototogisu*, screeching with its open beak as it flies in front of the low, grey rain clouds.

The hototogisu, often wrongly called the Japanese cuckoo, is the key to this print, for a famous love poem was associated both with the bird and Komakata Hall. This poem is attributed to the courtesan Takao II (1640–1659), who was glorified as a tragic heroine in the kabuki theatre and in legends. She was the lover of the feudal lord of Sendai, Date Tsunamune (1640–1711), who is said to have had a residence in the vicinity of Komakata. Takao died young, consumed with longing for Tsunamune, and had the following verse attributed to her:

"Are you now, my love, near Komakata? Cry of the cuckoo!"

Kimi wa ima, Komakata atari, Hototogisu.

The poem alludes onomatopoeically to the shrill cry of the hototogisu, which in Japanese poetry is a symbol of longing and loneliness.

Although Shin-Yoshiwara was totally destroyed in the 1855 earthquake, Hiroshige uses the red flag and the bird to emphasize the poetic aspect of the life of the courtesan. Far more prosaic is the print *Komakata* by Kunisada (i.e. Toyokuni III, 1786–1864), printed a year later, from the series *Famous Views of Edo with a Hundred Beauties* (*Edo meisho hyakunin bijo*, 1857/58). In his print, Kunisada alludes to Hiroshige's Komakata landscape, and as the central subject depicts a courtesan passing the time by preparing warm rice wine.

Die Halle Komakatadō und die Brücke Azumabashi

Der „berühmte Ort", der dieser Tafel den Titel gibt, ist die quadratische Halle Komakatadō. Über ihr Zeltdach hinweg blicken wir auf das Panorama des Flusses Sumidagawa bis zur Brücke Azumabashi vor dem Stadtviertel Asakusa (siehe Tafel 61). Dieser kleine Tempel, von dem es heute nur noch eine Nachbildung in Beton gibt, beherbergte einst die Statue des Bodhisattva Kannon mit Pferdekopf (*Batō Kannon*).

Der eigentliche Blickfang aber sind die – vermutlich vor einem Laden für Kosmetik – an einem Mast im Wind flatternde rote Fahne und ein schwarz-weißer Vogel (*hototogisu*), der mit geöffnetem Schnabel schreiend durch die grauen, tief hängenden Regenwolken am Sommerhimmel fliegt.

Der oft fälschlich als japanischer Kuckuck bezeichnete Vogel Hototogisu ist der eigentliche Schlüssel zur Darstellung, denn mit ihm und der Halle Komakatadō assoziierte man ein berühmtes Liebesgedicht. Es wird der Kurtisane Takao II. (1640–1659) in den Mund gelegt, die in Kabuki-Theaterstücken und Legenden als tragische Heldin verherrlicht wurde. Sie war die Geliebte des Feudalherrn von Sendai, Date Tsunamune (1640–1711), der in der Gegend von Komakata eine Residenz besessen haben soll. Der jung verstorbenen Takao, die sich in Sehnsucht nach Tsunamune verzehrte, wird folgendes Kurzgedicht zugeschrieben:

„Seid Ihr, mein Herr, schon bis Komakata gekommen? (Hört den Ruf des) Hototogisu!"

Kimi wa ima, Komakata atari, Hototogisu.

Das Gedicht spielt lautmalerisch auf den scharfen Schrei des Hototogisu an, in der japanischen Dichtung ein Symbol für Sehnsucht und Einsamkeit.

Obgleich Shin-Yoshiwara durch das Erdbeben von 1855 völlig zerstört worden war, betont Hiroshige mit der roten Fahne und dem Vogel die poetische Dimension des Kurtisanenlebens. Weitaus eindeutiger ist dieselbe Örtlichkeit in dem ein Jahr später erschienenen Blatt *Komakata* von Kunisada Toyokuni III. (1786–1864) aus der Serie *Berühmte Ansichten von Edo mit hundert Schönheiten* (*Edo meisho hyakunin bijo*, 1857–1858) behandelt. Kunisada spielt in der kleinen Vignette auf Hiroshiges Komakata-Landschaft an und zeigt davor als Hauptbildgegenstand eine Kurtisane, die sich mit der Zubereitung von warmem Reiswein die Zeit vertreibt.

Le pavillon Komakatadō et le pont Azumabashi

Le « lieu célèbre » qui donne son titre à cette planche est le pavillon carré Komakatadō. Par-delà son toit en forme de tente s'ouvre un panorama dans lequel la rivière Sumidagawa coule jusqu'au pont Azumabashi devant le quartier d'Asakusa (cf. pl. 61). Ce petit temple dont il n'existe plus aujourd'hui qu'une reproduction en béton, abritait autrefois une statue du bodhisattva Kannon à tête de cheval (*Batō Kannon*).

En fait, l'accroche visuelle réelle est donnée par le drapeau rouge – vraisemblablement placé devant une boutique de cosmétique – qui flotte au gré du vent au haut de son mât, et par un oiseau noir et blanc (*hototogisu*) qui vole bec ouvert parmi les nuages chargés de pluie d'un ciel d'été.

Souvent qualifié à tort comme le coucou japonais, l'oiseau hototogisu est la vraie clef de la représentation. C'est en effet à cet oiseau et au pavillon Komakatadō qu'est couramment associé un poème d'amour célèbre. Ce poème est attribué à la courtisane Takao II (1640–1659) glorifiée comme une héroïne tragique dans les légendes et les pièces de kabuki. Elle fut l'amante du seigneur féodal de Sendai, Date Tsunamune (1640–1711), qui est réputé avoir eu une résidence aux environs de Komakata. À la jeune Takao, qui se consumait d'amour pour Tsunamune, est attribué le court poème suivant :

« Êtes-vous, Seigneur, déjà venu jusqu'à Komakata ? (entendez-le cri du) hototogisu ! »

Kimi wa ima, Komakata atari, Hototogisu.

Ce poème est une allusion onomatopéique au cri aigu du hototogisu, symbole de la passion amoureuse et de la solitude dans la poésie japonaise.

Bien que Shin-Yoshiwara eût été entièrement détruit lors du grand séisme de 1855, avec le drapeau rouge, Hiroshige souligne la dimension poétique de la vie des courtisanes. La même valeur du lieu est traitée de manière encore bien plus claire dans la feuille *Komakata* de la série *Vues célèbres d'Edo avec cent beautés* (*Edo meisho hyakunin bijo*, 1857–1858) de Kunisada (Toyokuni III, 1786–1864) parue un an plus tard. Dans la petite vignette, Kunisada fait allusion au paysage de Komakata de Hiroshige et représente en avant-plan, comme motif principal, une courtisane préparant du saké chaud.

綾瀬川
鐘か淵

Ayasegawa Kanegafuchi
7–1857

The Ayase River and Kanegafuchi

Leaves and pink fan-shaped flowers of a mimosa tree (*nemunoki*) fill the top half of the print while criss-crossing reeds growing out of the banks of the Sumida River project above the horizon. A boatman in a geometrically patterned garment stands on his raft with his back to us, gazing towards the opposite bank, where the Ayase River joins the Sumida. Looking towards the north-east, we are at the most northern point on the Sumida River to be depicted by Hiroshige in his *One Hundred Famous Views of Edo*.

The decorative elements of this composition recall the industrial designs for fabrics and other utilitarian objects that were to appear in Japan only a few years later. It was these designs that encouraged an enthusiasm in the West for all things Japanese, known as Japonism, which in turn inspired Art Nouveau. In other words, this print was among the harbingers of Western commercial graphic art.

Der Fluss Ayasegawa und Kanegafuchi

Nah an den Betrachter herangerückte Blätter und rosafarbene, fächerförmige Blüten eines Mimosenbaumes (*nemunoki*) füllen die obere Blatthälfte, während sich kreuzende, lanzettartige Schilfgräser aus dem Fluss Sumidagawa von unten den Horizont überragen. Ein in geometrisch gemusterter Kleidung gewandeter Bootsmann steht in Rückenansicht auf seinem Floß und lenkt den Blick auf den in den Sumidagawa fließenden Fluss Ayasegawa in der Bildmitte. Wir schauen nach Nordosten und befinden uns hier an einem der nördlichsten Punkte des Sumidagawa, die Hiroshige in den *Hundert Ansichten* dargestellt hat.

In seiner ornamentalen Komposition erinnert dieser Druck an die wenige Jahre später in Japan entstandenen industriellen Entwürfe für Stoffe und andere Gebrauchsgegenstände. Es waren diese Muster, welche in Europa den Japonismus und später den Jugendstil beflügelten, für den der Holzschnitt ebenso wegweisend war wie die Gebrauchsgrafik.

La rivière Ayasegawa et Kanegafuchi

Des feuilles d'arbre fortement rapprochées du spectateur et les fleurs roses en éventail d'un mimosa (*nemunoki*) emplissent la moitié supérieure de la feuille, tandis que des roseaux lancéolés entrecroisés de la Sumidagawa s'élèvent d'en bas au-dessus de l'horizon. Un batelier vu de dos, vêtu d'un habit aux motifs géométriques se tient debout sur son radeau, le regard dirigé vers l'Ayasegawa, qui se jette dans la Sumidagawa au centre de l'image. La vue est orientée au nord-est, et cette portion de la Sumidagawa est l'une de celles qui se trouvent le plus au nord dans les *Cent Vues*.

De par la tendance ornementale de la composition, cette estampe rappelle les dessins industriels réalisés quelques années plus tard au Japon pour des tissus et des objets utilitaires. Ces motifs nourriront plus tard le japonisme et l'art nouveau en Europe, pour lesquels la présente estampe joua un rôle de précurseur autant que les arts graphiques appliqués.

堀切の花菖蒲

Horikiri no hanashōbu
15–1857

Horikiri Iris Garden

Hiroshige offers another demonstration of his predilection for unusual vantage points in this print: a low viewpoint through a screen of iris stalks confers a vertical, almost textile-like structure, while giving the viewer the impression of being a voyeur secretly observing the visitors beyond the riverbank. While the compositional frame reveals only part of the flower on the far left, the two other flowers are depicted in what can only be called a sensual clarity. In the seventh volume of Hiroshige's *Illustrated Souvenirs of Edo* (*Ehon Edo miyage*, 1857), irises are compared to the beautiful women admiring them, and such women are represented in the middle distance. It is certainly no coincidence that the grey and violet tones of their garments reflect the colours of the flowers.

The particular species of iris depicted here, known as the "flowering shōbu"

(*hanashōbu*), was first introduced to Europe by Engelbert Kaempfer (1651–1716) in his 1712 work *Flora Japonica*; from 1690 to 1692 he had worked as a physician for the Dutch trading company in Japan. The plant derives its botanical name, *Iris kaempferi*, from him. An iris plant was finally brought to Europe in the late 1850s, triggering a veritable iris craze from the 1870s, reflected in the founding of iris societies and in the motif repertoire of Art Nouveau. It is precisely the stylization of the plant illustrated here that we see also in Art Nouveau wall-plates, furniture and glassware, for example by Émile Gallé (1846–1904) around 1890.

The fact that this composition may not seem particularly daring to us in the 21st century is due in no small part to the influence of Hiroshige. To 19th-century eyes, it was extraordinary.

Irisgarten in Horikiri

Auf diesem Blatt demonstriert Hiroshige ein weiteres Mal seine bevorzugte Wahl eines ungewöhnlichen Betrachterstandpunktes: Dank des extrem niedrig angesetzten Blickpunktes wird das Bild mittels der filigran aufragenden Irispflanzen wie durch ein Gewebe vertikal strukturiert und der Eindruck beschworen, der Betrachter würde wie ein Voyeur das Geschehen jenseits des Flussufers beobachten. Während der Kompositionsrahmen so gewählt ist, dass die linke Blüte nur zur Hälfte sichtbar ist, sind die beiden anderen Blüten in einer geradezu lasziven Deutlichkeit herausgearbeitet. In Hiroshiges Werk *Illustrierte Mitbringsel aus Edo* (*Ehon Edo miyage*), Band 7, 1857, werden Irisblüten mit den sie bewundernden schönen Frauen verglichen, die im vorgestellten Blatt im Mittelgrund auch zu sehen sind. Es ist sicherlich kein Zufall, dass sich die Grau- und Violetttöne ihrer Kleidung mit denjenigen der Blüten decken.

Die spezifische Iris-Art „blühende *shōbu*" stellte der 1690–

1692 als Arzt für die holländische Handelsniederlassung in Japan tätige Engelbert Kaempfer (1651–1716) in seinem 1712 publizierten Werk *Flora Japonica* erstmals in Europa vor. Nach ihm heißt diese Art „Iris kaempferi". Ende der 1850er Jahre schließlich wurde die Pflanze selbst nach Europa eingeführt und löste ab den 1870er Jahren einen wahren Boom aus, der sich etwa in Gründungen von Iris-Gesellschaften oder auch im Bildrepertoire des Jugendstils niederschlug. Gerade die auf diesem Blatt vorgeführte Stilisierung der Pflanze findet sich unter anderem auf Wandtellern, Möbeln und Gläsern des Jugendstils (etwa von Émile Gallé (1846–1904), um 1890.

Wenn uns diese Komposition im 21. Jahrhundert nicht mehr als besonders gewagt erscheint, so ist das sicher auch darauf zurückzuführen, dass Hiroshiges Werk eine immense Wirkung entfaltete. Für die Betrachter im 19. Jahrhundert war dieser Holzschnitt dagegen außergewöhnlich.

Jardin d'iris à Horikiri

Dans cette feuille, Hiroshige montre à nouveau son intérêt pour les points de vues inhabituels : grâce à un point de vue surbaissé, l'image est marquée par un entrelacs d'iris jaillissants structuré comme une trame textile. La disposition de ces éléments place le spectateur dans la position d'un voyeur observant l'événement qui se déroule sur la rive opposée de la rivière. Alors que tout se passe comme si le cadrage de la composition avait été choisi pour que la fleur de gauche soit à moitié coupée par le bord de l'image, les deux autres iris ont été traités avec une clarté presque lascive. Dans le septième tome (1857) des *Souvenirs illustrés d'Edo* (*Ehon Edo miyage*), les iris sont comparés aux belles admiratrices qu'on aperçoit aussi au second plan de la présente estampe. Quant à la correspondance entre les tons gris et violets de leurs habits et des fleurs, elle ne saurait évidemment être un fruit du hasard.

La variété d'iris appelée « shōbu florissant » fut présentée pour la

première fois en Europe par Engelbert Kaempfer (1651–1716) – un médecin qui travailla entre 1690 et 1692 pour le comptoir hollandais au Japon – dans son ouvrage *Flora Japonica* paru en 1712. C'est d'après cet auteur que les iris de cette variété s'appellent « kaempferi ». À la fin des années 1850, la plante fut finalement introduite en Europe, déclenchant à partir des années 1870 un véritable engouement qui se constata par la création de sociétés de l'iris ou dans le répertoire visuel de l'art nouveau. La stylisation présentée dans cette estampe se retrouve ainsi notamment dans des assiettes décoratives, des meubles et des verres art nouveau (p. ex. vers 1890 chez Émile Gallé, 1846–1904).

Si cette composition ne nous semble plus aujourd'hui particulièrement audacieuse, ceci se doit assurément au fait que l'œuvre de Hiroshige a exercé une immense influence. Pour les spectateurs du XIXᵉ siècle, l'estampe avait en revanche un caractère tout à fait inhabituel.

65

亀戸
天神
境内

Kameido Tenjin keidai
7—1856

Inside Kameido Tenjin Shrine

This is one of the best-known prints in the series. Its effect on the Japanese collective memory is reflected in countless reproductions, of widely varying quality, including calendar illustrations. Even Claude Monet (1840–1926) was inspired to design his Japanese garden in Giverny according to the print.

The print shows one of the famous "drum bridges" (Taikobashi), based on Chinese models. This term derives from the circular form resembling a drum, which the semi-circular bridge forms together with its reflection. Unlike many of his imitators, Hiroshige does not depict the full circle of the "drum", concentrating instead on the timber construction. The copper, flame-shaped *gibōshi* on the pillars of the balustrade are unusual. In Edo, this decoration was reserved for the "high-ranking" Nihonbashi and Kyōbashi Bridges (see plates 43, 76). It was doubtless the close relationship with the Tokugawa dynasty that allowed the Kameido Tenjin Shrine, dedicated to the legendary courtier and famous poet Sugawara Michizane (845–903), to use this important decoration on its own bridge. Like Katsushika Hokusai (1760–1849), who

designed a print with a view of the same bridge around 1834, Hiroshige sets off the metal finials against a pale background.

The fact that it is summer is indicated by the cascades of purple wisteria admired by visitors in the foreground and middle distance; areas of dark-blue colour gradations on the water indicate the shadows cast by the trees.

The earliest impressions of this print, to which the one reproduced here belongs, display one of the few colouring errors in the series: the blue of the water continues above the horizon and fills out the entire arch of the bridge. The printer possibly misunderstood Hiroshige's colouring instructions; be that as it may, this misunderstanding demonstrates once more the important role of the printer in ensuring the quality of the final product.

After the devastating Meireki fire of 1657, efforts were made to settle the areas to the east of the Sumida River. One of the measures was the construction in the 1660s of the shrine that is cited in the title but not actually shown in the print.

Im Schrein Kameido Tenjin

Dieses Blatt gehört zu den bekanntesten der Serie. Seine Wirkung auf das visuelle Gedächtnis in Japan zeigt sich an den unzähligen Reproduktionen verschiedenster Qualität bis hin zu Kalenderblättern. Claude Monet (1840–1926) hat sich von diesem Holzschnitt für seinen japanischen Garten in Giverny inspirieren lassen.

Wir sehen hier eine der berühmten, auf chinesischen Vorbildern basierenden Trommelbrücken (Taikobashi). Diese Bezeichnung leitet sich von der einer Trommel gleichenden Kreisform ab, die die halbkreisförmige Brücke zusammen mit ihrem Spiegelbild im Wasser bildet. Hiroshige verzichtet im Gegensatz zu vielen seiner Nachahmer, auf die Darstellung des ganzen Rundes der „Trommel" und konzentriert sich auf die Holzkonstruktion. Ein Kuriosum sind die kupfernen, flammenförmigen *gibōshi* auf den Brückenpfosten. Diese Verzierung war in Edo den „rang-hohen" Brücken Nihonbashi und Kyōbashi vorbehalten (siehe Tafel 43, 76). Es ist wohl die enge Beziehung zum Haus der Tokugawa, welche es dem Sugawara Michizane (845–903) geweihten Schrein Kameido Tenjin erlaubte, dieses mit Bedeutung aufgeladene Zitat auf seiner Brücke zu verwenden. Ebenso wie Katsushika Hokusai

(1760–1849) in einer Darstellung derselben Brücke von ca. 1834 setzt Hiroshige die Metallkronen gegen einen hellen Hintergrund ab.

Auf die sommerliche Jahreszeit deuten die kaskadenartig herabfallenden violetten Glyzinienblüten im Vorder- und Mittelgrund hin, die dort von Besuchern bewundert werden. Auf der ausgedehnten Wasserfläche sind mittels dunkelblauer Farbgradierungen Baumschatten angedeutet.

Die frühesten Drucke dieses Holzschnittes, zu denen dieses Blatt gehört, zeigen einen der wenigen Farbfehler: Das Blau des Wassers ist über den Horizont hinaus erweitert worden und füllt das gesamte Rund der Brücke aus. Möglicherweise hat der Drucker Farbanweisungen von Hiroshige falsch verstanden; jedenfalls belegt dieses Missverständnis ein weiteres Mal, wie wichtig die Rolle des Druckers für das Endprodukt war.

Nach dem verheerenden Meireki-Feuer von 1657 war man bestrebt, die östlich des Flusses Sumidagawa gelegenen Gebiete zu besiedeln. Zu dieser Maßnahme gehörte auch der zwar im Titel benannte, auf dem Holzschnitt aber nicht dargestellte Bau des Schreins aus den 1660er Jahren.

Dans le sanctuaire Kameido Tenjin

Cette feuille est une des plus célèbres de la série. Son impact sur la mémoire visuelle du Japon est illustré par d'innombrables reproductions de toutes qualités – jusqu'aux feuilles de calendrier. Claude Monet (1840–1926) s'en est aussi inspiré pour son jardin japonais à Giverny.

Nous voyons ici un des fameux ponts-tambours (Taikobashi) dérivés de modèles chinois. Ce qualificatif rend compte de la forme circulaire, apparentée à un tambour, que le pont en plein cintre forme avec son reflet dans l'eau. Contrairement à nombre d'imitateurs Hiroshige renonce à la représentation intégrale du « tambour » et se concentre sur la construction en bois. Une curiosité du pont est donnée par les *gibōshi* en cuivre en forme de flamme fixés sur les montants du pont. À Edo, cette décoration était réservée aux seuls ponts « de haut rang », à savoir le Nihonbashi et le Kyōbashi (cf. pl. 43, 76). C'est sans doute aux liens étroits qui l'unissaient à la maison des Tokugawa que le sanctuaire Kameido Tenjin dédié à Sugawara Michizane (845–903) fut autorisé à arborer sur son pont cette citation chargée de sens. Tout comme l'a fait Katsushika Hokusai

(1760–1849) dans sa représentation du même pont (vers 1834), Hiroshige a démarqué les couronnements métalliques de l'ouvrage contre un fond clair.

La saison d'été est indiquée par les cascades de glycines violettes que des visiteurs admirent au premier et à l'arrière-plan. Sur le plan d'eau étendu, les ombres des arbres ont été évoquées par des dégradés bleus.

Les plus anciens tirages de cette estampe – cette feuille en fait partie – présentent une erreur de couleur peu visible : le bleu de l'eau a été étendu au-delà de la limite de l'horizon et emplit la totalité du rond formé par le pont. Il se peut que cette erreur se doive à une interprétation erronée des indications de ton données par Hiroshige ; en tout état de cause, ce malentendu est une nouvelle illustration de l'importance cruciale de l'imprimeur pour le résultat final.

Après l'incendie dévastateur de Meireki en 1657, l'on cherchait à coloniser les domaines situés à l'est de la Sumidagawa. C'est dans le cadre de ces mesures que le sanctuaire, situé en dehors du champ de l'image nonobstant sa citation dans le titre, avait été bâti dans les années 1660.

66

五百羅漢さゞゐ堂

Gohyaku Rakan Sazaidō
8–1857

The Sazaidō Hall at the Five Hundred Rakan Temple

Here we are in one of the eastern suburbs of Edo, in a district marked by a system of canals laid out in a grid pattern and integrated into Edo by the construction of the Ryōgoku and Shin-Ōhashi Bridges (plates 58, 59).

Together with the pilgrims on the balcony of the building of the title, we enjoy a famous panorama of green fields bordered on the horizon by the low houses and piles of timber lining the Tategawa Canal. Hiroshige thus contrasts the portentous presence of a culturally and symbolically important building with an extensive view of a flat and not particularly interesting landscape.

The building, emphasized in yellow, was actually called the "Hall of the Three Pilgrimages" (Sansōdō), a name that hints at its function: on its three storeys, the faithful could accumulate in a short time as much spiritual merit as would normally need three pilgrimages to acquire. On each storey there were replicas of the famous 33 statues of Bodhisattva Kannon from western Japan (Saikoku), the Kantō plain, and the Chichibu district in today's Saitama Prefecture. Having arrived on the top floor, the pilgrims were rewarded with an unusual view. This time-efficient way of acquiring good karma was typical of the rational and commercial approach to religion in Edo.

The hall was built in 1741 as part of the Temple of the Five Hundred Rakan, the Buddhist saints released from the eternal cycle of birth and rebirth. The temple itself was founded by a Zen priest of the Ōbaku School in 1695; it contained a full set of 500 statues of the *rakan*, completed in 1728.

Hiroshige takes up the motif of an earlier print in horizontal format in his series *Famous Views of Edo* (*Edo meisho: Gohyaku Rakan Sazaidō*), dating from about 1845. There, however, while likewise cropped by the right-hand margin of the print, the Hall in the previous version is viewed from a low vantage point, so that the view of the rural idyll is consequently less extensive.

Die Halle Sazaidō im Tempel der 500 Rakan

Wir befinden uns hier in einem der östlichen Vororte von Edo, in jenem von rechtwinklig angelegten Kanälen durchkreuzten Gebiet, welches durch die Konstruktion der Brücken Ryōgoku-bashi und Shin-Ōhashi (siehe Tafeln 58, 59) als Teil von Edo erschlossen worden war.

Mit Pilgern auf dem Balkon des angeschnittenen, titelgebenden Gebäudes genießen wir eine für ihren Panoramablick berühmte Aussicht auf grüne Felder, die am Horizont von – den Kanal Tategawa säumenden – niedrigen Häusern und Holzstapelstellen begrenzt wird. Hiroshige kontrastiert so die bedeutungsschwere Präsenz eines kulturell und symbolisch wichtigen Gebäudes mit dem weitläufigen Ausblick in die wenig aufregende flache Landschaft.

Das mit starkem Gelb hervorgehobene Gebäude hieß eigentlich „Halle der drei Pilgerreisen" (Sansōdō), womit seine Funktion angedeutet ist: Auf den drei Stockwerken des Gebäudes erwarben die Gläubigen in kurzer Zeit so viel religiösen Verdienst, wie dies normalerweise nur durch drei Pilgerreisen möglich war. In jedem Stockwerk standen jeweils Kopien der berühmten 33 Statuen des Bodhisattva Kannon aus Westjapan (Saikoku), der Kantō-Ebene und der Gegend von Chichibu in der heutigen Präfektur Saitama. Im dritten Stock angelangt, wurde man zusätzlich mit dem außergewöhnlichen Ausblick belohnt. Diese zeitsparende, effektive Art ein gutes Karma zu erwerben, ist typisch für die rationale und kommerzielle Behandlung des Themas Religion in Edo.

Die Halle wurde 1741 als Teil des Tempels der 500 Rakan – der vom ewigen Zyklus der Wiedergeburten befreiten buddhistischen Heiligen – erbaut. Ein Zen-Priester der Ōbaku-Richtung gründete 1695 den Tempel, der seinerseits die bis 1728 vervollständigten 500 Statuen der Rakan enthielt.

Hiroshige greift mit diesem Holzschnitt das Motiv eines früheren querformatigen Blattes aus der Serie *Berühmte Ansichten von Edo* (*Edo meisho: Gohyaku Rakan Sazaidō*) von etwa 1845 wieder auf. Dort allerdings wird die ebenso am rechten Bild angeschnittene Spiral-Halle von einem tieferen Standpunkt aus gesehen, und entsprechend weniger weitläufig ist die Aussicht auf die ländliche Idylle.

Le pavillon Sazaidō du temple des 500 rakan

Nous nous trouvons ici dans un des faubourgs situés à l'est d'Edo, dans le domaine sillonné de canaux croisés à l'orthogonale qui avait pu être colonisé comme partie intégrante d'Edo suite à la construction des ponts Ryōgokubashi et Shin-Ōhashi (cf. pl. 58, 59).

Avec des pèlerins qu'on peut voir au balcon de l'édifice coupé par le bord de l'image qui donne son titre à cette feuille, nous jouissons d'une vue célèbre pour son panorama, avec ses champs verdoyants limités par les maisons basses et ses entrepôts de bois de construction bordant le canal Tategawa à l'horizon. Hiroshige porte ainsi un regard contrasté sur la présence significative d'un édifice important culturellement et symboliquement d'une part, et d'autre part la vaste vue d'un paysage plant peu spectaculaire.

L'édifice souligné par sa couleur jaune vif avait en fait pour nom le « pavillon du triple pèlerinage » (Sansōdō) qui indiquait sa fonction : aux trois niveaux de l'édifice, les fidèles acquéraient autant de mérites que leur en auraient acquis trois pèlerinages. À chaque étage se trouvaient des copies des célèbres 33 statues du bodhisattva Kannon, respectivement de l'ouest du Japon (Saikoku), de la plaine de Kantō et de la région de Chichibu dans l'actuelle préfecture de Saitama. Parvenu au troisième étage, le pèlerin était en outre récompensé par une vue inhabituelle. Cette manière rapide et efficace d'accumuler un bon karma est caractéristique du traitement rationnel et commercial du thème religieux à Edo.

Le pavillon fut construit en 1741 comme partie du temple des 500 rakan – les saints bouddhiques libérés du cycle des renaissances. En 1695, un prêtre zen de la branche Ōbaku avait fondé le temple qui abritera les 500 statues des rakan achevées jusqu'en 1728.

Avec cette estampe, Hiroshige reprend le motif d'une ancienne feuille au format paysage de ses *Vues célèbres d'Edo* (*Edo meisho : Gohyaku Rakan Sazaidō*) créées vers 1845. Dans cette série, le pavillon, également coupé par le bord droit de l'image, est toutefois considéré à partir d'un point de vue placé plus bas, et la vue paysagère s'ouvrant sur l'idylle rustique en est donc d'autant moins vaste.

6

逆
井
の
わ
た
し

Sakasai no watashi
2–1857

The Ferry at Sakasai

This plate captivates us with its outstanding composition in luxuriant blue and green tones, dramatized by a perfect *bokashi*, from which the snow-white feathers of the herons stand out in great contrast. The luminous yellow thatched roof of the barge and those of three of the houses in the village of Shinmachi provide other bright colour accents. The gentle seamless transition from the green of the marshy riverbank to the blue of the "Middle River" Nakagawa at the bottom of the picture, along with the *karazuri*, the pigment-free embossed white of the birds, bear witness to the immense skill of the printers of that time, who made quite a crucial contribution to the success of the series.

Only a few people, depicted as tiny figures in the boats and in the village, appear in the middle distance of this natural scene. The massif in the distance hints at the mountains on the Chiba Peninsula, east of Edo.

Die Fähre bei Sakasai

Diese Tafel besticht durch ihre herausragende Komposition in üppigen Blau- und Grüntönen, dramatisiert durch ein perfektes *bokashi*, von dem sich das schneeweiße Gefieder der Fischreiher kontrastreich abhebt. Das leuchtend gelbe Strohdach des Frachtbootes setzt zusammen mit den drei gelben Hausdächern des Dorfes Shinmachi einen weiteren hellen Farbakzent. Der sanfte, nahtlose Übergang vom Grün des sumpfigen Ufers zum Blau des „Mittleren Flusses" Nakagawa am unteren Bildrand sowie das pigmentlose, embossierte (*karazuri*) Weiß der Vogelkörper bezeugen die enorme Kunstfertigkeit der Drucker jener Zeit, die ganz entscheidend zum Erfolg der Serie beitrugen.

Nur wenige Menschen, als kleine Figuren auf den Fähren und im Dorf dargestellt, erscheinen im Mittelgrund dieser Naturdarstellung. Das sich in der Ferne erhebende Massiv deutet die Berge der Halbinsel Chiba im Osten Edos an.

Le bac près de Sakasai

L'attrait particulier de cette planche réside dans la composition exceptionnelle de tons foisonnants de bleu et de vert dramatisés par un *bokashi* parfait sur lequel se détache le plumage blanc comme neige des hérons pêcheurs. Le toit de chaume jaune vif de la barque marchande pose un autre accent de couleur avec les trois toits du village Shinmachi. La transition subtile entre le vert du rivage marécageux et le bleu au milieu de la rivière Nakagawa, près du bord inférieur de l'image, ainsi que le *karazuri*, à savoir l'estampage à sec des corps blancs des oiseaux, illustrent l'immense savoir-faire des imprimeurs de l'époque, qui ont contribué de manière décisive au succès de la série.

Seuls quelques hommes sont représentés au second plan de cette scène naturelle sous forme de petites figures apparaissant sur les bacs et dans le village. Le massif montagneux qui s'élève au loin renvoie au relief de la presqu'île de Chiba, à l'est d'Edo.

68

深川
八まん
山ひらき

Fukagawa Hachiman yamabiraki
8–1857

Open Garden at the Hachiman Shrine in Fukagawa

Fiery red azaleas compete with pink cherry blossoms, and contrast with both the green of the hilly scenery and the gentle blue of the water. Men and women are strolling through the garden admiring the floral splendour. And yet the beauty of this scene contradicts nature: for in Edo/Tokyo, azaleas and cherry trees flower more than a month apart. Hiroshige was concerned with the possibilities of depicting a garden, not with a rendering according to nature. What at first sight looks like a natural landscape turns out to be a depiction constructed precisely for its visual effect and symbolic content of an artificially designed temple garden on a

piece of reclaimed land. This artificiality extends to the small hill in the distance, on which a path winds to the tree-crowned summit. This is one of the dozens of artificial Fujis (*fujizuka*) that gave pilgrims the opportunity to climb the mountain symbolically, without having to travel a long distance and then cope with a laborious ascent of the real thing. These artificial Fujis were between one and ten metres high, and were to be found scattered all over Edo (see plates 24, 25). Even today, according to a count made by one Shinto specialist, there are 58 such Fujis, which are as popular as ever.

Die Eröffnung des Gartens im Hachiman-Schrein von Fukagawa

Feuerrote Azaleen blühen mit rosa Kirschbäumen um die Wette und kontrastieren mit dem Grün der Hügellandschaft und dem zarten Blau des Gewässers. Männer und Frauen wandeln durch den angelegten Garten und bewundern die Blütenpracht.

Doch steht die Schönheit der dargestellten Landschaft im Widerspruch zur Natur, denn Azaleen und Kirschbäume blühen in Tokyo im Abstand von etwas mehr als einem Monat.

Es ging Hiroshige bei diesem Blatt um die Wiedergabe der Möglichkeiten eines Gartens, nicht um eine realitätsgetreue Momentaufnahme. Was auf den ersten Blick wie eine natürliche Landschaft aussieht, entpuppt sich also als eine auf visuelle Wirkung und symbolischen

Gehalt hin genau konstruierte Darstellung eines künstlich angelegten Tempelgartens auf einem Stück aufgeschüttetem Land. Zu dieser Künstlichkeit gehört auch der den Horizont überragende kleine Hügel mit seinen Serpentinen. Es handelt sich um einen der dutzendweise angelegten Fuji-Hügel (*fujizuka*), die Pilgern die Möglichkeit boten, den Berg symbolisch zu besteigen, ohne weit reisen und einen beschwerlichen Aufstieg auf sich nehmen zu müssen. Diese künstlichen Fujis waren zwischen einem und zehn Meter hoch und befanden sich überall in Edo verstreut (siehe Tafeln 24, 25). Auch heute noch existieren auf dem Gebiet von Tokyo nach der Zählung eines Shinto-Spezialisten 58 solcher Nachbildungen, die nach wie vor sehr beliebt sind.

L'ouverture du jardin dans le sanctuaire de Hachiman à Fukagawa

Des azalées rouge feu fleurissent de concert avec des cerisiers et contrastent avec le vert du paysage vallonné et le bleu délicat de l'eau. Des hommes et des femmes se promènent dans le jardin paysager et admirent la splendeur de cette foisonnante floraison. Mais la beauté du paysage est contraire à la nature, car les azalées et les cerisiers fleurissent en fait à Tokyo à plus d'un mois d'intervalle.

Dans cette feuille, le propos de Hiroshige porte sur la représentation des potentialités d'un jardin plutôt que sur une vue momentanée fidèle à la réalité. Ce qui apparaît d'abord comme un paysage naturel s'avère donc être la représentation, parfaitement construite en termes d'effet visuel et de signification sym-

bolique, du jardin d'un temple aménagé artificiellement sur une terre remblayée. De cet artifice participe également la petite colline qui se dresse au-dessus de l'horizon avec ses lignes serpentines. Il s'agit d'un des monts Fuji (*fujizuka*) aménagés par dizaines à Edo, et qui offraient aux pèlerins la possibilité de gravir symboliquement la montagne sans subir les peines d'un long voyage et d'une longue ascension. Ces Fuji artificiels avaient une hauteur d'un à dix mètres et étaient disséminés un peu partout dans Edo (cf. pl. 24, 25). Selon le comptage d'un spécialiste du shintoïsme, on trouve aujourd'hui encore dans le domaine de Tokyo 58 Fuji de ce type qui continuent de jouir d'une grande popularité.

69

深川
三十三
間堂

Fukagawa Sanjūsangendō
8–1857

Sanjūsangendō Hall in Fukagawa

Of the 33 bays in the Sanjūsangendō Hall, which was more than 120 metres (394 feet) long, this composition shows only about half, thereby suggesting the vast dimensions of the building, which is here placed diagonally across the picture. The Sanjūsangendō in Fukagawa was built in 1642 as a replica of its 12th-century namesake in Kyoto, which to this day houses 1,001 Kannon statues. The copy in Edo was not intended to house so many Kannon figures (it contains only a statue of a 1,000-armed Kannon). Instead, its long rear veranda was used for archery practice. From the southern end of the veranda, the archers had to hit a target at the northern end as often as possible without their arrows touching the building itself. Both archers and target are beyond the confines of this view, though women and samurai beneath the hall seem to be attentively following an imaginary arrow. The importance of the hall as a training ground for archers is confirmed by the explanation in the second volume of Hiroshige's *Illustrated Souvenirs of Edo (Ehon Edo miyage)*, dating from 1850. There, too, Hiroshige chose a diagonal composition, though in horizontal rather than vertical format.

In the river beyond the roadside stalls, we see building timber that has been amassed at the Kiba lumberyards in Fukagawa (see plate 106). The hall was transferred here by the new owner after a fire at the start of the 18th century. Notwithstanding the severe damage in the 1855 Ansei earthquake, the hall was important enough to be included in the *One Hundred Famous Views of Edo*. 15 years later, the Sanjūsangendō was finally demolished as part of the new Meiji regime's anti-Buddhist campaign.

Die Halle Sanjūsangendō in Fukagawa

Von den 33 Interkolumnien der mehr als 120 Meter langen Halle Sanjūsangendō zeigt dieses Blatt nur etwa die Hälfte und suggeriert somit die enormen Dimensionen des diagonal ins Bild gesetzten Baus. Die Sanjūsangendō im Stadtteil Fukagawa entstand 1642 als Replik des gleichnamigen Tempelgebäudes aus dem zwölften Jahrhundert in Kyoto, das bis heute 1001 Kannon-Statuen beherbergt. Die Nachbildung in Edo galt jedoch nicht der Unterbringung so vieler Kannon-Figuren – die Halle enthielt nur einen tausendarmigen Kannon –, sondern der Nutzung der langen Veranda an der Rückseite als Übungsplatz für Bogenschützen. Vom südlichen Ende der Veranda aus mussten die Schützen möglichst oft die Schießscheibe am Nordende treffen, ohne dass die Pfeile das Gebäude berührten. Schützen und Zielscheibe sind außerhalb des Blickfeldes, während Samurai und Frauen unterhalb der Halle aufmerksam einem imaginären Pfeil nachzuschauen scheinen. Die Bedeutung der Halle als Trainingsort für das Bogenschießen bestätigt die Erklärung im zweiten Band der *Illustrierten Mitbringsel aus Edo (Ehon Edo miyage)* von 1850. Deren diagonale Komposition im Querformat hat Hiroshige hier ins Hochformat übernommen.

Im Flussbett jenseits der Buden am Rand der Straße lagern die Bauhölzer des Lagerplatzes Kiba von Fukagawa (siehe Tafel 106). Dorthin war die Halle nach einem Brand zu Beginn des 18. Jahrhunderts von dem neuen Besitzer verlegt worden. Ungeachtet der Tatsache, dass die Halle während des Ansei-Erdbebens von 1855 schweren Schaden genommen hatte, war das Bauwerk bedeutsam genug, um unter die *Hundert Ansichten* aufgenommen zu werden. 15 Jahre später schließlich wurde die Sanjūsangendō im Zuge der Buddhismusverfolgung der noch jungen Meiji-Regierung (1868–1912) abgerissen.

Le pavillon Sanjūsangendō à Fukagawa

Des 33 travées du pavillon Sanjūsangendō qui mesure plus de 120 mètres de long, la présente feuille ne montre qu'environ la moitié, suggérant ainsi les formidables dimensions de l'édifice placé en diagonale dans l'image. Le Sanjūsangendō du quartier Fukagawa fut construit en 1642 comme réplique du temple homonyme fondé au XIIᵉ siècle à Kyoto et qui abrite jusqu'à ce jour 1001 statues de Kannon. La réplique d'Edo n'était cependant pas dédiée à la conservation d'autant de figures – le pavillon ne contenait qu'un Kannon aux mille bras –, mais à l'utilisation de la longue véranda adossée à la façade arrière comme lieu d'entraînement pour des archers. De l'extrémité sud de la véranda, les archers devaient atteindre la cible placée à l'extrémité nord sans que les flèches viennent à toucher l'édifice. Dans l'estampe, les archers et la cible sont situés hors du champ de vision, tandis qu'au pied du pavillon, des samouraïs et des femmes semblent suivre des yeux une flèche imaginaire. L'importance du pavillon comme lieu d'exercice pour l'archerie confirme l'explication donnée dans le deuxième tome (1850) des *Souvenirs illustrés d'Edo (Ehon Edo miyage)* de Hiroshige. Dans la présente estampe, la composition diagonale de la feuille correspondante a été transposée du format horizontal dans le format en hauteur des *Cent Vues*.

Dans le lit de la rivière, par-delà des baraques qui bordent la rue, sont entreposés les bois de construction de l'entrepôt Kiba de Fukagawa (cf. pl. 106), où le pavillon avait été déplacé par le nouveau propriétaire après un incendie du début du XVIIIᵉ siècle. Bien que le bâtiment eût subi de graves dommages lors du séisme d'Ansei de 1855, l'édifice était suffisamment important pour être accueilli dans la série des *Cent Vues*. 15 ans plus tard seulement, le Sanjūsangendō allait finalement être rasé dans le cadre des persécutions bouddhistes par le tout jeune gouvernement Meiji (1868–1912).

70

中
川
口

Nakagawaguchi
2–1857

The Mouth of the Nakagawa River

From a bird's-eye view, we look down on the lively traffic on the waterways of Edo. In the foreground, two boats are carrying passengers; in the middle, three raftsmen are transporting loads of timber, the major building material in Japan; while just beyond them, anglers in two other boats are hoping for a good catch. The thatched-roof boats by the canal bank on the top left have probably taken on cargoes of that vital commodity, salt, which was produced not far from here.

The title of the print is somewhat misleading, for the Nakagawa River, known for being rich in fish and scenically attractive, is the broad waterway in the middle of the scene, which flows into Edo Bay beyond our view to the right. The travellers in the boats below are on the Onagigawa Canal passing in front of one of the shogun's checkpoints. The purpose of these, set up immediately following the construction of the canal system in the 17th century, was to monitor the waterways closely. Originally serving a military function, by Hiroshige's day they had no more than a formal function, given the long intervening period of peace. Beyond the Nakagawa, the Shinkawa Canal flows eastwards. A bank of cloud lies over the idyllic landscape, and above it the typical gradated blue band of *ichimonji bokashi*.

Die Mündung des Flusses Nakagawa

Von einer hohen Vogelperspektive aus gewinnt der Betrachter einen Eindruck vom lebhaften Verkehr auf den Wasserwegen Edos. Ganz unten werden Passagiere in zwei Booten transportiert, in der Mitte befördern drei Flößer das wichtige Baumaterial Holz und in zwei weiteren Booten hoffen Angler auf einen guten Fang. Die mit Stroh überdachten Boote am Ufer des Kanals links oben haben wahrscheinlich das unweit erzeugte lebensnotwendige Salz geladen. Der Blatttitel ist irreführend, denn der als fischreicher und landschaftlich attraktiver Fluss bekannte Nakagawa ist der sich quer durch die Mitte ziehende breite Strom, der erst rechts außerhalb des Bildes in die Bucht von Edo mündet. Die Reisenden unten befinden sich auf dem Kanal Onagigawa, an dessen Ufer links unten die Dächer einer shogunalen Kontrollstelle angedeutet sind. Dort wurden unmittelbar nach dem Bau des Kanalsystems im 17. Jahrhundert strenge, vor allem militärisch motivierte Kontrollen durchgeführt, die nach der langen Friedenszeit in Hiroshiges Tagen nur noch formalen Charakter hatten. Jenseits des Nakagawa fließt der Kanal Shinkawa in östliche Richtung. Eine weiße Wolkenbank liegt über der idyllischen Landschaft und geht am oberen Blattrand in den typischen blau gradierten Streifen *ichimonji bokashi* über.

L'embouchure de la rivière Nakagawa

Une haute vue d'oiseau permet au spectateur de se faire une idée du trafic très dense des voies fluviales d'Edo. Tout en bas de l'image, deux barques assurent un transport de passagers, au milieu, trois bateliers transportent du bois, matériau de première importance, et dans deux autres barques, des pêcheurs attendent une bonne prise. Près de la rive du canal en haut à gauche, les barques à toits de chaume ont sans doute chargé l'indispensable sel produit dans les environs. Le titre de la feuille est ambigu, car la rivière Nakagawa, connue pour ses richesses poissonnières et très attrayante du point de vue paysager, est en fait le cours d'eau qui traverse le milieu de l'image et qui ne se jette dans la baie d'Edo qu'à droite, hors champ. Les passagers qu'on aperçoit au bas de l'image naviguent sur le canal Onagigawa, sur la rive duquel, à gauche, sont indiqué sommairement les toits d'un point de contrôle shogunal. Dès après le creusement du canal au XVIIe siècle, des contrôles sévères y étaient effectués pour des raisons essentiellement militaires ; après la longue période de paix de l'époque de Hiroshige, ces contrôles n'avaient plus qu'un caractère formel. Au-delà de la Nakagawa, le canal Shinkawa coule vers l'est. Un banc de nuages blanc flotte sur ce paysage idyllique et se transforme en un *ichimonji bokashi* caractérisé par ses bandes de dégradés bleus près du bord supérieur de l'image.

71

利根川
ばらばら
まつ

Tonegawa Barabara matsu
8–1856

Scattered Pines on the Tone River

This virtuoso example of the arts of the painter, woodblock carver and printer shows how an unspectacular river view can provide the motif for an exceptional woodblock print. Part of the river, the sail of a boat and the background are seen through a fisherman's net caught in mid-air. The texture of the snow-white sail is emphasized by the embossing technique of *nunomezuri* (see, for example, plate 6). With a subtle change in the colour of the blue water, of the boat and of the green tongue of land, here the printer has achieved a particularly striking naturalistic effect. This technical *tour de force* recalls the work of Dutch genre painters in the 17th century, who were superbly skilled, for ex- ample, at convincingly depicting the texture of a piece of cloth seen refracted by the water in a carafe.

Shown at the moment of being cast, the net, whose edge is hemmed with small lead weights, seems to create a flat surface. Hiroshige has complemented this image with the depiction of other fishermen at various stages of hauling in their nets in front of the reed-lined banks. The fishing net alludes to the famous carp in the Tone River, while the scattered pines of the title, grown into bizarre shapes as a result of the constant wind, stand unassumingly in the middle distance.

Verstreute Kiefern am Fluss Tonegawa

Dieses Bravourstück der Entwerfer-, Holzschneider- und Druckerkunst macht deutlich, dass eine unspektakuläre Flusslandschaft das Thema für einen einzigartigen Holzschnitt liefern kann. Der Fluss, das Segel einer Dschunke und der Hintergrund werden teilweise durch ein Fischernetz hindurch wiedergegeben, das schneeweiße Segel wird zudem durch die Blinddrucktechnik mit Stoffstruktur (*nunomezuri*) hervorgehoben (siehe Tafel 6). Mit einer subtilen Farbbänderung der hinter dem Netz liegenden blauen Wasserfläche, des Bootes und der Spitze der grünen Landzunge erzielte der Drucker einen besonders naturalistischen Effekt. Diese technische *tour de force* erinnert an holländische Genremaler des 17. Jahrhun- derts, die ein Stück Stoff durch die Lichtbrechung einer Wasserkaraffe hindurch haptisch überzeugend zu malen verstanden.

Das Netz wird im Moment des Auswurfs gezeigt, sodass der mit kleinen Bleigewichten gesäumte Rand völlig flach vor den Augen des Betrachters liegt. Die durch diese dynamische Bewegung erzeugte Spannung lockert Hiroshige durch die Darstellung verschiedener Stadien des Netzeinholens vor dem mit Schilf bewachsenen Ufer auf. Das Fischernetz als Blickfang spielt auf die berühmten Karpfen des Flusses Tonegawa an, während die im Titel genannten, durch den ständigen Wind bizarr gewachsenen, verstreuten Kiefern unscheinbar im Mittelgrund stehen.

Pins disséminés sur la rive de la Tonegawa

Ce morceau de bravoure du concepteur, du graveur et de l'imprimeur montre clairement qu'un paysage fluvial banal peut donner matière à une estampe tout à fait unique en son genre. La rivière, la voile de la jonque et l'arrière-plan sont en partie rendus au travers des mailles d'un filet de pêche, la voile blanche comme neige a en outre été soulignée par la technique d'estampage à sec avec application d'une trame textile (*nunomezuri*, cf. pl. 6). Par une subtile altération chromatique de la surface aquatique placée derrière le filet, de la barque et de la pointe de la langue de terre verte, l'imprimeur a su obtenir un effet particulièrement naturaliste. Ce tour de force technique n'est pas sans rappeler la peinture de genre hollandaise du XVIIe siècle, qui s'entendait à représenter les étoffes de manière particulière- ment convaincante et tactile par le truchement des altérations lumineuses produites par une carafe d'eau.

Le filet est montré au moment d'être jeté à l'eau, de sorte que le bord ponctué de petits plombs se déploie presque à plat dans le plan de la feuille devant les yeux du spectateur. Hiroshige a atténué la tension générée par cet élément dynamique en représentant plusieurs étapes de la récupération des filets de pêche sur la rive où foisonnent les roseaux. Le filet de pêche utilisé comme accroche visuelle est une allusion aux célèbres carpes de la Tonegawa, tandis que les pins disséminés évoqués dans le titre et auxquels le vent continuel a conféré des formes singulières, occupent le second plan de manière plutôt insignifiante.

72

はねたの
わたし
弁天の社

Haneda no watashi Benten no yashiro
8–1858

The Ferry at Haneda and the Benten Shrine

Few prints in the series evoked such contrasting reactions as this one. Basil Stewart (1880–?), the English author of *Subjects Portrayed in Japanese Colour-Prints*, a book published in 1922, thought that the depiction of the hairy legs of the ferryman "can only be attributed to premature senility" on Hiroshige's part. The contrast between the oversize motif in the foreground and the landscape in the background was criticized by the Japanese art historian Uchida Minoru (1894–?) as a "total blunder". Takahashi Seiichirō (1884–?), by contrast, saw it as "evidence of Hiroshige's unusual genius". The perspective, while remarkable, is nonetheless comparable with that in other prints of the series, for example, plate 86, in which the hind legs of a horse take up most of the right-hand half of the picture.

The close-up of the hairy leg effectively places the viewer in the position of the passenger in the boat, who is hinted at solely by a cropped parasol in the lower right-hand corner.

In the middle of the composition, projecting just above the horizon, we can see a lighthouse whose function was to warn ships of the sandbanks at the mouth of the river. On the wooded strip of land to its left, a shrine had been erected to the patron deity of water, Benten, such as we also see in a similar geographical location, in Shinagawa (see plate 83).

Today Haneda is home to an airport, the shrine having been lost to an expansion programme after World War II. Reluctant to offend the goddess, however, the developers put up a red *torii* gateway (see plate 83) in its place outside the entrance to the airport.

Die Fähre in Haneda und der Benten-Schrein

Wenige Tafeln der Serie haben so gegensätzliche Reaktionen hervorgerufen wie diese. Basil Stewart (1880–?), der englische Autor des 1922 erschienenen Buches *Subjects Portrayed in Japanese Colour-Prints*, sah in der Darstellung der haarigen Beine des Fährmanns einen Hinweis auf Hiroshiges „frühzeitig einsetzende Senilität". Der Kontrast zwischen übergroßem Motiv im Vordergrund und der Landschaft im Hintergrund wurde von dem japanischen Kunsthistoriker Uchida Minoru (1894–?) als „völliger Missgriff" kritisiert. Takahashi Seiichirō (1884–?) dagegen sah darin einen „Beweis für Hiroshiges ungewöhnliches Genie". Die Perspektive ist zwar bemerkenswert, aber durchaus vergleichbar mit anderen Blättern der Serie, etwa mit Tafel 86, auf dem die Hinterhand eines Pferdes die gesamte rechte Bildhälfte einnimmt.

Der Blick auf das zum Greifen nahe haarige Bein versetzt den Betrachter in die Person des Fahrgastes, der freilich nur durch einen Ausschnitt seines Sonnenschirms am rechten unteren Rand angedeutet ist.

Knapp über den Horizont hinausragend, ist in der Bildmitte ein Leuchtturm zu erkennen, der Schiffe in der Nacht vor den in die Flussmündung hineinragenden Sandbänken warnen soll. Auf der links daneben sichtbaren bewaldeten Landzunge wurde der Wasserschutzgottheit Benten ein Schrein errichtet, wie wir ihn in einer ähnlichen geografischen Situation in Shinagawa auf Tafel 83 wiederfinden.

Im Stadtteil Haneda befindet sich heute ein Flughafen, für dessen Erweiterung nach dem Zweiten Weltkrieg der Schrein weichen musste. Da man aber die Gottheit nicht verletzen wollte, wurde an seiner Stelle ein rotes Tor, *torii* (siehe Tafel 83), vor dem Eingang des Flughafens errichtet.

Le bac à Haneda et le sanctuaire de Benten

Peu de planches de la série des *Cent Vues* ont suscité des réactions aussi contradictoires parmi les critiques. Basil Steward (1880–?), l'auteur anglais du livre *Subjects Portrayed in Japanese Colour-Prints* paru en 1922, a vu dans la représentation des jambes poilues du passeur un symptôme de « sénilité précoce » chez Hiroshige. Le contraste entre un motif surdimensionné placé au premier plan et un paysage relégué à l'arrière-plan a été critiqué par l'historien de l'art japonais Uchida Minoru (1894–?) comme une « grossière erreur ». Takahashi Seiichiro (1884–?) y a vu pour sa part une « preuve de l'extraordinaire génie de Hiroshige ». Si cette vue est pour le moins frappante, elle ne représente pas un fait isolé, comme le montrent d'autres feuilles de la série, notamment la planche 86, dans laquelle l'arrière-train d'un cheval occupe presque toute la moitié droite de l'image.

La vue rapprochée de cette jambe qu'on pourrait presque toucher du doigt place le spectateur dans la position de l'usager du bac, lequel n'est, il est vrai, indiqué ici qu'au moyen d'un segment d'ombrelle apparaissant dans le coin inférieur droit.

Au centre de l'image, ne dépassant que légèrement l'horizon, on discerne un phare qui devait avertir les bateaux de la présence de bancs de sable dans l'embouchure de la rivière. Sur la langue de terre boisée à gauche près du phare avait été construit un sanctuaire dédié à Benten, la divinité protectrice des eaux, sanctuaire que la planche 83 nous montre dans une situation géographique similaire.

Après la Seconde Guerre mondiale, le sanctuaire a dû céder la place à une extension de l'aéroport qui se trouve aujourd'hui à Haneda. Pour éviter de s'attirer la colère de la divinité, une porte *torii* rouge (cf. pl. 83) fut érigée à son emplacement devant l'entrée de l'aéroport.

市中繁栄
七夕祭

Shichū han'ei Tanabata matsuri
7–1857

The City Flourishing, the Tanabata Festival

We are looking over the rooftops of a district in Edo, east of Mount Fuji, which during the hot summer days has lost its characteristic snow-cap. On the right, the gables of the shogun's castle are in the distance, though in reality the castle is only a few hundred metres away. Art historians such as Miyao Shigeo have argued that Hiroshige presents us here with the view from his own house. Rising up through the sea of roofs in Minami Denma-chō is a watchtower used for spotting fires; it was part of the fire brigade's living-quarters in Yayosu district, where Hiroshige grew up. This personal subject matter may also explain the absence of any figures, and the fact that this is the only print in the series that does not mention a place-name in its title. For Hiroshige's admirers, this biographical aspect lends the print a very special significance.

Among the print's most distinctive elements are the festival decorations of white, red and blue paper; fastened to green bamboo poles on the roofs, they flutter in the breeze against a bright sky. From the large bamboo pole on the left there hang, alongside numerous verse sheets in the same format as the series title and print cartouches, a red-and-yellow fishing net (which both literally and metaphorically stands for "a good catch"), along with a calabash and a *sake* bowl, which express the pleasure the owner (maybe Hiroshige himself) takes in alcohol. Attached to the pole below are an abacus and a ledger, the attributes of the merchant, while directly in front of the silhouette of Mount Fuji there hovers a yellow cash-box on which large characters express the wish for a large sum of money.

These festival decorations were dedicated to two stellar deities – a loving couple who, according to an ancient Chinese legend, were allowed to meet only once a year, on the seventh day of the seventh month.

In the Edo of the Tokugawa (1615–1868), the Tanabata Festival, like the Boys' Day Festival depicted on plate 48, was one of the five official seasonal festivals (*gosekku*) sanctioned by the government. Although it was celebrated during the hottest days of summer, according to the table of contents of *One Hundred Famous Views of Edo*, the print marks the start of the autumn section.

Die Stadt in voller Blüte, das Tanabata-Fest

Der Betrachter sieht sich über den Dächern Edos östlich des Berges Fuji, der in den heißen Sommertagen seine charakteristische Schneekrone verloren hat. Rechts tauchen in der Ferne die Giebel des shogunalen Schlosses auf, das tatsächlich nur ein paar hundert Meter entfernt stand. Kunsthistoriker wie etwa Miyao Shigeo haben die These aufgestellt, dass Hiroshige hier einen Blick vom Dach seines eigenen Hauses präsentiert. Aus dem Dächermeer des Stadtviertels Minami Denma-chō ragt schemenhaft ein Feuerwachturm empor; er gehört zu den Baracken im Distrikt Yayosu, wo Hiroshige aufwuchs. Diese persönliche Ansicht könnte auch die Abwesenheit jeglicher Menschen und das Fehlen einer Ortsbezeichnung im Titel, einmalig in der ganzen Serie, erklären. Jedenfalls verleiht der private Aspekt dem Druck in den Augen von Hiroshiges Verehrern eine ganz besondere Aura.

Zur Attraktion des Blattes gehört vor allem aber der aus weißen, roten, gelben und blauen Papieren geschnittene Festschmuck, der, an grünen Bambusstangen auf den Dächern befestigt, am hellen Himmel im frischen Wind flattert. Von der großen Bambusstange links wehen neben zahlreichen Gedicht-blättern in den Formaten des Serien- und Blatttitels ein rotgelbes Fischernetz, das – auch im übertragenen Sinne – für einen reichen Fang steht, sowie eine Kalebasse und eine Sake-Schale, die Freude des Besitzers (vielleicht Hiroshige selbst) am Alkoholgenuss ausdrücken. An der Stange darunter sind die kaufmännischen Attribute Rechenbrett und Kontobuch zu erkennen, direkt vor der Silhouette des Fuji schwebt eine gelbe Kasse, auf der in Schriftzeichen der Wunsch nach einem großen Geldbetrag aufgemalt ist.

Dieser Festtagsschmuck wurde dem Liebespaar zweier Sterngottheiten gewidmet, das sich einer alten chinesischen Legende nach nur einmal jährlich am 7. Tag des siebten Monats treffen durfte.

Das Tanabata-Fest gehörte wie das in Tafel 48 dargestellte Knabenfest im Edo der Tokugawa-Zeit (1615–1868) zu den fünf offiziellen, von der Regierung genehmigten Jahreszeitenfeste (*gosekku*). Es wurde zwar während der heißen Hochsommertage gefeiert, das Blatt markiert aber nach der Einteilung des Inhaltsverzeichnisses der *Hundert Ansichten* den Beginn der Herbst-Sektion.

La ville en pleine floraison, la fête de Tanabata

Ici, le point de vue du spectateur s'élève au-dessus des toits d'Edo, à l'est du mont Fuji qui a perdu son habituelle couronne de neige en ces chaudes journées d'été. Au loin à droite émergent les faîtes du château shogunal qui n'était en fait éloigné que de quelques centaines de mètres. Certains historiens de l'art comme Miyao Shigeo ont suggéré que cette estampe montrait une vue depuis le toit de la propre maison de Hiroshige. Dans l'océan de toits de Minami Denma-chō émerge, schématique, une tour de garde de la brigade du feu ; elle fait partie des baraques du district Yayosu où Hiroshige a passé une bonne partie de son enfance. Cette vue personnelle expliquerait aussi l'absence de toute présence humaine et de toute indication de lieu dans le titre, fait unique dans toute la série. En tout état de cause, pour les admirateurs de Hiroshige, l'aspect privé qu'elle pourrait avoir confère une aura particulière à cette vue.

L'attrait esthétique particulier de la feuille réside toutefois surtout dans les papiers découpés blancs, rouges, jaunes et bleus des décorations de fête qui flottent au gré du vent frais dans un ciel limpide, fixées aux perches de bambou dressées sur les toits. À la grande perche de bambou à gauche – outre les nombreuses feuilles de poésie qui présentent le même format que les titres de la série et les titres des feuilles individuelles – flottent aussi un filet de pêche jaune symbolisant une pêche abondante même au sens figuré, ainsi qu'une calebasse et une coupe de saké qui proclament fièrement le plaisir du propriétaire (peut-être Hiroshige lui-même) à consommer de l'alcool.

La perche placée dessous montre un boulier et un livre de comptes, attributs des marchands. Directement devant la silhouette du mont Fuji flotte encore un coffret jaune sur lequel on lit le vœu de recevoir une forte somme d'argent.

Cette décoration de fête était dédiée au couple d'amants de deux divinités stellaires qui, selon une ancienne légende chinoise, ne pouvaient se retrouver qu'une fois par an, le 7ème jour du septième mois.

Dans l'Edo de l'ère Tokugawa (1615–1868), tout comme la fête des garçons de la planche 48, la fête de Tanabata faisait partie des cinq fêtes saisonnières (*gosekku*) officielles approuvées par le gouvernement. Bien que cette fête fût célébrée pendant les plus chaudes journées d'été, la présente feuille a été placée en ouverture de la section d'automne selon le classement établi dans la table des matières des *Cent Vues*.

74

大伝馬町
こふく店

Ôdenma-chô gofukudana
7–1858

Silk Shops in Ôdenma-chô

Two months before his death, Hiroshige demonstrates with this print a sense of humour, a visual persuasiveness and a masterly talent for psychological empathy.

A procession of ceremonially dressed men with festival standards is moving close to the viewer along a shopping street. In spite of the formal samurai clothing – consisting of a jacket and trousers of the same patterned cloth (*kamishimo*) over a *kosode* – their facial expressions betrays a noisy cheerfulness. The standards refer to their guild: they are carpenters. After a topping-out ceremony with the ensuing alcohol indulgence, they are returning to the house of the guild master, who is leading the procession. The building trade was the leading beneficiary of the wave of reconstruction that followed the great Ansei earthquake of 1855, and contemporary reports indicate the extent to which this unexpected stroke of fortune went to the heads of many in the guild. The master himself carries the ritual standard with symbolically loaded festival ornamentation, followed by two oversize poles crowned with the symbols of longevity – the tortoise and the crane – carried on the shoulders of his retinue.

This dynamic demonstration of self-confident craftsmen is contrasted with the static alternate red and blue shutters of the Daimaru silk merchant's shop. Its striking logo also alludes playfully to the name: the Chinese character for "large" (*dai*) is in a circle (*maru*). At the same time, the emblem is framed on the right by the name of the founder, Shimomura (Hikouemon), and on the left by the full name "Daimaruya". The company was founded in Kyoto in 1717, and expanded to Edo in 1743, where it flourished until the early 20th century. Following the World War II, it became once more one of Tokyo's leading department stores.

Seidenladen in Ôdenma-chô

Zwei Monate vor seinem Tod beweist Hiroshige mit diesem Blatt Humor, visuelle Überzeugungskraft und eine meisterhafte psychologische Einfühlungsgabe.

Eine Prozession zeremoniell gekleideter Männer mit Festtagsstandarten zieht nahe am Betrachter durch eine Ladenstraße. Trotz der formellen Samurai-Kleidung – bestehend aus einer Jacke und einer Hose in gleichem Stoffmuster (*kamishimo*) über einem Kosode-Gewand – verrät ihr Gesichtsausdruck eine angeheiterte, laute Fröhlichkeit. Die Standarten weisen auf ihre Zunft hin: Es sind Zimmerleute, die nach einem Richtfest mit anschließendem Trinkgelage zum Haus des Meisters, der die Prozession anführt, zurückkehren. Das Baugewerbe profitierte am meisten von den Wiederaufbauarbeiten nach dem großen Ansei-Erdbeben von 1855, und aus zeitgenössischen Berichten geht hervor, wie sehr dieses unverhoffte Glück Vielen zu Kopfe stieg. Der Meister trägt selbst die Ritualstandarte mit symbolisch aufgeladenem Festtagsschmuck, gefolgt von zwei – mit den Langlebigkeitssymbolen der Schildkröte und des Kranichs bekrönten – überdimensionierten Pfeilen auf den Schultern seiner Leute.

Dieser Demonstration handwerklichen Selbstbewusstseins stehen die alternierend rot und blau gefärbten Ladenvorhänge des Seidenhandels Daimaru ruhig und klar gegenüber. Ihr plakatives Firmenzeichen gibt zugleich den Namen spielerisch wieder: Das Schriftzeichen für „groß" (*dai*) steht in einem Kreis (*maru*). Gleichzeitig wird das Emblem aber auch rechts vom Namen des Gründers Shimomura (Hikouemon) und links vom voll ausgeschriebenen Namen „Daimaruya" gerahmt. Dieses 1717 in Kyoto gegründete Handelshaus expandierte 1743 nach Edo, wo es bis Anfang des 20. Jahrhunderts florierte und nach dem Zweiten Weltkrieg wieder zu einem der zentralen Warenhäuser in Tokyo avancierte.

Boutique de soieries à Ôdenma-chô

Dans cette feuille créée deux mois avant sa mort, Hiroshige ne manque pas d'humour, de force de conviction visuelle et d'une grande maîtrise dans la description psychologique.

Une procession d'hommes en habits de cérémonie portant des étendards de fête passe près du spectateur dans une rue commerçante. Malgré leurs costumes formels de samouraïs – veste et culotte aux mêmes motifs (*kamishimo*) par-dessus un *kosode* – l'expression des visages trahit une bruyante jovialité. Les étendards renvoient à leur corporation : il s'agit en fait d'artisans retournant à la maison du maître charpentier, qui emmène la procession, après une « crémaillère » bien arrosée suivant l'achèvement d'un gros œuvre. La branche du bâtiment fut celle qui tira le plus large profit du grand séisme d'Ansei de 1855, et les récits de l'époque nous apprennent que cette chance inopinée fit tourner la tête à de nombreux ouvriers. Le maître porte lui-même l'étendard rituel chargé de décorations de fête symboliques, suivi de deux gigantesques flèches – couronnées des symboles de la longévité : la tortue et la grue – portées par ses employés.

À cette manifestation de fierté artisane s'opposent, clairs et calmes, les rideaux alternativement rouges et bleus de la maison de commerce de soieries Daimaru. En même temps, le « logo » de Daimaru traduit ce nom sous une forme ludique : l'idéogramme chinois pour « grand » (*dai*) est placé dans un cercle (*maru*). L'emblème de la maison est encadré, à droite, par le nom du fondateur Shimomura (Hikouemon), à gauche par le nom complet – « Daimaruya ». Cette maison de commerce fondée à Kyoto en 1717 s'implanta aussi à Edo à partir de 1743, où elle fut prospère jusqu'au début du XXᵉ siècle. Après la Seconde Guerre mondiale, elle redevint un des grands magasins du centre de Tokyo.

75

神田
紺屋町

Kanda Kon'ya-chō
11–1857

The Dyers' Quarter in Kanda

Among his many views of Edo, this print is an outstanding example of Hiroshige's wit in employing his compositional device of "blocking" the foreground with large motifs while the most important elements of the print are rendered in the background. In this case, the focus is not only the snow-capped Mount Fuji, but also the shogun's castle, which, with its striking watchtower and majestic roofs, looms out of the green of the surrounding trees.

The foreground is unmistakably dominated by a far more profane motif, namely the strips of cloth, with their printed patterns, hung out to dry by one of the dye works in the Kanda neighbourhood, which was well known for this particular trade. To the left and right hang the cotton fabrics for *yukata* kimonos, printed with check patterns in black and white, and abstract designs in indigo on a dark brown background. Between them, reaching almost to the top of the print, narrower strips of fabric flutter in the breeze. The first two, printed in blue and white, show the first character, *sakana* (meaning "fish"), in the name of Hiroshige's publisher, Sakanaya Eikichi. Hiroshige's own geometrically abstract monogram appears modestly on the fabrics behind. It contains the syllable *hi*, printed in white, framed by a blue lozenge, which can be read as *ro*. Lengths of fabric decorated in this way were cut up to make narrow towels (*tenugui*) or headbands, and were distributed to customers as advertising gifts. While painter and publisher are here jointly blowing their own trumpet, the motif itself also pays homage to Hiroshige's exemplar Katsushika Hokusai (1760–1849). As Henry D. Smith points out, Hokusai had already combined the motif of the Kanda dye works with the natural wonder of Mount Fuji in the second volume of *One Hundred Views of Fuji* (*Fugaku hyakkei*, 1830–1835) to create a composition of emblematic austerity.

When the first ukiyo-e painters, such as Okumura Masanobu (1686–1764), and subsequently Maruyama Ōkyo (1733–1795) and the painters in the "Dutch style" (*ranga*), applied linear perspective to native subjects, no one could have guessed the extent to which later Japanese masters would ignore the empirical constraints of Western spatial representation in order to fuse it with traditional pictorial techniques, such as the cropping of motifs and the use of multiple viewpoints.

Das Viertel der Färber in Kanda

Unter den Ansichten von Edo ist dieses Blatt ein hervorragendes Beispiel für Hiroshiges Witz bei der Anwendung des Kompositionsprinzips der „Vergitterung", das es erlaubt, von einem Objekt im Vordergrund auf das wichtigste Motiv in der Bildtiefe überzuleiten. In diesem Fall stehen der schneebedeckte Berg Fuji und der Palast des Shoguns im Mittelpunkt. Er ragt mit seinem markanten Wachturm und majestätischen Dächern aus dem Grün der ihn umgebenden Bäume hervor.

Den Vordergrund beherrscht unübersehbar ein weit profaneres Motiv, nämlich die zum Trocknen aufgehängten, verschieden bedruckten Stoffe einer Färberei in dem für dieses Gewerbe bekannten Viertel Kanda. Links und rechts außen hängen mit Schachbrett- und Streumustern locker eingefärbte Baumwollstoffe für Yukata-Kimonos in dunklem Braun und Indigo, während dazwischen, fast bis zum oberen Bildrand reichend, schmalere Stoffbahnen im Wind flattern. Die vorderen beiden blau auf weiß bedruckten Bahnen zeigen das Schriftzeichen für „Fisch" (*sakana*), das erste Zeichen im Namen des Verlegers Sakanaya Eikichi. Hiroshiges geometrisch abstrahiertes Monogramm erscheint bescheiden auf den hinteren Textilien. Es enthält in Weiß geschrieben die Silbe *hi*, die von einer blauen Raute, die *ro* gelesen werden kann, umfangen wird. Derart bedruckte Stoffbänder wurden zu schmalen Handtüchern (*tenugui*) oder Stirnbändern zerschnitten und als Werbegeschenke an Kunden verteilt. Während Maler und Verleger hier gemeinsam für sich Reklame machen, ist das Motiv selbst gleichsam eine Hommage an Hiroshiges Vorbild Katsushika Hokusai (1760–1849). Wie Henry D. Smith hervorhebt, hat bereits Hokusai in Band 2 seiner *Hundert Ansichten des Fuji* (*Fugaku hyakkei*, 1830–1835) das Bildmotiv der Färbereien von Kanda mit dem Berg Fuji zu einer Komposition von emblematischer Stringenz zusammengeführt.

Als die ersten Ukiyoe-Maler wie Okumura Masanobu (1686–1764) und nach ihnen Maruyama Ōkyo (1733–1795) sowie die Maler im „holländischen Stil" (*ranga*) die Linearperspektive auf einheimische Sujets anwandten, mochte noch niemand geahnt haben, mit welcher Nonchalance sich spätere Meister über die empirischen Zwänge der westlichen Raumdarstellung hinwegsetzen würden, um sie mit traditionellen Bildmitteln wie der Fragmentierung des Sujets und der Flächenkomposition zu verschmelzen.

Le quartier des teinturiers à Kanda

Parmi les vues d'Edo, cette feuille constitue un excellent exemple de l'humour dont fait preuve Hiroshige dans l'emploi du principe de composition du « clôturage » qui permet de faire passer le regard d'un objet placé au premier plan au motif principal situé dans la profondeur de l'image. Ici, le centre de l'image est occupé par le mont Fuji qui se dresse avec sa tour de garde très particulière et ses toits majestueux parmi des arbres verdoyants.

Le premier plan est dominé de manière frappante par un motif beaucoup plus quotidien, à savoir les draps d'une teinturerie séchant dans le quartier de Kanda, réputé pour cet artisanat. À l'extérieur, à gauche et à droite, sont accrochées des cotonnades teintées de motifs à damiers ou à fleurs pour des kimonos *yukata* brun foncé et indigo, tandis qu'entre eux, atteignant presque le bord supérieur de l'image, des bandes de drap plus étroites flottent au gré du vent. Les deux bandes imprimées en bleu et blanc présentent le premier caractère pour poisson, *sakana*, du nom de l'éditeur Sakanaya Eikichi. Le monogramme géométriquement abstrait de Hiroshige apparaît plus modestement sur les deux bandes postérieures. Il comporte, écrite en blanc, la syllabe *hi* entourée d'un losange bleu qui peut se lire *ro*. Ce genre de bandes de tissus étaient découpées en fines serviettes (*tenugui*) ou en bandeaux de tête et offerts aux clients comme cadeaux commerciaux. Alors que le peintre et l'éditeur font ici publicité commune, le motif lui-même est une sorte d'hommage à Katsushika Hokusai (1760–1849), le modèle de Hiroshige. Comme l'a fait observer Henry D. Smith, dans le deuxième tome de ses *Cent vues du mont Fuji* (*Fugaku hyakkei*, 1830–1835), Hokusai avait déjà réuni dans une estampe le motif des teintureries de Kanda et le mont Fuji pour former une composition d'une efficacité emblématique.

Quand les premiers peintres ukiyo-e comme Okumura Masanobu (1686–1764) et après eux Maruyama Ōkyo (1733–1795) et les peintres de « style hollandais » (*ranga*) appliquèrent la perspective linéaire à des sujets japonais, personne ne pouvait encore se douter avec quelle nonchalance les maîtres plus tardifs allaient s'affranchir des contraintes empiriques de la représentation spatiale occidentale, pour les faire fusionner avec des moyens iconiques traditionnels comme la fragmentation du sujet et la composition plane.

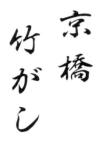

京橋
竹がし

Kyōbashi Takegashi
12–1857

Bamboo Quay by Kyōbashi Bridge

This print depicts one of the moonlit nocturnal scenes for which Hiroshige became so famous. We are looking eastwards down the Kyōbashi River, which is named after the bridge in the foreground. Pilgrims with lanterns are walking across this bridge from the right to the northern bank on the left. The silhouettes on that bank, which to modern eyes vaguely resemble skyscrapers as they loom into the night sky, are of the bamboo quay (Takegashi), where large quantities of bamboo rods were unloaded and subsequently dried in warehouses (they were brought to Edo as rafts, and so arrived waterlogged). Bamboo was used in a variety of ways, in architectural elements, objects of everyday use and in festival decorations.

Apart from the Nihonbashi Bridge, and the bridges leading to the gates of Edo Castle, only the Kyōbashi Bridge was allowed to sport *gibōshi* (see plate 43). In the present scene, these flame-shaped finials on the central pillars of the balustrade point directly to the full moon.

This print may well have served James Abbott McNeill Whistler

(1834–1903) as a model for his *Nocturne in Blue and Gold: Old Battersea Bridge*, dating from 1872–1875 (see ill. 1). Comparing the works, it is clear that both artists were more interested in capturing a mood than in topographical accuracy.

This print is also unusual in that it mentions the name of the woodblock cutter Yokogawa Horitake, though in an oblique way. The pilgrims returning from their climbing exercise on Mount Ōyama (see plate 60) are led by a figure carrying a red lantern, on which can be read, above and below the balustrade of the bridge, the characters *hori* and *take*, literally "engrave" and "bamboo". It is hardly a coincidence, then, that the "signature" of the woodblock engraver is to be found on precisely this print. In the mid-19th century, Yokogawa was one of the best-known practitioners of his craft, and in other works for Hiroshige, for example the series *Famous Views of Sixty-Odd Provinces* (*Rokujū yoshū meisho zue*, 1853–1856), often engraved his seal alongside the artist's signature cartouche.

Bambusquai an der Brücke Kyōbashi

Dieser Holzschnitt ist einer der ungewöhnlich düsteren, mondbeschienenen Nachtblätter, für die Hiroshige so bekannt wurde. Wir blicken nach Osten den Fluss Kyōbashi hinunter, der nach der im Vordergrund aufragenden Brücke benannt ist. Auf dieser zieht eine Prozession von Pilgern mit Laternen von rechts auf das nördliche Ufer zu. Die Silhouetten, die dort – für den heutigen Betrachter fast wie Wolkenkratzer – in den Nachthimmel ragen, gehören zum Bambusquai (Takegashi), an dem große Mengen Bambus von Schiffen abgeladen und anschließend in Lagerhäusern getrocknet wurden.

Die Stangen gelangten dorthin, nachdem sie sich durch das lange Flößen auf dem Weg nach Edo mit Wasser vollgesogen hatten. Bambus fand vielfältige Verwendung, etwa als Architekturelement, für Alltagsgegenstände oder als Festtagsdekoration.

Neben der Brücke Nihonbashi und den auf die Tore des Edo-Schlosses führenden Brücken war es nur an der Kyōbashi-Brücke erlaubt, die sogenannten *gibōshi* anzubringen (siehe Tafel 43). Diese flammenförmigen Metallkuppen auf den Mittelpfeilern des Geländers weisen hier direkt auf den Vollmond.

Dieses Blatt mag James Abbott McNeill Whistler (1834–1903) als Vorlage und Inspiration für sein Ölbild *Nocturne in Blue and Gold: Old Battersea Bridge* von 1872–1875 gedient haben (siehe Abb. 1). Beim Vergleich der Werke wird deutlich, dass es beiden Künstlern weniger um die konkrete Wiedergabe eines Ortes als vielmehr darum ging, eine Stimmung einzufangen.

Besonderen Wert hat dieser Holzschnitt auch wegen der für diese Serie einzigen, sehr versteckten Erwähnung des Holzschneiders Yokogawa Horitake. Die Pilger, die von der Besteigung des Berges Ōyama zurückkehren (siehe Tafel 60), werden von einer Figur angeführt, die einen roten Lampion trägt. Darauf sind ober- und unterhalb des Brückengeländers die Schriftzeichen *hori* und *take*, wörtlich „gravieren" und „Bambus", zu lesen – kaum ein Zufall, dass sich die „Signatur" des Holzschneiders ausgerechnet auf diesem Blatt findet. Yokogawa war um die Mitte des 19. Jahrhunderts einer der bekanntesten Holzschneider, der in anderen Werken für Hiroshige – etwa der Serie *Berühmte Ansichten von über sechzig Provinzen* (*Rokujū yoshū meisho zue*, 1853–1856) – häufig sein Siegel neben Hiroshiges Signaturenkartusche geschnitten hat.

Le quai au bambou près du pont Kyōbashi

Cette estampe, une des plus sombres, constitue une exception parmi les feuilles nocturnes éclairées par la lune qui ont assuré toute la célébrité de Hiroshige. Ici, la vue dirigée à l'est longe la rivière Kyōbashi, dont le nom est dérivé du pont qui l'enjambe au premier plan. Sur ce pont, un cortège de pèlerins munis de lanternes se dirige de la droite vers la rive nord. Les silhouettes qui se détachent sur le firmament – pour le spectateur d'aujourd'hui, elles s'apparent presque à des gratte-ciel – sont celles du Takegashi, le quai au bambou où cette plante était séchée en entrepôts après récolte. Les tiges de bambou y arrivaient gorgées d'eau suite à leur transport sous forme de radeaux sur les voies fluviales d'Edo. Le bambou servait pour de nombreuses utilisations, notamment comme élément d'architecture, pour des objets quotidiens ou comme décoration de fêtes.

À côté du pont Nihonbashi et des ponts menant aux portes du château d'Edo, seul le pont Kyōbashi était autorisé à porter sur les poteaux médians du parapet les fameux *gibōshi* (cf. pl. 43), chapeaux métalliques en forme de flamme qui pointent ici vers la pleine lune.

Cette feuille a pu servir à James Abbott McNeill Whistler

(1834–1903) de modèle et d'inspiration pour son tableau *Nocturne in Blue and Gold: Old Battersea Bridge* de 1872–1875 (cf. ill. 1). Une comparaison entre les deux œuvres montre clairement que le propos des deux artistes était moins la représentation concrète d'un lieu que l'évocation d'une atmosphère.

La présente estampe a aussi une valeur très particulière en raison de la mention, unique dans cette série et très cachée, du graveur Yokogawa Horitake. Les pèlerins revenant de l'ascension du mont Ōyama (cf. pl. 60) sont emmenés par une figure qui porte un lampion rouge sur lequel on peut lire les caractères *hori* et *take* au-dessus du parapet, littéralement « graver » et « bambou ». Ce n'est sûrement pas par hasard que la « signature » du graveur figure précisément dans cette feuille. Yokogawa était un des graveurs les plus célèbres depuis le milieu du siècle ; dans d'autres œuvres qu'il a gravées pour Hiroshige – notamment la série des *Vues des soixante et quelques provinces* (*Rokujū yoshū meisho zue*, 1853–1856) –, son sceau figure souvent à côté du cartouche de signature de Hiroshige.

鉄炮洲
稲荷橋
湊神社

Teppōzu Inaribashi Minato Jinja
2–1857

Inari Bridge and
the Minato Shrine in Teppōzu

The 14 prints bearing the censors' seal for the second month
of 1857 are at the beginning of
the most productive phase of the
*One Hundred Famous Views of
Edo*. In this print, Hiroshige
uses to great effect the compositional device that had by now
become a hallmark of the series:
a motif seen close up that opens
up rather than blocks a motif in
the middle distance or background. In the immediate foreground, the thick masts of a sea-
going cargo ship effectively
divide the print into three vertical sections. In the left-hand
section, Hiroshige places one of
the eponymous subjects of the
print: the Minato Shrine with its
distinctive red fence, and
beyond, Mount Fuji. The second
subject appears in the middle

section: the Inari Bridge, behind
which white warehouses line the
banks of the Hatchōbori Canal.
The piers of the bridge are rendered semi-transparent, which
helps to increase visually the
breadth of the canal: the strongly
gradated blue of the water
spreads out unrestricted.

The shrine was one of the oldest
in the city; its patron deity
watched over the harbour access
to Edo. Edo Bay was shallow, so
large ships could not dock at the
quayside, but had to lie at
anchor in the bay. Cargo was
transferred to smaller boats,
which we see in the foreground,
and then taken to the warehouses and markets of the
city via its many canals.

Die Brücke Inaribashi und
der Schrein Minato Jinja in Teppōzu

Die 14 Holzschnitte mit Zenso-
rensiegeln vom zweiten Monat
des Jahres 1857 läuten die pro-
duktivste Phase des Großunter-
nehmens *Hundert Ansichten*
ein. Den bereits zu einem Markenzeichen der Serie avancier-
ten Bildaufbau mit einem nah an
den Betrachter gerückten Motiv,
das den Blick auf eine Szene im
Mittel- und Hintergrund eher
eröffnet als verdeckt, setzt
Hiroshige hier effektvoll ein.
Direkt vor dem Auge des
Betrachters ragen die dicken
Masten eines Hochseefrachters
auf und strukturieren das Blatt
in drei vertikale Streifen. In den
Zwischenräumen platziert
Hiroshige die Protagonisten des
Holzschnitts: den vom Berg Fuji
hinterfangenen Schrein Minato
Jinja mit seinem roten Zaun
links und die Brücke Inaribashi

mit den weißen Lagerhäusern
am Ufer des Kanals Hatchōbori
in der Mitte. Die Brückenpfeiler
sind halb durchsichtig gestaltet,
wodurch der Kanal noch breiter
erscheint; das stark gradierte
Blau des Wassers dehnt sich
ungehindert aus.

Der Schrein war einer der ältesten der Stadt; seine Schutzgottheit bewachte den Zugang nach
Edo am Hafen. Die Edo-Bucht
war extrem seicht, sodass große
Schiffe nicht am Ufer anlegen
konnten, sondern in der Bucht
vor Anker gehen mussten. Von
den Frachtern wurden die
Güter auf die unten dargestellten kleineren Transportschiffe
verladen und über die zahlreichen Kanäle zu den Lagerhäusern und Märkten der Stadt
gebracht.

Le pont Inaribashi et le sanctuaire
Minato Jinja à Teppōzu

Les 14 estampes portant le
cachet de censure du deuxième
mois 1857 introduisent la phase
la plus productive de la grande
entreprise des *Cent Vues*. Déjà
devenue un emblème de la série,
la structure iconique présentant
un motif fortement rapproché
du spectateur et ouvrant la vue
– plutôt que la cachant – sur une
scène placée au second ou à l'arrière-plan, est ici employée de
manière particulièrement efficace. Directement sous les yeux
du spectateur, les mâts épais
d'un grand navire marchand se
dressent dans l'image et la structurent en trois bandes verticales. Hiroshige a placé les pro-
tagonistes de l'estampe dans les
intervalles générés par ces
bandes : à gauche, sur fond de
mont Fuji, le sanctuaire Minato
Jinja avec son enceinte rouge, au
milieu, le pont Inaribashi avec

les entrepôts blancs bordant le
canal Hatchōbori. Les poteaux
du pont ont été traités en semi-
transparence de manière à renforcer l'impression de largeur
du canal ; le fort dégradé bleu
réalisé sur l'eau s'étend ainsi
sans obstacles.

Le sanctuaire était l'un des plus
anciens de la capitale ; la divinité
protectrice gardait l'accès du
port d'Edo. La baie d'Edo était
très peu profonde, de sorte que
les gros navires ne pouvaient
aborder au rivage et devaient
jeter l'ancre dans la baie. Leurs
marchandises doivent donc être
chargées sur les barques de fret
plus petites qu'on peut voir en
bas de l'image, et amenées jusqu'aux entrepôts et marchés en
empruntant les nombreux
canaux d'Edo.

築地門跡 鉄炮洲

Teppōzu Tsukiji Monzeki
7–1858

Teppōzu and Tsukiji Monzeki Temple

Disproportionately large, the dark roof of Nishi Honganji rises up into the sky. This temple was an "offshoot" of the temple of the same name in Kyoto, one of the main temples of the Jōdo-Shinshū School of Amida Buddhism. The main hall, one of the largest buildings in Edo, was originally built in 1617 in Hamachō, to the south of Asakusa Gate. After the catastrophic Meireki fire of 1657, however, the government ordered a removal of large buildings, such as temples and daimyō residences, to locations where they had more open land around them. It was hoped this would prevent fires spreading so quickly. The building depicted here was transferred to Tsukiji ("Reclaimed Land"). It thus lay somewhat to the south of the view in plate 77. It was consecrated in 1680 and was known thereafter as Tsukiji Monzeki.

This woodblock print incidentally gives us an insight into the publishing strategy of Hiroshige and his publisher. One of the major goals of the *One Hundred Famous Views of Edo* was to meet the enormous demand for souvenirs of Edo. In 1854,

though, the main hall of the temple had been destroyed in a storm, and at the time of Hiroshige's composition in 1858 it was still being rebuilt. The buyers of prints, however, did not want a souvenir of "damaged reality", but attractive views that they could show off back home. This print took account of these wishes.

Like plate 79, this print bears the changed series title *Entertaining Supplements to the One Hundred Famous Views of Edo (Edo hyakkei yokyō)*. By the seventh month of 1858, when the censors approved the print, Hiroshige had already composed 110 prints, and possibly wanted to end the series. However, the publisher Sakanaya Eikichi probably insisted on continuing this successful and profitable undertaking. So the following month, Hiroshige resumed production of the series with three further compositions and the familiar series title. But he died in the ninth month of the same year and thus one of the most successful series of woodblock prints in Japanese art history came to an end.

Teppōzu und der Tempel Tsukiji Monzeki

Überproportional vergrößert ragt das dunkle Dach des Nishi Honganji in den Himmel. Dieser Tempel war ein „Ableger" des gleichnamigen Tempels in Kyoto, eines der Haupttempel der Jōdo-Shinshū-Richtung des Amida-Buddhismus. Die Haupthalle, eines der größten Gebäude in Edo, wurde ursprünglich 1617 im Stadtteil Hamachō südlich des Asakusa-Tors erbaut. Nach dem verheerenden Meireki-Feuer des Jahres 1657 befahl die Regierung, große Gebäude wie Tempel und Residenzen von Feudalherren an Örtlichkeiten zu versetzen, an denen mehr Umland zur Verfügung stand. So wollte man die Gefahr von sich schnell ausbreitenden Feuern eindämmen. Das hier abgebildete Gebäude wurde in das Viertel Tsukiji („Aufgeschüttetes Neuland") verlegt und lag damit etwas südlicher als die Komposition auf Tafel 77. Es wurde 1680 eingeweiht und seitdem auch Tsukiji Monzeki genannt.

Dieser Holzschnitt erlaubt uns einen Blick auf die Produktionsstrategie von Hiroshige und seinem Verleger. Eines der wesentlichen Ziele der *Hundert Ansichten* bestand darin, den enormen Bedarf an Souvenirs

von Edo zu decken. 1854 war nun aber die Haupthalle des Tempels durch einen Sturm zerstört worden, und als Hiroshiges Entwurf 1858 entstand, befand sie sich noch im Wiederaufbau. Die Käufer wollten allerdings als visuelle Erinnerung nicht eine „beschädigte Realität" mitnehmen, sondern zu Hause möglichst schöne Ansichten vorzeigen. Der Holzschnitt trägt diesem Wunsch Rechnung.

Das Blatt hat, wie auch Tafel 79, den abgeänderten Serientitel *Unterhaltsame Ergänzungen zu den Hundert Ansichten von Edo (Edo hyakkei yokyō)*. Im siebten Monat 1858, als der Holzschnitt von den Zensoren genehmigt wurde, hatte Hiroshige bereits 110 Blätter entworfen und wollte die Arbeit an der Serie möglicherweise abschließen. Wahrscheinlich wollte jedoch der Verleger Sakanaya Eikichi das erfolgreiche und profitable Unternehmen weiterführen. Im folgenden Monat nahm Hiroshige die Produktion der Serie mit drei weiteren Entwürfen und dem gewohnten Serientitel wieder auf, aber er starb schon im neunten Monat und beendete damit eines der erfolgreichsten Holzschnittserien der japanischen Kunstgeschichte.

Teppōzu et le temple Tsukiji Monzeki

Le toit sombre du Nishi Honganji se dresse agrandi et surdimensionné dans le ciel. Ce temple était un « surgeon » du temple homonyme de Kyoto, un des principaux lieux saints du courant Jōdo-Shinshū du bouddhisme Amida. En 1617, le pavillon principal, un des plus grands édifices d'Edo, fut d'abord construit à Hamachō au sud de la porte d'Asakusa. Après l'incendie dévastateur de Meireki en 1657, le gouvernement ordonna que des bâtiments comme les temples et les résidences seigneuriales fussent déplacés sur des sites entourés de plus grandes aires dégagées. L'on voulait ainsi pouvoir parer à l'extension rapide des feux. C'est ainsi que le bâtiment de la présente estampe fut déplacé à Tsukiji (« nouvelle terre remblayée ») et se trouvait donc un peu plus au sud que la composition de la planche 77 ; inauguré en 1680, il continua d'être appelé Tsukiji Monzeki.

La présente estampe nous donne un aperçu de la stratégie éditoriale de Hiroshige et de son éditeur. Un des propos principaux des *Cent Vues* consistait à couvrir l'immense demande de souvenirs d'Edo. En 1854, le

pavillon principal du temple avait été détruit par une tempête, et en 1858, au moment où Hiroshige réalisa ce projet, il était encore en voie de restauration. Cela dit, les acheteurs ne voulaient pas remporter les souvenirs d'une « réalité abîmée », mais pouvoir présenter de belles vues une fois rentrés chez eux. La présente estampe répond en tous points à ce désir.

Tout comme la planche 79, cette feuille porte le titre de série modifié *Compléments ludiques aux Cent Vues d'Edo (Edo hyakkei yokyō)*. Au septième mois 1858, au moment où la feuille fut approuvée par la censure, Hiroshige, qui avait déjà créé 110 feuilles pour les *Cent Vues*, voulut peut-être clore la série. De son côté, l'éditeur Sakanaya Eikichi entendait sans doute poursuivre avec Hiroshige cette entreprise lucrative couronnée de succès. Le mois suivant, Hiroshige reprit la production avec de nouveaux projets portant le titre habituel de la série, mais sa mort au neuvième mois de la même année allait mettre un terme à une des séries d'estampes les plus populaires de l'histoire de l'art japonais.

79

芝神明
増上寺

Shiba Shinmei Zōjōji
7–1858

Shiba Shinmei Shrine and Zōjōji Temple

The four women and four men approaching, headed by a travel guide, are not from Edo: they are visitors from the country who have come to the city to visit its sacred sites and places of interest. Following the peasants in a more sombre mood, the mendicant monks hidden under broad straw hats have also come a long way. Both groups have doubtless been visiting the Zōjōji Temple and are now going home, taking in the Shiba Shinmei Shrine on their way.

The Zōjōji, a temple belonging to the Pure Land School of Buddhism, was one of Edo's most majestic sacred buildings. Its axial arrangement of gates and halls was based on Chinese models. It was the funerary temple of the Tokugawa rulers, who had themselves buried in its precincts. The much older Shiba Shinmei Shrine in front of it to the right had stood here since the 11th century. With its forked finials (*chigi*) and wooden billets (*katsuogi*) placed atop the ridgepole, it reflected the archaic building style of the Ise Shrine, dedicated to the sun goddess Amaterasu.

As in plate 74, genre-like caricatures of the common people bear witness to Hiroshige's training in depicting all types of figures. A comparison with the small, fashionably dressed and elegantly posing citizens of Edo represented on most prints clearly shows that the idealization of the urban scene also extended to its inhabitants. Models of the samurai and the city ladies strolling in the streets and parks of Edo can be found among the bourgeois figures in European veduta, which the first views of Edo in the "Dutch style" in the early 19th century were based.

Der Schrein Shiba Shinmei und der Tempel Zōjōji

Die farbenfrohe Gruppe von vier Frauen und ebenso vielen Männern, die uns, angeführt von einem Reiseleiter, hier entgegenkommt, stammt nicht aus Edo, sondern ist vom Land in die Metropole gewandert, um deren Heiligtümer und Sehenswürdigkeiten zu besuchen. Von weit her kommen auch die unter breiten Strohhüten versteckten Bettelmönche, die den Bauern weniger gut gelaunt folgen. Beide Gruppen haben wohl den Tempel Zōjōji besucht und treten nun vorbei am Schrein Shiba Shinmei ihren Heimweg an.

Der Zōjōji, ein Tempel der Reinen-Land-Schule, gehörte in seiner aus China übernommenen axialen Anordnung von Toren und Tempelhallen zu den majestätischsten Kultbauten Edos. Er war der Grabtempel der Tokugawa-Herrscher, die sich in seinem Bezirk begraben ließen. Der viel ältere Schrein Shiba Shinmei rechts davor stand hier bereits seit dem 11. Jahrhundert. Mit seinen überkreuzten Dachbalken (*chigi*) und den Querhölzern (*katsuogi*) auf dem First gehört er zum archaischen Bautyp des der Sonnengottheit Amaterasu geweihten Ise-Schreins.

Ähnlich wie auf Blatt 74 beweist Hiroshige mit der genrehaft karikierenden Darstellung des Volkes seine Ausbildung in allen Bereichen der Figurendarstellung. Der Vergleich mit den kleinfigurigen, modisch gekleideten und elegant posierenden Bewohnern von Edo auf den meisten Blättern der Serie zeigt, dass die Idealisierung des städtischen Lebensraums sich auch auf dessen Bewohner erstreckte. Vorbilder für die Samurai und städtischen Damen, die in den Straßen und Parks von Edo flanieren, finden sich unter den bürgerlichen Figurentypen auf europäischen Stadt-Veduten, die den ersten Ansichten Edos im „holländischen Stil" aus dem frühen 19. Jahrhundert Modell standen.

Le sanctuaire Shiba Shinmei et le temple Zōjōji

Le groupe riche en couleurs de quatre femmes et autant d'hommes qui viennent à notre rencontre, conduits par un guide, n'est pas originaire d'Edo, mais est venu de la campagne à la capitale pour visiter ses sanctuaires et ses attractions. Un peu plus loin arrivent également des moines mendiants cachés sous leurs larges chapeaux de paille, suivant les paysans d'un air amusé. Les deux groupes viennent sans doute de visiter le temple Zōjōji et prennent le chemin du retour le long du sanctuaire Shiba Shinmei.

Avec son enfilade de portes et de pavillons héritée de la tradition architecturale chinoise, le Zōjōji, un temple de l'école de la Terre pure, faisait partie des édifices cultuels les plus imposants d'Edo. Il servait de temple funéraire aux shoguns Tokugawa qui s'y faisaient enterrer. Quant au sanctuaire Shiba Shinmei beaucoup plus ancien situé à droite devant lui, sa fondation remontait déjà au XIe siècle. Avec ses poutres croisées en façade (*chigi*) et ses poutres faîtières (*katsuogi*), il relève du type de construction archaïque du sanctuaire Ise dédié à la divinité solaire Amaterasu.

Un peu comme dans la planche 74, avec la représentation de genre légèrement caricaturale du peuple, Hiroshige démontre sa formation dans tous les modes de représentation des figures. La comparaison avec les petites figures habitant Edo, vêtues à la mode de l'époque, posant élégamment, telles qu'on les voit dans la plupart des feuilles de la série, montre que l'idéalisation de l'espace urbain s'étendait aussi à ses habitants. Les samouraïs et les mondaines qui flânent dans les rues et les parcs d'Edo ont pour modèles les types bourgeois des védutes européennes qui ont aussi servi de modèle aux premières vues d'Edo de « style hollandais » au début du XIXe siècle.

80

金杉橋
芝浦

Kanasugibashi Shibaura
7–1857

Kanasugi Bridge and Shibaura

In almost all the prints of the series, the title cartouche gives the names of locations. Here, however, the theme is not a place but a particular festivity: over the Kanasugi Bridge at the mouth of the Furukawa, a dense crowd of pilgrims moves southwards away from Edo, while another returns in the opposite direction, towards the city. The pilgrims are carrying objects that throw light on the purpose of the procession: *tenugui* towels suspended from poles, with the emblem of the Nichiren School of Buddhism – an orange blossom in a schematic rectangular well (*izutsu tachibana*). On the brown-and-white cloths around Hiroshige's signature (bottom left) is the personal abbreviation "Uoei", of the name of the publisher of the series, Sakanaya Eikichi, who was presumably an adherent of the school himself. The red banner on the bamboo pole crowned with a parasol is inscribed with the words "Namu Myōhō Rengekyō", which can be roughly translated as "Salvation is in thee, thou wonderful law of the Lotus Sutra". Above it, and on a drum in the crowd, is written: "Heaven and earth are subject to the Lotus Sutra."

The destination of the procession is the Honmonji funerary temple in Ikegami, where the founder of the school, Nichiren (1222–1282), died on the 13th day of the tenth month of 1282. The ceremonies and rites (*oeshiki*) performed annually on the anniversary of Nichiren's death in the Honmonji Temple attracted – and indeed still attract – large crowds of people.

In 1872, the first railway line linking Tokyo with western Japan was built along the narrow Shibaura coastal strip.

Die Brücke Kanasugibashi und Shibaura

Obgleich die Titelkartouche hier wie in fast allen Blättern der Serie die Namen von Örtlichkeiten angibt, ist nicht die Topografie, sondern ein bestimmtes festliches Geschehen das Thema des Blattes: Über die Brücke Kanasugibashi an der Mündung des Flusses Furukawa bewegt sich eine dicht gedrängte Menge von Pilgern gen Süden aus Edo heraus wie auch in entgegengesetzter Richtung zurück in die Stadt. Sie tragen Gegenstände, die über das Ziel der Prozession informieren: Es sind an Stangen aufgehängte Tenugui-Handtücher mit dem Wappenzeichen der buddhistischen Nichiren-Schule – einer Orangenblüte im schematisierten, viereckigen Brunnen (*izutsu tachibana*). Auf den weiß-braunen Tüchern rund um Hiroshiges Signatur ist das persönliche Namenskürzel „Uoei" des Verlegers der Serie, Sakanaya Eikichi, zu lesen, der vermutlich selbst ein Anhänger der Schule war. Das rote Banner an der mit einem Schirm bekrönten Bambusstange ist mit der magischen Formel „Namu Myōhō Rengekyō" beschrieben, die etwa mit „Das Heil ist in Dir, Du wunderbares Gesetz des Lotus-Sutra" übersetzt werden kann. Darüber und auf einer Trommel in der Menschenmenge steht: „Erde und Himmel unterstehen dem Lotus-Sutra."

Das Ziel der Prozession ist der Grabtempel Honmonji im Stadtviertel Ikegami, wo der Schulgründer Nichiren (1222–1282) am 13. Tag im zehnten Monat des Jahres 1282 starb. Die an Nichirens Todestag jährlich im Tempel Honmonji veranstalteten Zeremonien und Riten (*oeshiki*) lockten damals wie heute große Menschenmassen an. 1872 erbaute man an dem schmalen Küstenstreifen Shibaura die erste Eisenbahnlinie von Tokyo nach West-Japan.

Le pont Kanasugibashi et Shibaura

Bien que le cartouche de titre de la présente estampe contiennent des indications de lieux comme c'est le cas pour presque toutes celles de la série, le sujet n'est pas une topographie, mais une festivité particulière : sur le pont Kanasugibashi, près de l'embouchure de la rivière Furukawa, une foule dense de pèlerins se dirige à la sortie d'Edo vers le sud, mais aussi en sens contraire, retournant vers la capitale. Les pèlerins portent des objets qui nous renseignent sur l'objet de cette procession : il s'agit de serviettes *tenugui* accrochées à de grandes hampes et arborant le blason de l'école du bouddhisme nichiren – une fleur d'oranger dans une représentation schématique du puits carré (*izutsu tachibana*). Sur les pièces de tissus brun-blanc autour de la signature de Hiroshige, on peut lire l'abréviation personnelle « Uoei » de l'éditeur de la série, Sakanaya Eikichi, qui fut sans doute lui-même un adepte de cette école. La bannière rouge suspendue au bambou couronné d'une ombrelle porte l'inscription « Namu Myōhō Rengekyō », ce qui peut se traduire par « Le salut est en toi, ô loi merveilleuse du soutra du Lotus. » Au-dessus et sur un tambour parmi la foule, on peut lire : « Le ciel et la terre sont soumis au soutra du Lotus. »

Le but de la procession est le temple funéraire Honmonji à Ikegami, où Nichiren (1222–1282), le fondateur de l'école, mourut le 13ème jour du dixième mois 1282. Tout comme aujourd'hui, les rituels et les cérémonies (*oeshiki*) organisés au temple Honmonji le jour anniversaire de la mort du fondateur, attiraient alors de grandes masses humaines. Sur la fine bande côtière de Shibaura fut construite en 1872 la première ligne de chemin de fer reliant Tokyo à l'ouest du Japon.

81

高輪
うしまち

Takanawa Ushimachi
4–1857

Ushimachi in Takanawa

Takanawa was the official southern access to the city of Edo. We are looking across the Tōkaidō highway (Eastern Sea Road) over Edo Bay, which is accentuated by sailing boats and the *daiba* (earth ramparts) erected as defensive fortifications in 1853/54 (see plates 28, 83, 108). As Hiroshige indicates with the wheel and shafts in the foreground, we are in the "Ox Quarter" (Ushimachi). This name goes back to 1634, when oxen were brought to Edo to assist in the construction of the Zōjōji (see plate 53), the family temple of the Tokugawa shoguns. During the Tokugawa period (1615–1868), ox carts were used primarily for building projects inaugurated by the military elite, but as early as the Heian period (794–1185) they had also been regarded as an elegant means of transport for the court aristocracy and later for the social elite. As such, they lived on in the images and imaginations of the educated strata of society.

Motifs that seem assembled randomly in Hiroshige's compositions are often linked on a symbolic level. In this print, for example, he plays with the place-name Takanawa, which means "High Wheel", and which is symbolized by the cropped wheel on the right. The "high wheel" also appears, though, in the form of a pale rainbow spanning the sky and intersecting the shafts of the cart.

The low viewpoint allows a glimpse of things mostly overlooked and generally dismissed as unworthy of depiction: in plate 86, for instance, it is horse dung, while here it is melon rind, as well as a discarded straw sandal being gnawed at by a dog. Both hint at the presence of people, whose absence from the scene only enhances the print's poetic atmosphere.

The refreshing juxtaposition of things associated with everyday life, including excrement and refuse, with stately buildings and elegant gardens is an integral feature of Hiroshige's late work. This made him, along with Hasegawa Settan (1778–1843), who created the pictures for the 1834–1836 book *Illustrated Guide to Famous Places in Edo* (*Edo meisho zue*), one of the leading pioneers of modern Japanese printmaking.

Ushimachi in Takanawa

Takanawa war der offizielle südliche Eingang in die Stadt Edo. Wir blicken über die Hauptverkehrsstraße Tōkaidō (Ostmeerstraße) auf die Bucht von Edo, die von Segelbooten und den 1853/54 zur Verteidigung aufgeschütteten Erdwällen *daiba* (siehe Tafeln 28, 83, 108) akzentuiert wird. Wie Hiroshige mit Rad und Deichsel im Vordergrund andeutet, sind wir im „Viertel der Ochsen" (Ushimachi). Es geht auf das Jahr 1634 zurück, als Ochsen zur Konstruktion des Familientempels der Tokugawa-Shogune, des Zōjōji (siehe Tafel 53), nach Edo gebracht wurden. Ochsenwagen setzte man in der Tokugawa-Zeit (1615–1868) in erster Linie für Bauprojekte des Militäradels ein, bereits seit der Heian-Zeit (794–1185) galten sie aber auch als elegantes Transportmittel der Hofaristokratie und später der sozialen Elite. Als solches lebten sie in Bildern und in den Vorstellungen der gebildeten Schicht weiter.

Scheinbar zufällig zusammengeworfene Elemente sind in Hiroshiges Blättern oft auf einer symbolischen Ebene miteinander verbunden. Hier etwa spielt er mit dem Ortsnamen Takanawa, der „hohes Rad" bedeutet und mit dem angeschnittenen Rad am rechten Rand verbildlicht ist. Das „hohe Rad" erscheint aber auch in Form eines zarten Regenbogens, der den Himmel umspannt und von der Deichsel geschnitten wird.

Das Auge des Betrachters ist tief angesetzt und gewährt so einen Blick auf meist übersehene Dinge, die man gemeinhin als wenig bildwürdig beurteilt: In Tafel 86 etwa sind es Pferdeäpfel, hier sind es abgegessene Melonenschalen und eine zerfetzte Strohsandale, an der ein Hund knabbert. Beides deutet auf menschliche Präsenz hin, deren Abwesenheit den poetischen Gehalt des Bildes noch erhöht.

Das erfrischende Nebeneinander aller Dinge des menschlichen Alltags, zu denen Kot und Abfall ebenso gehören wie stattliche Gebäude und elegante Gartenanlagen, ist ein integraler Bestandteil in Hiroshiges Spätwerk. Er hat sich damit neben Hasegawa Settan (1778–1843), der die Bilder für den *Illustrierten Führer zu berühmten Ansichten von Edo* (*Edo meisho zue*) von 1834–1836 schuf, zu einem der wichtigsten Vorreiter der modernen japanischen Druckgrafik gemacht.

Ushimachi à Takanawa

Takanawa marquait l'entrée sud officielle de la ville d'Edo. Ici, la vue porte au-delà de la grande voie de circulation Tōkaidō (route de la mer orientale) pour s'ouvrir sur la baie d'Edo ponctuée de voiliers et de *daiba* (cf. pl. 28, 83, 108), remblais fortifiés construits en 1853/54 pour la défense du pays. Comme l'indique Hiroshige avec la roue et le timon au premier plan, nous nous trouvons dans le quartier dit « des bœufs » (Ushimachi), dont le nom remonte à 1634, année où des bœufs furent amenés à Edo pour la construction du Zōjōji, le temple privé des shoguns Tokugawa (cf. pl. 53). Pendant l'ère Tokugawa (1615–1868), les chars à bœufs servirent avant tout pour les constructions militaires de l'aristocratie. Dès l'ère Heian (794–1185), ils furent toutefois considérés aussi comme un moyen de transport élégant de la noblesse de cour et plus tard de l'élite sociale, et c'est en tant que tels qu'ils survivaient dans l'imagerie et l'imaginaire de la classe cultivée.

Chez Hiroshige, les éléments réunis de manière apparemment fortuite sont souvent liés par un plan symbolique. Ici, l'artiste joue par exemple sur le nom de lieu Takanawa (« haute roue ») que symbolise la roue coupée par le bord droit de l'image. Mais la « haute roue » apparaît encore sous la forme d'un arc-en-ciel diaphane qui s'arque sur l'ensemble du ciel et que coupe le timon.

Le point de vue du spectateur est placé bas et offre ainsi un regard sur des choses normalement ignorées, habituellement jugées indignes de figurer dans l'art : dans la planche 86 par exemple, il s'agit de crottin de cheval, ici, ce sont des écorces de pastèque jetées une fois la pulpe consommée, et une sandale de paille déchirée rongée par un chien. Les deux éléments renvoient à une présence humaine dont l'absence renforce le contenu poétique de l'image.

La fraîcheur de la juxtaposition de toutes ces choses de la vie quotidienne, dont font partie le crottin aussi bien que les constructions humaines et les élégants jardins paysagers, est une partie intégrante de l'œuvre tardif de Hiroshige. Cet aspect a fait de Hiroshige un des principaux précurseurs de l'estampe japonaise moderne avec Hasegawa Settan (1778–1843), qui fut l'auteur des illustrations du *Guide illustré des lieux célèbres d'Edo* (*Edo meisho zue*) de 1834–1836.

82

Tsuki no misaki
8—1857

Moon Viewing

This print, which presents approximately the same view as plate 83, achieves its effect primarily by suggestion. Through the wide-open sliding door of an establishment in Shinagawa, we are looking across Edo Bay, which is brightly illuminated by the full moon. A flock of birds is flying over the still, shallow water, while cargo ships lie at anchor, their rigging removed. All is silent.

The same tranquil mood also prevails in the room in the foreground. After an evening meal, guests have left the room. Two figures are cropped by the margins of the print: a geisha on the right has put down her musical instrument, a shamisen, while on the left we see the shadow of a prostitute, taking off her kimono.

The guests have left the room in some disorder. Hiroshige's com-position makes no bones about either this or the nature of the meal. On a large red lacquer tray stands a serving plate with left-over *sashimi* slices, doubtless of costly tuna; the *wasabi* is like-wise untouched. In the tall bowl to the side, a *sake* beaker is floating, a half-open fan is lying on the green tatami, and used napkins are lying around, apparently carelessly discarded.

From right to left – the direction in which Japanese is read – Hiroshige presents us therefore with a clear sequence of events: the music has fallen silent and the meal is over (past), we are watching the moon (present) and the shadow-figure is preparing herself for the immediate future. All this can be found in just one woodblock print that at first glance seems to be somewhat simplistic, even random.

Mondbetrachtung

Diese Tafel, die topografisch gesehen etwa die gleiche Sicht präsentiert wie Tafel 83, wirkt vor allem durch ihre Andeutungen. Wir blicken durch die weit geöffneten Schiebetüren eines Etablissements im Vorort Shinagawa auf die vom Vollmond hell erleuchtete Bucht von Edo. Ein Vogelschwarm zieht über das wellenlose, flache Wasser, abgetakelte Frachtboote liegen vor Anker, Stille ist eingekehrt.

Diese ruhige Stimmung herrscht auch im Inneren des nahe an den Betrachter gerückten Raumes: Nach einem Nachtmahl haben die Gäste das Zimmer verlassen. Am rechten und linken Bildrand sehen wir je eine angeschnittene Figur. Eine Geisha hat rechts ihr Instrument, eine Shamisen, abgestellt, links ist der Schatten einer Prostituierten zu erkennen, die ihren Kimono ablegt und sich für das Bett fertig macht.

Die Gäste haben eine Unordnung hinterlassen, die in Hiro-shiges Gestaltung klare Form annimmt und beredtes Zeugnis des Gelages ablegt. Auf einem großen roten Lacktablett steht ein Servierteller mit übriggebliebenen Sashimi-Scheiben, wohl vom teuren Thunfisch, und auch der Wasabi ist unangetastet. In der hohen Schale daneben schwimmt ein Sakebecher, ein halb geöffneter Fächer liegt auf den grünen Tatamis, und gebrauchte Handtücher wurden anscheinend achtlos hingeworfen.

So präsentiert uns Hiroshige von rechts nach links – in der Richtung, in der man japanische Texte liest, – einen zeitlichen Ablauf: Die Musik ist verklungen, die Mahlzeit beendet (Vergangenheit), wir betrachten den Mond (Gegenwart), und die Schattengestalt bereitet sich auf etwas Bevorstehendes vor. All dies finden wir in einem Holzschnitt, der auf den ersten Blick lapidar und etwas zufällig erscheint.

Contemplation de la lune

Cette estampe qui nous montre à peu près la même topographie que la planche 83, procède surtout par allusions. L'ouverture de deux portes coulissantes d'un établissement de Shinagawa y offre une vue de la baie d'Edo éclairée par un lumineux clair de lune. Un vol d'oiseaux passe au-dessus de l'eau parfaitement étale, des barques marchandes ont jeté leur ancre et le silence s'est fait dans la nuit.

La même ambiance paisible règne aussi à l'intérieur de la pièce fortement rapprochée du spectateur : après un tardif souper, des clients ont quitté la place. À gauche et à droite, on peut voir une figure coupée par les bords de l'image. À droite, une geisha a déposé son instrument de musique, un shamisen ; à gauche, on reconnaît l'ombre d'une prostituée qui s'est dévêtue de son kimono et se prépare à se mettre au lit.

De la droite vers la gauche, sens de l'écriture japonaise, Hiroshige nous montre ainsi un déroulement temporel : la musique a cessé, le repas a été achevé (passé), nous contemplons la lune (présent), et la silhouette se prépare à aller se coucher (futur) – tout ceci dans une estampe qui semble à première vue lapidaire et quelque peu fortuite.

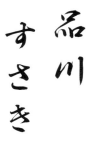

品川
すさき

Shinagawa Susaki
4–1856

Shinagawa Susaki

While in plate 82 Hiroshige chose a low viewpoint, in this print a bird's-eye view opens up a vista across the broad surface of Edo Bay, punctuated with white sails. But the location is more or less the same: the establishment depicted in *Moon Viewing* may well be identical to the building cropped by the left-hand and bottom margin of the present composition. Clearly recognizable here, by contrast, is the Benten shrine on the banks of the Meguro River, a bright red gate or *torii* ("where birds settle") standing in front of it, just to the right. Benten is an abbreviation of Benzaiti (in Sanskrit, "Sarasvati"), a Buddhist deity who was very important in Tokugawa Japan (1615–1868) in her capacity as deity of business success and patroness of rivers and lakes. (Other Benten shrines are depicted on plates 72, 87, 88, 117.) In the shrine precincts, a grave was prepared for the bones of a whale that became celebrated after becoming stranded in Edo Bay in 1798.

The horizon is characterized by a deep-red sky, which Hiroshige uses to suggest a clear sunset; he achieves this splendid colour effect through artistic licence: we are in fact looking not westwards, but to the north or northeast. To the right beneath the horizon, and surrounded by deep blue, two *daiba* project into the scene. These fortifications were built as a defence against foreign fleets after the first appearance of the so-called Black Ships of the American commodore Matthew Perry (1794–1858) in July 1853.

On high-quality impressions of this print, such as the one illustrated here, we see also the traces of the work of the printer. When the paper was pressed against the woodblock using a *baren* (a round rubbing instrument over which a bamboo leaf was stretched), the circular movements left scratch-like lines over the grain of the wood.

Shinagawa, in Hiroshige's day a southern suburb of Edo, was the first station on the famous Tōkaidō (Eastern Sea Road), the link between Edo and Kyoto, which started by the Nihonbashi Bridge in Edo (see plate 1). While Shinagawa was in fact only eight kilometres (five miles) away, that could well represent a day's journey. It was customary to accompany travellers as far as this first station and, before final farewells were said, to eat a lavish meal. In the case of male travellers, this was often followed by a joint visit to the local brothel.

Landzunge bei Shinagawa

Während Hiroshige in Tafel 82 einen niedrigen Betrachterstandpunkt wählt, öffnet sich hier der Blick aus der Vogelperspektive auf die weite, von weißen Segeln akzentuierte Wasserfläche der Bucht von Edo. Doch der Ort ist in etwa der gleiche: Das Etablissement des Holzschnittes *Mondbetrachtung* mag mit dem angeschnittene Gebäude links unten identisch sein. Deutlich hervorgehoben ist hingegen der Benten-Schrein jenseits des Ufers des Meguro-gawa, zu dem das hellrote Tor *torii* („wo sich Vögel niederlassen") rechts davor führt. Benten ist die Abkürzung für Benzaiten (Sanskrit „Sarasvati"), eine buddhistische Gottheit, deren Rolle als Göttin des Handelsglücks und als Schutzpatronin von Flüssen und Seen im Japan der Tokugawa-Zeit (1615–1868) eine große Rolle spielte (weitere Benten-Schreine auf den Tafeln 72, 87, 88 und 117). Im Schreinbezirk wurde ein Grab für die zu Berühmtheit gelangten Knochen eines Walfisches angelegt, der 1798 vor der Edo-Bucht gestrandet war.

Der Horizont wird von einem tiefroten Himmel geprägt. Hiroshige suggeriert damit einen Sonnenuntergang; er erzielt diesen großartigen Farbeffekt, indem er sich eine künstlerische Freiheit nimmt: Tatsächlich blicken wir nicht nach Westen, sondern nach Norden oder Nordosten. Rechts unter dem Horizont, von tiefem Blau umgeben, ragen zwei *daiba* ins Bild. Diese Befestigungsbauten wurden nach dem ersten Erscheinen der sogenannten „Schwarzen Schiffe" des amerikanischen Admirals Matthew Perry (1794–1858) im Juli 1853 zur Abwehr fremder Flotten erbaut.

Auf so qualitätvollen Exemplaren dieses Holzschnitts wie unserem sehen wir die Spuren des Druckers. Der mit einem Bambusblatt überspannte Reibetampon *baren* hinterließ beim kreisenden Andrücken des Papiers auf den Druckstock wie Kratzer anmutende Linien über der Holzmaserung.

Shinagawa, zur Zeit Hiroshiges ein südlicher Vorort von Edo, war die erste Station des berühmten Tōkaidō (Ostmeerstraße), der Verbindungsstrecke zwischen Edo und Kyoto, die an der Brücke Nihonbashi in Edo begann (siehe Tafel 1). Shinagawa lag zwar nur acht Kilometer entfernt, aber das konnte eine Tagesreise bedeuten. Reisende begleitete man bis zu dieser ersten Station, und vor dem endgültigen Abschied wurde ausgiebig getafelt. Oft mag sich für die Herren noch ein gemeinsamer Besuch im dortigen Bordell angeschlossen haben.

Langue de terre près de Shinagawa

Alors que dans la planche 82, Hiroshige a opté pour un point de vue placé très bas, ici, la vue s'ouvre à partir d'une perspective d'une étendue de la baie d'Edo ponctuée de voiles blanches. Mais le site est à peu près le même : l'établissement de l'estampe *Contemplation de la lune* est sans doute celui qu'on voit ici coupé par le bord inférieur gauche. Est en revanche plus fortement marqué le sanctuaire de Benten situé un peu au-delà de la rive opposée de la Meguro-gawa, et auquel on accède par la porte rouge dite *torii* (« où viennent se poser les oiseaux ») qu'on peut voir à sa droite. Benten est l'abréviation de Benzaiten (sanscrit « Sarasvati »), une divinité bouddhique qui jouait un rôle très important dans le Japon de l'ère Tokugawa (1615–1868) comme déesse de la chance en affaires et protectrice des rivières et des lacs (d'autres sanctuaires de Benten dans les planches 72, 87, 88 et 117). Dans le domaine du sanctuaire avait été aménagée la tombe du squelette d'une baleine qui s'était échouée dans la baie d'Edo en 1798.

L'horizon est marqué par un ciel d'un rouge profond qui permet à Hiroshige de suggérer un coucher de soleil. Ce spectaculaire effet de couleur a été obtenu par une licence artistique de Hiroshige : de fait, la vue est ici dirigée non pas à l'ouest, mais au nord ou nord-est. Sous l'horizon à droite, cernés d'un bleu profond, deux *daiba* se dressent dans l'image. Ces ouvrages fortifiés avaient été construits pour défendre le pays contre les flottes étrangères après la venue des « bateaux noirs » du commodore américain Matthew Perry (1794–1858) en juillet 1853.

Dans des tirages aussi excellents que la présente estampe, on peut relever les traces laissées par le procédé d'impression. Appuyé selon un mouvement circulaire contre la feuille posée sur le bois d'impression, le tampon *baren* enveloppé d'une feuille de bambou faisait ressembler les lignes des veinures du bois à des grattages.

Shinagawa, faubourg d'Edo à l'époque de Hiroshige, était la première étape de la célèbre Tōkaidō (route de la mer orientale), la grande voie de circulation qui reliait Edo à Kyoto en partant du pont Nihonbashi (cf. pl. 1). Même si Shinagawa n'était distante que de huit kilomètres, ce trajet pouvait demander une journée de voyage. Les amis accompagnaient les voyageurs jusqu'à cette première étape et l'on y festoyait dûment avant la séparation définitive. Les messieurs ne manquaient pas de faire un petit tour dans une des maisons de plaisirs de l'étape.

84

目黒
爺々が
茶屋

Meguro Jijigachaya
4–1857

"Grandpa's Teahouse" in Meguro

On his way south through Meguro, a traveller steps out between two hills on which pine trees grow and is suddenly confronted by the silhouette of Mount Fuji rising from a broad plain. On the right is a simple thatched cottage, doubtless the teahouse of the title run by an old man, while on the other side of the path is the even plainer primitive tea stall, roofed with a pergola and run by his wife.

Today one of the most opulent residential suburbs in the south of Tokyo, during the Tokugawa period (1615–1868) Meguro was one of the areas in which the shoguns used to go hawking. Hiroshige provided the motif, which appeared in the seventh volume of his *Illustrated Souvenirs of Edo* (*Ehon Edo miyage*), printed in 1857, with corresponding explanations. This beautiful spot had been depicted by Shiba Kōkan (1738/47–1818) in the European veduta style and he used its motifs for copperplate engravings that began to appear in 1783. *The Famous Views of Edo* (*Edo meisho*) conceived by this pioneer of Western-style painting were innovative in that they transferred Western perspective, popularized by perspective views seen through peep-boxes, to the Japanese landscape genre.

In this print, the landscape painter Hiroshige, who may well have frequented "Grandpa's Teahouse" himself, acknowledges his acceptance of the "realistic" landscape (*shinkei*) in the Western manner, both in style and iconography.

Teehaus „Zum Großvater" in Meguro

Auf seinem Weg durch den Bezirk Meguro gen Süden tritt der Wanderer zwischen zwei mit Kiefern bestandenen Hügeln in die Ebene und hat plötzlich die Silhouette des Berges Fuji vor sich. Rechts steht ein einfaches Häuschen mit einem Strohdach, wohl das im Titel genannte, von einem alten Mann geführte Teehaus. Auf der anderen Wegseite befindet sich der noch schlichtere, mit einer Pergola überdachte Teestand seiner Frau.

Heute eines der reichsten Wohnviertel im Süden Tokyos, gehörte Meguro während der Tokugawa-Zeit (1615–1868) noch zu den Gebieten, in denen die Shogune auf die Falkenjagd zu gehen pflegten. Hiroshige hat das Bildmotiv im siebten Band von *Illustrierte Mitbringsel aus Edo* (*Ehon Edo miyage*), 1857 erschienen, mit entsprechenden Erläuterungen versehen. Dieses Ausflugsziel zählte zu den landschaftlich reizvollen Örtlichkeiten, die bereits Shiba Kōkan (1738/47–1818) im Stil europäischer Veduten malte und als Motiv für seine ab 1783 erschienenen Kupferstiche auswählte. Die von diesem Pionier westlicher Malerei konzipierten *Berühmten Orte von Edo* (*Edo meisho*) brachten insofern etwas Neues, als sie die durch Guckkastenbilder populär gewordene westliche Perspektive auf die japanische Landschaft übertrugen. Der Landschaftsmaler Hiroshige, der das Teehaus „Zum Großvater" selbst inspiriert haben mag, bekannte sich in diesem Blatt ikonografisch und stilistisch zur Tradition der „realistischen" Landschaftsdarstellung (*shinkei*) im westlichen Stil.

La maison de thé « Au grand-père » à Meguro

Sur sa route vers le Sud, en traversant Meguro, le voyageur passe entre deux collines plantées de pins avant de déboucher sur une plaine où lui apparaît soudain la silhouette du mont Fuji. À droite se dresse une simple maisonnette couverte de chaume, sans doute celle évoquée par le titre, maison de thé dirigée par un vieil homme ; de l'autre côté de la route se trouve le stand à thé encore plus primitif, couvert d'une pergola, tenu par sa femme.

Pendant l'ère Tokugawa (1615–1868), Meguro, aujourd'hui un des quartiers les plus luxueux de Tokyo, faisait encore partie des domaines où les shoguns pratiquaient la fauconnerie. Dans le septième tome (1857) de ses *Souvenirs illustrés d'Edo* (*Ehon Edo miyage*), Hiroshige a assorti le même motif de quelques explications. Ce lieu d'excursion comptait parmi les sites les plus pittoresques que Shiba Kōkan (1738/47–1818) a dépeints dans le style des védutes européennes et choisis comme sujet de ses gravures sur cuivre publiées à partir de 1783. *Les vues d'Edo* (*Edo meisho*) conçues par ce pionnier de la peinture occidentale apportaient un élément nouveau dans la mesure où elles transposaient dans le domaine du paysage japonais la perspective occidentale popularisée par les boîtes optiques. Dans la présente feuille, le paysagiste Hiroshige, qui aura sans doute visité en personne la maison de thé « Au grand-père », se rattache iconographiquement et stylistiquement à la tradition de la représentation paysagère « réaliste » (*shinkei*) de style occidental.

85

紀の国坂
赤坂溜池
遠景

Kinokunizaka Akasaka Tameike enkei
9–1857

Kinokuni Hill and Distant View of Akasaka and the Tameike Pond

Samurai, recognizable by their two swords, are striding in rigid procession up Kinokuni Hill past the outer Benkeibori moat in the south-west of the precincts of Edo Castle. The jacket of the leader, who is carrying a standard cropped by the top margin of the print, bears an iris (*shōbu*) emblem; written with different characters, the word pronounced *shōbu* can also mean "appreciation of the martial spirit". In spite of their uniforms and their parade-ground movements, these somewhat caricatured warriors have individual facial features. Bearing in mind that just eleven years after this print was made, the samurai as a social stratum and a power to be reckoned with would be consigned to history, one is tempted to greet these grim and resolute warriors with a smile. Here Hiroshige reveals himself at the height of his skills in the humorous and psychological depiction of human figures.

In this print, his theme is an apparent contradiction in the society of his day: while the samurai dominate the foreground, the middle distance beyond the moat is occupied by the houses of the urban population (*chōnin*), which included the two lower estates comprising craftsmen and merchants. They accounted for more than half of the 1.5 to 2 million inhabitants of Edo, but were squeezed on to 21 per cent of the area of the municipality.

In spite of his samurai descent, Hiroshige earned his living exclusively as a painter and printmaker from 1832. This is just one of countless indications that the boundaries of the official four-estate system of the Tokugawa period (1615–1868), on which this print is a comment, were fluid.

Der Hügel Kinokunizaka und Akasaka sowie der Teich Tameike in der Ferne

Eine schnurgerade Prozession von Samurai, erkennbar an ihren zwei Schwertern, schreitet den Hügel Kinokunizaka hinauf, vorbei am äußeren Wassergraben Benkeibori im Südwesten des Edo-Schlosses. Die Jacke des Anführers, der eine über den oberen Bildrand hinausragende Standarte trägt, ist mit dem Emblem einer Schwertlilie (*shōbu*) versehen; mit anderen Schriftzeichen geschrieben, kann *shōbu* auch „Hochschätzung des kriegerischen Geistes" bedeuten. Trotz der gleichförmigen Kleidung und dem Gleichschritt tragen die leicht karikierend dargestellten Krieger individuelle Gesichtszüge. Bedenkt man, dass schon elf Jahre nach Entstehung dieses Holzschnitts die Samurai als Stand und als Machtinstanz der Vergangenheit angehören sollten, so muss man über die entschlossenen, mürrischen Krieger fast schmunzeln. Hiroshige erweist sich hier auf der Höhe seines Könnens in der humoristischen und psychologischen Figurendarstellung.

Dass Hiroshige trotz seiner Abstammung vom Stand der Samurai ab 1832 ausschließlich als Maler und Entwerfer von Holzschnitten tätig war, ist nur einer von unzähligen Belegen dafür, dass die Grenzen des offiziellen Vierständesystems der Tokugawa-Zeit (1615–1868) – das in diesem Blatt kommentiert wird – fließend waren.

Der Holzschnittmeister thematisiert auf diesem Blatt einen scheinbaren Gegensatz in der japanischen Gesellschaft seiner Zeit: Während die Samurai den Vordergrund beherrschen, erstreckt sich im Mittelgrund hinter dem Schlossgraben das Meer der Häuser für die Stadtbevölkerung (*chōnin*), zu der die beiden niederen Stände der Handwerker und Kaufleute gehörten. Sie stellten unter den anderthalb bis zwei Millionen Einwohnern von Edo mehr als die Hälfte, drängten sich aber auf nur 21 Prozent der Stadtfläche.

La colline Kinokunizaka et Akasaka avec l'étang Tameike dans le lointain

Des samouraïs défilant en bon ordre, reconnaissables à leurs deux sabres, montent la colline Kinokunizaka en longeant la douve extérieure sud-ouest du château d'Edo, la Benkeibori. La veste du chef de file, porteur d'un étendard qui dépasse le cadre supérieur de l'image, est dotée d'un emblème figurant un glaïeul (*shōbu*) ; écrit avec d'autres caractères, *shōbu* peut aussi signifier « exaltation de l'esprit guerrier ». Malgré l'uniformité des costumes et l'égalité du pas, les guerriers représentés sous une forme légèrement caricaturale dénotent des traits individuels. Quand on songe que onze ans seulement après la création de cette estampe, la classe sociale des samouraïs, levier séculaire du pouvoir au Japon, allait appartenir au passé, on ne peut s'empêcher de sourire en voyant leurs mines résolues et rébarbatives. Hiroshige est ici au sommet de son art dans la représentation humoristique et psychologique des figures.

Dans cette feuille, le maître de l'estampe illustre une apparente opposition au sein de la société japonaise de son époque : alors que les samouraïs dominent le premier plan de l'image, au second plan, derrière la douve, s'étend l'océan de maisons de la population urbaine (*chōnin*), à laquelle appartenaient les deux classes inférieures des marchands et des artisans. Ces deux classes représentaient plus de la moitié de la population d'Edo, c'est-à-dire entre 750 000 et un million d'habitants, mais n'occupaient que 21 pour cent de la superficie de la ville.

Le fait que malgré son appartenance à la classe des samouraïs, Hiroshige ait travaillé exclusivement à partir de 1832 comme peintre et concepteur d'estampes, n'est qu'une des nombreuses preuves du fait que les limites du système officiel des quatre classes en vigueur pendant l'ère Tokugawa (1615–1868) – et tel qu'il est commenté dans la présente estampe –, n'avaient rien d'hermétique.

86

四ツ谷
内藤
新宿

Yotsuya Naitō Shinjuku
11–1857

Naitō Shinjuku in Yotsuya

This print employs one of the extraordinary perspectives that make such an essential contribution to the popularity of Hiroshige's *One Hundred Famous Views of Edo*. The viewpoint here is located about half a metre above the ground, from where we have a close-up view of the straw-shod hooves, hind legs and elaborately knotted tail of a horse. The animal's dung is also clearly visible on the ground.

This naturalistic depiction provoked criticism of the print as vulgar, both in Europe and Japan, a judgement that was based on modern notions of hygiene and disregarded the importance of farming for a metropolis such as Edo. Not only animal but also human excrement had become an expensive commodity, sold as much-needed fertilizer to farmers in the hinterland.

We can reasonably assume that with this print Hiroshige was alluding to a quotation from the famous illustrated book *Master Flashgold's Splendiferous Dream* (*Kinkin sensei eiga no yume*), published in 1775. In this work, which ushered in a whole genre of satirical depictions in prose and pictures, prostitutes from the Shinjuku district, which is illustrated here, were described as "flowers thriving on the horse dung of Yotsuya".

The "new postal station" of Shinjuku was the first station on the main highway known as Kōshū kaidō, which led westwards from Edo to Shimo-Suwa (in today's Nagano Prefecture). Like similar stations, it became a semi-official centre for prostitution. For travellers coming from the west, Shinjuku was at the same time the gateway to the city of Edo, as Takanawa was for visitors from the south (see plate 81).

Naitō Shinjuku in Yotsuya

Dieser Holzschnitt bietet eine der außergewöhnlichen Perspektiven, die zur Beliebtheit von Hiroshiges *Hundert Ansichten* wesentlich beitragen. Der Betrachter befindet sich etwa einen halben Meter über dem Boden und blickt direkt auf die mit Strohschuhen bedeckten Hufe, die Hinterhand und den kunstvoll geknoteten Schweif eines Pferdes. Auf dem Boden liegen deutlich erkennbar die Hinterlassenschaften des Tieres.

Wegen dieser naturalistischen Darstellung wurde das Blatt in Europa wie auch in Japan als vulgär kritisiert – ein Urteil, das sich aus modernen Vorstellungen von Hygiene speist und die Bedeutung der Landwirtschaft gerade für eine Metropole wie Edo verkennt: Menschliche und tierische Fäkalien waren ein hochbezahltes Handelsgut. Sie wurden als dringend benötigter Dünger an Bauern im Umland verkauft.

Wir dürfen annehmen, dass Hiroshige mit diesem Blatt auf ein Zitat aus dem berühmten illustrierten Buch *Meister Goldgolds prächtiger Traum* (*Kinkin sensei eiga no yume*) von 1775 anspielt. In diesem Werk, das ein ganzes Genre satirischer Darstellungen in Prosa und Bild einläutete, werden Prostituierte aus dem hier abgebildeten Shinjuku als „auf dem Pferdemist von Yotsuya gedeihende Blumen" beschrieben.

Die „neue Poststation" Shinjuku war die erste Station auf dem Hauptverkehrsweg Kōshū kaidō, der von Edo Richtung Westen nach Shimo-Suwa (heutige Präfektur Nagano) führte. Wie vergleichbare Orte wurde es zu einem halboffiziellen Zentrum der Prostitution. Für Reisende, die von Westen kamen, war Shinjuku zugleich das Eingangstor zur Stadt Edo, so wie Takanawa für Besucher aus dem Süden (siehe Tafel 81).

Naitō Shinjuku à Yotsuya

Cette estampe présente une des perspectives inhabituelles qui ont fortement contribué à assurer la popularité des *Cent Vues*. Le point de vue du spectateur est abaissé à quelque 50 centimètres au-dessus du sol et son regard est directement dirigé sur les sabots couverts de paille, l'arrière-train et la queue joliment tressée d'un cheval. Au sol, on aperçoit très clairement le crottin laissé par l'animal.

Cette représentation naturaliste a fait que l'estampe a été jugée triviale en Europe comme au Japon – une critique nourrie des conceptions modernes de l'hygiène et qui méconnaît l'importance de l'agriculture justement dans une métropole comme l'était Edo : les fèces animales et humaines étaient une matière indispensable comme engrais pour les campagnes environnantes et donc vendues à bon prix.

On peut supposer que la présente feuille fait allusion à la citation d'un livre illustré célèbre paru en 1775 : *Le vain rêve de gloire du sieur Dorédor* (*Kinkin sensei eiga no yume*). Dans cet ouvrage qui lança tout un genre de descriptions satyriques mêlant l'image et la prose, les prostituées de Shinjuku – le quartier où ce déroule notre scène – sont appelées « fleurs poussant sur le crottin de Yotsuya ».

Le « nouveau relais de poste » de Shinjuku marquait la première étape de la Kōshū kaidō, la grande voie de circulation qui reliait Edo à la ville à Shimo-Suwa (actuelle préfecture de Nagano) à l'ouest. Comme d'autres lieux comparables, cette étape devint un centre semi-officiel de la prostitution. Pour les voyageurs venant de l'ouest, Shinjuku marquait en même temps la porte d'entrée de la capitale, comme Takanawa l'était pour les visiteurs du sud (cf. pl. 81).

井の頭
の池
弁天の社

Inokashira no ike Benten no yashiro
4–1856

Benten Shrine at the Inokashira Pond

Hiroshige employs a topographical view of a lake landscape to take the viewer to the most western point of the whole series, and at the same time the one farthest away from the centre of the city. The Inokashira Pond, depicted larger than it actually was, supplied the Kanda Aqueduct, which brought fresh water to the city; the pond itself was allegedly fed by seven springs. The Benten shrine on the island in the foreground takes account of this vital function of the pond. Hiroshige depicts the shrine frontally, positively inviting us to walk over a bridge and visit it. The goddess Benten (or, more formally, Benzaiten) was, among other things, venerated as the patron deity of water, and her cult sites form the central motif of a number of prints in the series (see plates 72, 83, 117).

The shrine depicted here is said to have been erected in 1197 by Japan's first military ruler, Minamoto no Yoritomo (1147–1199), while the main statue is even said to have been created by Dengyō Daishi (767–822) himself, the founder of the esoteric Tendai School of Buddhism. Its long history, and not least the scenic attraction of its surroundings, brought many visitors to this particular Benten shrine. The tall pine trees around it, arranged in a pair and one group of three, are part of the pictorial vocabulary Hiroshige frequently used. Groups of trees like this occur, for example, in the print *Shinagawa Susaki* (plate 83), which dates from the same time and likewise features a Benten shrine.

While Hiroshige renders the shrine and the island close to us, we survey the pond from a high vantage point as it stretches to the mountain range on the horizon as though it were tilted. Even the herons flying over the water are seen from above. These multiple viewpoints, which Hiroshige used in numerous prints in *One Hundred Famous Views of Edo*, are typical of traditional landscape compositions.

Der Benten-Schrein am Teich Inokashira no ike

Mit einem topografischen Blick auf eine Seelandschaft führt Hiroshige den Betrachter hier an den westlichsten und den am weitesten vom Zentrum der Stadt entfernten Punkt der gesamten Serie. Der überdimensional groß dargestellte Teich Inokashira no ike war der von angeblich sieben Quellen gespeiste Ursprung des Kanda-Aquädukts, das frisches Wasser in die Stadt leitete. Dieser vitalen Funktion des Teiches trägt der Benten-Schrein auf der Insel im Vordergrund Rechnung; Hiroshige hat ihn frontal dargestellt und lädt den Betrachter geradezu ein, über eine Brücke zu gehen und ihn zu besuchen. Die Gottheit Benten oder, formeller, Benzaiten wurde unter anderem als Schutzgottheit des Wassers verehrt; ihre Stätten bilden auf einigen Holzschnitten der Serie (siehe Tafeln 72, 83, 117) das zentrale Bildmotiv.

Der hier abgebildete Schrein soll vom ersten Militärherrscher Japans, Minamoto no Yoritomo (1147–1199), im Jahr 1197 errichtet worden sein, die Hauptstatue wurde angeblich von dem Gründer der esoterischen Tendai-Schule des Buddhismus, Dengyō Daishi (767–822), selbst erschaffen. Wegen seiner langen Geschichte, aber auch wegen der landschaftlichen Attraktion der Umgebung war dieser Benten-Schrein ein vielbesuchter Ort. Die hohen, in einer Zweier- und einer Dreiergruppe angeordneten Kiefern ringsum gehören zu dem Bildvokabular, auf das Hiroshige häufiger zurückgriff. Solche Baumgruppen tauchen zum Beispiel auf dem zeitgleich entstandenen, ebenfalls einen Benten-Schrein zeigenden Blatt *Landzunge bei Shinagawa* (siehe Tafel 83) auf.

Hiroshige rückt den Schrein und die Insel zwar ganz nah an den Betrachter heran, zugleich aber blickt dieser von hoch oben auf den von Reihern überflogenen Teich, der sich wie hochgeklappt bis zu den Bergmassiven am Horizont erstreckt. Diese multiplen Standpunkte sind typisch für traditionelle Landschaftskompositionen, die Hiroshige in zahlreichen Holzschnitten der *Hundert Ansichten* anwendete.

Le sanctuaire de Benten sur l'étang Inokashira no ike

Cette vue topographique d'un paysage lacustre place le spectateur à l'extrême limite occidentale et au point le plus éloigné du centre de la ville au sein de la série des *Cent Vues*. L'étang Inokashira no ike, représenté surdimensionné, était censé être alimenté par sept sources et marquait le début de l'aqueduc de Kanda, qui amenait de l'eau fraîche jusqu'à la ville. Cette fonction vitale de l'étang est attestée par la présence du sanctuaire de Benten édifié sur l'île au premier plan. Hiroshige l'a représenté frontalement, invitant manifestement le spectateur à franchir un pont pour le visiter. La divinité Benten – plus formellement Benzaiten – était notamment vénérée comme protectrice de l'eau ; ses sanctuaires constituent le motif central de plusieurs estampes de la série (cf. pl. 72, 83, 117).

Le sanctuaire de Benten de la présente feuille aurait été fondé en 1197 par le premier souverain militaire du Japon, Minamoto no Yoritomo (1147–1199), et sa statue principale serait l'œuvre du fondateur de l'école ésotérique tendai du bouddhisme, Dengyō Daishi (767–822). Du fait de sa longue histoire, mais aussi pour les charmes paysagers des environs, il était un lieu très visité. Les hauts pins organisés en groupes de deux ou trois autour du sanctuaire font partie du vocabulaire iconique auquel Hiroshige fait assez souvent appel. Ce genre de groupes d'arbres apparaît notamment dans la feuille *Langue de terre près de Shinagawa* créée à la même époque, laquelle montre également un sanctuaire de Benten (cf. pl. 83).

Si le sanctuaire et l'île ont été fortement rapprochés du spectateur, celui-ci se voit aussi offrir une vue d'oiseau de l'étang représenté comme replié vers l'avant, survolé par des hérons, et qui s'étend jusqu'aux massifs montagneux apparaissant à l'horizon. Ces points de vue multiples sont caractéristiques des compositions paysagères traditionnelles dont Hiroshige s'est inspiré pour de nombreuses estampes des *Cent Vues*.

88

王子
瀧
の
川

Ôji Takinogawa
4–1856

The Takinogawa in Ôji

The main seasonal attraction of this part of Ôji was the autumn foliage of the maple trees. They had been planted by the eighth shogun Tokugawa Yoshimune (1684–1751) in the 1730s for the general enjoyment of the public. Hiroshige frames the Shakujiigawa – which on account of its prominent waterfalls on this stretch was also popularly known as the Takinogawa ("Waterfall River") – with trees in their full autumnal colours. The pigment known as *tan*, used in his day for autumn foliage, was made out of either red lead or iron oxide, which in the course of time oxidized to a brownish-black in place of the original fiery orange (this process is apparent in all the impressions of this print, and also on plate 94). It can be prevented only by sealing the print in an airtight container immediately after printing.

In the river and by the waterfall, some men are undergoing a ritual cleansing, perhaps in preparation for entering the rock shrine, of which we see only the red *torii* or gateway at the entrance. The grotto was dedicated to the goddess Benten (Benzaiten), whose statue was inside; the site is part of the Matsubashi-Benten complex of shrine and temple buildings, which appears in the top right-hand corner behind the brow of the hill with its tall pine trees.

The simple wooden bridge over the Takinogawa linked the Nakasendô, the main highway to Kyoto, with the Ôji Gongen Shrine sponsored by the Tokugawa shoguns and the associated Temple of Kinrinji. On the opposite bank, two men walk along a path that leads up to the tea-houses sited picturesquely between the trees. There they will take a rest, like those already there, and will enjoy the view of the autumn foliage before proceeding to the temple and shrine complex beyond.

Der Fluss Takinogawa in Ôji

Die jahreszeitliche Hauptattraktion dieser Gegend von Ôji waren die im Herbst rot gefärbten Ahornbäume, die der achte Shogun Tokugawa Yoshimune (1684–1751) zur allgemeinen Erbauung in den 1730er Jahren pflanzen ließ. Hiroshige rahmt den Fluss Shakujiigawa, der wegen seiner prominenten Wasserfälle an dieser Stelle auch populär „Takinogawa" („Wasserfallfluss") genannt wurde, auf allen Seiten mit herbstlich verfärbten Bäumen ein. Das damals für das Herbstlaub verwendete Farbpigment *tan* wurde entweder aus Blei oder Eisenoxid hergestellt, das vom ursprünglich feurigen Orange im Lauf der Zeit in ein dunkles Braunschwarz oxidierte. Diese nur durch luftdichten Verschluss gleich nach dem Druck zu verhindernde Farbveränderung findet sich auf allen Abzügen dieses Blattes und ist auch auf Tafel 94 zu sehen.

In dem Fluss und am Wasserfall unterziehen sich einige Männer einer rituellen Waschung, vielleicht als Vorbereitung auf den Eintritt in den Felsenschrein, von dem wir nur das davor aufgestellte rote Tor *torii* sehen. Die Grotte war der Gottheit Benzaiten gewidmet, deren Statue darin aufgestellt war; die Stätte gehört zum Matsubashi-Benten-Komplex von Schrein- und Tempelgebäuden, die ganz oben rechts hinter der von hohen Kiefern bewachsenen Hügelkuppe auftauchen.

Die einfache Holzbrücke über den Takinogawa verband den nach Kyoto führenden Hauptverkehrsweg Nakasendô mit dem von den Tokugawa-Shogunen geförderten Schrein Ôji Gongen und dem dazugehörigen Tempel Kinrinji. Am gegenüberliegenden Ufer schreiten zwei Männer auf einem Weg, der sie nach oben zu den malerisch zwischen Bäumen erbauten Teehäusern führt. Dort werden sie, wie einige vor ihnen schon, wohl erst einmal eine Rast einlegen und den Blick auf die Bäume im Herbstlaub genießen, bevor sie zu dem dahinterliegenden Tempel- und Schreinbezirk weitergehen.

La rivière Takinogawa à Ôji

Les érables à feuilles rouges à l'automne que le huitième shogun Tokugawa Yoshimune (1684–1751) fit planter dans les années 1730 pour l'édification commune étaient la principale attraction saisonnière de la région d'Ôji. Hiroshige a encadré de tous côtés la rivière Shakujiigawa – populairement aussi appelée « Takinogawa » (« rivière aux chutes d'eau ») en raison de ses chutes d'eau, nombreuses à cet endroit – avec des arbres aux couleurs de l'automne. Le pigment *tan* utilisé à l'époque pour le feuillage s'obtenait à partir d'oxyde de plomb ou de fer et s'est oxydé au fil du temps, virant d'un orange vif à un sombre brun-noir. Cette altération chromatique que seul peut empêcher le scellage sous vide de la feuille immédiatement après impression, se retrouve dans tous les tirages de cette estampe comme dans la planche 94.

Dans la rivière et près de la chute d'eau, quelques hommes accomplissent une ablution rituelle, peut-être pour se préparer à entrer au sanctuaire rupestre dont seule la porte rouge dite *torii* apparaît dans l'image. La grotte était dédiée à la divinité Benzaiten, dont elle abritait une statue. Le lieu fait partie du complexe Matsubashi-Benten de bâtiments du temple-sanctuaire qu'on peut voir tout en haut à droite derrière la colline plantée de hauts pins.

Le simple pont de bois qui enjambe la Takinogawa reliait la grande voie de circulation conduisant à Kyoto (la Nakasendô) au sanctuaire Ôji Gongen protégé par les shoguns Tokugawa et au temple Kinrinji qui en dépendait. Sur la rive opposée, deux hommes marchent sur un chemin qui les conduit jusqu'aux maisons de thé pittoresquement bâties parmi les arbres à flanc de côte. Ils y feront sans doute une halte, comme d'autres l'ont fait avant eux, pour jouir de la vue des arbres noyés dans leurs feuillages d'automne – avant de poursuivre leur route jusqu'au domaine du temple-sanctuaire qui les surplombe.

89

上野山内
月のまつ

Ueno sannai Tsuki no matsu
8–1857

"Moon Pine" in Ueno

As in plates 56 and 86, Hiroshige employs a motif viewed as if through a telephoto lens as the structuring frame for his composition. In order to emphasize the unusual circular shape of the branch, the centre of the circle is entirely unspectacular. Beyond Shinobazu Pond, we see an unassuming mass of grey houses, over which three fire towers loom. The modern University of Tokyo is located in the area framed by the circle, which in those days belonged to the powerful feudal lord Maeda from K˜aga (in today's Ishikawa Prefecture).

Giving names to particular trees was a fashion in Edo (see also plates 26, 61, 110). The pine, which often attains a great age, and is venerated throughout East Asia as a symbol of longevity, often displays gnarled, bizarrely shaped branches. This is true also of the "Moon Pine" (Tsuki no matsu) depicted here, which we have already encountered on plate 11. In Hiroshige's day it was a famous tree, also known as the

"Rope Pine" (Nawa no matsu). Seen from various angles, the circular branch could also be perceived as a flattened ellipse resembling the crescent moon.

A remarkable feature of this print is the colour gradation lending volume to the tree trunk. The dark-green shimmer suggesting moss on the furrowed bark also contributes to this effect.

Dedicated to the water deity Benten, the shrine on the lower right was of great importance for the citizens of Edo. Another view of this shrine is in plate 117, and other Benten shrines can be seen on plates 72 and 83. The shrine was situated on an imitation of Chikubushima Island in Biwa Lake to the northeast of Kyoto. Along with other shrines dedicated to the seven gods of good fortune, the Benten shrine was a favourite destination for travellers, especially at New Year. Here they would pray for success and a long life.

„Mondkiefer" in Ueno

Hiroshige benutzt hier wie auf den Tafeln 56 und 86 ein wie mit einem Teleobjektiv herangezoomtes Motiv als strukturierenden Rahmen für seine Bildkomposition. Um die ungewöhnliche Form des kreisrunden Astes zu betonen, gestaltet er das Zentrum des Kreises völlig unspektakulär. Wir sehen jenseits des Teiches Shinobazu no ike eine gleichförmige Masse von grauen Häusern, die von drei Feuerwachtürmen überragt wird. Auf dem innerhalb des Astkreises umrahmten Gebiet des mächtigen Feudalfürsten Maeda aus Kaga (in der heutigen Präfektur Ishikawa) befindet sich heute die Universität Tokyo.

In Edo fanden die Menschen Geschmack daran, besondere Bäume mit Namen zu versehen (sieheTafeln 26, 61, 110). Die oft ein hohes Alter erreichende Kiefer, die in ganz Ostasien als Symbol der Langlebigkeit verehrt wird, verfügt häufig über knorrige, bizarr geformte Äste. Das gilt auch für die hier abgebildete „Mondkiefer" (Tsuki no matsu), die wir bereits auf Tafel 11 kennengelernt haben. Sie war zu Hiroshiges Zeit ein berühm-

ter Baum, den man auch „Seilkiefer" (Nawa no matsu) nannte. Aus verschiedenen Winkeln betrachtet, konnte der zum Kreis geformte Ast wie eine Mondsichel elliptisch verflacht wahrgenommen werden.

Bemerkenswert an diesem Blatt ist die dem Baumstamm Volumen verleihende Farbgradierung. Auch der dunkelgrüne, Moos suggerierende Schimmer auf der gefurchten Rinde trägt zu diesem Effekt bei.

Für die Bewohner Edos war der unten rechts angeschnitten dargestellte, der Wasserschutzgottheit Benten gewidmete Schrein von großer Bedeutung. Einen anderen Blick auf den Schrein gewährt Tafel 117; weitere Benten-Schreine sind auf den Tafeln 72 und 83 zu sehen. Das Heiligtum befand sich auf einer Nachbildung der Insel Chikubushima auf dem nordöstlich von Kyoto gelegenen Biwako-See. Vor allem um Neujahr war der Benten-Schrein mit weiteren Schreinen der sieben Glücksgötter ein beliebtes Ausflugsziel. Hier wurde für Erfolg und ein langes Leben gebetet.

Le «Pin de la lune» à Ueno

Dans cette estampe comme dans les planches 56 et 86, Hiroshige utilise un motif comme agrandi au zoom pour structurer le cadre de sa composition. Pour souligner la forme inhabituelle de la branche et le rond parfait qu'elle forme, l'artiste a conféré un aspect totalement anodin à l'espace iconique décrit à l'intérieur de ce cercle. Au-delà de l'étang Shinobazu no ike, nous voyons ainsi une masse uniforme de maisons grises que surplombent trois tours de garde de la brigade du feu. L'aire définie par le cercle appartient au domaine du puissant seigneur féodal Maeda de Kaga (dans l'actuelle préfecture d'Ishikawa), sur lequel se trouve aujourd'hui l'université de Tokyo.

À Edo, les gens trouvaient plaisir à donner des noms aux arbres (cf. pl. 26, 61, 110). Le pin, qui atteint souvent un grand âge et qui est vénéré comme un symbole de longévité dans tout l'Extrême-Orient, présente souvent des branches noueuses aux formes singulières. Ceci vaut également pour le « Pin de la lune » (Tsuki no matsu) déjà représenté dans la planche 11. À l'époque de Hiroshige, cet arbre

célèbre était aussi appelé « Pin à corde » (Nawa no matsu). Considérée sous différents angles, la branche formant un cercle pouvait en effet être aussi perçue comme un croissant de lune aplati en forme d'ellipse.

Un aspect très remarquable de cette estampe est le rare dégradé qui donne son volume au tronc de l'arbre. Le reflet vert sombre suggérant la présence de mousse sur l'écorce sillonnée de rides contribue encore à renforcer cet effet.

Pour les habitants d'Edo, le domaine du sanctuaire dédié à Benten, la divinité protectrice de l'eau, revêtait une très grande importance. La planche 117 nous offre une autre vue du même sanctuaire, et d'autres sanctuaires de Benten apparaissent encore dans les planches 72 et 83. Le sanctuaire se trouvait sur une réplique de l'île Chikubushima du lac Biwako situé au nord-est de Kyoto. Surtout pendant les fêtes de Nouvel An, le sanctuaire de Benten et d'autres sanctuaires des sept dieux du bonheur étaient un lieu d'excursion très populaire. On y priait pour la réussite et la longévité.

90

猿わか町
よるの景

Saruwaka-machi yoru no kei
9–1856

Night View of Saruwaka-machi

This night view of the street that was home to Edo's kabuki and puppet theatres is one of the most impressive prints from the *One Hundred Famous Views of Edo*. The exaggerated shadows of the figures in the foreground challenge all pictorial expectations – and not only for Hiroshige's contemporaries, but also for modern Westerners. The light of the full moon, falling diagonally from above, illuminates the passers-by, most of them seen from behind, making them seem like puppets on a stage. The long shadows convey the impression that the figures are moving across a reflecting surface. It is an experience that lends an unreal, utopian quality to a street scene like this. Hiroshige was keenly interested in three-dimensionality, light and shade, and experimented with Western pictorial techniques. This interest is evidenced by his series *Improvised Shadow Pictures* and triptychs such as *Summer Evening with Full Moon* from the series *Snow, Moon and Flowers* (*Yuki tsuki hana no uchi*). A fascination with the light-effects of evening and night, the mysterious mood created by moonlight or the brief flashes of artificial light from fireworks are leitmotifs in Hiroshige's work from the early 1830s onwards. He was concerned with a perception of complex reality, as comprehensive as possible and embracing all the senses, a reality that he subjects to a trenchant, subjectively coloured and often exaggerated interpretation in his pictures. In the present print, Hiroshige raised the street of the kabuki and the anonymous bustle of the urban populace on to an imaginary theatrical stage.

After the old theatre quarter was largely destroyed in the devastating fire of 1841, and amidst controversy over whether the theatre was the cause of moral decline, the shogunate approved the building of the new Saruwaka-machi. It consisted of the street named Saruwaka-chō, which was entered from the south through a large gate, which in this print is at the vanishing point. On the right-hand side of the street, we see the officially approved theatres with their *yagura* (turret-like structures on the roof). All the theatres are closed, with the exception of the brightly lit Morita Theatre in the foreground, which celebrated its reopening one month after the great earthquake of 1855.

Abendansicht des Viertels Saruwaka-machi

Die Abendansicht der Straße mit den Kabuki- und Puppentheatern Edos gehört zu den besonders eindrücklichen Blättern der *Hundert Ansichten*. Denn nicht nur für die Zeitgenossen von Hiroshige, auch für den modernen westlichen Betrachter, werden durch die übertriebenen Schlagschatten der Figuren im Vordergrund die gängigen Sehgewohnheiten auf den Kopf gestellt. Das schräg von oben einfallende Licht des Vollmonds beleuchtet die überwiegend in Rückenansicht wiedergegebenen Passanten wie Puppen im Raum. Im Gegenlicht vermitteln die langen Schatten den Eindruck, als würden sich die Figuren über eine reflektierende Oberfläche bewegen. Ein Seherlebnis, das dieser Straßenszene jedoch einen unwirklichen, utopischen Charakter verleiht. Der dreidimensionale Tiefenraum, Licht und Schatten und das experimentelle Spiel mit westlichen Darstellungsmethoden haben Hiroshige fasziniert. Dies bezeugen seine Serie *Improvisierte Schattenbilder* und Triptychen wie *Sommerabend bei Vollmond* aus der Serie *Schnee, Mond und Blumen* (*Yuki tsuki hana no uchi*). Die Auseinandersetzung mit den Lichtverhältnissen bei Abend und Nacht, mit der geheimnisvollen Stimmung des Mondlichts und dem kurzen Aufflackern der künstlichen Feuerwerksbeleuchtung zieht sich ab den frühen 1830er Jahren wie ein roter Faden durch sein Œuvre. Dabei geht es ihm um eine möglichst umfassende, alle Sinne einschließende Wahrnehmung der Wirklichkeit, die er in seinen Bildern einer pointierten, subjektiv gefärbten, oftmals übersteigerten Interpretation unterzieht. Mit diesem Blatt hat er die Straße der Kabuki-Theater und die anonyme Geschäftigkeit der Großstadtmenschen auf eine imaginäre Theaterbühne erhoben.

Nachdem die alten Theaterviertel bei dem verheerenden Feuer 1841 größtenteils vernichtet worden waren, genehmigte die Shogunats-Regierung nach Kontroversen über den durch das Theater verursachten Sittenverfall den Bau des neuen Theaterviertels Saruwaka-machi. Es bestand aus der Straße Saruwaka-chō, die im Süden durch ein großes Tor betreten wurde, das in diesem Druck im Zentrum der Fluchtlinien liegt. Auf der rechten Straßenseite sind die offiziell genehmigten Theater mit ihren *yagura* (Dachaufbauten) zu erkennen. Alle Theater sind geschlossen, mit Ausnahme des hell erleuchteten Morita-Theaters im Vordergrund, das einen Monat nach dem großen Erdbeben von 1855 seine Neueröffnung gefeiert hatte.

Vue vespérale du quartier Saruwaka-machi

La vue vespérale de la rue d'Edo où se trouvaient les théâtres de kabuki et de marionnettes est une des feuilles les plus frappantes des *Cent Vues*. Pour les contemporains de Hiroshige, mais aussi pour le spectateur occidental d'aujourd'hui, l'exagération des ombres portées des figures du premier plan met en effet sens dessus dessous les habitudes visuelles. Le clair de lune tombant à l'oblique dans l'image éclaire comme des poupées dans l'espace les passants majoritairement représentés de dos. Avec ce contre-jour et la longueur des ombres, on a le sentiment que les figures se déplacent sur une surface réfléchissante, expérience visuelle, qui confère à cette scène de rue un caractère irréel et utopique. La profondeur de l'espace et le jeu expérimental sur les méthodes de représentation occidentales ont toujours fasciné Hiroshige, comme l'illustrent notamment sa série des *Silhouettes improvisées* ou des triptyques comme *Soir d'été au clair de lune* de la série *Neige, lune et fleurs* (*Yuki tsuki hana no uchi*). À partir des années 1830, le travail sur les conditions d'éclairage vespéral ou nocturne, sur l'atmosphère mystérieuse du clair de lune ou l'éclat lumineux éphémère des feux d'artifice, parcourt tout l'œuvre de Hiroshige comme un fil conducteur. Dans ce contexte, le propos porte sur une perception du réel aussi complète que possible, englobant tous les sens, que les images de l'artiste soumettent à une interprétation pointée, teintée de subjectivité et souvent exacerbé. Dans la présente feuille, Hiroshige a transformé la rue des théâtres kabuki et l'affairement anonyme des habitants de la grande métropole en une scène de théâtre imaginaire.

Après la destruction des anciens quartiers des théâtres lors de l'incendie dévastateur de 1841 et après bien des controverses sur le déclin des mœurs associé au monde du théâtre, le gouvernement shogunal finit par autoriser la construction du nouveau quartier des théâtres Sarukawa-machi. Ce quartier était organisé autour de la rue Sarukawa-chō dont l'accès sud était marqué par une grande porte qui apparaît ici au point de convergence des lignes de fuite. Côté droit de la rue, on reconnaît les théâtres officiellement approuvés par le gouvernement, avec leurs *yagura* (mezzanines en toiture). Tous les théâtres sont fermés à l'exception du Morita fortement éclairé au premier plan, lequel avait pu rouvrir ses portes un mois après le grand séisme de 1855.

91

秋葉の境内

Ukeji Akiba no keidai
8–1857

In the Akiba Shrine at Ukeji

This print provides a bird's-eye view of the spectacular garden of the Akiba Shrine at Ukeji, whose deities offered protection against fire. The dominant element is the lake, which runs like a zigzag through the composition. Its clear water reflects the delicate orange and ochre of maple trees' autumn foliage and the green of the pines. The moss-covered banks are cropped so that in most cases only the trunks of the trees are visible.

Bottom left, a small tea pavilion projects into the scene. A monk with a shaven head sits down to drink a cup of tea, and has spread out his painting utensils to sketch the trees on the opposite bank. Henry D. Smith presumes that Hiroshige might have been portraying himself here: from behind – modestly, and in accordance with his social status, for he had become a monk in 1856 and taken the tonsure. This attractive idea seems perfectly credible. The woman and girl who have positioned themselves at a discreet distance from the pavilion, but seem to belong to the man, could be Hiroshige's wife, Yasu, who was 15 years younger than he, and whom he married in 1847, and their daughter, Tatsu, whom they adopted at the age of six in 1852. Even though all three figures are depicted from behind, the impression prevails that a certain energy emanates from this corner of the picture, and that the figures depart from Hiroshige's normal scheme of anonymous figure portrayal.

The particular relationship of Hiroshige's family to the Akiba Shrine is also evidenced by the fact that Hiroshige III, the last successor of the famous artist, and also the husband of Tatsu, had a carved stone plaque set up in this shrine to commemorate Hiroshige on the occasion of the 25th anniversary of his death. Alongside a portrait, which shows Hiroshige dressed in a monk's robe writing a poem, it also featured a farewell verse he wrote on his deathbed. The memorial plaque has not been preserved, and the question of why Hiroshige had such a close relationship to the Akiba Shrine is still unanswered.

Im Akiba-Schrein in Ukeji

Aus der Vogelperspektive blickt der Betrachter auf den spektakulären Garten beim Akiba-Schrein in Ukeji, dessen Gottheiten Schutz vor Feuersbrünsten gewähren sollte. Beherrschendes Element ist der See, der die Komposition wie ein Zickzackband durchzieht. Sein klares Wasser reflektiert die zart orange und ocker gefärbten Schatten der herbstlichen Ahornbäume und Kiefern. Die angrenzenden moosbedeckten Uferpartien sind angeschnitten und lassen größtenteils nur die Stämme der Bäume erkennen. Unten links ragt ein kleiner Teepavillon in die Komposition. Ein Mönch mit geschorenem Kopf hat sich bei einer Schale Tee niedergelassen und seine Malutensilien ausgebreitet, um die Bäume am gegenüberliegenden See zu skizzieren. Die von Henry D. Smith geäußerte Vermutung, Hiroshige könnte hier möglicherweise sich selbst – bescheiden und seinem sozialen Status entsprechend in Rückenansicht – wiedergegeben haben, nachdem er 1856 in den Mönchsstand getreten und die Tonsur erhalten hatte, erscheint mehr als verlockend und entbehrt auch nicht der Glaubwürdigkeit. Bei der Frau und dem Mädchen, die sich in diskreter Distanz neben dem Pavillon postiert haben, zugleich aber zu dem Mann zu gehören scheinen, könnte es sich um Hiroshiges zweite, 15 Jahre jüngere Frau Yasu handeln, die er 1847 geheiratet und mit der er 1852 die sechs Jahre alte Tatsu als Tochter adoptiert hatte. Auch wenn alle drei Figuren in Rückenansicht dargestellt sind, wird man sich nicht des Eindrucks erwehren können, dass von der Figurengruppe in der linken unteren Bildecke eine beherrschende, essentielle Spannung ausgeht und dass sie aus dem für Hiroshige typischen Raster anonymisierter Menschendarstellung herausfällt.

Die besondere Beziehung der Familie Hiroshiges zum Akiba-Schrein kommt auch darin zum Ausdruck, dass Hiroshige III, der letzte Nachfolger des berühmten Holzschnittmeisters und zugleich der zweite Ehemann seiner Adoptivtochter Tatsu, anlässlich des 25. Todesjahres von Hiroshige, eine in Stein gemeißelte Gedenktafel für den Verstorbenen im Akita-Schrein errichten ließ. Neben einem Porträt, das den in Mönchsrobe gekleideten Hiroshige beim Schreiben eines Gedichtes zeigte, gab sie auch sein auf dem Sterbebett verfasstes Abschiedsgedicht wieder. Die Gedenktafel ist nicht erhalten geblieben, und auch die Frage, wodurch Hiroshiges enge Beziehung zum Akiba-Schrein begründet sein könnte, ist bislang ungeklärt.

Dans le sanctuaire d'Akiba à Ukeji

Une vue d'oiseau fait plonger le regard sur le spectaculaire jardin proche du sanctuaire d'Akiba à Ukeji, sanctuaire dont les déités devaient protéger des incendies. L'élément dominant de cette estampe est le lac qui s'étire en un bandeau formant un zigzag à travers la composition. Son eau claire réfléchit les ombres délicatement ocres et orangées des érable et des pins automnaux. Les parties du rivage couvertes de mousse sont coupées par le bord de l'image et ne laissent plus entrevoir que les troncs de la plupart des arbres. En bas à gauche, l'angle d'un petit pavillon de thé s'avance dans la composition. Un moine au crâne rasé s'est assis près d'un bol de thé et a préparé ses ustensiles de peinture pour dessiner les arbres de la rive opposée. L'hypothèse émise par Henry D. Smith selon laquelle Hiroshige pourrait s'être éventuellement représenté lui-même – modestement de dos conformément à son statut social – après avoir pris l'état de moine et reçu la tonsure en 1856, est très séduisante et ne manque pas de crédibilité. Concernant la femme et la jeune fille qui se tiennent discrètement à quelques pas près du pavillon, mais qui semblent en même temps liées à cet homme, il pourrait s'agir de Yasu, la seconde épouse de Hiroshige, plus jeune de 15 ans, qu'il avait épousée en 1847 et avec qui il adopta la jeune Tatsu âgée de six ans. Même si les trois figures sont représentées de dos, on ne peut s'empêcher de ressentir qu'un lien essentiel émane du groupe représenté dans le coin inférieur gauche de l'image, et que la tension ainsi générée échappe aux schémas habituels qui caractérisent Hiroshige, à savoir la représentation humaine anonyme.

Le rapport particulier de la famille de Hiroshige avec le sanctuaire d'Akiba s'exprime aussi par le fait que Hiroshige III, dernier successeur du célèbre estampiste et second mari de sa fille adoptive Tatsu, y fit dresser une plaque en pierre gravée en mémoire de son beau-père défunt. À côté du portrait montrant Hiroshige en robe de moine écrivant un poème, cette plaque citait elle aussi le poème d'adieu composé par Hiroshige sur son lit de mort. La plaque ne s'est pas conservée, et la question de savoir ce qui pouvait motiver le lien particulier de Hiroshige avec le sanctuaire d'Akiba reste à ce jour sans réponse.

92

木母寺
内川
御前栽畑

Mokuboji Uchigawa Gozensaihata
12–1857

Mokuboji Temple and Vegetable Fields on Uchigawa Inlet

Mokuboji Temple on the Uchigawa Inlet of the Sumida River was one of the most popular destinations for the citizens of Edo. The temple was founded when a 10th-century itinerant monk erected a grave mound on this spot for an aristocratic boy named Umewaka. The boy, who came from Kyoto, had lost his way and fallen into the hands of a slave trader; he finally died of disease and exhaustion on the banks of the Sumida. The tragic story was taken up by writers and dramatists: the Nô play *Sumidagawa*, for example, describes his desperate mother's search for her son. Over the centuries, this grave mound developed into the Mokuboji temple complex, which, however, Hiroshige does not illustrate in this view. For in Hiroshige's day, the Uekiya Han'emon restaurant, known familiarly as "Uehan", whose elegant pavilion architecture projects invitingly into the picture from the right, was at least as famous as the temple next door. Hiroshige had already immortalized the restaurant, which specialized in sea food, in his series of 26 prints depicting the best restaurants and teahouses of Edo (*Edo kōmei kaitei*

zukushi), which appeared between 1835 and 1842: there, it is depicted in an atmospheric snowscape. The present print shows two affluent, smartly dressed ladies on a clear autumn day. They are disembarking from a roofed boat, and are making their way to the elegant establishment in order to savour its excellent food and enjoy the attractive views.

The vegetable garden (Gozensaihata) mentioned in the title alludes to the vegetables grown for the shogun by the local farmers. It is known that the cultivation of vegetables began around 1650 and that by 1780 about 36 different vegetables were being grown. Whether this practice continued down to Hiroshige's day, or whether the term *gozensaihata* had simply become a place-name, is uncertain. What is certain, though, is that the ruling shogun, Iesada (1824–1858), had passed by Mokuboji on an excursion just one month before the censors approved this print. According to Harashida Minoru, this was the opportunity for Hiroshige and his publisher to include this famous place in his *One Hundred Famous Views of Edo*.

Der Tempel Mokuboji und Gemüsefelder an der Bucht Uchigawa

Der Tempel Mokuboji an der Bucht Uchigawa des Flusses Sumidagawa zählte zu den beliebten Ausflugszielen der Städter. Seine Gründung ging auf einen Wandermönch des zehnten Jahrhunderts zurück, der für einen adeligen Jungen namens Umewaka an dieser Stelle einen Grabhügel errichtete. Der aus Kyoto stammende Knabe hatte sich verirrt und war in die Fänge eines Sklavenhändlers geraten; Krankheit und Erschöpfung sollen ihn am Ufer des Flusses Sumidagawa dahingerafft haben. Die tragische Geschichte fand auch Eingang in die erzählende Literatur und das Theater, so schildert das Nō-Drama *Sumidagawa* die Suche der verzweifelten Mutter nach ihrem Sohn. Im Laufe der Jahrhunderte entwickelte sich aus dem Grabhügel der Tempel-Komplex Mokuboji, den Hiroshige in diesem Blatt jedoch nicht illustriert. Denn zur Zeit Hiroshiges erfreute sich das unter der Bezeichnung „Uehan" bekannte Restaurant von Uekiya Han'emon, dessen elegante Pavillonarchitektur rechts verheißungsvoll in den Bildraum ragt, mindestens ebenso großer Berühmtheit wie der angrenzende Tempel. Hiroshige hatte das auf Fisch und Meeresfrüchte spezialisierte Restaurant bereits in nahezu identischer Komposition in seiner zwischen 1835 und 1842 erschienenen 26-teiligen

Serie der erstklassigen Restaurants und Teehäuser von Edo (*Edo kōmei kaitei zukushi*) in einer stimmungsvollen Schneeszenerie verewigt. Der hier vorgestellte Druck zeigt zwei wohlhabende, elegant gekleidete Damen an einem klaren Herbsttag. Soeben steigen sie aus einem überdachten Boot und steuern auf das feine Etablissement zu, um die guten Speisen zu kosten und die reizvollen Landschaftsausblicke zu genießen.

Der im Titel zitierte Gemüsegarten (Gozensaihata) spielt auf das für den Shogun von den Bauern der Umgebung kultivierte Gemüse an. Bekannt ist, dass der Anbau um 1650 begann und um 1780 rund 36 verschiedene Gemüsesorten umfasste. Ob diese Praxis auch zu Hiroshiges Zeit noch fortgesetzt wurde, oder ob der Begriff *gozensaihata* inzwischen zu einer Ortsbezeichnung geworden war, ist unklar. Sicher ist aber, dass der regierende Shogun Tokugawa Iesada (1824–1858) einen Monat vor Genehmigung des Blattes durch die Zensoren bei einem Ausflug am Tempel Mokuboji vorbeikam. Laut Harashida Minoru war das der Anlass für Hiroshige und seinen Verleger, den berühmten Ort zu diesem Zeitpunkt in die *Hundert Ansichten* aufzunehmen.

Le temple Mokuboji et des cultures potagères près de la baie d'Uchigawa

Le temple Mokuboji, situé près de la baie d'Uchigawa, embouchure de la rivière Sumidagawa, comptait parmi les lieux d'excursion les plus prisés des habitants d'Edo. Sa fondation remontait à un moine itinérant du Xᵉ siècle qui y édifia un tertre funéraire pour un jeune noble du nom d'Umewaka. Ce garçon originaire de Kyoto s'était égaré dans la campagne ; tombé aux mains d'un marchand d'esclaves, il serait mort d'épuisement et de maladie sur la rive de la Sumidagawa. Cette histoire tragique est aussi entrée dans la littérature et le théâtre, notamment dans un nó intitulé *Sumidagawa* qui évoque la mère éplorée partie à la recherche de son fils. Au fil des siècles, le tertre devint le complexe du temple-sanctuaire Mokuboji que Hiroshige n'a pas représenté pas dans cette feuille. À son époque en effet, le restaurant de Uekiya Han'emon, aussi connu sous le nom « Uehan », et dont l'élégante architecture pavillonnaire entre de manière alléchante dans l'espace de l'image, jouissait d'une réputation nom moins grande que le temple tout proche. Dans une scène enneigée évocatrice de son *Edo kōmei kaitei zukushi*, série en 26 parties consacrée aux meilleurs restaurants et maisons de thé d'Edo parue entre 1835 et 1842, Hiroshige

avait déjà immortalisé le restaurant connu pour ses spécialités de poissons et de fruits de mer. L'estampe reproduite ici montre deux dames élégamment vêtues par une claire journée d'automne. Elles quittent une barque couverte pour se diriger vers l'établissement distingué pour en goûter les spécialités gastronomiques et y jouir des charmes du paysage.

Le jardin potager (Gozensaihata) évoqué dans le titre est une allusion aux légumes cultivés aux environs pour le compte du shogun. On sait que ces cultures débutèrent vers 1650 et qu'en 1780, elles portaient sur quelque 36 sortes de légumes. L'on ignore en revanche si cette pratique était encore en vigueur à l'époque de Hiroshige ou si le terme *gozensaihata* n'était déjà plus qu'un toponyme. Une chose est sûre, c'est que le shogun Tokugawa régnant Iesada (1824–1858) passa près du temple Mokubōji lors d'une excursion entreprise un mois avant l'approbation de la présente feuille par la censure. Selon Harashida Minoru, c'est cet événement qui poussa Hiroshige et son éditeur à intégrer ce lieu célèbre aux *Cent Vues* précisément à cette époque.

に
い
宿
の
わ
た
し

Niijuku no watashi
2–1857

Niijuku Ferry

Although the Niijuku ferry across the Nakagawa River gave this print its title, Hiroshige leaves the boat itself relatively hidden, in the bottom right-hand corner; cropped by the margin of the print, it has just moored at a section of the bank, placed diagonally to the picture plane, that is lined by bizarrely shaped pine trees. Some travellers have already disembarked, and are making for a brightly lit two-storey restaurant. One of the travellers is still washing his horse's hooves in the shallow water, while a crouching angler at the mooring to the right of the restaurant is looking into the distance. On the opposite bank, the horizon is bathed in dark-red evening light, and we see the silhouette of a distant mountain range through the haze. The trees, by contrast, overprinted in green, are already sinking into shadow. The colour balance of the composition is maintained, however, by bright accents, for example the sails of the two cargo boats, the lit-up rooms of the restaurant and the horse's saddle blanket.

Niijuku Ferry is the northeast-ernmost of *One Hundred Famous Views of Edo*. This sense of being on the very edge of Edo is confirmed by the contrast between the detailed depiction of the Kameari bank of the river, which still belonged to Edo, and the comparative vagueness of the opposite, Niijuku, bank. Hiroshige also depicted the Niijuku ferry in the seventh volume of his *Illustrated Souvenirs of Edo (Ehon Edo miyage)*, which appeared in the same year as this print. The composition there, however, is different: the ferryboat, while small, is nonetheless central to the picture. The motif of the traveller washing his horse's hooves is in turn a topos that he took from his illustrated travel guide to Edo.

Die Fähre von Niijuku

Obwohl die Fähre von Niijuku zur Überquerung des Flusses Nakagawa dem Blatt seinen Titel verliehen hat, lässt Hiroshige das Fährboot in der rechten unteren Bildecke nur relativ versteckt und halb angeschnitten an der diagonal ins Bild gesetzten, von bizarren Kiefern gesäumten Uferpartie anlegen. Einige Reisende sind schon an Land gegangen und streben einem hell erleuchteten zweistöckigen Restaurant zu. Einer der Reisenden wäscht noch die Hufe seines Pferdes im seichten Wasser ab, während ein Angler auf der Anlegestelle rechts neben dem Restaurant kauert und in die Ferne blickt. Am gegenüberliegenden Flussufer ist der Horizont in dunkelrotes Abendlicht getaucht und lässt im Dunst die Silhouette einer fernen Bergkette erkennen, dagegen versinken die grün überdruckten Baumgruppen bereits im Schatten. Helle Farbakzente, etwa die Segel der beiden Frachtschiffe, die erleuchteten Räume des Restaurants und die Satteldecke des Pferdes halten die Komposition farblich im Gleichgewicht.

Das Blatt *Die Fähre von Niijuku* markierte nach Nordosten hin die äußerste Grenze des durch die *Hundert berühmten Ansichten von Edo* abgesteckten Terrains. Der Kontrast zwischen dem detailliert beschriebenen, noch zu Edo gehörenden Ufer bei Kameari und dem vergleichsweise nebulös wiedergegebenen gegenüberliegenden Ufer von Niijuku betont diesen Grenzcharakter. Hiroshige hat die Fähre von Niijuku auch in Band 7 seines Reiseführers *Illustrierte Mitbringsel aus Edo (Ehon Edo miyage)* dargestellt, der in demselben Jahr wie dieser Holzschnitt erschien. Die Komposition mit einem kleinen, aber zentral ins Bild gesetzten Fährboot weicht allerdings von dem hier vorgestellten Blatt ab. Das Motiv des Reisenden, der die Hufe seines Pferdes reinigt, ist wiederum ein Topos, den er aus seinem illustrierten Reiseführer zu Edo in die *Hundert Ansichten* übernahm.

Le bac de Niijuku

Bien que le bac de Niijuku qui traverse la rivière Nakagawa ait donné son titre à cette feuille, Hiroshige nous le montre seulement – dans le coin inférieur droit, relativement caché et coupé par le bord de l'image – au moment d'aborder la rive placée obliquement dans l'image et plantée de pins aux formes singulières. Quelques passagers ont déjà mis pied à terre et se dirigent vers un restaurant à deux étages clairement illuminé. L'un d'entre eux nettoie encore le sabot de son cheval dans l'eau peu profonde, tandis qu'un pêcheur à la ligne est accroupi, le regard perdu dans le lointain, sur le débarcadère aménagé à droite du restaurant. Sur la rive opposée, l'horizon est baigné des feux rouge foncé du couchant et laisse apparaître dans les brumes lointaines la silhouette d'un massif montagneux, tandis que les groupes d'arbres surimprimés de vert sont déjà plongés dans l'obscurité. Des accents de couleur comme les voiles des deux navires marchands, les salles éclairées du restaurant et la chabraque du cheval assurent l'équilibre chromatique de la composition.

Cette feuille *Le bac de Niijuku* marque la limite nord-est du territoire défini par les *Cent Vues célèbres d'Edo*. Le contraste entre la description détaillée de la rive proche de Kameari, qui fait encore partie d'Edo, et la rive opposée de Niijuku, relativement nébuleuse, souligne ce caractère limitrophe. Hiroshige a aussi représenté le bac de Niijuku dans le septième tome, paru la même année que cette estampe, de son guide de voyage *Souvenirs illustrés d'Edo (Ehon Edo miyage)*. Avec son bac placé au centre de l'image, la composition s'en distingue toutefois fortement de celle-ci. Quant au motif du voyageur nettoyant le sabot de son cheval, il s'agit d'un poncif que l'artiste a directement repris de cet ouvrage pour l'intégrer dans les *Cent Vues*.

真間の紅葉
手古那の社継はし

Mama no momiji Tekona no yashiro Tsugihashi
1–1857

The Maple Trees at Mama, the Tekona Shrine and Tsugihashi Bridge

The Guhōji Temple in the village of Mama was situated on the bank of the Edogawa River to the east of Edo. The beauty of the maple trees attracted many pilgrims to Mama, especially in the autumn. They came to visit the Buddhist temple, and above all the shrine erected in the temple precincts in 1501; this was dedicated to the legendary peasant girl Tekona, and promised both protection against chicken pox and safe childbirth. We see the small shrine on the left, immediately beyond the large trunk of the maple tree in the foreground.

The pretty peasant girl Tekona, surrounded and molested by suitors "as by moths", threw herself into the river near Mama and so ended her life. This story goes back to an 8th-century anthology of poems, the *Collection of Ten Thousand Leaves* (*Man'yōshū*). The Tsugihashi Bridge likewise alludes to a poem from the *Man'yōshū*, in which the grief of one of Tekona's suitors is described. Riding across the bridge to Mama, he laments his longing to ride to his beloved night after night.

The structure of the original Tsugihashi ("Linked Bridge") is unknown, but its name implies that it could have been composed of two or more sections. The bridge depicted in Hiroshige's view is slightly arched and shows no particular architectural characteristics. Yet the topos of the bridge by Mama was evidently sufficient to awaken memories of the tragic fate of Tekona and the poems in the *Man'yōshū*.

We view the scene, which is bathed in the red glow of evening light, from an elevated position through the gap in the forked trunk of a maple. The crossing branches with their originally flaming orange foliage, whose *tan* pigment has become brownish-black as a result of oxidization over time (see plate 88), block the pictorial space like a decoratively stylized vignette. This framing device, much used by Hiroshige, lends the whole scene an unreal, artificial character that corresponds to the many-layered poetic connotations of the place, and carries viewers into an imaginary world.

Ahornbäume von Mama, der Tekona-Schrein und die Brücke Tsugihashi

Der Tempel Guhōji in der Ortschaft Mama lag am Ufer des Flusses Edogawa östlich von Edo. Wegen der Schönheit seiner Ahornbäume wurde Mama besonders im Herbst von Pilgern frequentiert. Diese suchten nicht nur das buddhistische Heiligtum auf, sondern vor allem den 1501 auf dem Tempelareal errichteten Schrein, der dem legendären Bauernmädchen Tekona gewidmet war und Schutz vor Windpocken sowie Hilfe bei der Geburt versprach. Der kleine Schrein kommt im Bild links hinter dem überdimensionierten Stamm des Ahornbaums im Vordergrund zum Vorschein.

Die Geschichte des hübschen Bauernmädchens Tekona, das sich – von Freiern „wie von Motten" umschwärmt und belästigt – aus lauter Verzweiflung bei Mama in den Fluss stürzte und seinem Leben ein Ende setzte, geht auf die Gedichtanthologie *Sammlung von Zehntausend Blättern* (*Man'yōshū*) aus dem 8. Jahrhundert zurück. Die Brücke Tsugihashi spielt ebenfalls auf ein Gedicht aus dem *Man'yōshū* an, in dem die Trauer eines Freiers von Tekona beschrieben wird. Über die Brücke nach Mama reitend klagt er, wie sehr er wünschte, Nacht für Nacht zu seiner Angebeteten reiten zu können. Die Bauweise der ursprünglichen Brücke

Tsugihashi („fortgesetzte Brücke") ist unbekannt, ihr Name impliziert aber, dass sie aus zwei oder mehreren Elementen zusammengesetzt gewesen sein könnte. Die in der Ansicht von Hiroshige wiedergegebene Brücke ist leicht gewölbt und weist keine architektonische Besonderheit auf. Doch genügte offenbar der Topos der Brücke bei Mama, um die Erinnerung an das tragische Schicksal der Tekona und die Gedichte des *Man'yōshū* wachzurufen.

Der Betrachter blickt von einer Anhöhe durch den Zwischenraum des verzweigten Stammes eines Ahornbaums, der die in rotes Abendlicht getauchte Szenerie. Die einander kreuzenden Äste mit ursprünglich leuchtend orange gefärbtem Laub, dessen Farbe *tan* sich aufgrund eines chemischen Prozesses zu einem Braunschwarz verändert hat (siehe Tafel 88), verstellen den Bildraum wie eine dekorativ stilisierte Vignette. Dieses von Hiroshige häufig eingesetzte Stilmittel der Vergitterung verleiht der gesamten Szenerie einen unwirklichen, ins Künstliche übersteigerten Charakter, der den vielschichtigen poetischen Konnotationen des legendären Ortes entspricht und den Betrachter in eine imaginäre Traumwelt entrückt.

Les érables de Mama, le sanctuaire de Tekona et le pont Tsugihashi

Le temple Guhōji dans la localité de Mama, était situé à l'est d'Edo au bord de l'Edogawa. Mama attirait plus particulièrement les pèlerins à l'automne en raison de la beauté de ses érables. Les pèlerins n'y visitaient pas seulement le sanctuaire bouddhiste, mais surtout le sanctuaire bâti en 1501 dans le domaine du temple et dédié à la fille de paysans Tekona. Le petit sanctuaire promettait la protection contre la varicelle et l'aide aux accouchements. Il apparaît à gauche, derrière le tronc surdimensionné de l'érable du premier plan.

L'histoire de la jolie fille de paysans Tekona, qui se jeta de désespoir dans la rivière près de Mama pour mettre fin à ses jours – entourée et molestée comme elle l'était par des prétendants aussi nombreux « que des mouches » –, remonte au *Recueil de dix mille feuilles* (*Man'yōshū*), une anthologie poétique du VIIIe siècle. Le pont Tsugihashi se réfère lui aussi à un poème du *Man'yōshū* dans lequel est décrit le deuil d'un prétendant de Tekona. Chevauchant sur la route de Mama et traversant ce pont, il se lamente sur son sort et clame son désir de pouvoir se rendre toutes les nuits auprès de sa bien-aimée. Le mode de construction du premier pont Tsugihashi (« pont prolongé ») est inconnu, son nom indique toutefois qu'il aurait pu être constitué de deux ou plusieurs parties. Dans la présente estampe, il est légèrement arqué et ne présente aucune particularité architecturale. Reste que le poncif du pont près de Mama suffisait apparemment à conserver la mémoire du destin tragique de Tekona et les poèmes du *Man'yōshū*.

D'une hauteur, dans l'intervalle ménagé par le double tronc de l'érable, la vue s'ouvre sur une scène plongée dans la lumière rouge du couchant. Les branches entrecroisées qui portaient initialement un feuillage orange dont la couleur *tan* a viré au brun sombre suite à un processus d'oxydation (cf. pl. 88), déforment l'espace de l'image en vignette décorative. Ce moyen stylistique du cadrage particulier, fréquent chez Hiroshige, confère à l'ensemble de la scène un caractère irréel qui confine à l'artifice et qui rend compte des connotations du site légendaire, emportant le spectateur dans un monde imaginaire et onirique.

鴻の臺
とね川
風景

Kōnodai Tonegawa fūkei
5–1856

View of Kōnodai and the Tone River

The steep and rocky bluff at Kōnodai overlooking the Tone River (today known as the Edogawa) had for a long time played an important defensive role, as its heights commanded the Kantō plain. This explains why Kōnodai over the centuries was on several occasions the scene of violent military confrontations. To the citizens of Edo, including Hiroshige, this place was very familiar from historical literature, in particular the heroic epic written by Takizawa Bakin (1767–1848) between 1814 and 1841, *Biographies of the Eight Dogs (Nansō Satomi hakkenden)*. In it, Bakin reports how, with the help of the so-called "Eight Dog Warriors" (whose surnames all began with the character for "dog"), the Satomi family succeeded in restoring the social order on Confucian and Buddhist principles and so helping to bring about the victory of good over evil.

In Hiroshige's depiction, a rocky escarpment topped by bizarrely shaped pines and broad-leaved trees in their autumnal colours juts into view in the Chinese manner. The three tiny figures make it look all the more imposing as a foreground motif. They also provide a narrative context, and at the same time open up the view of the river and the broad plain, on which Mount Fuji rises majestically from the mist and the sketchily indicated vegetation.

The heavily laden boats are on their way to Edo. The delicate yellow of the horizon and the reddish foliage of the trees convey a sense of the freshness and the readiness for action felt on a crisp autumn morning.

Blick auf Kōnodai und den Fluss Tonegawa

Das steile Felsenufer Kōnodai am Fluss Tonegawa (heute Edogawa genannt) spielte seit alters eine wichtige Rolle als Verteidigungsstützpunkt, da seine Höhe eine Kontrolle der Kantō-Ebene erlaubte. Dies erklärt, warum Kōnodai im Laufe der Geschichte mehrfach Schauplatz heftiger kriegerischer Auseinandersetzungen wurde. Der Stadtbevölkerung von Edo – und sicherlich auch Hiroshige – war dieser Ort aus der historischen Literatur, insbesondere dem von Takizawa Bakin (1767–1848) zwischen 1814 und 1841 verfassten Heldenepos *Biographien der Acht Hunde (Nansō Satomi hakkenden)* bestens vertraut. Darin berichtet Bakin, wie es der Familie Satomi gelang, mit der Unterstützung der sogenannten „Acht-Hunde-Krieger", deren Nachname jeweils mit dem Schriftzeichen für „Hund" begann, die gesellschaftliche Ordnung nach konfuzianischen und buddhistischen Normen wieder herzustellen und dem Guten zum Sieg zu verhelfen.

Hiroshige lässt einen mit bizarr geformten Kiefern und herbstlich verfärbten Laubbäumen bestandenen Felsvorsprung in chinesischer Manier seitlich in die Komposition ragen und bevölkert ihn mit drei kleinen Figuren, die das Bergmassiv als Vordergrundmotiv umso gewaltiger erscheinen lassen. Als Identifikationsfiguren bieten sie dem Auge des Betrachters einen narrativen Fixpunkt; zugleich öffnen sie den Blick auf den Fluss und die weite Ebene, aus der die Silhouette des Berges Fuji hinter Nebelbänken und summarisch angedeuteter Vegetation majestätisch aufragt.

Die schwer beladenen Frachtboote befinden sich auf dem Weg nach Edo. Der zart gelb gefärbte Horizont und das rötlich angedeutete Laub vermitteln die Assoziation von Frische und unbeschwertem Tatendrang an einem klaren Herbstmorgen.

Vue de Kōnodai et de la rivière Tonegawa

La rive rocheuse escarpée de Kōnodai au bord de la rivière Tonegawa (aujourd'hui Edogawa), a joué de tous temps un rôle important comme point d'appui défensif, car sa hauteur permettait de contrôler la plaine de Kantō. C'est ce qui a fait de Kōnodai l'objet de bien des conflits militaires tout au long de son histoire. La population urbaine d'Edo – et assurément aussi Hiroshige – connaissait au mieux ce site par la littérature historique, en particulier par les *Vies des huit chiens (Nansō Satomi hakkenden)*, épopée écrite entre 1814 et 1841 par Takizawa Bakin (1767–1848). Dans ce livre, l'auteur rapporte comment la famille Satomi soutenue par les huit « chiens de guerre » dont le nom de famille commence respectivement par le signe « chien », parvint à rétablir l'ordre social selon les conceptions confucianistes et bouddhistes et à faire triompher le bien du mal.

Un surplomb rocheux planté de pins aux formes singulières et d'arbres portant un feuillage aux teintes automnales, entre latéralement dans l'image ; Hiroshige y a placé trois petites figures qui font apparaître le massif montagneux d'autant plus imposant au premier plan. Comme figures d'identification, ces personnages offrent un point d'appui anecdotique au regard, ouvrant en même temps la vue sur la rivière et sur une vaste plaine d'où la silhouette du mont Fuji émerge majestueusement derrière des bancs de nuages et une végétation sommairement indiquée.

Les navires marchands lourdement chargés sont en route vers Edo. L'horizon délicatement teinté de jaune et les tons rougeâtres du feuillage évoquent un mélange de fraîcheur et d'affairement insouciant par un clair matin d'automne.

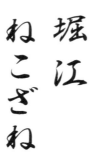

堀江
ねこざね

Horie Nekozane
2–1856

Horie and Nekozane

The two villages of Horie and Nekozane, which are located on either side of a branch of the Edogawa River, were well known to the citizens of Edo for their outstanding seafood. We are looking west across Edo Bay, with Mount Fuji in the distance rising above a horizon bathed in the red glow of evening. The two peaceful villages nestle among pine woods. In the foreground, a strip of land projecting diagonally into the picture provides us with an insight into an unusual method of catching birds: two peasants have buried a net in the sand on which unsuspecting birds have gathered, lured there by a whistle; the idea was to catch the birds in the net by giving a sudden tug on the rope. Their fate was to end up as culinary delicacies.

The print bears a censors' date seal for the second month of 1856. It is thus one of the earliest prints in *One Hundred Famous Views of Edo*, and this narrative element, illustrating the mundane task of bird catching, distinguishes it from later works in the series.

Horie und Nekozane

Die zu beiden Seiten eines Nebenarms des Flusses Edogawa gelegenen Dörfer Horie und Nekozane waren den Stadtbürgern von Edo wegen ihrer hervorragenden Meeresfrüchte wohlbekannt. Die friedliche, durch Kiefernwälder geschützte dörfliche Szenerie öffnet sich nach Westen hin zur Bucht von Edo und lässt in der Ferne den Kegel des Berges Fuji vor dem in rotes Abendlicht getauchten Horizont erkennen. Die diagonal ins Bild ragende Landzunge im Vordergrund bietet dem Betrachter Einblick in eine ungewöhnliche Methode des Vogelfangs: Zwei Bauern haben ein Netz im Sand vergraben, auf dem sich ahnungslos Vögel tummeln, die durch eine Pfeife angelockt werden. Durch plötzliches ruckartiges Ziehen an dem Seil sollen die Vögel unter dem Netz gefangen werden, um später als kulinarische Leckerbissen zu enden.

Das Blatt trägt einen auf den zweiten Monat des Jahres 1856 datierten Zensurstempel und zählt damit zu den frühesten Drucken aus der Serie *Hundert berühmte Ansichten von Edo*. Stilistisch hebt sich die Darstellung durch ihren erzählerischen Charakter, etwa die Beschreibung des Vogelfangs, gegenüber den späten Arbeiten der Serie ab.

Horie et Nekozane

Situés de part et d'autre d'un affluent de la rivière Edogawa, les deux villages Horie et Nekozane étaient bien connus des habitants d'Edo pour l'excellence de leurs fruits de mer. La scène rustique paisible à l'abri des pinèdes s'ouvre à l'ouest, vers la baie d'Edo, et laisse voir au loin le cône du mont Fuji placé devant un horizon baigné par la lumière rouge du couchant. Au premier plan, la langue de terre qui entre à l'oblique dans l'image montre au spectateur une technique de capture d'oiseaux inhabituelle : deux paysans ont enterré dans le sable un filet sur lequel déambulent innocemment des oiseaux attirés par un appeau. En tirant brusquement sur la corde, les oiseaux sont pris dans les mailles du filet avant d'être préparés comme spécialités gastronomiques.

Cette feuille porte un cachet de censure daté du deuxième mois 1856 et compte ainsi parmi les premières estampes de la série des *Cent Vues*. Sur le plan stylistique, la représentation se distingue des réalisations plus tardives par son caractère anecdotique, notamment avec la description d'une chasse aux oiseaux.

小奈木川
五本まつ

Onagigawa Gohonmatsu
7–1856

"Five Pines" and the Onagi Canal

The branches of an ancient pine tree supported by wooden poles project abruptly into our view from the left. The bizarre pattern of poles, boughs and the bunches of needles rendered in various green hues forms a three-dimensional grid, which Hiroshige boldly and strikingly places in front of the actual landscape. The tree was called the "Five Pines" (Gohonmatsu). According to a source dating from 1732, originally five pine trees grew on the Onagi Canal at this location, but only one survived. In Hiroshige's day, this tree, still known as "Five Pines", stood in the grounds of the estate of the feudal lord of Ayabe. The name Gohonmatsu finally came to refer to the surrounding residential neighbourhood.

Hiroshige is inventive in the way he lends the composition atmosphere, not only in the depiction of the famous pine, but also in the way he represents the canal and the boat. In reality, the Onagi Canal was not curved, but ran straight in an easterly direction. We could therefore hardly expect to see the horizon tinted red by the evening sun. The boat, laden with all kinds of baggage, and with the travellers relaxing after a strenuous day, is a set motif that Hiroshige evidently borrowed from a work by Katsushika Hokusai (1760–1849). In any case, we find the same detail of a man casually trailing a cloth in the water in Hokusai's *Sunset over the Ryōgoku Bridge* from his series *Thirty-Six Views of Mount Fuji* (*Fugaku sanjūrokkei*).

Die „Fünf Kiefern" und der Kanal Onagigawa

Unvermittelt ragen die Äste einer alten, durch Holzstangen gestützten Kiefer von links in den Bildraum. Das bizarre Astwerk und die in unterschiedlichen Grüntönen wiedergegebenen Nadelkissen bilden ein dreidimensionales Gitter, das Hiroshige kühn und plakativ vor die eigentliche Landschaftskomposition setzt. Bei dem Baum handelt es sich um eine unter der Bezeichnung „Fünf Kiefern" (Gohonmatsu) bekannte Sehenswürdigkeit. Laut einer Quelle aus dem Jahr 1732 sollen ursprünglich fünf einzelne Kiefern am Kanal Onagigawa gestanden haben, von denen aber nur eine erhalten blieb. Zu Hiroshiges Zeiten gehörte dieser nach wie vor als „Fünf Kiefern" bezeichnete Baum zum Anwesen des Feudalfürsten von Ayabe. Der Name Gohonmatsu diente schließlich sogar als Ortsbezeichnung für die umliegenden Wohnquartiere.

Nicht nur bei der Darstellung der berühmten Kiefer, auch bei der Wiedergabe des Kanals und des Bootes ging Hiroshige erfindungsreich vor, um der Komposition atmosphärische Spannung zu verleihen. Der Onagigawa-Kanal hatte in Wirklichkeit keine Krümmung, sondern verlief schnurgerade in östlicher Richtung. Er dürfte daher kaum den Blick auf den von der westlichen Abendsonne rot erleuchteten Horizont freigegeben haben. Das mit allerlei Gepäckstücken beladene Boot, auf dem sich Reisende nach einem anstrengenden Tag entspannen, ist ein Versatzstück, das Hiroshige offenbar aus einem Werk von Katsushika Hokusai (1760–1849) entlehnt hat. Jedenfalls findet sich das gleiche Detail eines Mannes, der lässig ein Tuch in das Wasser hängen lässt, in Katsushika Hokusais Ansicht *Sonnenuntergang über der Brücke Ryōgokubashi* aus seiner Serie der *36 Ansichten des Berges Fuji* (*Fugaku sanjūrokkei*).

« Cinq pins » et le canal Onagigawa

Les branches d'un vieux pin soutenu par des perches entrent inopinément par la gauche dans le champ de l'image. Le branchage aux formes biscornues et les touffes d'aiguilles rendues par différents tons de vert forment une trame tridimensionnelle que Hiroshige a posée audacieusement et efficacement devant la composition paysagère proprement dite. Concernant l'arbre lui-même, il s'agit d'une attraction connue sous le nom « cinq pins » (Gohonmatsu). Selon une source de 1732, cinq pins se dressaient autrefois au bord du canal Onagigawa, mais un seul s'était ensuite conservé. À l'époque de Hiroshige, cet arbre que l'on continuait d'appeler « cinq pins » faisait partie du domaine du seigneur féodal d'Ayabe. Quant au nom Gohonmatsu, il finit par désigner les quartiers d'habitation environnants.

Pour conférer sa tension et son ambiance à la composition,

Hiroshige a fait preuve d'une invention particulière non seulement pour le célèbre pin, mais aussi dans le traitement du canal et de la barque. En réalité, le canal Onagigawa était tracé en droite ligne d'est en ouest, et il est fort improbable qu'il ait pu offrir une telle vue sur l'horizon occidental éclairé par la lumière du couchant. La barque chargée de toutes sortes de bagages sur laquelle des voyageurs se délassent après une longue journée est un accessoire inventé que

Hiroshige semble avoir emprunté à une œuvre de Katsushika Hokusai (1760–1849). Quoi qu'il en soit, le détail d'un homme laissant négligemment pendre une pièce de tissu dans l'eau du canal se trouve aussi dans la vue de Hokusai *Coucher de soleil sur le pont Ryōgokubashi* de la série des *36 Vues du mont Fuji* (*Fugaku sanjūrokkei*).

98

両

国

花

火

Ryōgoku hanabi
8–1858

Fireworks by Ryōgoku Bridge

Hiroshige depicted the firework displays by Ryōgoku Bridge over the Sumida River more than 50 times, each time from a different perspective. In so doing, he raised them to the status of an unmistakable topos relating to the pleasures of a summer night.

In this print, Hiroshige shows himself to be a master of atmospheric evening and night scenes. With great precision, he displays light effects not only in the sky, but also on the opposite bank, where buildings and vegetation are faintly silhouetted against the dark sky. Other striking features include the burst of whitish-grey light in the top right-hand corner, itself containing numerous individual points of light; and also the black *bokashi* gradations above the horizon and at the top of the sky, against which a rocket stands out in its steep but stuttering parabolic trajectory. The bright red cartouche on the left bearing Hiroshige's signature, and the two red cartouches on the top right, which give the title of both the series and of this particular print, accentuate the brilliant chiaroscuro of the composition.

The first official firework display by Ryōgoku Bridge, commissioned by the eighth Tokugawa shogun, Yoshimune (1684–1751), was staged in 1733. The symbolic "opening of the river" (*kawabiraki*) on the 28th day of the fifth month was part of a purification ritual designed to drive away the evil spirits.

But fireworks at the bridge were not limited to this annual official ceremony. Throughout the hot summer months, boat-hire operators and restaurateurs sponsored numerous displays, as the exciting spectacle provided by the pyrotechnics was good for business. Alongside simple and roofed boats (*yanebune*) were also so-called palace boats (*yakatabune*), which provided space for large functions and were mostly hired by rich merchants. Food and drink could be bought from tradesmen operating from boats illuminated by a single lantern (*urourobune*), which moved between the other boats, plying their wares. In this print, Hiroshige has depicted all four types of boat.

Feuerwerk bei der Brücke Ryōgokubashi

Hiroshige hat die Feuerwerke bei der Brücke Ryōgokubashi über dem Fluss Sumidagawa mehr als fünfzigmal und jeweils aus unterschiedlichen Perspektiven thematisiert und sie so in den Rang eines unverwechselbaren Topos erhoben, der stets mit den Vergnügungen heißer Sommernächte assoziiert wird.

Hiroshige erweist sich in diesem Druck als Meister der stimmungsvollen Abend- und Nachtdarstellung. Mit größter Genauigkeit zeigt er die Lichteffekte am Himmel, aber auch an der gegenüberliegenden Uferseite, auf der sich schemenhaft Gebäude und Vegetation aus dem Dunkel lösen. Besondere Aufmerksamkeit verdienen die Farbgradierungen (*bokashi*), etwa in dem grauen Farbstreifen, der die aus vielen einzelnen Lichtkörpern zusammengesetzte weißlichgraue Lichtkugel oben rechts umgibt, und in den schwarzen Farbverläufen zum Horizont und zum oberen Bildrand hin, vor denen sich das linke Feuerwerk in steilem, spannungsvoll zuckendem Bogen abhebt. Die leuchtend rote Kartusche links mit der Signatur Hiroshiges und die beiden roten Kartuschen rechts, die den Titel der Serie und der Sehenswürdigkeit tragen, akzentuieren den feurigen Helldunkelkontrast der Komposition.

Das offiziell vom achten Tokugawa-Shogun Yoshimune (1684–1751) in Auftrag gegebene erste Feuerwerk bei der Brücke Ryōgokubashi fand im Jahr 1733 statt. Die symbolische „Öffnung des Flusses" (*kawabiraki*) am 28. Tag des fünften Monats hatte den Charakter eines Reinigungsrituals, durch das die bösen Geister vertrieben werden sollten. Aber auch außerhalb dieser alljährlichen offiziellen Zeremonie gab es während der heißen Sommermonate zahlreiche Feuerwerksveranstaltungen bei der Brücke, die von den Bootsverleihern und Restaurants der Umgebung finanziert wurden, da sich das abendliche Schauspiel überaus günstig auf deren Geschäft auswirkte. Neben einfachen und überdachten Booten (*yanebune*) gab es auch sogenannte „Palastboote" (*yakatabune*), die Raum für große Gesellschaften boten und meist von reichen Kaufleuten gemietet wurden. Für Verpflegung sorgten die mit einer einzelnen Laterne bestückten Händlerboote (*urourobune*), welche sich zwischen den übrigen Booten hin- und herbewegten und Speisen und Getränke verkauften. Hiroshige hat in diesem Druck alle vier Typen von Booten wiedergegeben.

Feu d'artifice près du pont Ryōgokubashi

Dans son œuvre, Hiroshige a représenté plus de cinquante fois les feux d'artifices donnés près du pont Ryōgokubashi qui enjambe la Sumidagawa, et ce à partir de points de vue toujours différents. L'artiste a ainsi élevé ce thème au rang de poncif tout à fait unique en son association avec les divertissements des chaudes nuits d'été.

Hiroshige nous apparaît ici comme un maître de la représentation vespérale et nocturne. Il nous montre avec une extrême précision les effets de lumière qui se déploient dans le ciel et sur la rive opposée, où des bâtiments et des végétations schématiques se détachent de l'obscurité. Méritent ainsi une attention toute particulière, en haut à droite, la zone de couleur grise qui entoure la boule lumineuse gris-blanc composée d'une multitude d'éclats de lumière isolés, ainsi que les dégradés de couleur (*bokashi*) des zones de l'horizon et du bord supérieur de l'image, devant lesquelles le feu d'artifice de gauche se détache en une haute courbe animée de frémissements passionnants. À coté des barques couvertes (*yanebune*) et des simples barques sans toit, il existait aussi des « bateaux-palais » (*yakatabune*) qui offraient de l'espace pour des groupes de plaisanciers plus nombreux, et que louaient généralement de riches marchands. Le ravitaillement des barques pendant ces spectacles était assuré par des barques marchandes pourvues d'une seule lanterne (*urourobune*), qui vendaient des mets et des boissons en allant d'une barque à l'autre. Dans cette estampe, Hiroshige a représenté ces quatre types de barques.

flamboyant contraste clair-obscur de la composition.

Le premier feu d'artifice officiel commandé près du pont Ryōgokubashi par le shogun Tokugawa Yoshimune (1684–1751) fut donné en 1733. La symbolique « ouverture de la rivière » (*kawabiraki*) le 28ème jour du cinquième mois avait un caractère de rituel de purification destiné à chasser les mauvais esprits. Mais de semblables spectacles étaient aussi organisés près du pont en dehors de ce cadre officiel et annuel, spectacles que finançaient les loueurs de barques et les restaurants de la zone, vu qu'ils avaient un effet positif sur les affaires.

99

浅草
金龍山

Asakusa Kinryūzan
7–1856

Kinryūzan Temple in Asakusa

The Kinryūzan Temple in Asakusa, dedicated to the Bodhisattva Kannon, was another of the famous sites of Edo that Hiroshige repeatedly depicted from various perspectives and in various seasons. In many of his snowscapes, dense crowds of people gather in front of the temples for fairs, or on the occasion of the Buddhist celebrations to mark the year's end. In this print, by contrast, we see what became a hallmark of Hiroshige's bold late work: a focus not on people, but on the composition itself and the atmosphere created.

An imposing and festive framework for this view of the Niōmon Gate and the pagoda is created by part of the bright red and blue-green bay of "Thunder Gate" (Kaminarimon), which projects into the print on the left, and the huge paper lantern suspended from above. In large black calligraphy on a bright red background of the lantern, we read the last character in the address of its donors, namely "Shinbashi". The middle distance is dominated by the white snow and the pale-blue shadow of the entrance gate, which convey an impression of profound silence. The path is lined by visitors seen from behind, with snow-covered umbrellas and hats, making for the bright red "Gate of the Two Guardian Kings" (Niōmon), which we see behind snow-laden trees whose size diminishes in accordance with the rules of linear perspective.

The censors approved the print in the seventh month of 1856, two months after the pagoda had been restored and solemnly re-dedicated following damage suffered in the great earthquake of 1855. As so often, Hiroshige moves the central building into the middle distance, and shows it partly concealed. He doubtless illustrated this view when he did to commemorate this important event.

Der Tempel Kinryūzan in Asakusa

Auch der volkstümliche, dem Bodhisattva Kannon geweihte Tempel Kinryūzan im Stadtteil Asakusa gehört zu den Sehenswürdigkeiten Edos, die Hiroshige wiederholt aus unterschiedlichen Blickperspektiven und zu verschiedenen Jahreszeiten dargestellt hat. Dabei zählen die Schneeszenen zu den geläufigsten, in denen sich dichte Menschenmengen anlässlich der buddhistischen Feierlichkeiten zum Jahresende oder auf den Jahrmärkten vor den Tempeln zusammenfinden. Ganz anders erscheint hingegen die Komposition dieses Blattes, das zu einem Markenzeichen für Hiroshiges kühnes Spätwerk geworden ist, in dem weniger die Sehenswürdigkeit oder das Treiben der Menschen das eigentliche Thema darstellen, sondern vielmehr die Bildgestaltung selbst und die dadurch erzeugte Stimmung.

Der links suggestiv ins Bild gerückte Türflügel des kräftig rot und blaugrün gefärbten „Donnertores" (Kaminarimon) und die riesige, von oben ins Bild ragende Papierlaterne, liefern die imposante und zugleich feierliche Rahmenkulisse, die den Blick auf das Tor Niōmon und die Pagode freigibt. Auf der Laterne steht in großem schwarzem Schriftzug auf leuchtend rotem Grund das letzte Zeichen der Adresse ihrer Stifter, nämlich „Shinbashi". Der Schnee und der blassblaue Schatten des Eingangstors beherrschen den Mittelgrund und vermitteln den Eindruck von Stille. Vereinzelte, in Rückenansicht wiedergegebene Besucher mit schneebedeckten Schirmen und Hüten säumen den Weg und streben zu dem „Tor der beiden Wächterkönige" (Niōmon), das leuchtend rot hinter verschneiten Bäumen zum Vorschein kommt. Ihre Größe nimmt – entsprechend der Zentralperspektive – mit zunehmender Distanz ab.

Das Blatt wurde von den Zensoren im siebten Monat des Jahres 1856 genehmigt, zwei Monate, nachdem die Pagode infolge von Schäden nach dem großen Erdbeben von 1855 wieder restauriert und feierlich eingeweiht worden war. Wie so oft rückt Hiroshige auch hier das zentrale Gebäude leicht verdeckt in den Mittelgrund. Zum Gedenken an dieses wichtige Ereignis thematisierte Hiroshige diese Sehenswürdigkeit wohl genau zu diesem Zeitpunkt.

Le temple Kinryūzan à Asakusa

Le très populaire temple Kinryūzan à Asakusa dédié au bodhisattva Kannon fait partie des attractions d'Edo que Hiroshige a représentées de plusieurs points de vue et en différentes saisons. Les scènes enneigées sont en l'occurrence les plus fréquentes, dans lesquelles les solennités bouddhistes donnent lieu à des rassemblements de foules devant les temples, à l'époque du Nouvel An ou lors des grandes foires. Il en va en revanche tout autrement de la présente composition, qui est devenue une référence signalétique de l'œuvre tardif audacieux de Hiroshige, et dont le thème est moins déterminé par des attractions touristiques ou des activités humaines que par la création visuelle elle-même et l'atmosphère particulière qui en découle.

Le battant de la « Porte du tonnerre » (Kaminarimon) peinte en rouge vif et bleu-vert qui entre de manière suggestive dans l'image par la gauche et l'immense lanterne en papier dans le coin supérieur droit définissent le cadre frappant et solennel qui ouvre la vue sur la porte Niōmon et la pagode du temple. La lanterne porte dans une grande écriture noire sur fond rouge vif le dernier caractère de l'adresse du fondateur du temple, « Shinbashi ». La neige et l'ombre bleu pâle de la porte d'entrée dominent le second plan et communiquent un sentiment de paix. Des visiteurs isolés montrés de dos, portant des parapluies et des chapeaux enneigés, bordent le chemin et s'avancent vers la « Porte des deux rois-gardiens » (Niōmon) peinte en rouge vif qui apparaît derrière les arbres enneigés. Leur grandeur diminue en fonction de la distance, conformément à la perspective centrale.

Cette feuille a été approuvée par les censeurs au septième mois de 1856, c'est-à-dire deux mois après que la pagode eut été restaurée et solennellement inaugurée suite au grand séisme de 1855. Comme si souvent, Hiroshige place une fois de plus le bâtiment central au second plan en l'occultant légèrement. C'est sans doute pour commémorer l'importance de l'événement que Hiroshige a illustré cette attraction précisément à cette époque.

100

よし原
日本堤

Yoshiwara Nihontsutsumi
4–1857

Nihon Embankment and Yoshiwara

A half-moon lights this nocturnal scene, which focuses atmospherically on the final stretch of the way to the pleasure quarter of Shin-Yoshiwara. The Nihon Embankment is lined on both sides by thatched tea-houses, each representing an individual "establishment" in the quarter. Indecisive guests who have not yet made a final choice are being persuaded by the advantages of this or that brothel. Others, by contrast, their faces in some cases concealed, are moving decisively and without wasting time, just like the bearers of palanquins carrying their affluent customers. They are streaming to the brothels beyond the embankment, whose roofs are hinted at behind the trees, the clouds above shaded an enticing pink. When one considers that Shin-Yoshiwara was totally destroyed in the great earthquake of the tenth month of 1855, and temporarily replaced by quickly established substitute brothels, the lively goings-on depicted in this print must surely be celebrating the quarter's phoenix-like resurrection.

The high quality of this particular impression is evident in the carefully differentiated reproduction of the trees; the finely nuanced colours of the shore and the edge of the embankment, overprinted in green; and the green accents of the weeping willow at the end of the embankment. This willow could be the famous "Willow of Looking Back" (Mikaeri Yanagi), where brothel visitors liked to stop and take their leave, a motif which, like the flight of wild geese and the semi-shrouded half-moon, evokes a mood of lyrical melancholy.

Der Deich Nihontsutsumi und Yoshiwara

Die vom abendlichen Halbmond beschienene Szene rückt die letzte Strecke des Weges zum Vergnügungsviertel Shin-Yoshiwara stimmungsvoll ins Blickfeld. Beide Seiten des Deiches Nihontsutsumi werden von strohbedeckten Teebuden gesäumt, die einzelne Etablissements vertreten. Unschlüssige Gäste, die noch keine feste Buchung vorgenommen haben, können sich hier von den Vorzügen des einen oder anderen Etablissements überzeugen lassen. Die Passanten, die ihre Gesichter zum Teil unter dunklen Tüchern verborgen halten, bewegen sich jedoch wie die Sänftenträger, die wohlhabende Kunden zu befördern haben, zielstrebig und ohne Zeit zu verlieren. Sie strömen zu den Bordellen jenseits des Deiches, deren Dächer skizzenhaft zwischen verheißungsvoll rosa schattierten Wolkenbänken zum Vorschein kommen. Bedenkt man, dass Shin-Yoshiwara während des großen Erdbebens im zehnten Monat 1855 total zerstört worden war und von anderen – wie Pilze aus dem Boden sprießenden – Freudenhäusern provisorisch ersetzt wurde, so sollte das lebhafte Treiben der Kunden hier sicherlich das wieder auferstandene Viertel feiern.

Für die hohe Druckqualität des Blattes sprechen, neben der differenzierten Wiedergabe der Bäume, die nuancenreichen Farbverläufe der Uferpartie, der grün überdruckte Deichrand und die grün akzentuierte Trauerweide am Ende des Deiches. Bei der Trauerweide dürfte es sich um den berühmten „Weidenbaum des Zurückblickens" (Mikaeri Yanagi) handeln, an dem Freudenhausbesucher gerne innehielten, um zurückzublicken und Abschied zu nehmen, ein Motiv, das wie die fliegenden Wildgänse und der von einer Schleierwolke umwehte Halbmond eine lyrisch-melancholische Stimmung evoziert.

La digue Nihontsutsumi et Yoshiwara

Cette scène très évocatrice éclairée par le dernier quartier de lune présente la fin du chemin qui mène au quartier des plaisirs de Shin-Yoshiwara. Les deux côtés de la digue sont bordés de gargotes de thé couvertes de chaume servant d'avant-postes à différents établissements du quartier. Des clients indécis n'ayant encore aucune « réservation » se laissent séduire par les avantages de tel ou tel établissement. D'autres passants – certains ont le visage partiellement caché sous des pièces de tissu sombres –, se déplacent en revanche comme des porteurs de palanquins transportant diligemment des clients fortunés : avec un but précis, sans se laisser distraire. Ils se hâtent vers les maisons de plaisirs situées après la digue, et dont les toits sommairement esquissés apparaissent au travers de bancs de nuages aux prometteuses ombres rosées. Lorsqu'on songe que Shin-Yoshiwara fut entièrement détruit lors du grand séisme de 1855 et que le quartier fut d'abord remplacé par des établissements temporaires sortant de terre comme des champignons, on comprend que l'affairement de la clientèle a été représenté pour célébrer la renaissance du quartier.

La haute qualité de ce tirage est attestée non seulement par le traitement subtil des arbres, mais aussi par les riches dégradés de couleurs de la rive, de la bordure de la digue surimprimée de vert, et des accents verts du saule pleureur représenté à la fin de la digue. Cet arbre est vraisemblablement le fameux « saule des regrets » (Mikaeri Yanagi), sous lequel les visiteurs des maisons de plaisir aimaient à s'arrêter pour jeter un regard en arrière et prendre congé ; tout comme le vol d'oies sauvages et le quartier de lune auréolé d'un nuage, ce motif évoque une atmosphère à la fois poétique et mélancolique.

101

浅草田甫
酉の町詣

Asakusa tanbo Torinomachi mōde
11–1857

Asakusa Rice Fields and Torinomachi Festival

In the distance, Mount Fuji, reduced to a stylized outline, appears small in the red glow of sunset. Its regular conical shape is framed symmetrically by two of the vertical laths of a wooden framework that takes up almost the whole height of the print.

The wooden bars, visible because the *shōji* doors have been slid to the sides, are the clue that we are in a teahouse in Yoshiwara. The prostitutes were not allowed to leave the quarter, and frequently not even the teahouse in which they worked. The white cat looking through the bars into the open air is raised three-dimensionally from the surface of the print using the *kimedashi* printing technique (see plate 35). It represents the courtesan who has just finished her work.

A client has just left the room: this is shown not only by the bowl of water, which has just been used, and the towel that has been left casually lying on the ledge, but also by the *onkotogami*, the "paper towels for the honourable act", which are peeking out on the left, largely concealed by the back of a folding screen.

In front of the paper towels lies a gift brought by the client: so-called bear's-paw hairpins (*kumate kanzashi*), wrapped in paper. This motif links the interior with the Torinomachi Festival of the title, taking place outside in the fields.

It is early evening on the "Day of the Cockerel" in the eleventh month, and in the background the festival procession can just be seen making its way to Chōkokuji Temple. The pilgrims are holding up rakes in the form of bears' paws. Since the 12th century, rakes like these had served as weapons to seize enemies in war. Here they have become a symbol of good luck: with their aid, company employees were supposed to be successful in attracting customers.

19th-century Europeans were also fascinated by this print: it was published as early as 1889 as a black-and-white drawing in an article on Hiroshige by William Anderson in the magazine *Le Japon Artistique*.

Reisfelder in Asakusa und das Torinomachi-Fest

Ein zur Silhouette stilisierter Berg Fuji steht klein im roten Licht der eben untergegangenen Sonne. Seine regelmäßige Kegelform ist symmetrisch in die vertikalen Stäbe eines fast die Bildhöhe durchmessenden Holzgitters eingepasst.

Das durch die zur Seite geschobenen Shōji-Türen sichtbare Gitter deutet an, dass wir uns in einem Teehaus in Yoshiwara befinden. Die Prostituierten durften das Viertel kaum verlassen und häufig nicht einmal die Teehäuser, in denen sie tätig waren. Die hinter Gittern ins Freie schauende weiße Katze ist mit der Kimedashi-Drucktechnik (siehe Tafel 35) dreidimensional aus der Blattoberfläche herausgehoben und steht für die Kurtisane, die ihre Arbeit gerade beendet hat.

Ein Kunde hat das Etablissement vor kurzem verlassen: Die eben benutzte Wasserschale und das achtlos liegen gelassene Handtuch zeugen ebenso davon wie die *onkotogami*, die „Papiertücher für den ehrenvollen Akt", die am linken Blattrand, von der Rückseite eines Stellschirms weitgehend verdeckt, hervorlugen.

Davor liegt das Gastgeschenk des Freiers: die in Papier gewickelten sogenannten „Bärentatzen-Haarnadeln" (*kumate kanzashi*). Dieses Motiv verbindet die Szene im Interieur mit dem titelgebenden Fest Torinomachi draußen auf dem Feld.

Es ist früher Abend am Tag des Hahns im elften Monat, und im Hintergrund ist schemenhaft der Festtagszug auf seinem Weg zum Tempel Chōkokuji zu erkennen. Die Pilger tragen hoch aufgereckte Rechen in der Form von Bärentatzen mit sich. Seit dem zwölften Jahrhundert dienten solche Rechen im Krieg als Waffe, mit denen Feinde ergriffen wurden. Hier sind sie zu einem Glück bringenden Symbol geworden: Mit ihrer Hilfe soll es den im Gewerbe Beschäftigten gelingen, Kunden anzulocken.

Dieser Druck faszinierte auch die Europäer des 19. Jahrhunderts, denn er wurde bereits 1889 in einer schwarz-weißen Umzeichnung in einem Artikel zu Hiroshige von William Anderson in der Zeitschrift *Le Japon Artistique* publiziert.

Rizières à Asakusa et la fête Torinomachi

La petite silhouette stylisée du mont Fuji se dresse dans la lumière rouge du couchant. Son cône régulier est placé symétriquement derrière un des barreaux verticaux d'une grille en bois qui occupe presque toute la hauteur de l'image.

La grille visible à travers les portes à glissières (*shōji*) ouvertes de part et d'autre indique que nous nous trouvons dans une maison de thé de Yoshiwara. Les prostituées n'étaient guère autorisées à quitter le quartier et souvent pas même les maisons de thé pour lesquelles elles travaillaient. Le chat blanc qui contemple la liberté derrière les barreaux est accentué par un effet d'estampage à sec en relief appelé *kimedashi* (cf. pl. 35) et symbolise la courtisane qui vient de terminer son travail.

Un client a quitté l'établissement : le bol d'eau tout juste utilisé et la serviette négligemment laissée à terre en témoignent tout autant que les *onkotogami*, c'est-à-dire les « serviettes en papier pour l'acte honorable » largement cachées derrière un paravent près du bord gauche de l'image. Devant se trouve le cadeau du client : des épingles à cheveux en patte d'ours (*kumate kanzashi*) enveloppées dans du papier. Ce motif associe la scène d'intérieur avec la fête dite Torinomachi qui se déroule à l'extérieur dans les champs, et qui donne son titre à l'estampe.

L'heure est le début de soirée, le jour celui du coq du onzième mois ; à l'arrière-plan, on reconnaît un cortège de fête schématique en route vers le temple Chōkokuji. Les pèlerins portent des râteaux levés en forme de patte d'ours. Depuis le XIIe siècle, ce genre de râteaux servait aussi comme arme de guerre pour agripper l'ennemi. Ici, ils se sont transformés en signes de bon augure : c'est avec leur aide que les artisans doivent attirer des clients.

Cette estampe a aussi fasciné les Européens du XIXe siècle, car elle fut publiée dès 1889 en contours noirs dans un article sur Hiroshige publié par William Anderson dans la revue *Le Japon Artistique*.

102

簑輪
金杉
三河しま

Minowa Kanasugi Mikawashima
15–1857

Minowa, Kanasugi and Mikawashima

A crane, diving steeply, its wings outspread, dominates the upper section of this print. Only half of its body can be seen, but its snow-white plumage, its head and red crown, and its long grey bill are depicted in fine detail. Another red-crowned crane (tanchōzuru) stands in shallow water in the foreground and seems to be greeting its partner with its open bill.

All three villages named in the title lie to the north-west of Shin-Yoshiwara and close to the Ōshū kaidō highway. In winter, the shogun went on "crane excursions" (tsuru no onari) to the area around Mikawashima, where the birds were hunted with falcons. In order to attract the cranes to the area, food was left out for them. On the right is a straw-covered feeding station, which the crane feeder farther to the left has presumably just left.

In East Asia, the crane is seen as a harbinger of good fortune. The fact that it has become a symbol of longevity, fidelity and marital bliss is the result of close observation: cranes as a rule pair for life, and reinforce their bonds with dances.

Hiroshige's depiction of a pair of cranes is one in a long line of representations of this subject, which was taken from Chinese ink painting. The birds are depicted sometimes flying, sometimes standing, with closed and open bills, and seen from close up and afar.

The embossing technique known as karazuri ("empty printing") is applied in the plumage of the cranes. This involves using a baren, a flat, disc-shaped rubbing tool, to press an area of the paper face down into the carved area in the woodblock. No pigment is applied, however. This results in this case in the birds' plumage having a three-dimensional effect.

For the final illustration of the fifth volume of his Illustrated Souvenirs of Edo (Ehon Edo miyage), Hiroshige depicted a single crane as a symbol of the area of Mikawashima. It is accompanied by a satirical poem alluding to winter: "Melted by the call of the crane: the thin ice."
Tsuru no naku kata kara tokete – usu kohori.

Minowa, Kanasugi und Mikawashima

Ein Kranich im Sturzflug auf eine Ebene umspannt mit seinen ausgebreiteten Flügeln den oberen Bildrand. Sein Körper ist nur halb zu sehen, dafür sind das schneeweiße Gefieder, der Kopf mit seiner roten Krone und der lange graue Schnabel detailliert dargestellt. Ein weiterer Mandschuren-Kranich (tanchōzuru) stakt durch ein Gewässer im Vordergrund und scheint mit geöffnetem Schnabel den Partner zu begrüßen.

Alle drei im Titel genannten Orte liegen nordwestlich von Shin-Yoshiwara und nahe dem Hauptverkehrsweg Ōshū kaidō. Der Shogun machte im Winter einen „Kranichausflug" (tsuru no onari) in die Gegend um Mikawashima, wo die Vögel mit Falken gejagt wurden. Man war deswegen bemüht, sie hier anzulocken und versorgte sie mit Futter. Vom Bildrand rechts angeschnitten ist eine mit Stroh abgedeckte Futterstelle erkennbar, die der Kraniche fütternde Mann weiter links im Bild offenbar gerade verlassen hat.

In Ostasien gilt der Kranich als Glück bringendes Tier. Dass er zum Symbol für langes Leben, Treue und Eheglück wurde, zeugt von genauer Beobachtung: Ein Kranichpaar bleibt in der Regel ein ganzes Leben lang zusammen und festigt seine Bindung durch spezifische Tänze.

Hiroshiges Darstellung eines Kranichpaares folgt unzähligen Vorbildern zu diesem Motiv, das aus der chinesischen Tuschmalerei übernommen wurde. Die Vögel werden dabei meist in unterschiedlichen Posen, mal fliegend, mal stehend, mit geschlossenem und geöffnetem Schnabel, von nah und von fern wiedergegeben.

Das Gefieder der Kraniche ist eines der besten Beispiele für die Anwendung der Blinddrucktechnik karazuri („leerer Druck"). Das vorgesehene Muster wird in die Holzplatte geschnitten und anschließend das Papier mit der baren genannten Scheibe darauf gepresst. Durch diesen Druck ohne Pigmente entstehen auf der Vorderseite erhabene Partien, die hier die Vogelfedern plastisch hervorheben.

Nur einen vereinzelten Kranich, der stellvertretend für die Gegend von Mikawashima steht, zeigt Hiroshige als letzte Illustration des fünften Bandes von Illustrierte Mitbringsel aus Edo (Ehon Edo miyage). Dazu spielt ein Scherzgedicht auf die Wintersaison an: „Vom Rufen der Kraniche geschmolzen: das dünne Eis."
Tsuru no naku kata kara tokete – usu kohori.

Minowa, Kanasugi et Mikawashima

Une grue plongeant vers la plaine déploie ses ailes sur toute la largeur de l'image près du bord supérieur. Si son corps n'est qu'à moitié visible, le plumage blanc comme neige, la tête, la crête rouge et le long bec gris ont été représentés en détails. Au premier plan, une autre grue de Mandchourie (tanchōzuru) déambule près de la rive d'un étang et semble saluer du bec ouvert sa congénère.

Les trois lieux cités dans le titre sont situés au nord-est de Shin-Yoshiwara, près de la voie de circulation principale Ōshū kaidō. En hiver, le shogun faisait une « sortie aux grues » (tsuru no onari) dans la région de Mikawashima, où il chassait ces oiseaux au faucon. L'on s'efforçait donc de les attirer en leur offrant de la nourriture. Coupée par le bord de l'image, une mangeoire recouverte de paille apparaît à droite : l'homme à gauche au second plan qui nourrit les grues semble l'avoir tout juste quittée.

Dans tout l'Extrême-Orient, la grue est considérée comme un animal de bon augure. Le fait que la grue plus soit devenue plus qu'une autre espèce animale le symbole de longévité, de fidélité et de bonheur conjugal, repose sur une observation exacte : les couples restent généralement fidèles toute leur vie et renforcent leurs liens par des danses spécifiques.

La représentation d'un couple de grues par Hiroshige suit d'innombrables modèles de motifs dérivant de la peinture à l'encre chinoise. Les oiseaux y sont généralement représentés dans différentes poses, tantôt volant, tantôt debout, bec ouvert ou fermé, de loin ou en vue rapprochée.

Dans la série des Cent Vues, le plumage des grues est une des meilleures illustrations de la technique d'estampage à sec dite karazuri (« estampage vide »). Le motif prévu est gravé dans le bois d'impression, contre lequel le papier est ensuite pressé à l'aide du tampon appelé baren. De cette impression sans encre résultent sur la face avant des parties en relief qui font ici ressortir le plumage des oiseaux.

Une seule grue isolée, qui sert ici d'emblème de la région de Mikawashima, tel est aussi le motif que Hiroshige nous montre dans la dernière illustration du cinquième tome de ses Souvenirs illustrés d'Edo (Ehon Edo miyage). Un poème humoristique sur la saison d'hiver y fait allusion : « Fondu par les cris des grues : la glace fine. »
Tsuru no naku kata kara tokete – usu kohori.

千住の
大はし

Senju no Ōhashi
2–1856

Senju Great Bridge

One striking feature of this print is its use of dual viewpoints. On the one hand, we look over a broad river landscape from an elevated position, while on the other hand, we see the people on the bridge as if they were moving in front of us. Hiroshige uses these differing perspectives to construct a panoramic yet richly detailed view. In this print, he is already staking out the territory he planned to depict in his *One Hundred Famous Views of Edo*.

This composition is one of the very first in the series, the date seal at the top indicating that it was made in the second month of 1856.

In the extreme north of Edo, Senju Great Bridge for a long time provided the only way of crossing the Arakawa River for travellers wishing to use the Ōshū kaidō highway to reach the province of Ōshū. It was built as early as 1594, four years after the warlord Tokugawa Ieyasu (1542–1616) was forced to choose the then remote Edo as his base. The bridge withstood various natural disasters, not least on account of its robust timber construction, which Hiroshige depicts in this print. In addition to the load-bearing structure, the bridge is characterized by details such as the wooden panels whose little "roofs" were designed to protect the structural beams from rain and wind. The bridge survived until the great flood of September 1885, when it was washed away and had to be replaced.

For security reasons, very few bridges crossed the rivers surrounding Edo. The road to the north was so important, however, that reliance on a ferry was considered too risky. Even the shoguns used the Senju no Ōhashi in the 17th and 18th centuries for their politically and symbolically important pilgrimages to Nikkō to pay their respects at the grave of their ancestor Tokugawa Ieyasu, the founder of the Tokugawa dynasty.

Die Große Brücke in Senju

Diese Tafel besticht durch zwei Betrachterstandpunkte: Von einem stark erhöhten Standpunkt schweift der Blick über die Flusslandschaft, während sich die Menschen auf der Brücke vor den Augen des Betrachters zu bewegen scheinen. Dies erfordert eine größere Nähe zum Motiv. Hiroshige nutzt die unterschiedlichen Perspektiven, um daraus eine detailreiche Gesamtansicht zu konstruieren. Er steckt mit diesem Holzschnitt bereits das Territorium ab, das er in seinen *Hundert berühmten Ansichten von Edo* darzustellen beabsichtigte.

Es handelt sich bei dem Blatt um einen der allerersten Drucke der gesamten Serie, denn das Datumssiegel am oberen Bildrand gibt an, dass es im zweiten Monat des Jahres 1856 entstanden ist.

Im äußersten Norden von Edo bot die Große Brücke in Senju, lange Zeit die einzige Möglichkeit, den Fluss Arakawa zu überqueren, wenn man über die Hauptstraße Ōshū kaidō in die nördliche Provinz Ōshū reisen wollte. Sie wurde bereits 1594 gebaut, vier Jahre, nachdem der Feldherr Tokugawa Ieyasu (1542–1616) das seinerzeit abgelegene Edo als Stützpunkt für sein Hauptquartier hatte wählen müssen. Nicht zuletzt wegen ihrer robusten Holzkonstruktion, die Hiroshige in diesem Druck sichtbar macht, überstand die Brücke verschiedene Naturkatastrophen. Neben dem tragenden Gerüst zeichnen besonders Details wie etwa Holztafeln, deren kleine „Dächer" die tragenden Querbalken vor Feuchtigkeit und Wind schützen sollten, diese Brücke aus. Erst die große Flut vom September 1885 spülte die Brücke fort, und sie musste ersetzt werden.

Aus Sicherheitsgründen führten nur wenige Brücken über die Flüsse, die Edo umgaben. Die Straße in Richtung Norden war jedoch so wichtig, dass man sich zur Überquerung des Flusses nicht allein auf den Fährverkehr hatte verlassen wollen. Sogar die Shogune benutzten im 17. und 18. Jahrhundert die Brücke Senju no Ōhashi auf ihrer politisch und symbolisch wichtigen Pilgerreise nach Nikkō zum Grab ihres Ahnherrn Tokugawa Ieyasu, des Gründers der Tokugawa-Dynastie.

Le grand pont à Senju

Cette planche présente un attrait particulier par son double point de vue : d'un site élevé, le regard embrasse le vaste paysage fluvial, tandis que sur le pont, les hommes semblent se déplacer sous les yeux du spectateur, ce qui obligeait à rapprocher fortement le motif. Hiroshige se sert des différentes perspectives pour construire un panorama détaillé. Avec cette estampe, il délimitait déjà le territoire qu'il entendait représenter dans les *Cent Vues célèbres d'Edo*.

Cette estampe est une des premières à avoir été réalisée pour la série ; le cachet de datation près du bord supérieur de l'image indique qu'elle a vu le jour pendant le deuxième mois de l'année 1856.

À l'extrême nord d'Edo, le grand pont de Senju fut longtemps le seul ouvrage permettant de franchir la rivière Arakawa pour se rendre dans la province d'Ōshū par la route dite Ōshū kaidō. Sa construction remontait déjà à 1594, quatre ans après que le général Tokugawa Ieyasu (1542–1616) eut été contraint d'installer son quartier général à Edo, alors éloignée de tout. Le pont survécut à plusieurs catastrophes naturelles, notamment grâce à sa robuste construction en bois, que Hiroshige détaille dans cette estampe. À côté de la structure porteuse, des détails particuliers caractérisent ce pont, comme les plaques en bois dont les petits « toits » servaient à protéger les traverses de l'humidité et du vent. Il fallut attendre la grande inondation de septembre 1885 pour voir un nouveau pont remplacer l'ancien ouvrage emporté par les eaux.

Pour des raisons de sécurité intérieure, seuls de rares ponts étaient construits sur les cours d'eau des environs d'Edo. La route vers le nord revêtait toutefois une telle importance qu'on n'avait pas voulu confier la circulation aux seuls bacs. Les shoguns des XVIIe et XVIIIe siècles empruntaient eux-mêmes le pont Senju no Ōhashi lors du pèlerinage, si important au plan politique et symbolique, qui les conduisait à Nikkō sur la tombe de leur ancêtre Ieyasu, fondateur de la dynastie Tokugawa.

104

小梅堤

Koumetsutsumi
2–1857

Koume Embankment

In this view we are on the eastern side of the Sumida River, to the north of the district of Honjo, near the village of Koume. The canal in the picture, the Yotsugi dōri, was used for transporting goods and people by towboats (see plate 33), but in the section shown here, no boats are visible; instead, we have a rural idyll featuring a number of bridges.

In this high-quality impression, the *bokashi* colour gradation runs from pale to very deep blue towards the middle of the waterway, but ends abruptly on the right at a bend in the canal.

A typical feature seen on this print is the way the various figures in the foreground bottom right, lightly dressed children are playing with puppies beneath the Japanese alders (*hannoki*) that span the height of the picture. The boy in the light-blue *haori* jacket is lifting his still defenceless animal, while the one in red has just put his down again. In contrast to this lively scene, two ladies wrapped in dark, warm winter *haori* are walking in dignified fashion over the wooden bridge, and an angler is sitting lost in thought by the edge of the water. On the embankment, we see all kinds of ordinary people making their way along the country road, thereby underscoring the sense of pastoral remoteness.

In order to lend depth and structure to the reddish sky, Hiroshige, as so often, has added a flight of birds.

Am Deich Koumetsutsumi

Wir befinden uns hier auf der Ostseite des Flusses Sumidagawa, nördlich des Stadtteils Honjo, in der Nähe der Ortschaft Koume. Der dargestellte Kanal Yotsugi dōri wurde, wie wir auf Tafel 33 gesehen haben, von Treidlern als Transportkanal benutzt; der Abschnitt hier ist dagegen ohne Boote dargestellt und wird dafür brückenreich und idyllisch präsentiert.

Die Farbgradierung (*bokashi*) ist auf diesem qualitätvollen Druck zur Flussmitte hin sehr dunkel, endet aber abrupt an der Flussbiegung am rechten Rand der Komposition.

Typisch an dem Blatt sind die Darstellungen unterschiedlicher Figuren: Unten rechts im Vordergrund spielen unter den bildumspannenden japanischen Erlen (*hannoki*) auffällig leicht gekleidete Kinder mit jungen Hunden. Der Junge mit der hellblauen Haori-Jacke hebt das noch wehrlose Tierchen auf, der rot bekleidete Junge hat sein Hündchen eben wieder losgelassen. Im Kontrast zu dieser bewegten Szene schreiten zwei in dunkle, warme Winter-Haoris gehüllte Damen würdevoll über die Holzbrücke, und ein Angler sitzt gedankenversunken am Wasserrand. Daneben bevölkern allerlei einfache Leute die ländliche Straße und unterstreichen die pastorale Abgeschiedenheit.

Um dem rötlichen Himmel Tiefe und Struktur zu verleihen, setzt Hiroshige, wie so häufig, mit leichter Hand die Formation eines Vogelschwarms hinein.

Près de la digue de Koumetsutsumi

Nous sommes ici sur la rive est de la Sumidagawa, au nord du quartier Honjo, près du village de Koume. Comme on l'a vu dans la planche 33, le canal Yotsugi dōri de la présente estampe servait de voie de transport aux haleurs ; sans aucune barque sur son eau, agrémentée de nombreux ponts, la présente section du canal est en revanche présentée sous une forme idyllique.

Dans ce tirage de grande qualité, le dégradé de couleurs appelé *bokashi*, très sombre au milieu de la rivière, se termine de manière abrupte au niveau du tournant, près du bord droit de la composition.

Un des aspects caractéristiques de cette feuille est la représentation des différentes figures : en bas à droite, sous les aulnes japonais (*hannoki*) qui s'élèvent au premier plan sur toute la hauteur de l'image, des enfants manifestement court vêtus jouent avec de jeunes chiens. Le garçon qui porte la veste *haori* bleu clair soulève le petit animal encore sans défense, tandis que le garçon vêtu de rouge vient de relâcher son jeune chien. Cette scène animée contraste avec les deux dames emmitouflées dans des *haori* d'hiver sombres et chauds qui franchissent le pont de bois dans une attitude empreinte de dignité ; un pêcheur perdu dans ses pensées est assis sur la rive. Toutes sortes de gens simples peuplent par ailleurs la route de campagne et soulignent l'isolement pastoral de cette vue.

Pour conférer au ciel sa profondeur et sa texture, Hiroshige y a jeté d'une main légère un vol d'oiseaux.

105

御厩河岸

Oumayagashi
12–1857

Oumayagashi

Hiroshige has used this unusually dark print to present a stark image of the lowest form of prostitution in his day. The two young women in the boat were known as "night hawks", *yotaka*. Their pimp may well have been their brother or father. Many of them carried straw mats so as to be able to provide their services anywhere, even where there was nothing but a bridgehead or small copse to provide scanty protection from prying eyes. The faces of these girls were often disfigured by disease, forcing them to apply their make-up very thickly. Hiroshige takes up this aspect: the faces of the two girls in the boat look like masks, and the crude strokes of their eyebrow make-up stands out clearly against the pale white.

Just as Henri de Toulouse-Lautrec (1864–1901) a few decades later created provocative images of the street-girls of Paris, who fascinated the bourgeoisie and played a significant role in his own life, Hiroshige depicted everything that interested both him and the mass of consumption-oriented citizens of Edo who constituted his customer base.

In this composition, Hiroshige contrasts sharply with famous predecessors such as Katsukawa Shunshō (?–1792) or Kitagawa Utamaro (1753–1806), who depicted the world of Yoshiwara devoid of social context, and presented it instead in a glorified, almost abstract way.

Oumayagashi

Auf diesem außergewöhnlich dunklen Holzschnitt zeichnet Hiroshige ein drastisches Bild der niedersten Form von Prostitution seiner Zeit. Die beiden jungen Damen auf dem Boot werden „Nachtfalken" *(yotaka)* genannt. Sie waren oft in Begleitung eines Bruders oder mit dem Vater als Zuhälter unterwegs. Viele von ihnen trugen eine Strohmatte bei sich, auf der sie ihre Dienste überall anbieten konnten, selbst dort, wo nur ein Brückenkopf oder ein kleines Wäldchen dürftigen Schutz vor neugierigen Blicken bot. Die Gesichter dieser Mädchen waren oft von Krankheiten entstellt, und das zwang sie, die Schminke besonders dick aufzutragen. Hiroshige greift dies auf: Die Gesichter der beiden Mädchen im Boot sehen aus wie Masken, und vom fahlen Weiß heben sich die groben Striche der Augenbrauentusche deutlich ab.

Wie Henri de Toulouse-Lautrec (1864–1901) wenige Jahrzehnte später die leichten Mädchen von Paris, die das Bürgertum faszinierten und die auch in seinem eigenen Leben eine wichtige Rolle spielten, auf provozierenden Plakatdrucken wiedergab, so stellte auch Hiroshige alles dar, was ihn selbst und seine Kunden, die große Zahl der konsumfreudigen Städter, bewegte.

Hiroshige setzt sich mit seiner Komposition hingegen deutlich von berühmten Vorgängern wie Katsukawa Shunshō (?–1792) oder Kitagawa Utamaro (1753–1806) ab, die die Welt von Yoshiwara losgelöst von sozialen Kontexten, verklärt und gewissermaßen abstrakt dargestellt hatten.

Oumayagashi

Dans cette estampe inhabituellement sombre, Hiroshige livre une image cruelle de la forme la plus basse de la prostitution à son époque. Les deux jeunes dames dans les barques sont appelées « faucons de nuit » *(yotaka)*. Elles étaient souvent accompagnées d'un frère ou d'un père qui leur servait de souteneur. Beaucoup avaient avec elles une paillasse sur laquelle elles pouvaient offrir leurs services en tous lieux, même là où seuls l'arche d'un pont où un petit bosquet pouvaient protéger des regards indiscrets. Les visages de ces filles étaient souvent défigurés par les maladies, ce qui les obligeait à s'appliquer d'épaisses couches de fard. Hiroshige évoque ici cet aspect : les visages des deux filles debout dans la barque ressemblent à des masques, et sur la pâleur du blanc se détachent nettement les traits grossiers du fard à sourcils.

Tout comme Henri de Toulouse-Lautrec (1864–1901) allait le faire quelques décennies plus tard dans ses affiches et dessins provocants des filles légères qui fascinaient la bourgeoisie parisienne et qui jouèrent aussi un rôle important dans sa propre vie, Hiroshige a dépeint tout ce qui l'intéressait lui-même et ses clients, les nombreux consommateurs de plaisirs de la capitale.

Avec cette composition, Hiroshige se démarque en revanche clairement de ses précurseurs célèbres comme Katsukawa Shunshō (?–1792) ou Kitagawa Utamaro (1753–1806), qui ont représenté le petit monde de Yoshiwara dissocié de tout contexte social, transfiguré comme une sorte d'abstraction.

106

深川木場

Fukagawa Kiba
8–1856

The Fukagawa Lumberyards

On the snow-covered umbrella in the foreground we see the cut-off character *sakana* ("fish"), the first character in the name of the publisher of this series, Sakanaya Eikichi. Beyond the umbrella is an enchanted winter landscape characterized by bold diagonals. From left and right, lengths of lumber, covered in fresh snow, project into the grey sky, and the rafters' canal, elaborately coloured with gradated blue tones, snakes in a picturesque zigzag through the scene. The dominant colours blue and white give the print an atmosphere of wintry cold. This silent snowy scene is enlivened by two sparrows above a dark-grey cloud (which, like the blue gradations of the canal, is absent from later impressions); by two workers on the right bank using poles to propel the lumber across the water; and by two dogs in the left foreground.

The small, distant lumberyard workers with their snow-covered straw cloaks are positioned in such a way that they stand out against the deep-blue *bokashi*. This device, frequently used by Hiroshige to direct attention to even the smallest figures, emphasizes that they too have a role to play in the total composition.

Timber was the most important building material for the city, which in those days almost exclusively (and today still to a considerable extent) consisted of wooden dwellings. It was not long after the establishment of Edo as the seat of the shoguns that the military ruler decreed that a lumberyard should be set up in the city centre. However, after a devastating fire in 1641, which also destroyed the yard, the government decided to transfer the yard to a site outside the city, east of the Sumida River. This place, which was home to timber merchants and rafters, is still known simply as "Kiba" ("Wood Place"). The lumberyards were again relocated in the mid 1970s, this time to reclaimed land in Tokyo Bay.

Das Bauholzlager in Fukagawa

Auf dem schneebedeckten Schirm am unteren Bildrand ist das angeschnittene Schriftzeichen *sakana* ("Fisch") zu erkennen, das erste Zeichen im Namen des Verlegers dieser Serie, Sakanaya Eikichi. Über den Schirm hinweg blickt die Betrachterin auf eine bizarre, von Diagonalen beherrschte Winterlandschaft. Von links und rechts ragen mit frischem Schnee bedeckte Holzsparren in den grauen Himmel, und der aufwändig mit abgestuftem Blau kolorierte Flößerkanal zieht in einem malerischen Zickzack durchs Blatt. Die dominierenden Farben Blau und Weiß verleihen dem Holzschnitt den Eindruck winterlicher Kälte. Die stille Schneeszene wird belebt von zwei Spatzen oberhalb der dunkelgrauen Wolke (die ebenso wie die Blaugradierung des Flusses in Nachdrucken fehlt), von zwei das Holz im Fluss mit Stangen verschiebenden Arbeitern am rechten Ufer und von zwei Hunden im linken Vordergrund.

Die Holzarbeiter mit ihren schneebedeckten Strohumhängen sind so platziert, dass ihre Oberkörper in das tiefblaue *bokashi* hineinragen. Dies ist eine von Hiroshige oft angewendete Technik, um die Aufmerksamkeit auch auf kleinste Figuren zu lenken und zu verdeutlichen, dass selbst sie in der Gesamtkomposition des Bildes eine Rolle spielen.

Holz war das wichtigste Baumaterial in einer Stadt, die damals (wie zum Teil noch heute) fast ausschließlich aus mit Holz gebauten Häusern bestand. Schon kurz nach der Gründung Edos als Hauptsitz der Tokugawa-Shogune wurden auf Geheiß des Militärherrschers im Stadtzentrum Holzlager angelegt. Nach einem verheerenden Brand im Jahr 1641, der auch die Lager vernichtete, beschloss die Regierung, diese außerhalb der Stadt östlich des Flusses Sumidagawa anzulegen. Man nennt diesen Ort, wo die mit Bauholz handelnden Kaufleute und die Flößer lebten, bis heute schlicht "Kiba" ("Holzplatz"), obwohl die Holzlager seit Mitte der 1970er Jahre in die aufgeschüttete Tokyo-Bucht verlegt wurden.

L'entrepôt de bois à Fukagawa

Sur l'ombrelle enneigée coupée par le bord inférieur de l'image, on reconnaît le caractère coupé *sakana* (« poisson »), qui est le premier caractère du nom de Sakanaya Eikichi, l'éditeur des *Cent Vues*. Depuis l'ombrelle le regard de la spectatrice plonge sur un paysage d'hiver bizarre dominé par des diagonales. Par la gauche et la droite, des madriers couverts de neige fraîche entrent dans le ciel gris, tandis que le canal coloré d'un riche dégradé de bleu zigzague de manière pittoresque à travers l'image. Les couleurs dominantes bleu et blanc confèrent à cette estampe une impression de froideur hivernale. La scène silencieuse est animée par deux moineaux figurés au-dessus du nuage gris sombre (absent des tirages ultérieurs tout comme le dégradé bleu du canal), par deux ouvriers sur la rive droite qui déplacent du bois dans la rivière à l'aide de perches, et par deux chiens figurés au premier plan à gauche.

Vêtus de paille, tout enneigés, les ouvriers du bois ont été placés de sorte que leurs torses se détachent sur le bleu profond du *bokashi*. Il s'agit là d'une technique fréquemment employée par Hiroshige pour diriger l'attention du spectateur même vers les figures les plus insignifiantes et montrer qu'elles jouent elles aussi un rôle dans la composition générale.

Le bois était alors le premier matériau de construction dans une ville constituée (et en partie aujourd'hui encore) presque exclusivement de maisons en bois. Peu après la fondation d'Edo, devenue le siège principal des shoguns Tokugawa, des entrepôts de bois avaient été aménagés au centre de la ville à l'initiative du gouvernement militaire. Après un incendie dévastateur qui détruisit jusqu'aux entrepôts en 1641, le gouvernement résolut de les déplacer hors de la ville, à l'est de la rivière Sumidagawa. De nos jours encore, ce lieu est simplement appelé « Kiba » (« lieu du bois »), bien que les entrepôts aient été déplacés depuis le milieu des années 1970 dans la baie de Tokyo remblayée.

107

Fukagawa Susaki Jūmantsubo
15 – 1857

Fukagawa Susaki and Jūmantsubo

The contrast between a flying eagle depicted at close range and the deserted white-and-blue expanse of snow below has made this print, along with plates 58 and 118, one of the most popular in the series. From the *Fukagawa Lumberyards* of plate 106, of which we see the vertical timber projecting from the left margin of the print, we have been lifted to the airy heights over Edo Bay, looking into the eye of a fierce and majestic eagle. Its plumage is elaborately and expensively printed with mica particles and meticulous colour gradations, and its three black talons are printed with animal glue (*nikawa*) to produce a deep shine. The eagle stares fixedly at potential prey beneath, and seems to be about to swoop. The black-and-grey coloration of the wings, which occupy the whole breadth of the picture, is taken up in the small barrel floating in the water far below – Hiroshige's method of creating compositional tension.

The only "famous" element in this otherwise unspectacular scene of Fukagawa Susaki east of the Sumida River is the silhouette of the snow-covered Mount Tsukuba on the horizon. The Jūmantsubo of the title is the name given to a piece of land reclaimed in the 1720s to the north-east of Susaki, which formed part of the estates of a daimyō from outside the city – and at the same time indicates the size of the plot: a jūmantsubo (100,000 tsubo) is about 33 hectares.

Fukagawa Susaki und Jūmantsubo

Der einzigartige Kontrast zwischen einem aus unmittelbarer Nähe dargestellten fliegenden Adler und der einsamen weiß-blauen Winterlandschaft in der Ebene hat dieses Blatt neben den Tafeln 58 und 118 zu einem der beliebtesten der Serie gemacht. Vom *Bauholzlager in Fukagawa* von Tafel 106 – an das die vertikalen Holzstangen am linken Rand erinnern – ist der Betrachter nun in die Nähe der Edo-Bucht und hinauf in luftige Höhen gerückt, Auge in Auge mit dem furchterregenden, majestätischen Adler. Sein Gefieder ist mit Glimmerdruck und Gradierungen aufwändig gestaltet; die drei schwarzen Krallen sind mit Tierleim (*nikawa*) gedruckt, mit dem ein tiefglänzender Effekt erzielt wird. Der Raubvogel blickt starr auf ein Beutetier und scheint zum Sturzflug anzusetzen. Die schwarzgraue Farbigkeit der die gesamte Bildbreite umfassenden Flügel wird in der kleinen, auf dem Wasser schwimmenden Tonne aufgenommen – so erzeugt Hiroshige eine kompositorische Spannung.

Das einzig „berühmte" an dem ansonsten wenig spektakulären Ort Fukagawa Susaki östlich des Flusses Sumidagawa ist die Silhouette des schneebedeckten Berges Tsukubasan am Horizont. Das im Titel erwähnte Jūmantsubo bezeichnet ein in den 1720er Jahren aufgeschüttetes Stück Land nordöstlich von Susaki, das zum Grundbesitz eines Daimyō außerhalb der Stadt gehörte – und gibt zugleich die Größe der Länderei an: Jūmantsubo (100 000 Tsubo) entspricht etwa 33 Hektar.

Fukagawa Susaki et Jūmantsubo

Le contraste tout à fait unique entre un aigle représenté en vue fortement rapprochée et en plein vol d'une part, et d'autre part la désolation d'un paysage d'hiver blanc-bleu dans la plaine, a fait de cette feuille une des plus populaires de la série avec les planches 58 et 118. De l'*Entrepôt de bois à Fukagawa* de la planche 106 – que rappellent les perches de bois verticales près du bord gauche de l'image –, le spectateur s'est rapproché de la baie d'Edo en vue d'oiseau, les yeux dans les yeux avec l'aigle terrible et majestueux. Le plumage de l'oiseau de proie est enrichi de poussière de mica et de riches dégradés de couleurs ; les trois serres ont été imprimées à l'aide d'une colle animale (*nikawa*) permettant d'obtenir un effet de profond brillant. L'aigle jette un regard acéré sur une proie et semble s'apprêter à fondre vers le sol. Le chromatisme bleu-noir des ailes, qui couvrent toute la largeur de l'image, est repris par le tonneau que charrie la rivière – ce qui permet à Hiroshige de générer une tension dans la composition.

Le seul aspect « célèbre » du lieu-dit Fukagawa Susaki – par ailleurs peu spectaculaire – situé à l'est de la rivière Sumidagawa, est la silhouette du mont Tsukubasan enneigé qui apparaît à l'horizon. Le Jūmantsubo évoqué par le titre désignait une terre remblayée dans les années 1720 au nord de Susaki, terre qui faisait partie du domaine d'un daimyō à l'extérieur de la ville – le terme renseigne sur la taille des terres : Jūmantsubo (100 000 Tsubo) correspond en effet à une superficie d'environ 33 hectares.

108

芝うらの
風景

Shibaura no fūkei
2–1856

View of Shiba Coast

Two formations of seagulls in the foreground help to frame this view. The large wooden structure on the far left marks the edge of the navigation channel running through the inshore reaches of Edo Bay. By repeating the marker, smaller as a result of perspective, Hiroshige conveys depth to the picture. The same compositional technique is also employed, somewhat clumsily, using the four boats that form the diagonal in the middle distance. The fortification wall on the right was part of the embankment of the shogun's villa, Hama, whose extensive grounds consisted of reclaimed land.

In the middle distance on the left we see the earth ramparts (*daiba*) that were hastily erected after the arrival of the so-called Black Ships of commodore Matthew Perry (1794–1858) in July 1853. The cannons placed on them were intended to serve as a defence against attack by foreign ships.

In the second volume of his *Illustrated Souvenirs of Edo* (*Ehon Edo miyage*), printed in 1850, Hiroshige deals with the same stretch of coast in two compositions. In those prints, however, the coastal scenery is enlivened by many heavily laden sailing boats, while Hama and the ramparts are absent. Perhaps the change in the present composition points to a politically more explicit picture: the shogun is metaphorically confronted with the foreign threat. There is also an allusion to the desperate situation just four months after the great earthquake of the tenth month of 1855.

The censors approved this print, one of the first five prints in the series, in the second month of 1856. An indication of its early date is the seal, in the bottom left-hand corner, of the wood-block cutter "Horisen" (Hori Sennosuke, doubtless the same person as Sugawa Sennosuke). This is the only occurrence of his seal directly on a print in *One Hundred Famous Views of Edo*. Two and three months later, respectively, we find it again in plates 17, 28 and 83, but this time outside the margin of the image; and then it disappears altogether. Evidently the publisher Sakanaya decided to single out Hiroshige as the sole creator of the series.

Die Landschaft an der Küste Shibaura

Ein Schwarm Möwen durchzieht das Blatt in zwei Formationen. Ein großes A-förmiges Seezeichen links dient der Markierung einer Fahrrinne in den küstennahen Bereichen der Edo-Bucht. Hiroshige wiederholt es perspektivisch verkleinert und erzeugt dadurch Bildtiefe. Dasselbe Kompositionsmittel kommt etwas unbeholfen auch bei den vier Booten zum Einsatz, die von rechts diagonal in die Bucht gesetzt sind. Die Befestigungsmauern daneben gehören zu den Uferpartien der shogunalen Villa Hama, deren großes Areal aus aufgeschüttetem Land besteht.

Im linken Mittelgrund sind die Erdwälle (*daiba*) zu sehen, die nach der Ankunft der Schwarzen Schiffe des amerikanischen Admirals Matthew Perry (1794–1858) im Juli 1853 hastig errichtet worden waren. Mit den eingelassenen Kanonen wollte man angreifende ausländische Schiffe abwehren.

Im zweiten Band seiner *Illustrierten Mitbringsel aus Edo* (*Ehon Edo miyage*) von 1850 thematisiert Hiroshige denselben Küstenabschnitt in zwei Kompositionen. Dort beleben allerdings viele reich beladene Segelboote die Bucht, während die Villa Hama und die gegenüberliegenden Erdwälle fehlen. Möglicherweise deutet die Änderung im Blatt der *Hundert Ansichten* auf ein politisch expliziteres Bild: Dem Shogun sind metaphorisch die ausländischen Eindringlinge gegenübergestellt, und auch auf die desolate Situation nur vier Monate nach dem großen Erdbeben vom zehnten Monat 1855 wird angespielt.

Als einer der ersten fünf Holzschnitte der Serie wurde dieses Blatt im zweiten Monat des Jahres 1856 von den Zensoren genehmigt. Ein Anzeichen für eine frühe Entstehung findet sich in der linken unteren Ecke: das Siegel des Holzschneiders „Horisen" (Hori Sennosuke, wohl identisch mit Sugawa Sennosuke). Es ist das einzige *auf* der Bildfläche eines Holzschnittes der *Hundert Ansichten*. Zwei beziehungsweise drei Monate später findet sich noch dreimal (siehe Tafeln 17, 28, 83) sein Siegel am Blattrand, dann verschwindet es ganz. Offensichtlich entschied sich der Verleger Sakanaya, Hiroshige als einzigen Schöpfer dieser Serie herauszustellen.

La côte à Shibaura

Un vol de mouettes traverse l'image en deux formations. À gauche, un grand signal maritime en forme de « A » sert à marquer un chenal dans la zone côtière de la baie d'Edo. Hiroshige le reprend plus loin en raccourci et confère ainsi de la profondeur à l'image. Le même moyen de composition revient de manière un peu maladroite dans les quatre barques alignées en diagonale qui entrent dans la baie par la droite. Les murs fortifiés qu'on aperçoit à leur droite font partie de la zone côtière de la villa shogunale dite Hama, dont le vaste domaine est constitué de terres remblayées.

À gauche au second plan, on aperçoit des *daiba*, remblais de terre fortifiés qui avaient été levés à la hâte en juillet 1853 après la venue des « bateaux noirs » du commodore américain Matthew Perry (1794–1858). Les canons dont ils étaient armés étaient censés protéger le pays contre une attaque navale ennemie.

Dans le deuxième tome (1850) des ses *Souvenirs illustrés d'Edo* (*Ehon Edo miyage*), Hiroshige avait représenté la même partie de la côte dans deux compositions. Il est vrai que de nombreux voiliers fortement chargés y animaient la baie, tandis qu'y manquaient la villa Hama et les *daiba* levés le long de la côte. Il se peut que les modifications apportées dans la feuille des *Cent Vues* relèvent d'une volonté politique plus explicite : au shogun s'opposent métaphoriquement les intrus étrangers, et l'image contient aussi des allusions à la situation de désolation quatre mois seulement après le grand séisme du dixième mois 1855.

Cette feuille, une des cinq premières de la série, fut approuvée par la censure au deuxième mois 1856. Un autre signe de cette réalisation précoce apparaît dans le coin inférieur gauche de l'image avec le sceau du graveur « Horisen » (Hori Sennosuke, sans doute Sugawa Sennosuke). Il s'agit du seul sceau apparaissant à *l'intérieur* d'une image des *Cent Vues*. Deux ou plus exactement trois mois plus tard, on retrouve encore par trois fois le même sceau – cette fois-ci dans la marge (cf. pl. 17, 28, 83) –, puis il disparaît complètement. L'éditeur Sakanaya résolut visiblement de faire ressortir Hiroshige comme le seul créateur de la série.

109

南品川
鮫洲海岸

Minami Shinagawa Samezu kaigan
2–1857

Minami Shinagawa and Samezu Coast

This print provides us with a bird's-eye view over Edo Bay near Shinagawa. In the southern part of this settlement stood the Zen Temple of Kaianji, founded in the 13th century, whose entrance gate can vaguely be made out between the dense but sketchily indicated clumps of trees on the left. Beyond, the curve of the bay draws the eye to the profile of Mount Tsukuba rising out of a bank of mist. Samezu means "Shark Sandbank" and refers to a legend in which a shark was washed ashore on this stretch of coast. In its belly the fishermen found a golden statue of the Bodhisattva Kannon. In Kamakura, the regent Hōjō Tokiyori (1227–1263) was so impressed by the miraculous find that he endowed the Kaianji Temple in order to house the icon.

The stretch of Edo Bay by Shinagawa was known nationwide as the source of the best seaweed. In the autumn, fishermen would submerge tree trunks and branches in the shallow inshore waters so that the seaweed would grow on them. From winter to spring the crop was harvested and processed into the thin, tasty sheets of seaweed known as *nori*, which are used in Japanese cuisine both to flavour food and to wrap *sushi*. The present print shows seaweed gatherers at low tide, guiding their boats through the dense rows of branches.

Minami Shinagawa und die Küste bei Samezu

Aus der Vogelperspektive blickt der Betrachter über die Bucht von Edo bei Shinagawa. Im südlichen Teil dieser Siedlung lag der im 13. Jahrhundert gegründete Zen-Tempel Kaianji, dessen Eingangstor zwischen den dichten, summarisch dargestellten Baumgruppen links vage auszumachen ist. Dahinter setzt sich die Bucht bei Samezu fort und leitet zu dem hinter Nebelbänken aufragenden Profil des Berges Tsukubasan über. Samezu bedeutet „Haifisch-Sandbank" und bezieht sich auf eine Legende, nach der an dieser Stelle ein Hai an Land gespült worden sein soll. In seinem Bauch fanden die Fischer eine goldene Statue des Bodhisattva Kannon. Der wundersame Fund beeindruckte den Regenten Hōjō Tokiyori (1227–1263) in Kamakura dermaßen, dass er den Zen-Tempel Kaianji als Aufbewahrungsort für die Figur stiftete.

Der hier gezeigte Abschnitt der Edo-Bucht bei Shinagawa war im ganzen Land für die Gewinnung der besten Algen bekannt. Im Herbst vergruben die Fischer Bäume und Äste zur Kultivierung der Algen in den seichten Küstenpartien. Vom Winter bis zum Frühling wurden die Algen geerntet und zu schmackhaften dünnen Algenblättern (*nori*) verarbeitet, wie man sie zur Würzung von Speisen, aber auch zur Zubereitung von Sushi verwendet. Der Holzschnitt zeigt Algensammler, die bei Ebbe ihre Boote durch die dichten Reihen der Äste steuern, um die Algen abzuernten.

Minami Shinagawa et la côte près de Samezu

Une vue d'oiseau offre au spectateur un panorama de la baie d'Edo près de Shinagawa. Dans la partie sud de ce lotissement se trouvait le temple zen Kaianji fondé au XIIIᵉ siècle, temple dont la porte d'entrée se distingue vaguement parmi les bosquets touffus sommairement indiqués à gauche. Plus loin, la baie s'étend de Samezu jusqu'au profil du mont Tsukubasan émergeant parmi des bancs de nuages. Samezu signifie « banc de sable du requin » et se réfère à une légende selon laquelle un requin y aurait été rejeté par la mer. Dans son ventre, les pêcheurs trouvèrent la statue en or du bodhisattva Kannon. Cette découverte miraculeuse impressionna tellement le régent Hōjō Tokiyori (1127–1263) de Kamakura qu'il institua le temple zen Kaianji pour conserver la figure.

La portion de la baie d'Edo proche de Shinagawa qui nous est montrée dans cette estampe était réputée dans tout le pays pour la culture des meilleures algues. À l'automne, les pêcheurs enterraient des arbres et des branches dans l'eau peu profonde de la côte pour favoriser la croissance des algues. Les algues étaient récoltées de l'hiver au printemps et transformées en fines feuilles (*nori*) savoureuses utilisées comme assaisonnement, mais aussi pour la préparation de sushis. Ici, on voit les barques des cultivateurs se frayant un chemin parmi les branches pour récolter les algues à marée basse.

110

千束の池
袈裟懸松

Senzoku no ike Kesakakematsu
2–1856

"Robe-Hanging Pine" at Senzoku no ike

In this print, Hiroshige depicts two lesser-known pilgrimage sites, the Hachiman shrine at Senzoku and the "Robe-Hanging Pine". He clearly knew the location from personal experience, but for this print, one of the earliest in *One Hundred Famous Views of Edo*, he resorted to an earlier depiction in the second volume of the *Illustrated Guide to Famous Views of Edo* (*Edo meisho zue*) of 1834.

The Hachiman shrine can be seen on the left, in a small copse on the opposite bank of the lake. The focus of the composition, however, is the lake itself; into it, on the right, projects a spit of land on which grows a lone pine tree. According to legend, its name, "Robe-Hanging Pine" (Kesakakematsu), goes back to the famous monk Nichiren

(1222–1282), who stopped off here for a rest and hung his monk's robe on its branches. Later, followers of Nichiren erected the Myōfukuji Temple in the immediate vicinity, which, like the pine, became a destination for pilgrims. In the foreground, we can see travellers on foot, on horseback and in a palanquin. They have taken refreshment at a food stand decorated with red paper lanterns. Pilgrims are looking at the imposing fenced-in pine on the spit of land and are preparing to visit the stone stele bearing a memorial inscription. Because of the arc of dark-blue water around the peninsula, the auspicious cranes flying over the lake and the narrative element provided by the pilgrims, the print has something of the character of a picture-postcard idyll.

Die „Kiefer zum Aufhängen der Mönchsrobe" am See Senzoku no ike

Hiroshige stellt in diesem Blatt zwei weniger bekannte Pilgerziele vor, den Hachiman-Schrein von Senzoku und die „Kiefer zum Aufhängen der Mönchsrobe". Offenbar hatte er den Ort selbst besucht. In dieser Komposition – einer der frühesten der *Hundert Ansichten* – stützt er sich jedoch auf den zweiten Band des *Illustrierten Führers zu berühmten Ansichten von Edo* (*Edo meisho zue*) von 1834.

Der Hachiman-Schrein kommt links am gegenüberliegenden Ufer zwischen einem kleinen Wäldchen zum Vorschein. Im Zentrum der Komposition steht jedoch der See, in den eine von einer einzelnen Kiefer bestandene Landzunge ragt. Ihr Name „Kiefer zum Aufhängen der Mönchsrobe" (Kesakakematsu) geht einer Legende zufolge auf den berühmten Mönch Nichiren (1222–1282) zurück, der hier

Rast machte und bei dieser Gelegenheit seinen Mönchsumhang an ihr aufhängte. Später errichtete die Nichiren-Schule in unmittelbarer Nähe den Tempel Myōfukuji, der ebenso wie die Kiefer zu einem Pilgerziel wurde. Im Vordergrund sind Reisende zu Fuß, zu Pferd und in einer Sänfte unterwegs. Sie haben sich an dem mit roten Papierlaternen geschmückten Imbissstand gestärkt. Auch auf der Landzunge sind Pilger auszumachen. Sie betrachten die imposante, eingezäunte Kiefer und steuern auf die mit einer Gedenkinschrift versehene Steintafel zu. Das um die Landzunge in schwungvollem Bogen dunkelblau schattierte Wasser, aber auch die über den See fliegenden, Glück verheißenden Kraniche ebenso wie das narrative Element der emsigen Pilger verleihen der Szenerie den Charakter einer Ansichtskartenidylle.

Le « Pin pour accrocher la robe de moine » au bord du lac Senzoku no ike

Dans cette estampe, Hiroshige nous montre deux lieux de pèlerinage moins connus : le sanctuaire de Hachiman à Senzoku et le « Pin pour accrocher la robe de moine ». L'artiste avait apparemment visité ce lieu en personne. Pour la présente composition – une des toutes premières des *Cent Vues* – Hiroshige est toutefois parti du deuxième tome (1834) du *Guide illustré des vues célèbres d'Edo* (*Edo meisho zue*).

Le sanctuaire de Hachiman apparaît à gauche, parmi les arbres d'un petit bois sur la rive opposée. Le centre de la composition est néanmoins occupé par un lac dans lequel s'avance une langue de terre plantée d'un pin isolé appelé « Pin pour accrocher la robe de moine » (Kesakakematsu). Une légende rapporte que ce nom remonte au célèbre moine Nichiren

(1222–1282), qui fit une halte sous les branches de l'arbre et y accrocha son pardessus de moine. Aux abords immédiats, l'école Nichiren construisit plus tard le temple Myōfukuji, qui devint un lieu de pèlerinage tout comme le pin lui-même. Au premier plan, on aperçoit des voyageurs à pied, à cheval et dans un palanquin, et d'autres pèlerins se reconnaissent sur la langue de terre. Ils contemplent l'arbre imposant entouré d'une clôture et se dirigent vers la plaque de pierre gravée d'une d'inscription commémorative. L'eau ombrée présente un *bokashi* bleu foncé dont la courbe s'adapte à la langue de terre. Les grues de bon augure qui volent au-dessus du lac et l'élément anecdotique des pèlerins dévoués confèrent à ce décor paysager un caractère de carte postale.

111

目黒
太鼓橋
夕日の岡

Meguro Taikobashi Yūhi no oka
4–1857

Meguro Drum Bridge and Sunset Hill

Hiroshige depicts the path to a famous temple in Meguro, dedicated to the "king of esoteric knowledge" (Fudō Myōō), that leads over the "Drum Bridge" (Taikobashi). Its arched shape, and the fact that it was built of stone rather than the usual wood, presumably following Chinese models, made it a tourist attraction for pilgrims. The Shōgatsuya teahouse, famous for its sweet-bean soup (*shiruko mochi*), was also a destination. Hiroshige has depicted the teahouse only indirectly, by means of the roof projecting into the print in the bottom right-hand corner, beneath his signature cartouche. To the left in the background is the tree-covered Sunset Hill (Yūhi no oka), which provided an attractive view of the Meguro River valley.

With their snow-covered hats and umbrellas, pilgrims and peasants are crossing the bridge as snow falls. The bridge itself is aligned diagonally to the picture plane. The clear Prussian blue of the Meguro River stands out radiantly against the gentle grey-brown and grey-blue tones of the snowy landscape and sky, where snowflakes are represented by unprinted spots on the paper. Not only the composition and style of this print, but also this method of representing falling snow, show how effortlessly Hiroshige had mastered the techniques and imagery of Chinese ink painting.

Together with three other prints (plates 24, 25, 84) in the series, all with the same date seal, this print depicts the area around Meguro. In the fourth month of 1857, this quarter was host to an exposition of the Rōzenji Temple's Fudō icon, popularly known also as the "Meguro Fudō". While the temple itself was never a motif in *One Hundred Famous Views of Edo*, the four contemporaneous compositions relating to Meguro indicate that Hiroshige and his publisher had seen the exposition as a timely opportunity to issue a print.

Trommelbrücke von Meguro und Sonnenuntergangshügel

Das Blatt beschreibt den Weg zu einem berühmten, dem König esoterischen Wissens (Fudō Myōō) geweihten Tempel in Meguro über die sogenannte „Trommelbrücke" (Taikobashi). Ihre gewölbte Form und die Tatsache, dass es sich nicht um eine der üblichen Holzbrücken, sondern um eine aus Stein gemauerte Brücke wohl nach chinesischem Vorbild handelte, machte sie für die Pilger zu einer touristischen Attraktion. Davon profitierte auch das Teehaus Shōgatsuya, das für seine Suppe aus süßen Bohnen (*shiruko mochi*) bekannt war. Hiroshige hat das Teehaus nur indirekt – durch das unten rechts ins Bild ragende Hausdach, über das sich die rote Kartusche mit seiner Signatur erstreckt, – in die Komposition einbezogen. Links im Hintergrund ist der baumbestandene Sonnenuntergangshügel (Yūhi no oka) zu erkennen, der einen schönen Ausblick auf das Tal des Flusses Megurogawa bot.

Mit schneebedeckten Hüten und Schirmen ausgestattet, überqueren einzelne Pilger und Bauern im Schneetreiben die diagonal ins Bild gesetzte Brücke. Das klare Preußischblau des Flusses Megurogawa hebt sich strahlend gegen die zart graubraun und graublau schattierte Schneelandschaft und den Himmel ab, in dem die Schneeflocken weiß ausgespart sind. Nicht nur Komposition und Stil dieses Blattes, auch die Methode der Schneedarstellung durch Aussparung des weißen Papiergrundes zeigen, wie mühelos und routiniert Hiroshige das Bildvokabular der chinesischen Tuschmalerei beherrschte.

Gemeinsam mit drei weiteren Blättern der Serie, die alle mit dem gleichen Datumssiegel versehen sind, zeigt dieser Holzschnitt die Gegend von Meguro (siehe Tafeln 24, 25, 84). Im vierten Monat 1857 wurde in diesem Stadtviertel die Fudō-Ikone des Tempels Rōzenji ausgestellt – populär auch „Meguro Fudō" genannt. Zwar wurde der Tempel selbst nie Gegenstand der *Hundert Ansichten*, aber die vier zeitgleich fertiggestellten Entwürfe zu Meguro verraten, dass Hiroshige und sein Verleger an die Ausstellung als Anlass für dieses Blatt gedacht hatten.

Le pont-tambour de Meguro et la Colline du soleil couchant

Cette feuille décrit le chemin qui mène à un temple de Meguro consacré au roi de la connaissance ésotérique (Fudō Myōō) en franchissant un « pont-tambour » (Taikobashi). La forme arquée du pont et le fait qu'il ne s'agissait pas d'un habituel pont en bois, mais d'un ouvrage en pierre bâti sur le modèle chinois, en faisaient une attraction touristique pour les pèlerins. La maison de thé Shōgatsuya en retirait tous les bénéfices ; elle était réputée pour sa soupe de haricots doux (*shiruko mochi*). Dans sa composition, Hiroshige ne montre qu'indirectement la maison de thé – avec le toit entrant dans l'image par le coin inférieur droit, et sur lequel vient se superposer le cartouche de signature rouge. À gauche à l'arrière-plan, on reconnaît la Colline du soleil couchant (Yūhi no oka) plantée d'arbres, d'où l'on avait une vue magnifique sur la vallée de la rivière Megurogawa.

Sous les rafales de neige, des pèlerins isolés et des paysans vêtus de chapeaux enneigés et portant des parapluies traversent le pont placé à l'oblique dans l'image. Le clair et lumineux bleu de Prusse de la Megurogawa se démarque du paysage enneigé ombré de tons délicats de gris-brun et gris-bleu, mais aussi du ciel dont les flocons de neige ont été représentés par des épargnes blanches. La composition et le style de cette feuille, mais aussi et surtout le mode de représentation de la neige par épargne du fond blanc, montre avec quelle suprême aisance routinière Hiroshige maîtrisait le vocabulaire iconique de la peinture à l'encre chinoise.

Avec les trois autres feuilles de la série portant le même cachet de datation (cf. pl. 24, 25, 84), cette estampe dépeint la région de Meguro. Au quatrième mois 1857, une exposition de l'icône de Fudō du temple Rōzenji – que l'usage populaire appelait aussi « Meguro Fudō » – était présentée dans ce quartier. Si le temple n'a jamais été pris à proprement parler comme sujet dans les *Cent Vues*, les quatre projets autour de Meguro réalisés à la même époque montrent que Hiroshige et son éditeur avaient pris cette exposition comme prétexte pour éditer la présente feuille.

112

愛宕下
藪小路

Atagoshita Yabukōji
12–1857

Atagoshita and Yabu Lane

The name Atagoshita means, literally, "beneath Atago", and refers to Atago Hill, which thus gave its name to this quarter, with its numerous daimyō residences. The brilliant red gatehouse in the background leads to the Atago Shrine. In front, we see the residence of daimyō Katō from Minakuchi, while the large, long building on the left is the residence of daimyō Hijikata from Komono (in today's Mie Prefecture). Yabu Lane is not actually depicted, only a part of the bamboo thicket (*yabu*) lining it. Hiroshige deploys snow-covered bamboo branches as a decorative foreground motif. Combined with sparrows, bamboo in snow is a symbol of placidity and friendship, and has an auspicious meaning.

Cheerful colour accents are provided by the powerful blue of the canal; the saturated green of the bamboo beneath a thick blanket of snow; the corn yellow of the umbrellas and hats; the luminous red of the cartouches and the small building in the distance; and the gradations of the sky from black via pale-blue and white to russet. Yet if one imagines the print in black-and-white, this lane, along which the people are trudging, silent and absorbed, through the snow between the closed-up daimyō residences, can seem somewhat oppressive. An impression not dispelled even by the very animated sparrows in the foreground.

Atagoshita und die Straße Yabukōji

Der Name Atagoshita bedeutet wörtlich „unter dem Atago" und bezieht sich auf den Hügel Atagoyama, der dem Viertel mit seinen zahlreichen Daimyō-Residenzen den Namen gab. Der leuchtend rot gestrichene Torbau im Hintergrund führt zum Schrein Atagosha, davor ist das Anwesen des Daimyō Katō von Minakuchi auszumachen. Das große, längliche Gebäude links ist die Residenz des Daimyō Hijikata von Komono (heutige Präfektur Mie). Die Straße Yabukōji ist im Bild nicht wiedergegeben, sondern nur ein Teil des Bambusdickichts (*yabu*), das sie säumte. Hiroshige setzt einige schneebedeckte Bambuszweige als dekoratives Vordergrundmotiv in die Komposition. In Kombination mit Sperlingen gilt der Bambus im Schnee als Symbol für Sanftmut und Freundschaft und hat eine Glück verheißende Bedeutung.

Das kräftige Blau des Kanals, das satte Grün des unter einer dicken Schneedecke zum Vorschein kommenden Bambus, das Maisgelb der Schirme und Hüte ebenso wie der von Schwarz über Hellblau und Weiß zu Braunrot gradierte Himmel und die leuchtend roten Schriftkartuschen setzen heitere Farbakzente. Doch wenn man sich diese fröhlichen Farben wegdenkt, wirkt die Straße, auf der die Menschen schweigsam und in sich gekehrt zwischen den hermetisch abgeriegelten Daimyō-Residenzen durch den Schnee stapfen, eher bedrückend. Diesen Eindruck können auch die betont lebhaften Sperlinge im Vordergrund nicht zerstreuen.

Atagoshita et la rue Yabukōji

Le nom Atagoshita signifie littéralement « sous l'Atago » et se réfère à la colline Atagoyama qui a donné son nom à ce quartier où se trouvent de nombreuses résidences de daimyōs. La porte peinte en rouge à l'arrière-plan marque l'accès au sanctuaire Atagosha ; devant elle, on aperçoit la propriété du daimyō Katō de Minakuchi, le long bâtiment qu'on peut voir à gauche étant la résidence du daimyō Hijikata de Komono (actuelle préfecture de Mie). La rue Yabukōji n'est pas représentée dans l'image, hormis par un bambou (*yabu*) foisonnant qui la bordait. Au premier plan, Hiroshige a placé comme motif décoratif quelques rameaux de bambou enneigés. Associé aux passereaux, le bambou dans la neige symbolise l'amitié et la douceur de caractère et est considéré comme une promesse de bonheur.

Le bleu profond du canal et le vert saturé du bambou apparaissant sous l'épaisse couche de neige, le jaune maïs des parapluies et des chapeaux, le ciel avec son dégradé du noir au bleu clair et du blanc au rouge-brun ainsi que les cartouches d'écriture rouge vif ponctuent la composition d'accents de couleur joyeux. Si on les laisse un moment de côté, la rue dans laquelle les passants marchent dans la neige, intériorisés, silencieux parmi les hermétiques résidences des daimyōs, est d'un effet plutôt oppressant, impression que ne parviennent pas non plus à effacer les passereaux qui animent le premier plan.

虎
の
門
外

あ
ふ
ひ
坂

Toranomon-soto Aoizaka
11–1857

Aoi Slope outside Toranomon Gate

On a starry winter's evening, two artisan apprentices return from ascetic exercises in the Konpira Shrine, which was situated on territory belonging to the feudal lord Kyōgoku, from the port of Marugame on the north-west of Shikoku Island. During the late Tokugawa period (1615–1868), ships with pilgrims travelling to the Konpira Shrine to the south anchored here.

On the 13th day of each month, this shrine in Edo was open to the public, which supplied the daimyō with a welcome source of income. The young men seen here have exposed themselves to the icy water at the shrine in order to strengthen their characters, but above all to purge themselves of negative mental attitudes that might stand in the way of the development of their skills. Dressed in nothing but loincloths, and carrying lanterns before them, the two heroes are marching up Aoi Slope. No less impervious to the cold than the two young men, on the right two cats are lying at the foot of the slope, next to Hiroshige's red signature cartouche. The pointed confrontation of man and beast, mostly cats or dogs, is a device often deployed by Hiroshige as a means of ironic commentary. He himself obviously sympathized with the animals, humorously making fun of the fussy assiduity of human beings (see plate 90).

Two portable noodle stalls are on the right by the outer moat of the castle. One stall, which is being carried home by the proprietor, bears a sign with the inscription *nihachi* ("Two times Eight"): it is offering buckwheat noodles at 16 *mon* – about the price of a Hiroshige print. The other specializes in *ohira shippoku*, noodles with fried egg, mushrooms, water chestnuts or fishcakes. Some distance away are several figures, including two women being led by men holding paper lanterns. The horizon is bathed in a magical light, against which stand out the houses and temple buildings, but above all the pines and the Chinese hackberry trees (*enoki*), their branches strangely forking like the claws of a crab. The perfectly calculated chiaroscuro of this print effortlessly evokes spatial depth, and makes this print another masterpiece in the depiction of twilight.

Der Hang Aoizaka außerhalb des Tores Toranomon

In einer sternenklaren Winternacht kehren zwei Handwerkslehrlinge von asketischen Übungen im Schrein Konpira zurück. Der Schrein befand sich auf dem Anwesen des Daimyō Kyōgoku. Der Feudalherr stammte aus der Hafenstadt Marugame im Nordwesten der Insel Shikoku, wo in der späten Tokugawa-Zeit (1615–1868) die Schiffe mit Pilgern anlegten, die von dort in Richtung Süden zum Hauptschrein Konpira wanderten.

Am 13. Tag jeden Monats war der Schrein in Edo für die Öffentlichkeit zugänglich, was dem Feudalherrn willkommene Nebeneinnahmen einbrachte. Die jungen Männer haben sich in der Kälte dem eisigen Wasser beim Schrein ausgesetzt, um ihre Disziplin zu stärken, vor allem aber, um sich von negativen Geisteshaltungen zu reinigen, die der Entwicklung ihrer Fertigkeiten im Wege stehen könnten. Nur mit einem Lendenschurz bekleidet und eine Laterne vor sich tragend, marschieren die beiden Helden über die Straße des Hangs Aoizaka. Teilnahmslos und vollkommen unbeeindruckt von ihren heroischen Anstrengungen, aber ebenso unempfindlich gegenüber der Kälte, lagern zwei Katzen am Fuß des Hangs rechts neben der leuchtend roten Signaturenkartusche Hiroshiges. Die pointierte Gegenüberstellung von Mensch und Tier, meist Hund oder Katze, ist ein Stilmittel, das Hiroshige häufig im Sinne eines humorvoll-ironischen Kommentars einsetzt, wobei er offenbar mit der Position des Tiers sympathisiert und die Geschäftigkeit der Menschen scherzhaft ins Lächerliche zieht (siehe Tafel 90).

Zwei tragbare Nudelgarküchen sind rechts am äußeren Schlossgraben zu erkennen. Der eine Nudelstand trägt ein Schild mit der Aufschrift *nihachi* („zwei mal acht"). Er bietet Buchweizennudeln zum Preis von 16 *mon* an – etwa so viel wie ein Holzschnitt Hiroshiges kostete. Der andere Stand ist auf *ohira shippoku*, Nudeln mit gebratenem Ei, Pilzen, Wasserkastanien oder Fischkuchen spezialisiert. In einiger Entfernung sind mehrere hell erleuchtete Personen auszumachen, darunter zwei Frauen, die von Männern mit Papierlaternen geleitet werden. Der Horizont ist in ein magisches Licht getaucht, vor dem sich die Häuser und Tempelgebäude, vor allem aber die Kiefern und die Nesselbäume (*enoki*) mit ihren krebszangenartigen Ästen geheimnisvoll abheben. Die perfekt kalkulierten Helldunkelkontraste evozieren räumliche Tiefe und machen das Blatt zu einem weiteren Meisterwerk der Abenddarstellung.

La montée d'Aoizaka à l'extérieur de la porte Toranomon

Par une claire nuit d'hiver étoilée, deux apprentis artisans reviennent de leurs pratiques ascétiques au sanctuaire de Konpira. Le sanctuaire faisait partie du domaine du daimyō Kyōgoku, un seigneur féodal originaire de la ville portuaire de Marugame, au nord-ouest de l'île Shikoku. Vers la fin de l'ère Tokugawa (1615–1868), les pèlerins y débarquaient avant de poursuivre leur route plus au sud jusqu'au sanctuaire de Konpira.

Le sanctuaire était ouvert au public le 13ème jour de chaque mois, ce qui assurait au seigneur féodal des rentrées d'argent secondaires opportunes. Les jeunes hommes se sont exposés à l'eau glaciale pour se fortifier dans la discipline, mais surtout pour se purifier des attitudes d'esprit négatives qui pourraient faire obstacle à leur progression sur la voie. Vêtus seulement d'un pagne et munis d'une lanterne, les deux joyeux drilles marchent sur la route de la montée d'Aoizaka. Insouciants, totalement indifférents à leurs efforts héroïques, mais tout aussi insensibles au froid, deux chats sont couchés au pied de la côte, à droite du cartouche de signature de Hiroshige. La juxtaposition délibérée de l'homme et de l'animal – le plus souvent un chien ou un chat – est un moyen stylistique dont Hiroshige se sert souvent comme d'un commentaire mi-humoristique, mi-ironique, sachant qu'il sympathise visiblement avec la position de l'animal, et qu'il confère ainsi une note plaisante de ridicule aux activités humaines (cf. pl. 90).

Deux cantines portables se reconnaissent à droite, le long de la douve extérieure du château d'Edo. L'une porte un écriteau avec le mot *nihachi* (« deux fois huit »), elle propose des nouilles de sarrasin pour 16 *mon* – à peu près le prix d'une estampe de Hiroshige à l'époque. L'autre est spécialisée dans les *ohira shippoku*, des nouilles aux œufs, aux champignons, châtaignes d'eau ou à la quiche de poisson grillée. À quelque distance de là, on reconnaît plusieurs personnes fortement éclairées, notamment deux femmes précédées par des hommes portant des lanternes en papier. L'horizon est baigné d'une lumière magique devant laquelle les maisons, les bâtiments du temple, mais surtout les pins et les micocouliers (*enoki*) et leurs branches en pinces de crabes se détachent mystérieusement. Les contrastes de clair-obscur parfaitement calculés produisent une grande profondeur spatiale et font de cette feuille un nouveau chef-d'œuvre de la représentation vespérale.

114

びくにはし
雪中

Bikunihashi setchū
10–1858

Bikuni Bridge in Snow

On the right, a steep wall is hinted at, part of the fortifications of the outer moat of the shogun's castle. In other words, the Bikuni Bridge was centrally situated, but in the 19th century was in a run-down district of cheap restaurants and brothels. The word *bikuni* had been used since about the 14th century for an itinerant nun. In Hiroshige's day, though, the name was also applied to prostitutes who, disguised as nuns, circumvented the ban on prostitution outside the licensed pleasure quarter of Yoshiwara.

On the bridge were simple restaurants that offered popular winter specialities, such as the *yakiimo*, roast sweet potatoes, which are still sold on the streets of Tokyo today. On the edge of the street to the right we can just see baskets of raw potatoes. The large characters next to them advertise the fact that the *imo* here are roasted whole and are even tastier than chestnuts. Also on the right, directly above Hiroshige's signature, is a wheel, cropped by the margin of the

print, which suggests a *yakiimo* shop on wheels, typical of this district.

The large sign of the shop on the left advertises in bold characters that it sells "mountain whale" (*yama kujira*), a euphemism for the meat of wild animals. The eating of fish was permitted, though as late as the 18th century the Buddhist ban on the consumption of meat was still largely adhered to. By Hiroshige's day, however, the eating of red meat was a status symbol, though the euphemistic description "mountain whale" was nevertheless retained. In fact this meat was in particular demand, as consuming it was thought to give the eater some of the animal's strength.

It is believed that this print, like plates 12 and 41, is the work of Shigenobu (1826–1869), the future Hiroshige II. The largely empty foreground, the unconvincing depiction of the wall and the schematic arrangement of snowflakes suggest a different hand from that of Hiroshige.

Die Brücke Bikunihashi im Schnee

Am rechten Rand des Holzschnittes ist eine steile Mauer angedeutet, die zum Schutzwall am äußeren Graben des shogunalen Schlosses gehört. Die titelgebende Brücke Bikunihashi war zentral gelegen, stand aber in einer im 19. Jahrhundert heruntergekommenen Gegend mit billigen Essgelegenheiten und Bordellen. Als *bikuni* bezeichnete man etwa seit dem 14. Jahrhundert eine umherziehende Nonne. Zu Hiroshiges Zeiten wurden aber auch Prostituierte so genannt, die, als Nonnen verkleidet, das Verbot der Prostitution außerhalb des lizensierten Vergnügungsviertels Yoshiwara umgingen.

An der Brücke standen einfache Restaurants, die beliebte Winterspezialitäten anboten, wie die bis heute auf der Straße verkauften *yakiimo*, geröstete Süßkartoffeln. Wir sehen rechts am Straßenrand Körbe mit rohen Kartoffeln. Die großen Schriftzeichen daneben werben damit, dass die *imo* hier als Ganzes geröstet würden und noch leckerer seien als die ebenfalls beliebten Kastanien. Direkt über der Signatur Hiroshiges ist ein angeschnittenes Rad zu sehen, das den für diese Gegend

typischen Laden für *yakiimo* auf Rädern andeutet.

Das fest etablierte Geschäft links bietet mit seinem Aushängeschild in schwungvoller Schrift „Walfische aus den Bergen" (*yama kujira*) an, ein Euphemismus für wilde Tiere. Der Genuss von Fisch war erlaubt, wohingegen noch im 18. Jahrhundert das buddhistische Verbot des Verzehrs von anderem Fleisch weitgehend eingehalten wurde. Zur Zeit Hiroshiges galt Fleisch bereits als kostspieliges Statussymbol. Die euphemistische Bezeichnung „Walfische aus den Bergen" blieb allerdings erhalten. Dieses Fleisch war besonders begehrt, da man durch seinen Genuss etwas von der Kraft dieser Tiere in sich aufzunehmen hoffte.

Man vermutet, dass dieses Blatt wie die Tafeln 12 und 41 von Shigenobu (1826–1869) stammt, dem späteren Hiroshige II. Der weitgehend ungestaltete Vordergrund, die wenig überzeugende Darstellung der Mauer und die schematisch angeordneten Schneeflocken deuten auf eine andere Hand als die Hiroshiges hin.

Le pont Bikunihashi sous la neige

Près du bord droit de cette estampe est indiqué un mur escarpé qui fait partie de l'enceinte protectrice longeant la douve extérieure du château shogunal. Le pont Bikunihashi qui donne son titre à l'image était situé dans une zone centrale qui avait décliné au XIVᵉ siècle et où l'on pouvait trouver des restaurants bon marché et des prostituées. Depuis le XIVe siècle environ, le terme *bikuni* désignait une nonne errante. À l'époque de Hiroshige, c'est aussi le nom qu'on donnait aux filles publiques qui se déguisaient en nonnes pour contourner l'interdiction de se prostituer hors du cadre légal du quartier des plaisirs de Yoshiwara.

Près du pont se trouvaient de modestes restaurants qui proposaient des spécialités d'hiver très prisées, comme les *yakiimo*, patates douces grillées qu'on peut encore trouver aujourd'hui dans les rues de Tokyo. Au bord de la rue, on voit des corbeilles remplies de patates crues. Les grands idéogrammes à leur gauche proclament qu'ici les *imo* sont grillées entières et qu'elles sont encore plus savoureuses que les châtaignes également très prisées. Directement au-dessus de la signature de Hiroshige, coupée

par le bord de l'image, on peut voir une roue qui renvoie à la vente de *yakiimo* dans les magasins roulants caractéristiques de cette zone.

L'enseigne du magasin solidement établi à gauche propose en écriture cursive des « baleines des montagnes » (*yama kujira*), euphémisme désignant les bêtes sauvages. La consommation de poisson était autorisée, sachant que l'interdiction bouddhiste de consommer toute autre chair était largement respectée au XVIIIᵉ siècle. À l'époque de Hiroshige, la viande était déjà considérée comme un coûteux symbole social. Le terme euphémique « baleines des montagnes » restait néanmoins en usage. Cette chair était particulièrement recherchée dans la mesure où l'on espérait retirer de sa consommation un peu de la force des animaux concernés.

On suppose que l'auteur de cette feuille – comme les planches 12 et 41 – fut en fait Shigenobu (1826–1869), le futur Hiroshige II. Le premier plan presque vide, la représentation peu convaincante du muret et l'organisation schématique des flocons de neige suggèrent effectivement le travail d'une autre main que celle de Hiroshige.

115

Takata no baba
2–1857

The Takata Riding Grounds

These riding grounds in the north-west of Edo were laid out in 1636; it was here that the warrior aristocracy could practise their equestrian and archery skills. In the middle distance, and below the silhouette of Mount Fuji, two horsemen are galloping in opposite directions along a grey track, while further to the right, a group of archers have met at a shooting bunker; three of the men have bared their shoulders in order to gain the freedom of movement needed to aim. What they are aiming at is the round target covered in white leather and fastened by cords to two posts. The surface of the target is literally raised above the rest of the scene by the *nunomezuri* technique of blind printing (see plate 6). It is also placed strikingly in the foreground, even though it is

cropped, like the arrows, by the coarse grey-brown bark of a pine, which is itself cropped by the margin of the print.

With highly limited means, Hiroshige thus focuses on the core ethic of the warrior aristocracy: the contrast between nature and culture, between natural qualities and cultivated abilities. For the cultivation of both civilian and military virtues and skills was the declared aim of the Confucian ethical code of the samurai.

The strong colour contrasts, and the lack of transition between foreground, middle distance and background, seem contrived and give the composition a somewhat artificial character.

Der Reitplatz Takata no baba

Im Nordwesten von Edo befand sich der 1636 angelegte Reitplatz, auf dem die Angehörigen des Schwertadels Reiten und Bogenschießen trainieren konnten. Im Mittelgrund, vor der Silhouette des Berges Fuji, galoppieren zwei Reiter in entgegengesetzter Richtung über eine graue Reitbahn, während sich weiter rechts eine Gruppe von Bogenschützen an einem Schießunterstand zusammengefunden hat, darunter drei Herren, die ihre rechte Schulter entblößt haben, um die zum Zielen erforderliche Bewegungsfreiheit zu gewinnen. Ihr Ziel ist eine kreisrunde, mit weißem Leder bespannte Scheibe, die durch Schnüre an zwei Pfählen befestigt ist. Hiroshige rückt die mit der textilen Blinddrucktechnik *nunomezuri* (siehe Tafel 6) hervorgehobene Zielscheibe dekorativ und zugleich plakativ in den Vordergrund,

indem er sie ebenso wie die Pfeile nur zum Teil hinter der groben, braun und grau schattierten Borke eines angeschnittenen Kiefernstammes zum Vorschein kommen lässt. Mit aufs Äußerste reduzierten Mitteln bringt er so den Kern der Ethik des Schwertadels auf den Punkt: den Kontrast zwischen Natur und Kultur, zwischen natürlicher Beschaffenheit und kultivierter Fähigkeit. Denn die Kultivierung der zivilen wie auch der militärischen Tugenden und Fertigkeiten war das erklärte Ziel der konfuzianisch geprägten Samurai-Ethik.

Die kräftigen Farbkontraste, aber auch der unvermittelte Gegensatz zwischen Vorder-, Mittel- und Hintergrund wirken konstruiert und verleihen der Komposition einen artifiziellen Charakter.

Le manège équestre Takata no baba

Au nord-ouest d'Edo se trouvait un manège équestre qui existait depuis 1636 et sur lequel les membres de la noblesse d'épée pouvaient exercer l'équitation et le tir à l'arc. Au second plan, devant la silhouette du mont Fuji, deux cavaliers galopent en sens inverse sur une piste grise, tandis qu'un peu plus loin à droite, un groupe d'archers s'est retrouvé près d'un stand de tir. Trois seigneurs ont dénudé leur épaule droite pour avoir la liberté de mouvement nécessaire à la visée. Leur cible est un grand cerceau tendu de cuir blanc fixé à deux poteaux par des cordes. Hiroshige a placé de manière aussi décorative que voyante la cible mise en valeur par la technique d'estampage à sec appelée *nunomezuri* (cf. pl. 6) et n'en laisse apparaître qu'une partie, ce qui vaut égale-

ment pour les flèches partiellement cachées derrière l'écorce rugueuse, ombrée de gris et de brun, du tronc d'un pin coupé sur toute sa hauteur par le bord de l'image. Par l'extrême réduction des moyens, Hiroshige fait ressortir le noyau de l'éthique chevaleresque de la noblesse d'épée : le contraste entre nature et culture, entre conformation naturelle et culture de l'adresse. La pratique des vertus et habiletés civiles autant que militaires était le but déclaré de l'éthique des samourais marquée par le confucianisme. Les forts contrastes de couleurs, mais aussi l'opposition directe entre premier, second et arrière-plan font l'effet d'une construction detoutes pièces et confèrent à la composition un caractère artificiel.

116

高田姿見
のはし
俤の橋
砂利場

Takata Sugatami no hashi Omokage no hashi Jariba
1–1857

Sugatami Bridge, Omokage Bridge and Jariba at Takata

The rice fields of Hikawa near the Takata Riding Grounds (see plate 115) stretch out in the middle distance. It is winter, and the fields, covered in yellow stubble, are represented by yellow areas overprinted patchily in grey. They are named after the Hikawa Shrine further to the right, to which visitors gained access via a simple wooden bridge, the Sugatami no hashi. The dominant foreground motif is the other bridge of the title, the Omokage no hashi, whose high arch spans the Kanda Aqueduct, and which Hiroshige set diagonally to the picture plane. It was a timber-plank bridge, with a moss-covered layer of earth on each side. The actual footpath is, like the path to the shrine itself, surfaced with grey gravel. It was across this bridge that shogun Iesada (1824–1858) walked on his way home from an excursion to Ōji in the same month the censors approved this print. Two other prints in this series (see plates 17, 115) demonstrate once more that Hiroshige and his publisher reacted quickly to such events.

The composition of this topographical print is not unusual. What makes it memorable are the brilliant colours, for example the golden yellow of the fields, partially overprinted in grey, the red and purple of the banks of mist and finally the orange of the horizon – all of which form a striking contrast to the saturated blue and green of the water and vegetation. Hiroshige modelled the pictorial space of this print primarily through colour.

Die Brücken Sugatami und Omokage und Jariba bei Takata

Der Blick fällt auf die winterlichen, mit goldgelben Stoppeln bedeckten, hier aber summarisch durch gelbe und grau überdruckte Farbflächen wiedergegebenen Reisfelder von Hikawa in der Nähe des Reitplatzes Takata no baba (siehe Tafel 115). Sie sind nach dem weiter rechts gelegenen Schrein Hikawa benannt, zu dem die Besucher über eine einfache Holzbrücke, die Brücke Sugatami no hashi, gelangten. Beherrschendes Motiv im Vordergrund ist die in hohem Bogen über das Kanda-Aquädukt führende Brücke Omokage no hashi, die Hiroshige diagonal in die Komposition setzt. Es handelt sich um eine Holzplanken-Brücke, auf der eine an den Seiten bemooste Erdschicht liegt. Der eigentliche Gehweg ist wie der Weg zum Schrein Hikawa mit grauem Kies bedeckt. Diese Brücke hatte der Shogun Tokugawa Iesada (1824–1858) auf dem Heimweg von einem Ausflug nach Ōji in demselben Monat überquert, in dem dieses Blatt von den Zensoren genehmigt wurde. Zwei weitere Holzschnitte der Serie (siehe Tafeln 17, 115) belegen einmal mehr, dass Hiroshige und sein Verleger schnell auf solche Ereignisse reagierten.

Ungewöhnlich ist nicht das Kompositionsschema dieser topografischen Ortsbeschreibung, es sind vielmehr die leuchtenden Farben – etwa das zum Teil grau überdruckte Goldgelb der Felder, das Rot und Violett der Nebelbänke und schließlich das Orange des Horizontes –, die einen fulminanten Kontrast zu dem satten Blau und Grün von Wasser und Vegetation bilden und dem Betrachter nachhaltig in Erinnerung bleiben. Hiroshige hat den Bildraum bei diesem Druck im Wesentlichen durch die Farbe modelliert.

Les ponts Sugatami et Omokage et Jariba près de Takata

Le regard tombe sur les rizières de Hikawa, près du manège équestre Takata no baba (cf. pl. 115). Les rizières hivernales couvertes de chaumes dorées sont rendues ici sommairement par des surfaces de couleur jaunes et grises. Leur nom leur vient du sanctuaire Hikawa situé un peu plus loin à droite, et vers lequel les visiteurs se rendaient en franchissant le simple pont de bois Sugatami no hashi. Le motif dominant du premier plan est le pont Omokage no hashi qui jette son grand arc sur l'aqueduc de Kanda et que Hiroshige a placé diagonalement dans la composition. Il s'agit d'un pont en planches de bois couvert d'une couche de terre bordée de mousse sur les côtés. Le chemin proprement dit est couvert de graviers gris tout comme celui qui mène au sanctuaire Hikawa. Ce pont fut emprunté par le shogun Tokugawa Iesada (1824–1858) lors de son retour d'une excursion qu'il fit à Ōji au mois même où la présente estampe fut approuvée par la censure. Deux autres estampes de la série (cf. pl. 17, 115) montrent une fois de plus que Hiroshige et son éditeur ont réagi sans tarder à ce genre d'événements.

L'aspect inhabituel de cette estampe n'est pas donné par le schéma de composition de la description topographique, mais bien plutôt par les couleurs vives – le jaune d'or partiellement surimprimé de gris des rizières, le rouge et le violet des bancs de brouillard, enfin, l'orangé de l'horizon. Ce couleurs forment avec le bleu saturé et le vert de l'eau et de la végétation un contraste fulminant qui reste durablement gravé dans la mémoire du spectateur. Ici, Hiroshige a modelé l'espace de l'image essentiellement par la couleur.

117

湯しま
天神坂上
眺望

Yushima Tenjin sakaue chōbō
4–1856

View from the Hilltop of Yushima Tenjin Shrine

The hill of Yushima Tenjin Shrine offers a fabulous view of the Shinobazu Pond in Ueno. On a small island is a temple dedicated to the goddess Benten, and the main halls of Kan'eiji Temple behind. The red walls of the temple buildings are luminous beneath the snow-covered roofs and, together with the red of the horizon and the clear blue of the pond, form a radiant winter backdrop. In the foreground, Hiroshige has not depicted the actual shrine, but only the steps leading to it and the cropped *torii* gate, which as *pars pro toto* marks the shrine precincts. There were two ways of reaching the shrine: steep "men's steps", and less steep "women's steps". This can be gathered from the inscription on the stone (*otokozaka*, "Hill for Men") at the top of the steps meant for men, which are being climbed by two figures just coming into the picture bottom right, their heads wrapped in thick scarves. Two figures are climbing the women's steps, approaching head on. Beneath them spreads out a broad sea of houses with grey snow-covered roofs and sketchily indicated grey-blue façades. Their appearance on the scene at this point, facing the *torii* and with the houses spread out far below them, emphasizes the sharp juxtaposition of two pictorial planes. The tension is further increased by the teahouse projecting suggestively into the picture behind the *torii*, its veranda decorated with luminous red lanterns. We might ask where the visitors are actually making for on a crisp winter's day like this – first to the shrine, or to the teahouse? This speculation may well have occupied the purchasers of Hiroshige's prints, too. They would have been well informed about the places to visit in and around Edo, and would enthusiastically discuss the scenic qualities of the various locations, the merits of their restaurants and teahouses and the social status of their respective clientele. The present print provided plenty of material for such discussions.

Ausblick von der Anhöhe des Schreins Yushima Tenjin

Die Anhöhe mit dem Schrein Yushima Tenjin bietet eine hervorragende Sicht auf den Teich Shinobazu no ike in Ueno, mit dem der Gottheit Benten geweihten Tempel auf einer kleinen Insel sowie den dahinter liegenden Haupthallen des Tempels Kan'eiji. Leuchtend kommen die roten Fassaden der Tempelgebäude unter den schneebedeckten Dächern zum Vorschein und bilden zusammen mit dem Rot des Horizonts und dem klaren Blau des Sees eine strahlende Winterkulisse. Hiroshige hat nicht den eigentlichen Schrein in Szene gesetzt, sondern nur die Treppen, die zu ihm führen, und das angeschnittene Tor *torii*, das als Pars pro toto den Schreinbezirk markiert. Es gab zwei Aufstiegsmöglichkeiten dorthin: Man konnte die Anhöhe über eine steile „Treppe für Männer" und eine weniger steile „für Frauen" erreichen. Dies geht aus der Steininschrift (*otokozaka*: „Hügel für Männer") unten rechts, am Ende der für die Männer bestimmten Treppe hervor, die zwei in dicke Kopftücher gehüllte Gestalten erklimmen. Über die Treppe für Frauen geraten zwei dem Betrachter frontal zugewandte Figuren ins Blickfeld. Sie werden durch die Ebene, zu der sie hinaufsteigen, jäh abgeschnitten. Unter ihnen erstreckt sich ein weites Häusermeer mit grau schattierten, schneebedeckten Dächern und summarisch angedeuteten graublauen Fassaden. Im Zusammenspiel mit der dem *torii* zugewandten Figur pointiert ihr Auftauchen das Aufeinanderprallen zweier Bildebenen. Das Spannungsmoment wird zusätzlich gesteigert durch das hinter dem *torii* suggestiv ins Bild ragende Teehaus, dessen Veranda mit leuchtend roten Lampions geschmückt ist. Der Betrachter mag sich fragen, wohin die Besucher an einem solchen strahlenden Wintertag streben – ob zuerst zum Schrein oder zum Teehaus. Diese spekulative Frage dürfte auch die Käufer von Hiroshiges Drucken beschäftigt haben, die über die Ausflugsziele der Stadt Edo bestens informiert waren. Mit Begeisterung tauschten sie sich über deren landschaftliche Vorzüge, die Qualität ihrer Restaurants und Teehäuser und das Niveau ihres jeweiligen Publikums aus. Das hier vorgestellte Blatt bot dazu reichlich Anlass.

Vue depuis les hauteurs du sanctuaire Yushima Tenjin

La hauteur sur laquelle est bâti le sanctuaire Yushima Tenjin offre une vue magnifique de l'étang Shinobazu no ike à Ueno, du temple dédié à la divinité Benten qui se dresse sur sa petite île et des pavillons principaux du temple Kan'eiji situés sur la rive opposée. Les lumineuses façades rouges des bâtiments du temple apparaissent parmi les toits enneigés et forment un lumineux décor d'hiver avec l'horizon rougeoyant et le bleu limpide du lac. Hiroshige n'a pas mis en scène le sanctuaire à proprement parler, mais seulement les escaliers d'accès et la *torii* qui représente le domaine du sanctuaire comme une partie pour le tout. Le sanctuaire possédait deux voies d'accès distinctes : on pouvait gravir la hauteur soit par l'« escalier des hommes » escarpé, soit par un escalier moins pentu appelé « escalier des femmes ». Ceci ressort de l'inscription gravée dans la pierre (*otokozaka* : « colline des hommes ») qu'on voit en bas à droite, au sommet de l'escalier des hommes que gravissent les deux figures coiffées d'épais couvre-chefs. Deux figures féminines tournées frontalement vers le spectateur entrent dans le champ de vision sur l'escalier des femmes, coupées abruptement par l'esplanade qu'elles vont atteindre. Au-dessous d'elles s'étend une vaste étendue de maisons aux toits enneigés, ombrés de gris, et de façades gris-bleu indiquées sommairement. Dans le dialogue avec la figure tournée vers la *torii*, leur apparition marque la collision entre deux niveaux iconiques. Ce facteur de tension est encore renforcé par la maison de thé émergeant de manière suggestive dans l'image derrière la *torii*, maison dont la coursive est décorée de lampions rouge vif. Le spectateur peut se demander vers où se dirigent les visiteurs par une radieuse journée d'hiver comme celle-ci. Se rendent-ils d'abord au sanctuaire ou à la maison de thé ? Cette spéculation a sans doute aussi préoccupé les acheteurs des estampes de Hiroshige, qui étaient parfaitement informés des lieux d'excursions d'Edo, et qui avaient des discussions passionnées sur leurs avantages paysagers, sur la qualité de leurs restaurants et maisons de thé comme sur le niveau des différents publics de visiteurs. La présente feuille fournissait ample matière à ce genre de discussion.

118

王子装束
ゑの木
大晦日の
狐火

Ōji Shōzoku enoki Ōmisoka no kitsunebi
9–1857

Foxfire on New Year's Night under the Enoki Tree near Ōji

Hiroshige produces a dramatic setting of an ancient legend, according to which New Year's Night saw a gathering, beneath an *enoki* tree (Chinese hackberry), of foxes with magical powers, who worshipped the rice deity Inari. They would then proceed to the Ōji Inari (also known as Shōzoku Inari) Shrine, where they would receive instructions from Inari for the coming year.

The peasants of the region claimed to be able to forecast the harvest prospects from the number of magic foxes, and from the form taken by their ghostly "lights".

On a cold and starry night, the foxes have gathered beneath the lone, bare *enoki* tree and a neighbouring pine. Their luminous breath resembles will o' the wisps. More foxes with flaming breath approach from the distance, where the shrine lies hidden in the grey-black overprinted woods. The composition is based on a depiction in the fifth volume of the *Illustrated Guide to Famous Views of Edo (Edo meisho zue)* dating from 1836. Hiroshige has even taken over the motif of the haystacks and the pine just visible behind the *enoki*. A surprising feature

of this print is the manner in which he has translated the composition into the medium of the colour woodblock print and in doing so created a scene of incomparable painterly density. Only the foxes in the foreground and their "foxfires" are outlined sharply and precisely, while all other elements appear indistinct in the dark of the night.

The pale pink of the foxes' bodies and the red-to-pink shaded flames they are exhaling create the impression that their bodies are indeed the source of the light that is illuminating the mound with the two bizarre trees. The smaller foxfires on the plain behind convey a sense of spatial depth and lead our gaze to the horizon, where the outlines of houses and roofs are suggested vaguely and schematically. The nuances of the colour scheme are remarkable, changing as they do between black, grey, blue-green and grey-green, and allowing the bark and roots of the *enoki* to be clearly differentiated. It is doubtless primarily the tension between the naturalism of the landscape and the unreality of the fantastical, almost ghostly event that holds us under its spell.

Fuchsfeuer in der Neujahrsnacht unter dem Enoki-Baum bei Ōji

Hiroshige setzt auf diesem Holzschnitt eine mit dem Neujahrsbeginn in Zusammenhang stehende Legende dramatisch in Szene. Gemäß einer alten Sage versammelten sich in der Neujahrsnacht mit magischen Zauberkräften ausgestattete Füchse, die dem Reisgott Inari huldigten, an einem bestimmten Enoki-Baum, um sich dann gemeinsam zu dem Schrein Ōji Inari (auch Shōzoku Inari) zu begeben. Dort erhielten sie von dem Reisgott Anweisungen für das neue Jahr. Die Bauern der Gegend behaupteten, aus der Anzahl der magischen Füchse und den Formen ihrer Irrlichter die Ernte des bevorstehenden Jahres vorhersehen zu können.

In einer sternenklaren Frostnacht haben sich die Füchse um den einsamen, kahlen Nesselbaum (*enoki*) und die benachbarte Kiefer versammelt. Ihr heller Atem gleicht Irrlichtern. Weitere Scharen von Füchsen mit flammendem Atem kommen aus der Ferne, wo der Schrein in den grauschwarz überdruckten Wäldern versteckt liegt. Die Komposition stammt aus dem Band 5 des *Illustrierten Führers zu berühmten Ansichten von Edo (Edo meisho zue)* von 1836. Hiroshige hat sogar das Motiv der Heuhaufen und der hinter dem Enoki-Baum zum Vorschein kommenden Kiefer übernommen. Überraschend

auf diesem Blatt ist aber die Art und Weise, wie er die Komposition in das Medium des Vielfarbendrucks übersetzt und eine Szene von unvergleichlicher malerischer Dichte geschaffen hat. Nur die Füchse im Vordergrund und ihre Irrlichter sind mit scharfen, präzisen Linien konturiert, alle übrigen Bildelemente verschwimmen im Dunkel der Nacht. Tatsächlich erwecken das zarte Rosa ihrer Körper und die rot bis rosa schattierten Flammen vor ihren Mäulern den Eindruck, als seien ihre Körper die Lichtquelle, welche die Anhöhe mit den beiden bizarren Bäumen beleuchtet. Die kleineren Fuchsfeuer in der weiten Ebene vermitteln räumliche Tiefe und leiten über zu dem Horizont, der nur vage und schemenhaft die Umrisse von Häusern und Dächern erahnen lässt. Bemerkenswert ist der Nuancenreichtum der zwischen Schwarz, Grau, Blaugrau und Graugrün changierenden Farbpalette, durch die etwa die Rinde und die Wurzeln des Enoki-Baums äußerst differenziert wiedergegeben werden. Es ist wohl vor allem die Spannung zwischen der naturalistisch dargestellten Landschaft und der Unwirklichkeit des fantastischen, nahezu gespenstisch anmutenden Geschehens, die den Betrachter in den Bann zieht.

Feux de renards dans la nuit du Nouvel An sous l'enoki près d'Ōji

Hiroshige présente dans cette estampe la mise en scène dramatique d'une légende liée au Nouvel An. Conformément à cette ancienne légende, des renards dotés de forces magiques, adorateurs d'Inari, le dieu du riz, se réunissaient la nuit du Nouvel An près d'un certain arbre avant de se rendre au sanctuaire Ōji Inari (aussi appelé Shōzoku Inari), où le dieu leur donnait des instructions pour l'année nouvelle. Les paysans de la région affirmaient pouvoir prédire la récolte de l'année à partir du nombre des renards magiques et des formes de leurs feux follets.

Dans le froid glacial d'une claire nuit étoilée, les renards se sont réunis autour du micocoulier (*enoki*) et d'un pin mitoyen. Leur haleine claire s'apparente à des feux follets. D'autres hordes de renards arrivent du lointain où le sanctuaire est caché parmi les bois traités dans un ton gris-noir. La composition dérive de la représentation correspondante du cinquième tome (1836) du *Guide illustré des vues célèbres d'Edo (Edo meisho zue)*. Hiroshige en a même repris le motif des meules de foin et du pin apparaissant derrière le micocoulier. N'en reste pourtant pas moins surprenante dans cette feuille la manière dont Hiro-

shige a traduit la composition dans le médium de l'estampe et créé une scène d'une incomparable densité picturale. Seuls les renards du premier plan et leurs feux follets présentent des contours précis ; tous les autres détails de l'image apparaissent flous et noyés dans l'obscurité de la nuit. De fait, le rose délicat de leurs corps et les flammèches ombrées de tons allant du rouge au rose devant leurs gueules sont la source lumineuse qui éclaire la hauteur où sont plantés les deux arbres aux formes singulières. Dans la vaste plaine, les plus petits feux de renards confèrent une profondeur spatiale à l'image et assurent la transition vers l'horizon qui ne laisse discerner que vaguement les contours schématiques des maisons et des toits. La richesse de tons de la palette, qui évolue entre des tons de noir, de gris, de bleu-gris et de gris-vert, est tout à fait remarquable ; l'écorce et les racines du micocoulier notamment sont rendues par des nuances particulièrement subtiles. De fait, la fascination exercée par cette estampe se doit sans doute avant tout à la tension entre la représentation naturaliste du paysage et l'irréalité de l'événement fantastique, voire fantomatique.

119

赤坂桐畑
雨中
夕けい

Akasaka Kiribatake uchū yūkei
4–1859

Night Rain in the Paulownia Garden at Akasaka

A number of passers-by run through the pouring rain along the Paulownia-lined Tameike Pond (see plate 52). Their blue, red and yellow clothes produce, in combination with the green of the two banks, a garish effect that contrasts with the greyish-black coloration of the background, where people under umbrellas can be vaguely made out ascending the steep road to the Akasaka Gate of Edo Castle. The majestic trees behind, recognizable through the mist only as silhouettes, belonged to the stately residences of the powerful Ii daimyō family, and the two branches of the Tokugawa from Owari (in today's Aichi Prefecture) and Kii (in today's Wakayama Prefecture). Some incongruities in the composition (for example no rain is visible in the foreground, the reservoir fades out into nothing on the left and the path there has no beginning and seems to be hovering in the air); the combined censors' seal outside the top margin of the print consisting of *aratame* ("examined") and the date (fourth month of 1859), usual between 1859 and 1871; and not least the signature "Nise Hiroshige" (Hiroshige II, 1826–1869) – all indicate that this is the work of Hiroshige's pupil and successor.

Accordingly, this print is not usually included in reproductions of the *One Hundred Famous Views of Edo*, although it bears the same series title. The thesis that it was made to replace a lost woodblock for *The Paulownia Garden at Akasaka* (see plate 52), composed by Hiroshige exactly three years earlier, is unconvincing, for often both prints appear in complete editions of the series. The ukiyo-e expert Asano Shūgō thinks, by contrast, that Hiroshige II was commissioned by the publisher Sakanaya Eikichi to execute this print in order to celebrate his adoption of the name and seal of the master in the spring of 1859.

As was usual in the studios of painters and woodblock-print masters, Hiroshige II worked on many projects in close collaboration with the master. Thus he not only completed the last three volumes of the ten-volume *Illustrated Souvenirs of Edo (Ehon Edo miyage)*, but also composed at least three (see plates 12, 41, 114) of the *One Hundred Views of Edo*, most probably on the basis of sketches by the master after the latter's death.

Nachtregen am Paulowniengarten in Akasaka

Einige Passanten laufen in strömendem Regen entlang des von Paulownienbäumen gesäumten „Teichreservoirs" Tameike, dem wir schon in Tafel 52 begegnet sind. Ihre blaue, rote und gelbe Kleidung ergibt mit dem starken Grün der beiden Ufer einen knalligen Effekt, der mit der grauschwarzen Palette des Hintergrunds kontrastiert. Dort sind schemenhaft Menschen unter Regenschirmen auszumachen, die eine zum Tor Akasakamon des Edo-Schlosses führende, steile Straße erklimmen. Die dahinter durch die feuchte Luft lediglich als Silhouetten erkennbaren majestätischen Bäume gehörten zu den stattlichen Residenzen der mächtigen Daimyō-Familie Ii und der beiden Zweigfamilien der Tokugawa aus Owari (heutige Präfektur Aichi) und Kii (heutige Präfektur Wakayama). Einige Unstimmigkeiten der Komposition – zum Beispiel sind keine Regentropfen im Vordergrund zu sehen, das Reservoir verläuft links ins Nichts, der dort ansteigende Weg hat keinen Ursprung und scheint in der Luft zu schweben –, das zwischen 1859 und 1871 übliche Kombinationssiegel der Zensoren aus *aratame* („geprüft") und Datum (vierter Monat 1859) am oberen Bildrand und nicht zuletzt die Signatur „Nise Hiroshige" (Hiroshige II, 1826–1869) bezeugen die Autorschaft von Hiroshiges Schüler und Nachfolger.

Dieses Blatt wird deswegen üblicherweise in Reproduktionen der *Hundert berühmten Ansichten von Edo* nicht mitberücksichtigt, obwohl es denselben Serientitel trägt. Die These, dieses Blatt sei als Ersatz für die verlorengegangene Druckplatte des genau drei Jahre zuvor von Hiroshige entworfenen *Paulowniengarten in Akasaka* (siehe Tafel 52) entstanden, ist wenig überzeugend. Häufig finden sich nämlich beide Blätter in kompletten Serien. Der Ukiyo-e-Spezialist Asano Shūgō vermutet dagegen, dass Hiroshige II das Blatt zur Feier der Übernahme des Namens und Siegels seines Meisters im Frühjahr 1859 im Auftrag des Verlegers Sakanaya Eikichi anfertigte.

Wie in Ateliers von Holzschnittmeistern und Malern üblich, arbeitete Hiroshige II in vielen Projekten eng mit seinem Lehrer zusammen. So hat er nicht nur die letzten drei der zehnbändigen *Illustrierten Mitbringsel aus Edo (Ehon Edo miyage)* vervollständigt, sondern auch wenigstens drei Drucke der *Hundert Ansichten* wohl auf der Grundlage von Vorzeichnungen nach dem Tod seines Meisters gestaltet (siehe Tafeln 12, 41, 114).

Pluie nocturne près du jardin de paulownias à Akasaka

Quelques promeneurs courent sous une pluie diluvienne le long de l'« étang-réservoir » Tameike bordé de paulownias qu'on a déjà pu voir dans la planche 52. Avec le vert vif des deux rives, leurs vêtements bleus, rouges et jaunes produisent un effet de couleurs éclatant qui contraste avec la palette gris-noir de l'arrière-plan, où l'on reconnaît des figures humaines schématiques s'abritant sous des parapluies et gravissant la route escarpée qui mène à la porte Akasakamon du château d'Edo. Les arbres majestueux, que l'humidité ambiante transforme en pures silhouettes, font partie de la luxueuse résidence de la puissante famille de daimyōs Ii et des deux branches Tokugawa d'Owari (actuelle préfecture d'Aichi) et de Kii (actuelle préfecture de Wakayama). Quelques maladresses dans la composition – aucune goutte de pluie au premier plan, réservoir ne donnant sur rien à gauche, chemin pentu sans vrai point de départ et semblant flotter dans les airs –, mais aussi, près du bord supérieur de l'image, le sigle de censure en usage entre 1859 et 1871, et qui combine l'*aratame* (« vérifié ») et la date (quatrième mois 1859), enfin, la signature « Nise Hiroshige » (Hiroshige II, 1826–1869), attestent la paternité de l'élève et successeur de Hiroshige.

C'est pour cette raison que, bien qu'elle porte le même titre de série, cette feuille ne figure pas habituellement dans les reproductions intégrales des *Cent Vues célèbres d'Edo*. La thèse selon laquelle elle aurait été créée en remplacement du bois d'impression perdu du *Jardin de paulownias à Akasaka* (cf. pl. 52) conçu exactement trois ans plus tôt, n'est guère convaincante, car bien des séries complètes les contiennent toutes deux. Le spécialiste de l'ukiyo-e Asano Shūgō suppose plutôt que Hiroshige II créa cette feuille commandée par l'éditeur Sakanaya Eikichi pour célébrer l'adoption du nom et du sceau de son maître au printemps 1859.

Comme cela se faisait couramment dans les ateliers des graveurs et des peintres, Hiroshige II avait travaillé en étroite collaboration avec son maître pour de nombreux projets. Ainsi, le successeur de Hiroshige n'a pas seulement complété les trois derniers des dix volumes des *Souvenirs illustrés d'Edo (Ehon Edo miyage)*, mais a aussi créé au moins trois estampes pour les *Cent Vues* (cf. pl. 12, 41, 114), vraisemblablement sur la base de dessins préparatoires.

Acknowledgements
Danksagung
Remerciements

We should like first and foremost to thank the ukiyo-e expert Orii Takae, formerly curator at the Nakagawa-machi Bato Hiroshige Museum of Art, who played a decisive role in obtaining material. Together with the art historians Asana Shūgō and Kobayashi Tadashi, she also gave us important hints and advice.

Our book is seriously indebted to Henry D. Smith's research into Hiroshige and the *Meisho Edo hyakkei*, as well as to Harashida Minoru's new thesis on the historical context of the series.

We should like to thank Doris Croissant and Adele Schlombs for kindly contributing descriptions of some individual plates.

Wir danken vor allem der Ukiyoe-Expertin Orii Takae, ehemals Kuratorin am Nakagawa-machi Bato Hiroshige Museum of Art, die entscheidend bei der Beschaffung von Material geholfen hat. Zusammen mit den Kunsthistorikern Asano Shūgō und Kobayashi Tadashi gab sie uns zudem wichtige Ratschläge und Hinweise.

Die Forschungen von Henry D. Smith zu Hiroshige und den

Meisho Edo hyakkei sowie Harashida Minorus neue These zum historischen Zusammenhang der Serie sind ein roter Faden, der sich durch unser Buch zieht.

Frau Doris Croissant und Adele Schlombs haben freundlicherweise einzelne Tafelbeschreibungen übernommen.

Nous remercions en premier lieu l'experte Ukiyo-e, Orii Takae, ancienne conservatrice du musée Nakagawa-machi Bato Hiroshige, pour le matériel fourni, qui nous a considérablement aidés. Nous lui devons également des indications et des conseils précieux, tout comme aux historiens d'art Asano Shūgō et Kobayashi Tadashi.

Les recherches de Henry D. Smith sur Hiroshige et le *Meisho Edo hyakkei* ainsi que la nouvelle thèse de Harashida Minorus sur le contexte historique de la série constituent le fil directeur de ce livre.

Mesdames Doris Croissant et Adele Schlombs ont aimablement réalisé la description de certaines planches.

Photo credits
Fotonachweis
Crédits photographiques

The copy used for printing belongs to the:

Der Druck erfolgte nach dem Exemplar vom:

L'impression a été effectuée d'après l'exemplaire du:

Ota Memorial Museum of Art, Tokyo
© 2007, Ota Memorial Museum of Art, Tokyo
© akg-images/Erich Lessing: p. 8 left
Bayerische Staatsbibliothek München, Munich: p. 35 left
© Chazen Museum of Art, Bequest of John H. Van Vleck, Madison (WI): pp. 31, 32, 35 right, 36 left and right, 47 right

© Collections Baur Genève, Geneva: pp. 40, 43
© Courtesy Fukushima Kiyotake, Unsōdō Publishers, Tokyo/Kyoto: p. 44
© Freer Gallery of Art, Smithsonian Institution, Gift of Charles Lang Freer, F1904.75. Washington (DC): p. 39
© Van Gogh Museum, Vincent van Gogh Foundation, Amsterdam: p. 11 left and right
© Tōkyō National Museum. Image: TNM Image Archives Source: http://TNMArchives.jp/. Tokyo: p. 27
University of Cambridge, University Library, Cambridge: p. 24 left and right

Imprint
Impressum
Copyright

© 2009 TASCHEN GmbH
Hohenzollernring 53,
D-50 672 Köln
www.taschen.com

This 2009 edition published by Barnes & Noble, Inc., by arrangement with TASCHEN GmbH.

Project managing: Petra Lamers-Schütze, Cologne

Project editing: Ute Kieseyer, Cologne

The following plate descriptions were written by: Adele Schlombs, Cologne: 90–100, 109–113, 115–118 Doris Croissant, Heidelberg: 18, 22, 51, 61, 62, 69, 75, 79, 80, 84

English translation: Michael Scuffil, Leverkusen

French translation: Wolf Fruhtrunk, Asnières-sur-Seine

Production: Horst Neuzner, Cologne

Design: Sense/Net, Andy Disl and Birgit Eichwede, Cologne
Cover: Angelika Taschen, Berlin
Cover typography: Sense/Net, Andy Disl and Birgit Eichwede, Cologne

Front cover: Detail from Plate 35. *The Grove at the Suijin Shrine and Massaki on the Sumida River*

Back cover: Detail from Plate 34 *Night View of Matsuchiyama and the San'ya Canal*

Barnes & Noble, Inc.
122 Fifth Avenue
New York, NY 10011

ISBN: 978-1-4351-1942-0
Printed in China

1 3 5 7 9 10 8 6 4 2

Editorial Notes

ROMANIZATION

Japanese words are given in the standard revised Hepburn romanization, Chinese words in the Pinyin romanization. For classical poems, the traditional romanization, as used in lexicons of Japanese literature, has been adopted.

NAMES

Japanese personal names are given with the surname preceding the given name or artist name.

ORDER OF CHARACTERS

Japanese script is traditionally read from top to bottom, and the columns from right to left.

PRONUNCIATION

The vowels in the Hepburn romanization system have approximately the values they have in Italian. They are pronounced short unless they have a macron. The macron has been omitted in words that have been anglicized (e. g. Tokyo, shogun). Two vowels in succession are sometimes pronounced separately (e. g. ukiyo-e), sometimes as diphthongs. Consonants are pronounced much as in English; double consonants are pronounced double, as in Italian. The consonant "g" is always pronounced as in "get"; the Japanese "r" is pronounced with a single flap of the tongue.

TRANSLATIONS

Where not otherwise indicated, quoted textual sources and verses are taken from the standard translations given in the bibliography.

TITLES

The title of each woodblock print is given in English, German and French translation, and in Japanese (Hepburn romanization). Also given is the date of approval by the censors (month, year). The months in the lunar calendar used until 1872 do not correspond with those of the Gregorian solar calendar, hence in the text we use the expression "first month" (for example) rather than "January." Intercalary months are indicated by the letter "i."

CARTOUCHES

Each print contains three cartouches:
1. The cartouche at top right, always on a red ground, in the format of a *tanzaku* vertical poem sheet, contains the series title *Meisho Edo hyakkei*;
2. The square cartouche to the left of it imitates the *shikishi* poem sheet and contains the title of the print in question;
3. The signature cartouche, usually placed in the bottom left of the picture, reads "Hiroshige *ga*" (painted by Hiroshige).

SEALS OUTSIDE THE FRAME OF THE PICTURE

1. In many cases, one of five different seals used by the publisher Sakanaya Eikichi is placed at the bottom left. The most frequent seal is an abbreviation of his address in Shitaya Shinkuromonchō (near Ueno) and his name "Shitaya Uoei."
2. The censors' seal, as a rule placed top right, reads *aratame* ("examined"), while the date seal beside it, also deriving from the censors, gives the cyclical year character and the month. The year 1856 was the year of the dragon (*tatsu*), 1857 was the year of the snake (*hebi*) and 1858 the year of the horse (*uma*). In 1858 the responsibility for censorship was transferred to the publisher, which is why the ten prints dating from 1858 include no *aratame* seal.

Editorische Anmerkungen

UMSCHRIFT

Japanische Wörter wurden in der üblichen revidierten Hepburn-Umschrift transkribiert, das Chinesische in der Pinyin-Umschrift wiedergegeben. Für die Wiedergabe klassischer Gedichte wurde die historische Transliteration verwendet, wie sie in Wörterbüchern zu japanischer klassischer Literatur erscheint.

NAMEN

Bei der Nennung japanischer Namen wird der Nachname dem Vor- bzw. Künstlernamen vorangestellt.

LESERICHTUNG

Die japanische Schrift wird traditionell von rechts nach links und von oben nach unten gelesen.

AUSSPRACHE

Die Vokale werden wie im Deutschen kurz ausgesprochen, wenn sie nicht durch ein Längungszeichen gekennzeichnet sind. Bei japanischen Namen, die im Deutschen geläufig sind (z. B. Tokyo, Shogun), wird auf das Längungszeichen verzichtet. Doppelvokale werden zum Teil als Diphthonge ausgesprochen (z. B. „ukiyoe"), Konsonanten annähernd wie im Englischen, Doppelkonsonanten ähnlich wie im Italienischen. Ausnahmen stellen die Konsonanten „g" (Aussprache wie im Deutschen) und „r" dar (zwischen Zungen-r und l).

ÜBERSETZUNGEN

Wenn nicht anders angegeben, so sind zitierte Textquellen und Gedichte den Standardübersetzungen entnommen, die in der Literaturliste angegeben sind.

TITEL

Der Titel jedes Holzschnitts enthält die englische, deutsche und französische Übersetzung, die Transkription des japanischen Titels und die von den Zensoren angegebene Datierung (Monat/Jahr). Der Monat des bis 1872 gültigen Mondkalenders stimmt nicht mit dem Gregorianischen Sonnenkalender überein, deshalb wird im Text zum Beispiel „erster Monat" und nicht „Januar" angegeben. Die Schaltmonate werden abgekürzt als „i" (intercalary) gekennzeichnet.

KARTUSCHEN

Jeder Holzschnitt enthält drei Kartuschen:
1. Die stets rot unterlegte Kartusche rechts oben, im Format eines vertikalen Gedichtblattes *tanzaku*, enthält den Serientitel *Meisho Edo hyakkei*.
2. Die quadratische Kartusche links daneben ahmt das Gedichtblatt *shikishi* nach und enthält den Titel des jeweiligen Blattes.
3. Die zumeist am linken unteren Bildrand angebrachte Signaturenkartusche liest sich „Hiroshige *ga*" (gemalt von Hiroshige).

SIEGEL AUSSERHALB DES BILDRAHMENS

1. Oft ist am linken unteren Rand eines von fünf verschiedenen Siegeln des Verlegers Sakanaya Eikichi angebracht. Das häufigste Siegel gibt seine Adresse in Shitaya Shinkuromonchō (nahe Ueno) und seinen abgekürzten Namen „Shitaya Uoei" an.
2. Das Zensorensiegel, in der Regel oben rechts angebracht, liest sich *aratame* („geprüft"), und das ebenfalls von den Zensoren vergebene Datumssiegel daneben gibt das zyklische Jahreszeichen und den Monat an. Das Jahr 1856 stand im Zeichen des Drachens (*tatsu*), 1857 war das Schlangenjahr (*hebi*) und 1858 das Jahr des Pferdes (*uma*). 1858 wurde die Ausübung der Zensur auf den Verleger übertragen, daher fehlt das Siegel *aratame* auf den zehn im Jahre 1858 entstandenen Holzschnitten.

Remarques de l'éditeur

TRANSCRIPTION

Les termes japonais sont donnés dans l'habituelle transcription Hepburn modifiée, les termes chinois en transcription pinyin. Pour les poèmes classiques, on a retenu la translittération historique, telle qu'elle est utilisée dans les dictionnaires de littérature classique japonaise.

NOMS DE PERSONNES

Pour les noms de personnes japonais, le nom de famille est cité avant le prénom ou le nom d'artiste.

SENS DE LECTURE

L'écriture japonaise se lit traditionnellement de droite à gauche et de haut en bas.

PRONONCIATION

La prononciation des voyelles est brève, sauf lorsqu'elles portent des macrons (accents d'allongement). Pour les noms japonais couramment utilisés en français (Tokyo, shogun etc.), on a renoncé aux macrons, hormis dans les noms propres. Certaines doubles voyelles sont prononcées en faisant la diérèse, la prononciation des consonnes suit à peu près celle de l'anglais, les doubles consonnes celle de l'italien. Deux exceptions à cette règle : la consonne « g », qui se prononce « gu » comme dans « guépard », la consonne « r », qui se prononce entre « r » lingual et « l ».

TRADUCTIONS

Les sources – textes et poèmes – ont été traduites à partir des traductions standard référencées dans la bibliographie.

TITRES

Les titres des estampes sont donnés en traduction anglaise, allemande et française avec la transcription du titre japonais et la datation indiquée par les censeurs (mois/année). Les mois du calendrier lunaire en vigueur jusqu'en 1872 ne coincident pas avec les mois du calendrier solaire grégorien ; c'est pourquoi on trouvera dans le texte, à titre d'exemple, « premier mois » et non « janvier ». Les mois intercalaires sont indiqués par l'abréviation « i ».

CARTOUCHES

Chaque estampe présente trois cartouches :
1 Le cartouche à fond rouge uni en haut à droite, au format d'une feuille de poème verticale *tanzaku*, contient le titre de la série *Meisho Edo hyakkei*.
2 Le cartouche carré placé à sa gauche imite le format d'une feuille de poème *shikishi* et contient le titre de l'estampe.
3 Le cartouche de signature, généralement placé en bas de l'image, près du bord gauche, se lit « Hiroshige *ga* » (peint par Hiroshige).

CACHETS HORS DU CADRE DE L'IMAGE

1 On trouvera souvent, apposé en bas dans la marge de gauche, un des cinq sceaux de l'éditeur Sakanaya Eikichi. Le sceau le plus fréquent est celui de l'abréviation de son adresse à Shitaya Shinkuromonchō (près d'Ueno) et de son nom en « Shitaya Uoei ».
2 Le cachet de la censure apposé le plus souvent en haut à droite se lit *aratame* (« vérifié »), et le cachet de datation également apposé par les censeurs indique le signe cyclique de l'année et le mois. L'année 1856 fut placée sous le signe du dragon (*tatsu*), 1857 sous celui du serpent (*hebi*), et 1858 fut une année du cheval (*uma*). En 1858, l'exercice de la censure fut transféré aux éditeurs ; le cachet *aratame* ne figure donc pas sur les dix estampes de 1858.

Bibliography
Bibliographie
Bibliographie

Anderson, William. "Hiroshighé I, II". *Le Japon Artistique* 16 (1889), 33–40 and 45–52.

Asakura Teruhiko, ed. *Edo no maki I* [Tome on Edo, vol. 1], Nihon meisho fūzoku zue 3 [Illustrated Guides to Famous Places in Japan, vol. 3]. Tokyo: Kadokawa Shoten, 1979.

Asakura Teruhiko, ed. *Edo no maki II* [Tome on Edo, vol. 2], Nihon meisho fūzoku zue 4 [Illustrated Guides to Famous Places in Japan, vol. 4]. Tokyo: Kadokawa Shoten, 1980.

Asano Shūgō and Yoshida Nobuyuki, eds. *Hiroshige, Ukiyo-e wo yomu* 5 [Reading ukiyo-e, vol. 5]. Tokyo: Asahi shinbunsha, 1998.

Asano Shūgō. "Tōyō bunko no ehon to ukiyoe: Hiroshige 'Meisho Edo hyakkei' wo chūshin ni" [Illustrated books and ukiyo-e prints from the Tōyō bunko collection. Focusing on Hiroshige's 'One Hundred Famous Views of Edo'], in *Tōyō bunko meihinten — Chiyoda-ku Edo kaifu 400nen kinen jigyō: Treasures of the Tōyō Bunko: Commemorating the 400th Anniversary of the Edo Shogunate*. Tōyō bunko and Nihon Keizai Shinbun, eds. Tokyo: Nihon Keizai Shinbun, 2003, 9–15.

Clark, Timothy. "Utagawa Hiroshige and the Maruyama-Shijō School," in Amy Reigle Newland, ed. *The Commercial and Cultural Climate of Japanese Printmaking*. Amsterdam: Hotei Publishing, 2004, 143–161.

De Becker, J. E. (Joseph Ernest). *The nightless city of the geisha: the history of the Yoshiwara*. New York: ICG Muse, Inc., 2000.

Edo Tōkyō daichizu: chizu de miru Edo Tōkyō no konjaku [Enlarged Maps of Edo and Tokyo: Past and Present of Edo and Tokyo as seen in maps], Masai Yasuo, general editor. Tokyo: Heibonsha, 1993.

Fiévé, Nicolas and Paul Waley, eds. *Japanese Capitals in Historical Perspective. Place, Power, and Memory in Kyoto, Edo, and Tokyo*. London: Routledge Curzon, 2003.

Forrer, Matthi, ed. *Hiroshige: prints and drawings*. London: Royal Academy of Arts. Munich: Prestel, 1997.

Forrer, Matthi. "The Art of Hiroshige," in Forrer, Matthi, ed. *Hiroshige: prints and drawings*. London: Royal Academy of Arts. Munich: Prestel, 1997, 11–27.

Forrer, Matthi. "The Relationship between Publishers and Print Formats in the Edo Period", in Amy Reigle Newland, ed. *The Commercial and Cultural Climate of Japanese Printmaking*. Amsterdam: Hotei Publishing, 2004, 171–205.

Hillier, Jack. *The Japanese Print. A new Approach*. London: G. Bell and Sons, Ltd., 1960.

Harashida Minoru and Kitahara Itoko. "Jishin no konseki to 'Meisho Edo hyakkei' no atarashii yomikata: Hiroshige's One Hundred Famous Views of Edo after the Earthquake", in *Nenpō jinrui bunka kenkyū no tame no himoji shiryō no taikeika: The Annual Report, Systematization of Nonwritten Cultural Materials for the Study of Human Societies*, vol. 1. Yokohama: Kanagawa daigaku 21seiki COE puroguramu, 2004, 62–104.

Harashida Minoru. "Shinshaku 'Meisho Edo hyakkei': An Interpretation of 'One Hundred Famous Views of Edo', *Ukiyo-e Geijutsu* 150 (2005), 85–94.

Harashida Minoru. "Ukiyo-e ha dekigoto wo dono yō ni toraete kita ka" [How did ukiyo-e depict current events?], in *Kanagawa daigaku 21seiki COE puroguramu shinpojiumu hōkoku, dai kai kokusai shinpojiumu pureshinpojiumu "Hanga to shashin' — 19seiki kōhan dekigoto to imēji no sōshutsu—"* [First Report of the 21st Century Center of Excellence symposium at Kanagawa University: Preperatory symposium for the First International Symposium: "Prints and photography: Current incidents of the second half of the nineteenth century and the creation of images]. Yokohama: Kanagawa daigaku 21seiki COE puroguramu, 2006, 15–31.

Kobayashi Tadashi and Tōkyō dentō mokuhanga kōgei kyōkai,

eds. *Ukiyo-e 'Meisho Edo hyakkei' fukkoku monogatari* [Ukiyo-e 'One Hundred Famous Views of Edo': A story of revival]. Tokyo: Unsōdō, 2005.

Köhn, Stephan. *Berichte über Gesehenes und Gehörtes aus der Ansei-Zeit (Ansei kemmonshi): Kanagaki Robuns (1829–1894) Bericht über das große Ansei-Erdbeben 1855 als Repräsentant des Genres der „Katastrophendarstellungen."* Wiesbaden: Harrassowitz, 2002.

Miyao Shigeo. *Meisho Edo hyakkei I* [One Hundred Famous Views of Edo, vol. 1]. Ukiyo-e taikei, vol. 16, Gotō Shigeki, ed. Tokyo: Shūeisha, 1975.

Miyao Shigeo. *Meisho Edo hyakkei II* [One Hundred Famous Views of Edo, vol. 2]. Ukiyo-e taikei, vol. 17, Gotō Shigeki, ed. Tokyo: Shūeisha, 1976.

Naito, Akira. *Edo, The City That Became Tokyo. An Illustrated History*. Tokyo: Kodansha International, 2003.

Naitō Masato. *Ukiyo-e saihakken: daimyōtachi ga medeta ippin, zeppin* [Renewed discoveries of ukiyo-e: Rare and superb works loved by feudal lords]. Tokyo: Shōgakkan, 2005.

Nishiyama, Matsunosuke. *Edo Culture. Daily Life and Diversions in Urban Japan, 1600–1868*. Honolulu: University of Hawai'i Press, 1997.

Noguchi, Yone. *Hiroshige*. Paris: G. van Oest, 1926.

Ono Tadashige. *Edo no yōgaka* [Painters in the Western Style in Edo]. Tokyo: Sansaisha, 1968.

Orii Takae. "Hiroshige to meisho-e [Hiroshige and paintings of famous places]. in Kobayashi Tadashi and Tōkyō dentō mokuhanga kōgei kyōkai, eds. *Ukiyo-e 'Meisho Edo hyakkei' fukkoku monogatari* [Ukiyo-e 'One Hundred Famous Views of Edo': A story of revival]. Tokyo: Unsōdō, 2005, 24–26.

Perzynski, Friedrich. *Der japanische Farbenholzschnitt:*

seine Geschichte, sein Einfluss. Berlin: J. Bard, 1903.

Pissarro, Camille: *Correspondance de Camille Pissarro*, vol. 3, 1891–1894. Janine Bailly-Herzberg, ed. Paris: Editions du Valhermeil, 1988.

Schwan, Friedrich B. *Handbuch Japanischer Holzschnitt*. München: Iudicium Verlag, 2003.

Seidensticker, Edward. *Low City, High City. Tokyo from Edo to the earthquake: How the Shogun's ancient capital became a great modern city, 1867–1923*. New York: Alfred A. Knopf, 1983.

Seidlitz, Woldemar von. *Geschichte des japanischen Farbenholzschnitts. Mit 95 Abbildungen*. Dresden: G. Kühtmann, 1897.

Seigle, Cecilia Segawa. *Yoshiwara: The glittering world of the Japanese courtesan*. Honolulu: University of Hawaii Press, 1993.

Smith, Henry D. and Amy G. Poster. *Hiroshige: One Hundred Famous Views of Edo*. New York: George Braziller, 1986.

Smith, Henry D. "Hiroshige in History," in *Hiroshige: prints and drawings*, Forrer, Matthi, ed. London: Royal Academy of Arts; Munich: Prestel, 1997, 33–45.

Stewart, Basil. *A guide to Japanese woodblock prints and their subject matter*. New York: Dover, 1979.

Strange, Edward F. *The colourprints of Hiroshige*. New York: Stokes, 1925.

Suzuki Jūzō. *Hiroshige*. Tokyo: Nihon keizai shinbunsha, 1970.

Suzuki Jūzō, ed.: *Hiroshige I: Edo meisho mono* [Hiroshige, vol. 1: Series of Famous Views of Edo]. Meihin Soroimono Ukiyo-e [Famous series of ukiyo-e prints], vol. 10. Tokyo: Gyōsei, 1991.

Suzuki, Jūzō. "Some Observations on Hiroshige", in *Hiroshige: prints and drawings*, Forrer, Matthi, ed. London: Royal Academy of Arts; Munich: Prestel, 1997, 28–32.

Uhlenbeck, Chris. "Production constraints in the World of the Ukiyo-e: An Introduction to the Commercial Climate of Japanese Printmaking," in Amy Reigle Newland, ed. *The Commercial and Cultural Climate of Japanese Printmaking*. Amsterdam: Hotei Publishing, 2004, 11–22.

Uspenski, Michail. *Hundert Ansichten von Edo: Farbholzschnitte von Ando Hiroshige*. Bournemouth: Parkstone, 1997.

Waley, Paul. *Tokyo Now and Then. An Explorers Guide*. New York: Weatherhill, 1984.

Yamaguchi Keizaburō. *Hiroshige*, Ukiyo-e taikei, vol. 11, Gotō Shigeki, ed. Tokyo: Shūeisha, 1974.

Yamaguchi Keizaburō, ed. *Hiroshige III: Shokoku meisho mono* [Hiroshige, vol. 3: Series of Famous Views of All the Provinces], Meihin Soroimono Ukiyo-e [Famous series of ukiyo-e prints], vol. 12. Tokyo: Gyōsei, 1992.

Internet Sources

http://eos.kokugakuin.ac.jp/modules/xwords
last accessed on June 13, 2007

http://www.woodblock.com
last accessed on June 13, 2007

Chronology of Japanese Historical Periods

Kofun	c. 3rd century–AD 538
Asuka	538–710
Nara	710–794
Heian	794–1185
Kamakura	1185–1333
Nanbokuchō	1333–1392
Muromachi	1392–1573
Momoyama	1573–1615
Tokugawa	1615–1868
Meiji	1868–1912
Taishō	1912–1926
Shōwa	1926–1989
Heisei	1989–present

Zeittafel der japanischen Epochen

Kofun	ca. 3. Jh. – 538
Asuka	538–710
Nara	710–794
Heian	794–1185
Kamakura	1185–1333
Nanbokuchō	1333–1392
Muromachi	1392–1573
Momoyama	1573–1615
Tokugawa	1615–1868
Meiji	1868–1912
Taishō	1912–1926
Shōwa	1926–1989
Heisei	1989–heute

Chronologie des époques historiques du Japon

Kofun	env. IIIᵉ siècle à 538
Asuka	538 à 710
Nara	710 à 794
Heian	794 à 1185
Kamakura	1185 à 1333
Nanbokuchō	1333 à 1392
Muromachi	1392 à 1573
Momoyama	1573 à 1615
Tokugawa	1615 à 1868
Meiji	1868 à 1912
Taishō	1912 à 1926
Shōwa	1926 à 1989
Heise	1989 à aujourd'hui

APPENDIX

Bibliography
Bibliographie
Bibliographie

Chronology of Japanese Historical Periods
Zeittafel der japanischen Epochen
Chronologie des époques historiques du Japon

Editorial Notes
Editorische Anmerkungen
Remarques de l'éditeur

Acknowledgements
Danksagung
Remerciements

Photo credits
Fotonachweis
Crédits photographiques

Imprint
Impressum
Copyright